When the newly consecrated m̶ ̶ ̶ ̶ ̶ ̶ ̶ ̶ ̶ ̶
ited his seminary in 1929 he ̶ ̶ ̶ ̶ ̶ ̶ ̶
dictine spirituality. "There is no such thing," he replied. "It
is nothing other than the spirituality of the Church: the
praying of the Sacred Liturgy." For Blessed Ildefonso Schuster—monk, abbot, cardinal and archbishop—that reality was
a constant. The Sacred Liturgy was the source and summit of
his entire Christian life and work, as these volumes testify.

Scholarship has progressed in the century since higher
duties called Schuster from the classroom, certainly. Yet in
these pages his thirst for learning is as palpable as is the true
liturgical spirit—indeed sanctity—that animates his exposition of the nature of the liturgy and his meditations on the
seasons and feasts of the liturgical year. From these we can
learn a great deal, not only in respect of our approach to
liturgical study and celebration, but also regarding the fundamental nature of Christian life and spirituality. That these
volumes are once again in print is a singular grace.

—DOM ALCUIN REID, Prior, Monastère Saint-Benoît,
Fréjus-Toulon, France, Author, *The Organic Development of the
Liturgy*

In addition to having been a worthy son of Saint Benedict
and, later, successor of Saint Ambrose, Blessed Ildefonso
Schuster (1880–1954) was a notable figure of the early Liturgical Movement, one whose scholarship deserves to be better known in the anglophone world. Arouca Press has done
a great service toward that end by republishing the English
translation of his long out-of-print seminal work. Although
scholarship has progressed in some areas in the last century,
it remains a valuable commentary on the living tradition that
is the older Roman Rite, on a par with Dom Guéranger's magnum opus, *The Liturgical Year*.

—FR. THOMAS KOCIK, KHS, Author, *Singing His Song:
A Short Introduction to the Liturgical Movement*

The achievement of Blessed Ildefonso's Schuster *Liber sacramentorum* was to build a bridge between liturgical scholarship
and spiritual commentary on the Mass. The reprint of this great
contribution to liturgical renewal in the twentieth century is
most welcome at a time when the older form of the Roman Rite
is rediscovered by new generations of Catholics. Anyone diving
into this monumental work of erudition and piety will find it
an inspiring guide to the riches of the liturgical year.

—FR UWE MICHAEL LANG, Cong.Orat., Mater Ecclesiae
College, St Mary's University, Twickenham, London

Ildefonse Schuster was among the towering figures of the Liturgical Movement in its healthy phase, where the overriding concern was to study the family history in the spirit of descendents keen to know their glorious heritage, so that they might carry on long-standing customs with grateful understanding, and rediscover lost, forgotten, or neglected treasures. In his own life, he combined a scholar's diligent attention to primary sources with a pastor's warm-hearted embrace of all the gifts the Holy Spirit has bestowed on the Church over the ages. This carefully limned commentary, spacious and leisurely, plunges us into the pure font of tradition and intensifies our participation in the life-giving mysteries of Christ.

—DR. PETER KWASNIEWSKI, author of *Noble Beauty, Transcendent Holiness: Why the Modern Age Needs the Mass of Ages*

THE SACRAMENTARY

The Sacramentary

(LIBER SACRAMENTORUM)

Historical & Liturgical Notes on the Roman Missal

BY ILDEFONSO SCHUSTER

Abbot of the Monastery of St Paul's Without the Walls. Translated *from the Italian by* ARITHUR LEVELIS-MARKE, M.A.

VOLUME II

(PARTS 3 AND 4)

AROUCA PRESS

Volume 2 originally translated from the Italian
by Arthur Levelis-Marke
© Burns Oates & Washbourne Ltd.
1927

Reprinted by Arouca Press 2020

All rights reserved
No part of this book may be reproduced or transmitted,
in any form or by any means, without permission

ISBN: 978-1-989905-05-0 (pbk)
ISBN: 978-1-989905-06-7 (hardcover)

Arouca Press
PO Box 55003
Bridgeport PO
Waterloo, ON N2J3G0
Canada
www.aroucapress.com

Send inquiries to info@aroucapress.com

NIHIL OBSTAT:

    Fr. INNOCENTIUS APAP, S.Th.M., O.P.
                  Censor Deputatus.

IMPRIMATUR:

    EDM. CAN. SURMONT,
                 Vicarius Generalis.

WESTMONASTERII
    die 1 *Octobris,* 1925.

Made and Printed in Great Britain

CONTENTS

PART III

THE NEW TESTAMENT IN THE BLOOD OF THE REDEEMER

(THE SACRED LITURGY FROM SEPTUAGESIMA TO EASTER)

INTRODUCTION

THE SACRED LITURGY FROM SEPTUAGESIMA TO EASTER

APPENDIX

PART IV

BAPTISM BY THE SPIRIT AND BY FIRE

(THE SACRED LITURGY DURING THE EASTER CYCLE)

INTRODUCTION

Contents

THE SACRED LITURGY DURING THE EASTER CYCLE

EUCHOLOGICAL APPENDIX

PART III
THE NEW TESTAMENT IN THE BLOOD OF THE REDEEMER
(THE SACRED LITURGY FROM SEPTUAGESIMA TO EASTER)

ECCLESIAE · MISERICORDIAM · CONSECVTAE · IN · MAGNIFICENTIA

PATRIS · ALTISSIMI · ET · IESV · CHRISTI

ECCLESIAE . DILECTAE · ET · ILLVMINATAE

QVAE · ETIAM · PRAESIDET · IN · LOCO · REGIONIS · ROMANORVM

DIGNA · DEO · DIGNA · DECORE · DIGNA · QVAE · BEATA · PRAEDICETVR

VNIVERSO · COETVI · CHARITATIS · PRAESIDENS

CHRISTI · HABENS · LEGEM · PATRIS · NOMEN

IGNATII EPIST · AD ROMAN.

INTRODUCTION

CHAPTER I

THE LENTEN LITURGY AT ROME

THE Saturday night vigil in expectation of the *Parousia* of the Lord contributed from very early times to the substitution of the Christian Sunday for the Jewish Sabbath, and even from the times of the Apostles the two weekly fasts of Wednesday and Friday were regarded as the principal foundations of the liturgical week. We find the first mention of these in the *Didache,* in the *Pastor* of Hermas, and in the writings of Tertullian, according to whom the *statio* included an early rising with the threefold prayer of Terce, Sext, and None, followed at sunset by the eucharistic oblation.

Hermas attests that this observance was known in his day by the military term *statio;* but, as we learn from Tertullian, this watch kept by the Christian band was of a purely voluntary character, so much so that it became the first cause of the disputes between the Montanists and the Catholics. The former maintained that these fasts were obligatory, and that they should be prolonged until sunset; the latter, that they might end at None, after the offering of the Sacrifice, and, moreover, that no one was under compulsion to take part in them.

The very spirit and supernatural character of Christianity must, even before the canons of the Councils existed, have given rise to special observances in preparation for Easter. Otherwise it would be difficult to explain the different rules of the various churches in this matter. Thus, whilst originally the fast lasted a week at Alexandria, at Rome, and in Gaul, other churches kept as a fast only the last two days of Holy Week, from the Lord's Supper on Maundy Thursday until Easter morning, precisely as was done, we are told, by the Apostle St James *the Just.*

We do not know the reasons which caused Rome in the third century to prolong the fast for three weeks, but it was certainly the example of our Lord's forty days' fast in the desert which impelled the Fathers at the Council of Nicaea to fix the duration of the fast ordained by them at exactly forty days. From then onwards the Fathers, in accordance with the civil legislation of Byzantium, simply enjoin the observance, determine the rites, and explain the motives of this penitential time, and the benefits to be derived from it. Thus through many centuries, almost down to our own times, Lent was regarded as the support of Christian training, the " truce of God," during which period even the law-courts and the places of amusement were closed, the whole body of the faithful put aside all other concerns, and endeavoured by practices of penance and by liturgical instruction to renew their spiritual energy in order to rise to a holier life with Christ risen and triumphant over death.

The Byzantines, who looked upon all Saturdays and Sundays, with the exception of Holy Saturday, as festival days, and consequently exempt from fasting, anticipated the paschal fast by two or three weeks, in order to make up the full number of the Lenten fast-days which they had taken away. At Jerusalem, Lent began eight weeks before Easter, a custom which was imitated to a certain degree by the Latins, when they, too, began the fast on the Wednesday of Quinquagesima—afterwards known as Ash Wednesday—in order to make up the four days lacking to their Lenten fast of thirty-six days.

The very first idea of a penitential period in preparation for Easter seems to have arisen with regard to the catechumens, who prepared themselves by prayer and fasting to receive holy baptism on the night before Easter. A great part of the Lenten liturgy is inspired by the idea of the *baptismum poenitentiae,* so that it would be difficult to find a better way of reawakening in ourselves the grace of our baptism, and of strengthening our resolution to fulfil our baptismal promises, than that of following step by step the teaching which the Church imparts, at this season, in the Missal.

At Jerusalem, as a sign of penance and mourning, the divine Sacrifice was not offered up on weekdays in Lent, but at Rome only the last two days were considered as aliturgical.[1] All other days had their distinctive rites, their processions, their special chants; so that, in harmony with the character of the Latin eucharistic anaphora,[2] the Western Churches, and Rome in particular, would seem to have sought, by the splendour of their Lenten liturgy, to obey faithfully the command of the divine Master who teaches us to hide the rigour of our penance under the appearance of rejoicing.

Ash Wednesday has now for many centuries marked the beginning of the *jejuniorum veneranda solemnia,* but in the Roman Liturgy it is still possible to discern through subse-

---

[1] *i.e.,* days on which Mass was not said.
[2] This is the ancient name given by the Eastern Christians to the prayers now called *Canon Missae.*

quent changes different formulas for the beginning of Lent, which at various times superseded one another. After the Sacrifice *quadragesimalis initii* on the First Sunday in Lent, the significance of the ancient Roman solemnity of the *dominica mediante (die festo)*, or *mediana,* three weeks before Easter, becomes of great importance. The Pope, wearing on his head the *regnum*,[1] as on all great festivals, passed from the Lateran to the stational basilica of Santa Croce in Gerusalemme, carrying in his hand a golden rose sprinkled with balsam, which he afterwards presented to the prefect of the city.

In the time of St Gregory the true paschal fast began on the first Monday of Lent, as we learn from the *secreta* of the first Sunday, which makes mention of the *sacrificium quadragesimalis initii,* the beginning, that is, of the holy fast. Further, the *cursus*[2] of the divine Office, the hymns, versicles, and responsories, do not vary at all during the entire week of Quinquagesima. Moreover, the same holy pontiff, in a homily on the Gospel pronounced on the First Sunday *in Quadragesima,* declares that, although from this day six weeks will elapse before the joys of Easter begin, yet, as the six Sundays are deducted from the forty-two days of fasting, so in reality only thirty-six are devoted to rigorous penance. He makes no mention of the four fast-days of Quinquagesima week. Besides the Thursday, on which day the stational Mass was omitted at Rome, the Sunday, too, after the great nocturnal vigil of Ember Saturday, was considered " vacant " (*Dominica vacat*), the reason being that the Mass was celebrated at dawn, at the end of the night office.

Under Gregory II (715-31), however, the stations of the Thursdays in Lent were instituted, the sung portions of the offices being gleaned here and there from the Antiphonary. Later, especially out of Rome, in places where the solemn papal vigils were not kept, the Second Sunday in Lent was also distinguished by its proper stational Mass. This completed the Lenten office.

One most important point in the ancient observance of Lent was the custom of not taking either food or drink until sunset. During the day both clergy and people followed their usual avocations; but when in the forum the *meridiana* marked the hour of None, the faithful hastened from every part of the city to the stational church, where the Pope himself very often appeared in order to celebrate the divine Sacrifice. Usually the stational procession set forth from a

---

[1] This was the name formerly given to the papal tiara when it consisted of a single crown. The *triregnum* dates from the late Middle Ages.

[2] The order of arrangement.

neighbouring basilica, where the people, as they gradually assembled, awaited the arrival of the Pontiff and of the high officials of the Lateran Palace, who brought with them the banners and the precious vessels for the Mass. As soon as the celebrant had finished the collect, the procession, devoutly chanting the Litany, moved towards the stational church, where the holy Sacrifice ended as the sun was sinking. It seemed an evening oblation offered by the whole Christian family at the end of a busy day, sanctified by prayer, work, and self-denial.

The *Ordines Romani*[1] thus describe the rite of the *feria IV cinerum.* After None, the people and clergy assembled in the Basilica of St Anastasia at the foot of the Palatine, where the Pontiff, surrounded by the deacons, went up to the altar and intoned a prayer. Towards the tenth century the ancient ceremony of sprinkling the head with ashes, instituted, as a matter of fact, for public penitents, became more and more general, until the *Ordo Romanus XI* ended by applying it to all the faithful without distinction. This mournful rite being ended, a subdeacon raised aloft the precious stational cross,[2] and all present set forth in procession to the singing of litanies and antiphons suited to the occasion, and ascended the Aventine Hill to the Basilica of St Sabina, where Mass was celebrated. According to the same Roman rite, the Pope and the deacons walked in the procession barefooted, a custom common to the penitential liturgy of medieval Rome.

The Mass had neither *Kyrie* nor Litany, this latter having been recited on the way, but the Introit was repeated, and all the other ceremonies of the papal Mass were carried out as usual. Before the Communion a subdeacon of the *regio* announced to the people *Crastina die veniente, statio erit in ecclesia sancti Georgii martyris ad Velum aureum,* and the *schola* replied, *Deo gratias.* Then, after the Communion and the collect *super populum,* which took the place of the final blessing, the faithful were dismissed (*ite missa est*), and the clergy withdrew to their own abodes. There is no mention made of Vespers, because in Rome during the Middle Ages, except on great festivals, they were sung only in the monasteries.

On these occasions, when the Pope did not take part in the stational feast, an acolyte was sent to him, bearing as a devotional offering a small piece of flax dipped in the oil of

---

[1] These form a collection of ceremonial statutes by means of which we are able to trace step by step the development of papal Liturgy in Rome from the sixth to the sixteenth centuries.

[2] So called because it was carried aloft in the processions to the stations.

the sanctuary lamp. The acolyte said : *Jube, domne, bene-dicere*, and, having received the blessing, continued : *Hodie fuit statio ad sanctam Sabinam, quae salutat te.* The Pope replied *Deo gratias*, and, kissing the flax reverently, he handed it to the *cubicularius*, in order that it might be care-fully preserved and placed, at his death, in the funeral cushion.

It has not been possible to discover exactly the system which guided the choice of stational churches for the Lenten season. The basilicas at the catacombs of the martyrs are always excluded, which seems to point to an order established after the fifth century, when, owing to the unsafe condition of the devastated Roman Campagna, the popular devotion to the extra-mural catacombs had somewhat lessened. Excep-tions are made only for the great basilicas of the Apostles, and for the tomb of St Lawrence, which at certain solemn times—during the preparation for Lent, for instance, in Easter Week, and on the three days following Pentecost—formed the natural objective of the faithful and the neophytes in their pilgrimages beyond the city walls. Especially after baptism had been administered in the Lateran during the solemn vigil of Easter it seemed a pious duty for the entire Church, clergy and people, to accompany the neophytes to those famous sanctuaries and to present them, as it were, to the three great patrons of Rome—St Peter, St Paul, and St Lawrence.

The Ember Days also had their special stations—on the Wednesday at the Liberian Basilica, on the Friday at the *Apostoleion* of Pope Pelagius, and on the Saturday night at St Peter's, where the ordinations took place. The sacred Orders, however, were conferred in an oratory adjoining the Vatican Basilica; that is to say, within the monastery of St Martin, it being regarded as the exclusive privilege of the Popes to be consecrated at the actual tomb of the Apostle.

In the Roman Liturgy the station often assumed the character of a festival in honour of the titular saint of the church where the synaxis was held, as is still seen in the Missal of the present day on Sexagesima Sunday, when the station was at the Basilica of St Paul, and on the Thurs-day before the Sunday *in mediana*, when Mass was celebrated in the Church of SS Cosmas and Damian.

The remembrance of the titular saints has also influenced in some degree the choice of the Lenten lessons, and careful study of the portions of Scripture prescribed by the Roman Missal reveals many historical details of great value. Thus the Mass of the Thursday following Ash Wednesday at the Church of St George *in Velabro*, by its Gospel narrative of the centurion of Capharnaum, calls to mind St George, whom tradition presents to us as the pattern of a valiant soldier. The next day the stational Mass is at the Church of Pammachius close to the *Xenodochium* of the Valerii on the Coelian Hill; and the scriptural lessons there read teach us that alms are of no value unless given with a pure conscience and a single intention.[1] The following Monday the station is at the Basilica of St Peter ad Vincula on the Esquiline, and the remembrance of the *Pastor Ecclesiae* inspires the choice of the classic description of the Good Shepherd taken from the Book of Ezechiel. On the next Wednesday the stational festival is at the Liberian Basilica, and the Liturgy finds in the Gospel lesson a delicate way of conveying to our minds the praises of the Blessed Virgin.

It would be easy to multiply these examples and to insist on the importance of the local colouring which pervades the whole of the ancient liturgy of Rome, giving to it that intensely popular character, that variety, that strong sense of actuality, and that delicacy of feeling by which it penetrates so deeply into our souls. For this reason, if we desire to appreciate the exquisite beauty, both religious and æsthetic, of the liturgical patrimony of Rome, we cannot afford to neglect altogether the external surroundings amongst which it arose and developed; not to speak of the spiritual conditions required of us—especially a lively and active faith, without which *animalis homo non percipit ea quae spiritus sunt.*[2]

But besides the cult of the saints in their stational churches another great thought dominates the whole Lenten liturgy of the Roman Church. The institution of Lent was first inspired by the preparation of the catechumens for baptism, and the Liturgy of that holy time could not but be powerfully influenced by the grand conception of the resurrection of humanity through Christ rising from the dead.

At the beginning of Lent, or towards the *Dominica in mediana,*[3] the more fully instructed and best disposed among the catechumens gave in their names to the bishop, in order to be admitted to baptism. *Ecce Pascha est,* repeats St Augustine, *da nomen ad baptismum.*

The names having been entered on the register, the station was celebrated on the following Wednesday, in the vast Basilica of St Paul, when the great scrutinies were held. Even now the liturgy of that day is permeated with the thought of baptism, and the Roman Church places before the catechumens as an example of the sincere convert the Apostle of the Gentiles, who spent the three days before his baptism

---

[1] For a further explanation of this see *Feria VI post Cineres.*—Tr.

[2] 1 Cor. ii 14.

[3] This corresponds to the Fourth Sunday in Lent.

in prayer and fasting.   Therefore the choice of the Gospel lesson of the man born blind, besides signifying that through original sin all men are born blind to the light of faith, alludes also to the physical blindness of the Apostle, from which he was cured instantly at the moment of his baptism.

The ceremony began towards the hour of Terce.   An acolyte called the catechumens by name, placing them in two rows, the boys on the right and the girls on the left.   Then a priest passed through their ranks, and, laying his hands on the head of each in turn, recited the formula of exorcism, and placed some blessed salt on their lips.   The catechumens having retired, the Mass began; but after the first collect they were called back, and, at the invitation of the deacon, recited some prayers on their knees.   The deacon then said to the sponsors, *Signate illos,* and they made the sign of the cross on their foreheads.   Three acolytes followed and again performed the imposition of hands, the signing with the cross, and the exorcism, after which the deacon exclaimed, *Catechumeni recedant; si quis catechumenus est, recedat; omnes catechumeni exeant foras,* and the catechumens withdrew.   At the offertory the sponsors presented oblations to the Pope, as well for themselves as for their future god-children, whose names were read out publicly during the Canon.   After the Communion the Pope made known to the people the day of the second scrutiny, which began with the same rites as the first.   This second ceremony, however, had a special name at Rome—*in aurium aperitione*—for on that day the ears of the catechumens heard for the first time the public reading of the holy Gospels.

After the Gradual had been sung four deacons appeared, bearing the Gospels, which they placed at the four sides of the holy table.   The Pope then delivered a homily on the character and importance of the Evangelic Law, after which a deacon read the first verses of the Gospel of St Matthew and then delivered the book into the hands of a subdeacon, who, wrapping it reverently in a veil, deposited it in the *sacrarium.*   The Pope commented on the first verses of the four Gospels successively in the order in which they had been read by the deacons, and afterwards explained the Creed, which until then had been unknown to the candidates.   The discourse being ended, an acolyte came forward holding in his arms a little Greek child, of whom there were many in Rome during the Byzantine period.   The Pope asked : *Qua lingua confitentur Dominum nostrum Jesum Christum?— Graece.—Annuntia fidem illorum.*   And the acolyte sang, Πιστεύω εἰς ἕνα . . . in the name of the Byzantine children, sons and daughters of the imperial functionaries.   Another acolyte did the same for the Latin children, after which the

Pope, having given a short address to the catechumens, taught them the Lord's Prayer.

There were at first three scrutinies at Rome, but later these were increased to seven, the last being on the morning of Holy Saturday, when no other ceremony took place. At this last scrutiny a priest again signed each of the candidates on the forehead with the cross and laid his hands on them, pronouncing as he did so the formula of exorcism; then he touched their ears and their upper lip with saliva—*Ephpheta, quod est, adaperire, in odorem suavitatis*—and, again laying his hands upon them, made them recite the Creed—*Redditio symboli*. After a last prayer recited together, the catechumens were dismissed to await the setting of the sun, when the solemn paschal vigil commenced, the only one which from the third century was obligatory on all Christian people.

Some of the most beautiful passages of the Bible which foreshadow the final triumph of the Christian people through the grace of holy baptism having been read, the Pope, accompanied by a number of priests, deacons, and lesser clergy, went in procession to the magnificent Lateran baptistery, the rest of the clergy and people remaining in the church to sing the Litany of the Saints. First the Pope blessed the baptismal font, pouring perfumed chrism on the water; then he administered baptism to some of the catechumens, and whilst the priests, deacons, and acolytes, who had descended barefooted into the sacred font, were baptising the rest, he entered the *consignatorium* and confirmed with chrism each of the neophytes as they were presented before him.

The first rays of the sun were already gilding the summits of the Alban Hills, whose noble outlines are so clearly seen from the piazza of the Lateran, when the procession of white-robed neophytes, followed by their sponsors and the Pope, returned to the church to celebrate the eucharistic sacrifice of the paschal feast, at which they received Holy Communion for the first time. This was for them a day of wondrous experiences; all was new, and everything revealed the magnificence and fulness of their redemption—the heavenly teaching, the holy sacraments, the divine Liturgy of the Church, who must indeed have appeared to them on that day, as she did to Hermas, under the form of a glorious Mother radiant with splendour and eternal youth.

The baptismal feast continued at Rome for an entire week. Every day, after Vespers, the procession again escorted the neophytes to the baptistery up to the following Sunday, when, having laid aside their white garments, they took part in the station at the extra-mural church of the youthful martyr Pancratius, who was chosen in the liturgy as the

model to be imitated by these young recruits of the army of
Christ. On that day, which still bears the title *in Albis,* in
reference to the white baptismal robes soon to be laid aside,
the Mass seems to be attuned to the enthusiasm and joyous-
ness natural to youthful vigour—*quasi modo geniti infantes*—
and must have filled the neophytes with the brightest hopes
and fairest promises of grace and blessing.

Such is, in its main outline, the splendid stational liturgy
of the Roman Church, in which this divine Mother and
Teacher of the Christian peoples reveals a unique genius for
training in holiness her faithful children, and impressing on
their minds by means of processions, rites, and sacred songs
her sublime and fruitful precepts. The sacred Liturgy of the
Church in those days, when it was fully understood by the
people, took the place of our pictures, statues, and illustrated
catechisms, nor was the religious instruction then imparted
any less profound, as is shown by the inspired defence made
before the pagan tribunals by some of the early martyrs for
the Faith. This primitive teaching, conveyed chiefly through
liturgical forms, remained firmly impressed on the hearts of
the people in such a manner that the Christian doctrine was
not merely understood and believed, but—what is far more
important—was transformed into action in their daily life.

It was Gregory I, the great restorer of the Christian spirit,
especially by means of the Liturgy, who reorganised the
stational functions in Rome. History shows him to us at the
head of his people, leading the procession to one or other of
the sanctuaries of the martyrs, feeding his flock by his
example, his words, and the holy sacraments.

It is certain that—even setting aside, if this were possible,
the supernatural efficacy of these rites and prayers offered to
God by a whole people—there could be nothing more beautiful and touching than the sight of this multitude of the
faithful of all ages and of every condition—working folk,
patricians, monks, and dignitaries of the Church, who, the
day's labour over, refreshed their souls, athirst for God and
heavenly things, at the stational feast. Here the unity of one
flock under one Shepherd was visibly represented by one holy
table, one Host, and one chalice offered to God in the name
of all by the supreme Pastor.

Nowadays the changed conditions of social life have caused
the Church herself to introduce some minor alterations into
her rites. The preparatory ritual for catechumens has long
fallen into disuse, but this does not mean that the Lenten
liturgy has lost its living force, for even in these latter times
many souls outside the fold of the Catholic Church await the
touch of heavenly grace, and it is the duty of the Church to
hasten by her prayers the hour of their conversion—*Oremus*

et pro catechumenis nostris—as we are taught to say in the Office for Good Friday.

Lent, moreover, is the season of penitence, of amendment of life, of preparation for Easter, and these conditions of the spiritual pilgrimage transcend the ages and still continue the common duty of all the faithful.

The holy joys of Easter will shine more radiantly and will touch the heart of the Christian more intimately if, purified by penance, he shall have rendered himself worthy to live a supernatural life given entirely to God, after the likeness of the risen Christ, of whom St Paul writes : *Mortuus est semel, quod autem vivit, vivit Deo.*[1]

[1] Rom. vi 10.

CHAPTER II

THE EASTER TRIDUUM IN THE
ROMAN MISSAL

WE are about to speak of the ceremonies of the last three days of Holy Week, and we shall describe this period as the Easter Triduum, in accordance with the ancient usage which amplified the significance of the Christian Easter so that the liturgical cycle should conclude the whole mystery of man's redemption from the Last Supper to the dawn of the Resurrection. It was in this sense that the early Christians designated Holy Thursday by the name of Pasch; and even now the first day of the Lenten fast is described in the Secret of the Missal as " the beginning of the venerable Paschal Sacrament itself "—*ipsius venerabilis sacramenti celebramus exordium.*

These last days of Lent have preserved their original liturgical character far less altered than any others, nor has the antiquity of the rite suffered very greatly from any successive modifications. We find additions, indeed, but no real changes or transformations, as in some other parts of the Missal. The study of the rites of the Easter Triduum will prove very useful, as they serve to illustrate those of the ordinary sacramental synaxes held by our forefathers during the course of the year. The penitential observance of this Triduum was the first nucleus, or, we might almost say, the original cell around which the entire existing system of abstinence during this holy space of forty days came afterwards to group itself.

The Rites of " Feria V in Coena Domini "

At Rome, Thursday in Holy Week is more commonly called after the *Coena Domini,* whereas in the Frankish countries it already takes its name from the paschal solemnity.

As the Pope usually resided in the Lateran, the Basilica Salvatoris was naturally chosen for the station of this day; the more so as the long duration of the ceremonies would not have permitted of a procession to any of the other urban titular churches. Contrary to the ordinary custom which prescribed that there should be only one Mass in each church, in earlier times there were three eucharistic synaxes on Holy Thursday—one in the morning for the public reconciliation of penitents, the second for the consecration of the holy oils, while the third *in Coena Domini* towards the close of day was the time chosen for the Easter Communion.

We must remember that originally the administration of all the sacraments was bound up with the celebration of the divine Sacrifice, so that the *Liber Sacramentorum,* which we shall now call the Roman Missal, contained in reality the rites of all the seven sacraments, so closely were they linked with the celebration of Mass. In these days, the ceremonies being shorter, and the rule of public penance having ceased to be enforced, at least as regards that part reserved for the bishop, the holy oils are consecrated at the Mass of the Easter Communion.

The Reconciliation of Penitents

The custom of reconciling penitents on the occasion of the paschal solemnity was universal, and dates back to very ancient times.

The spirit of the ancient Roman Liturgy was, generally speaking, much averse from those pious exaggerations so dear to the Irish and Frankish peoples, among whom canonical penances of dozens upon dozens of years were common, with as many additional quarantines. These excesses—endurable only in the first ardour of conversion—from the very impossibility in which the penitent usually found himself of being able to accomplish them, contributed largely to bring about the abolition of the whole system of public penances.

On the other hand we find that in Rome in the sixth century canonical penances did not last longer than forty days. At the beginning of Lent the transgressor presented himself before the penitentiary, who, from the fourth century onwards, was to be found at the principal basilicas of the city, and received from him a hair-shirt sprinkled with ashes, with which to clothe himself. Occasionally the forty days would be spent in a monastery secluded from the world, but in any case the penance ended with the commencement of the paschal solemnity on Holy Thursday, when public absolution was given and the penitent was once more admitted to Holy Communion. This was the mode of procedure related by St Jerome in the case of Fabiola.

The solemn rites of this reconciliation described in the Roman Pontifical are derived chiefly from the Gallican use. In the Mozarabic rite, too, the absolution of penitents is eminently dramatic, whereas the Roman mentality preserves its primitive austere dignity until the end of the early period, being characterized by its great sobriety and its consistent avoidance of scenic effect.

The *missa poenitentium* must have finally fallen into disuse during the twelfth century, for the *Ordo Romanus X* prescribes that the Pope shall merely have the list read out towards midday of those who were announced *in Coena Domini* as being under censure, and shall then grant to the people the customary absolution.[1]

THE CONSECRATION OF THE HOLY OILS

The *missa chrismalis,* the formulas of which are in part preserved in the rite for the consecration of the holy oils, described in the Roman Pontifical now in use, is of very ancient origin. The blessing of the oil appears in the so-called *Canones Hippolyti* as a ceremony common to any festival Mass celebrated by a bishop. Before the end of the Canon of the Mass, at the moment of the blessing of the first-fruits of the season, vegetables, pulse, and fruit, the oil was also blessed, so that it might be used for the anointing of the sick, both as an act of private devotion and also in the ritual administration of the sacrament of Extreme Unction.

There is preserved intact in the Missal at this point of the Canon the ultimate form of that primitive benediction : *Per quem haec omnia, Domine, semper bona creas, sanctificas, vivificas, benedicis, et praestas nobis.* The words *haec omnia* refer to the grain, fruit, and oil brought to the altar, and not, as might now perhaps be imagined, to the eucharistic oblations, which it would scarcely be reverent to designate collectively as *haec omnia . . . creas . . . vivificas, benedicis.*

The *Ordines Romani* describe the rite observed by the Pope at the blessing of the holy oils. Some of the vessels containing the oil were placed on the altar itself, but owing to the great concourse of people, whilst the Pontiff was reciting the prayers prescribed in the Sacramentary for the blessing of the oil for the sick, the bishops and priests, who celebrated together with the Pope on solemn festivals, advanced to the *podium* and there repeated the same formulas over the phials brought by the faithful.

In early times everyone wished to possess some of this blessed oil; the more so because the form of consecration then in use not only referred ,to the oil destined for the sacramental administration of Extreme Unction, but also invoked in a general sense a health-giving grace—*Omni ungenti, gustanti, tangenti tutamentum mentis et corporis*

---

[1] *P.L.* LXXVIII, col. 1009.

. . . *ad evacuandos omnes dolores, omnem infirmitatem, omnem aegritudinem.*

Thus the faithful in those days used the oil as they now use that of the lamps of some especially venerated sanctuary, or Lourdes water. When, however, the sickness became serious and the unctions used in private were deemed insufficient, the priests were called in, and the blessed oil, which had hitherto served merely as a vehicle of private devotion, became the matter necessary to the sacrament of Extreme Unction. Something of the same kind is still found in the East, where, after Extreme Unction has been administered to the sick person, those present, and even the walls of the dwelling where the ceremony takes place, are anointed out of pure devotion with the remainder of the holy oil.

The consecration of the chrism took place between the Pope's Communion and that of the clergy. The Pontiff first breathed on the phial of perfumed oil, tracing over it the sign of the cross; then, as in all consecrations at Rome, he chanted a long eucharistic prayer or Preface which still exists in the Pontifical. In this prayer is traced the history of the scriptural symbolism connected with this anointing with olive oil from the olive branch brought to Noe by the dove to the anointing of Aaron by the hand of Moses and the appearance of the dove after the baptism of Christ in the Jordan. This *consecratio chrismatis,* as it is called, has a true epicletic form, since the prayer is addressed to God the Father that he, through the merits of the Saviour, will send the Holy Ghost to consecrate the fragrant oil so that it may become for the baptized a chrism of salvation.

The blessing of the oil for the anointings which took place before the baptism of catechumens was more simple. In the ancient Liturgy these unctions recalled those used by the wrestlers in the games, which were intended to render the limbs more supple, and to strengthen the combatants for the contests. The catechumens, being about to sustain the last and decisive combat with the Evil One, received, at the moment in which they were solemnly preparing to renounce all his works and pomps, these symbolical anointings with holy oil on the breast and on the shoulders—in the East they were extended over the whole person—to strengthen them, as it were, in the fight.

The collect which the Pope recited over the oil for the catechumens expressed the desire that the virtue of the Holy Ghost should inwardly prepare those aspiring to the sacrament of spiritual regeneration, frustrating the wiles of the Devil, and purifying their minds and bodies in order that *Sancti Spiritus operatione . . . sit unctionis hujus prae-*

paratio utilis ad salutem. Hence the custom, derived from the Gallican use and introduced into the Roman Pontifical, of anointing the hands of those being ordained as priests with the oil intended for the unction of the catechumens, appears wholly unmeaning.

We may note with reference to this that the anointing of bishops on the head with chrism, and the unctions used in the blessing of bells, are ceremonies which the *Ordines Romani* refused to admit until many centuries later. The papal tradition in the Liturgy during the early Middle Ages ignored these unctions so greatly cherished in countries of the Gallican rite, and to a fantastic and imaginative ritual preferred one which expressed theological truths with force and precision. It is a ritual endowed with that same gift by which the *Summa Theologica* of St Thomas Aquinas, conceived by an intellect devoid of sentimentalism but of angelic lucidity, resembles one of those classical buildings of the Renaissance, sober and elegant, stately and severe, to the perfection of which nothing is wanting.

THE MASS OF THE PASCHAL COMMUNION

The two preceding offices must have occupied the greater part of Holy Thursday; it was therefore excusable that the third or evening Mass *in Coena Domini* should be celebrated according to the archaic rite of the *Pannuchis*—that is to say, the holy Sacrifice began immediately at the Canon. We know that all the first part of the eucharistic Liturgy with the three lessons, the interposed psalmody, the sermon, and the final litany, are derived from the Jewish worship of the synagogue, and have no essential relationship to the Mass.

There were also other offices of a non-sacramental character with the same rites. The offering of the divine Sacrifice might or might not follow this *didascalia* of Jewish origin; but frequently, as was once the custom every Friday in Rome, the congregation dispersed after the Litany, without either Consecration or Communion having taken place. The Mass of the Presanctified on Good Friday, as we shall presently see, is of later and foreign origin.

In order to save time, the lessons and psalms were omitted at the evening Mass of the *Coena Domini*, which thus began at the Preface. This arrangement is ancient, and is borne out by the *Ordines Romani;* moreover, we find a trace of it in the Missal of our own days. In fact, the first part of the Mass of Holy Thursday has no definite character of its own, for the Introit is taken from the preceding Tuesday, the collect from Good Friday, the Epistle from the vigil of the day itself, and the Gospel (from St John) also from the Tuesday.

In the Missal of Pius V, the reading of the Passion according to St Luke is assigned to Tuesday in Holy Week; but this ordering is much later; since in the Roman Lectionaries of the later Middle Ages the lesson from St John, relating the washing of the feet, is always assigned to the station of the Tuesday. That the introduction of this Gospel into the Mass of Holy Thursday was by chance and was of later date is proved by the fact that it is not intimately connected with the *Coena Domini,* the thought of which entirely dominates the liturgy of this evening.

Of interest and importance is the collect said over the Oblations, which we now call the Secret, and which in the ancient Roman Liturgy was a preparation of the spirit before proceeding to the consecration and offering of the Sacrifice in the Canon. "We beseech thee, O holy Lord, Father almighty, eternal God, that he may render our service acceptable to thee, who by this day's tradition directed his disciples to do this in remembrance of him."

Anciently the eucharistic Canon began with that which we now incorrectly call the *Preface.* The Gregorian Sacramentary contains a most beautiful one for the Mass *in Coena Domini,* and it is very much to be deplored that the faulty taste of the later Middle Ages in matters liturgical transmitted to the Missal of St Pius V only a few of the more common of the Prefaces, which are repeated with great monotony during the course of the year; whilst so much of the original wealth of the Liturgy lies wellnigh forgotten in the Roman codices. The Preface for to-day dwelt on the treachery of Judas and the goodness of his Lord, who through the eucharistic banquet made a last but fruitless effort to soften the hardened heart of his faithless disciple.

The word *Preface,* as we have already said, tends to mislead us; for it appears to describe the hymn *Vere dignum et justum est,* which precedes the *Te igitur* of the Canon, whereas the true Preface is that brief duologue between priest and people recited before the sacerdotal hymn *Vere dignum.* Thus the *Canon Missae* begins, properly speaking, with the words: *Vere dignum et justum est,* and ends with the doxology *Omnis honor et gloria.*

There was originally no break in the unity of this eucharistic anaphora. From the Trisagion, through the *Te igitur* and the episcopal diptychs, whilst the deacon recited the *memento* of the living, it passed on at once to the epiklesis before the Consecration. Then followed the account of the Last Supper, the anamnesis, the oblation, the second part of the prayer called by the Greeks *the great intercession,* which accompanied the reading by the deacon of the diptychs of the dead, and finally the fraction of the sacred Species.

The text of the invocation of which Pope Pelagius (555-560) speaks, has suffered too many alterations for us to be able to reconstruct it in its entirety. The following may, however, give the reader some idea of the general tenor of the epiklesis of the *Coena Domini: Hanc oblationem servitutis nostrae* (the entire company of the *Servi Dei*) *sed et cunctae familiae tuae, quam tibi offerimus ob diem in qua Dominus noster Jesus Christus tradidit discipulis suis corporis et sanguinis sui mysteria celebranda; quaesumus Domine, ut placatus accipias. (Descendat[1] etiam, Domine, super eam illa Sancti Spiritus tui incomprehensibilis maiestas, sicut quondam in hostias Patrum descendebat) qui et oblationem nostram benedictam, adscriptam, ratam, rationabilemque facere dignetur, ut nobis Corpus et Sanguis fiat dilectissimi Filii tui Domini nostri Jesu Christi, qui pridie quam pro nostra omniumque salute pateretur, hoc est hodie, accepit panem,* etc.

The antiphon *ad Communionem*, which is in harmony with the Gospel of the washing of the feet, is also not of great antiquity. After the Mass the sacred Host consecrated for the following day is removed to a chapel suitably decorated. This rite, too, dates only from the end of the Middle Ages, and came into use during the residence of the Popes at Avignon. It was the custom at Rome at every papal Mass, and also in Gaul and in the East, to carry in procession a casket containing the sacred species—consecrated at a preceding Mass. This was to indicate the continuity, the *juge sacrificium* which the Church offers from the first Holy Thursday down to the last Mass, that shall salute the dawn of the *Parousia (donec veniat).*

When it became customary for the Pope to receive Holy Communion on Good Friday, it sufficed that the sacred particle should be brought as usual from the Lateran to the stational church of Santa Croce in Gerusalemme to be placed at the conclusion of the litany in the wine of the chalice and consumed by the celebrant. The custom of reserving it beforehand in a chapel adorned as for the Quarant'ore, and of bearing it processionally to the altar where the Liturgy of the Presanctified was celebrated, was introduced from the Court of Avignon.

In the twelfth century, according to the *Ordo Romanus XI,*

---

[1] This reconstruction, although hypothetical, is not entirely arbitrary. The invocation introduced into the text is still to be found in a prayer in the Breviary erroneously attributed to St Ambrose, but really the work of Ambrose Autpert, Abbot of Volturnum. In it the author has paraphrased and amplified an ancient anaphora no longer in use.

the Pope went immediately after the Mass of the Presanctified to the Oratory of St Lawrence, called also *Sancta Sanctorum,* and there washed the feet of twelve clerics, during which time the Cardinals recited the Vesper Office. Afterwards there took place the usual distribution of the *presbyterium,* or gifts of money, to the higher and lower clergy of Rome. When this was over, the pontifical court proceeded as it began to grow dark to the basilica-like Triclinium of Pope Theodore, where they dined.

The absolution of sinners, the chrism of joy for the neophytes, the oil of strength on the limbs of the sick, the divine Eucharist in the hearts of the faithful; all these unspeakable mysteries of love are the gifts bestowed on this feast-day of the *Coena Domini.* The Saviour, being about to die, pours forth all the treasures of his heart, and having loved us from all eternity, loves us unto the end—*in finem dilexit*—even to the laying down of his life for us.

FERIA VI IN PARASCEVE

The Stational Procession.

Christ had foretold that a prophet should not die except in Jerusalem, therefore to-day's station is celebrated in the Basilica of Santa Croce, known also as *Sancta Hierusalem,* where a large portion of the true cross is preserved.

It is extremely probable that in the plan of this sanctuary and the chapel below it it was intended to reproduce the *Martyrium* erected by Constantine on Calvary; so that, while the Lateran Basilica with its circular baptistery should represent at Rome the *Anastasis* at Jerusalem, the Sessorian Basilica, on the other hand, with its oratories *ante* and *post crucem,* should correspond to the *Martyrion* of Constantine, of which Etheria speaks in the account of her pilgrimage to the holy places.

At one time the Pope used to walk to the Good Friday station barefoot, swinging a censer before the relic of the true cross, which was carried by a deacon, whilst the choir sang the psalm *Beati immaculati in via* as they went along. Formerly, as a sign of deep mourning, the holy Sacrifice was not offered on this day, for the rigorous fast of the *Coena Domini* had to be continued until the announcement of the Resurrection.

It was not until towards the seventh century that the Church mitigated to some extent the severity of her ancient discipline, when, the celebration of stational Masses on the Fridays of Lent having already been introduced at Rome, the people were allowed to receive Communion in the urban titular churches also on Good Friday. The Pope and his deacons adhered for many centuries to the older rule of abstaining completely from participation in the sacred mysteries, and therefore also from food, on a day dedicated to mourning and the strictest fasting, but the *Ordines Romani* of the tenth century show that the pontifical court itself had at last fallen in with the general custom.

According to this later ritual, all the faithful in Rome received Holy Communion on Good Friday—*communicant omnes sub silentio*[1]; therefore the present custom of abstaining from Communion on this day as a universal liturgical law is of much later date and represents a feeble—indeed, one might almost say a distorted—reflection of what was the primitive rule of the Roman Church.

The ceremony which we now call by the Byzantine name of the *Mass of the Presanctified* has been in use among the Greeks since the seventh century at least, and is celebrated by them on all days of fasting in Lent. It has resulted from the fusion of three distinct rites—the Adoration of the Cross, the usual instructional office of lessons, psalms, and litanies preceding the eucharistic anaphora, and the Communion of the Presanctified. In our Missal these three rites are so closely intermingled as to disturb and obscure somewhat the due ordering of the ceremony, but in the ancient *Ordines Romani* they are described with all precision and exactitude.

The Pope first of all repaired in procession from the Lateran to Santa Croce, and there presented the relic of the true cross to the people to kiss, imitating in this the rite at Jerusalem described by Etheria. This adoration being ended, the lessons began as in any office, eucharistic or otherwise.

After the Gospel there followed the great litany, *Oremus dilectissimi,* etc., which from the days of Justin formed part of the sacred *actio,* so much so that in the present Missal of St Pius V the people are still invited at the Offertory to join in the litany by the *Oremus* of the priest as he turns towards them. No collect, however, now follows the invitation, so it is evident that at this point the rite is interrupted and a hiatus produced by the absence of the great intercessory prayer which once filled it.

At the conclusion of the litany the Pope used formerly to dismiss the congregation, and, without receiving Communion, return to the Lateran, just as was done in Rome on the Wednesday in Holy Week. But from the Roman rituals of the twelfth century it appears that the Adoration of the Cross, which at first preceded the stational office, and closed

[1] *Ordo Romanus, I, P.L., LXXVIII,* col. 963.

the procession, was now deferred until after the great litany, and placed between the first ceremony and the Communion of the Presanctified.

In practice the one arrangement may appear as good as the other, but the ancient Roman custom seems more logical. After carrying the cross in procession, it is adored according to the custom of Jerusalem; then the Mass begins with the usual lessons, psalms, and litanies. As, however, on this day there is no consecration of the sacred species, the celebrant passes on at once, after the great intercessory prayer, to the *Pater Noster,* which before the reform of St Gregory was said immediately before the Communion.

The Adoration of the Cross is derived, as we have said, from the rite used at Jerusalem, which was described by the pilgrim Etheria at the end of the fourth century. This rite soon spread throughout Christendom, and became one of the most characteristic ceremonies of Good Friday. According to the Roman use, the Pope first of all sprinkled the holy cross with sweet-smelling balsam in the Chapel of St Lawrence at the Lateran; then, during the procession from the Lateran to the stational basilica, he himself—contrary to the Western custom—swung the censer before the holy relic, a sign that this ceremony had been introduced from the East, where the office of thurifer is sometimes filled by a bishop or by a priest.

THE OFFICE AT THE SESSORIAN BASILICA

The first part of the Mass for to-day preserves untouched the ancient character of the Roman synaxis as it was before the *schola* arose about the time of Celestine I (423-432), with its great antiphonal psalmody which altered in some measure the primitive simplicity of the stational offices. On this day, therefore, there is no singing of the Introit, nor any litany preceding the reading of the Scriptures, but, as in the ancient synagogues in which Paul and Barnabas preached, three lessons interspersed by the responsory solos and by the collect said by the presiding official. The first lesson, from Osee vi, speaks of the divine plan of the coming redemption. After three days of expectation in the sepulchre of sin humanity shall rise again at the voice of Christ, triumphing over death and hell, and in the place of the ancient law of sacrifices and bloody holocausts in the national Temple of the Jews, the Redeemer shall establish the universal worship of faith and love.

The responsorial canticle of Habacuc follows, which ecclesiastical tradition had already destined to the office of Friday. In it the soul contemplates with wonder, amazement, and deep emotion these fresh instances of God's almighty power, who in the fulness of time shows forth on Calvary, in all his awful majesty, the infinite holiness of his nature, which demands from a sinful world so terrible a sacrifice of reconciliation. The mystery which fills the heart of the prophet with dread is one of fearful justice, but at the same time a mystery of ineffable love, since it is God in very deed who takes upon himself the punishment meted out to the guilty.

The next lesson is from Exodus xii, and describes the manner of eating the paschal lamb. It would be impossible to find a more perfect and more appropriate figure, for it is evident from the Gospel narrative that at the very hour in which the trumpet gave the signal in the Temple for the slaughter of the paschal lambs, Jesus, the true Lamb of the eternal Pasch, expired upon the cross.

Then comes the responsorial Psalm cxxxix with its eloquent interpretation of the feelings of the divine Victim of Golgotha, the desolation of his soul, the bitterness of his enemies, and his entire trust in God, who shall raise him up and fill him with joy in the glory of his countenance.

The third lesson is that of the Passion according to St. John, as is seen in the *Ordines Romani* of the ninth century. This was usually followed in early times by the homily of the principal ecclesiastic, as in the time of St Leo and St Gregory, this sermon of the bishop bringing to a close the first or catechetical part of the office—that to which the catechumens also were admitted.

After these had been dismissed, only those of the faithful who had been completely initiated into the mysteries remained in the church, and, having first exchanged the Kiss of Peace, they took part in the common intercessory prayer in the form of a litany of which we have already spoken. The text of this prayer, preserved for us in the Missal on Good Friday, is, in its origin, of great antiquity, but the present rendering can hardly go back beyond the fifth century, as its terminology and mentality distinctly bear the stamp of the Leonine age.

In the religious hierarchy the last place but two is given to the *confessores*. By this name it was not intended to denote those who had suffered for the faith without actually dying under the tortures, as was still meant in the fourth century by the same word, but according to the terminology of the Leonine Sacramentary, simply the monks, who by the austerity of their lives, without shedding their blood, made a constant sacrificial confession of the true faith.

The collect for the Roman Empire, too, is full of significance, and becomes clearer in the light of similar examples in the Leonine Sacramentary, which show how the fate of the universe seems inseparably bound up with that of the *Res*

, of the Eternal City. Tertullian also asserts that it
itomary to pray *pro mora finis*, in the belief that it was
the preservation of the *pax romana* which was delaying the
end of the world, which, were it not for the power of the
Capitol, would inevitably rush to its destruction. Some have
given the same interpretation to the obscure words addressed
by St Paul to the Thessalonians regarding the influence
which holds back Satan from triumphing completely over
Christianity.

Unlike a well-known Ambrosian prayer in which intercession is made even for those *confessores* condemned to
penal servitude *ad metalla*[1]—the true *confessores* in the
ordinary sense of the word—the Roman litany merely calls
upon the divine mercy that *aperiat carceres*. According to
the ancient Roman idea, the *carcer* was intended as a place
of detention for the accused while awaiting trial rather than
of punishment for the guilty; hence the grace here asked
for is that the prisoner, having established his innocence,
may recover his liberty, not that the prisons should be
thrown open and the malefactors let loose upon the land.

The litany being ended, it would have been more regular
if, leaving out the consecratory anaphora altogether, the
eucharistic *actio* had been resumed at the *Pater Noster*. It
would have sufficed to bring the consecrated Host to the
altar, and, having placed a particle in the chalice in accordance with the customary rite of " infusion "—which dates
from the second century at least, and of which a trace is
still existent in our private Mass—to have proceeded at
once to the Communion. The great gap occasioned by the
absence of the eucharistic anaphora would certainly have
been felt, but the regular order at least would not have
been disturbed. In the later Middle Ages, however, the
rite of the Adoration of the Cross was interpolated at this
point, with the result that the great litany of intercession
was separated from the presentation of the presanctified
oblations on the altar.

THE ADORATION OF THE CROSS

The ritual and formula for the Adoration of the True
Cross (for in those days the relic itself was the object of
devotion, and not, as is now allowed, a wooden or metal
representation of the Crucified) are of some antiquity and
are entirely Eastern in origin. They were introduced into
Rome somewhat late, as the earlier *Ordines Romani* merely
mention the verse *Ecce lignum* with the processional Psalm
cxviii *Beati immaculati in via*. In Greek the ceremony was

---

[1] *i.e.*, to the mines.—TR.

called the " Exaltation of the Holy Cross," which clearly explains the name and origin of the feast held at Jerusalem on September 13, when the *Encaenia* of the *Martyrion* was celebrated and the cross shown to the people.

The Greek and Latin *Trisagion* interposed in the singing of the *improperia*, which were partly inspired by the apochryphal book of Esdras, is ancient, so much so that the Monophysites attempted to detract from the testimony it bears to the Blessed Trinity by adding the words " Thou who wast crucified for us." This addition was condemned as being heretical, and the Roman Church purposely continued to sing the *Trisagion* during the Adoration of the Cross in order to emphasize the Trinitarian signification of the invocation, since the sacrifice of Calvary represents the highest and most perfect act of homage rendered by the High Priest of Creation to the august Three-in-One. Never did the ineffable sanctity of the Three Persons in one God and the glory of the crucified Lord shine forth more brightly than on Calvary, when the Redeemer gave up his spirit, uttering the hymn of the Resurrection—that sublime Psalm xxi, with its Alleluia of thanksgiving to the Lord.

The hymn of Venantius Fortunatus—*Lustris sex*—which is sung during the Adoration of the Cross, is taken from the Gallican use, and, although full of devotion, represents but an interpolation in the Missal of the Roman Church, in which hymnody was not admitted in the Divine Office until the late Middle Ages.

According to the *Ordines*, during the Adoration of the Cross the priests—and later the Cardinal deacons—placed on the altar the casket containing the consecrated species which had been brought from the Lateran for the Communion. At Avignon, among surroundings entirely different from those in which the stational ritual had originated, the French Popes preferred to go themselves to the chapel where the sacred species were reserved, and to carry them thence in procession to the high altar. The hymn *Vexilla regis*, which is now sung during the procession, has no connection whatever with the Blessed Sacrament, but was introduced from Avignon.

THE COMMUNION

According to the *Ordines Romani*, the sacred species having been placed on the altar—as was the usual custom at the beginning of every papal Mass—the prayer in preparation for Communion—*i.e.*, the *Pater Noster*—was said, and the Blessed Sacrament consumed. In later times, for greater reverence, the incensing both of the presanctified oblations and of the Holy Table was introduced. Then followed the Lavabo, the Elevation, and the breaking of the Host, with other prayers, which gave to this rite the appearance of a Mass.

THE PASCHAL VIGIL

The night vigil preceding the paschal solemnity may be considered as the beginning of all the night offices during the year. In the time of Tertullian, the faithful were free to attend the ordinary Sunday *Pannuchis* or not, as they chose; but no one could exempt himself, without incurring blame, from being present at the nocturnal office of Easter Eve; the more so as in some quarters the hope was not excluded that the *parousia* would take place during that very vigil. St Jerome has described how the assembly waited in expectation until midnight, and when the hour was past and Christ had not come, it was deemed that the *parousia* had been deferred yet another year, so the Easter festival was celebrated instead.

In spite of their complexity, the rites described in the Roman Missal may all be reduced to a very simple and systematic plan. First come the prayers of the *Lucernarium,* then the vigil itself, and lastly the baptism of the cate-chumens, the whole ceremony ending with the celebration of Mass.

THE PRAYERS OF THE LUCERNARIUM

The rite of the *Lucernarium,* or *Eucharistia Lucernaris,* in which the evening light kindled at the beginning of the night office was offered to God, although widely spread in the East and in use in many churches in Gaul and Italy— where we still find it at Milan—was destined after the third century to disappear entirely from the Roman Liturgy, together with the evening office, of which it was the customary prelude.

The *Lucernarium,* therefore, of the *Vigilia Paschae* described in the Missal owes its place to a belated revival after at least four centuries of oblivion, and in this case the prodigal son is hardly to be recognized in the strange garb in which he presents himself. In fact, the blessing of the fire, according to the Missal of St Pius V, of the incense and of the candle, all refer to an identical rite—that is, to the lighting of the *lucerna,* which was to illuminate the ambo during the reading of the nocturnal lessons, so that this triple benediction now represents merely three alternative formulas.

According to the text of the collects still existing in the

Missal, these prayers do not refer to the holy fire, nor to the grains of incense to be inserted in the candle, but the *novus ignis* is truly the *lumen Christi,* while the *incensum* signifies not the perfumed gum of Arabia, but rather the *nocturnus splendor* of the *lighted* candle which represents Christ the "Light of the World."

Although the words of these ceremonies may have been erroneously interpreted in later times, it cannot be denied that they embody all the deepest and most beautiful thoughts inspired by the Easter festival. The Preface especially, recited by the deacon on this occasion only, as originally it was his duty to light the *lucerna,* is so sublime in its conception as in itself to equal an entire theological treatise on the mystery of Redemption.

St Jerome, writing to a deacon of Piacenza, strongly condemns the deacons of his time, who in the Easter *praeconium* gave rein to their imagination and actually went so far as to introduce into the sacred text Vergil's verses in praise of the *apis mater* which produces the wax. The form in use in our present Missal dates undoubtedly from that epoch, but although it shows a certain youthful enthusiasm, it has a graceful dignity, and from the theological point of view only a narrow mind could misunderstand or be scandalized by the enthusiastic expressions *O felix culpa, o certe necessarium Adae peccatum,* which, however, in some places —as at Cluny, for instance—were omitted from the Sacramentary.

THE VIGIL

After the offering of the lighted candle, which was placed beside the *Lectorium* on the ambo, the vigiliary rite commenced, which at Rome consisted entirely of a series of readings in Latin and Greek, interspersed with responsories and collects. This type of night watch is much older than that of the actual nocturns given in the Breviary, which derive their origin from the monastic devotions.

At Rome the lessons were twelve in number, read both in Latin and in Greek, out of consideration for the mixed population of the city during the Byzantine period. The responsories are not taken from the Psalter, as in the Mass, but from the prophetic morning *Odes* already in use among the Jews.

In order to reconstruct the ceremony as it was in olden days, it is necessary to take into consideration the homilies of the priests and of the Pope, which were meant from the first to explain the sacred Scriptures to the people, nor must we pass over the meditations and private prayers of each person, for which the deacon gave the signal with the words

Flectamus genua. Kneeling on the ground, all prayed in silence, until after a certain space of time the leader announced *Levate,* and uniting in a single prayer the desires of the congregation—*collecta*—he offered them up together to God.

THE BAPTISM

The greater part of the night had passed thus when towards daybreak the procession of the catechumens and the higher orders of clergy " descended " to the baptistery, with the exception of the *schola,* who remained in the church with the rest of the faithful to sing the litany which habitually brought the vigil to an end.   The word "descend" is still used in the Missal, whether because it referred originally to the apostolic baptistery *ad Nimphas, ubi Petrus baptizabat,* in the Nomentano-Salarian district, or because it denoted the baptismal *piscinae* constructed by Pope Damasus in the Vatican, the level of which was much below that of the basilica where the vigil took place, and from where the procession "descended" *ad fontes.*

The blessing of the font was accompanied in Rome by the chanting of a long eucharistic prayer or thanksgiving of the same type as the one used at the consecration of the chrism mentioned above.   It is addressed to God the Father, and, after having called to mind all the types in Holy Scripture connected with water and with the rite of baptism instituted by Jesus Christ in the Jordan, it invokes the grace of the Holy Ghost (*Epiklesis*), that he may descend upon the font and sanctify the water of regeneration.   At this point in the ceremony, from about the ninth century onwards, two assistant ministers, and later the celebrant himself, dipped the paschal candle in the water before pouring therein the phial of consecrated chrism.

At Rome baptism was originally administered by immersion and infusion together, and as the water in the font did not reach above the ankles, there were fountains or jets under which the priest placed the catechumen, in order that the water should fall from the head over the whole body. Towards the thirteenth century many dioceses in Italy still retained the ancient usage of baptism by immersion, but later the present form by infusion became general.   Of this the first mention is made in the Διδαχή—at the end, that is, of the first century.

In early times Confirmation was administered at the same time as Baptism ; and the former, following on the sacrament of Christian regeneration, held, as it were, the place of the invocation of the Holy Ghost after the Consecration in the Mass, so that it came to be called *confirmatio,* which was the name given to the eucharistic epiklesis in the Mozarabic Liturgy—*confirmatio sacramenti.*

The imposition of hands by the bishop, the unction with chrism, and the signing of the cross on the forehead—*consignatio*—are thus three sacramental acts which complete each other and form a single sacrament, called by the Byzantines *Signaculum doni Sancti Spiritus.* This gift of the Paraclete is as a seal set on the sacred love which espouses the soul to God, an inward unction dedicating and consecrating it to be the temple of the most blessed Trinity.

THE MASS

These rites being finished, the procession, now accompanied by the white-robed band of neophytes, returned to the basilica, which still re-echoed with the invocations of the litany, each repeated seven, then five, and lastly three times.

The Introit was superfluous in this paschal Mass, as the congregation had been already present at least eight hours. It is also doubtful whether the *Gloria in excelsis* formed part of the original rite, although at Rome it was regarded as being the true paschal hymn. It can hardly have held at first the place now given to it in the vigiliary Easter Mass, as even the two existing lessons from the Epistle of St Paul and from the Gospel of St Matthew, with the announcement of the Resurrection, are an unnecessary addition to the preceding vigiliary office. The Easter Mass, like the Mass for the *Coena Domini,* should have commenced directly with the Preface *Sursum corda.*

During the later Middle Ages, when the night office of the paschal vigil was held in the afternoon of the Saturday, another short office was added to this Easter Mass, which took the place of the Vespers of Holy Saturday. The Roman Liturgy held out as long as possible against this innovation, which takes no heed of the anachronism it creates by commemorating the sorrowful ending of Holy Saturday after having already several hours previously by the mouth of the deacon joyfully saluted the dawn of the Sunday of the Resurrection.

THE SACRED LITURGY
FROM SEPTUAGESIMA TO EASTER

SEPTUAGESIMA SUNDAY

Station at St Lawrence Without the Walls.

THE Eastern usage regarded Saturday and Sunday as festival days, and therefore as exempt from the Lenten fast; so, in order to complete the forty days of Lent, the Greeks anticipated the penitential season by some weeks, and from this Sunday onward abstained from the use of meat. In the following week they abstained also from milk and similar foods, and finally on the Monday of Quinquagesima they commenced the rigid fast in preparation for Easter.

Among the Latins the custom varied at different times. By beginning the Lenten cycle with the First Sunday in Lent, there remain indeed, as St Gregory remarks, forty days of preparation for Easter, but of these only thirty-six are devoted to fasting. In order to supply the four missing days, pious persons and ecclesiastics began, in quite early times, to abstain from meat on the Monday after Quinquagesima (*In carnis privio* or *in carne levario* = Carnival); but it is not until the time of St Gregory that we find in the antiphonary the liturgical consecration of the *caput jejunii* on the Wednesday of Quinquagesima.

The piety of the more devout, however, was not satisfied by these four supplementary days. The Greeks began earlier, and, living as they did beside them in Rome during the Byzantine period, the Latins could do no less. St Gregory therefore instituted, or at least gave definite form to, a cycle of three weeks' preparation for Lent, with three solemn stations at the patriarchal Basilicas of St Lawrence, St Paul, and St Peter, as though to begin the Easter fast under the auspices of the three great patrons of the Eternal City.

The order of the stational cycle has been reversed, and begins on this day with the station at St Lawrence, which holds the fourth place only among the papal basilicas, the reason for this change being that it was not considered advisable to remove the first Lenten station from the Lateran, where ever since the fourth century the Popes had been in the habit of offering the *sacrificium quadragesimalis initii*, as the Sacramentary calls it.

It would seem that the three Masses of Septuagesima, Sexagesima, and Quinquagesima date from the time of St Gregory, since they reflect the terror and grief that filled the minds of the Romans in those years during which war, pestilence, and earthquake threatened the utter destruction of the former mistress of the world.

The Introit is taken from Psalm xvii: "The groans of death surrounded me, the sorrows of hell encompassed me: and in my affliction I called upon the Lord, and he heard my voice from his holy temple."

From this Sunday until Maundy Thursday the *Gloria in Excelsis* is omitted in Masses *de tempore*. Originally it was sung only at Christmas and Easter, but later it came to be used on all Sundays, except those in Lent, and also on the feasts of martyrs, but only by special privilege. The collect, which immediately follows the litany on days of fasting and penance, truly represents, therefore, the ordinary and normal form of the litany as used in the ancient liturgy of the Mass and of the divine office.

The collect betrays the deep affliction which weighed on the soul of St Gregory at the sight of the desolation of Rome and of all Italy during his pontificate. "O Lord, we beseech thee, graciously hear the prayers of thy people; that we who are justly afflicted for our sins may for the glory of thy name be mercifully delivered."

The Epistle is from 1 Cor. ix 24-27 and x 1-5. It may be a mere coincidence, or it may be by intent, that after the long pilgrimage by the faithful to that extra-mural station in the Campus Veranus, for which some other basilica within the city was sometimes substituted in the Middle Ages, on account of the distance, this epistle was chosen, in which the Christian is compared to the athlete, who by his endurance and agility wins a crown in the contests of the stadium.

In concluding, the Apostle tells us that we are not saved merely because we are counted among the followers of Christ or of Moses. The Israelites all received those same gifts—the miraculous bread, the water bursting from the rock, the safe passage of the Red Sea, etc.—which were symbols of the sacraments of the New Covenant; yet out of so vast a multitude only two entered the Promised Land. It is not, therefore, the caste to which we belong which gains for us the favour of God, but our own good works, our struggle against evil, our courage, and our constancy in doing that which is right.

The Gradual comes from Psalm ix: "Thou art a helper in due time in tribulation: let them trust in thee, who know thee: for thou dost not forsake them that seek thee, O Lord.

For the poor man shall not be forgotten to the end: the patience of the poor shall not perish for ever: arise, O Lord, let not man prevail."

Instead of the alleluiatic verse, which, perhaps, was originally only an exclamation of praise after the Gospel, and therefore distinct from the psalmody, or after the second New Testament lesson, we have to-day the *psalmus tractus*. This in early times, before St Gregory had extended the use of the *Alleluia* to all Sundays except those in Lent, formed part of the psalmody of every festival office. Psalm cxxix: " From the depths I have cried to thee, O Lord: Lord, hear my voice. Let thine ears be attentive to the prayer of thy servant. If thou shalt observe iniquities, O Lord, Lord, who shall abide it? For with thee there is propitiation, and because of thy law I have waited for thee, O Lord."

The Gospel parable (Matt. xx 1-16) of the householder who went out to hire labourers into his vineyard, has reference to the calling of the Gentiles. These have been brought in at the eleventh hour of the history of humanity, but by the inscrutable decree of divine mercy, have received the same abundant reward, neither more nor less, as the patriarchs and prophets of the third, sixth, and ninth hours. St Gregory, when expounding this parable to the people assembled in the Basilica of St Lawrence, touched upon the deep mystery of the gratuitous bestowal of grace, to which God alone holds the clue. In this connection, the holy Pontiff spoke of three of his aunts who had all consecrated themselves to God with equal fervour, and of whom two, Tersilla and Emiliana, persevered and are venerated as saints, while the third, Gordiana, broke her vows and ended miserably.

The Offertory is from Psalm xci: " It is good to give praise to the Lord, and to sing to thy name, O most High."

The Secret is the same as that of the Octave of the Nativity, and bears a general application.

The Communion is derived from Psalm xxx: " Make thy face to shine upon thy servant, and save me in thy mercy: let me not be confounded, O Lord, for I have called upon thee."

The Post-Communion is as follows: " May thy faithful, O God, be strengthened by thy gifts, that by partaking of them they may still continue to seek after them, and by seeking them constantly partake of them."

How great is the uncertainty of eternal salvation! *Cum metu et tremore vestram salutem operamini,* as the Apostle says (Phil. ii 12); this is the fruit of to-day's meditation on the Epistle of St Paul and on the parable of the vineyard.

How many and how striking were the miracles worked by almighty God during the forty years that Israel wandered in the desert! The heavenly food, the miraculous water, the cloud and the column of fire, the Red Sea and the Jordan parting before them; and yet out of the many thousands for whom these wonders were worked, the greater number fell away, and only two reached the final goal.

Thus, it is not enough for us to have been baptized, to have been called by God to a holy state, to the dignity of the priesthood, to have become the object of his special predilection by the frequent opportunities he has given us of receiving the holy sacraments and of hearing his gracious word. It is necessary to labour diligently—*operamini*—to follow the narrow way that leads to life eternal; it is necessary to imitate the chosen few—that is, the saints—in order to be saved together with them. Never can we apprehend these divine truths with greater clearness than when we meditate upon them, as in to-day's station, beside the tombs of the martyrs, who, in order to gain their heavenly reward, were ready to sacrifice wealth, youth, and even life itself.

SEXAGESIMA SUNDAY

Station at St Paul.

The rigour of winter is nearly over, and the milder air of a springlike morning seems to invite the fortunate dwellers *urbis aeternae gentemque togatam,* to take a walk under the colonnade which leads almost from the centre of Rome to the Basilica of St Paul. The Lenten fast, of course, has not yet begun. To-day's Mass, therefore, combines a melancholy strain of penitence with notes of rejoicing in honour of the Apostle of the Gentiles. The first incentive to the choice of this station may have been given by the enigmatical *Translatio sancti Pauli,* found in the martyrology of St Jerome under January 25, of which Rome keeps the last trace in to-day's synaxis.

There was a marked tendency in Rome towards the seventh century to postpone local feasts of minor importance which fell on a weekday until the following Sunday; and it is also to be observed that in various ancient Eastern and Gallican Liturgies a feast of greater or lesser importance in honour of the holy Apostles Peter and Paul is always to be found at the Christmas season, either during the days immediately following the Nativity or during the month of January.

The choice of St Paul's for to-day's station is also necessitated by the order prescribed in honouring before Lent the titular saints of the great Roman patriarchal basilicas. First comes Lawrence the cross-bearer, then follow Peter and Paul, and last of all the divine Redeemer himself.

The Introit is solemn and sad, in keeping with the time of the institution of this station, in the days when the Lombards were carrying fire and sword throughout Italy, and were already threatening the Eternal City itself. It comes from Psalm xliii : " Arise, why sleepest thou, O Lord? arise and cast us not off to the end. Why turnest thou thy face away, and forgettest our trouble? our belly hath cleaved to the earth. Arise, O Lord, help us and deliver us."

The Collect, which is one of the many collects contained in the Sacramentaries for times of calamity, has an addition in honour of the Apostle whose memory may be said to pervade and to give a special character to this Mass : " O God, who seest that we put not our trust in anything that we do of ourselves; mercifully grant that by the protection of the Doctor of the Gentiles we may be defended against all adversities."

The passage which follows from St Paul's Epistles (2 Cor. xi 19-33; xii 1-9) is almost an autobiography of the Apostle; all the more valuable in that it partly fills in the gaps in the Acts, and describes for us vividly the incredible trials endured by St Paul in his apostolate among the Gentiles. These our Lord had foretold to him in the early days of his conversion on the road to Damascus, saying to Ananias : " I will show him how great things he must suffer for my name's sake."[1] This is a law in the kingdom of grace, which in the present order of divine Providence admits of no exception. Suffering is the supernatural atmosphere in which every Christian must live, baptized as he is into the death of Christ.

In to-day's Epistle the Apostle is obliged to defend himself against that powerful Judaizing party which was desirous of subjecting the Churches of the Gentiles to the rites of Israel. The Corinthians regarded these teachers—direct descendants of Abraham—as supermen beside Paul, who, on account of his plain and simple speech, was looked upon by them as a mere nonentity. St Paul accepts this position, and, in contrast to the proud titles of his opponents, sets forth his own as confirmatory of his apostolic mission : " They are Hebrews; so am I. They are Israelites; so am I. They are the seed of Abraham; so am I. They are the ministers of Christ (I speak as one less wise); I am more."

Then he goes on to point out how heavily the service of Christ weighs upon his shoulders, already bowed down by

[1] Acts ix 16.

the labours, the persecutions, the scourgings endured for the faith, and by the solicitude he bears amongst so many sufferings for the government of the Church of the West. And what of his visions, of the rapture which bore him even to the third heaven, and revealed to him things which the tongue of man may not utter? Of these gifts he makes but small account, prizing rather the tribulations and sorrows which show forth the power of God's grace in making perfect his temple on the ruins of the *superbia vitae*.

The Gradual is part of Psalm lxxxii, and is like a mighty cry of defiance against the enemies of the people of God: " Let the Gentiles know that God is thy name : thou alone art the Most High over all the earth. O my God, make them like a wheel, and as stubble before the face of the wind."

The Tract is derived from Psalm lix, and is inspired by the same feeling : " Thou hast moved the earth, O Lord, and hast troubled it. Heal thou the breaches thereof, for it has been moved. That thy elect may flee from before the bow; that they may be delivered."

The parable of the sower (Luke viii, 4-15) is aptly chosen by the Church for this feast of the Apostle Paul, who scattered the seed of the good tidings from Damascus and Arabia in the East even unto the Pillars of Hercules in the West. As then, so now, his word which we hear every day at Mass does not bear everywhere the same fruit, for shallowness of mind, excessive love of worldly things, and the hardness of a heart voluntarily closed to the promptings of grace often render profitless the labour of the sower. The wayside, the stony soil, the thorns, represent the many obstacles which hinder the successful working of the word of God in the human soul.

St Gregory likewise commented upon this parable to the Roman people who were gathered together on this day at the tomb of St Paul. Even down to the late Middle Ages, the Romans continued to attend this station in great numbers, and we are told that St Frances of Rome once chose one of these occasions of popular assembly in order to mingle with the crowd of beggars who asked alms on this day at the doors of the Ostian Basilica.

The Offertory is taken from Psalm xvi : " Perfect thou my goings in thy paths, that my footsteps be not moved : incline thy ear, and hear my words : show forth thy wonderful mercies, thou who savest them that trust in thee, O Lord."

The Secret, of a general character, is the same as that for the Sunday within the Octave of the Epiphany.

The Communion is from Psalm xlii : " I will go in to the altar of God : to God who giveth joy to my youth."

The Post-Communion is as follows : " We humbly beseech

thee, almighty God, that thou wouldst grant that those whom thou refreshest with thy sacraments may serve thee worthily by a life well pleasing to thee."

Many are the evils that threaten our eternal salvation, in the midst of the world. The good seed falls, indeed, on the highway, and not only is it in danger of being trodden under foot by wayfarers, devoured by birds, or choked by thorns, but, as our Lord clearly warns us, the devil comes and takes the word of God from our hearts, lest believing we should be saved.

In a work of such importance, on which our eternal happiness depends, no preparation can be too great, and each one of us should resolve at the foot of the altar to make use, as St Peter would have us do, of every means to ensure our final salvation. It was this thought taken seriously into consideration which gave rise to so many thousands of monasteries in days of old, and which drew to the cloister so great a number of the faithful of both sexes and of all ages and conditions. What shall it profit us to gain the whole world, if by so doing we imperil our own soul?

QUINQUAGESIMA SUNDAY

Station at St Peter.

This solemn assembly at the *confessio* of the Vatican brings to a close the Triduum in preparation for the great solemnity of the coming fast. Having assured ourselves of the patronage of St Lawrence, St Paul, and St Peter, we shall be ready with full confidence to commence next Sunday at the Lateran Basilica the holy cycle of penance. In imitation of the Greeks, all religious communities and the more devout amongst the laity began, in early times, to abstain from meat from this week onwards. The Church has adopted this use to a certain extent by beginning Lent on the following Feria IV (Ash Wednesday).

The Introit is taken from Psalm xxx : " Be thou unto me a God, a protector, and a place of refuge, to save me; for thou art my strength and my refuge : and for thy name's sake thou wilt lead me, and nourish me."

Sin is the cause of all human misery; wherefore in the Collect the Church prays that, the bonds of sin being loosed, we may be preserved from all adversity.

St Paul, who, in the lesson read last Sunday, told us how he had been rapt even to the third heaven and had heard secret words, which it is not granted to man to utter, in the sublime words of to-day's Epistle (1 Cor. xiii 1-13) attempts to raise a corner of the veil which hides the Eternal Love from the eyes of mortals. God is the primary and immediate object of the precept of charity, as he is the final end to which the creature tends. Nevertheless, the Apostle dwells rather upon his illuminative intercourse with men, in so far as they are created in his likeness and are the mystical members of Christ; for it is not possible for anyone easily to persuade himself into thinking that he loves the invisible God, if at the same time he does not love him through those creatures who visibly represent him on earth.

The Gradual is taken from Psalm lxxvi. It is less subdued than those of the two preceding stations, for here the soul already foresees that her hope in the help of the Lord will be crowned with victory. " Thou art the God that alone dost wonders : thou hast made thy power known among the nations. With thy arm thou hast delivered thy people, the children of Israel and of Joseph."

The Tract is a beautiful hymn of thanksgiving to God for his divine attributes of Father and Shepherd of his people : " Sing joyfully to God, all the earth : serve ye the Lord with gladness. Come in before his presence with exceeding great joy : know ye that the Lord he is God. He made us, and not we ourselves : but we are his people, and the sheep of his pasture."

The Gospel (Luke xviii 31-43) gives us the definite announcement of the approaching Sacrifice. Our Lord is proceeding towards the city whose sad prerogative it was to be the place where the Prophets should be slain—*Non capit prophetam perire extra Jerusalem*—and when Peter in his impetuous affection tries to restrain the Redeemer from exposing himself to such a danger, our Lord repulses him, and, addressing him as Satan, assures him that he who despises the cross has no knowledge of things divine. The miracle of the blind man of Jericho confirms the wavering faith of the disciples, showing them that though the human nature of Christ was to be voluntarily surrendered to the violence of his enemies, yet his divine nature which worked all these wonders would raise his human body again after three days, incorrupt and glorious.

In the Offertory, which is from Psalm cxviii, the psalmist praises God for having given him grace to testify to him boldly before the great ones of the earth and before the unbelievers, and begs him to continue to enlighten him as to his commandments.

The Secret is the same as that of the Third Sunday after the Epiphany.

The Communion is derived from Psalm lxxvii, and in its literal sense alludes to the food (the quails) with which the Israelites were miraculously fed in the desert; but it is also applicable to the Holy Eucharist, of which those wonders of the Old Covenant were prophetic figures. " They did eat and were filled exceedingly, and the Lord gave them their desire : they were not defrauded of that which they craved."

In the Post-Communion we pray that the heavenly food of which we have partaken may protect us against all adversities.

The mystery of the cross is so difficult for the mind of man to understand that even the Apostles, who had studied for three years in the school of Christ, had not yet penetrated it. They did not understand it now as they journeyed to Jerusalem, nor yet on the evening of the paschal feast, at which they were consecrated the Pontiffs of the New Testament. One short hour later, *omnes, relicto eo, fugerunt,* leaving Jesus to go up to Calvary alone. How necessary, then, is it for us to meditate upon Christ crucified, lest we should fail in a matter of the highest moment, towards which the whole of our spiritual life should be directed—that is, the mystery of expiation through suffering.

The Gregorian antiphonary contains the proper chants only of the Masses of Wednesday and Friday of Quinquagesima, whilst on the Thursday and Saturday, even to this day, the melodies belonging to other Masses are repeated. This anomaly is, perhaps, to be accounted for by the fact that the weekday stations of Ferias IV and VI were observed even as early as the second century in Africa and in Rome. The anticipated Lenten fasts of the last four days of Quinquagesima week could easily be added to the two stational fasts without greatly disturbing the order of the antiphonary. Lent had its clearly established daily stations, but for these supplementary and, at first, merely voluntary fasts the two traditional Masses, which even from the time of the Apostles had sanctified the weekly fast on each Wednesday and Friday throughout the year, might well suffice.

ASH WEDNESDAY

This day, which from the time of St Gregory has inaugurated at Rome the forty holy days of Lent, was also called *in capite jejunii.* In the fourth century it marked the beginning of the canonical penance which public penitents had to undergo in order to be absolved on Maundy Thursday.

According to the rituals of the seventh century, the penitents presented themselves on the morning of this day before the appointed priests at the various titular churches and at the patriarchal basilicas. Having confessed their sins, they received—in cases of grave and notorious transgressions—from the hand of the penitentiary a garment of rough hair-cloth sprinkled with ashes. They were then ordered to withdraw to some monastery, of which there were about a hundred in the city of Rome, and there to do penance for forty days. This is the origin of the quarantines which we find in ancient forms of indulgences.

Our Missal of to-day still keeps, in the rite of the blessing of the ashes, a last trace of the ceremony of the imposition of canonical penance on public penitents. In early days a high conception of the special sanctity of the sacerdotal state excluded priests from this category. It was only towards the eleventh century that, the disciplinary rule of public penance being done away with, instead of the penitents of former days, the Pope, the clergy, and the Roman people took part indiscriminately in this function, and began to walk barefoot, with ashes sprinkled on their heads, to the Basilica of St Sabina.

In the ninth century the imposition of the ashes was still a separate penitential ceremony, and was not in any way connected with the eucharistic station. Towards the seventh hour—at the time, that is, when the Roman ended his day's work and went to bathe at the Thermae, getting ready later for his *coena*, which was the principal meal of the day—the people, headed by the Pope and the clergy, assembled at the Church of St Anastasia in the narrow valley between the Palatine and the Aventine, and from there went in procession, singing the Litany, to St Sabina. On arriving there the eucharistic sacrifice was offered, the Introit being omitted, as it had already been sung during the *collecta* at St Anastasia, and after the last blessing, at the invitation of the deacon—*ite, missa est*—the people returned to their homes and broke their fast.

This rite was very much more developed in the twelfth century, as we see in the *Ordo Romanus* of the Canon Benedict. The Pope first distributed the ashes at St Anastasia; then the procession, barefooted and in penitential garments, ascended the gentle slope of the Aventine to the Basilica of St Sabina, where Mass was celebrated. Before the Communion one of the regionary subdeacons announced to the people, *Crastina die veniente, statio erit in ecclesia sancti Georgii Martyris ad velum aureum*, and all replied, *Deo gratias*.

Collecta, or Assembly, at St Anastasia.

This is the real meaning of the word *collecta*, which is noted regularly in the ancient *Ordines Romani* for each day in Lent.

The Introit, with the antiphon, is from Psalm lxviii: "Hear us, O Lord, for thy mercy is kind: look upon us, O Lord, according to the multitude of thy tender mercies."

Then follow these four prayers :

"Almighty and eternal God, spare those who are penitent, be merciful to those who implore thee, and vouchsafe to send thy holy angel from heaven, to bless and hallow these ashes, that they may be a wholesome remedy to all who humbly implore thy holy name, and, conscious of their sins, accuse themselves, deploring their crimes before thy divine clemency, or humbly and earnestly beseeching thy bountiful loving-kindness; and grant through the invocation of thy most holy name, that whoever shall be sprinkled with them, for the remission of their sins, may receive both health of body and safety of soul."

"O God, who desirest not the death, but the repentance of sinners, favourably look down upon the frailty of human nature, and in thy mercy vouchsafe to bless these ashes, which we purpose to put upon our heads in token of our humility, and to obtain forgiveness; that we who know that we are but ashes, and for the punishment of our wickedness must return to dust, may deserve to obtain of thy mercy the pardon of all our sins, and the rewards promised to the penitent."

"O God, who art moved by humiliation and appeased by satisfaction, incline the ear of thy clemency to our prayers, and mercifully pour forth upon the heads of thy servants, sprinkled with these ashes, the grace of thy blessing; that thou mayest both fill them with the spirit of compunction, and effectually grant those things which they have justly prayed for; and ordain that what thou hast granted may be established and remain unmoved for ever."

"Almighty and eternal God, who didst grant the remedy of thy pardon to the Ninevites doing penance in ashes and sackcloth, mercifully grant that we may so imitate their penance, that we may follow them in obtaining forgiveness."

These prayers are not to be found in the old Roman Sacramentaries, from which it may be concluded that they were introduced into the Missal at a later date from the Frankish liturgies.

In accordance with a medieval tradition, the ashes are formed from the branches of olive blessed on the preceding

Palm Sunday. The priest, having recited the prayers over them, sprinkles them with holy water and incenses them; then he signs the people with them on the forehead, saying : " Remember, man, that thou art dust, and unto dust thou shalt return."[1]

During the distribution of the ashes, the *schola* sings the following antiphons and responsories taken from the Lenten night office :

(*a*) " Let us change our garments for ashes and sackcloth : let us fast and lament before the Lord : for our God is plenteous in mercy to forgive our sins.

(*b*) " Between the porch and the altar the priests, the Lord's ministers, shall weep and shall say, Spare, O Lord, spare thy people : and shut not the mouths of them that sing to thee, O Lord.

(*c*) " Let us amend for the better in those things in which we have sinned through ignorance : lest suddenly overtaken by the day of death, we seek space for penance and are not able to find it.

" ℟. Hear, O Lord, and have mercy : for we have sinned against thee.

" ℣. Help us, O God, our Saviour : and for the honour of thy name, O Lord, deliver us. Attend, O Lord.

" ℣. Glory be to the Father, to the Son, and to the Holy Ghost. Attend."

Having administered the ashes, the priest recites the following prayer :

" Grant us, O Lord, to begin our Christian warfare with holy fasts, that as we are about to fight against the spirits of wickedness, we may be defended by the aids of self-denial. Through Christ our Lord."

In the *Ordines Romani* of the later Middle Ages, it is prescribed that after the general imposition of ashes on the heads of the clergy and people, all shall go in procession barefoot up the Aventine Hill to St Sabina, in the *atrium* of which there was in those days a small cemetery. In such a place those tombs at once recalled the thought of death, and therefore the *schola* sang the funeral responsory: *Immutemur habitu . . . ne subito preoccupati die mortis . . .* still preserved in the Missal. The procession then stopped for a few moments while the Pope repeated an absolution over the tombs, and then entered the great Aventine Basilica, singing the responsory : *Petre, amas me?* with the verse *Simon Joannis . . .* in honour of the Prince of the Apostles.

[1] Gen. iii 19.

The commemoration of St Peter at this part of the ceremony seems strange, but this may be a papal custom derived
from the Vatican Basilica whenever it was entered processionally across the courtyard which was used as a place of
burial; or it may have arisen from the circumstance that in
the thirteenth century the Pope resided at St Sabina, and the
basilica was therefore considered as being the habitual seat
of the successor of St Peter.

Station at St Sabina.

This basilica was founded or rebuilt under Celestine I
(423-32) by an Illyrian priest of the name of Peter, but there
must have also contributed to its erection a certain Sabina
of that time, as the church was known by this name even
before the relics of the martyred St Sabina were brought
thither from the *area Vindiciani.*

Gregory the Great instituted there his famous *septiformis*
litany of penance, and in the Middle Ages the dwelling
adjoining the basilica was often occupied by the Pontiff.
Pope Silverius (536-38) was living there when he was exiled
from Rome by Belisarius. Honorius III (Savelli, 1216-17)
fortified it with walls and towers still existing in part, and
at the death of Honorius IV (1285-87) the Cardinals met
there in a conclave which lasted about a year. After that
time, the importance of the papal residence on the Aventine
gradually lessened, until the ancient fortified palace became
finally the peaceful retreat of the Friars Preachers, who to
this day reverently show to visitors the cells sanctified by
having been the abodes of St Dominic and St Pius V. Under
the high altar, beside the bones of St Sabina and St Serapia,
lie the bodies of the martyrs of Ficulea on the Via Nomentana, Alexander, Eventius, and Theodulus.

The Introit of the Mass is from the book of Wisdom
(xi 24-25), and declares that no sinner, however vile, is ever
shut out from the divine mercy, which looks not so much at
the sin, which is man's handiwork, as at the creature, who
is the masterpiece of God. "Thou hast mercy upon all,
O Lord, and hatest none of the things which thou hast
made, overlooking the sins of men for the sake of repentance,
and sparing them, for thou art the Lord, our God."

The following prayer consecrates the beginning of the
fast: "Grant to thy faithful, O Lord, that they may begin
the venerable solemnities of fasting with suitable piety, and
perform them with tranquil devotion."

Then follow two other collects of some antiquity and of
deep theological meaning, especially the second, which touches

upon the profound mystery of predestination. The first of these two prayers implores the intercession of the saints : " Defend us, we beseech thee, O Lord, from all dangers of mind and body ; and by the intercession of the blessed and glorious Mary ever Virgin, Mother of God, of blessed Joseph, with thy blessed Apostles Peter and Paul, and blessed N. and all the saints, mercifully grant us safety and peace ; that all adversities and errors being destroyed, thy Church may serve thee with secure liberty."

The second prayer is for the special necessities of all Christians, and in the MSS. is often attributed to St Augustine : "O almighty and eternal God, who hast dominion over the living and the dead, and art merciful to all whom thou foreknowest shall be thine by faith and good works ; we humbly beseech thee that they for whom we have determined to offer up our prayers, whether the present world still detains them in the flesh, or the future has already received them out of the body, may by the intercession of all thy saints, and the clemency of thy pity, obtain the pardon of all their sins."

The fruit of this first day of fasting is the spirit of inward contrition and of a true return to God, outward signs of penitence being useless unless the heart has resolutely renounced sin. This is what the Lesson from Joel (ii 12-19) teaches us. The Jews used to rend their garments, tear their hair, and sprinkle dust on their heads in sign of mourning and grief ; but this is not what God demands when he sends chastisements upon his people. By depriving them suddenly of those temporal blessings by the abuse of which they were becoming still more hardened in sin, he desires to call them to a complete change of life.

The Gradual is taken from Psalm lvi : " Have mercy on me, O God, have mercy on me ; for my soul trusteth in thee. He hath sent from heaven, and delivered me ; he hath made them a reproach that trod upon me."

As a general rule the daily Masses had no Tract. The one given for this day in the Missal, which will be repeated three times a week during Lent, is of a later and irregular composition, for it consists of fragments of verses from various psalms. It appears to have been introduced into the Liturgy by Pope Hadrian I (772-95), who ordered it to be recited by desire of Charlemagne.[1] Psalm cii : " O Lord, repay us not according to the sins we have committed, nor according to our iniquities." Psalm lxxviii : " O Lord, remember not our former iniquities : let thy mercies speedily prevent us, for we are become exceeding poor."

Here all kneel.

[1] Cf. *Ord. Rom. I*, *P.L.* LXXVIII, col. 949.

"Help us, O God our Saviour: and for the glory of thy name, O Lord, deliver us: and forgive us our sins for thy name's sake."

The Gospel follows from Matt. vi 16-21, in which our Saviour himself teaches us how to render our fast meritorious. A humble sincerity of heart, a holy cheerfulness of spirit, and the avoidance of vain ostentation, these are the essential qualities of Christian penitence. Our Lord also exhorts us to gather up treasures for eternal life rather than those which can be taken from us. For to toil day and night and suffer hardships in order to amass riches; to live in constant fear lest they should be stolen from us by thieves, to be tormented by the thought of having one day to abandon them for ever, is not all this thankless toil, and in the words of Ecclesiastes, nothing but *vanitas et afflictio spiritus?*

The Offertory is from Psalm xxix: "I will extol thee, O Lord, for thou hast upheld me; and hast not made my enemies to rejoice over me; O Lord, I have cried to thee, and thou hast healed me."

In the Secret we ask God to give us the right disposition in which to offer to him the solemn Sacrifice that inaugurates the paschal season. For in the ancient liturgical terminology Easter commenced on Maundy Thursday with the *Coena Domini,* hence a particularly suitable phrase describes the Sacrifice of this first day of Lent as the opening rite of the paschal cycle—*Ipsius venerabilis sacramenti celebramus exordium.*

The following collects are added to the Secret:

To obtain the intercession of the saints: "Graciously hear us, O God our Saviour, and by virtue of this sacrament defend us from all enemies of mind and body, bestowing upon us grace now, and glory hereafter."

For the living and the dead: "O God, who alone knowest the number of the elect who are to enjoy the happiness of heaven, grant, we beseech thee, that by the intercession of all the saints the names of all those who have been commended to our prayers and of all the faithful may be kept in the book of blessed predestination."

This last prayer, which found its way into the Roman Missal through the Frankish liturgies, is a precious memorial of the *oratio post nomina,* or the prayer of the priest which ended the reading of the diptychs before the Canon, in Gaul and in some parts of Italy. It is well known that in ancient times the names of those making offerings, of the bishops, and of distinguished personages who had a special claim on the prayers of each church, were inscribed on the diptychs, which were read aloud by the deacon after the Offertory, so that the eucharistic Canon suffered no interruption thereby.

The present Roman usage, though an innovation, dates from the time of Innocent I (402-17), who, writing to Bishop Decentius of Gubbio concerning it, maintains its legitimacy to the rigid exclusion of any other. Yet, notwithstanding the protests of the Pontiff against the supposed liturgical innovation of the Church of Gubbio, it is permissible to doubt whether it was not Rome herself who had changed the order of her diptychs.

The Communion is from Psalm i, that beautiful poem which forms, as it were, the introduction to the entire Psalter : " He who shall meditate upon the law of the Lord day and night, shall bring forth his fruit in due season." The Psalmist says " in due season " because Lent is the time in which we sow the seed of fasts and of penance, but Easter is the season when we shall reap the fruit and shall be initiated into the mysteries of spiritual union with God.

The series of antiphons *ad Communionem,* for the weekday Masses of Lent, is taken from the Psalter in consecutive order, and forms a cycle in itself. The exceptions are very rare and are later additions. Cagin, who has studied the question carefully, has come to the conclusion that the two Masses of Ferias IV and VI of Quinquagesima, with the antiphons *ad Communionem* drawn from Psalms i and ii, belong really to the primitive Gregorian cycle of Lenten Masses.

In the Post-Communion we pray that the divine sacrament may so strengthen us that our fasts may be pleasing to God and a healing remedy to ourselves.

Here follow two collects :

The one to beg the prayers of the saints : " May the gift of this divine sacrament which we have offered cleanse and defend us, we beseech thee, O Lord, and by the intercession of the blessed Virgin Mary, Mother of God, of blessed Joseph, with thy holy Apostles Peter and Paul and blessed N., and all the saints, purify us from all sins, and deliver us from all adversities."

The other for the living and the dead : " May the mysteries which we have received purify us, we beseech thee, O almighty and merciful God : and by the intercession of all thy saints grant that this thy sacrament may not be to us a means of condemnation, but of pardon and salvation ; may it be the washing away of sins, the strength of the weak, protection against all the dangers of the world, and remission of all the sins of the faithful, living and dead."

It was a very ancient rite in all liturgies, including those of the East, to recite at the end of each synaxis special forms of blessing upon the catechumens, the penitents, the faithful, the virgins, etc., before dismissing them. Often, as at Jerusalem, these invocations were accompanied by the imposition of the hands of the bishop, so that, as St Augustine says, the three expressions—benediction, *oratio super homines,* and imposition of the priest's hands—became synonymous terms. In the Roman sacramentaries this last collect is called *ad complendum,* and the preceding invitation of the deacon, *Humiliate capita vestra Deo,* recalls its primitive euchological meaning.

In the Roman Liturgy these forms of dismissal *ad complendum* have been preserved only in the weekdays of Lent, for on account of their solemn and episcopal character they were easily omitted by the *amanuenses* in private synaxes, and every time that there was no station, when a single formula sufficed, which the priest knew by heart and repeated daily. From the same cause we have lost the different *Missae* or prayers with which the penitents, catechumens, and those possessed of devils were formerly dismissed at Matins and at the Offertory.

We have already mentioned elsewhere how much the people held to these blessings; so much so that when Pope Vigilius (538-55) was dragged from the altar of St Cecilia whilst he was celebrating the Christmas station at the martyr's basilica in Trastevere, the populace rose up and demanded that the boat which was to convey the prisoner to Ostia and carry him thence into exile at Constantinople should not depart until he had recited the collect *ad complendum,* leaving in this way his benediction to the people of Rome.

The actual blessing now given to the faithful after the form of dismissal represents a later phase. It is derived from the circumstance that when the Pope returned to the *secretarium* from the altar the bishops, clergy, monks, etc., prostrated themselves before him, begging his blessing, and he, making the sign of the cross, replied: *Dominus nos benedicat.*

The form of prayer *ad complendum* for to-day is full of significance: "Turn, O Lord, the ear of thy mercy to thy people who lie prostrate before thy majesty; that we who have been refreshed by the divine gift may ever be sustained by heavenly aids."

℣. Let us bless the Lord.

℟. Thanks be to God.

THURSDAY AFTER ASH ,WEDNESDAY

Collecta at St Nicholas in Carcere.   Station at St George in Velabro.

The Basilica of St Nicholas stands in the ancient *forum olitorium* near the theatre of Marcellus, and, owing to its central position, became very celebrated in the Middle Ages, and was raised to the status of a deaconry.

The station at St George's was instituted by St Gregory II (715-31), when the *cultus* of the great Cappadocian martyr had become exceedingly popular in Rome. A titular church already existed here in 482, as an inscription of that date mentions an *Augustus lector de Belabru,* but the dedication to St George was certainly of later date.

To-day's Gospel, telling of the Centurion of Capharnaum, alludes to the military character ascribed by tradition to St George, which caused him to be specially invoked during the Middle Ages as the armed champion of the Christian family.

The Introit is taken from Psalm liv : " When I cried to the Lord, he heard my voice from them that draw near to me, and he humbled them, who is before all ages, and remains for ever : cast thy care upon the Lord, and he shall sustain thee."

The Collect implores almighty God, who by sin is offended, and by penance pacified, to receive favourably the prayers of his suppliant people, and to turn away the scourges of his wrath, which they have deserved by their sins.

The present Mass, composed in the time of Gregory II, is a mere collection of chants and lessons taken from other offices and adapted as we see it to-day. The scene from Isaias (xxxviii 1-6), in which the prophet warns King Ezechias of his approaching death, was very popular in ancient times, and we find it reproduced also in painting, in the neighbouring Basilica of *Sancta Maria Antiqua* in the Forum Romanum. As it in no wise relates to St George, we may suppose that it contains some allusion to Pope Gregory II, who, having miraculously recovered from a dangerous illness, but ever dreading the approach of the Lombards, is said to have instituted the stations of the Thursdays in Lent, comparing himself at the same time with Ezechias, who was struck down by a mortal sickness at the very moment in which the Assyrian army was surrounding Jerusalem.

It is in any case certain that when, about the thirtieth year of the eighth century, these words were read at Rome—" I will deliver thee and this city out of the hand of the King of the Assyrians and I will protect it "—the thoughts of the people must have turned to Luitprand and his *nefandissima gens langobardorum,* as the Romans called the barbarian foe which was laying siege to the capital of the world.

At the announcement of the nearness of death, Ezechias, although a just and devout man, wept, for the violence of death is a penalty against which human nature rebels. He wept, too, because none may dare to appear before the judgement-seat of almighty God unless he be truly penitent. God heard his prayer, and granted him a reprieve of three lustres, not indeed that this present life is a better gift than life immortal, but because the years of this earthly pilgrimage afford us time in which to sow the seed of life eternal, the fruit of which is to be garnered in glory. He who labours most and sows more diligently will gather a greater harvest, and will thus give greater glory to God in heaven.

The Gradual is closely connected not only with the lesson, but also with the Introit; so much so that these two antiphons are often taken from the same psalm, more especially on the Sundays after Pentecost, to-day's Gradual, for instance, being from Psalm liv, as is the Introit. " Cast thy care upon the Lord, and he shall sustain thee. When I cried to the Lord, he heard my voice from them that draw near to me."

The Gospel (Matt. viii 5-13), in relating the story of the centurion who deemed himself unworthy to receive Jesus under his roof, but begged him to speak just one word that his servant might be healed, foretells the calling of the Gentiles, who, though separated from the Messias by race, customs, and country, receive the privileges of the children of Abraham, by their faith in his divine nature, and thus obtain salvation. The example of the centurion, as also of St George, who were both bound by military discipline, in surroundings often conducive to unbridled licence, shows that virtue is not the privilege of any one caste, as the Pharisees claimed in their pride, but that the humble confidence of a heathen soldier was as pleasing to God as that of Matthew or of Nicodemus.

The Offertory is that of the First Sunday in Advent (Ps. xxiv), and is a sublime lifting up of the soul towards God, in whom she places all her confidence, in spite of the onslaught of her enemies.

The Secret is that of Ember Saturday in Advent : " Look down propitiously on these sacrifices, we beseech thee, O Lord, and grant that they may be profitable both to our devotion and salvation."

The Communion breaks the series of these eucharistic chants, for—the Mass of this Thursday being an addition— instead of being from Psalm ii, which is kept for **the Friday,** it is taken from Psalm 1: " Thou wilt accept the sacrifice of justice, oblations, and whole-burnt offerings upon thy altar, O Lord."

The Post-Communion has a graceful classical style: " Having received the blessing of the heavenly gift, we humbly beseech thee, almighty God, that through it we may receive both a sacrament and salvation."

The blessing of the people before their dismissal bears a markedly penitential character. It was appropriate to the condition of the Romans at that time, who were being struck down by plague, famine, and war. " Spare, O Lord, spare thy people, that whereas they have been deservedly chastised, they may find rest in thy compassion."

The thought of death is a powerful inducement to us to change our mode of life. Thus the devout Ezechias, seeing the moment draw near in which he must set in order his affairs and prepare for death, turned his face to the wall which separated the royal palace from the temple, and wept bitter tears of repentance. If we would only realize that the moment of our passing from this world to eternity may come unawares, and that, as the Apostle says, it is a terrible thing to fall into the hands of the living God, how much more keenly should we feel the necessity of imploring a *spatium verae poenitentiae* and of resolutely making good use thereof.

FRIDAY AFTER ASH WEDNESDAY

Collecta at Sta Lucia in Septizonio. Station at SS John and Paul.

Sta Lucia in Septizonio is an ancient deaconry which stood at the southern corner of the Palatine, near the *Septizonium* of Septimius Severus, but which was demolished under Sixtus V (1585-90). The *Liber Pontificalis* makes mention of it in the biographies of Leo III (795-816) and Gregory IV (827-44), who made donations to it, and we know that it was of considerable size and beauty.

The stational Mass was on the Coelian Hill, in the Basilica of Bizante, erected by that senator and his son Pammachius within the house of SS John and Paul. The two martyrs had suffered death on this spot for the faith, and had been secretly buried in a crypt beneath the building. Thus it came about that of all the Roman martyrs, who as a rule were buried according to the law in extra-mural cemeteries, SS John and Paul alone lay in the very heart of the Eternal City, a special privilege to which the Leonine Sacramentary draws particular attention in the preface of the feast of these two saints.

The Introit is from Psalm xxix: " The Lord hath heard and hath had mercy on me : the Lord became my helper."

The Collect asks that God will bless the fast which has been begun, so that abstinence from food may be accompanied by the purification of the soul.

The lesson from Isaias (lviii 1-9) dwells upon the emptiness of external ceremonies where these are not accompanied by a real desire to please God, and by an internal spirit of true repentance, which will turn us away from sin and call us back to him. Without these it is useless to fast, to wear a hairshirt, and to show other outward signs of grief, as Isaias reproached the Jews with doing.

The Gradual is from Psalm xxvi: " One thing I have asked of the Lord, this will I seek after, that I may dwell in the house of the Lord. That I may see the delight of the Lord, and be protected by his holy temple." The Psalmist suffers violence at the hands of his enemies, probably those of the levitical class, who would cast him out as unworthy from the service of the temple, in the same manner that Christ was declared a blasphemer and deserving of death by the high priests and the members of the Sanhedrim. The Psalmist in the person of Christ prays, and God grants his prayer, conferring on him an eternal priesthood.

The Gospel of to-day (Matt. v 43-48; vi 1-4) sets forth the Christian law of love and good-will towards our neighbour. To return the courtesy of others with equal grace is a rule of good manners that even pagans may practise, but in order to be able to pardon injuries, to do good without hope of return, to deprive ourselves secretly even of the necessaries of life in order to help others; for all such things we need the example, the command, and the grace of Jesus Christ.

The choice of this passage from St Matthew may, perhaps, have been inspired by memories of the place where the sacred rite was being solemnized on this day. Pammachius gave all his substance to the poor, and, after having converted his house into a church, he founded at Porto one of the earliest hospitals for pilgrims and sick persons. The Christian family of the Valerii followed his example, and on the spot where once stood the magnificent palaces of Melania, of Pinianus, of the Gordiani, and of the martyrs SS John and Paul, there arose in the fourth century the *Xenodochium Valerii,* which was afterwards joined to a famous monastery dedicated to St Erasmus.

The Offertory is taken from Psalm cxviii: " O Lord, enliven me according to thy word, that I may know thy testimonies."

In the Secret we pray that the sacrifice which accompanies our Lenten fast may render us acceptable to God and obtain for us the grace of a holy zeal in the observance of our abstinence.

The Communion is derived from Psalm ii, and is a proof that yesterday's station was a later addition : " Serve ye the Lord with fear and rejoice unto him with trembling, embrace discipline lest you perish from the just way."

The Post-Communion is imbued with the spirit of St Paul. As bread is formed by many grains of corn being ground and blended together into one mass, so the eucharistic food produces and represents the unity of the Church bound together by one ideal of faith and love.

The Prayer over the people before their dismissal is as follows : " Protect, O Lord, thy people, and mercifully cleanse them from all sins ; for no harm shall hurt them, if no wickedness be found in them."

God desires us not only to be good, but to be perfect after the example of his infinite and divine holiness. He has given us abundant means of attaining to this, and has willed that our redemption should be not merely sufficient, but abundant and all-embracing, for it was to this end that he poured forth his precious blood on the cross.

There are some who by a perverse error hold that only a few chosen souls, the religious and the clergy at most, are called to perfection. Yet what greater ingratitude can one imagine than that of saying, " I will love thee thus far, to the avoidance of grave sin, but no farther," to that God who has so loved us, as St Paul says, even to the making himself as of no account for our sakes?

SATURDAY AFTER ASH WEDNESDAY

Collecta at St Lawrence in Lucina. Station at St Trypho.

St Lawrence in Lucina stands on the Via Lata in the Campus Martius, and perhaps owes its origin to a matron named Lucina, who is mentioned frequently in the Acts of Pope St Marcellus (304-9), and of St Sebastian, and who probably left the Church heir to her great wealth in the fourth century. The title of Lucina still stands first in hierarchical rank among the presbyteral titles, and besides many other relics of early martyrs, a large portion of the gridiron on which St Lawrence was burnt is preserved in the spacious basilica, consecrated by Pope Celestine III in 1196.

The title of St Trypho, on the other hand, is of medieval origin, and appears to have been built and restored in the tenth century by the famous Crescenzi family, whose stronghold was near by. Under the altar were the bodies of the martyrs Trypho, Respicius, and Nympha, whose *natalis* is celebrated on November 10; but when Clement VIII was Pope (1592-1605), the building being then in a ruinous condition, both the station and the relics were transferred to the neighbouring Church of St Augustine.

In the days of St Gregory, although the Lenten fast began four days earlier, there were held, as we have said, in Quinquagesima week, only the two traditional synaxes of Ferias IV and VI; hence the antiphonary contains no chants for this Mass, but those of the previous day are repeated.

The Collect is as follows: " Give ear, O Lord, to our supplications; and grant that we may celebrate with devout service this solemn fast, which thou hast ordained as a salutary remedy both for our souls and bodies."

The Lesson from Isaias (lviii 9-14) is the continuation of that of yesterday; consequently its theme is the same. If Israel desires to receive the divine graces, let him break the bonds of his sins, let him perform works of mercy, and let him render to God not merely outward and formal worship, but that which is inward and spiritual. The Sabbath which is most pleasing to God is that on which man abstains from sin, and practises self-denial. The Church, in these first days of Lent, insists constantly on the importance of the spiritual side of our penitence, which has nothing in common with the observances of the Pharisees, or of the followers of Mohammed.

The Gospel (Mark vi 47-56) describes how our Lord, after approaching the Apostles across the tempest-tossed waves, returned with them to the land of Genesareth, where he healed all those who came to him and crowded about him that they might touch but the hem of his garment. The choice of this passage of Scripture has reference to the numerous miracles obtained by the faithful at the tomb of St Lawrence.

The Secret is the following: " Receive, O Lord, this sacrifice, by the offering of which thou hast vouchsafed to be appeased; and grant, we beseech thee, that we may be cleansed through its virtue, and may offer to thee the acceptable affection of our mind."

The Post-Communion is thus conceived: " Being quickened by the gift of a heavenly life, we beseech thee, O Lord, that what is in this life a mystery, may become to us a help for eternity."

The Sabbath is symbolical of the peace of God, and of the repose of the soul after the tempests of this life. Many desire this Sabbath, but few attain to it, because they will not accept the truth that in order to reach it they must first endure the dereliction of Good Friday. He who would rest with Christ must first climb the mount of Calvary and die upon the cross before he can find peace in the tomb of Joseph of Arimathea.

THE FIRST SUNDAY IN LENT

Station at St John Lateran.

On some of the most solemn feasts of the year the Roman Liturgy celebrates the station in the basilica of the ancient house of Fausta, which under Nero was the property of the Laterani. Constantine gave it to Pope Melchiades (311-14), and from that time onwards through the whole of the Middle Ages the palace became the usual residence of the Popes, the *episcopium,* or seat, of the Lateran Patriarchate. St Peter's is the ancient liturgical cathedral of the Roman Pontiffs, who repair there to officiate on all the great festivals, but the habitual seat, the normal residence of the Popes, is the Lateran, and for this reason the *Basilica Salvatoris* can claim the title of Mother and Head of all the churches of the city and of the world.

It is therefore fitting that the first sacrifice of the holy season of Lent should be offered on this day in the Lateran, in the glorious basilica dedicated to the Saviour, which only in later days came to be called after St John. In fact, only two small oratories near the baptistery were dedicated, one to St John the Evangelist and the other to St John the Baptist. These were erected by Pope Hilary (461-8), as a votive memorial of his fortunate escape in 449 from the violence of that heretical assembly which history has designated by the name of *latrocinium Ephesinum.*

Many precious relics of the martyrs are preserved under the high altar of the Lateran, and in the oratories of St Venantius, St Lawrence, etc., for which reason the ancient papal chapel of the Patriarchate is still called *Sancta Sanctorum.* In the Middle Ages no less than four monasteries, with a numerous choir of singers, were engaged by day and by night in the performance of the office in the Lateran Basilica.

As to-day is not a day of fasting, there is no *collecta* previous to the stational procession, this being a rite of a distinctly penitential character, and therefore not in keeping with the Sunday festival.

In the Mass for this Sunday great prominence is given to Psalm xc, that psalm which was quoted by Satan when tempting our Lord. It is repeated in the Introit, the Gradual, the Offertory, and the Communion, as though in protest and reparation for the sacrilegious suggestion of the

Evil One. On the other hand, this psalm so well expresses
the return of the soul to God through penitence and confidence in his mercy that the Church has chosen it as her
favourite Lenten chant.

The Introit expresses the wondrous promises made by God
to the soul that turns to him : " He shall call upon me, and
I will hear him; I will deliver him and glorify him; I will
fill him with length of days."
The Collect is as follows : " O God, who dost purify thy
Church by the yearly fast of Lent; grant to thy household
that what we strive to obtain from thee by abstinence, we
may secure by good works."
The Fathers of the Church, and St Leo I (440-61) in particular, dwell upon the fact that Lent is the time especially
acceptable to God, as the Apostle so well explains in the
lesson for the day (2 Cor. vi 1-10), a time of grace, in
which all the faithful, together with the catechumens and
penitents, are called upon to amend their lives. In olden
days, indeed, Lent was like a time of annual retreat for all
Christians. Therefore the words of St Paul which are
read to-day contain a great plan of inward reformation
which should be carefully meditated on, particularly by the
clergy, to whom it is specially addressed. The Apostle
describes from his own experience the double signification
of the profession of the Christian faith : the negative meaning—that is, poverty, calumny, persecution, mortification of
mind and body—and the positive meaning, which is the
result of the former; spiritual favours, generosity towards
the needy, gladness of soul, edification of others, possession
of all things in God.
The Gradual foretells the reverential homage of the angels
to Jesus Christ, that same homage which they all owe to
the *Caput hominum et angelorum*, and from which Satan
will draw a motive of temptation, as we shall presently
see in the Gospel for to-day : " God hath given his angels
charge over thee, to keep thee in all thy ways. In their
hands they shall bear thee up, lest thou dash thy foot against
a stone." This verse refers to Christ in his sacred humanity
and in his mystical body. The service rendered by the
angels to his humanity is a service of adoration due to him,
not of assistance, for the Redeemer could not need the help
of the angelic spirits.
The care of the Church and of the faithful entrusted to
the angels is an act of true condescension on the part of
Jesus, by which he allows those blessed spirits to co-operate
with him in the glorious work of the salvation of mankind.
This guardianship on the part of the angels, besides being

a service which they fittingly render to the Redeemer in his mystical body, is an office to which they are eminently adapted, in that they thus reflect upon creatures a little lower than themselves that light and that grace which they themselves draw from divine sources.

On the other hand, to us the ministry and guardianship of the holy angels is a matter of necessity, and their help is proportionate to our need. As we have to wage war against the powers of darkness, *spiritualia nequitiae in coelestibus,* as St Paul calls them, it is necessary that other spiritual beings, holy and more powerful, should assist us, and that their might should equal, nay, exceed, that of our terrible foes.

Further, the Fathers tell us that those who are pre-destined shall fill the places left empty in the ranks of the angels by the defection of Lucifer and his followers. Thus it is just that the good angels should co-operate with Jesus Christ in restoring the number of their hosts.

The Tract, too, is from Psalm xc : " He that dwelleth in the aid of the Most High shall abide under the protection of the God of heaven. He shall say unto the Lord, Thou art my upholder, and my refuge : my God, in him will I hope. For he hath delivered me from the snare of the hunters, and from the sharp word. He will overshadow thee with his shoulders; and under his wings shalt thou hope. His truth shall compass thee with a shield : thou shalt not be afraid of the terror of the night. Of the arrow that flieth by day; of the business that walketh in the dark; of invasion, or of the noonday devil. A thousand shall fall at thy side, and ten thousand at thy right hand : but it shall not come nigh thee. For he hath given his angels charge over thee, to keep thee in all thy ways. In their hands they shall bear thee up : lest thou dash thy foot against a stone. Thou shalt walk upon the asp and the basilisk : and thou shalt trample underfoot the lion and the dragon. Because he hath hoped in me, I will deliver him : I will protect him because he hath known my name. He shall cry to me, and I will hear him : I am with him in tribulation. I will deliver him and will glorify him : I will fill him with length of days : and I will show him my salvation."

It should be noticed here that originally the Gradual and the Tract not only had two distinct places—that is, after the first and second scriptural lessons—but that they dif-fered completely in the nature of the psalmody employed. To-day's Tract is one of the few examples remaining of the original length of this chant, which usually consisted of an entire psalm.

The Gospel (Matt. iv 1-11) describes the temptation of

Christ in the desert, when Satan, rendered suspicious by seeing his marvellous life, and desiring to assure himself that this was indeed the promised Messias, suggested to our Lord that he should prove his divine power first by changing stones into bread, then by casting himself down from the pinnacle of the Temple, and lastly that he should fall down and adore him as lord of the world.

Christ deigned no direct answer, replying to the first suggestion that man does not live by bread alone but by the divine word, wherefore the miracle asked for would be unnecessary. As to the second, it would be tempting God by presuming to demand a miracle at the mere caprice of the Evil One; while at the third temptation Christ no longer tolerated the audacity of Satan, but drove him away with the words : " Begone, Satan, for it is written, The Lord thy God shalt thou adore, and him only shalt thou serve."

The Fathers of the Church, and notably St Gregory, in a famous homily delivered on this day to the people assembled at the Lateran, ask why Christ consented to be tempted by Satan, and remark that he did so in order to partake of the infirmity of our nature, and in that nature to defeat and humble the tempter on our behalf and to obtain for us the grace of overcoming our temptations by the merits of his victory. Our Lord also wished to teach us that there is no sin in being tempted, but only in giving way to the tempter. The temptations of Christ were furthermore entirely external, as his sacred humanity could not possibly take pleasure in them, far less consent to them.

The faithful should contemplate with special devotion this mystery of Christ tempted in the desert, for there is no other which shows more clearly how the divine Providence makes even the wiles of the devil serve to our sanctification by using temptation as a crucible in which to purify our virtue, and by causing it to be an occasion of greater grace and profit to the soul in its spiritual life.

The Offertory is the following : " The Lord will overshadow thee with his shoulders, and under his wings thou shalt trust : his truth shall compass thee with a shield."

To-day Lent begins, so the Church consecrates it by means of that perfect sacrifice which is complete in itself, and sanctifies every other act of worship rendered to God through all ages, according to the word of the Apostle : *Una enim oblatione consummavit in sempiternum sanctificatos.*[1]

Now we have this very beautiful Secret : " We solemnly offer the sacrifice of the beginning of Lent, and we beseech thee, O Lord, that while we restrain our carnal feasting, we may likewise abstain from all hurtful pleasures."

[1] Heb. x 14.

Although the faithful have already been fasting for five days, it is only to-day that the Liturgy celebrates the beginning of Lent, for until this Sunday nothing has been changed either in the divine Office or in the Mass. The two stations of Ferias IV and VI are a survival of the original weekly fast of Wednesday and Friday, first mentioned in the Διδαχή where they are set against the *jejunio bis in sabbato* of the Pharisees, who abstained on Monday and Thursday. The Masses of Thursday and Saturday of Quinquagesima week represent a later addition of the time of Gregory II. St Gregory the Great is explicit on this point when he remarks in the Homily XVI *in Evang.* that, as a matter of fact, the Roman Lent at that time consisted only of thirty-six fasting days.

The Secret mentioned above is found in the Gelasian Sacramentary. The phrase *sollemne sacrificio—solemniter immolamus* is of interest. As a general rule, the Masses described in the Sacramentaries have the solemn stational character of the public offices, in which the whole body of the faithful took part with the clergy. In private Masses—*cotidianae,* as they were sometimes called—being rather of a votive nature, a more simple formulary was probably in use.

The Communion is the same as the Offertory.

The following is the text of the Post-Communion : " May the holy libation of thy sacrament refresh us, O Lord, and, purifying us from our old life, make us pass on to the fellowship of thy saving mystery." In this Collect we find the idea—a very common one in ancient liturgies—that Lent, inasmuch as it is a prelude to the great paschal drama, is a period of inward renewal after the image of Christ risen from the dead. The Gelasian Sacramentary in these first days of Lent comes back constantly to this idea, as these few examples will show : *Sacrificium, Domine, observantiae paschalis exserimus* . . . (Feria VI in Quinquagesima); *Aufer a nobis* . . . *ut ad Sancta Sanctorum* (= Easter) . . . *mereamur* . . . *introire* (at Quinquagesima, at Quadragesima); *jejuniis paschalibus convenienter aptari* (Feria VI in Quinquagesima); *Paschalibus actionibus inhaerentes* (Feria VII in Quinquagesima).

In the existing Missal of St Pius V, the Preface proper to this first Sunday in Lent is missing, as well as the last collect before the dismissal of the people. This latter, however, we find both in the Gelasian and in the Gregorian Sacramentary; the Leonine Sacramentary is defective. It runs as follows : " Graciously pour down, we beseech thee, O Lord, thy blessing upon thy people, that it may fill us with all consolation, confirm in us the true faith, and strengthen in constant well-doing those who by thee have been redeemed."

The people of God could not begin the paschal fast under happier auspices. Christ precedes them into the desert of expiation. The Apostle follows, and in one of the noblest of his epistles shows them how fastings, persecutions, and bodily sufferings are outweighed by the gifts of the Holy Ghost, longanimity, meekness, joy in suffering for love of God, happiness in serving one's fellow-men, in such ways sharing with Christ the sublime ministry of the redemption of mankind.

MONDAY AFTER THE FIRST SUNDAY IN LENT

Collecta at SS Cosmas and Damian.   Station at St Peter ad Vincula.

The basilica where the *collecta* in honour of the two celebrated Eastern doctors (Anargyri) takes place to-day was constructed by Felix IV (526-30) in the *aulae* of the *templum Romuli* and the *templum sacrae urbis* (the place of the archives of the city). During the Byzantine period it was held in very great veneration, and crowds flocked to the sanctuary of the two martyred physicians as to a sure source of health. To this the lines placed by order of Felix IV under the absidal mosaic bear witness :

Martyribus medicis, populo spes certa salutis
Fecit, et ex sacro crevit honore locus.
Optulit hoc Domino Felix antistite dignum
Munus ut aetheria vivat in arce poli.

After the inauguration of the Lenten fast at the Lateran, the station meets to-day at the basilica *in exsquiliis*, dedicated by Sixtus III (432-40) to the Apostles Peter and Paul, the great patrons of Rome. Although their tombs were quite distinct and separated one from the other by the whole extent of the city, Rome has always venerated them together ; and in her Liturgy, when she celebrates the memory of the one, she immediately joins thereto the commemoration of the other.

The insistence should be noted with which the Pontiff who founded the basilica unites the glories of the two Princes of the Apostles.

Haec Petri Paulique simul nunc nomine signo
Xystus, Apostolicae Sedis honore fruens.
Unum quaeso, pares, unum duo sumite munus
Unus honor celebrat quos habet una fides.

Later, however, the title of St Peter *ad Vincula* was adopted from the Chains of St Peter preserved there. Those of St Paul, according to St Gregory the Great, are kept at the Ostian Basilica.

The Lessons from Ezechiel and from St Matthew, which are read at this Mass, recall the *munus pastorale* of the two Apostles *quos operis vicarios . . . eidem* (that is, at Rome) *contulisti praeesse pastores.*

The relics of the seven martyred Machabees are preserved under the altar.

The Introit is taken from Psalm cxxii. We must endeavour to impress on our minds once and for all that the psalmody of the Mass was intended to be clothed with the marvellous melodies contained in the Gregorian antiphonary. If, therefore, we wish to appreciate the full artistic beauty of the Roman Liturgy, it is not enough to read, nor even to meditate upon the words of the Missal, for these are like the text of some great drama, the full significance of which cannot be fully grasped until one sees it interpreted on the stage. In the same manner, the Roman Liturgy must be seen and heard in the basilicas, with the music, the sacred vestments, the ritual, and the processions which render it so rich and varied, so sublime and impressive. When carried out as the *Caerimoniale Episcoporum* and the *Missale Romanum* prescribe, the liturgy is seen to be so great a masterpiece of heavenly grace and beauty that no art can ever produce its equal.

The words of the Introit are as follows: " As the eyes of servants are on the hands of their masters, so are our eyes unto the Lord our God, until he have mercy on us : have mercy on us, O Lord, have mercy on us."

The Collect begs almighty God to illuminate our minds with his heavenly light, so that the Lenten fast may not only discipline our bodies, but may render our souls both contrite and earnest. Then follows the beautiful lesson from Ezechiel (xxxiv 11-16) wherein the Lord God compares himself to the good Shepherd lovingly feeding his flock, which he leads through flowering meadows and by running waters; and if some sheep strays away and loses itself, he goes in search of it and brings it back to the fold.

The docility with which the soul entrusts itself to the care of the divine Shepherd keeps it from all danger and renders it the object of his heart's tenderest solicitude. The scene here described by Ezechiel has been constantly reproduced in the *cubicula* of the ancient cemeteries and perhaps in the apse of the Esquiline Basilica itself, so that when these words of the prophet were read the people may have had this very

representation before their eyes, a first page, as it were, of
that famous and illustrated *Biblia pauperum* of the late
Middle Ages which contributed so much to the catechetical
instruction of the people.

The Gradual is taken from Psalm lxxxiii : " Behold, O
God our protector, and look upon thy servants. O Lord God
of hosts, attend to the prayers of thy servants."

The Gospel from St Matthew (xxv 31-46) dwells again on
the figure of the good Shepherd who separates the sheep on
his right hand from the goats on his left. The divine Master
insists on the absolute necessity of our faith being effective,
otherwise it is dead and cannot save us. In truth the elect
are rewarded and the reprobate condemned; not indeed
because they have, or have not, accepted the Gospel, but
according as to whether they have lived up to its precepts or
not. Christianity, therefore, is not merely a philosophy, an
abstract thought, but a life which reveals itself in action and
sacrifice.

The Offertory is derived from Psalm cxviii : " I will lift up
my eyes and consider thy wonders, O Lord, that thou mayest
teach me thy justices; give me understanding, and I will
learn thy commandments."

In the Secret, while we ask God to hallow our oblation, we
pray that he will also cleanse us from all stain of sin.

The Communion antiphon, which should rightly be from
Psalm iii, was replaced in ancient times by one taken from
the Gospel of to-day : " Amen I say to you : what you did to
one of my least ones, you did to me : come, ye blessed of my
Father, possess the kingdom prepared for you from the
beginning of the world." The series of antiphons from the
psalms is consequently incomplete, since, owing to the omission of Psalm iii, we go on to-morrow to Psalm iv. So very
ancient, then, are these steps in the construction of the
Roman Liturgy.

The Post-Communion collect is a very fine one : " Being
filled with the gift of thy salvation, we humbly beseech thee,
O Lord, that as we rejoice in tasting thereof, we may also be
renewed by its result."

The prayer over the people is as follows : " Loosen, O
Lord, we beseech thee, the bonds of our sins; and mercifully
turn from us whatever we have deserved for them."

The sheep is chosen as an emblem of docility and meekness to be imitated by those striving to follow him who is
meek and humble of heart. The good Shepherd watches
tenderly over his flock, but the sheep who wander away from
him in pursuit of their own will, being deprived of his loving
care, fall victims to the wolf and perish miserably.

TUESDAY AFTER THE FIRST SUNDAY IN LENT

Collecta at St Nicholas in Carcere. Station at St Anastasia.

We have already mentioned the diaconal Basilica of St Nicholas in the *forum olitorium,* which during the Middle Ages became one of the most central and important of the Roman churches, at the time when the Pierleoni, the Orsini, the Frangipani, and others had, so to speak, quartered themselves about the Capitol. In this neighbourhood Urban II expired in 1099, whilst a guest of the Pierleoni, and his funeral was celebrated with much ceremony at St Nicholas in Carcere. The name *in Carcere* goes back to the Middle Ages, but the prison *ad Elephantum* in the *forum olitorium* is not to be confused with the *latomiae* of the Tullianum underneath the Capitol.

The popularity of the veneration paid to St Anastasia, which in Rome is perhaps older than the feast of Christmas itself, brought it about that under the influence of Byzantine imperialism her titular church, which was looked upon as a court church, being at the foot of the imperial *Palatium,* was chosen for the second Christmas Mass and for the second Lenten station. Indeed, it hardly seems a mere coincidence that after the Esquiline Basilica of SS Peter and Paul there should immediately follow the imperial basilica close to the *Palatium.*

A tradition asserts that the *titulus Anastasiae* mentioned in a synod of 499 marks the spot of the martyr's dwelling, but on the other hand it is quite possible that it is only a case of identity of name between the foundress of the basilica and the titular saint. St Leo I delivered a vigorous homily in St Anastasia against the heresy of Eutyches, probably at Christmas-time. The church is enriched with very precious relics.

The antiphon of the Introit to the fifth tone from Psalm lxxxix has such grace and spirit in the Gregorian antiphonary that it should certainly be heard. " Lord, thou hast been our refuge from generation to generation : from eternity thou art."

The following are the words of the first prayer after the litany : " Look down, O Lord, upon thy family, and grant that our minds, which are chastened by the mortification of the flesh, may glow with desire of thee."

The Lesson from Isaias (lv 6-11) describes the nature of true repentance, which, in order to be real, must be accompanied by a firm resolve of change of heart. Man cannot

understand the whole mystery of mercy hidden in the desire
of God to forgive the sinner.   His grace is compared to a
life-giving rain which refreshes and fertilizes the soil, and
causes it to bring forth fruit.

The Gradual comes from Psalm cxl, which in all oriental
liturgies belongs to the night office of the *Lucernare*. " Let
my prayer be directed as incense in thy sight, O Lord. The
lifting up of my hands as an evening sacrifice."

The liturgical importance of this psalm *Lucernare* should
be noted, for it was used—with the exception of Rome—
almost universally.   If, indeed, in the third century the
evening office *ad incensum lucernae* was known in the Eternal
City, it soon fell into disuse; so much so that St Benedict, in
his day, freely arranged his own *cursus* of vesper psalms
without any regard whatever to Eastern traditions, precisely
for the reason that such traditions were wholly unknown in
Rome.

In the Benedictine rite Psalm cxl forms part of the vesper
office on Thursdays only, whereas in the Gregorian antiphonary we find the Gradual taken from this same psalm both
in the evening Mass of to-day, and also in the night Mass of
the vigil following on Ember Saturday. We must bear in
mind that for many centuries Rome did not use the canonical
office of Vespers, its place being taken by the stational Mass
celebrated either during Lent or on the eve of some solemn
feast, at the very hour of sunset, when the Eastern Church
was reciting the office of the *Lucernare*.

The Gospel (Matt. xxi 10-17) describes how our Lord,
amid the hosannas of the children, drove out the money-
changers as profaners of the Temple. The ruling party, the
Pharisees and the Sanhedrim, were moved with indignation,
and desired him to silence the crowd, but he pointed out to
them that those acclamations were the fulfilment of the
Messianic prophecy contained in the Psalmist's words that
from the lips of little children should come forth a true hymn
of praise.[1]

Seeing that during the Byzantine era St Anastasia was, as
it were, the Palatine church, it is probable that the choice of
this Gospel was occasioned by some abuse giving rise to lack
of respect due to the holy place, and which had necessitated
the interference of the ecclesiastical authorities.

The Offertory is from Psalm xxx : " In thee, O Lord, have
I hoped : I said, thou art my God, my times are in thy
hands."

The Secret is as follows : " Be appeased, O Lord, we
beseech thee, by the gifts we offer; and defend us from all

[1] Ps. viii 3.

dangers." Here in a few words we have the propitiatory and supplicatory fruits of the Communion.

The Communion is taken from Psalm iv : " When I called upon thee, thou didst hear me, O God of my justice : when I was in distress, thou hast enlarged me : have mercy on me, O Lord, and hear my prayer."

The Post-Communion is that of the Fifth Sunday after the Epiphany.

The following is the prayer over the people : " Let our prayers rise up to thee, O Lord, and drive away all wickedness from thy Church."

To-day the Gospel mentions four classes of people who come in contact with Christ in the Temple—the merchants, the sick, the children, and the members of the Sanhedrim— each being affected thereby according to the state of their souls. The sacrilegious traffickers and the haughty scribes became more obstinate in their malice, while the innocence of the children and the humility of the sick moved to compassion the heart of Jesus, who poured forth upon them the treasures of his love. Thus we learn how important it is after careful preparation to approach the sacraments, or to give one's self to prayer and meditation.

EMBER WEDNESDAY AFTER THE FIRST SUNDAY IN LENT

Collecta at St Peter ad Vincula. Station at St Mary Major.

It seems quite superfluous to speak of Ember days in Lent, as the three days out of this week which are devoted to the fast *IV Temporum* are merged in the other days of Lent, from which they do not differ in any way. In fact, the ancient Roman sources speak of the fasts of the fourth, seventh, and tenth months, and the *Pontificale* relates how Pope Callixtus *Hic constituit jejunium die sabbati ter in anno fieri,*[1] without making any mention of the three fasts of the *Tempora* in March.

Lent was a special fast of its own, and had no relationship with the cycle of the *III Temporum,* unless the first of these Ember weeks was made to coincide with Quinquagesima, or the actual fixing of the fast in the sixth week before Easter dates from a time when the paschal fast began only three weeks before the great festival. In conclusion, then, either these Ember fast-days are a patchwork addition devoid of any particular significance, or else a place should be found for them apart from the paschal fast.

[1] Ed. Duchesne, I, 141.

The ordinations *mense martio* do not date from the earliest times. The first mention of them occurs in a letter of Pope Gelasius I (492-6) to the bishops of Lucania,[1] whilst in the time of St Leo I (440-61) they were allowed on the first day of Easter.[2] Be this as it may, it is customary at Rome on the Wednesday preceding the ceremony to hold the scrutinies of the candidates for the priesthood in the Liberian Basilica, where the station is held, as though to place them under the patronage of her whom Proclus of Constantinople (d. 447) invoked in the words : " *O templum, in quo Deus sacerdos factus est.*"

The Liberian Basilica on the summit of the Esquiline was originally adapted by Pope Liberius (352-66) from a classical *aula* named after Sicininus, for which reason Ammianus Marcellinus calls it the *Basilica Sicinini*. In the time of Pope Damasus I (366-84) it was occupied by the schismatics belonging to the party of the antipope Ursicinus. Sixtus III (432-40) caused it to be restored and decorated with mosaics representing the life of the Blessed Virgin, and it is possible that the shrine of the *praesepe,* a small Roman reproduction of the sanctuary of the Nativity at Bethlehem, dates from the same time. Under the high altar rest the bodies of St Matthias and of St Epaphras, a disciple of St Paul at Colosse.[3]

The Introit from Psalm xxiv is full of confidence, not-withstanding its marked sadness, and the art of the Gregorian composer has succeeded marvellously in expressing both these sentiments in the melody of the antiphonary : " Remember, O Lord, thy bowels of compassion, and thy mercies that are from the beginning of the world ; lest at any time our enemies rule over us : deliver us, O God of Israel, from all our tribulations."

After the litany the deacon calls upon the faithful to prostrate themselves—*flectamus genua*—then, after a brief interval of private prayer, he gives them the signal to rise—*levate*—so that the priest may *collect*—this is the true meaning of the word—the desires of each one in order to present them together to God.

To-day's Collect is as follows : " Mercifully hear our prayers, we beseech thee, O Lord ; and stretch forth the right hand of thy majesty against all our adversaries."

The Lenten fast and the *catechesis* given to the candidates for baptism evoke the remembrance of Mount Horeb (Exod. xxiv 12-18), where Moses dwelt for forty days, fasting and

---

[1] *P.L.* LIX, col. 47.   [2] *Ep. ad Diosc., P.L.* LIV, col. 626.
[3] *Cf.* Col. i 7; Philem. 23.

conversing with Jehovah on the rugged heights of Sinai, in order to receive from him the Tables of the Law.

Prayer, fasting, solicitude, clouds, fire, and lightning, together with penitence and humility, were to purify the soul of the great leader of Israel, and to instil into him the fear of God and a high conception of the sanctity and majesty of Jehovah. Yet on Sinai it was only an angel who appeared as the messenger of God. What a high degree of sanctity will there not be asked of us who minister at the altar, on which rests, not the shadow, but the reality of the mysteries prefigured in the Old Law !

The Gradual, like the Introit, is from Psalm xxiv : " The troubles of my heart are multiplied : deliver me from my necessities, O Lord. See my abjection and my labour, and forgive me all my sins."

The second collect follows, being closely connected with the preceding lesson, and with the Gradual, of which it is, as it were, the conclusion. " Mercifully look down, we beseech thee, O Lord, upon the devotion of thy people, that they whose bodies are mortified by fasting, may through the fruit of good works be refreshed in mind."

In the evening hymn of Lent is sung with reference to the holy fast :

> Lex et Prophetae primitus
> Hoc praetulerunt. . . .

After Moses the lawgiver comes Elias the prophet. In a moment of unspeakable distress Elias experienced all the misery of isolation and of the persecution of Jezabel, but being sustained by grace and by the bread *subcinericius* of fasting, he walked in the strength of that food forty days and forty nights, unto the Mount of God, Horeb, whence the Law was originally given (3 Kings xix 3-8). The wonder-working bread which fortified the prophet was a type of the Eucharist, the true unleavened bread of mortification which, as the Scripture says, purifies the soul and leads it to the height of Calvary.

The Tract also is taken from Psalm xxiv, following the rule in the most ancient Masses, where all the chants, whether antiphonal or responsorial, are derived from one and the same psalm. It is worthy of remark that to-day's Tract, being separated from the Gradual, is in its proper place— that is, after the second lesson. " Deliver me from my necessities, O Lord : see my abjection and my labour, and forgive me all my sins. To thee, O Lord, have I lifted up my soul : in thee, O my God, I put my trust, let me not be ashamed, neither let my enemies laugh at me. For none of them that wait on thee shall be confounded : let all them be confounded that do vain things."

II.

The station to-day being at the principal basilica dedicated to our Lady in Rome, the Gospel (Matt. xii 38-50), by a delicate allusion to the Blessed Virgin, testifies to her holiness and to the intimate union which joins the heart of the Mother to that of her divine Son. Christ was teaching the multitude when a message was brought to him that his Mother and his kinsfolk were without, seeking him. Our Lord took advantage of the occasion to point out that the inner virtues, together with complete submission to the divine will, bind the soul much more closely to God than even the ties of human relationship.

The Offertory comes from Psalm cxviii : " I will meditate on thy commandments, which I have loved exceedingly : and I will lift up my hands to thy commandments, which I have loved."

The Secret is the same as on the Fifth Sunday after the Epiphany.

The Communion is derived from Psalm v : " Understand my cry, hearken to the voice of my prayer, O my King and my God, for to thee will I pray, O Lord."

This is the striking Post-Communion collect : " By receiving thy sacrament, O Lord, may we both be cleansed from our hidden sins, and delivered from the snares of enemies."

The prayer over the people is insistent upon the necessity of the divine light, in order that we may find out all the evil which hides itself in the secret places of our conscience : " Enlighten our minds, we beseech thee, O Lord, by the light of thy brightness, that we may be able to see what we ought to do, and have power to do what is right."

It is characteristic of every frivolous and unbelieving age, such as our own, to manifest a certain inquisitive desire for religious experiences, as they are called, but which, on account of an evil disposition of mind, though they may tend to soften the heart, yet never succeed in bringing it back to God. Such unbelieving persons, who, like Herod, when confronted with Jesus,[1] seek supernatural and miraculous manifestations for the sake of excitement—thus in our own days spiritualism and theosophy have become the vogue—as a vent for their morbid curiosity, are altogether on the wrong road.

God hides himself from the idle curiosity of the inquisitive and from the arrogant investigations of those scientists who claim to scrutinize the footprints of the divine Master on the sands of creation, and conceals his glory under the veil of humility and of the annihilation of the cross and the

---

[1] Luke xxiii 8-9.

sepulchre. This is the sign, prefigured by the prophet Jonas, which alone, as the Gospel of to-day attests, will be granted to a sceptical and unbelieving generation.

THURSDAY AFTER THE FIRST SUNDAY IN LENT

Collecta at St Agatha in Monasterio. Station at St Lawrence in Panisperna.

St Agatha is the patron saint of the famous deaconry of the Suburra. The titular church, once adorned with mosaics by Ricimer (472), was given over later to the Arians by the Goths. It was restored to Catholic worship by Gregory the Great, who dedicated it to the celebrated Sicilian martyr Agatha, to whom the Romans had such great devotion. In the eighth century a monastery was attached to it, which was afterwards converted into a collegiate community.

To-day's station at St Lawrence in Panisperna on the Viminal was instituted by Gregory II, who took the Introit from the festive Mass of St Lawrence. With a graceful allusion to the splendour of his sepulchral basilica, called the *Speciosa,*[1] the Introit celebrates the sanctity of the great archdeacon, to whose prayers the early Fathers especially attributed the final triumph at Rome of the cross over paganism. For this reason we find St Lawrence represented in ancient mosaics as carrying the sign of redemption, as though he held the office of cross- or standard-bearer of the Roman Church. Tradition has it that the martyr endured his fiery torment near to-day's stational church, known as *in Formoso.* The adjoining monastery was, in the Middle Ages, one of the twenty privileged abbeys of the Eternal City.

The Introit is from Psalm xcv: "Praise and beauty are before him; holiness and majesty in his sanctuary. Sing ye to the Lord a new canticle: sing to the Lord all the earth."

The Collect is the same as the second collect of yesterday, and entreats almighty God that he will favourably regard the devotion of his people, so that whilst they mortify their bodies by fasting, their spirit may be nourished by good works.

The sacred Liturgy dwells frequently during these days on the chastisement of the body by means of fasting: *Qui per abstinentiam macerantur in corpore;* and, indeed, fasting in those days was anything but a mere ritual ceremony, as it has become for many Christians of our own time, for it

[1] St Lawrence Without the Walls.—Tr.

entailed abstinence from every kind of food or drink until the evening. At sunset—that is, after the stational Mass—the tables were spread, but even on Sundays only such things were allowed as were consistent with strict abstinence; wine, meat, eggs, and milky foods being absolutely forbidden. It is easy to understand that so rigid a fast must have been a great physical strain.

The lesson from Ezechiel (xviii 1-9) explains that our merits or demerits are entirely personal, and not like a title of nobility, inherited from our ancestors.

It was therefore necessary that the Jews should not take any part in the idolatrous rites which were celebrated on the hill-tops and in the sacred groves that had been planted everywhere in the kingdom of Israel, in honour of the heathen gods, after the schism of the ten tribes. This was their duty towards God. With regard to their neighbours, they had the sixth and the ninth commandments of the Decalogue, that law which regulated loans between Israelites, and the various works of mercy. He who practises these things, says the Prophet, he is just, and shall surely live in the sight of the Lord.

We should notice here the first place given to the practice of good works, without which faith alone cannot save us, being lifeless like a withered trunk, which produces neither fruit nor flowers.

The Gradual is taken from Psalm xvi. It is the martyr Lawrence who, in his anguish, calls on the judgement of God: "Keep me, O Lord, as the apple of thy eye; protect me under the shadow of thy wings. Let my judgement come forth from thy countenance: let thine eyes behold equity."

The choice in the Gospel of to-day of the episode of the woman of Canaan who, by humility and perseverance in prayer, obtained the cure of her daughter, though our Lord, in order to try her faith, treated her with apparent harshness, was suggested by Gregory II by a magnificent responsory of the night office in this first week of Lent. *Tribularer, si nescirem misericordias tuas . . . qui Cananeam et publicanum vocasti ad poenitentiam. . . .*

It is interesting to note the wonderful development of the Roman Liturgy, which even after the golden age of Gregory continued to unfold its treasures and to produce new masterpieces. The responsory in question was probably derived from a Greek source; but from this Eastern theme Rome acquired first a grand responsorial melody, and then the motive of one of the most touching Gospel lessons (Matt. xv 21-28) for the stational solemnity of St Lawrence.

The troubled Canaanite is a symbol of the Gentiles, who,

without having the privilege of the Jewish circumcision, obtain salvation by virtue of their faith. It is through this faith that Christian Rome occupies the place forfeited by Jerusalem the deicide, for God does not regard a man's worldly lineage, but his humility and simplicity of heart.

The Saviour's first refusal to perform a miracle in favour of a Gentile woman, besides the reasons given above, was also intended to show that God is the Lord of order, and that therefore he did not desire to forestall the moment determined by his Providence for the calling of the Gentiles to the faith, but to wait until such time as the Jews should have rendered themselves unworthy of this grace by voluntarily closing their eyes to the light of the Gospel.

Furthermore, Christ wished to avoid furnishing his enemies with a fresh motive for attempting his life before the destined hour, through taking notice of a Gentile, whom the fanaticism of the Jews would have described in the words still in use among the Arabs of to-day, as "a dog of an unbeliever."

The Offertory from Psalm xxxiii bears an allusion to St Lawrence, of whom we read in the acts of his martyrdom that an angel comforted and succoured him whilst he lay on the red-hot gridiron. "The angel of the Lord shall encamp round about them that fear him, and shall deliver them : taste and see that the Lord is sweet."

The Secret is as follows : "May these sacrifices, we beseech thee, O Lord, which are instituted with wholesome fasts, save us by thy mercy."

The Antiphon for the Communion in the Masses of Gregory II often has a eucharistic character. To-day it comes from the Gospel of St John, and therefore differs in two ways from the general rule which formerly governed the psalmody of the Mass in the golden period of the Roman Liturgy. In those days the antiphons were always taken from the Psalms and never from the Gospels. A little later the antiphon *ad Communionem* was, on the contrary, derived from the Gospel of the day, as in the common of saints. In the present instance, however, the antiphon is from the Gospel of St John, and has not the slightest reference to the preceding lesson from St Matthew, with its story of the Canaanite woman.

In the Post-Commuunion we see that the mind of the Church is marvellously balanced between two extremes : on the one hand, materialism, which recognizes only the laws of matter ; and on the other hand, gnostic enlightenment, which is but the aberration of a morbid mind. The Church has always opposed these heretical exaggerations, which do not acknowledge the dual nature of man, but which either reduce him to the level of the brute, or raise him up like some fantastic edifice, which totters to its fall because it has no solid base. The substratum of grace is human nature, which is, indeed, raised up by the action of the Holy Ghost, but never destroyed. " By the bountifulness of thy gifts, O Lord, do thou support us by temporal aids, and renew us by those that are eternal."

The Prayer over the people also has a eucharistic character : " Grant, we beseech thee, O Lord, to all Christian people, that they may acknowledge what they profess, and love the heavenly mystery which they frequent."

Moses, in the last Canticle of Deuteronomy,[1] says that God acts towards the soul as the eagle towards its young when encouraging them to fly. Of this, we have an example in our Lord's demeanour towards the Canaanite. At first he treats her with much severity, but underneath his discouraging words lie hidden such compelling sympathy and pity that the poor mother, instead of being rebuffed, feels her faith so much strengthened that at last she merits to hear from the Saviour's lips those welcome words of praise : " O woman, great is thy faith."

This is always the end which God has in view when he seems to deal harshly with us, when he withdraws or hides himself from us. He is ever seeking to urge us forward on the road to perfection, compelling us, as it were, to take breath in order to hasten our steps, so that we may reach the goal before the twelfth hour, the hour of our death, shall have sounded.

EMBER FRIDAY AFTER THE FIRST SUNDAY IN LENT

Collecta at St Mark. Station at the Twelve Holy Apostles.

A *Lector de Pallacine* is already mentioned in an inscription of the year 348, for the church built by Pope Mark (337-40) is reckoned among the first erected in Rome. It is possible that the dedication to the Evangelist of Alexandria is of later date; the *titulus Marci* would, in time, have become the Basilica of St Mark, just as the titular churches of Sabina, Balbina, etc., became sacred to the martyrs bearing those names.

The two celebrated deacons of Sixtus II (260-6), Felicissimus and Agapitus, represented in the mosaic of the apse dating from the time of Gregory IV (827-44), were specially

---

[1] Deut. xxxii 11.

venerated in the basilica *ad balneas pallacinas;* also the two
Persian martyrs, Abdon and Sennen, whose bodies lie under
the altar of the *confessio.*

On this day, in the ancient Roman Liturgy, the second
scrutiny of the candidates for the priesthood and diaconate
took place; it was therefore proper that after the station of
the Wednesday at the Basilica of our Lady on the Esquiline,
the Church should invoke the protection of the whole Apostolic College for those who continue their great mission upon
earth.

In the venerable Basilica of the Holy Apostles—built by
Pelagius I (555-60), and dedicated by John III (560-73) as a
votive offering for the deliverance of Rome from the Goths
by Narses—are preserved under the altar the relics of
St Philip and St James. In the Middle Ages, many bodies
of saints were brought hither from the Apronian Cemetery
on the Via Latina, amongst them that of the martyr Eugenia,
in whose honour the station of the Fourth Sunday in Advent
was celebrated in this church.

The Introit is taken from Psalm xxiv : " Deliver me from
my necessities, O Lord; see my abjection and my labour,
and forgive me all my sins."

The Collect is the following : " Be merciful, O Lord, to
thy people; and as thou makest them devout to thee, in thy
mercy cherish them by thy kind help."

Among the early Christians, especially when, as in the time
of Tertullian, *Christiani non nascuntur sed fiunt,* and when
baptism was administered to adults, it was expected that the
sacrament should effect in the catechumen a complete change
of heart. For this reason the Lenten Liturgy, especially
during these first days, insists on the necessity of a reformation of life.

The Lesson for to-day is the continuation of that of yesterday (Ezech. xviii 20-28). Works and responsibilities are
strictly personal matters, nor does God consider the claims
of one's ancestry, and in this we see a foreshadowing of
the catholicity of the New Covenant, in distinction to the
nationalism of the Old. Yet the man who, by misuse of his
free-will, has separated himself from God and broken his
holy law, may still retrace his steps and return to the Lord,
through penitence and contrition.

The Gradual is from Psalm lxxxv : " Save thy servant, O
my God, that trusteth in thee. With thy ears, O Lord,
receive my prayer."

The Pool of Bethsaida, of which the Gospel (John v 1-15)
speaks, symbolizes the baptismal font of the catechumens,
and is, to all the faithful, a figure of the adorable Heart of

Jesus, through whose wounded side they pass into an ocean of love and compassion. The Fathers saw in the five porches of the Probatica a type of the five wounds of the Crucified, of which St Augustine said : *Vulnera tua, merita mea.*

The infirm man who had been for thirty-eight years in that sad condition, without having found any kindly disposed person to assist him into the water, when the angel came to disturb it, teaches us that we must not lean exclusively on human friendship, which often cannot or will not help us, and that we are to regard the *piscina probatica* as a symbol of grace, which exceeds the power and requirements of man, and alone can be bestowed on us by him who is called in the Scriptures *Vir oriens, Vir, Filius hominis*—the perfect man.

The Offertory is derived from Psalm cii : " Bless the Lord, O my soul, and forget not all his benefits ; and thy youth shall be renewed like the eagle's."

The Secret is the following : " Receive, we beseech thee, O Lord, the offerings made by our service, and mercifully sanctify thy gifts." The Roman conception of the prayer over the oblations (the Secret) is made known to us by Pope Innocent, who writes thus to Decentius of Gubbio : *Oblationes sunt commendandae;* not that the eucharistic transubstantiation needs any other intercessory prayers by the priest, for the sacraments derive their value from their divine institution, but in order that the minister and the faithful who offer the Sacrifice may also find favour in the sight of God, and that it may profit them to their common salvation.

The Communion is taken from Psalm vi : " Let all my enemies be ashamed and be very much troubled, let them be turned back and be ashamed very speedily." The curses and chastisements so often invoked by the Psalmist in Holy Scripture may be considered as directed against the impenitent enemies of Christ at the last judgement, or merely as threats to hasten their conversion.

The Post-Communion is that of the Sunday within the Octave of the Nativity.

The Prayer over the people before their dismissal asks God to enlighten the darkness of our hearts and our souls, that we may learn to know ourselves and him—*Noverim me, noverim te,* as St Augustine prayed.

How blind are those who set their hopes on creatures ! After years of anxious waiting we have at last to admit that we have found none who can or will succour us—*Hominem non habeo.* When shall we, too, break the enchantment which binds us to earthly things? When shall we be convinced, like the celebrated Chancellor Gerson, that *omnis copia quae Deus tuus non est, tibi inopiae est?*

EMBER SATURDAY OF THE TWELVE LESSONS AFTER THE FIRST SUNDAY IN LENT

Collecta at St Mary in Transpontina. Station at St Peter.

St Mary *in Transpontina* stood, as ancient writers tell us, in *capite porticus;* that is to say, between the Ælian Bridge and the colonnade which led to St Peter's. Near by was the *terebinthus Neronis,* whence the clergy moved in procession, when they escorted the new Emperor as he went to receive the crown in St Peter's from the hands of the Pope. The church was destroyed, perhaps, under Pius IV (1559-65), and the one which now bears its name is not an ancient building, nor does it stand on the original site, but about three hundred yards nearer the Vatican.

In former days this Saturday was aliturgical, as it had to be spent in strict fasting, and Mass was not said until the end of the vigil preceding the Sunday, which took place at St Peter's. But for many centuries now the Church in her motherly condescension has allowed the rites of the vigil to be anticipated on the morning of the Saturday.

The station at the Vatican Basilica was prompted by the eminently Roman idea that every transmission of ecclesiastical power, through the conferring of one of the sacred orders, was derived from the supreme power of Peter. Therefore ordinations in Rome must take place at the Vatican, with this distinction, that whereas it was the prerogative of the Pope to receive consecration at the altar which was over the tomb of the Prince of the Apostles, in other cases the ceremony took place in one of the adjoining oratories. The surroundings were especially inspiring. That ancient basilica, whose destruction in order to make room for the existing building of Bramante and Michelangelo can never be sufficiently deplored, was the monument of the victory of Christianity over Paganism, on the very spot where Nero crucified the first Pope. Around the tomb of the Galilean fisherman, whom Christ had raised to the dignity of being the foundation-stone of his Church, a noble band of Pontiffs slept the sleep of death. All the Catholic nations had built hospices for their pilgrims around this spot, and it could be said with truth that the sepulchre of St Peter was the goal of the desires of all Christianity, the centre of the Catholic world.

In olden times the faithful spent the whole of this night in prayer, singing psalms, and listening to the reading, both in Greek and in Latin, of twelve lessons from Holy Scripture. The ceremony was enlivened by the beautiful melodies of the *schola,* by the brilliant light from the silver lamps which dispelled the shadows of the night, and by the perfume of incense and Eastern aromatics, with which the tomb of St Peter was incensed at the reading of each lesson. St Gregory the Great reduced the twelve lessons of the Roman *Pannuchis* to six, and in our days the five lessons which precede the Epistle are the last relics of this most ancient nocturnal solemnity.

The Introit derives its antiphon from Psalm lxxxvii, which we might almost call the evening hymn, for, by reason of the words *In die clamavi et nocte coram te,* it is repeated each time that the *Pannuchis* is celebrated.

The *Liber Pontificalis,* in the life of Pope Callixtus, seems to imply that originally in Rome only three Ember fasts were celebrated, corresponding to the ancient rural festivals of the harvest, the vintage, and the drawing off of the new wine— at the beginning, that is, of summer, autumn, and winter. There was no special fast in the spring, as it would always have coincided with the holy season of Lent. When, how- ever, towards the golden age of St Leo I it was desired to make the Jewish fast of the first month coincide with the beginning of Lent and with the spring, the Liturgy had necessarily to be somewhat modified, and the lessons appointed for the vigils were specially chosen so as to harmonize with the rural character of these ancient Roman festivals.

The Collect after the first litany beseeches God to look favourably on his people, and mercifully to turn away from them the scourge of his anger.

A passage from Deuteronomy (xxvi 12-19) follows, relative to the giving of tithes to the Levites and to the poor. A kind of contract is formed between Jehovah and his people. The latter undertake to obey his law and to worship the true God only, among all the idolatrous nations that surround them, whilst on the other hand God promises to exalt Israel above all nations and to enrich it with every spiritual and material blessing.

As St Paul explains in his Epistle to the Galatians, the idea of a contract is the very essence of the Old Law; but not- withstanding this the lesson has a deep significance which can be fitly applied to the catechumens, who by their baptismal promises undertake to observe the teaching of the Gospel, and thus inherit in a higher sense the Messianic promises made to those whom the Apostle calls *Israel Dei,* in contrast to the *Israel secundum carnem.*

The Gradual is from Psalm lxxviii, in which the protection of God is invoked against the Gentiles,

During Lent, on Monday, Wednesday, and Friday, a *tractus* appears in the Missal with an absolutely different melody, but with very nearly the same words. These represent two quite independent kinds of psalmody, although the introduction of the tract *Domine non secundum,* etc., in the Lenten Masses dates only from the early Carlovingian period.

After the Gradual follows a collect, in which we pray God to free us from the weight of our sins, a burden all the more hard to bear since it is the consequence not only of the weakening of our spiritual powers due to evil passions, but also of the chastisement which these bring upon us even in this life.

The second Lesson is also taken from Deuteronomy (xi 22-25). The Lord God lays before his people the choice between his blessing or his curse. If Israel will keep the *Torah* and the pact made with God, they shall receive every blessing, symbolized by all the material prosperity which would appeal to that rough and sensual people. If, on the other hand, the nation abandons God, it will itself be abandoned by Jehovah to its fate.

The Gradual *Protector* is the same as that of the Mass of the preceding Monday.

The Collect implores almighty God to impress upon our conduct that prudent moderation which our forefathers deemed the most excellent of gifts, and which is described by Cassian as the queen of all virtues, so that we may be humble in prosperity and steadfast in adversity. This is the state of a soul which has successfully sustained the hardest trials, and which, being firmly established on the rock of conformity to the will of God, possesses a peace which the chances and changes of human fortune cannot touch.

The third lesson is derived from 2 Machabees i 23-27, and contains the prayer of Nehemias when, after the return of the Jews from exile, the worship of the Temple was restored, and the fire from heaven descended on the sacrifice.

The Gradual comes from Psalm lxxxix, which from early times was one of the morning psalms. In it we pray God to look with favour on his servants, whose refuge he has been from generation to generation.

The Collect is the same as that of Septuagesima Sunday.

The fourth lesson follows, being taken from Ecclesiasticus (xxxvi 1-10), generally called " Wisdom," as was usual in Rome when speaking of all such books of learning. It is a touching prayer, but one which shows unmistakably the servitude of fear which was the characteristic of the Old Law; for, while it desires the blessing of Jehovah on the people of Israel, it invokes at the same time his judgement on the *Goyim.* It asks that, as the Gentiles had been the instruments of his judgement on the Jewish nation, so they in their turn may receive the punishment they have deserved, and may learn to fear the true God—the God of Israel.

The Gradual is that of the preceding Tuesday, and as we have already seen a similar instance in the Mass of the Monday, it points to the probability that the office of the Spring *Pannuchis* was composed at a later time, and that the various parts were drawn from more ancient Masses.

The Collect is in itself worth a whole treatise on Grace, such as those of the time of the Pelagian controversy. It invokes the divine assistance, in order that our actions may be suggested by heavenly inspiration and our wills sustained to carry them out. This assistance, both *prevenient* and *concurrent*, as the scholastics say, if it is of value for human action in the purely natural order, becomes absolutely essential in the supernatural; inasmuch as nature and grace receive the first impulse from God, and with his continued assistance attain their proposed aim.

The fifth and last Lesson—as on Ember Saturday in Advent —is from Daniel, and tells us of the three youths in the fiery furnace of Babylon. Then follows, as was usually the case at the end of the vigil, the canticle of the *Benedictiones*—for so it was anciently called—which takes the place of a hymn of transition from the night office to the Mass itself.

In the late Middle Ages, the Pope retired during the reading of the lessons to the oratory of St Andrew, near the *Confessio* of St Peter, and there consecrated the new priests and deacons. The ordinations being ended, he returned to the great basilica, amid the triumphant strains of the *Benedictiones*, and there offered the divine Sacrifice, bringing therewith to an end the long and rigorous fast which the faithful had kept since Friday night.

The two Lessons which follow—that is, those from the Epistle to the Thessalonians and the Gospel of St Matthew— are a repetition of the former office; for, as we know, the whole of the first part of the actual Mass reproduces in an abbreviated form the rite of the vigil which in older times always preceded the Sunday Mass. Therefore, in accordance with a very ancient ecclesiastical custom, the consecratory anaphora should immediately follow the canticle of the *Benedictiones*.

In to-day's passage from the first Epistle to the Thessalonians (v 14-23), St Paul draws a picture of the perfect Christian life, alluding especially to the gifts of the Spirit, one particularly suited to the new candidates for the priesthood. Now, indeed, more than ever before, is it a time when the clergy must act and be diligent. *Spiritum nolite exstinguere*: the great social upheaval or revolution, which we are witnessing, may need to be met by new forms and methods of propaganda and evangelization. The clergy, however, in their sacred ministry must not adopt the methods employed by lay proselytism. That which has the appearance of being new and good and helpful is not to be at once accepted and introduced into the Church; it must first be examined by competent authorities, *Omnia probate;* the Church, therefore, alone can choose that which is really good out of all these modern systems—*Quod bonum est tenete.*

The Tract follows from Psalm cxvi, a psalm of thanksgiving, forming, as it were, the conclusion of the rite of Ordination. The Roman Liturgy always placed it at the end of the night vigil and before the solemn chanting of the Gospel.

It is in accordance with the spirit of the ancient liturgy that the Gospel should have more or less connection with the titular saint of the stational church. On this occasion, the *Pannuchis* being celebrated at the tomb of St Peter, the account of the Transfiguration (Matt. xxvii 1-9) is chosen, in which, of the three Apostles mentioned, St Peter, who was later to be the chief witness of this divine manifestation, takes the leading part.

The solitary height on which Jesus clothes himself in splendour is typical of the sacerdotal state, which demands a complete detachment from earthly things, an intense interior life, and a sublime spirit of contemplation. As in heaven, God in his majesty is seated upon the Cherubim, so, on earth, their sublime office is filled by his priests.

The Offertory is, as usual, from Psalm lxxxvii: " O Lord, the God of my salvation, I have cried in the day and in the night before thee, let my prayer come in before thee, O Lord." This psalm occurs regularly each time that the *Pannuchis* of the night preceding the Sunday is celebrated in Rome.

In the Secret, we ask that God will hallow our fasts by the merits of the holy Sacrifice, so that our outward abstinence may be accompanied by the inward sacrifice of all that is displeasing to him.

The psalms chosen for the Communion during Lent form a series by themselves in the Gregorian antiphonary, and follow the order given in the Psalter. When an antiphon *ad Communionem* differs from this order, we may be sure either that it is an interpolation or an addition to the original arrangement made by St Gregory. To-day the Communion comes from Psalm vii, which, with its antiphon, fills the heart with hope : " O Lord my God, in thee have I put my trust; save me from all them that persecute me, and deliver me."

The Post-Communion prays that the divine Sacrament may be to us a remedy against our vices, and procure for us an eternal recompense.

The final Prayer of benediction over the people is as follows : " May the desired blessing strengthen thy faithful people, O God; may it cause them never to depart from thy will, and ever to rejoice in thy benefits."

The Gospel of to-day shows us how deeply imbedded was the thought of the cross in the heart of Jesus. Even amid the glory of Mount Thabor he spoke with Moses and Elias of his approaching death, in order to make known the force of the love which impelled him to sacrifice himself for us.

THE SECOND SUNDAY IN LENT

Station at St Mary in Domnica.

Properly speaking there should be no stational Mass to-day, as it has already been celebrated at St Peter's on the termination of the *Pannuchis*. In fact, in the ancient Sacramentaries, this day is marked *Dominica vacat;* the people, too, were weary after the prolonged fast and vigil. When the Roman Sacramentary was introduced into other places outside Rome, where there were neither stations nor vigils, it was found necessary to make up the liturgy for to-day with portions taken from other Masses, and this was finally accepted even in Rome itself. The name given to the Basilica of St Mary on the Coelian Hill, *in domnica,* is of very ancient origin—of the fourth century, at least—when the Lord's house was generally called the *Dominicum,* as it is to this day among nations of Anglo-Saxon and Germanic race.

The Introit is that of the preceding Wednesday.

In the Collect we ask God to behold our poverty, our weakness and our need, and implore his help that our bodies may not succumb to outward evils, and our souls to sin.

The passage from the first Epistle to the Thessalonians (iv 1-7) precedes in the text yesterday's lesson. To the early Christians of Asia and of Greece, affected as they were by the extreme corruption of the surroundings in which they lived and of which they themselves had once formed part, the chief danger was that arising from the prevalent sin of immorality, raised by idolatry to a form of religious worship. The Apostle, with a plain-spoken frankness necessitated by the circumstances, explains to those to whom he was writing the purpose and the holiness of matrimony. " Each one of you possesses his own wife, so that in her he may have a help towards holiness. Marriage, therefore, is enjoined as regards each of the faithful with the object that no one shall covet his neighbour's wife, for God is the defender of conjugal fidelity."

The Gradual is taken from Psalm xxiv : " The troubles of my heart are multiplied; deliver me from my necessities, O Lord. See my abjection and my labour, and forgive me all my sins."

The Tract is from Psalm cv, and is a beautiful hymn of thanksgiving : " Give glory to the Lord, for he is good : for his mercy endureth for ever. Who shall declare the powers of the Lord, who shall set forth all his praises? Blessed are they that keep judgement, and do justice at all times. Remember us, O Lord, in the favour of thy people : visit us with thy salvation."

The Gospel is the same as that of the Mass of the preceding *Pannuchis* (Matt. xvii 1-9). In the Middle Ages many churches and monasteries, in imitation of the Greeks, instituted a special festival for the celebration of the mystery of the Transfiguration. Rome did not adopt this custom until 1457, when Callixtus III introduced the feast in commemoration of a great victory over the enemies of the Faith.[1] Up to that time the traditional liturgy of this Second Sunday in Lent, which formerly was celebrated with great pomp and solemnity, had amply satisfied the desires of the people.

The early Roman Liturgy did not, it is true, devote many festivals to celebrating even the most important mysteries of the life and Passion of our Saviour, but in its annual cycle it offered to the faithful full opportunity of meditating, at the proper season, on all the solemn mysteries of the Redemption. Therefore the homilies of St Leo I on the Transfiguration, delivered on this same night at St Peter's, are a masterpiece of their kind.

Later on, when the spirit of the Roman Liturgy was no longer clearly understood—in its dedicating, for instance, the whole of the fifteen days before Easter to the commemoration of the Passion of our Lord, the Second Sunday in Lent with the preceding Saturday to the Transfiguration, the first of January to the Holy Name of Jesus, the Invention of the Holy Cross to the honouring of the instrument of Redemption, in the midst of all the paschal rejoicings—there were added as many more feasts in memory of the Passion, of the sacred lance, etc., which, although devotional in themselves, disturb the harmonious lines of the Roman Liturgy. These form a needless repetition which detracts from the beauty of the

[1] *i.e.*, the Ottoman Turks.—TR.

original design; they are additions intended to fill up the older *lacunae,* but they show a lack of comprehension of the wealth of the liturgical treasure of the Roman Church, in reference to which we may repeat : *Floribus eius nec rosae nec lilia desunt.*

The Psalm for the Offertory is that of the preceding Wednesday; the Secret is the same as that of the other *dominica vacat* after the *Pannuchis* of December; the Communion is also from the Mass of Wednesday, while the Post-Communion is taken from Sexagesima Sunday.

Thus the patchwork composition of this Sunday's Mass confirms two important principles. The first is liturgical— namely, that the Mass of the *Pannuchis* dispensed originally with the celebration of any other Mass, so that in some places the holy Sacrifice was not offered even on Easter Day. The second principle is theological—to wit, that the ecclesiastical spirit, especially in the matter of liturgy, which to the ordinary Catholic is as a part of his Catechism, is strongly opposed to that hankering after novelty so dear to the secular mind.

Pious and simple souls are disturbed by any kind of innovation, as though they feared it would shatter the edifice of their faith, fortified by the buttress of patriotic tradition. To pray to God in those same formulas dedicated by the Fathers, to sing those same hymns which comforted them in their sorrows and labours for the Church ; all this helps us to enter more completely into their devotion, and to be sharers with them in their hopes and their ideals.

MONDAY AFTER THE SECOND SUNDAY IN LENT

Collecta at SS Cosmas and Damian.   Station at St Clement.

The basilica of the two holy physicians (*Anargyri*) stands in the Forum, having been adapted by Felix IV in the ancient *aulea* of the *Eroon* of Romulus, and the temple *Sacrae urbis* where the catastal archives of the city were kept. In the Byzantine period it was celebrated as a famous sanctuary where the two martyrs worked all manner of marvellous cures for their clients.

The Basilica of St Clement rises on the site of an ancient Roman *domus,* which a well-founded tradition connects with the Pope of that name. There is nothing unlikely in the story that Clement, in the days following the Neronian persecution, gathered together the scattered flock of Christians under the very roof of the house which we visit to-day, and encouraged them to persevere in the faith. It appears that later, during the final persecution, there was a deliberate attempt to profane the spot sanctified by Christian worship, by erecting here an altar to Mithras, which, however, under Constantine, gave place once more to the cross of Christ. A careful study of the plan of the basilica allows us to infer that the architect wished to make the position of the altar correspond with that of an ancient *aula* beneath it, which was probably known to be the one used by Clement.

St Jerome particularly mentions the *dominicum Clementis*, and as in early days basilicas were not erected in Rome to the martyrs except over their tombs, or on the site of their dwellings, the tradition concerning the house of Clement does not appear to be in any way doubtful.

The actual basilica was built on a higher level by Paschal II (1099-1118), after the first had been seriously damaged in the great conflagration on the entry of Robert Guiscard into Rome in 1084.

The Introit is derived from Psalm xxv, and is in perfect harmony with the place and the traditions concerning it. Let us call to mind that we are in the house of a martyr, and, in addition, in one of the chief ecclesiastical buildings of Rome. " Redeem me, O Lord, and have mercy on me, for my foot hath stood in the direct way." It is the martyr himself who is speaking in the person of the Psalmist. " In the churches will I bless the Lord "—that is, in those assemblies which were brought together by Clement in his own house, and which were the forerunners of our stational synaxes. " Judge me, O Lord, for I have walked in my innocence, and hoping in the Lord I shall not be weakened."

In the Collect we beseech God that we may not only afflict the flesh by fasting, but may also abstain from sin and follow justice. Thus we ask for two gifts, the one negative—*declina a malo*—the other positive—*et fac bonum*—without which piety would not be a virtue. Every virtue, in fact, disposes us to do good; indeed, it is not possible to conceive a virtue which does not tend to produce tangible result.

The lesson from Daniel (ix 15-19) describes in sorrowful words the sad condition of Rome in the seventh century, when the city was more than once surrounded by its enemies, devastated by war, famine, plague, and earthquake, so that Gregory the Great expected nothing less than the end of the world. But an immovable confidence in God and an unbounded hope lie under the pathetic lament, so the Romans, like Daniel in Babylon, doubt not that the merits of their great Apostles will avail to save the holy city, and that the great destiny promised to her by the divine Redeemer will surely be fulfilled.

The Gradual comes from Psalm lxix : " Be thou my helper and my deliverer ; O Lord, make no delay. Let my enemies be confounded and ashamed that seek my soul."

What became of Clement after his apostolate and episcopate in Rome? An ancient tradition says that he died in the Chersonesus, and perhaps the Gospel of to-day (John viii 21-29) is intended to allude to this in the words of our Lord to the Jews, when he announces his departure from Judea and the impossibility of their following him : " Whither I go, you cannot come." For Clement was an exile from Rome, even after death, and the pagan world which refused his teaching and drove him into banishment in the mines of the Crimea could not follow him to the sublime regions of faith and celestial glory.

The Offertory, from Psalm xv, renders thanks to almighty God for having given us understanding, and dwells upon the thought of his constant presence at our side, lest we should waver in face of temptation.

The Secret asks that our sacrifices of praise and propitiation may render us worthy of the divine protection.

The Communion is taken from the first verse of Psalm viii : " O Lord, our Lord, how admirable is thy name in all the earth !" He who represents on earth this name of God is, first of all, Jesus Christ, the eternal Word of God, and, in his human nature, the perfect image of the Father. Secondly, it is ourselves, as being created to the likeness of God and raised by grace to participate as far as we are able in the divine nature, and to renew it in Christ by the sanctity of our Christian life.

The Post-Communion is common to many Masses : " May this Communion, O Lord, cleanse us from guilt, and make us partakers of a heavenly remedy."

In the Prayer over the people we beg that as God has put into our hearts the hope of pardon, so he will bestow upon us also the grace of his accustomed mercy.

Terrible are the crimes caused by envy, so vividly described by St Clement in his epistle to the Church of Corinth, when he attributes to this ignoble passion even the martyrdom of St Peter and St Paul, and the immolation of numerous victims of Nero in the *Circus Vaticanus*. The Gospel of to-day describes the envy of the Synagogue—that implacable stepmother of the Church throughout the ages—against the divine Redeemer, and at the same time it announces its punishment : " You shall see me—in your hatred and despair —but you shall not find me, nor can your malice touch me ; and you shall die in your sin."

TUESDAY AFTER THE SECOND SUNDAY IN LENT

Station at St Balbina.

There was no *collecta* on this day, perhaps because the Basilica of St Balbina stood alone, far away on the Aventine, there being no other church in its vicinity from which the stational procession could set out.

The foundress of the *titulus Balbinae*—dedicated at first to the divine Redeemer, before it took the name of the martyr Balbina, who was buried in the cemetery of Prae-textatus—was perhaps the matron Balbina, after whom a portion of the vast necropolis of St Callixtus was called. It appears, indeed, as though to-day's liturgy intended, by the narrative of the widow of Sarephta, in whose house the prophet Elias was lodging, to render homage to the faith of this Balbina, who towards the end of the fourth century transformed her palace into a church, and there received the Saviour.

The Introit is derived from Psalm xxvi. The soul longs ardently to contemplate the face of God, and will not be satisfied with anything less: "My heart hath said to thee, I have sought thy face: thy face, O Lord, will I seek: turn not away thy face from me." The desire is excellent; but how pure those eyes must be that seek to look on the brightness of God.

In the Collect we ask God to grant us the grace to persevere in the fast we have undertaken, and thus to carry out the observance of which he first gave us the example.

The lesson, telling us of the widow of Sarephta of the Sidonians, comes from 3 Kings (xvii 8-16) and symbolizes the rejection of the Redeemer by Israel, and his reception by the Gentile nation, desolate after many fruitless unions. The poor woman, when the prophet met her, was gathering two sticks, just the number requisite to form a cross, for it was through the wood of the cross alone that salvation was to come to Jews and Gentiles alike.

The Gradual is the same as that of the Thursday after Ash Wednesday; the Mass for that day dates, as we have already seen, from the time of Gregory II, but the original place of the Gradual *Jacta* (Psalm liv) is in to-day's liturgy.

The Gospel is taken from St Matthew (xxiii 1-12), and warns us not to imitate the empty ambition of the Rabbis of Israel who displayed great zealousness in the knowledge of the *Torah*, out of mere ostentation, in order to be given the first places in the assemblies, and to be honoured and reverenced by the people. We are all disciples in the school of Christ, and he is the only true teacher and father of our souls. It is true that we give in his honour these names to those, too, who represent him on earth, but the veneration which we profess for the sacred hierarchy is like that which we show to holy images. The honour we render them, is not addressed to the picture or to the statue itself, but to the person represented thereby.

The Offertory is from the beginning of Psalm l—one of the penitential psalms : " Have mercy on me, O Lord, according to thy great mercy : O Lord, blot out my iniquities."

In the Secret, we beseech God to accomplish our sanctification by means of the sacred mysteries, and by purifying us from earthly vices, to render us worthy of his heavenly gifts.

The Communion comes from Psalm ix, with its joyous antiphon : " I will relate all thy wonders : I will be glad and rejoice in thee : I will sing praise to thy name, O thou most High."

The Post-Communion to-day is full of beauty : " That we may be made worthy, O Lord, of thy sacred gifts, grant us, we beseech thee, ever to obey thy commandments."

In the final Benediction of the people, we pray that the divine mercy may favourably accept our supplications, and heal the diseases of our souls, so that having obtained the forgiveness of our sins, we may truly rejoice in the blessing of God.

There is a morbid tendency in persons disposed to melancholy, and but little filled with the love of God, to approach Jesus with fear and trembling, as though in the presence of an inexorable and pitiless judge—his Heart, on the contrary, contains such a wealth of compassion for our miseries, that no one will ever be able to exhaust it, for the more wretched we are rendered by sin, the more is he drawn to pity us. St Paul says that the Pontiff of our faith is not of such a nature as not to be able to feel compassion for us, and is therefore in this far removed from the Pharisees in the Gospel, who laid insupportable and fantastic burdens on the people, which instead of assisting them to advance, crushed them in the way. Experience shows that the most faulty and imperfect souls are always those who expect the most of others, whilst those who are truly full of the love of God are ever loving and compassionate towards their neighbour.

WEDNESDAY AFTER THE SECOND SUNDAY IN LENT

Collecta at St George.   Station at St Cecilia.

The basilica where the people met to-day for the *collecta* before the procession still stands on the further side of the *pons Senatorum,* in the *regio* of the Velabrum.

The *titulus Caeciliae* is in Trastevere, in the actual house of the martyr.   Recent discoveries have brought to light a great part of this ancient Roman dwelling, where St Cecilia first converted to the faith her husband, Valerian, together with his brother Tiburtius, and which she afterwards hallowed by her martyrdom.   In 1595, the sarcophagus under the high altar containing her relics was opened, and the body of the holy virgin was found in the same position as it had assumed after the fatal blow of the executioner, lying on one side, with the knees slightly bent and her arms stretched along her side.   She was clad in costly robes woven with gold, but under the silken folds the rough hair-shirt, with which, according to her *Acta,* she chastised her flesh, could be plainly felt.   Beside her, in separate tombs, Paschal I (817-24) laid the bodies of the martyrs Tiburtius, Valerian and Maximus, and of the Popes Lucius and Urban.

The Introit, taken from Psalm xxxvii, is the appealing cry of the martyr, who amidst her torments calls upon God not to abandon her, but to come to her aid.

In the Collect we beseech almighty God favourably to regard his people who are mortifying themselves in the hope that his grace may give them strength to abstain from sin. The representation of Cecilia, who, adorned with golden ornaments and Byzantine gems, is resplendent in the apsidal mosaic of Paschal I, evokes the memory of Esther imploring from the Persian king the salvation of her people.   The prayer of Mardochai in to-day's lesson (Esther xiii 8-17) might well have been uttered by the inhabitants of Rome in the seventh century, when the Eternal City was more than once besieged, with the result that the cemeteries of the martyrs and the extra-mural basilicas were abandoned to the depredations of the Lombards, and the once joyful chants of the Liturgy seemed to have perished, choked by the tears and lamentations of the people.   Truly there was need to say with Mardochai : " Shut not the mouths of them that sing to thee, O Lord our God."   These words apply also to St Cecilia—the patron of sacred music—who, whilst the harps of the mystical banquet sounded in her ears, sang to the Lord in her heart : " Keep thou my heart unspotted, that it may not suffer evil."

The Gradual comes from Psalm xxvii : " Save thy people, O Lord, and bless thine inheritance. Unto thee have I cried, O Lord; my God, be not thou silent to me, lest I become like them that go down into the pit."

The usual Tract *Domine non secundum,* etc., follows.

Like the Mother of James and John, of whom the Gospel of to-day speaks (Matt. **xx** 17-28), Cecilia presents her petition to the Lord, and asks that her two spiritual children, Valerian and Tiburtius, who through her have received the faith, may be enthroned with him in heaven. Her prayer is granted, but on one condition—that they drink the chalice of martyrdom. This condition they accept. Valerian and Tiburtius bow their necks to the sword of the executioner, and whilst their bodies lie in peace under the altar beside that of the virgin martyr, their souls are for ever united to hers in heaven.

The Offertory is the same as that of the First Sunday of Advent. It is the uplifting of a troubled soul to God, in the steadfast hope that he will save her from her enemies.

The Secret is as follows : " Graciously regard the sacrifices which we offer thee, O Lord, and by this holy intercourse loosen the bonds of our sins."

The Communion is from Psalm x : " The Lord is just, and hath loved justice ; his countenance hath beheld righteousness."

In the Post-Communion, we pray that the holy Sacrifice may profit us to that eternal redemption in which Christ has caused us also to have our part.

Jesus feeds among the lilies, and is the restorer and lover of innocence. His blood cleanses the garments of the penitent ; thus in the Prayer over the people the priest to-day begs for this purification, so that the faithful, inflamed by holy fervour, may be steadfast in the faith, and zealous in all good works.

The privilege which Jesus concedes to his chosen friends is that of drinking his chalice. The draught is bitter, but it gives strength to the soul. Love is nourished on sacrifice and pain. The more we love Jesus, the more we shall suffer for him. We suffer because we love, and we love because pain feeds the pure flame of love. Thus the Seraph of Assisi, with his hands and feet and side pierced by love, taught the people how to love and suffer in the words :

> " So great the good I have in sight,
> It changeth pain into delight."[1]

---

[1] " Tant'è il bene ch'io m'aspetto,
Che ogni pena m'è diletto."

THURSDAY AFTER THE SECOND SUNDAY IN LENT

Collecta at St Chrysogonus. Station at St Mary in Trastevere.

The Basilica of St Chrysogonus in Trastevere stands on the same spot as the former house of the martyr, of which the rooms were used to form the sanctuary or crypt under the high altar. The church is claimed to have been built under Constantine, and the veneration paid to St Chrysogonus was so widely spread in Rome in the fourth century that his name is still to be found in the diptychs of the Roman Canon.

The stational Basilica of St Mary in Trastevere is one of the most ancient in the city, and may be considered as a continuation or enlargement of the *titulus Callisti,* which is quite near it.

We know for a fact on the authority of Lampridius that Alexander Severus confirmed by a legal decree the right of the Christians to the possession of a meeting-place in the Trastevere, which had been contested by the *popinarii* of the *Taberna emeritoria.* Ancient documents identify this place with the *titulus Callisti,* from which, strictly speaking, the actual *Basilica Julii* built *juxta Callistum* by Pope Julius I (341-52) should be distinguished, though the two buildings were so close together that in the Middle Ages they formed but one edifice, whilst the site had already been named *Area Callisti,* after the first founder of the *titulus.*

An ancient tradition says that on this spot Pope Callixtus (219-24) died for the faith, being thrown into a well. Hippolytus, in his pamphlet against Callixtus, is altogether silent on this point, which, however, is rendered very probable by the fact that the Pontiff was buried in the cemetery of Calepodius on the Via Aurelia, instead of being placed— as was customary in the case of the Popes of the third century—in the great cemetery on the Via Appia, which he himself had enlarged and which accordingly bears his name. Grave reasons must have necessitated this course, and we should probably not be far from the truth in inferring that the Pope, who was well known in Trastevere before his admission to the ranks of the priesthood, perished in a popular riot, and that the faithful considered it more prudent to lay his body in the neighbouring cemetery of the Via Aurelia than to risk exciting the fury of the pagans by carrying it as far as the second milestone on the Via Appia.

The body of Callixtus, together with those of the martyred priest Calepodius and Pope Julius I, now lies under the high altar of the splendid Basilica of our Lady, at which the station is held to-day.

The Introit is from Psalm lxix, so dear to the early Fathers of the desert, who frequently made use of the first verse as an ejaculatory prayer at every action of the day, in moments of temptation, and in the hour of danger : " O God, come to my assistance; O Lord, make haste to help me : let my enemies be confounded and ashamed that seek my soul."

In the Collect we pray that, as we apply ourselves to fasting and prayer, we may keep far from us that terrible foe, who, as the Gospel tells us, can be cast out only *oratione et jejunio.*

The Lesson from Jeremias (xvii 5-10) prepares the way for the parable of Lazarus and Dives. Here, too, we see two types of persons : the one who finds his paradise in this world, and rests all his hope on created things and on the pleasures of this life; the other who leans on the arm of the Lord as on a pillar of strength. He who places his trust only in his fellow-men will fall with them, whilst he who hopes in the Lord will not be confounded for ever.

The Gradual *Propitius* is the same as that which comes after the first lesson of the *Pannuchis* of Ember Saturday in Lent.

Whether the remembrance of the *Taberna emeritoria* suggested the choice of the parable of the rich reveller or not, it could not have been more appropriate. The idolater, like those of whom the Apostle says " their god is their belly," spends his life in the enjoyment of every worldly good, whilst the Christian, oftentimes deprived of temporal comforts, goes on his way in poverty, want, and affliction, bowed down beneath the weight of the cross. This is the story of the Church during the nineteen centuries and more that have passed since her foundation. Her very existence emanates from the cross of Christ, and it would not be possible for those who live the Christian life so to change their nature as to be happy according to the ideas of the world. The hour of judgement will come and will restore the balance of justice. Lazarus is carried by the hands of angels to Abraham's bosom, while the proud worldling is buried in hell.

The Offertory is the same as that of the Twelfth Sunday after Pentecost, but the words, sublime as they are, do not give any idea of its beauty, unless clothed in the harmonies of the Gregorian chant : " Moses prayed in the sight of the

Lord his God, and said, Why, O Lord, art thou angry with thy people? let the anger of thy soul be appeased. Remember Abraham, Isaac, and Jacob, to whom thou sworest that thou wouldst give the land flowing with milk and honey. And the Lord was appeased from the evil which he said he would do to his people."

This passage (Exodus xxxii 11-14) is very important also from the theological point of view, for it shows (contrary to Protestant opinion) how efficacious are the merits of the saints when invoked by the faithful, in propitiating divine justice.

In the Gospel the rich man is reminded of Moses and the prophets, whose teaching should suffice and render unnecessary any such prodigy as the return of one from the dead; while Gregory II, too, recalls once more in the Offertory the memory of these ancient Patriarchs.

The Secret keeps before us the object of the stational sacrifice, which is that of consecrating the fast, for which reason it was accepted as a principle in Rome from earliest times that there should be no fast unless it could be at once followed by the offering of the eucharistic oblation. The Mass and the fast are in strict relationship to one another. The celebration of the one marked the termination of the other; wherefore there was no Mass throughout the duration of the fast, and there was never any fast that was not concluded by the holy Sacrifice. Moreover, to-day's Secret clearly reflects this feeling of the early Church: " May the fast we have devoted to thy name, O Lord, sanctify us by means of this sacrifice; that what our observance professes exteriorly, it may effectually operate internally."

The Communion, as is often the case in these Masses of the time of Gregory II, is derived from the Gospels; but, contrary to the usual custom, the passage is not from that read in the Mass of to-day—it is a eucharistic antiphon: " He that eateth my flesh and drinketh my blood, abideth in me, and I in him, saith the Lord " (John vi 57).

In the Post-Communion we pray that the grace of God may not forsake us, but that we may devote ourselves still more earnestly to the divine service, and thus obtain the happy effects of a closer union with God.

The final Blessing over the people asks that God would deign to accept the prayers of his people, and as these glory in being the work of his hands, and of being governed by his Providence, so he, by this same Providence, would make good all the deficiencies of the household of the faith, and rendering it worthy of the truths it professes, would maintain it for ever one, holy, catholic, and apostolic in the fulness of divine love.

The rich man dies and is buried in hell. What a fearful warning for those who allow themselves to be carried away by the lure of earthly pleasures! *Recepisti bona in vita tua.* This is the share which divine justice reserves for Esau and for all those who, whilst they do not actually forfeit eternal life by reason of their sins, yet expect a temporal reward for the few virtues they have acquired and for the trifling good they have done.

FRIDAY AFTER THE SECOND SUNDAY IN LENT

Collecta at St Agatha in Monasterio. Station at St Vitalis.

The meeting-place to-day is in the deaconry of St Agatha " of the Goths " in the Suburra, which was restored to Catholic worship by Gregory the Great. From there the procession went to the neighbouring Church of Vestina, dedicated under Innocent I (402-17) to the martyr Vitalis. Who was this Vitalis? Probably a Roman martyr, confused by Ado in his martyrology with the saint of the same name at Ravenna, and if so, this church records the place where his house once stood.

In the celebrated *Litania septiformis* of St Gregory, at the time of the plague, the Basilica of Vestina was chosen as the place of assembly whence the procession of the widows was to move towards St Peter's. In ancient times the priests of this church had the administration of the cemetery *in agello* in the Via Nomentana where St Agnes was buried.

In the Mass, the choice of the lesson of Joseph let down by his brothers into an empty well, and the Gospel of the wicked husbandmen who stoned their master's son, was suggested by the *Acta* of St Vitalis, which tell us how the martyr was first buried up to the waist in a pit and then stoned to death.

The Introit comes from Psalm xvi : " As for me, I shall appear with justice in thy sight : I shall be satisfied whilst thy glory shall be made manifest." It is the martyr who speaks, and as the sun of his life sets in tribulation, already greets by faith the dawn of his triumph.

In the Collect we pray that we may be cleansed by the holy fast from all fleshly stain, and thus enabled to celebrate with pure hearts the Paschal Sacrament which is to come.

The Lesson is taken from Genesis (xxxvii 6-22). Joseph, sold by his brethren to the Ishmaelite merchants and carried off by them into Egypt, where he was raised by God to the dignity of ruler and saviour of the people, is a type of Jesus Christ delivered by those of his own race to the Roman governor to be crucified; but God exalts the humble obedience of his Son, and, raising him up, bestows on him the glory of a name which is above every name.

In the Gradual it is still the just man who suffers persecution—the martyr—who calls on Jehovah in his tribulation and is heard. " Deliver my soul, O Lord," he cries with the Psalmist (Ps. cxix) "from wicked lips and a deceitful tongue."

The Gospel of the wicked husbandmen follows (Matt. xxi 33-46), in which is clearly foretold the rejection of the Synagogue as unworthy, and the election of the Gentiles in its place, a terrible sentence which for nineteen centuries and more has weighed on Israel and on all the enemies of Christ. He is indeed the stone which the builders rejected, but which is become the head of the corner. He who shall fall upon this stone shall perish, and he upon whom it shall fall shall be crushed.

The history of nineteen centuries of Christianity has confirmed the truth of this prophecy. Nero, Galerius, and Diocletian have passed like a hurricane which rages for a time but is soon spent; all the idols of pagan Rome lie beneath the blue waters of the Mediterranean, where the vessels of the Vandals sank, laden with the treasures of the Eternal City, which they had pillaged for fifteen days in succession. At the beginning of the fourth century Lactantius wrote his book *De mortibus persecutorum,* but, besides the names of those persecutors who followed, how many blank pages still remain on which to record the chastisements of the future enemies of Christ ! All the centuries pass in review before him, he alone *vincit, regnat, imperat, heri, hodie, ipse et in saecula.*

The Offertory from Psalm xxxix is the cry of the oppressed calling God to his aid. His enemies may deprive him of life, but God will receive the soul of the martyr in glory, whilst the shame of the sacrilege will recoil upon his murderers.

The Secret is brief and concise. In it we ask for two things : firstly, that the holy Sacrifice *actione permanet et operatione firmetur*—in other words, that the efficacy and mystical working of the Sacrifice may be fully and lastingly realized in the souls of the communicants—and, secondly, that their effect may be intensified by an assiduous correspondence to grace on the part of the faithful.

The Communion is from Psalm xi : " Thou, O Lord, wilt preserve us and keep us from this generation for ever."

Keep us, that is, not only in our bodily life, but also in thy grace and thy love, for, without the constant support of thine arm, we cannot move one step nor even stand upright before thee.

The Post-Communion has the charm of classical antiquity : "Grant, we beseech thee, O Lord, that having received the pledge of eternal salvation, we may in such manner tend towards it as to be able to arrive thither."

In the prayer of Benediction over the people the priest invokes the divine grace, that it may preserve the faithful in mind and body. It is, in a better sense, the *mens sana in corpore sano* of the heathen poet; for an exaggerated spiritualism which separates that which God has joined together is as inimical to true piety as is sensual materialism. Soul and body have both shared the guilt of sin; it is therefore necessary that both should have part in the expiation, the sanctification, and in the final glorification of each.

The Church, as though she feared that the very splendour of her liturgy might lead simple folk into thinking that Christianity consisted merely in holding functions and receiving the sacraments, insists continually in her Lenten formulas that we should, by our good works, give reality to what is so sublimely expressed in the liturgy. Without this personal and intimate realization, brought about by constant effort, the liturgy would become a kind of magic formula. This fact clearly explains the words of the Gospel that many who during this life hold a high place among the followers of Christ, who even prophesy and work wonders in his name, will after death be rejected and condemned by our Lord himself. *Nescio vos*—"I know you not—depart from me all ye that work iniquity." It is not ritual forms nor a sterile faith, but the good deeds inspired by a living faith, that will gain for us everlasting salvation.

SATURDAY AFTER THE SECOND SUNDAY IN LENT

Collecta at St Clement. Station at SS Peter and Marcellinus.

The church of the *Collecta* is already well known to us; it is the *dominicum Clementis,* about three hundred yards distant from the *titulus* of SS Peter and Marcellinus. This basilica was built during the lifetime of Pope Siricius (385-98), and, according to the Roman custom, it probably marks the dwelling-place on that spot of one at least of the two martyrs whose names it bears. We know from Pope

Damasus (366-84) that as a boy he learnt the circumstances of their martyrdom from the lips of the executioner himself.

Percussor retulit mihi Damaso cum puer essem.

As the liturgy of this day lays great stress on the contrast between the two brothers, Esau and Jacob, and between the faithful son and the prodigal, it is possible that underneath there lies an allusion to that executioner, who expiated his crime by baptism and penitence.

The Introit, taken from Psalm xviii, praises the law of God, which is perfect and unalterable, and, while it enlightens the intellect as to the claims of duty, also arouses the heart and strengthens the will to accomplish that duty. This is the difference between the mild evangelical law and the laws of men—and, for the most part, those, too, of the Synagogue. Men preach and speak well, indeed, but without making sufficient allowance for the weakness of human nature, which cannot rise to higher things unless God himself lifts it up and infuses into it the desire to will what he wills.

The Collect expresses the usual sentiment of the Lenten fast, desiring that the chastisement of the flesh may promote the vigour of our souls.

The Lesson from Genesis (xxvii 6-40), relating how Jacob took the place of the first-born son Esau and obtained his father's blessing, alludes to the Gentiles, who in the divine economy of redemption take the place of the Jewish people, being protected by the merits of our Lord Jesus Christ, typified by the skins of the kids which covered the neck and hands of Jacob.

The Gradual is derived from Psalm xci : " It is good to give praise to the Lord, and to sing to thy name, O most High. To show forth thy mercy in the morning, and thy truth in the night." The just man feels the need of raising his thoughts to God and communing with him in prayer at all times. Therefore in the early morning he gives thanks for the mercy which awaits him ere the sun has gilded the mountain-tops with its rays, and again in the evening, when all is quiet around him and nature is wrapped in shadow, he, too, following the example of Jesus, who *erat pernoctans in oratione Dei,* lifts up his soul to the Lord and obtains from above that light and strength which he needs for the labours of the coming day. So, too, does the Church act, of which it is written in the Book of Proverbs, *De nocte surrexit deditque praedam domesticis suis . . . non exstinguetur in nocte lucerna eius*[1]*;* and this has been the practice of all the

[1] **xxxi** 15, 18.

great apostles and saints—as, for instance, of St Francis
Xavier, who laboured by day among the heathen Indians,
and by night communed with our Lord in the Blessed Sacrament of the Altar concerning the affairs of his apostolic
ministry.

The parable in the Gospel (Luke xv 11-32) of the prodigal
son carries on the allegory begun in the preceding lesson.
The prodigal represents the Gentile people, who have squan-
dered their inheritance of natural virtues by giving way to
their evil passions, and because they have not willed to
recognize God as they should have done by the light of
reason, were abandoned by God's justice, as St Paul teaches
us, *in reprobum sensum et in passionem ignominiae.* The
self-righteous son, who is angry because his father rejoices
over the return of the poor prodigal in penitence to the
paternal home, represents the Jewish people, who tried every
means in their power to prevent the Apostles from opening
the gate of redemption to the heathen around them.

The Offertory is from Psalm xii: " Enlighten my eyes,
that I may never sleep in death; lest at any time my enemy
say, I have prevailed against him." The sleep of death
signifies not only the death of the body, but also that of the
soul which is sunk in the lethargy of final impenitence. Such
a soul no longer feels either shame or remorse; it glories in
its wrongdoing, for outwardly it is prosperous and successful.
This condition is a prelude to final reprobation, and Jeremias
compares those who are enjoying this apparent happiness to
a flock of sheep fattening in fertile meadows in preparation
for the hour of slaughter.

The sleep of death represents also lukewarmness and indifference, which of all spiritual evils is one of the most
difficult to cure. It is necessary to ward it off with great
diligence, and to that end the soul must constantly seek the
light which comes from on high, for the twilight of devotions,
monotonously performed from mere force of habit, easily
induces this dangerous somnolence of the spirit.

The Secret is inspired by the following verse from Psalm
xviii: *Ab occultis meis munda me, et ab alienis parce servo
tuo,* according to the text of the Septuagint and of the
Vulgate, which probably is inexact. Instead of *alienis* or
strangers, we should aparently read and translate: *From
the proud* preserve thy servant, O Lord. The Secret modifies
to some extent the expression of the Psalmist, and implores,
through the merits of the eucharistic sacrifice, the remission
not only of personal sins, but also of those which are collective, external, and general, such as we sometimes commit
through omission in cases where we are bound to prevent evil
and do not do so.

This is a somewhat unusual but truthful aspect of the responsibility which we have before our conscience and before God for the sins which our dependants, or even the whole community, may commit through our acquiescence, or through our solidarity with those who are violating the laws of divine justice. Especially in these days, when the nations govern themselves by a representative system, how many crimes may be committed, even by abstention, in political elections and in parliamentary sittings, of which the guilt falls not on one individual alone, but on the whole people.

The Communion comes from the Gospel of to-day : " Thou oughtest to rejoice, my son, because thy brother was dead and is come to life again ; he was lost and is found."

In the Post-Communion we pray that the power of the Sacrament may penetrate our inmost being, but in order to obtain this result we must open wide the door of our soul, and keep no secret and hidden places where our Lord cannot enter.

In the Prayer over the people the priest beseeches almighty God mercifully to preserve his family—that is, the Church militant ; and as, unlike the Church triumphant, which consists entirely of the saints in heaven, the Church on earth depends solely on his merciful forgiveness of our sins, we ask him so to assist us with his grace that our confidence in him may not be in vain.

Let us not show ourselves harsh towards those who, like the prodigal son, return home from a great distance. We ourselves were once a long way off, and if we now belong to the household of the faith it is because the good Shepherd has brought us back to the fold. We must try to smooth away difficulties, to help on conversions, and to imitate the angels of God, who rejoice with Jesus in heaven over one repentant sinner.

THE THIRD SUNDAY IN LENT

Station at St Lawrence Without the Walls.

The Laurentian basilica owes its foundation to Constantine, but, being considered too small, a large upper *aula* was added to it by Pelagius II (578-90) and dedicated to the Blessed Virgin. For this reason Leo IV (847-55) decreed that the station of the Octave of the Assumption should be held there, and the Gospel of to-day alludes to this dedication by praising the great Mother of God, who not only gave her own substance to form the sacred humanity of the Lord's Anointed, but was, on her part, nourished spiritually by the divine Word and lived thereby. The other portions of the Mass have been chosen in connection with the martyr after whom the Basilica Tiburtina is named.

The Introit is from Psalm xxiv : " My eyes are ever towards the Lord, for he shall pluck my feet out of the snare : look thou upon me, and have mercy on me, for I am alone and poor." It is Lawrence, the cross-bearer of the Roman Church, who, surrounded by enemies and placed on the fiery gridiron, calls upon God for help, obtains it, and conquers.

The Collect is of a general nature. It prays that God may look upon us, and, seeing our misery, may stretch forth his right arm to help us. According to the *Acta* of St Lawrence, whilst the intrepid martyr was enveloped by the red glare of the fire, another light from on high filled his soul. Pelagius II, having finished his great work of transforming the original Basilica of St Lawrence, and having brought it to the level of the cemetery of Cyriaca, thereby letting into it the light which flooded the upper *aula*, took this thought as a motive for the graceful distich which can still be read around the mosaic of the great triumphal arch :

Martyrium olim flammis Levita subisti
Jure tuis templis lux beneranda redit.

In the Epistle to the Ephesians (v 1-9), read as the lesson for to-day, St Paul speaks very appropriately of the divine light and its fruits, which are first described in their negative aspect, when he warns his hearers against sensual pleasures, evil-speaking, and covetousness, and then in their positive aspect *in omni bonitate, justitia et veritate*. Goodness and justice are exercised through the will, and truth through the intellect. The first two virtues should balance each other, lest the one or the other be excessive. Truth enlightens the mind, in order that the judgement which precedes an action may conform to the divine will. It is precisely in this conformity that truth consists.

The Gradual is taken from Psalm viii, and invokes the help of the Lord that, in spite of the apparent triumph of the tyrant over the martyr, the final victory may rest with God. Indeed, St Lawrence already foresees that glorious day, and beholds the enemy retreating, losing strength, and vanishing before the coming of the Lord. Prudentius has magnificently expressed in his *Peristephanon* these sentiments of St Lawrence on the gridiron, when he makes the martyr see a distant vision of Constantine giving peace to the Church and raising glorious basilicas to those who shed their blood for the faith.

The Tract, originally the conclusion of the second lesson preceding the Gospel, comes from Psalm cxxii. It tells how the soul, oppressed by the tribulations of this life, lifts up her gaze to heaven, and as the eyes of the servant and the hand-maid watch for the slightest sign from their master, so does she keep her eyes ever fixed on the Lord.

The Gospel of to-day could not be more appropriate. Before the coming of Christ the devil tyrannized over the world, and his strongholds were those of idolatry and sensuality. The Messias came, and by the sacrifice of the cross freed humanity from the cruel yoke. The house of which the Gospel speaks symbolizes the whole world, but more especially pagan Rome, the strong fortress of the empire of Satan, but which God overcame by his martyrs. St Lawrence, from the earliest times, was honoured as the standard-bearer of these hosts, and as such is represented in ancient mosaics with a cross in his hand. As he lay dying he hailed already the monogram of Christ, reproduced *ad Saxa Rubra* on the triumphant *labarum,* and foretold the conversion of the first Christian Cæsar.

A woman in the multitude took occasion from the discourse of our Lord to praise his blessed Mother. Jesus did not forbid it, but, passing over the privilege of being the Mother of God according to the flesh—a privilege upon which it was not fitting that that carnal and sensual people should dwell overmuch—insists rather on the meritorious worth of those who receive spiritually the divine Word and retain it in their heart.

The Offertory from Psalm xviii sings the praises of this divine Word, the eternal law of holiness which rejoices the heart and does not oppress it, for grace bends the will to obey, whilst leaving it full freedom of action. The Word of God is sweeter than the honey that drops from the honey-comb.

The Secret is that of the Third Sunday after the Epiphany.

The Communion is taken from Psalm lxxxiii: "The sparrow hath found herself a house, and the turtle a nest where she may lay her young: thy altars, O Lord of hosts, my King and my God; blessed are they that dwell in thy house, they shall praise thee for ever and ever." These are more especially the feelings of a pious soul dwelling under the same roof as Jesus in the Blessed Sacrament, who day and night, in the canticles of the sacred Liturgy, vies with the Seraphim in heaven in singing praises to the majesty of almighty God.

The Post-Communion follows: "Mercifully absolve us, we beseech thee, O Lord, from all guilt and danger, on whom thou bestowest the participation of so great a mystery.'' Indeed, as the Council of Trent teaches us, the Holy Communion is not only an antidote against the renewal of sin, but a salutary fount, a bath of fire, in which the soul is cleansed from the stains contracted day by day through its imperfections.

The Church celebrates her solemn stations in the sanctuaries of the martyrs in order to remind us that we are the heirs of their spiritual patrimony. Their blood cemented the first Christian edifice, and we, as children of the martyrs, possess their sepulchres and the places sanctified by their confession, inasmuch as we succeed them in the profession of the same faith.

MONDAY AFTER THE THIRD SUNDAY IN LENT

Collecta at St Adrian. Station at St Mark.

The church of the deaconry of St Adrian is in the Forum in the former *aula* of the Senate. It was dedicated by Pope Honorius I (625-38) to the memory of this famous martyr of Nicomedia, who, during the Byzantine era, was the object of much devotion in Rome, where churches and monasteries were built in his honour.

The stational basilica *de Pallacine*, dedicated later on to St Mark the Evangelist, was erected by the Pope of that name (337-40), and is the only church in Rome sacred to the memory of this devoted disciple of St Paul and faithful interpreter of St Peter, who, besides sharing with these Apostles the first evangelization of the Eternal City, wrote his Gospel after their death, at the request of the faithful in Rome. Under the high-altar of the *titulus Marci* rests the body of the founder with the relics of the martyrs Abdon and Sennen. We find ourselves here, as it were, in an Eastern sanctuary in the very heart of the city, with Mark the founder of the Patriarchate of Alexandria on the one hand—for the Egyptian element was strong in Rome—and the Persians Abdon and Sennen on the other.

The scriptural passage read to-day has in mind the Eastern origin of the titular patrons of the basilica, and tells us, therefore, of the Syrian Naaman, who, rejecting the grander rivers of Damascus, was cleansed from his leprosy in the lesser waters of the Jordan.

This extract is well adapted to the catechumens who yesterday began their course of instruction preparatory to baptism. Peter, observes Tertullian, baptized in the Tiber, and if the aspirants desire to be healed from the leprosy of infidelity and original sin, they must humble themselves, and, abandoning the rivers of Damascus—that is, the attractions of their former worldly life, must wash themselves clean in the pure waters of holy baptism.

The Introit is derived from Psalm lv. With the glory given by men, the psalmist contrasts the glory he will receive from God, whose word will never be made void, nor can all the threats of man prevail against those to whom the Lord has promised salvation.

In the Collect the Church insists again on the quality of our fast, which must have nothing in common with that of the followers of Islam nor with that of the Jews. The Christian fast consists essentially in curbing our passions and avoiding sin.

The Lesson from 4 Kings (v 1-15) follows, with the story of the healing of Naaman by Eliseus the prophet, through his bathing seven times in the Jordan. The Syrian, covered with leprosy but full of pride in spite of his terrible condition, was angry because the seer of Israel had not made use of solemn rites and special formulas to heal him, and had not even come out of his house to speak to him, but merely ordered him by a messenger to wash in the waters of the Jordan.

Yet it is thus that God acts when overcoming the devil in his pride, by employing humble means, such as the sacraments and sacramentals, in order that Satan's defeat shall be the more humiliating. Naaman, therefore, if he wished to be cured, had first to lay aside all pride, to acknowledge his uncleanness, and to wash himself in the Jordan, in those very waters where, some centuries later, John baptized with the baptism of penance, in preparation for our Christian baptism.

The Gradual—as is the rule—is taken from the same psalm as the Introit : " O God, I have declared to thee my life : thou hast set my tears in thy sight. Have mercy on me, O Lord, for man hath trodden me under foot : all the day long he hath afflicted me, fighting against me."

The Gospel of to-day is suggested by the preceding lesson from the fourth Book of Kings. Our Saviour in the Synagogue of Nazareth reproaches his countrymen with having imitated the incredulity of their ancestors of the time of Eliseus, which obliged the prophet to work miracles only in favour of strangers, a terrible example which may well give us food for reflection. The divine graces poured forth so abundantly sometimes on certain favoured souls, meet with such very insufficient co-operation that there supervene indifference and a turning away from holy things. Those sacraments, those sermons, and those devotional exercises which sometimes touch the heart of the sinner so deeply, have no longer any effect on those pious souls who have become lukewarm and apathetic through the very abundance of divine gifts, and are like those sick persons who can no longer digest the food they take.

The Offertory is from Psalm liv : " Hear, O God, my prayer, and despise not my supplication : be attentive to me and hear me." God always hears the prayer of a humble and sincere heart. Even when the unworthiness of the suppliant renders certain special graces which he dares to ask for inopportune, God does not let the prayer go unanswered, but grants him that which is more important, a return to sanctifying grace through a sincere conversion.

The Secret of to-day is a very beautiful prayer : " Grant, O Lord, that the offering of our homage which we make unto thee may be made to us a sacrament available to our salvation."

The Communion, too, from Psalm xiii, resembles a cry of victory : " Who shall give salvation to Israel out of Sion ? when the Lord shall have turned away the captivity of his people, Jacob shall rejoice and Israel shall be glad."

The Post-Communion repeats in other words a thought which is often seen in similar prayers in the Roman Liturgy : " Grant, we beseech thee, almighty and merciful God, that what we take with our mouths we may receive with clean minds."

The Blessing over the people is expressed thus : " Let thy mercy, O Lord, assist us, that by thy protection we may deserve to be delivered from the threatening dangers of our sins, and to be saved by thy deliverance."

Rome was continually being attacked by the Goths, Visigoths, and Lombards, shaken by earthquakes and decimated by famine and pestilence during the fifth, sixth, and seventh centuries.

If Venice boasts of possessing the relics of St Mark, Rome may with greater justice address to him the salutation used by the " Serenissima "[1] : *Pax tibi, Marce, Evangelista meus.*[2] " Meus," indeed, by the very best of rights, for St Mark and St Luke exercised their apostolate in the Eternal City immediately after the two Princes of the Church, St Peter and St Paul ; it was there that they wrote their Gospels, and Christian antiquity loved to give to St Mark the glorious title of " Interpreter of Peter."

[1] *i.e.,* the Republic of Venice.
[2] Tradition has it that St Mark was saluted at Venice by an angel with these words, which were consequently added by the Venetian Republic to its arms.—Tr.

TUESDAY AFTER THE THIRD SUNDAY IN LENT

Collecta at SS Sergius and Bacchus.   Station at
St Pudentiana.

The church where the assembly meets to-day owes its origin to the zeal of the Byzantines, who built at least five churches in Rome to the honour of the martyrs Sergius and Bacchus.   One of these, the *Canelicum,* with the adjacent monastery, where the people collected for the stational procession to the Basilica of Pudens, stood in the *regio* of the *Montes.*   The *domus Pudentiana* or the *titulus sancti Pudentis* was one of the oldest of the urban titular churches, and, so far, nothing has appeared to disprove the truth of the ancient ecclesiastical tradition which asserts that it was sanctified by the sojourn of Peter in the house of the senator Pudens.   The memories of Pope St Pius I (158-67), of his brother Hermas, the mystic author of the *Pastor,* those of Priscilla, Pudentiana, Praxedes, Justin the Philosopher, Hippolytus the Doctor—all these are connected with the Viminal and with the history of the house of the Pudenti in such a way as to make it appear that in the second century this was really the papal residence.

The sacred Liturgy has re-echoed this local tradition, and the Gospel for to-day, containing the passage in which Peter interrogates our Lord concerning the forgiveness of sins, has been chosen on purpose, in order to recall the memory of the Apostle in the very place where he was the guest of the Pudenti.

The Introit, from Psalm xvi, beautifully expresses the hope that the Lord will guard under the shadow of his wings all those that trust in him.   This verse of the psalm should be borne in mind when examining the apsidal mosaic of the Basilica of St Pudentiana, in which we see the Saviour stretching out his hand to protect the apostolic church and ancient residence of the Popes of the second century.   He holds an open book in which we may read the words : *Dominus conservator Ecclesiae Pudentianae,* to express a special tutelage over this basilica, which in olden times was a visible token and monument of the apostolate and primacy of St Peter.

The Collect again implores that the fruits of the fast expressed in the Lenten Preface may be granted : *corporali jejunio vitia comprimis, mentem elevas, virtutem largiris et praemia.* . . .

The Lesson from 4 Kings (iv 1-7) relates the miracle wrought by Eliseus in favour of a poor widow, when, by multiplying the vessels of oil, he saved her sons from being carried off by her creditor into slavery. This may have reference to St Peter, whose presence in the house of Pudens was the cause of all manner of prosperity and abundance.

The Gradual comes from Psalm xviii : "From my secret sins cleanse me, O Lord, and from those of others cleanse thy servant. If they shall have no dominion over me, then shall I be without spot; and I shall be cleansed from the greatest sin." This alludes to the idolatrous Gentiles, with whom the psalmist wishes to have nothing to do, lest they should contaminate him, for the company of the corrupt is too often a source of danger to the righteous.

The Gospel, from Matthew xviii 15-22, brings out clearly three very strong bonds which preserve to the Church her mystical unity in the love of God and in charity towards one's neighbour. These are : the sacrament of penance in the remission of sins, the mutual forgiveness of injuries which we have done one to another, and the union of all the members of the mystical body of Christ in one spirit. A Catholic never acts singly and alone. In virtue of the Communion of Saints, he lives, suffers, prays, and works in the Church and with the Church—that is to say, with Christ.

The Offertory is the same as on the Third Sunday after the Epiphany, but to-day it becomes a hymn of triumph in honour of the *domus Pudentiana,* whose *conservator* is the Redeemer himself.

The Secret begs for the fruits of our redemption so that, by restraining our vicious passions, nothing may hinder the working of the eucharistic grace.

The Communion is from Psalm xiv : "Lord, who shall dwell in thy tabernacle? or who shall rest in thy holy hill? He that walketh without blemish, and worketh justice." How pure, indeed, must we be before we can attain to heaven, where no stain of sin or guilt, however small, can enter !

The Post-Communion is a continuation of the thought expressed in the preceding verse : "Having been cleansed by these sacred mysteries, we beseech thee, O Lord, that we may obtain both pardon and grace."

The form of the last Benediction over the people is full of beauty : "Defend us, O Lord, by thy protection; and preserve us ever from all iniquity." All other evils, indeed, are only apparent, or at least reparable and of short duration; sin alone separates the soul from God and should be terribly feared.

Once more we will repeat the words of Pope Siricius in the mosaic of the Basilica of St Pudentiana—the dedication to the saint of that name came later—*Dominus conservator*

Ecclesiae Pudentianae. Charity and hospitality never impoverished anyone, and when the needy are given shelter for the love of God it draws down upon that roof the blessings of divine Providence.

WEDNESDAY AFTER THE THIRD SUNDAY IN LENT

Collecta at St Balbina. Station at St Sixtus.

We already know the Church of St Balbina on the Aventine; that of St Sixtus is at no great distance on the Via Appia, and before the body of the martyr Pope Sixtus II (260-6) was carried thither from the cemetery of St Callixtus, it was known as the *titulus* of Tyridis after the name of its foundress. A convent of virgins was attached to it which was afterwards given by Honorius III (1216-27) to St Dominic.

In ancient times the scrutiny of the catechumens who wished to be admitted to holy baptism on Easter Eve began to-day; the Mass, therefore, has a distinctly catechetical character, especially in the lessons.

The Introit is taken from Psalm xxx. The soul exults in the Lord because her hope in him has not been in vain.

The Collect prays that by uniting our corporal fast with the interior purification of the spirit, which keeps us free from all sin, we may more readily hope to obtain pardon. It is well always to bear in mind the penitential character which Lent assumed in those days for such as were preparing to receive baptism. They were, as a rule, adults or *convertiti,* and therefore Lent was for them more especially the time for doing penance, for bewailing their sins, and for preparing themselves for the life-giving ablution in *remissionem peccatorum.*

The Lesson, from Exodus xx 12-24, with the solemn announcement of the Decalogue, is intended especially for the catechumens.

The New Testament presupposes the Old Testament, of which it is the continuation, and the Gospel law of love is but the confirmation and final perfection given by the Word made flesh to the Mosaic law. Christian teaching therefore begins with the Decalogue and ends with the sermon preached by our Lord at the Last Supper.

It is necessary to note that the original order of the lessons on the days of the baptismal scrutinies has been somewhat altered; the Roman documents of the eighth century prescribe for to-day's lesson the passage from Ezechiel xxxvi—*Effundam super vos aquam*—which in our present Missal is read on the following Wednesday, when the second scrutiny took place. The Gospel for to-day, instead of being from Matt. xv, as in the Missal of Pius V, was the passage *Confiteor tibi Pater,* from Matt. xi, which is now that of the feast of St Matthias. Probably these alternative extracts used at the scrutinies had no fixed place, but varied, as did the scrutinies themselves, which from being only three in the seventh century became seven.

The Gradual is from Psalm vi : " Have mercy on me, O Lord, for I am weak ; heal me, O Lord. All my bones are troubled : and my soul is troubled exceedingly." St Paul describes this state as the *stipendium peccati,* the wages of sin—viz., affliction and death.

The Gospel (Matt. xv 1-20) recalls the previous lesson from Exodus. Our Lord answers the futile questions of the Pharisees concerning the observance of the traditions of the Sanhedrim, by accusing them of having perverted the Decalogue, and instances the case of those sons who, acting on the traditions of the Talmud, which were intended to benefit the ministers of the Temple, allowed their parents to die of starvation. The sanctity of the Pharisees was wholly exterior, and consisted in the rigid performance of certain rites, whereas Jesus Christ insisted on the spiritual quality of our worship ; not that outward rites are to be neglected, for it is necessary that our entire being, both body and soul, should adore and serve God according to its proper nature ; but it is evident that the soul must take the chief part as being called to worship the Father *in spiritu et veritate.* The body should merely be its instrument and servant.

The Offertory comes from Psalm cviii : " O Lord, be merciful to me for thy name's sake, because thy mercy is sweet." This is the ultimate and decisive motive of the love which God bears to man. It is not our merits, nor is it our worth which impels him to love us, but he loves gratuitously : he loves because he is Love, and by loving us he creates in us those virtues which correspond to his love ; he makes us good—*imagini bonitatis suae conformis.*

In the Secret we beseech God to accept our sacrifice and our prayers, that his grace may defend us from all dangers. These last words may be noted in connection with the history of Sixtus II and his six deacons who were surprised in the neighbouring cemetery of St Callixtus whilst they were celebrating the eucharistic synaxis, and were decapitated on the sacred altar, thus uniting their own sacrifice to that of Christ.

The *ways of life* of which the antiphon for the Communion (Ps. xv) speaks are those of the cross, of the sepulchre, and of the descent into Limbo, by which Christ passed to the glory of the resurrection. God tries a soul in the crucible of suffering before revealing himself in his heavenly splendour.

The Post-Communion asks that the heavenly banquet may sanctify the faithful, obtain the pardon of their sins, and dispose them to merit that which God has promised.

In the final Blessing the priest—as though still moved by the cruel death of Sixtus II and his deacons who were martyred not far from there—again implores the protection of God, that being freed from danger we may with an untroubled mind devote ourselves to his holy service. Respect and deference to parental authority, which is the first of all natural authorities, are the essential conditions and the basis of all social order. The child—and in many ways humanity is still a child—before he can understand must believe in the authority of those who teach him and guide him. Without this obedience all education and progress is impossible. If modern society is now beginning to realize all the horror of the state of anarchy into which it has fallen, it must seek the first cause of this evil in the fact that the foundations of social order have been demolished, and that the law of egoism and the worship of the State have taken the place of the Decalogue.

THURSDAY AFTER THE THIRD SUNDAY IN LENT

Collecta at St Mark. Station at SS Cosmas and Damian.

To-day the place of meeting is at the Basilica of St Mark, which, richly ornamented with gold and precious marbles, rises near the famous *balnea pallacina,* where, according to Cicero, the murder of Sextus Roscius took place. For us Catholics the church is far more important, because under its venerable altar rest the bodies of the martyrs Abdon, Sennen, and Hermes, transferred thither by Gregory IV (827-44).

The stational basilica we have already noticed as the place of the *collecta* on the second Monday in Lent.

The Greeks were in the habit of celebrating a day of festival in honour of the holy cross in the middle of Lent, making a break, as it were, in the long period of fasting. In Rome this solemnity is deferred to the Sunday following, but Gregory II instituted this station at the Church of SS Cosmas and Damian, in order not altogether to deprive the faithful of that innocent satisfaction in the very middle of Lent. The two martyrs are known as " Anargyri " (moneyless)—that is, they belonged to that class of pious Byzantine doctors who despised money and gave their healing services gratis. More-

over, considering the rigour of the Lenten fast in those days,
it is easy to understand that many persons must have needed
to have recourse to these heavenly physicians. The Mass has
been adapted to the occasion; it refers chiefly to the anniversary of their martyrdom, and the frequent mention of
health, sickness, and healing recalls the great popularity of
the veneration paid to the holy Anargyri in those early days.

The Introit is scriptural in spirit, but does not seem to be
derived from any particular text; it belongs to a cycle of
non-psalmodic introits proper to the last Sundays after Pentecost, and was adapted by Gregory II to the feast of the
martyrs Cosmas and Damian. "I am the salvation of the
people, saith the Lord: from whatsoever tribulation they shall
cry to me, I will hear them; and I will be their Lord for ever."
The Collect refers to the *natalis* of the two saints: "May
the blessed solemnity of thy saints Cosmas and Damian
magnify thee, O Lord; by which thou hast both granted
eternal glory to them, and help to us by thy ineffable
Providence."
The Lesson from Jeremias (vii 1-7) follows, in which are
described the conditions of purity of heart which God
demands of the faithful if they wish to experience the efficacy
of his presence in the Ark of the Covenant. It is vain to
boast of the glory of his sanctuary, and to suppose that a
mere outward symbol of religion is the best that we can give
to the Lord. He wills that we should pay him exterior
worship, and in the Book of Leviticus he has deigned to
dictate its ritual; but above all he loves the religion of the
spirit.
The Gradual (Ps. cxliv) is taken from the Twentieth Sunday
after Pentecost, and later was adapted also to the Mass of
Corpus Christi: "The eyes of all hope in thee, O Lord; and
thou givest them meat in due season. Thou openest thy
hand and fillest every living creature with blessing."
The Gospel from St Luke (iv 38-44) describes the healing
of Peter's mother-in-law and other miracles worked by Jesus
on the sick and on those possessed by devils at Capharnaum.
Whilst the Doctors of the Law make a show of not recog-
nizing the Messias and of not understanding his mission, the
needy and the suffering press round him and beg him to help
them and not to depart from them. How blessed is our
necessity, which evokes in us humility and lowliness of
spirit, the two virtues that above all others move the heart
of Jesus to pity!
This touching scene of Capharnaum was repeated at Rome
in the fifth century at the shrine of the Anargyri.
The Offertory (Ps. cxxxvii) is that of the Nineteenth

Sunday after Pentecost. The faithful no longer fear tribulations and calamities, for God has made known to them his protection through the intercession of his martyrs. He will deliver them from peril, and, stretching forth his hand, will bring them to safety.

The following beautiful Secret commemorates the *natalis* of the martyrs: "In the precious death of thy just ones, O Lord, we offer to thee that sacrifice from which martyrdom received its whole beginning."

The Communion is from Psalm cxviii: "Thou hast commanded thy commandments to be kept exceedingly: O that my ways may be directed to keep thy justifications."

In the Post-Communion we again find the same certainty that the sacrifice will obtain for us a sure salvation, which we implore to-day through the merits of the martyrs Cosmas and Damian.

The Prayer over the people begs God that whilst his heavenly mercy increases the number of the faithful, it may also sanctify their minds that they all may obediently follow the divine commandments.

Why is it that the ancient sanctuaries of the martyrs, the very tombs of the Apostles themselves, are no longer the scenes of such miracles and graces as those of the early days of Christianity? The Lord treats us as he treated the people of Israel. On account of our sins, and especially on account of disbelief, he is silent as the Saviour was silent in the house of Herod. Therefore the sanctuaries once dear to Christian hearts fall into ruins, and are even profaned, just as befell the sanctuaries of Shiloh and of Sion: the cause and the result in both cases are the same.

FRIDAY AFTER THE THIRD SUNDAY IN LENT

Collecta at St Mary ad Martyres. Station at St Lawrence in Lucina.

St Mary *ad Martyres* is the name given to the beautiful Pantheon of Agrippa when it was turned into a Christian Church by Boniface IV (608-15). The Romans of the Middle Ages loved this majestic sanctuary, where among other relics was preserved in a casket locked with thirteen keys the image of the holy face, and in the thirteenth century the *Senator Urbis*, when taking possession of his office, swore to defend and preserve for the Pope *Mariam Rotundam*.

The Basilica of St Lawrence in Lucina dates from the fourth century; but unfortunately the personality of Lucina has been so obscured by legends, which first relate that she took her part in the *Acta* of St Peter and St Paul, and then afterwards mention her as a contemporary of St Lawrence, St Sebastian, and St Marcellus, that it is difficult to decide how much historical truth is contained therein.   Most probably the subject of these legends was a matron living in the time of Pope Marcellus (304-9), who placed her houses in the Via Lata at the disposal of the ecclesiastical authorities; these erected there the *titulus Marcelli,* and, when the church was confiscated, built another not far off, *in Lucina.*

In the list of churches St Lawrence in Lucina is the first of the presbyteral titles; Pope Celestine III (1191-98), who consecrated it on May 26, 1196, placed under the altar a large piece of the gridiron on which St Lawrence was martyred. The most ancient document which guarantees the authenticity of this holy relic is a sermon by St Leo the Great, who, on the feast of St Lawrence, speaks of it as an object of veneration to all Romans.   The martyrs of the Via Nomentana, Alexander, Eventius, and Theodulus, the Popes Pontian and Eusebius, with the saints Vincent, Peregrinus, Gordian, Felicola, and Sempronius, all rest in this venerable basilica.

In the Introit from Psalm lxxxv the Psalmist calls upon God for a token of his protection, not for himself indeed, for he has perfect faith in Jehovah, but in order to confound his adversaries, who are also the adversaries of the glory of God.

The Collect repeats once more the prayer that God would assist our fasts, so that we may not only abstain from bodily food, but may also restrain our evil passions.

To-day's Lesson (Num. xx 1-13), describing how Moses caused water to spring forth from the rock, was very familiar to the early Christians, for it was constantly reproduced in paintings on the walls and *arcosolia* of the extra-mural cemeteries.   In primitive Christian art at Rome, Moses sometimes bears the lineaments of Peter; indeed, there are examples in the catacombs, especially in glass, where the word PETRVS is written around the head of the figure which is striking the rock with his rod, as though to point out that the scene described in the Book of Numbers was a symbol of the Christian baptism of regeneration, whose first minister was the Prince of the Apostles himself.

This comparison drawn in early Christian art between Moses and Peter is of exceptional importance from a theological point of view in the history of the papal primacy.   As Moses was the first prophet and lawgiver of the Old Testament, so the Galilean fisherman is the first Pontiff and Vicar of Jesus Christ, in whose name and by whose authority all the other pastors of the Church feed each one his own flock.

At Rome baptism is connected especially with St Peter. He is said by Tertullian to have baptized in the Tiber, and in the fourth century an ancient tradition pointed out a chair in the cemetery of the Via Nomentana as having been used by the Apostle, while the neighbouring *Nymphae* retained the memory of his having administered baptism on this spot. The Popes of the fourth century baptized near the tomb of St Peter at the Vatican, long before they did so at the Lateran; indeed, this fact of the sacrament of regeneration being administered near the sepulchre of the Prince of the Apostles, and by his authority, appeared to be of such great importance and to confer such great honour on the Roman Church, that it was commemorated in the following verses formerly carved in marble in the baptistery of St Damasus at the Vatican :

Auxit Apostolicae geminatum Sedis honorem
Christus et ad coelos hanc dedit esse viam ;
Nam cui siderei commisit limina regni,
Hic habet in terris altera claustra poli.

Christ willed to give increased honour to the Roman See, rendered illustrious by the two great Apostles, Peter and Paul, by making this the path to heaven; so that he to whose care he had already committed the threshold of paradise should also guard here on earth the first door of heaven.

The Gradual comes from Psalm xxvii, and alludes to the sufferings of Jesus, and to his glory in his resurrection : " In God hath my heart trusted, and I was helped; my flesh flourished again, and with my will I will give praise to him. Unto thee, O Lord, have I cried; O my God, be not thou silent, depart not from me."

The Liturgy now becomes permeated with the thought of baptism. After hearing of the water gushing from the rock in the desert, we now read in the Gospel (John iv 5-42) of the living water which our Lord promised to the Samaritan woman. This second scriptural scene was also familiar to the faithful as a type of the sacrament of baptism, and we see it represented as early as the second century in the cemetery of Praetextatus.

The whole of St John's narrative is full of the greatest charm. Jesus goes forth first to seek the sinful soul, then for three-and-thirty years he treads the weary path of redemption, and towards midday, that is, when the oppression of earthly cares drives the tired heart to seek refreshment in the things of the spirit, he awaits the wanderer by the wayside well and offers her the living water which allays all thirst for human affections.

Let us learn from one who had drunk deeply of that water

of life, the great St Ignatius of Antioch, who wrote : "I feel within me as it were a fountain springing up on high, and I hear a voice which says : Come to the Father."

The Offertory from Psalm v is a humble prayer : "Hearken to the voice of my prayer, O my King and my God ; for to thee will I pray, O Lord." God is always mindful of our prayers as often as we, on our part, are mindful of them, and ask from him with lively faith those things which will forward our eternal salvation.

The prayer over the oblations—the Secret—which also serves as a prelude to the anaphora of thanksgiving—*prae-fatio*—is as follows : "Look down favourably, we beseech thee, O Lord, upon the offerings we consecrate ; that they may be pleasing to thee, and ever prove salutary to us."

The Antiphon *ad Communionem*, with the promise of the Redeemer that the water of grace shall be to him who drinks it as a fountain jet raising him on high, is one of the few Lenten antiphons which break in on the usual psalmodic cycle and are derived from the Gospels. The same thing occurs in to-morrow's Mass. If, however, we take note that the Communion of last Wednesday was taken from Psalm xv —that of Thursday, having been introduced later, does not count—whilst the Communion for next Monday is from Psalm xviii, we must come to the conclusion that the beautiful Gospel antiphons of to-day and to-morrow are not the original ones, but that they have taken the place of two other antiphons from the psalms which have disappeared from the series.

The Post-Communion is of a general character, and asks that through the participation of the divine sacrament God will purify us from sin and lead us to eternal life.

In the final Prayer the priest prays God that, trusting in his protection, we may be given grace to overcome all adversities.

Jesus announces to the woman of Samaria the new commandment for the true worshippers of God, who are to adore the Father in spirit and in truth, whether on Mount Zion or on Mount Garizim. This perfect worship belongs to Jesus Christ alone, the Pontiff of the New Testament. He alone adores the Father in truth, because he knows him perfectly. He alone adores the Father in spirit, because on him alone the Holy Ghost has rested with the plenitude of his gifts. Therefore all Christians, in order to render to God a perfect worship, must unite themselves to Jesus Christ and offer the sacrifice of their spirit and their hearts to the Father through him. It is for this reason that the Church ends all her collects with these words addressed to the Father : "Through Jesus

Christ our Lord "—this is the adoration in the truth—"who liveth and reigneth with thee in the unity of the Holy Ghost "—this is the adoration of the spirit.

SATURDAY AFTER THE THIRD SUNDAY IN LENT

Collecta at St Vitalis " ad duas domos." Station at St Susanna.

St Vitalis, which is also known from the name of its foundress as the *titulus Vestinae,* was dedicated by Innocent I (412-17) to the martyrs Vitalis, Gervase, and Protase. The Basilica of St Susanna is the ancient *titulus Gaii,* called also after the saints Gabinius and Susanna, the brother and the niece of the Pontiff who performed the dedication. It rises on the ruins of an ancient Roman building—*ad duas domos,* mentioned in the Bernese martyrology—and its titular clergy appear in the Roman Council of the year 497, under Pope Symmachus (498-514). Leo III (795-816) restored it from the foundations, and placed in the church the body of St Felicitas, the mother of the seven martyred brothers.

In the late Middle Ages, the second scrutiny of the candidates for baptism took place on this day, and the *Ordines Romani* therefore prescribe appropriate chants and lessons, which differ from those given in the Missal.

The Introit is from Psalm v : " Give ear, O Lord, to my words, understand my cry : hearken to the voice of my prayer, O my King and my God."

This appeal goes on increasing in power and in fervour. It is the cry of an oppressed soul seeking escape from its burden of anguish in prayer ; lonely and forsaken, it knocks insistently at the door of heaven ; it cries out, it groans, it clamours for the help of Jehovah. Who then is this soul, if not he of whom the Gospel says that in the Garden of Gethsemani, *factus in agonia, prolixius orabat?*

The Collect is one of the type which is so common in the Gregorian Sacramentary : " Grant, we beseech thee, almighty God, that they who in afflicting their flesh abstain from food, may, by following justice, fast from sin." This expresses the negative side of the Lenten abstinence—that is, corporal fasting and the mortification of our senses ; the positive side is the practice of the virtues.

The story of Susanna described in the Book of Daniel (xiii 1-62) was well known to the early Christians, for it was often represented in the *cubicula* of the catacombs. The figure of Susanna was typical of the Church, which was persecuted and calumniated by the Jews, in the first place, and then by pagans and heretics. When every human hope of safety fails, then is the moment chosen by God to show his power. Susanna prays and is saved. Her story teaches us to fear nothing so much as sin and to put all our trust in God. The choice of this passage from the Old Testament was evidently suggested by the name of the martyr to whom the basilica is dedicated.

The Gradual of to-day, taken from Psalm xxii, is full of sweetness and is the aspiration of a fervent soul to God: " If I should walk in the midst of the shadow of death, I will fear no evil, for thou art with me, O Lord. Thy rod and thy staff they have comforted me."

Then follows the scene from the Gospel, where the woman taken in adultery is brought before Christ. It is reminiscent of the preceding lesson, but if the accusation of sin is the same in both cases, the conditions of the accused are very different. God protects the innocence of Susanna and saves her; in the Gospel story, by an act of divine wisdom and compassion, he abashes the accusers of the adulteress, whom he converts and pardons. Human justice is inflexible towards certain sins for which the world has no pity. How much more gentle is the grace of the Holy Ghost, which takes away the stain of sin, regenerates the soul, restores it to its former dignity, and changes a wretched sinner into a Mary Magdalen, a Pelagia, or a Margaret of Cortona.

Why did Christ say to the adulteress in the Gospel: " Neither will I condemn thee "? Does his law, then, not condemn sins of impurity? It does condemn them, and, as long as the sinner cherishes an affection for sin, God will not receive him, but when he repents and detests his wrongdoing, his contrition brings him back to God, who no longer condemns him but grants him pardon and reconciliation. How great a consolation it is to the fallen ones, to those who can never hope to regain the esteem of their fellowmen, to hear the voice of God within them saying: " Neither will I condemn thee."

The Offertory is taken from Psalm cxviii: " Direct my steps according to thy word: that no iniquity may have dominion over me, O Lord."

The Secret is the same as that of the Fourth Sunday after the Epiphany.

The Communion is from the Gospel of the day. It expresses the compassion of Jesus and, at the same time, the condition requisite for forgiveness and reconciliation with

God : " Woman, hath no man condemned thee? No man, Lord. Neither will I condemn thee; go, and now sin no more." The resolve to abandon sin is essential in the penitent, for without it even sacramental confession would but be like that made by Judas in the Sanhedrim, when, throwing down before them the money he had received as the price of his treachery towards his divine Master, he exclaimed: " *Peccavi, tradens sanguinem justum.*" The confession was complete, but Scripture adds that going out he hanged himself from a tree. Judas, therefore, was wanting in the purpose of amendment, he was wanting in hope and wanting in love.

In the Post-Communion we implore God that the Communion of the body and blood of Christ may strengthen us in the Communion of the mystical body of the Church with its Head, causing us to participate more intensely in his life and in his spirit.

In the last Blessing we pray that God would extend towards us the right hand of his heavenly aid, and would grant us the grace of seeking him with all our heart. To seek God—what a noble aim! We seek God when we desire him alone, and the road by which we must seek him is the way of the divine commandments and the evangelical counsels of perfection.

The story of Susanna, so familiar to the early Church, and so ofter reproduced in the paintings of the catacombs, should fill our souls with loving confidence. Susanna prefers to fall a victim to the vengeance of her accusers rather than sin against God. She places all her trust in the Lord, and her prayer becomes her salvation.

THE FOURTH SUNDAY IN LENT

Station at Holy Cross in Jerusalem.

Following the example of the Byzantine churches, which celebrated a feast in honour of the true Cross on the Fourth Sunday in Lent, the Roman Liturgy dedicates this Sunday, originally called *in vigesima,* to celebrating the wondrous triumph of the Sign of Redemption. Ever since the time of St Helen, a large portion of the true Cross has been preserved in the basilica *in aedibus sessoriis,* and for this reason the station is held there to-day. This venerable building with its two sanctuaries—*ante Crucem* and *post Crucem*—was supposed in Rome to be a reproduction, more or less exact, of the *Martyrion* at Jerusalem. Its earliest designation was *Basilica Heleniana,* or more commonly

Sancta Hierusalem, whence we have those frequent allusions to Jerusalem in to-day's Mass.

In the Middle Ages, the Pope used to proceed to the station at Sta Croce in Gerusalemme holding in his hand a golden rose, the mystical significance of which he afterwards explained to the people. On his return he presented it to the Prefect of Rome, and this gave rise to the custom, which continues to this day, of sending the golden rose blessed by the Pope as a gift to one of the Catholic princes. It is difficult to trace the origin of this ceremony, which at Rome gives a special distinction to the Fourth Sunday in Lent. It may be derived from the Byzantine feast of Mid-Lent, but the hypothesis cannot be entirely rejected that in to-day's solemnity, under the name of *Dominica in vigesima,* is recorded the ancient Roman *caput jejunii* which occurred three weeks before Easter.

The Introit comes from Isaias (lxvi 10-11) where the prophet, foreseeing the future destinies of the Church, exhorts Jerusalem to rejoice, and invites those also who mourned with her to be glad, for the Lord will fill her with all consolation. The verse that follows is from Psalm cxxi, which was chosen because of its many allusions to Jerusalem. To-day is indeed the feast of *Sancta Hierusalem.*

In the Collect we confess that the scourges which fall upon us are indeed deserved by our sins. They are our just due, but we cannot forget that mercy and compassion befit the Lord, therefore with filial confidence we pray in all humility and contrition as the prophet prays in Psalm l : *redde mihi laetitiam salutaris tui.*

The Lesson is taken from St Paul's Epistle to the Galatians (iv 22-31). It is fitting that on a festival such as this the Church should proclaim before the triumphal sign of her redemption her own deliverance from the bondage of sin as represented by the Synagogue, and that glorious freedom to which she was called by Christ from the cross. As Ishmael once persecuted the *Son of the Promise,* so the world persecuted the Redeemer and nailed him to the cross ; yet this shameful death did but prepare the way for the triumph of the victim, while the murderers, like the son of Agar, lie crushed under the curse of God. The victory of evil is brief and superficial ; the future belongs to Christ and his Church.

The Gradual, in praise of Jerusalem, is from Psalm cxxi. The mere announcement of the return from the exile of Babylon to the holy city fills the faithful soul with such joy that it already feels itself loosed from the bonds of the flesh, and free to take flight upwards towards heaven.

The Tract comes from Psalm cxxiv, and is very similar in conception to Psalm cxxi. The position of Jerusalem with its surrounding hills is taken as a type of the soul which trusts in the Lord. Its faith is as immovable as Mount Sion, for its hope is in God, whose grace is about his people, even as the hills encircle Jerusalem, so that the enemy shall not prevail against them.

The fast is suspended to-day on account of the Sunday—not, however, abstinence from flesh meat, for in early days this was strictly observed all through Lent at Rome, just as it is now by the Russian and Oriental Churches—and the Church invites us, as it were, to take a little rest in order to recruit our strength before proceeding with renewed fervour on the road of penance. The Liturgy, therefore, reminds us of how our Lord multiplied the loaves and the fishes in the desert, and fed therewith five thousand persons (John vi 1-15). That food represents the Word of God, which is the food of the soul, but it also represents the material blessings with which the divine Providence unfailingly sustains our human nature.

It is not fitting through an exaggerated piety to put asunder that which God has joined together. Nature is the support and foundation on which both grace and the supernatural order rest; therefore, whilst mortifying our desires, we must always satisfy the legitimate requirements of our frail humanity. As a general rule, except in special cases of privileged souls sustained by grace, the Fathers of the spiritual life insist strongly on the necessity of discretion, which is the golden mean between two contrary excesses. There have been examples of persons who, rashly trying to dispense with it in spiritual matters, have justified the saying : " He who would set himself up to be an angel, ends by falling to the level of the brutes."

The Offertory is taken from Psalm cxxxiv : " Praise ye the Lord, for he is good : sing ye to his name, for it is sweet : whatsoever he pleased he hath done in heaven and in earth." The infinite power of God is very terrible, but in him it is closely allied with infinite love and tenderness, hence we should always keep both these attributes before us in contemplating him. An infinite justice fills us with dread, yet when we consider that this justice is at the same time both lovingkindness and mercy, we are filled with that filial reverence which is a happy mingling of love and holy fear.

The Secret is the same as that of the Fourth Sunday in Advent, which originally had no proper Mass.

The verse from Psalm cxxi which is chosen for the Communion proclaims once more the glories of the mystical city of God, the heavenly Jerusalem. It is built on the hill of faith like a walled city, and its streets are connected with one another, just as the blessed are united together in the Communion of Saints. Through its twelve apostolic gates all the tribes of the Lord enter in to glorify the name of Jehovah.

The Post-Communion desires to obtain from almighty God that frequent participation in the Sacrament may confer on us right dispositions—that is, the grace to receive our Lord with a clean heart and a submissive mind. The best preparation that we can make for our Communion to-morrow is to receive Communion fervently to-day.

How different is the providence of man from that of God! Philip and the other Apostles realized the difficulty of feeding so great a multitude in that desert place, but made no further effort to solve it. Many good but languid souls stop short at the first difficulty. Jesus, on the contrary, never refuses his aid, and when natural resources are exhausted, he exerts his divine power, and sooner than abandon his creatures, works a miracle on their behalf.

MONDAY AFTER THE FOURTH SUNDAY IN LENT

Collecta at St Stephen on the Coelian Hill. Station at the Four Holy Crowned Martyrs.

We have already spoken of the circular church of the Protomartyr Stephen on the Coelian Hill, where the station of December 26 is celebrated. It is situated less than three hundred yards from the Basilica of the Four Holy Crowned Martyrs, which rises fortress-like on the hill-side.

The legend of these four martyrs presented until lately a confused skein, which has only now been disentangled. In the first place, we have a group of Roman martyrs—Clement, Simpronianus, Claudius, and Nicostratus, who were buried *ad duas lauros* on the ancient Via Labicana; not far, therefore, from the imperial residence—whose tomb decorated with *graffiti* was discovered not long ago. To these we must add a second group of stone-cutters from Pannonia who met their death as martyrs in the river Save, and lastly a third group of four other martyrs from Albano.

The relics of the titular saints are preserved in the crypt under the high altar, but the present building is not the original church of the fifth century, which was almost destroyed by the conflagration caused by the Normans, and was rebuilt by Paschal II (1099-1118) on a much smaller scale. The head of St Sebastian is also kept here in an ancient reliquary of great value.

The Introit is from Psalm liii : " Save me, O God, by thy name, and in thy strength deliver me : O God, hear my prayer : give ear to the words of my mouth. For strangers have risen up against me : and the mighty have sought after my soul." Already on the distant horizon the heights of Calvary can be discerned, and the words of the divine Victim, who asks God so earnestly for help against his enemies, serve as introduction to the drama of the Passion.

In the Collect we pray that the devotion with which the faithful celebrate year by year the Lenten fast may merit for them the grace that not only their outward works, but also their spiritual ones may always be pleasing to God.

The Lesson from the third Book of Kings (iii 16-28) follows, with the story of the judgement of Solomon, of which we find a representation even in the paintings at Pompeii.

As the tenderness of one of the women towards the living child revealed to Solomon which of the two was the true mother, so the Church shows herself, rather than the Synagogue, to be in truth the Mother of souls, by her loving care for their well-being. It matters little, says the Jewish Sanhedrim, that a sword should cleave humanity in two— the heirship of Abraham must have nothing in common with the *Goyim,* who all are destined to perdition. But it is Christ, the true Solomon, who delivers the sentence. The Synagogue, which has shown itself to be a cruel step-mother, is rejected, whilst the tender feelings of the Church plead in favour of her Motherhood; to her, therefore, let the child— that is, the world—be given.

The Gradual derives its first verse from Psalm xxx and its second verse from Psalm lxx. Christ, as the hour of his Passion draws near, calls for help : " Be thou unto me a God, a protector and place of refuge to save me. O God, I have hoped in thee : O Lord, let me never be confounded." In what manner did God fulfil those words? By raising up his Son and making him the Saviour of the whole human race.

The paschal fast, which included the three weeks before Easter, began at Rome on this day in the third century; and the last trace of this special liturgical period is to be seen in the series of lessons from St John's Gospel, which continue from now until Easter. The few Masses which form an exception to this rule only serve to prove it, as either they are those of stations instituted afterwards by Gregory II, or the scriptural passages contained in them were added at a later date.

In to-day's Gospel (John ii 13-25) our Lord, after driving the money-changers and traffickers from the Temple, disputes with the representatives of the Sanhedrim, to whom he foretells in veiled language his death and resurrection, as a proof of his divine nature. The Jews did not forget this confession of his Messianic mission, but later made use of it to accuse him before Caiphas, by giving to his words a material signification. The spiritual temple of which Jesus spoke was his sacred humanity, which was raised up by God to a glorified life on the third day after his crucifixion; but it also signifies the Catholic Church, which after the resurrection took the place of the ancient Synagogue, destroyed by the hands of its own sons.

The Offertory is that of the First Sunday after the Epiphany. It is a true *jubilus* with its flowing Gregorian melody, which was well suited in olden times to this first day of the great paschal fast, when a special note of gladness was to dominate the whole liturgy. God, says the Apostle, loves a cheerful giver, and St Francis de Sales adds that a sad saint makes a poor saint.

The Secret is likewise taken from the First Sunday after the Epiphany, and in it we pray that the divine Sacrifice which we are about to offer may awaken and confirm in us that grace which is the life of the soul.

The Communion comes from Psalm xviii: "From my secret sins cleanse me, O Lord; from those sins which self-sufficiency hides from me and which negligence prevents me from finding out. Keep me also far from the disobedient, and from association with those who may lead me into evil, and who may be a stumbling-block and a cause of sin both to myself and to others."

In the Post-Communion we pray that participation in the divine Sacrament may intensify in us the work of our redemption, delivering us from the slavery of our passions, and directing our feet in the way of eternal salvation. The Blessed Sacrament, inasmuch as it communicates to us the spirit of Christ crucified, is to the soul a principle of life and a principle of death. Of death, because it gives death to sin and to the corrupt part of our nature; of life, because through it we share in the life of Christ, a life of perfect holiness, a life wholly in God, for God and of God. This is what was meant by St Paul when speaking of our Lord he said: *Quod mortuus est peccato, mortuus est semel, quod autem vivit, vivit Deo.*

The *missa,* or Prayer of Benediction over the people before their dismissal, begs the divine clemency that, having granted us the grace of raising our supplications to God in order to obtain protection from the dangers that threaten us, we may duly attain to the salvation for which we pray.

The grace of prayer is one of the highest favours that God imparts to the human soul. Prayer is indeed the atmosphere in which holiness develops and flourishes; it enables the Holy Ghost to communicate himself to the soul and to bind it to himself with the bonds of love. The whole essence of asceticism is contained in this one word "prayer." We first pray in order to obtain the help of God's grace in our struggles in the path of purification; and, when we are engaged in the path of meditation, again we have recourse to prayer. In heaven itself we shall do nothing else but pray, so we may consider prayer as the beginning of our future state of blessedness.

TUESDAY AFTER THE FOURTH SUNDAY IN LENT

Collecta at the Monastery of " Santa Maria Domnae Rosae." Station at St Lawrence in Damaso.

The church of the *collecta* corresponds to the present Sta Caterina dei Funari, and the foundress of the monastery may have been the *nobilissima foemina* whose father in 967 granted a piece of land to the adjacent monastery. At one time *Sancta Maria domnae Rosae* was the residence of the Dean of the Lateran *Schola,* and in 1536 Paul III granted it to St Ignatius Loyola, who founded there an institution for poor girls.

The Basilica of St Lawrence in Damaso takes its name from the great Pontiff of the catacombs, who caused it to be built beside the ancient Archives of the Roman Church, on the spot where his father had ended his long ecclesiastical career, and where he himself had begun his own. It is therefore full of memories connected with his family, especially as, according to an ancient tradition, the family of Pope Damasus (366-84), like that of the martyr St Lawrence, was of Spanish origin, and there may be some truth in the hypothesis of those archæologists who would identify the celebrated Bishop Leo, who is buried at the Campo Verano, near the tomb of the Archdeacon Lawrence, with the husband of Laurentia, the mother of Pope Damasus. Whatever may be the truth of this, we know from documentary evidence that the family of Damasus had been established in Rome for a long period, while the high ecclesiastical office held by his father made it easy to suppose that the son, too, would in time attain to the highest honours, so

in a famous inscription we find the following designation
bestowed upon Damasus in his quality of being born a Pope :

Natus qui antistes Sedis Apostolicae.

Under the high-altar of the stational basilica rest the sacred
relics of its founder, transferred thither from his tomb near
that of Pope Mark (337-40) in the Via Ardeatina.

The Introit is taken from Psalm liv (the martyrs' psalm) :
" Hear, O God, my prayer, and despise not my supplication :
be attentive to me, and hear me. I am grieved in my exercise ; and am troubled at the voice of the enemy, and at the
tribulation of the sinner." This is the cry of the Just One,
the prayer of Jesus in the Garden of Gethsemani, when for
our sake he endured the assault of the tempter, who vaunted
over him, innocent and holy, the power of sin and death and
hell.

In the Collect we pray God that the observance of the fast,
while it enables us to subdue the body and to increase in true
piety, may also procure for us the pardon we desire.

The Lesson (Exod. xxxii, 7-14) contains the beautiful
prayer of Moses for his people, who had fallen into the sin
of idolatry. This is perfect love—to be willing that one's
name be struck off from the book of life rather than let one's
own brethren perish beneath the justice of God. It was
through love that Moses, as the Scriptures tell us, wrestled
with this divine but terrible justice, and love prevailed.

The Gradual comes from Psalm xliii, and, following the example of the great lawgiver, Moses, who invoked the merits
of the early Patriarchs in order to propitiate the divine anger,
asks God to help us as he helped our fathers in the days of
old. The wonders worked by almighty God in past times
should fill us with confidence, for his arm is not shrunken
through length of years, nor has his love grown cold towards
us.

The rebellion of the Israelites against Moses, narrated in
the foregoing lesson, whilst it may contain an allusion to the
schism which broke out in Rome on the occasion of the
election of Damasus as Pope, when even a great part of
the clergy abandoned him, most certainly is a type of the
treatment which our Lord received from his own people when
he went up to Jerusalem for the feast of Tabernacles, and of
which we read in the Gospel of to-day (John vii, 14-31). The
kinsfolk of Jesus desired that he should attract attention to
himself by signs and wonders, especially in the Holy City
and on a festival day, but he preferred to go up to Jerusalem
secretly and quietly, avoiding all outward show, and making

no attempt to reveal himself as the Messias. This was because he did not seek glory for himself, but only the honour of his Father.

Nevertheless, he gave one of the strongest proofs of his divine nature to the Jews, who were always asking for signs, in the fact that, notwithstanding all the hatred borne to him by the Sanhedrim, he was able to defy them by appearing in public, by preaching and by healing the sick, without their being able to harm one single hair of his head until the hour should come which he himself had appointed. When, however, this hour did at last come, the Jews, even in his very Passion itself, could do to him no more than that which had already been foretold by the Holy Ghost through the mouths of the prophets many centuries before. Every minute circumstance of time, place, and person had been foreseen in such a manner that St Peter was able to say that the Sanhedrim had conspired against Christ: *facere quae manus tua et consilium tuum decreverunt fieri.*

It should be noted that in the Roman liturgical terminology this first week of the second half of Lent was known as *mediana;* and from the Gospel of to-day *die festo mediante,* which was, however, deferred in other churches until the middle of the paschal season.

The Offertory is from Psalm xxxix: " With expectation I have waited for the Lord, and he looked upon me : and he heard my prayer : and he put a new canticle into my mouth, a song to our God." What is this new canticle of praise? The hymn of the resurrection, the *Eucharistia* of the New Testament in the blood of Christ.

The Secret is that of the Third Sunday after the Epiphany.

Psalm xix provides the verse for the Communion : " We will rejoice in thy salvation, and in the name of our Lord God we shall be exalted." The name of God is the Word; it is Jesus, he who declares all the glory, the beauty, the power, and the goodness of the Father; he is the salvation sent by God to man; the fount of bliss in whom alone we should rejoice.

The Post-Communion, or thanksgiving after the Communion, is that of the preceding Friday. The order of the collects in the ancient sacramentaries is less precise than that of the lessons, because there was a large number of alternative ones; some selected one, some another, which explains the fact that in our present Missal, notwithstanding this great variety, we meet with gaps which have been filled in by the repetition of the same collect.

In the *missa* over the people the priest calls down upon them the divine compassion, to the end that the chastisements from which they suffer—in days of old this meant barbarian invasions, earthquakes, plague, famine, and the subversion of public order—may cease, and that they may mercifully be granted relief.

The primary cause of all unhappiness, not only of individual, but also of social and public troubles, is sin; for, as Holy Scripture tells us, *miseros facit populos peccatum.* If sin were done away with from among us, there would no longer be any necessity for the instruments of divine justice, death, sorrow, and disease, etc.—all those evils, in fact, which St Paul calls *stipendia peccati.*

In the incident of Jesus going up to the feast of Tabernacles only when the festival was well begun we may perceive a veiled purpose. In this way he not only wishes to teach us to love and reverence the sacred Liturgy and the rites of religion, but shows us that he himself is the centre of creation and of all history. Everything culminates in him, and the order and harmony of all creatures consist in this final relationship of every created being with the Word of God. Woe to those who overturn this divine ordering of the world and sacrifice the creature to the worship of self! God alone is all, and he it is *in quo vivimus, movemur et sumus.*

WEDNESDAY "IN MEDIANA" AFTER THE FOURTH SUNDAY IN LENT

Collecta at St Mennas.   Station at St Paul " in aperitione aurium."

The Church of St Mennas was probably built in the fourth century by the Alexandrian colony in Rome. It stood on the left bank of the Tiber at the first milestone on the Via Ostiensis, nearly opposite, therefore, to the other Alexandrian sanctuary of the martyrs Cyrus and John, which was on the other bank of the river in the Via Portuensis. The devotion of his fellow-countrymen caused the Egyptian saint to become popular in Rome, so much so that his *natalis* on November 11 was still honoured in the seventh century by the celebration of the station at his sanctuary, where on one occasion St Gregory the Great himself delivered the sermon.

To-day's station is held at St Paul's because he is the prototype and model of catechumens, on account of his conversion on the way to Damascus, where he was blinded by the light from heaven.

The ceremony is also known as *in aperitione aurium,* because the miracle which Christ worked upon the deaf man was renewed in a spiritual sense upon the candidates for baptism, to whom the Pontiff explained for the first time with solemn rites the Creed, the Lord's Prayer and the beginning of the four Gospels. Thus the ears of the catechumens, deaf hitherto to the words of truth, were opened at length to hear the tidings of eternal life.

The entire Mass is inspired by the thought of the sacrament of baptism.

The Introit comes from Ezechiel (xxxvi 23-26), where God promises to his people that when he shall be sanctified in them he will gather them again from every land in which they have been scattered, and will pour upon them a cleansing water and fill them with a new spirit.

This Collect follows : " O God, who grantest the reward of their merits to the just, and pardon to sinners through their fasts; have mercy on thy suppliants, that the confession of our guilt may prepare us to receive the forgiveness of our sins."

In early times after this collect the deacon invited the catechumens to enter the basilica for the *aperitio aurium.* We will describe this ceremony according to the *Ordines Romani.*

The Deacon : *Catechumeni procedant (Let the catechumens advance).* The acolyte proceeds to call out the names of the candidates.

The Deacon : *Orate, electi, flectite genua.* Placing the men on the right and the women on the left, he says : *Kneel, O chosen ones, and pray.*

The Catechumens : *Pater Noster,* etc. This was probably recited by one in the name of all.

The Deacon : *Levate. Complete orationem vestram in unum et dicite: Amen (Rise. Conclude your prayer together and say: Amen).*

The Catechumens : *Amen.*

The Deacon (turning to the godparents) : *Signate illos (Sign them with the sign of the cross).* (Turning to the catechumens) : *Accedite ad benedictionem (Draw near to receive the blessing).*

The godfathers and godmothers, making the sign of the cross with the thumb on the foreheads of their respective godchildren, say : *In the name of the Father, and of the Son, and of the Holy Ghost.*

The acolyte, or perhaps originally the exorcist, repeats the same rite on the men, saying : *In the name of the Father,* etc., lays his hands upon each of them, and with a commanding gesture recites in a loud voice the following form of exorcism :

I Exorcism

O God of Abraham, God of Isaac and God of Jacob, O God who didst appear on Mount Sinai to thy servant Moses, and didst lead Israel forth from Egypt, appointing the angel of thy mercy to guard them by day and by night; send, we beseech thee, O Lord, thy holy angel to guard also these thy servants and bring them unto the grace of thy baptism.

Therefore, O cursed devil, remember thy sentence and give honour to the living and true God; give honour to Jesus Christ his Son, and to the Holy Ghost, and depart from these servants of God. For our Lord Jesus Christ hath vouchsafed to call them to his holy grace and blessing and to the font of baptism. And this sign of the cross which we make on their foreheads mayst thou, cursed devil, never dare to violate.

The same rite was performed for the women, except that for them the exorcism was as follows : *O God of heaven and of earth, God of the angels and of the archangels, God of the prophets and of the martyrs, God of all the just, O God whose glory the tongues of all in heaven, in earth and under the earth confess, I beseech thee, O Lord, that thou wouldst deign to guard these thy handmaids and bring them unto the grace of thy baptism. Therefore, O cursed devil, etc.*

II Exorcism

At the words of the deacon, *Orate electi,* etc., the first part of the ceremony is repeated, and a second acolyte makes the sign of the cross on the foreheads of the catechumens, lays his hands upon them, and says : *Hear, O cursed devil, I adjure thee in the name of the eternal God and of our Saviour Jesus Christ that thou depart in sorrow and mourning, a victim of thine own envy. Thou hast no longer anything in common with these servants of God whose thoughts are already turned to heavenly things and who are ready to renounce thee and the world in order to live in immortal bliss. Give honour to the Holy Ghost who is about to come; may he descend from on high and make these hearts the temple and dwelling-place of the Divinity after they have been purified and sanctified in the holy font. So shall these servants of God, freed from all stain of former guilt, render perpetual thanks to God, and eternally bless his holy Name. Through our Lord Jesus Christ, who shall come to judge the living and the dead and the world by the final fire.*

The same rite was performed for the women with the following exorcism :

O God of Abraham, God of Isaac and God of Jacob, O God who didst teach the tribes of Israel, and deliver Susanna from her false accusers, I pray and beseech thee, O Lord, that thou wouldst deliver these thy handmaids, and deign to bring them into the grace of thy baptism.

Therefore, O cursed devil, etc.

III EXORCISM

For the third time an acolyte repeats the rite already described, but the exorcism is different : *I exorcise thee, O unclean spirit, in the name of the Father, and of the Son, and of the Holy Ghost, that thou go out and depart from these servants of God. For it is he that commandeth thee, O cursed fiend, who walked upon the sea, and stretched forth his hand to Peter when he was about to sink.*

Therefore, O cursed devil, etc.

For the women the exorcism was as follows : *I exorcise thee, O unclean spirit, by the Father, the Son, and the Holy Ghost, that thou depart from these handmaids of God. For it is he who commandeth thee, O cursed devil, who opened the eyes of the man born blind, and who raised Lazarus to life after he had been dead four days.*

Therefore, O cursed devil, etc.

IV EXORCISM (*by the Priest*)

After the third exorcism by the acolytes, follows that by the priest :

Deacon : *Pray, O chosen ones,* etc. The godfathers again sign their godchildren on the forehead with the cross ; one of the priests also traces the sign of the cross, and laying his hands upon the head of each one, recites the following prayer :

O Lord most holy, Father almighty, eternal God, the author of light and truth, I beseech thy everlasting and just mercy on behalf of these thy servants and handmaids, that thou wouldst vouchsafe to enlighten them with the light of thy knowledge: cleanse and sanctify them; give them true wisdom; that being made worthy to receive the grace of thy baptism, they may persevere in firm hope, righteous designs, and holy doctrine.

We may note that, unlike the exorcists, who threaten the devil, the priest does not deign to speak a single word to Satan, but addresses himself direct to God, whose minister he is.

Deacon : *Pray, O chosen ones,* etc. (as above). To the sponsors : *Sign them with the cross. Arise, stand in your places and be silent.*

As early as the ninth century there were read in Rome on this day, as on the most solemn occasions, the two lessons from the Old Testament given in our present Missal. Originally, however, as they had already been read at the first scrutiny in the preceding week, the *Ordines Romani* prescribed for to-day's station these other lessons *In aurium aperitione;* " *Audite audientes me, et comedite bonum,* " from Isaias, and " *Exspoliantes vos veterem hominem* " from the Epistle to the Colossians.

In the first of these Lessons the prophet describes the sweetness of the counsels of God to the soul, counsels of compassion and more than maternal solicitude.

At its conclusion, the Gradual, taken from Psalm xxxiii, is sung, which is eminently suited to the catechumens, to whom it promises light, safety, and a filial spirit of a holy fear of God as a result of their baptism. *Come, children, hearken to me: I will teach you the fear of the Lord. Come ye to him, and be enlightened; and your faces shall not be confounded.*

The prayer of the priest follows the responsorial psalmody of the Gradual: " Grant, we beseech thee, almighty God, that we who are chastised by votive fasts may also be gladdened with holy devotion, that, our earthly affections being weakened, we may more easily grasp heavenly things." It was such a prayer as this which gave strength to the martyrs, to the solitaries of old and to the penitents : they suffered great things for Christ, but they were sustained by grace and by the interior joy of the heart, which is indeed one of the gifts of the Holy Ghost.

In the second lesson from St Paul's Epistle to the Colossians (iii 9-17) the Apostle explains the symbolism of the baptismal rites. The old man with his perverse inclinations is put off, and the new man is put on, which is Christ. The virtues which belong to this new life are humility and patience, but above all charity, which is the bond of holiness. The Christian life should be like a beautiful melody inspired by the Holy Ghost, of which the key-note is Christ.

Then follows another Gradual from Psalm xxxii which describes the happiness of that people whom the Lord has chosen for his inheritance : " Blessed is the nation whose God is the Lord : the people whom he has chosen for his inheritance. By the word of the Lord the heavens were established; and all the power of them by the spirit of his mouth."

In the meanwhile four deacons come out from the sacrarium, carrying the books of the holy Gospels, which they place at the four corners of the altar. The Pontiff then begins to initiate the candidates for baptism into the knowledge of the Gospel teaching.

Priest: " Dearly beloved sons, before making manifest to

you the Gospel, that is, the story of the works of God, we must explain to you its character: what this Gospel is, whence it comes, whose words it contains, why the Gospels are four in number and no more, who were their authors, what manner of men were those four persons who had already been preannounced by the Prophet through the inspiration of the Holy Ghost. All this we must briefly declare unto you, for without this explanation a doubt might remain in your minds, and having come here this day in order that your ears might be opened to the truth, you might instead be dazed and bewildered by the novelty of the things we tell you.

"The word 'Gospel' means 'good tidings': and these good tidings are the announcement of the coming of our Lord Jesus Christ. We call them the 'Gospel' because they announce and show forth how he, who in olden times spoke through the Prophets, has at the last clothed himself in human flesh, and has come, as the Scripture saith: 'For I myself that spoke, behold I am here' (Isa. lii 6).

"Now to explain briefly to you what this Gospel contains, and who are the four persons foretold by the Prophet, we will identify them by their names and by the symbols through which they were prefigured.

"Ezechiel says: 'This was their appearance: the first on the right had the face of a man, the second of a lion, the third on the left of an ox, and the fourth that of an eagle.' There is no doubt that the four types represent the four Evangelists. The names of the authors of the Gospels are: Matthew, Mark, Luke and John."

Deacon: "Be silent and listen attentively: The beginning of the holy Gospel according to Matthew, etc. . . . and he shall save his people from their sins."

Priest: "Dearly beloved sons, in order not to keep you any longer in doubt, we will explain to you the symbol and the mode of writing of each of the Evangelists. Why is Matthew prefigured by the symbol of a man? Because from the beginning of his Gospel he describes fully the birth of our Saviour and gives minute particulars of his genealogy. He begins thus: 'The book of the generation of Jesus Christ, the son of David, the son of Abraham.' You see for yourselves that it is not without good reason that a man is the type of this Evangelist, as he begins at once to tell of the human birth of Christ. Therefore this symbol was justly attributed to Matthew."

Deacon: "Be silent," etc. "The beginning of the holy Gospel according to Mark, etc. . . . but he shall baptize you with the Holy Ghost."

Priest: "The Evangelist Mark is represented by the lion

because he begins his account by describing the life of John
in the desert. He says in speaking of John : ' A voice of one
crying in the desert : prepare ye the way of the Lord.' The
lion is a symbol of Mark also because it is the king of beasts
and none can overcome it. This symbol of the lion is frequently used in Scripture with various meanings, as, for
instance, we read : ' Juda is a lion's whelp ; to the prey, my
son, thou art gone up, resting thou hast couched as a lion
. . . who shall arouse him ?''[1]

Deacon: " Be silent," etc. " The beginning of the holy
Gospel according to Luke, etc. . . . to prepare unto the
Lord a faithful people."

Priest: " The ox is the symbol of the Evangelist Luke, and
was also typical of our Saviour himself sacrificed as an
innocent victim for the sins of his people. Luke begins his
Gospel with the narration of the history of Zachary and
Elizabeth, who, though advanced in years, gave birth to
John the Baptist. The ox justly represents the Evangelist
Luke, for the two horns are typical of the Old and New
Testaments, whilst the four hoofs are symbolical of the four
Gospels, which appear indeed to originate from a feeble
beginning, yet contain in themselves all completeness and
wisdom."

Deacon: " Be silent," etc. " The beginning of the holy
Gospel according to John, etc. . . . full of grace and truth."

Priest: " John is compared to the eagle because of the
height to which he rises in his Gospel, which begins with
the words : ' In the beginning was the Word and the Word
was with God, and the Word was God. The same was in
the beginning with God.'

" David, too, says of Christ : ' Thy youth shall be renewed
like the eagle ' (which renews its plumage), meaning that the
youth of our Lord Jesus Christ was renewed when he rose
again from the dead and ascended into heaven.

" Therefore does the Church, who has given you life, and
still carries you in her bosom, now rejoice, and with good
cause, for all her desires and longings are for the renewal
of the Christian faith, which will be realized when, on the
paschal feast, you shall be born again to grace through the
waters of baptism. So shall you, with all the saints, obtain
the reward promised to those who become as little children,
by Jesus Christ our Lord, who liveth and reigneth for ever
and ever."

The catechumens, having been initiated into the knowledge
of the Gospels, were then taught the Creed, which originally
was a formula of the Christian faith, intended to be learnt

---

[1] Gen. xlix 9.

by heart by the candidates for baptism, and recited by them publicly on Holy Saturday. As long as the rule of the *arcanum* was in force, it was forbidden to write the Creed on parchment or on papyrus; but it had to be committed to memory and used as a spiritual shield of defence in temptations and dangers. Even now the Church orders it to be recited several times a day; that is, in the Mass and at the beginning and end of the divine Office. It was also the custom in the Middle Ages to recite it especially when assisting the dying.

TRADITIO SYMBOLI

Priest: " Dearly beloved, before receiving the sacrament of baptism, and before being born again by the power of the Holy Ghost, embrace with all your heart that faith by means of which you must be sanctified. Let your hearts be changed by a sincere conversion, and turn to God who fills our souls with his light; more especially now that you have been initiated into the sacred mystery of the Gospel teaching and have learnt the formula which was inspired by God and taught by the Apostles.

" It is brief and simple in expression, but profound in meaning. Indeed, the Holy Ghost, who taught it to the early Fathers of the Church, defined this life-giving faith with such clearness of thought and precision of language in order that those things which you must believe and on which you must always meditate should neither be hidden from your intelligence nor be wearisome to your memory. Devote yourselves therefore with great attention to learning the symbol of the Faith and all else that we may teach you as we ourselves have been taught. Do not write it on corruptible material, but write it on your heart. This is the beginning of the profession of the Faith which you have now embraced."

In the sixth century, when baptism was administered to everyone as infants, and no longer to adults, except in rare instances, an acolyte took one of the youthful catechumens in his arms or by the hand and presented himself before the Pontiff.

Priest: " In which language do they confess our Lord Jesus Christ?"

Acolyte: " In Greek."

Priest: " Declare then their Faith which they profess."

There were, at that time, in Rome, a large number of Byzantine officials and courtiers, for whose benefit the acolyte recited the Nicene Creed in Greek.[1]

Acolyte: " I believe," etc.

---

[1] The " Filioque " clause being omitted.

Priest (addressing the Byzantine candidates): "Dearly beloved sons, you have heard the Creed in Greek; now listen to it in Latin."

The acolyte then presented the Latin catechumens.

Priest: "In which language do they confess our Lord Jesus Christ?"

Acolyte: "In Latin."

Priest: "Declare then their faith which they profess."

The acolyte then recited the Creed in Latin. "I believe," etc.

Priest: "This, dearly beloved, is the summary of our faith. This is the text of the Creed, composed not by skill of human language, but ordained by God. No man can plead that he is incapable of understanding or of realizing these things. Herein we declare the unity, and the equality in power, of the Father and of the Son; here we show that the only-begotten Son of God after the flesh was born of the Virgin Mary and of the Holy Ghost, and that he was crucified and buried and that he rose again the third day. We proclaim his ascension into heaven and assert that he sits at the right hand of the Father in majesty, from whence he shall come one day to judge the living and the dead. In this our Creed we confess the same undivided Divinity in the Holy Ghost as in the Father and the Son, and in it we teach the divine Mission of the Church, the remission of sins and the resurrection of the body.

"Therefore, O beloved sons, from being the children of Adam you are now to be remade in the likeness of the new man—that is, Jesus Christ; from being carnal you are to become spiritual; from earthly you are to be heavenly. With firm and unshaken faith you truly believe that, as Christ rose from the dead, so also we shall rise again, for that which is done in the head must be done also in the members.

"Indeed, the very sacrament of baptism which you are preparing to receive expresses this hope by its rites, for in it is foreshadowed in a measure both death and resurrection. The old man is cast aside, and the new man arises; the sinner goes down into the water and comes forth from it justified. He who led us to death is rejected, and he who brought us back to life is welcomed. It is through him that you are made sons of God, begotten, not by the flesh, but by the power of the Holy Ghost.

"Impress then in such a manner upon your hearts this brief but comprehensive profession of faith that you may be able to strengthen yourselves by its protection in whatever dangers may befall you. The true soldiers of Jesus Christ always avail themselves of this invincible weapon against all the snares of the enemy. May the devil, who never ceases to tempt us, find you always armed with this holy symbol, so that, having vanquished the foe whom you now renounce, you may be able by the divine assistance of him whom you confess to keep the grace of God incorrupt and perfect unto the end. Thus may you arrive at the glory of the resurrection through him by whose mercy you obtain the remission of your sins.

" You have listened, dearly beloved, to the symbol of the Catholic faith; and when you now go hence, learn it by heart without altering a syllable of it. The mercy of God can do all things; may it lead you thirsting to the faith and to baptism, so that we who teach you these divine mysteries, and you also who listen to them, may together reach the kingdom of heaven. Through the same Jesus Christ our Lord," etc.

Deacon: " Be silent and listen attentively."

Then there probably followed a lesson from the Gospel, containing the text of the Lord's Prayer.

Priest: " Jesus Christ, our Lord and Saviour, among other precepts of salvation, at the request of his disciples who one day asked him how they should pray, taught them the form of prayer which you have now heard and understood. Listen then to the manner in which Jesus bade his followers pray to God the Father almighty.

" ' When thou shalt pray,' he said, ' enter into thy chamber, and having shut the door, pray to thy Father in secret.' In speaking of the chamber, Jesus does not mean a secret place in the house, but wishes to remind us that to him alone are known the secrets of our heart. He tells us also to shut the door when we pray to the Father, because as with a mystical key we must close our heart against all evil thoughts; and though our lips may make no sound, we must converse with God by means of a pure and undefiled spirit.

" Our God, in truth, regards the faith of the soul, and not the sound of the voice. Let the key of faith therefore close our heart against the snares of the evil one, and may it remain open only to God whose temple it is. May he who dwells within our heart plead our cause when we pray. Jesus Christ himself who is the very Word and Wisdom of God taught us these words in order that we should pray in this manner."

The priest now gives an explanation of the Lord's Prayer :

" *Our Father, who art in heaven.*

" This is a cry of freedom and of perfect confidence. Let your conduct show that you are indeed sons of God, and brothers of Jesus Christ. For how can any man dare to call God his Father, unless he strives to do his will? Therefore, dearly beloved, endeavour to show yourselves worthy of this divine adoption, since it is written that as many as believed in him were made worthy to become the sons of God.

Hallowed be thy name.

" This does not mean that God, himself the source of all sanctity, may become holy because we acknowledge him as holy; on the contrary, we ask that his name may be sanctified in us, so that we, having become holy by means of his baptism, may always persevere in this purity of life.

" *Thy kingdom come.*

" God, whose dominion is without end, reigns for ever. Therefore, when we say, ' Thy kingdom come,' we ask that our kingdom also may come, that Messianic kingdom promised to us by God and bought by the Passion and the precious Blood of the Redeemer.

" *Thy will be done on earth as it is in heaven.*

" That is to say, may thy will be accomplished, and those things which thou dost will in heaven be carried out by us here on earth.

" *Give us this day our daily bread.*

" By these words is meant our spiritual food. Our bread indeed is Christ, who said : ' I am the living bread which came down from heaven.' We speak of our *daily* bread because we must pray to be kept continually far from sin, in order to be worthy of the heavenly food.

" *And forgive us our trespasses, as we forgive them who trespass against us.*

" This precept teaches us that we cannot obtain pardon for our sins, unless we first forgive those who have sinned against us, as our Lord says in the Gospel : ' If you will not forgive men, neither will your Father forgive you your offences.'

" *And lead us not into temptation.*

" That is, let not the author of evil, the tempter, drive us into sin. Holy Scripture, indeed, says that it is not God who tempts us but the devil, against whom Christ tells us to watch and pray lest we enter into temptation.

" *But deliver us from evil. Amen.*

" This is added because as St Paul says : ' You know not that for which you should pray.' We must therefore pray the one and all-powerful God that he would give us strength to avoid those things into which our human weakness might lead us, through Jesus Christ our Lord," etc.

Deacon: " Stand in order, be silent and attentive."

Priest: " You have heard, dearly beloved, the profound and sacred meaning of the Lord's Prayer. Go now and ponder it in your hearts, that you may become perfect in Jesus Christ, and may obtain the mercy which you implore. Our God is able to do this; may he lead you who desire to embrace our holy faith to the waters of regeneration; and may he grant us who have instructed you in the sacred mysteries the grace of attaining with you to the heavenly kingdom, he who with the Father," etc.

Here ends the first part of the Mass. The tremendous mysteries are about to begin, and, according to the rule of the *arcanum,* the excommunicated, the penitents and the catechumens are dismissed. The doorkeepers stand on guard at the entrances of the church, the subdeacon watches the *vima* and the deacon proclaims : " Let the catechumens retire ; he who is still a catechumen, let him retire ; let all cate- chumens go forth."

The catechumens being gone, the holy Sacrifice begins. The parents and the future godparents were admitted that they might present the oblation in the name of their god- children, whose names were afterwards read by the deacon from the diptychs.

The Offertory is taken from Psalm lxv, and is a hymn of thanksgiving to God for having been called to the grace of baptism and to a holy Christian life : " O ye Gentiles, bless the Lord our God, and make the voice of his praise to be heard ; who hath set my soul unto life, and hath not suffered my feet to be moved : blessed be the Lord, who hath not turned away my prayer, nor his mercy from me."

The Secret is as follows : " We humbly beseech thee, almighty God, that by these sacrifices our sins may be cleansed away ; for thus thou bestowest upon us true health of mind and body."

The Communion is from St John's narrative of the cure of the man born blind, which is read in to-day's Gospel. The spittle with which our Lord made clay and gave sight to the eyes of the blind man is a symbol of the waters of baptism, which illuminate the soul of the neophyte. " The Lord made clay of spittle, and anointed my eyes : and I went, and I washed, and I saw, and I believed in God."

After the Communion the archdeacon announced the day and the place of the next scrutiny.

The Post-Communion is the following : " May the sacraments we have received, O Lord our God, both fill us with spiritual food and defend us by bodily succour."

The Blessing over the people is invoked in these words : "Let the ears of thy mercy, O Lord, be open to the prayers of thy suppliants; and that thou mayest grant the desires of those who seek, make them to ask what is pleasing to thee."

One often speaks nowadays of a vocation to the priesthood or to the religious life, but too little is said of the call to the Christian life, which is bestowed on us through the grace of holy baptism. Yet the religious vocation itself does but develop and realize in us to the fullest extent the call to a Christian life, by means of the counsels of perfection. These are not two separate forms of Christianity, as some modern Protestants have supposed, for the Christianity of the Gospel and that of the monastic rule are but one and the same Christian profession, in which the baptismal promises are ratified and more perfectly carried out in the religious state. The monk or religious is therefore merely a perfect Christian, one who, having taken to heart the call to follow Christ which he received at his baptism, walks in his footsteps on the narrow road of the counsels of perfection.

This does not mean, however, that the simple layman is not to live in a holy state, nor that he is dispensed from aiming at perfection in his own sphere of life. On the contrary, the more he is surrounded by the dangers and temptations of the world, the more must he jealously guard his Christian vocation by carrying out to the utmost of his power the promises he made in baptism.

The sacrament of regeneration holds for each one of the faithful the place of the religious profession; the catechumenate is equivalent to the noviciate; the promises made at baptism represent the vows of the clergy; the white robe is the religious habit; while the Gospel is the rule of life which each one takes upon himself faithfully to observe.

THURSDAY AFTER THE FOURTH SUNDAY IN LENT

Collecta at St Quiricus. Station at St Martin "ad montes."

The Church of St Quiricus at the foot of the Quirinal was dedicated by Pope Vigilius probably to the holy deacons Stephen and Lawrence, but later, under Byzantine influence, its title was changed, and it took that of the Oriental martyrs Quiricus and Julitta, who are especially venerated in the oratory of Sta Maria Antiqua in the Forum Romanum.

The stational basilica is the ancient *Titulus Equitii*, erected in the time of Pope St Silvester. Afterwards two celebrated oratories arose beside it, through the zeal of Pope Symmachus, the one dedicated to St Martin of Tours, and the other to Pope St Silvester, the first two confessors after the martyrs to whom liturgical *cultus* was paid. These soon attracted all the popular devotion, so that the ancient founder of the title being completely forgotten, the church became known simply as the Basilica of SS Silvester and Martin.

Sergius I (687-701) undertook extensive restorations of the building, but his death occurring whilst the work was in progress, they were completed under Leo IV, who also annexed a monastery to the church so as to provide for the divine Office.

COENOBIVMQVE · SACRVM · STATVIT · MONACHOSQVE · LOCAVIT
QVI · DOMINO · ASSIDVAS · VALEANT · PERSOLVERE · LAVDES

The basilica is enriched by the bodies of many ancient martyrs brought thither in the ninth century from the extramural cemeteries. The Blessed Cardinal Tommasi (d. 1713) was titular priest of the church, and was by his desire buried there.

As to-day's station dates only from the time of Gregory II, the sung parts of the Mass are borrowed from those of other feasts.

The Introit is that of the Friday in the September Ember week, and is taken from Psalm civ : " Let the heart of them rejoice that seek the Lord : seek the Lord and be strengthened : seek his face evermore." To seek the Lord means to make his glory the end of all our actions ; to live and work in his presence, for him only and not for ourselves.

In the Collect, which is the same as that after the first lesson of yesterday, we invoke for those who mortify their flesh by fasting, the joy of the Holy Ghost and of a fervent devotion. It is impossible to unite the consolations of the spirit and those of the senses, their desires are diametrically opposed to each other. When the senses are pleased, the spirit becomes as it were clouded by the physical satisfaction, whereas the more the soul imprints on the flesh the stigma of the cross, so much the more does it feel itself become free and pure, and its vision clear and penetrating.

The two Lessons tell us of two miracles, one worked by Eliseus and the other by our Lord, in raising the dead to life. Whilst the choice of these lessons may perhaps have been inspired by thoughts of the neighbouring cemetery of the Via Merulana, they contain also an interesting allusion to St Martin of Tours (316-400), who was greatly celebrated among the early Christians, because in *fide Trinitatis trium mortuorum suscitator meruit esse magnificus.* The miraculous restoration of the dead to life reminds us further that the sacred fast and Holy Communion give us a special right to the glorious resurrection of the body at the last day.

The first lesson comes from the Fourth Book of Kings (iv 25-38), in which it is related how the child, who could not be brought back to life by the staff of Eliseus, was nevertheless raised up by the breath of the prophet. This should be a lesson to superiors, and indeed to all of us in our dealings with our neighbour, that the strongest methods are not always the most efficacious; for, as the holy Bishop of Geneva[1] wittily said: " More flies can be caught with a spoonful of honey than with a barrel of vinegar."

The Gradual, from Psalm lxxiii, is borrowed from the Thirteenth Sunday after Pentecost: " Have regard, O Lord, to thy covenant, and forget not to the end the souls of thy poor. Arise, O Lord, judge thy own cause: remember the reproaches of thy servants." The covenant of Jehovah is the promise of the Messiah made to Abraham and to the Patriarchs, and, unlike the ancient joint pact made between God and Israel by the mouth of Moses, is purely voluntary and irrevocable.

The Gospel narrative (Luke vii 11-16) of the raising to life of the widow's son at Naim has also been borrowed from the Fifteenth Sunday after Pentecost. The widowed mother is a type of the Church, who by her prayers and her tears obtains from God the conversion of sinners and their return to grace. The bearers of the bier represent our senses and our passions; these greatly disturb and confuse the soul, which, thinking itself to be alive, is really dead. The first grace which we receive from God is that which causes these evil powers to halt, and in the calm and quiet which ensue the soul begins to reflect on its own condition. How much then is the grace of God needed to drive away all those illusions that blind us to that which we really are. In this we are like the angel of the Apocalypse to whom God said: *Nomen habes quod vivas, et mortuus es* (Apoc. iii 1).

The Offertory is from Psalm lxix, and was a special favourite with the Fathers of the desert, who used to recite this verse as an ejaculatory prayer many times during the day: " O Lord, make haste to help me: let all those be confounded that desire evils to thy servants." The tender heart of the Father cannot resist the voice of a son who calls for help, and God is ever at our side in whatever hour we call lovingly upon his name.

The prayers and the sacrifice offered by the Church, the mystic bride of Christ, are always pleasing and efficacious in the sight of God. But when accompanied also by the

[1] St Francis de Sales.

devotion of the faithful, the eucharistic sacrifice becomes still more pleasing to God and of greater benefit to the faithful. This is the thought so gracefully expressed in to-day's Secret. In other words, the Eucharist and the other sacraments derive their power indeed from divine institution, but the benefit we receive from them depends very much on our own disposition, just as a nourishing and delicious food may be less salutary and suitable in its effects on a weakly and disordered constitution.

The Communion is taken from Psalm lxx : " O Lord, I will be mindful of thy justice alone : thou hast taught me, O God, from my youth : and unto old age and grey hairs, O God, forsake me not." As the years pass by, we learn by bitter experience that all in this world is vanity and affliction of spirit apart from God, and seeing everything that we cherish slip away from us—youth, health, fame and fortune— being moreover wearied and prematurely old, we turn at last to the Saviour and cling to him whom alone we never wish to lose. He is the one faithful friend, the same in prosperity and in adversity, as Holy Scripture says : *Omni tempore diligit qui amicus est.*

In the Post-Communion we pray that our coldness and unworthiness in receiving the heavenly food may not cause the sacrament instituted for the remission of sins to turn to our judgement and condemnation. This prayer is inspired by the well-known words of St Paul in his first Epistle to the Corinthians, in which he says of those who receive the Holy Eucharist unworthily : *judicium sibi manducant et bibunt.*

In the Prayer over the people the priest begs God to take away from his faithful children those sins which now weigh heavily upon them, so that in the future their conduct may always be pleasing to him and that they may be assured of the grace of his protection. This is the perfect order established by God—first our sins must be taken away, then we must live in accordance with his commandments, for thus only may we rely on the divine favour.

Let us consider again the beautiful story of the prophet Eliseus raising the child of the Sunamite woman to life. He lays himself gently upon him, his face against the dead child's face, his hands upon his hands, his feet upon his feet and, adjusting himself so as to cover the little body, he thus brings it back to warmth and life. Here we have an example of the discretion needed by superiors in dealing with those under their care. Above all there is necessary a spirit of prudent toleration to weigh carefully that which they demand of others, and to judge the powers of those who receive their commands. We must not consider only that which ought to be done; it is equally essential to realize how much it is possible for ourselves, or for others, effectively to accomplish.

FRIDAY AFTER THE FOURTH SUNDAY IN LENT

Collecta at St Vitus " in Macello Liviae." Station at St Eusebius.

The church on the Esquiline appointed for to-day's assembly was also known by the name *ad Lunam*, and perhaps owes its foundation to Pope Hilary (461-8); later it was raised to the rank of a deaconry under the name of St Vitus, when during the seventh century the *cultus* of this martyr became so popular in Italy that a great number of churches were erected to his honour. A monastery was attached to the deaconry, the monk Philip, who was raised to the papacy for a single day by the party opposing Stephen IV (768-71), being a member of this community.

The *dominicum Eusebii* marks the site of the house of St Eusebius, that heroic Roman priest who was a victim of the cruel measures of the Arian Emperor Constantius II (353-61). It was converted into a church immediately after the death of the saint, and in the Gelasian Catalogue of 894 we find among the signatories a certain *Valentinus archipresbyter in titulo Sancti Eusebii in Esquilinis*. More ancient still is the inscription on a tomb in the cemetery of SS Peter and Marcellinus :

OLYMPI LECTORIS DE DOMINICO EVSEBII LOCVS EST

which takes us back to the fourth century.

Near this spot was the ancient burying-ground of the Via Merulana, which circumstance may have influenced the choice of the two lessons of to-day's Mass, in which the raising of the widow's child from the dead by Elias and the resurrection of Lazarus are narrated.

The Introit is derived from Psalm xviii : " The meditation of my heart is always in thy sight, O Lord, my helper and my redeemer." The very thought of God is to us a tower of strength in which we can always take refuge from the temptations and troubles of life.

In truth, when temptations assail us, when the glamour of this world threatens to stifle that higher aspiration to an infinite good which is present in all of us, when the weight of our past sins causes us almost to despair of ever reaching the port of salvation, when especially in the hour of death

Satan makes a final effort to gain possession of our souls, it is enough to think of God, to call upon him with all our heart, and lo ! the storm ceases, the enemy is routed and the soul becomes filled with the sweetness which the name of God alone can bring, when invoked with faith and with fervour. In a word, all our trouble arises from our forgetfulness of God, whereas the prophet says : *Memor fui Dei et delectatus sum.*

The Collect already hints at the coming paschal regeneration, when the spiritual life of Christ received by us in holy Communion will accomplish in our souls the mystery of his spiritual resurrection. This new birth, however, is at present only spiritual, so the Church continues to be a visible society, composed of suffering and mortal men, whose material needs also have to be satisfied. The Church, taking into account both the aspirations of our soul and the necessities of our bodily nature, is careful not to separate that which God has joined together, so she prays that her children whilst seeking to treasure up eternal riches may not be deprived of temporal help.

The Lesson, telling of the restoration to life by Elias of the widow's son (3 Kings xvii 17-24) is suggested by the account in the Gospel of the resurrection of Lazarus. Those great friends of God, Abraham, Moses and Elias, show in their dealings with him a confidence born of love, which is infinitely pleasing to him. It is the mark of a soul which believes, as St John expresses it, in the love of God and therefore dares all things. In all its needs it turns to him, and with perfect simplicity and fearless words like those of Elias in to-day's lesson, demands that which seems to it to be for the greater glory of God and the more worthy of his infinite goodness.

The Gradual comes from Psalm cxvii, which is one of the ancient canticles of the paschal feast. " It is good to trust in the Lord, rather than to have confidence in man." The latter, indeed, even though willing, may not always be able to help us. The love of God alone can never fail, and has both the power and the will to save us.

The Gospel describes the resurrection of Lazarus (John xi 1-45), thus anticipating by a week the Greek Church, which celebrates it with great solemnity on the day preceding Palm Sunday.

The raising up of Lazarus after he had lain four days in the grave is the most marvellous of the miracles worked by our Saviour. Not indeed on account of the magnitude of the prodigy—for to the omnipotence of God it is as easy to raise to life the whole human race at the last day as it is to cause the smallest flower of the field to unfold its petals—

but because of the circumstances which accompanied it. The miracle, tangible and undeniable, was worked at the very gates of Jerusalem, and in the presence of a multitude of witnesses. The enemies of Jesus were so convinced of the decisive power of this new proof of his Messianic mission that they even planned to do away with Lazarus and put him back again into his tomb, as though by killing him they could, says St Augustine, prevent our Lord from restoring him a second time to life.

Jesus loved Mary, Martha and Lazarus, and in their home found comfort for the sorrows caused him by the Jews. This little family is a symbol of all religious houses, and a proto-type of those loving souls who are bound to Jesus by a more intimate union. Persecuted and rejected by the world, he takes shelter in the cloister, and seeks compensation in the love of a few chosen friends. He weeps and shudders beside the grave of him whom he loved, not only to show us how great was his love, but also to teach us that the death of Lazarus is a figure of the sentence of death which has been pronounced upon all the seed of Adam. Jesus the friend of our fallen race suffers death for us in his own person, he weeps tears of blood for our sakes, and at last by the word of his Gospel calls us from the tomb to a newness of life, so that henceforth each one of us may live to God—*vivat Deo.*

The verse chosen for the Offertory from Psalm xvii may well be applied to the multitude who sleep in the grave : " Thou wilt save the humble people, O Lord, and wilt bring down the eyes of the proud; for who is God beside thee, O Lord?" The liturgical application of this verse indicates that our Lord's mission as the Messiah will be fulfilled in the resurrection of the dead. The first consequence of the sin into which humanity was beguiled by the devil, whom the Scriptures therefore call *homicida ab initio,* was death; now the Saviour is come into the world to destroy the effects of sin, hence the day of his Parousia, when he shall raise up the human race and shall share the glorified life with his faithful friends, will be the day of his final victory.

The Secret asks that the expiation of the eucharistic sacri-fice may purify us from sin and appease the anger of God.

The Communion, contrary to the usual Lenten custom, is drawn from the Gospel of the day. It belongs to the Ambro-sian Liturgy, which shows a more archaic taste in the selection of its chants compared to that of Rome. The *videns Dominus* with the syllabic melody of the Gregorian antiphonary is wonderfully striking, especially in the force of the *Lazare, veni foras,* in which the composer has en-deavoured to express the fulness of the love of Jesus for his friend.

In the Post-Communion we pray that our participation in the holy Sacrament may ever cleanse us from our own faults and may defend us from all adversity.

The Church in her eucharistic collects always places before us one or other of the fruits of the Blessed Sacrament. The Eucharist, in fact, is everything to us, for it is Jesus himself; and Jesus is not only our grace and propitiation for past sins, but he is the antidote which preserves the soul from the corruption of temptation, and sows in our flesh the seed of immortality.

In the final Blessing over the people, the priest implores almighty God that we, who, knowing our own weakness, trust in his strength, may by his grace ever rejoice in his loving-kindness.

This is the spirit which is pleasing to God. He suffers for a time the proud man who boasts that he can do without his help, and when he does strike him down, it is to teach him that without the grace of God no one can prosper. When, however, a soul in true humility acknowledges its absolute need of divine assistance, God condescends to its unworthiness, and stretching forth his hand to succour it, he raises it up to the height of heaven.

The resurrection of Lazarus may be regarded by us also as a type of the Sacrament of Penance. Jesus alone has the power to convert the heart, but he delegates to his apostles and ministers the office of freeing Lazarus from the bands and the winding-sheet which envelop him, so that he may henceforth be able to walk easily in the way of the divine precepts.

SATURDAY AFTER THE FOURTH SUNDAY IN LENT

(Station at St Lawrence)

Collecta at St Angelus " in piscibus." Station at St Nicholas in Carcere.

Ever since the time of Gelasius I (492-6) this day has been devoted in Rome to the conferring of Holy Orders. As, however, this necessitated the great fast together with the *Pannuchis* at the tomb of St Peter, and as Holy Orders were not usually conferred until dawn on the Sunday, it is probable that originally this Saturday was " aliturgical," as was always the case in Rome when the vigil for the Sunday followed. The station at St Lawrence marked in the ancient Sacramentaries was, therefore, held only in those years in which the Pope did not ordain any titular priests or deacons, for, in any case, the consecration of the ministers of the

Church could take place only at the tomb of the Apostles at the Vatican.

The synaxis at the Ager Veranus, when it could be held, seems to have been connected with the preparation of the catechumens for baptism. When the scrutinies had taken place at St Paul's, these new recruits of the Church were conducted to the tomb of St Lawrence, the glorious crossbearer of the Apostolic See. After their initiation they will return thither on Easter Wednesday, but it was fitting that they should at once be placed under his patronage.

During the later Middle Ages, when the disciplinary measures regulating the catechumenate had become obsolete, and the procession to the Ager Veranus in the showery weather of March was found to be inconvenient, the Church of St Nicholas in Carcere was substituted for that of St Lawrence. This church was one of the most popular in Rome, especially after the Pierleoni had erected their fortress in its vicinity.

Among the sixty or so churches and chapels formerly dedicated to St Nicholas the Wonder-worker of Myra,[1] this one, situated in the Forum Olitorium, was the most celebrated, because it was also a diaconal title. It stands on the ruins of a temple of Piety, erected 165 B.C. by the duumvir Acilius Glabrio, and is called *in carcere,* because from the time of Pliny down to the eighth century at least, a public prison existed there—sometimes erroneously confused with the *Tullianum* on the Capitoline Hill. Under the high altar repose relics of Faustinus and Viatrix, the martyrs of the Via Portuensis. The church was reconsecrated by Honorius II on May 12, 1128.

The basilica in which the *collecta* meets to-day was originally dedicated to St Paul, but later it took the name of St Angelus with the addition of *in piscina* or *in piscibus,* on account of the fish-market, which was held until quite recently in that neighbourhood. The church was certainly in existence before the eighth century, for we know that Theodore, the uncle of Adrian I (772-95), rebuilt it from its foundations. Many holy relics are preserved there, including the bodies of the martyred sons of St Symphorosa of Tibur (Tivoli).[2]

The Mass of to-day is inspired by the holy feelings which must have filled the hearts of the catechumens as the day of their baptism drew nigh. The Gospel speaks again of the inner light of the New Covenant, a subject which seems to

---

[1] The modern Dembre in Asia Minor, where St Nicholas died in 342. He is also called St Nicholas of Bari in Southern Italy, whither his body was transported in 1097.—TR.

[2] St Symphorosa was put to death, together with her seven sons, under the Emperor Hadrian in 120.—TR.

have been treated habitually when the station took place at the tomb of the saint, the flames of whose funeral pyre dispelled the darkness of idolatry in Rome.

The Introit is taken from Isaias (lv 1): "O you that thirst"—that is, you in whom the pleasures of life and earthly possessions have increased, instead of extinguishing, within your breast your thirst for true happiness—"come to the waters" of divine grace which alone can satisfy your longings. Let not your wretchedness hinder you, come and draw water freely and joyfully; quench your thirst at the pure fountain of grace, which an infinitely merciful and loving God has given you without regard for human imperfections. Psalm lxxvii follows, which is a hymn of thanksgiving for the many benefits bestowed by God upon the patriarchs of old.

In the Collect we ask that God would grant us the spiritual fruit for which our devotion craves, for our fast will then indeed be profitable when all our Christian life shall reflect the divine perfections.

In the first Lesson Isaias (xlix 8-15) predicts, with the vision of a seer, the Messianic mission which will restore to the souls of men their spiritual freedom, which will illuminate them with the rays of a faith derived from the source of all truth, and will give them to drink of the fresh waters of the sacraments. Idolatry, legal rites and ceremonies were all as bonds fettering the body and encumbering the spirit; in their place has been substituted the adoration of the heart. It is indeed true that the world by its wrongdoing had forfeited the mercy of God, but a mother—and here Isaias likens God to the tenderest of mothers—does not forget nor turn away from her child, notwithstanding its many transgressions.

The Gradual is taken from Psalm ix. It is the poor man who speaks, the victim of the oppressor in his pride, nor has he any to succour him. He compares himself to an orphan, having no father here below except God his heavenly Father, whose aid he invokes. Who is this poor man, this orphan, but Jesus Christ himself, who, feeling the hour of his Passion draw near, and foreseeing the sufferings that he must endure at the hands of the Synagogue, calls upon his Father to help him in the day of victory, at the dawn of the resurrection?

In the Roman Lectionaries of the ninth century, there followed here a second lesson from Isaias: *Omnes sitientes venite ad aquas,* which, like the Introit, exhorted the catechumens to hasten to the baptismal font.

The reading of the Gospel of St John, begun on the day of the great scrutinies at St Paul's, is now continued. To-day the Evangelist speaks of the inward illumination of the soul, by means of faith, and narrates how, when the Pharisees refused to accept the testimony of Christ, he appealed to the authority of the Father who had sent him. This discussion took place in the treasury, called in Greek γαζοφυλάκιον, perhaps to convey to us that charity and compassion towards the poor are the roads that lead to Jesus. Blessed indeed is he who finds Jesus, for he finds a treasure above all treasures. Thus a saint has said: "My Jesus, he who desires aught beside thee knows not what he desires."

The Offertory comes from Psalm xvii: "The Lord is become my firmament and my refuge and my deliverer: and in him will I put my trust." He has become my firmament because his grace strengthens me against the assault of my spiritual enemies; my refuge, because I find rest in him from the persecution of my adversaries, who, when I invoke the name of Jesus, flee away in terror; my deliverer, because the Lord only permits me to be tempted by the devil in order to reward me with the joy and triumph of victory.

In the Secret we pray God to accept our offering, and to turn away his anger—this is the propitiatory effect of the Sacrifice—and because our evil will is the chief obstacle to the grace of God, we implore him to change by the efficacy of his power these rebellious and distorted dispositions of our soul into responsive and obedient instruments of the Holy Ghost.

The Communion is taken from Psalm xxii, which is the joyful hymn of one whom the divine shepherd feeds amid fresh pastures and flowing streams: "The Lord ruleth me and I shall want nothing: he hath set me in a place of pasture"—that is, the Catholic Church, the holy sacraments, the interior grace which ever nourishes the faith of a believing soul—"and he leadeth me to the water of refreshment" to the place where the thirst for worldly joys ceases and only the desire for heavenly things remains.

In the Post-Communion we ask that the holy Sacrament may purify us—this is the satisfying effect of the Sacrifice—and may by its efficacy adorn our souls with such virtues as will render them pleasing to God. Holy Communion is assuredly the true school for saints. It at once causes God to look favourably upon us; it purifies our souls; it obtains for us the gift of those virtues which we need; and it finally draws us to him by the gentle ties of a uniting and transforming love; so that feeding in truth upon him, we also live by him. This is the crowning effect in the soul of Holy Communion.

In the Benediction over the people the priest prays thus: "O God, who choosest rather to pity than to be angry with those who hope in thee; grant us worthily to lament the evils we have done, that we may deserve to find the grace of thy consolation." In this life, the tears of the penitent not only extinguish the flames of hell, but quench also the fire of the righteous anger of God.

If, as Christ has said, the house of God on earth is not to be turned into a house of traffickers—still less can we expect to purchase our entrance into heaven. The grace of God is not bought but is freely given to all. In order, there-fore, to become saints, it is sufficient to respond generously to the call from God given to us in holy baptism, seeking with joy the fountains of grace which flow from the blessed Eucharist : *bibite cum laetitia.* In to-day's Mass the divine Saviour renews his invitation to his holy table.

PASSION SUNDAY, OR SUNDAY "IN MEDIANA"

Station at St Peter.

The station at the Vatican to-day is the last remaining trace of the *Pannuchis* which, in the time of Pope Gelasius, was celebrated at the tomb of the Prince of the Apostles during the night previous to the solemn Ordination of the priests and deacons of Rome.

To-day begins the fortnight of immediate preparation for Easter, which, in the third century, included a twelve days' fast preceding the dawn of the Resurrection. In the sacred Liturgy, and more especially in the Breviary, we can still distinguish the special cycle formed by this holy Passion-tide. Whereas during Lent, which, as we have said above, was of later institution, the Church is chiefly occupied in the instruction of the catechumens and in the preparation of the penitents for their solemn reconciliation on Holy Thursday, all this during the last fortnight before Easter takes a secondary place. From now onward during these two weeks but one thought predominates in the Missal and in the Breviary—the thought of the Just One, who realizes the bitter persecution which his enemies are plotting against him. He is innocent, but is so encompassed by the hatred of his adversaries that he has none to defend him. He therefore turns to his heavenly Father, calls him to witness that he is innocent, and entreats him not to abandon him in the day of trial.

The liturgical cycle of the Passion begins with the Mass at the Vatican, where Nero crucified the first Vicar of Christ and where Symmachus had built an oratory named *Sancta Hierusalem,* as the Sessorian Basilica was originally called, in honour of the triumphant Standard of Redemption. It was from that oratory near St Peter's that the following verses were introduced into the Liturgy :

Salva nos, Christe Salvator, per virtutem Crucis;
Qui salvasti Petrum in mari, miserere nobis.

The Mass of this Sunday is entirely dominated by the memory of the Sacrifice on Golgotha, and is one of the most beautiful and pathetic in the whole Roman Antiphonary. During this fortnight, in which the Liturgy illustrates with dramatic force the ever-growing hate of the Sanhedrim against our Lord, the early *Ordines Romani* forbid the final doxology to be said after either the antiphonic or the responsorial psalmody. Psalm xlii, *Judica me,* is also omitted at the beginning of the Mass, but this is not a very ancient custom, nor has it any special significance, for the prayers which the priest now recites at the foot of the altar before beginning the Introit were first introduced into Frankish countries about the eighth century. As in to-day's Mass the *Judica me* is sung at the Introit, it is therefore omitted previous to the Confession before the priest goes up to the altar.

In the Introit, from Psalm xlii, Christ appeals to the judgement of his Father against the sentence of death which his treacherous and deceitful enemies are plotting against him, so that he may justify him in the day of his resurrection. That is indeed the day when the light and the truth spoken of by the Psalmist shall be fully revealed.

In the Collect we pray that God will look mercifully upon his family, the Church, so that by his providence the bodies of its members may be preserved in health while his grace guards their souls from all evil; a magnificent synthesis which recognizes the natural as well as the spiritual element in man. Sanctity is innate in the soul, but before it can be clothed with this glorious vesture it is necessary that both the body and the senses obey and follow closely the precepts of the Gospel.

In the Lesson, from the Epistle to the Hebrews (ix 11-15), St Paul declares the greater excellence of the New Testament as compared with the Old, because of the completeness of the sacrifice of Calvary. For while, in the Old Law, it was necessary to repeat without ceasing the same sacrifices for the sins of the people—the High Priest himself also entered every year into the Holy of Holies to offer up therein the blood of innocent victims—Jesus Christ, by the shedding of his own blood, redeemed once for all the whole race of Adam, and entered the heavenly sanctuary at the head of the unending company of the redeemed.

The Gradual is taken from Psalms cxlii and xvii. As the day of his Passion draws near, Christ fears and calls upon his Father to save him from the malice of the wicked. He does not lose courage, for he is confident that on the day of his resurrection God will deliver him from the hands of those cruel men, and from the gates of death, and will glorify him in the sight of all nations.

The *psalmus in directum,* or Tract (Psalm cxxviii) is inspired by the same conception, but alludes more definitely to the Passion of the Saviour. "Often have Herod and the Synagogue fought against me from my youth, but they could not prevail over me. The wicked have wrought upon my back, as in the terrible scourging at the pillar in the hall of the *praetorium* of Pilate. They have lengthened their iniquities, but the Lord is just. In his inscrutable wisdom he permits that the wicked shall prevail for a time over the innocent, but in the day of his triumph at the Easter dawn, he will cut the necks of sinners."

The rupture between Christ and the Sanhedrim is now imminent; indeed, it has been definitely announced and proclaimed in all the three hundred or more synagogues of Jerusalem. Jesus is banished from the inheritance of Israel, and anyone who is seen in his company shares in this excommunication. The Jews accuse the Saviour of being possessed by the devil, whilst he on his part defies them to convince him of a single sin. Passing then from defence to accusation, he shows that his adversaries are not of God, as otherwise they would hearken to his words. This is a terrible judgement, and one which every Christian should take as a test to see whether he has the spirit of Christ or not. "Out of the fulness of the heart the mouth speaketh." Only if our heart is full of the spirit and love of God shall we find consolation in thinking and speaking of him.

The Offertory comes from Psalm cxviii, which expresses the joy of the just in walking in the way of the commandments of God, in spite of the threats of the enemy. Jesus, that Just One of whom the Psalmist sings, implores his Father again and again *ut vivam,* more especially now that the Jews have resolved to seek his life. He does not, however, pray to be saved from temporal death, for he is come to die for us, but he desires the risen life which, by means of grace and of glory, he is to communicate to his mystical body.

In the Secret we ask that the merits of the eucharistic sacrifice may both unloose the bonds of our wickedness and procure for us the gifts of the divine mercy, for we are indeed bound and fettered by sin, as Christ has said : *Omnis qui facit peccatum, servus est peccati.* The sinner who breaks the law thinks to gain liberty by so doing, whereas he forges for himself the heaviest possible chain, becoming thereby the slave of his passions and so of Satan himself.

The verse for the Communion, by an infringement of the regular usage, is not taken from one of the Psalms nor from the Gospel of the day, but, with some slight alterations, from St Paul (1 Cor. xi 24-25), for it testifies to the fact that the eucharistic sacrifice is commemorative of the Passion of our Lord, of which the liturgical celebration begins to-day. It is for the same reason that St Ambrose remarked that the Church celebrates daily the death and burial of Jesus Christ, in that the whole Christian life with its sufferings, its austerities, and its sacrifices, is but the continuation and completion of the one drama of salvation begun on Calvary; the accomplishing of one only sacrifice, that of Jesus Christ, which concentrates within itself, sanctifies and consecrates all our sacrifices. *Una enim oblatione consummavit in sempiternum sanctificatos.*[1]

In the Post-Communion or *Eucharistia*—not to be confused with the original and ancient *Eucharistia,* or thanksgiving, which was the consecratory anaphora itself—we beseech almighty God to continue to protect by his grace those whom he has refreshed with his mysteries. It is not enough to approach the holy Sacrament; we must also correspond with divine grace and develop those seeds of eternal life which Jesus has sown in our hearts in Holy Communion.

One of the greatest evils of our time is the want of spiritual vigour, which makes even the preachers of the Gospel hesitate sometimes to declare to this frivolous generation how wide a gulf lies between the doctrine of Christ and the aims of the worldly-minded. Even the faithful demand mitigations of the rules of the Church and compromises which often end by obscuring the Gospel teaching. No heed is given to the four last things; the intangible rights of God and his Church may not be alluded to for fear of wounding the susceptibilities of men; in a word, it would appear that it is no longer Christianity which is to convert the world, but the world which is fashioning Christianity anew after its own heart. Yet our Lord and his martyrs for our sakes did not hesitate to declare the Gospel in all its fulness, though they knew that by so doing they would incur the penalty of death.

[1] Heb. x 14.

MONDAY AFTER PASSION SUNDAY

Collecta at St George. Station at St Chrysogonus.

We have already spoken of the Church of St George *de Belabru* at the foot of the Palatine, where the four-sided arch of Janus stands, and where, from remote antiquity, the pagan populace used to seek divinations. Hither, too, even down to our own days, the more superstitious among the Romans were in the habit of coming, in order to obtain from the spirits of criminals who had been executed the numbers which would be drawn at the coming " lotto."

The Basilica of St Chrysogonus in Trastevere, near the classical guard-house of the *Vigiles,* still preserves under the sanctuary the remains of the dwelling-place of the martyr of that name, which dates back to the time of Constantine. The Byzantine period no doubt increased the popularity of the veneration paid to this saint of Aquileia, whose name by a special privilege was placed in the Diptychs of the Roman Mass.

Gregory III restored the church about the year 731, and founded a monastery beside it which he dedicated to the martyrs Stephen and Lawrence. Later, towards 1123, the titular Cardinal Giovanni da Crema rebuilt the church on a smaller scale and raised the floor so that the remains of the original basilica are now on a lower level than the present pavement.

The Introit is from Psalm lv, and is the cry of the Just One oppressed by the ungodly man, or rather by a multitude of enemies, since all the sins of the entire human race have been laid upon him and clamour for his death.

In the Collect we ask two things of God : firstly, that he would so sanctify our lenten fast that our interior dispositions may harmonize with our bodily abstinence; and, secondly, that our penitence and contrition of heart may obtain for us the pardon of our past shortcomings.

The Lesson, taken from Jonas (iii 1-10), was very familiar to the early Christians, for we often find the story which it relates pictured on the walls of the catacombs or carved on the marble sarcophagi. The Ninevites, who by their fasts and penances saved their city from the destruction which threatened it, are an example to Christians to follow in their footsteps. We know that some Oriental peoples, such as the Armenians, the Abyssinians, and others, keep a special fast before Lent which is known as the " Fast of Ninive." This was vigorously combated by the Greeks, but, in any case, the various liturgies, including the Latin, have always regarded the fast of the Ninevites as a type of the Christian season of penance.

We should note the official character of the penitential fast at Ninive, which was proclaimed by Jonas on the authority of the king and his nobles. It is not, indeed, enough that religion and religious worship should simply be a personal and private tribute to God, but these should also be collective and social, for the family, the municipality, the nation, etc., are all living entities, and, as such, should render to God that worship which is his due.

Further, God has not created man to stand alone, but has made him a member of a society, both in the natural and in the supernatural order, and it is only by means of this two-fold society that man can reach the perfection at which he aims. It follows, then, especially in matters concerning the soul, that we should deem of the first importance and adhere scrupulously to all those acts of worship which express the perfect and supernatural homage rendered by the Church to God. We must pray and meditate, we must fast and mortify ourselves, in all things striving after holiness in one mind with the Church; for it is from the body that the life, the happiness, and the well-being of the members are derived.

The Gradual comes from Psalm liii, in which the Just One appeals to the judgement of God to deliver him from the calumnies of his enemies.

The Gospel is from St John (vii 32-39), in which Jesus, taking an illustration from the ceremony of drawing water by the priests for the service of the Temple, announces the mission of the Holy Ghost and the preaching of the Gospel to the Gentiles. Grace is here compared to water, because, like water, it extinguishes the fire of the passions, refreshes the spirit, quenches the thirst of immoderate desires, and gives life and growth to the beauteous flowers of virtue.

The Offertory is derived from Psalm vi: "Turn to me, O Lord, and deliver my soul; O save me for thy mercy's sake." That is, turn and look mercifully upon me, after thy justice shall have been satisfied, O Thou who on account of the sins which bow me to the ground hast turned away thy face from me. Deliver me and grant me that plenitude of life which I desire and which will free me for ever from the cruelty of my enemies.

In the Secret we beg that the Host of Salvation which we are about to offer may cleanse us from our sins and obtain for us the divine mercy. This is the established order of things; first comes the propitiation and then the generous bestowal of graces.

The Communion is taken from Psalm xxix: "The Lord of hosts, he is the king of glory." It is well that we should impress this on our hearts, for within a few days we shall see the same king veil his glory under the ignominy of the Passion, and the Lord of hosts fall beneath the weight of the cross. Herein lies the *Mysterium Fidei.* He who, hanging on the cross, is derided by the multitude, is at the same moment acclaimed by myriads of angels who, trembling with awe, sing the Trisagion during the tragedy of Calvary. He who yields up his soul in unspeakable agony and humiliation is the strong Lion of Juda, the true Samson who in his death crushed the hordes of the Philistines.

To the eyes of faith Jesus Christ never appeared more glorious and more terrible than on the cross when he addressed Death in the words of Osee : *O mors, ero mors tua, morsus tuus ero, inferne.*

The Post-Communion is as follows : " May the saving reception of thy Sacrament, we beseech thee, O Lord, bestow upon us purification and healing." Holy Mass and Communion not only possess a propitiatory efficacy, but are an antidote against the poison of sin. We are the children of a corrupt race, and there is a taint in the blood of our veins which can be cleansed only by a health-giving remedy— that is, by the sacred blood of Christ, who has said : "He that eateth me, the same also shall live by me."[1]

In the Prayer over the people we beseech God to give strength not only to our souls, but also to our bodies, which cannot always do that which the spirit wills—*Spiritus quidem promptus est, caro autem infirma*—in order that the constant practice of good works may obtain for us the grace of his protection from the fierce assaults of the adversary. Neither faith nor fair words alone, without good works, will avail to build up the kingdom of God within us.

How much do we owe to the devoted care of the Roman Church, which has so jealously preserved the memory of those who have cemented with their blood the stones of the City of God? When it was not possible to possess the tomb of a martyr, as in the case of St Chrysogonus, his house was venerated instead, as being the place where the future athlete had prepared himself for the combat on behalf of the faith. Rome has consecrated as churches many of the ancient homes of her martyrs, and what could be more inspiring to the faithful than a martyr's empty house! Those rooms once beautified with paintings and mosaics, of which some traces still remain, are silent and empty for the very reason that the martyrs voluntarily abandoned all things in order to follow Christ on the road to Calvary.

---

[1] John vi 58.

TUESDAY AFTER PASSION SUNDAY

Station at St Cyriacus at the Baths of Diocletian.

The *Ordines Romani* observe that no station was held on this day, which rule occurring in Passion week, with its venerable usages, may be a survival of the very ancient regulation prohibiting the procession and the stational Mass on Mondays, Tuesdays and Thursdays throughout the year, except on the feasts of the martyrs.

The origin of the *titulus Cyriaci* goes back to the beginning of the fourth century, but its founder should in all probability be distinguished from the other Cyriacus, the martyr who was buried in the Via Ostiensis, and who, by reason of his bearing the same name, eventually became the patron saint of the Basilica of Cyriacus on the Quirinal.

The church was successively restored under Adrian I, Leo III and Gregory IV. Bruno, also, the celebrated founder of the Carthusians, sanctified this spot by his presence and gathered together here a band of his monks, whose successors continued to inhabit the monastery almost down to our time. The venerable church, being now dilapidated, was replaced by a new and splendid one dedicated to our Lady, Queen of Angels, which the genius of Michelangelo constructed within the ancient halls of the Baths of Diocletian, whilst to-day's station was transferred to the Basilica of Sta Maria in Via Lata. St Cyriacus must long have been venerated at this latter church, near which a celebrated convent of nuns existed from the ninth century, for it would appear that the head of the famous martyr was brought here in the later Middle Ages from the cemetery on the Via Ostiensis.

The Introit comes from Psalm xxvi : " Expect the Lord, and do manfully : let thy heart take courage, and wait thou for the Lord." Not all our days are alike, but God attains his sublime ends by co-ordinating the most various and untoward circumstances ; in nothing does his divine providence shine forth more magnificently than in this—that he makes events which seem to be most contrary serve to the accomplishment of his own designs. " There is a time to build," says the Holy Ghost in the Book of Coheleth—*i.e.*, Ecclesiastes, or the Preacher—" and a time to destroy ; a time of love and a time of hatred ; a time to weep and a time to laugh.[1] All things have their season,"[2] and in life's dark days we must be steadfast and ever trust in the Lord, who.

---

[1] Eccles. iii 3, 4, 8.   [2] *ibid.*, iii 1.

in the words of the prophet, brings us to the very gates of hell and then draws us back to safety.

In the Collect we pray that God will accept our fasts, so that through their efficacy we may obtain such an abundance of grace that the final *aeterna remedia* may be assured to us after the sorrows of our earthly pilgrimage.

We should note the order followed in the prayer. In the first place comes the expiation, for *qui non placet, non placat,* and God may refuse special graces to him who has still a heavy debt to pay to divine justice. When satisfaction has been made, and the friendship of the soul with God fully re-established, we can then confidently ask of him those particular favours which friendship alone can embolden us to ask, for they are vouchsafed to friends alone : *Et adjicias quod oratio non praesumit.* As, however, every grace which we receive here is but the prelude to the final grace, that of eternal glory in heaven, we must pray without ceasing that the favours granted to us on earth may be crowned by that which is their proper end and fruition—viz., the beatific vision in paradise.

The story of Daniel in the lions' den (Dan. xiv 27-42) was widely known in the early days of Christianity, for it is reproduced in many of the catacombs, a very fine example of the first half of the second century being in that of Priscilla, in the so-called *Cappella Greca.* This lesson may have been chosen because, according to the legend, St Cyriacus, like Daniel, first exercised his apostolate at the Persian Court, that of King Sapor. Later on he was condemned to death for the faith by the Emperor Diocletian, whom a painter of the fourth century likened to Nabuchodonosor in the crypt of the martyr Crescentius in the cemetery of Priscilla.

Daniel among the lions is a figure of the early Church persecuted to death by the whole world, and against whom even the law was commissioned to carry out this cruel sentence : *Non licet esse vos.* But, like Daniel, the Church raised her hands and her heart in supplication to God, and God did not abandon those who trusted in him. We must follow the example of Daniel and go down fearlessly into the lions' den, whenever it may please God to try us, and there await with confidence the hour of our deliverance. Sorrows and troubles do not harm the soul, so long as we do not allow them to disquiet us.

The Graduals at Mass all refer henceforth to the divine Victim who appeals to his heavenly Father against the judgement of his impious persecutors who have condemned him to death, imploring him that he would give back to him his life on Easter morn. To-day's Gradual is derived from

Psalm xlii. The light and truth which are invoked by the Psalmist refer to the mission of the Paraclete, which, according to the words of the Gospel, is especially that of convincing the world of unrighteousness and malice. The Paraclete indeed came, and by pouring forth his gifts upon the disciples of the Crucified, whilst abandoning the obstinate Jews to their blindness, clearly proved the divine origin of the mission of our Lord.

The Gospel is the continuation of St John's narrative, and tells us (vii 1-13) how our Lord went up to the feast of Tabernacles in the month of *Tishri*. To the invitation of his kinsfolk, Jesus replied that he would not go up to the festival, meaning that he did not wish to join the noisy caravan which was then proceeding to Jerusalem, making merry. He therefore did not take any part in the feast, having, as he said, no wish to do so; but he went up secretly to the holy City after the festival had begun, in order that he might teach the people who usually assembled in great numbers on this occasion.

The fact that our Lord habitually attended all the great ceremonies of the Law should be a lesson to us to cultivate a lively spirit of devotion to the liturgy of the Church, by being present at its functions, especially on feast days, thus helping by our numbers to increase the splendour of the worship which the Church pays to the honour and glory of God.

The desolation of the sanctuary abandoned and neglected by the people, who in so many lands no longer flock to the services of the true religion, is one of the grave disasters which Jeremias deplores in his *Lamentations* when he says : *Viae Sion lugent eo quod non sit qui veniat ad solemnitatem.*

In the Offertory, taken from Psalm ix, is expressed the steadfast confidence of Jesus, even in that fateful hour in which the justice of his Father abandons him to the hatred of his foes. " Let all those trust in thee who know thy name, O Lord," he says, " for thy name expresses ineffable love. Thou dost not forsake them that seek thee, or rather, thou dost not forsake any man, for even when the sinner flies from thee, thou dost follow after him to bring him back to repentance. How then canst thou fail those who seek thee?" The divine Victim knows that he will rise again in glory, and in the midst of his Passion, he already sings the paschal hymn : " Sing ye to the Lord who dwelleth in Sion : for he hath not forgotten the cry of the poor." Christ himself is here meant, of whom St Paul writes : " *Propter nos egenus factus est cum esset dives, ut nos illius inopia divites essemus* "; whilst the cry spoken of by the Psalmist is our

Saviour's last word on the cross : " *Eloi, Eloi, lamma sabac-thani:* My God, my God, why hast thou forsaken me?"

In the Secret we ask that the victim which we are about to offer to God may obtain for us such temporal consolations as are necessary for our existence; yet not in superfluity, lest they should stifle within us the desire for heavenly blessings. Thus does the Church, the prudent director of the spiritual life, discern the necessities both of the body and of the soul. We should bear in mind the twofold nature of man and avoid excess on either side, says the Wise Man : *Divitias et paupertatem ne dederis mihi, sed tantum victui meo tribue necessaria . . .* and for this reason, that poverty when it becomes grinding tempts man to blasphemy and despair, whilst an abundance of the good things of this life easily inclines the heart to forgetfulness of God.

In the Communion (Psalm xxiv 22) we hear again the voice of Christ, who, bowed under the weight of our sins and the rage of his enemies, earnestly prays to his Father that he would deliver him from the power of death. He prays thus rather for us than for himself, who, being the very fount of life, could not remain bound for long by the chains of death, whereas we have absolute need of the resurrection of Christ, as being the beginning and visible proof of the resurrection of the whole human race.

In the Post-Communion we beseech God that our frequency in drawing near to the holy Table may be for us both a token and a pledge of our approaching each day nearer to the celestial altar and the eternal prize.

The Church militant is to some extent a symbol and prophetic type of that which will one day be accomplished in the heavenly Church, especially after the whole expiatory work of Jesus Christ has been fulfilled on the day of his final *parousia.* If external good works and the position held in the household of the faith are accompanied by a spirit of faith and fervent charity, the place of each one in the glory of heaven and his eternal reward will be certainly proportionate to the amount of grace which has enriched his soul on earth.

In the final Prayer before the dismissal of the people, we ask God, the author of all merit, the first cause of the movements of our free will, to support by his grace the weakness and inconstancy of this same will, so that our example may help to increase not only the numbers, but also the merits of those who believe. It would truly be vain for the Church to attain a great exterior development if the sanctity of her followers did not increase in like manner, for God does not consider *quantum, sed ex quanto.*

The Church makes use of the Psalter during these last days of Lent, in order to reveal to us the innermost thoughts of the Redeemer, as the hour of his Passion draws near. The Psalms form indeed the chief of all books of prayer. The holy Gospels relate the life of Jesus in all its details and expound his teaching, but the psalms of David show us the mind of our Saviour, and make known to us his preferences, his feelings, his struggles and his anxieties, and tell us of the accents of deep love in which he prayed to his heavenly Father. Throughout his life, Jesus addressed him in the words of the Psalter, and on the cross, during his last agony, the twenty-first psalm was on his lips. We might almost liken the Psalter to a sacerdotal book of prayers which the eternal Pontiff recited whilst offering up to his Father the sacrifice of his own life.

For these reasons the ascetics of old studied the Book of Psalms assiduously, and recited it in its entirety every day. Even in our own times the Coptic and Abyssinian chiefs not only in their houses, but on journeys and during their halts in the desert, never let this book out of their sight— a tradition which they share with the Jews, who also for many centuries had no other prayer-book but that containing the songs of David.

The private piety of present-day Catholics would gain much, if, letting themselves be influenced by the example of our common Mother, the Church, who appoints for her ministers the weekly recital of the Psalter, they too would make more use of this prayer-book, which was inspired by the Holy Ghost and adopted for our example by our Saviour Jesus Christ himself.

WEDNESDAY AFTER PASSION SUNDAY

Collecta at St Mark.   Station at St Marcellus.

The *titulus de Pallacine,* built by Pope Marcus in the first years of the Peace of Constantine, is already known to our readers. That of Marcellus stands on the Via Lata, on the site once occupied by the house of a matron named Lucina, who is said to have converted it into a parochial church. Recent excavations have corroborated the data furnished by the *Acta* of St Marcellus, so that we may hold for a certainty that the church was erected during the pontificate of the martyr who was afterwards buried there.

The Introit is from Psalm xvii, and is a hymn of praise for the deliverance of the Just One. " My deliverer from the angry nations : thou wilt lift me up above them that rise up against me, from the unjust man thou wilt deliver me, O Lord." In what manner did God reply to this steadfast hope of his dying Son? By freeing him from the bonds of death, and setting him as judge—from whom there is no appeal— over the whole human race, including those who, sitting formerly in the *Lithostrotos*[1] or in the seats of the Sanhedrim, had cried out : *Reus est mortis ;* by delivering him from the gates of hell; and finally by glorifying him as being the firstborn among all the dead who shall rise again, the source and fount of life unending.

The Lenten fast is now drawing to its close, wherefore we pray in the Collect that the abstinence which we have practised, being sanctified by the mortification of all our evil passions, may serve to enlighten the hearts of the faithful. God himself has placed this desire in our hearts, so we trust that he will graciously accept it and will grant it abundant fruit.

In a short time, the catechumens will be called upon to take a solemn vow in public that they will observe the Law of God, for which reason the Church, with more than her usual insistence, dwells on the teaching of the Decalogue in the lesson of to-day (Lev. xix 1, 2, 3, 11-19, 25). The ten precepts of the *Torah* are indeed comprised in the New Testament in a single word, " Love," for, as St Paul explains, the law of love having no limit, embraces God as well as our neighbour, and is the chief motive of all dutiful service. We must desire to serve God because he is our Father and our neighbour because he is our brother. The will to serve others is true charity, therefore love is the master-key of the entire Christian edifice.

The Gradual comes from Psalm xxix, and, as usual, anticipates the triumph of the resurrection amid the sorrows of the Passion. Our Lord himself did the same during the Last Supper—and the Liturgy faithfully follows his example —in order to strengthen our hope when faced with the " scandal of the cross "; " I will extol thee, O Lord, because thou hast delivered me from the darkness of hell, nor hast thou permitted my enemies to triumph over me, who, having slain me, had sealed my tomb and set their guard about it. Thou hast brought forth my soul from hell, and hast saved me as I was about to go down into the pit, and hast not suffered that my body should be subject to the common law of nature and see corruption; but, hearing my cry, hast raised it from death, healing its wounds and glorifying them with the sublimity of heavenly light."

The feast of the *Encaenia*—as the Hellenist Jews called the new dedication of the temple—was being celebrated at

[1] John xix 13 *sqq.*

Jerusalem (John x 22-38). The weather was rainy,[1] so Jesus walked in the Temple in Solomon's porch teaching the people after the manner of the peripatetics and stoics of Athens.

Our Lord's presence at the feast of the *Encaenia* again teaches us that we should take frequent part in the solemn festivals of the Church, in order that they may be in truth the social and collective expression of the mystical union which binds all the faithful to the person of the Redeemer in a common bond of faith, hope and charity.

The question asked by the Jews, and the suspense in which they professed to be held, were not genuine but feigned and cunning; for in reality they wished to extort some word from Christ, by which he would be compromised in the sight of the Sanhedrim. Our Lord will not give his confidence and friendship to those who do not approach him with straightforwardness and candour. If those who questioned him were really desirous of learning the truth concerning his Messianic mission and his divine nature, they would have found abundant proof of both in his teaching and his miracles. This, however, was not what they wanted; they sought a pretext which would avail to bring Jesus to judgement before the Sanhedrim, but he refused to afford them such a pretext, and appealed instead to the testimony of his works.

The Offertory is derived from Psalm lxiii: " Deliver me from my enemies, O my God, and defend me from them that rise up against me, O Lord." Save me, O Father, not indeed by delivering me from the cross, for I am come to die for all mankind, but by not permitting that death and hell should triumph over me—that is, over my mystical Body, the Church.

In the Secret we pray that we may bring to God the sacrifice of propitiation and praise with sincere devotion. The grace of piety is one of the seven gifts of the Holy Ghost, and, as St Paul says, it is needed by us in every circumstance of life, for it supplies a supernatural motive to all our words, our acts and our judgements. Considered in this sense, piety is a special attitude of the soul which enables it to work in the light of God and under the guidance of his grace.

The Communion is from Psalm xxiv, and speaks to us of that purity of heart with which we should draw near to the altar of God. An absolute freedom from every stain of venial sin is not required of us, for our God is a purifying and a

---

[1] Although the Evangelist wrote in Greek, yet he thought in Syriac, in which language the same word is used for " winter " as for " rain "; but from the context it is clear that the word " rain " is more consistent with the narrative, for the fact that it was winter would have no connection with our Lord's walking in the porch.

consuming fire, and will destroy in the flames of his love the chaff of our imperfections, and all else that is not in accordance with his divine will. It is, however, expedient that the soul should not be inclined to sin, but should freely allow itself to be enwrapped by the flames of divine love.

The Post-Communion is the same as that of the Thursday after Ash Wednesday. We here ask of God that, as the sacramental species are the visible sign of the *res sacra*—that is, of the body of Christ—so the communion of this sacred body may also be the symbol of our union with him who is the cause and source to us of all salvation.

Jesus worked a great many miracles in the sight of the Jews to prove his divine nature and to show that he was indeed the Messiah, but they were not convinced, and complained that he left them in great uncertainty. This is always the case with sceptics. The truths more positively affirmed by Scripture and taught by the Church will always appear confused and doubtful to such, because they use their intellect not in finding grounds for belief, but in criticizing and detracting from the truth. It is vain to trust alone to our own intelligence in examining into the doctrine of the Church. The first step is to believe in God who speaks to us, and in his Church which teaches us according to the saying of Isaias so often repeated by St Anselm of Aosta : *Nisi credideritis, non intelligetis.*

THURSDAY AFTER PASSION SUNDAY

Collecta at Sta Maria " in Via Lata." Station at St Apollinaris " in Archipresbyteratu."

The Church of the deaconry of Sta Maria in Via Lata was erected about the time of Sergius I (687-701), and a medieval tradition, confusing perhaps the name of Pope Paul I (757-767), who further embellished it, with that of the Apostle St Paul, asserted that this was the site of the house hired by the Apostle when, at the time of his first captivity, he spent two years in Rome in the company of St Luke. History, however, gives us no clue to the whereabouts of this dwelling-place of the Apostle.

Under the high altar is preserved with all veneration the body of Agapitus, the famous martyr of Praeneste (Palestrina), together with some relics of St Cyriacus, the martyr of the Via Ostiensis.

The basilica " *in Archipresbyteratu* " is dedicated to St Apollinaris, the patron saint of Ravenna, a city of such importance in the Middle Ages, consequent on the presence there of the Byzantine Exarchs, that its archbishops, copying the œcumenical patriarchs of Constantinople, began to arrogate to themselves papal honours. It was therefore necessary to treat these prelates with great consideration, and it was during their ascendancy—at the time when even Gregory the Great assigned a place of distinction to the *apocrisarius* of the metropolitans of Ravenna at the papal functions in Rome—that many churches and chapels were built in honour of St Apollinaris. There was one at the Vatican, another at the Lateran, a third—at which to-day's station is held—near the Baths of Severus, and another on the Via Appia.

Rome, whilst showing this special veneration for St Apollinaris, was careful to point out (and for this she had excellent reasons) that the saint had been a disciple of Peter, from whom he had received a mission to evangelize the Romagna; but there were certain patriarchs of Ravenna who tried to emancipate themselves entirely from papal jurisdiction, so much so that the Roman Missal does not fail to inculcate in its lessons on the Feast of St Apollinaris the necessity of humility and of avoiding that spirit of domineering arrogance which characterizes secular authority.

Under the high altar of the Basilica of St Apollinaris *in archipresbyteratu* repose the relics of the Armenian martyrs Eustacius, Mardarius, Eugenius, Orestes, and Eusentius, who were greatly renowned among the Greeks.

The Introit is derived from Daniel (iii 31); Azarias being cast into the furnace at Babylon, confesses that the evils which oppress the people are the just retribution of their misdeeds, since they refused to obey the commandments of God and therefore deserved to be abandoned by him. Yet, as the divine justice is ever tempered by compassion, the martyr implores God not to regard the sins of Israel, but rather to give glory to his name by pardoning those who have rightly merited chastisement, and by dealing with them according to the multitude of his mercies. The choice of this Introit by Gregory II is a vivid comment on the pitiable condition of Rome during the first half of the eighth century.

In the Collect we humbly confess that it was through the sin of intemperance and greed that human nature fell from its original dignity of grace, and as this malady can be cured only by its opposite remedy, we pray that our fast may serve both as an expiation and an antidote.

In the Lesson from Daniel (iii 25, 34-45) is read the lament of Azarias over the sad fate of his nation, who were without a leader, without a priesthood, and without a temple. But the martyr does not lose his confidence in God, for a contrite heart and a humble spirit will avail more than the sacrifice of bullocks in the sight of the Lord, who regards the sincerity of those who call upon him for help in their adversity, rather than the outward ceremonies of the law.

These words of Holy Scripture should be meditated upon carefully, especially by religious. It is not the habit which makes us saints and renders us pleasing to God; the inner dispositions must be in harmony with the outward appearance, which is too liable to become a mere formality. For this reason, St Bernard, in rebuking the arrogant bearing of some of his monks of Clairvaux towards those of Cluny, said to them : " We wear a cowl and are proud, despising those who wear a tippet, as though humility concealed under a tippet were not more worthy than pride under a cowl."

The Gradual is taken from Psalms xc and xxviii, and instructs us in the dispositions with which we should enter to-day into the church of the great martyr of Ravenna. We should never come before God empty-handed, but should bring him gifts and sacrifices, not indeed of brute beasts, but of ourselves and of our own will. The power of the Lord is over all : " He will discover the thick woods and in his temple all shall speak his glory." This acclamation of praise is now begun by the Church militant in the Liturgy, but it will continue throughout all eternity in the heavenly liturgy, for in the Apocalypse St John tells us that he heard the Blessed in Paradise ever singing *Amen, Alleluia.*

The Gospel (Luke vii 36-50) narrates the conversion of Mary of Magdala, whom widespread tradition, as early as the time of Tertullian, identifies with the sister of Martha and Lazarus. God does not heed the past sins of the penitent, and in the Magdalen he wishes to give us an example of the way in which he will receive a sinner who returns to him with true contrition. The fire of the Holy Ghost, says St Chrysostom, envelops the poor penitent, sanctifies her and raises her up, even above the virgins. *Vides hanc mulierem?* Jesus desires that all humanity should behold this woman and follow her example. Much is forgiven her because she loves much. We are not all able to fast, nor can we all be apostles, but everyone of us has a heart to consecrate to the love of God alone.

The Offertory is from Psalm cxxxvi, in which the soul mourns, being wearied with its exile, but refuses to join in the worldly pleasures of the children of Babylon.

The Secret bears the mark of great antiquity : " O Lord our God, who from these creatures which thou hast created for the support of our weakness, hast likewise commanded gifts to be set apart and dedicated to thy name : grant, we beseech thee, that they may procure for us aids in this present

life, and be to us also an eternal sacrament." Jesus instituted the divine Sacrament under the species of bread and
wine in order that we might understand that, as these
creatures are the daily food of man, so the holy Eucharist is
the heavenly food on which the soul maintains its supernatural life. Thus St Ambrose said :

> *Christusque nobis sit cibus,*
> *Potusque nobis sit fides;*
> *Laeti bibamus sobriam*
> *Ebrietatem spiritus.*

The Communion is taken from Psalm cxviii : " Be thou
mindful of thy word to thy servant, O Lord, in which thou
hast given me hope : this hath comforted me in my humiliation." What is this word of consolation and comfort? It is
Jesus, in whose name is contained all grace and hope and love.

The Post-Communion is ancient, and was chosen in the
Middle Ages as a prayer of private devotion, which the priest
used to recite immediately after having participated in the
sacred mysteries. In this way it came to form part of the
Ordinarium Missae in the present Roman Missal. " Grant,
O Lord, that what we have taken with our mouth, we may
receive with a clean mind, and that from a temporal gift it
may become for us an everlasting remedy."

We must not deceive ourselves : it is one thing to receive
the Blessed Sacrament, and quite another thing to receive
the *rem et virtutem sacramenti,* as St Thomas says. The
first may be received by sinners, or even by those no better
than brute beasts, as, alas ! has sometimes happened; but in
order to partake of the divine efficacy of the Body and Blood
of Christ, a fitting preparation is required, as well as a
fervent love and a lively desire, which will unite our souls
with the life and death of Christ.

In the Prayer of Benediction over the people, we beg that
God will give us grace to scorn the vain allurements of the
senses—such as that concerning which St Agatha prayed
before her martyrdom, *Gratias tibi ago, Domine, quia ex-
stinxisti a me amorem saeculi*—and that he will fill us with
the joy of the Holy Ghost, that interior unction which accompanies obedience to God's commands, which upheld Stephen
in his stoning and sweetened the sufferings of all those who
were martyred for the Faith.

Rome replied to the usurpations of the Patriarchs of
Ravenna in the Middle Ages with lessons on humility drawn
from the Gospels. She multiplied temples and altars in
honour of St Apollinaris, in order that those in the capital
of Emilia who were inclined towards schism might learn that
the true greatness of their episcopal see consisted in its

having been founded and sanctified by a disciple of Peter, by an emissary from Rome. This is the law ordained by God : the papal blessing consolidates and gives increase to the position of her sons, but if one of these rises up against the See of Peter, he will infallibly be crushed by the majesty of Rome.

FRIDAY AFTER PASSION SUNDAY

Collecta at SS John and Paul. Station at St Stephen on the Coelian.

We have already spoken of the Basilica of SS John and Paul, built by Bizante and Pammachius over the very house where the two martyrs suffered death for the Faith. That of St Stephen, which stands at a short distance from the former, and was called *in Coelio monte,* in order to distinguish it from the many churches dedicated to him in the city itself, was finished by Pope John I (523-26), who also adorned it with mosaics.

Towards the year 645, when Nomentum[1] had been devastated by the Lombards, and there seemed but little hope of that ancient city returning to normal conditions, Pope Theodore I (642-9) transferred the bodies of the two local martyrs, Primus and Felician,[2] from there to St Stephen on the Coelian Hill, where he embellished a small chapel in their honour, the mosaic apse of which still remains. These were the first martyrs who were brought from extra-mural cemeteries into the city—for the law forbidding burial within the city walls was generally observed under the Empire—and whose bodies were carried triumphantly into Christian Rome.

The Introit is taken from Psalm xxx, and again alludes to the mental anguish of Jesus as the hour of his Passion draws near. "Have mercy on me, O Lord, for I am troubled—laden with the sins of the whole world, I have become the object of implacable hatred on the part of my enemies and of them that persecute me, and a sign of the offended justice and holiness of God—deliver me from the hands of my enemies; O Lord, let me not be confounded, for I have called upon thee."

The prayer of Christ was answered; for the Eternal Father delivered him and the whole human race from the bonds of death in the day of the resurrection, when the fulness of the glorious life of Christ was transmitted also to his mystical

---

[1] In Sabinum. Renowned for its martyrs; also known as La Mentana.—Tr.

[2] These were brothers; martyred *circa* 286.—Tr.

body in such a manner as to make the spiritual resurrection of souls the beginning of their future glory. It was in this sense that the Apostle says that Christ *mortuus est propter delicta nostra, resurrexit propter justificationem nostram,* inasmuch as the glorious resurrection of the head is shared with the members through the grace which remits the sin and merits an eternal reward.

In the Collect we beseech God to infuse into our hearts the spirit of contrition, so that, expiating our sins in this life by means of penance, we may escape everlasting punishment. The preaching of penance formed an important part of the teaching of the Gospel. *Poenitentiam agite et credite evangelio.* This spirit of penance which prepares the way for grace and for the reconciliation of the soul to God is a special gift from him for which we must diligently ask in prayer. The Church sings in one of her finest Lenten hymns :

> *Dans tempus acceptabile,*
> *Et poenitens cor tribue;*
> *Convertat ut benignitas*
> *Quos longa sufferi pietas.*

The prophet Jeremias is a type of Christ persecuted by the Synagogue, therefore the Church places on the lips of the Redeemer in the divine offices of this last fortnight of Lent words of bitter sorrow and of desolation, yet of hope, which the prophet has expressed in his Lamentations. To-day the lesson is from chapter xvii 13-18, and represents the Just One confronted with his adversaries. Jeremias never places his hope in human aid, but utters the sublime words *diem hominis non desideravi,* words in which another great soul, Blessed Nicholas of Prussia, O.S.B., revealed himself in his last moments. The prophet knows that all things which are of the earth are scattered like dust before the wind, or become as words written in the sand. It is God alone who suffices for the soul. As long as God be not against us, what do the judgements of the world matter?

The Gradual, from Psalm xxxiv, describes the duplicity and malice of the enemies of the Just One : " My enemies spoke peaceably to me; and in anger they were troublesome to me. Thou hast seen, O Lord, be not thou silent; depart not from me." The Sanhedrim not being able to lay hands on Jesus openly for fear of the people, who were devoted to him, have recourse to the treachery of Judas, suborn false witnesses, accuse the Holiest of blasphemy and violate every legal form in the trial of the Saviour, condemning to death one who is wholly innocent, even their Creator, under the cloak of zeal for the honour of God and the rights of Cæsar.

The entire trial was one great crime against truth; God

saw, and was not silent. The more the Jews strove to besmirch the holiness of Jesus, the more clearly it shone forth, confessed even by those who took part in the deicide. Thus was the innocence of the Son of Man testified to, in turn, by Judas, Herod and Pilate, by the centurion, and by the very earth itself, which trembled to its foundations at the death of its Lord.

The Gospel (John xi 47-54) relates how the Sanhedrim assembled to devise the death of Jesus, Caiphas, turning arrogantly to the rest, taunts them with their ignorance : *Vos nescitis quidquam nec cogitatis;* but in prophesying the death of Christ and declaring it to be expedient, he speaks, not of himself, but as high priest, for God never fails to grant the graces necessary to our state. Whosoever is permitted to hold the office of superior, speaks in the name of God, even though he be as Caiphas. Jesus, then, must die for all mankind; Caiphas has spoken thus in prophecy, being moved thereto by the power of the Holy Ghost, quite otherwise than was intended by the crafty high priest himself. Christ is to die in order to bring together all the children of God dispersed throughout the world in one great family, which shall be neither Jew nor Greek nor Gentile, but only one holy Catholic Church, the *Ecclesia Sancta Dei.*

Stephen, the titular saint of to-day's station, receives this last wish of his divine Master, and boldly announces it to the Hellenist Synagogues of Jerusalem. The holy deacon himself falls a victim to the nationalist fury of the Jews, but the result of his last prayer will be the conversion of Paul, that Apostle who will proclaim the catholicity of the Christian faith far beyond the confines of Palestine.

Jesus therefore died, not for the Jews alone, but also for the Gentiles. Let us not therefore take too much into account geographical boundaries or mere nationality. God calls his own from the uttermost parts of the earth, and his grace makes us all brothers. Even those who to-day profess a different faith from our own may be converted and return to-morrow to the bosom of the Church. We should therefore lay aside our prejudices, and be careful not to despise anyone nor to despair of another's conversion, however unlikely it may appear. God holds the souls of all men in his hands, and we should welcome with open arms those whom he has brought back from a long way off, remembering how we, too, had once strayed far away, but are now converted to the Shepherd of our souls.

The Offertory comes from Psalm cxviii : " Blessed art thou, O Lord ; teach me thy justifications "—by means of the Gospel and the Sacraments which cause us to participate in this divine holiness. " Deliver me not up to the proud who calumniate me;" grant that, though I may be exposed to temptations which are sent to prove and purify my faith, I may never yield to them; "I will answer a word to those who upbraid me." I will not be silent before their accusations, but will convince them of falsehood and blasphemy, showing them by word and example with whom the Truth dwelleth.

This is the line of action taken by the Church when attacked by the hatred and calumnies of unbelievers, of Jews, and also of many heretics who, perverting the Gospel of Christ, preach another, which is not that of the "kingdom" entrusted by our Lord to his Apostles, more especially to Peter. It may be the Gospel of Marcion, of Arius, of Luther, of Henry VIII, of Marx, but it is not that Gospel which the Apostles received from Christ. To all these false teachers we put, with Tertullian, the simple question : *Qui estis vos?*

Our faith is one which has been safeguarded by an unbroken ecclesiastical tradition, and testified to by a line of infallible teachers, of whom Peter was the first. To Peter Christ committed the preaching of his Gospel, but you, who after two or fifteen or even nineteen centuries suddenly begin to preach a so-called Christian Gospel, who are you? Who has sent you? Who authorizes you, after so many years, to usurp the office bestowed on the Catholic Church—that of guarding and interpreting the holy Scriptures?

In the Secret we beseech God that his grace may render us worthy to fulfil the sacerdotal ministry at the altar, in order that we may perfect in eternity, through the beatific vision, that eucharistic union with God which was begun in the Liturgy here on earth. This sacerdotal ministry of which the Secret speaks is, in a manner, shared by the laity, for they too, the *regale sacerdotium,* as St Peter calls them, together with the priest and by his hands, offer to God the holy Sacrifice, and truly participate in it in Holy Communion.

The Communion is derived from Psalm xxvi : "Deliver me not over to the will of them that trouble me." Christ prays by the mouth of the Psalmist that he may not be delivered definitely into the power of his enemies, without hope of future triumph. Jesus speaks thus chiefly on our account, for whom his resurrection was an absolute necessity. "Unjust witnesses have risen up against me"—those suborned by the Sanhedrim—"and iniquity hath lied to itself"—that is, in confirmation of its own assertion, or rather, for its own protection, since all we who crucified Christ through sin did so in order that his precious blood might wash away our guilt.

In the Post-Communion we pray that the efficacy of the Sacrament in which we have participated may never fail us, on account of our sloth or our dissipation—and that it may drive away from us all that might be hurtful to the soul. We should continue to live in the spirit of thanksgiving after having received Holy Communion, so as to maintain this spiritual union of the soul with Jesus during our whole life. It is this which the Church desires when she teaches us to pray for the grace *ut in gratiarum semper actione maneamus*. To "persevere in the Eucharist" means to be transformed in it, to become a sacrifice for Jesus, even as he became a sacrifice for us.

The final Prayer over the people is the same as that of the Wednesday after the Third Sunday in Lent.

The question which arose in Jerusalem, immediately after the death of the divine Teacher, was that of the character of Christianity; whether, that is, it should represent merely a spiritual movement within the Synagogue, like those of the Essenes and of the Pharisees, or, whether it was to be a new religion surpassing the ancient national form of worship. St Peter decided the matter in the first place by the baptism of Cornelius; but it was Stephen who, more particularly among the Jews themselves, was foremost in carrying the question out of the immediate circle of the Apostles, and bringing it to the notice of the Hellenists, who, having been used to living amongst the Gentiles of the *Diaspora,* were less narrow in their views than their co-religionists.

Yet the Hellenists, too, shared many of the prejudices of the Sanhedrim, so they were scandalized by what appeared to them an intolerable innovation on the part of the disciple of the Galilean. Stephen, however, stood forth fearlessly before the council, and confirmed the doctrine of catholicity, declaring that he beheld the heavens opened, and the Son of Man standing on the right hand of God.[1]   Then, clothed in the purple of his blood shed for Christ, he fell asleep in the Lord to awaken in the splendour of eternal glory.

SATURDAY AFTER PASSION SUNDAY

Collecta at St Peter " quando Dominus Papa eleemosynam dat." Station at St John before the Latin Gate.

In the early Middle Ages, this Saturday preceding Holy Week in which the great ceremonies began, was aliturgical: *sabbatum vacat.*   This was in order that the people might be able to take some rest, whilst the Pope, too, in the Vatican *Consistorium,* or the Lateran *Triclinium,* having distributed the paschal alms to the poor, consigned the consecrated Host

---

[1] Acts vii 55.

to the titular priests.   This latter rite signified their close
connection with the Apostolic See; and during the following
week they could begin their Mass at whatever time they preferred, without having to wait every day for the acolyte to
bring the particle consecrated by the Pope for them to place
in their chalice.   It was sufficient that, after the ritual breaking of the Host, they should place in the chalice a particle of
that Host sent to them on this Saturday by the Pope.

To this ceremony, with its profound significance, was
joined the distribution of abundant alms—in imitation of the
Saviour who, on the occasion of the Pasch, was wont to
entrust Judas with the duty of giving alms to the poor.

In course of time both these ceremonies became obsolete,
and in their place a new station was instituted at the Church
of St John before the Latin Gate, which was first connected
by Ado in his Martyrology with the martyrdom suffered at
Rome by the Apostle under Diocletian.   The tradition which
relates that St John was miraculously preserved from death
when plunged into a caldron of boiling oil is very ancient,
as it is vouched for by Tertullian; but that this scene took
place before the Latin Gate precisely on the spot where the
Church of St John now stands, is a conjecture of Ado *sine
idoneis tabulis.*

However this may be, the important fact is the coming of
the Apostle John to Rome some ten years after the martyrdom of SS Peter and Paul.   As the Lateran basilica was
originally called the Basilica of the Saviour, and St John was
merely the name of a small chapel in the baptistery, built by
Pope Hilary (461-8), the stational Church of St John before
the Latin Gate is the most ancient and venerable monument
which records for the faithful the apostolate at Rome of the
disciple whom Jesus loved so well.

The Mass has no Proper except the Collects and the
Lessons, for in the early Middle Ages so great was the
respect for the Antiphonary of St Gregory, that no one
would have dared to insert in it any new musical compositions.   Hence the chants for to-day's Mass are all borrowed
from that of yesterday.

In the Collect we beseech God that the people who are
dedicated to him may increase in the affections of pious
devotion and may develop by good works that seed of holiness which was sown in their hearts at holy Baptism.   The
school in which they must learn this lesson of perfection is
the Church herself with her Sacraments and her Liturgy; so
that the Christian life may become one long chain of graces
connected one with another, each grace serving to prepare
and dispose us to receive another.

The Lesson from Jeremias (xviii 18-23) forms a sequel to that of yesterday, and predicts the terrible chastisements which will follow on the deicide. It is Jesus who, typified by the prophet of the Lamentations, calls them down on the Jews through his Father, but in so doing he does not act in contradiction to his own words, when from the cross he implores pardon for his executioners. During our present life every chastisement sent by God is for our correction, as he himself has spoken in the Apocalypse : *Ego quos amo, arguo et castigo.* As temporal happiness becomes to many an excuse for neglecting their spiritual welfare, so sorrow and adversity lead back to God many souls disillusioned by the emptiness of the promises held out by the world.

Further, in the case of the Jews, the theocracy of the Old Testament had a distinctly prophetic character which was to prepare the way for the New Testament, as the fulfilment of all the symbols and promises of the Old. Jesus Christ, having come into the world, and having established the new Covenant, it became necessary that the old Covenant should be abrogated.

The good of humanity required this; for, as long as the ancient Temple stood as a *palladium* of Jewish nationalism, the Apostles always found themselves opposed by Jewish prejudice, actively supported by a strong Christian party with pro-Jewish tendencies. These latter wished to combine the Law with the Gospel, circumcision with baptism, the religious rites of the temple with the sacrifice of Calvary, and it was against their crafty machinations that St Paul was obliged, more than once, to warn the faithful. The whole question is fully discussed in his Epistles to the Galatians and the Romans.

The Gospel (John xii 10-36) describes in anticipation of to-morrow the entrance of Christ into Jerusalem. Our Lord desires that his Messianic mission should be openly and clearly manifested before the Sanhedrim, so, for this purpose, he allows his triumphal entry to take place in the identical circumstances described by the prophets. The hosannas of the multitude and of the children were caused by the miracle of the resurrection of Lazarus, which had just been witnessed at Bethania, so the Jews could no longer profess themselves to be in perplexity and doubt, because Jesus did not openly declare his divine nature.

The light now shines forth in all its fulness. In complete harmony with our Lord's repeated declarations appear his marvellous works, and the fulfilment in him of all the Messianic prophecies. Amongst these there is one, soon to be realized, which concerns the Gentiles, who are to share the privileges and blessings of Abraham; for the two Gentiles who come to Philip, desiring to see Jesus, are the first-fruits of the Greek and Roman world which the divine Saviour is about to draw unto himself.

There remains, it is true, the scandal of the cross, which confounds the Jews and arouses the contempt of the Gentiles; but, in the counsel of God, it is the necessary condition of redemption, not only for Jesus, but also for ourselves. It is not enough that he should bear the cross for us; if we wish to be saved, we must take our burden on our own shoulders, and bear it for love of him. As the grain of wheat, unless it first fall into the ground and die, cannot bring forth fruit, so the soul, unless it die with Jesus, cannot share in his divine life.

In the Secret we beseech the divine mercy to preserve the faithful, who are to be partakers in so great a mystery, from all sin and danger—sin which harms the soul, and danger which threatens the body. The graces which God gives us are not indeed without due order and connection; they all form part of one plan of predestination, and it is for this reason that God does not dispense his favours at haphazard, nor only when we feel moved to ask him for them.

From the very first moment of our being, he has been carrying out a marvellous plan, which his love alone has inspired. All will be fulfilled in its own time with a splendour and a magnificence worthy of God and of our high destiny as the sons of God. He treats us, as he himself tells us in the holy Scriptures, with great regard; but in the plan of our predestination, there is nothing superfluous, nothing disordered, nothing wasted. A marvellous harmony, a perfect rhythm binds together all the graces which God has granted to us.

In the Post-Communion we pray that, as God has already filled us with the abundance of the divine gift—that is to say, not with any particular grace, but with the very fulness of grace, with Jesus himself who is the author of all grace, now become *donum nostrum*—he would also grant us to participate therein for ever in heaven. The Blessed Sacrament is indeed the token of future glory, and the union which takes place in Holy Communion between the soul and God will be perfected in the Beatific Vision.

In the last Blessing before the dismissal of the people we ask God that his strong right hand may defend his suppliant people, purify them from sin, and duly instruct them in spiritual things, so that, by present consolation, they may arrive at future rewards. The Church asks in this prayer for four things—first of all for the special help of God that will enable the soul to make the acts of contrition and love which must precede its reconciliation and forgiveness; then comes the purification from sin by the infusion of sanctifying grace. All this forms part of that which ascetics call the purificative way.

Next follows the illuminative way, which consists in the training of the soul by the light of the Holy Ghost, especially in prayer and meditation. Lastly comes the unitive way, when the soul, though still a pilgrim in this land of exile, anticipates and experiences to some extent a foretaste of complete union with God. Christ espouses her for ever to himself in such a manner that the nuptials contracted in this life preserve by their grace the fidelity of the soul to her Crucified Spouse, who from the cross calls her to the wedding feast of eternity in his Father's house.

It is a striking confession which the Pharisees make in to-day's Gospel: "We prevail nothing! The whole world is gone after him." This truth, proved through the centuries, should strengthen us especially in moments of discouragement, when we see the evil forces of this world obtain a momentary triumph over the Church of God. He has spoken, and his word shall never be made void; Christ conquers, reigns, and triumphs, though in a few days' time he will be lifted up on the cross, whence he will draw all men unto himself.

PALM SUNDAY

Station at the Basilica of the Saviour in the Lateran.
(Station at St Peter.) Collecta at Sta Maria " in Turri."

The great ceremonies of the "paschal" week—as this solemn period of seven days on which we are now entering was originally called—took place, as a rule, during the Middle Ages, in the pontifical residence in the classical palace of the Lateran. For this reason the procession of the palms or olive branches and the stational Mass are celebrated to-day in the venerable Basilica of the Saviour; that lasting monument of the victories of the Roman Pontiffs over idolatry, heresy, and the gates of hell, which for more than nineteen centuries have conspired against the Church, but which have ever been repulsed and defeated. *Non praevalebunt adversus eam;* Christ has said, and before one word of his lips shall be made void, both heaven and earth shall pass away.

In the late Middle Ages, to-day's station was sometimes, at the desire of the Pope, celebrated at the Vatican, and the blessing of the palms then took place in the Church of Sta Maria "in Turri," which stood in the *atrium* of the basilica.

We find preserved, in the blessing of the palms, the

ancient type of the liturgical synaxes, of those assemblies, that is, for the recitation of the Divine Office, the instruction of the faithful, and so on, which were not followed by the celebration of Mass. This type of synaxis was taken from the Jewish rite used in the Synagogues of the Diaspora and formed part of the Christian ritual from the time of the Apostles.

The procession of the olive branches is derived from the ceremony witnessed by the pilgrim Etheria in Jerusalem at the end of the fourth century. In the West it was customary from the first to hold olive twigs in the hand during the reading of the Gospel; in Gaul a special blessing was first given, not indeed to the branches, but to the people who rendered this act of reverence to the Word of God. Later, there was added the procession before the Mass, which gave a greater show and importance to the olive twigs, and these finally, in their turn, received the sacerdotal blessing.

THE BLESSING OF THE PALMS

Collecta at St Silvester in the Lateran.

According to the *Ordines Romani* of the fourteenth century the palms were first blessed by the Cardinal of St Lawrence, and were then carried by the clergy into the patriarchal basilica to the oratory of St Silvester, where the acolytes of the Vatican Basilica proceeded to distribute them to the people. The Pope himself performed the distribution among the clergy in the *Triclinium* of Leo IV, whence the stational procession moved towards the Basilica of the Saviour.

The Pope, having reached the porch, seated himself on a throne, and whilst the doors of the sacred building still remained closed, the *primicerius* of the cantors and the prior of the basilica at the head of their assistants intoned the hymn *Gloria, laus,* etc., which is still retained in the Missal. Then, at last, the doors were opened, and the procession made its triumphal entrance into the church and the great drama of the redemption of mankind began with the celebration of Mass. The Pope put on sacred vestments in the *secretarium,* but as a sign of mourning, in keeping with the sadness which pervades the whole Liturgy of this week, the *basilicari* did not on this day extend over his head the traditional *mappula* or *baldachino,* which was one of the marks of veneration and respect among the ancient peoples.

The *collecta* for the blessing of the palms begins with the Introit : " Hosanna to the Son of David : blessed is he that cometh in the name of the Lord. O King of Israel : Hosanna in the highest." This is the Messianic salutation which

Christ, acclaimed to-day by the Gentiles, the children, the multitude, and the simple folk, awaited in vain from the Synagogue. Jesus, therefore, casts off the obstinate Sanhedrim, and turns instead to the nations of the Gentiles, who hail him as their God and their redeemer. But the mercy of God is infinite, so Israel itself may hope for salvation if it too will go forth to meet the Messias, exclaiming with the Psalmist and the children : " Blessed is he that cometh in the name of the Lord."

We should feel a great devotion for this act of faith in the Messias, so much desired by our Lord. The Church repeats it at the most solemn moment of the Mass, when Jesus Christ, at the call of his minister, is about to descend as Victim upon our altars.

Then follows the Collect of benediction upon the assembled people : " O God, whom to love above all is righteousness, multiply in us the gifts of thy ineffable grace ; and since thou hast given us in the death of thy Son to hope for those things which we believe, grant us by the resurrection of the same to attain the end to which we aspire." The form of the prayer is very fine, and the meaning clear and definite. The death of Jesus merits for us eternal life, but we attain to it through his resurrection, because the glorified Christ transfuses into his body—the Church—and its mystical members that holiness and that blessedness which fills the Head in the day of his triumph over sin and death.

The lesson from Exodus (xv 27 ; xvi 1-7), with the narrative of the revolt of the Israelites against Moses, does not appear to be in keeping with to-day's mystery. It was introduced by the Gallican liturgists of the Middle Ages, on account of the reference to the fountains of water and the seventy palm-trees, under the shade of which the chosen people rested. The Israelites, delivered in such a marvellous manner from slavery, murmur against Jehovah and sigh after the flesh-pots of Egypt. In this they were the forerunners of those who acted in like manner against the true Moses, their true deliverer from the slavery of hell, who was cursed and denied by them at the very moment that he was about to lay down his life for their redemption.

The two alternative Graduals which follow have no bearing whatever on the ceremony of the blessing of the palms, and have been inserted here merely to fill in the gaps and to separate the two scriptural lessons. It is easy to see that the whole arrangement of to-day's function, in spite of its apparent antiquity, is somewhat artificial ; consisting, as it does, of various parts differing greatly both in inspiration and in origin, which have been joined together anyhow, without any real unity of design.

The first Gradual is taken from St John (xi 47-53), and describes the meeting in the house of Caiphas at which, after the Pharisees had observed that Jesus was drawing the multitude after him, and was thereby exposing the Sanhedrim to the danger that the Romans—ever jealous for their rights—would sooner or later crush by force such insurrectionary movements for national independence, Caiphas declared that it was expedient for one man—that is, Jesus— to die for the people, rather than that the whole nation should perish. The Evangelist insists on the fact that the words of the crafty pontiff had a far higher meaning than he was aware of, and that by reason of his office they were placed in his mouth by the Holy Ghost.

The second Gradual is used only as an alternative responsory, and is borrowed from the first Nocturn of Maundy Thursday. It is from the Gospel of St Matthew (xxvi 39-41), and tells us of the appeal of Jesus to his Father in his agony on Mount Olivet, of his submission to his Father's will and of his admonition to the sleeping disciples to seek strength in prayer against the temptations and trials which were drawing near.

It is not enough that the habitual dispositions of the will be upright; human nature is weak, and without the help of grace it will succumb. We must therefore pray without ceasing and never grow weary of asking for this succour of which we stand so much in need. The saints, and especially St Alphonsus, thus sum up the Catholic teaching concerning the necessity of prayer: " He who prays will be saved, and he who does not pray will be lost."

To-day's Gospel from St Matthew (xxi 1-9), with the account of the solemn entry of Jesus into the holy City, is known to have been used in the Liturgy at Jerusalem from the second half of the fourth century. In accordance with the prophecy of Zacharias, the Redeemer enters into Sion sitting upon an ass, to show the meekness and gentleness of this his first Messianic appearance. He does not wish to cause alarm by the rays of his glory, but desires to draw all men to his heart by the attraction of his presence. The ass and her colt—which, according to the Gospel, were tied outside the walls of a village near the Mount of Olives, whence they were loosed by the Apostles and brought to Jesus—represent the people of the Gentiles, excluded from the heirship of Abraham, deprived of the heritage of Israel, and held fast by the fetters of idolatry. The task of setting them free from their errors and of bringing them back to the true God was the great mission entrusted to the Apostles.

The following Collect, according to the usage of the Roman Liturgy in the case of prayers of special importance, serves as a prelude to the consecratory anaphora of the olive branches. It therefore holds the same place as the Secret before the Preface of the Mass :

Prayer: " Increase the faith of those that hope in thee, O God, and mercifully hear the prayers of thy suppliants : let thy multiplied mercy descend upon us; may these branches of palm or olive be blessed; and, as in a figure of thy Church thou didst multiply Noe going forth out of the ark, and Moses going out of Egypt with the children of Israel; so may we go forth to meet Christ with good works, bearing palms and branches of olive; and through him may we enter into eternal joy. Who liveth and reigneth with thee, world without end. R̰. Amen." This prayer, so beautiful in form, and of such profound devotion, clearly explains the symbolism of the procession which is about to take place, and gives the reason why the lesson from Exodus about the seventy palm-trees was chosen for to-day. The palm is awarded to the victor, and he who comes in safety out of Egypt well deserves the triumph of a conqueror.

Priest: ℣. " The Lord be with you."
R̰. " And with thy spirit."
Priest: ℣. " Lift up your hearts."
R̰. " We have lifted them up to the Lord."
Priest: ℣. " Let us give thanks to the Lord our God."
R̰. " It is meet and just."

The anaphora follows, which, in accordance with its primitive significance, is to-day a veritable eucharistic hymn, a song of praise and thanksgiving to God for his transcendent holiness and the exceeding tenderness of his mercy towards men.

Priest: " It is truly meet and just, right and available to salvation, that we always and everywhere give thanks to thee, O holy Lord, Father almighty, eternal God; who dost glory in the assembly of thy saints. For thy creatures serve thee; because they acknowledge thee as their only creator and God : and thy whole creation praiseth thee, and thy saints bless thee. For with free voice they confess that great name of thy only-begotten Son, before the kings and powers of this world. Around whom the angels and arch-angels, the thrones and dominions stand; and with all the army of heaven, sing a hymn to thy glory, saying without ceasing : Holy, holy, holy, Lord God of Sabaoth. The heavens and earth are full of thy glory. Hosanna in the highest. Blessed is he that cometh in the name of the Lord. Hosanna in the highest."

Then follows a number of collects of ancient origin and inspired conception, in which the Church seems to wish to pour out all her love for her Redeemer about to sacrifice himself for her. These various prayers originally formed a series of alternative collects; nowadays, however, the ceremony is much longer, for all these different forms of blessing, the Preface, the collects, etc., which were formerly substituted for, or rather excluded, each other, now constitute in our present Missal an integral part of the ceremony of the blessing of the palms. The result has been a function which doubtless is devout, but is somewhat lacking in proportion and harmony, a sure sign that it did not originally form part of the Roman Liturgy.

The following Collect refers exclusively to the branches of olive, without any mention of palms, for these had become very scarce in Europe in the Middle Ages.

Prayer: " We beseech thee, O holy Lord, almighty Father, eternal God, that thou wouldst vouchsafe to bless and sanctify this creature of the olive-tree, which thou hast caused to spring from the substance of the wood, and which the dove, returning to the ark, brought in its mouth; that all those who receive of it may be protected in soul and body : and may it become, O Lord, a saving remedy, the sacred sign of thy grace. Through Christ our Lord. R̂. Amen."

God is pleased to humble the pride of Satan by hindering him from harming Christians by virtue of the sacramentals, which consist mostly of small objects of devotion blessed by a priest and reverently kept by the people. The palms belong to this kind of sacramental.

Prayer: " O God, who dost gather what is dispersed, and preserve what is gathered together; who didst bless the people who went forth to meet Jesus, bearing branches of palms; bless likewise these branches of palm and olive, which thy servants receive faithfully in honour of thy name; that into whatever place they may be brought, those who dwell in that place may obtain thy blessing, and, all adversities being removed, thy right hand may protect those who have been redeemed by our Lord Jesus Christ, thy Son. Who liveth and reigneth with thee," etc.

In the following prayer all the symbolism of to-day's ceremony is explained. As the multitude went forth with palms to meet the conqueror of death and hell, so to-day God anticipates for us the gift of the palm, in order to inspire us to fight more strenuously so that we may gain for all eternity that other palm of victory which will never fade nor wither.

Prayer: " O God, who by a wonderful order and disposition hast been pleased to manifest the dispensation of our salvation even from things insensible; grant, we beseech thee, that the devout hearts of thy faithful may profitably understand what is mystically signified by the fact that on this day the multitude, taught by a heavenly illumination, went forth to meet their Redeemer, and strewed branches of palm and olive at his feet. The branches of palms, therefore, signify his triumphs over the prince of death; and the branches of olive proclaim, in a manner, the coming of a spiritual unction. For that blessed company of men understood that these things were then prefigured; that our Redeemer, compassionating human miseries, was about to fight with the prince of death for the life of the whole world, and, by dying, to triumph. For which cause they dutifully ministered such things as signified in him the triumphs of victory and the richness of mercy. And we also, with full faith, retaining this as done and signified, humbly beseech thee, O holy Lord, Father almighty, eternal God, through the same Jesus Christ our Lord, that in him and through him we, whose members thou wert pleased to make us, may become victorious over the empire of death, and may deserve to be partakers of his glorious resurrection. Who liveth and reigneth with thee," etc.

There is no mention in the following collect of palms, but of olives, to which are added other trees as well; for, in northern countries, where this rite was specially developed, neither the palm nor the olive can grow on account of the cold.

Prayer: "O God, who didst command the dove to proclaim peace to the earth by an olive branch; grant, we beseech thee, that these branches of olive and other trees may be sanctified with thy heavenly blessing, and so may profit all thy people unto salvation. Through Christ our Lord. Amen."

The external rite is indeed a vain thing if the adoration of the heart does not accompany the words of the lips.

Prayer: "Bless, we beseech thee, O Lord, these branches of palm or olive, and grant that what thy people this day bodily perform for thy honour, they may perfect spiritually with the greatest devotion, by gaining a victory over the enemy, and ardently loving every work of mercy. Through Christ our Lord."

Here the priest sprinkles the palms three times with holy water and offers incense.

Priest: ℣. "The Lord be with you."

℟. "And with thy spirit."

Prayer: "O God, who didst send thy Son, Jesus Christ our Lord, into this world for our salvation, that he might humble himself for us and call us back to thee; before whom also, when he entered into Jerusalem, that he might fulfil the Scripture, a multitude of believers, with most faithful devotion, strewed their garments in the way, with branches of palms; grant, we beseech thee, that we may prepare for him the way of faith, from which the stone of offence and rock of scandal being removed, our works may flourish before thee with branches of justice, that so we may deserve to follow his footsteps. Who liveth and reigneth with thee," etc.

During the distribution of the palms or olive branches, the cantors sing the following antiphons taken from the Gospel which has just been read:

"The Hebrew children bearing branches of olive went forth to meet the Lord, crying out and saying, Hosanna in the highest."

The children are given the place of honour to-day because God loves innocent and simple souls, and it is to them that he reveals his mysteries.

"The Hebrew children spread their garments in the way and cried out, saying, Hosanna to the son of David; blessed is he that cometh in the name of the Lord."

After having distributed the consecrated palms, the following Collect is recited before forming the procession.

Prayer: "O almighty and everlasting God, who didst ordain that our Lord Jesus Christ should sit upon an ass's colt, and didst teach the multitude to spread their garments or branches of trees in the way and sing Hosanna to his praise; grant, we beseech thee, that we may imitate their innocence, and deserve to obtain their merit. Through the same Christ our Lord. ℞. Amen."

Deacon: ℣. "Let us go forth in peace."
℞. "In the name of Christ. Amen."

The procession then sets forth, and although on this occasion it has a special significance, and is intended to commemorate the triumphant entry of Jesus into Jerusalem, it is in reality a survival of the ancient stational Sunday procession, which in the Middle Ages, and especially in Benedictine abbeys, regularly preceded the Mass. During the procession the cantors sing the following antiphons:

Ant. (Matt. xxi): "When the Lord drew nigh to Jerusalem, he sent two of his disciples, saying: Go ye into the village that is over against you; and you will find the colt of an ass tied, upon which no man hath sat; loose it, and bring it to me. If any man ask you any questions, say: The Lord needeth it. They untied, and brought it to Jesus, and laid their garments upon it; and he seated himself on it. Others spread their garments in the way; others cut branches from the trees; and those who followed cried out, Hosanna, blessed is he that cometh in the name of the Lord; and blessed be the reign of our father David: Hosanna in the highest: O Son of David, have mercy on us."

Ant. (John xii) : " When the people heard that Jesus was coming to Jerusalem, they took palm branches, and went out to meet him; and the children cried out, saying : This is he who hath come for the salvation of the people. He is our salvation, and the redemption of Israel. How great is he whom the thrones and dominions go out to meet ! Fear not, O daughter of Sion : behold thy King cometh to thee, sitting on an ass's colt, as it is written : Hail, O King, the creator of the world, who art come to redeem us."

Ant.: " Six days before the solemnity of the Passover, when the Lord was coming into the city of Jerusalem, the children met him, and carried palm branches in their hands, and they cried out with a loud voice, saying : Hosanna in the highest, blessed art thou who art come in the multitude of thy mercy : Hosanna in the highest."

Ant.: " The multitude goeth out to meet the Redeemer with flowers and palms, and payeth the homage due to a triumphant conqueror : the Gentiles proclaim the Son of God : and their voices thunder through the skies in the praise of Christ : Hosanna in the highest."

Ant.: " Let the faithful join with the angels and children, singing to the conqueror of death : Hosanna in the highest."

Ant.: " A great multitude that was met together at the festival cried out to the Lord : Blessed is he that cometh in the name of the Lord : Hosanna in the highest."

Then follows the hymn *Gloria, laus et honor,* together with the ceremony of the cross-bearer knocking on the door of the church for it to be opened to the procession. Rome adopted this rite only at a much later time. The two choirs who answer one another from the interior and exterior of the church represent the divine praises which are for ever sung alternately by the Church triumphant and the Church militant.

THE MASS

Station at St John Lateran.

The Mass begins upon the return of the procession, but its character is quite different from that of the blessing of palms, being more closely connected with the liturgy of the preceding days. For, while the prayers and antiphons of the former ceremony hail the Redeemer as victor over death and hell, the stational Mass, entirely Roman in composition, dwells chiefly upon his humiliation, his sufferings and his sorrows, as the Victim of expiation for the sins of the world.

The sacred liturgy of these last days of Lent does not separate the remembrance of the Saviour's Passion from that of his triumphant Resurrection, and this is the reason why the name *hebdomada paschalis* was formerly given to this week, and why mention is so frequently made of the Resurrection in the Mass and in the Divine Office both to-day and on Good Friday. Indeed, if the *Pascha nostrum immolatus Christus* begins on the evening of Maundy Thursday and continues throughout Good Friday, it finds its true fulfilment on the morning of the Resurrection, when he who was *mortuus propter delicta nostra, resurrexit propter justificationem nostram*. In the eyes of the early Christians the *Paschale Sacramentum* included this triple mystery, for which reason, even on Good Friday before the cross itself, they preannounced the glory of the risen Saviour. *Crucem tuam adoramus . . . et sanctam resurrectionem tuam laudamus et glorificamus.*

The Introit comes from Psalm xxi, that psalm which was on our Lord's lips as he hung upon the cross, and expresses so truly his sufferings and humiliations, the anguish of his heart and his hope of a very near and joyful Resurrection. " O Lord, remove not thy help to a distance from me; look towards my defence : deliver me from the lion's mouth, and my humility from the horns of the unicorns."

The beautiful phraseology of the Collect shows that it belongs to the golden period of Roman liturgy. "Almighty and everlasting God, who didst cause our Saviour to take upon him our flesh, and to suffer death upon the cross, that all mankind should imitate the example of his humility; mercifully grant that we may deserve both to keep in mind the lessons of his patience, and also to be made partakers of his resurrection."

These words explain the full meaning of the sacred rites which will be carried out during the coming week. Jesus Christ crucified is, at it were, a book in which the soul may read all that God desires it to do in order to be perfect.

They signify that we must realize in our own life those lessons of patient suffering and of expiation which Jesus teaches us from the cross. Lastly, we must keep before our mind the hope of the Resurrection which the Church always links together with the agony of Golgotha.

The Lesson is from the Epistle of St Paul to the Philippians (ii 5-11), in which he reminds us how Christ, laying aside for love of us the glory of his consubstantiality with the Father, took upon him the form of a servant and was obedient unto death, even the most cruel and ignominious death upon the cross. The expiation being thus complete, it is followed at once by his triumph and the inauguration of the Messianic kingdom. God sends forth his divine fire to bring warmth to the lifeless limbs of Jesus, which had been offered up to him on the cross. He breathes into them his own life, and to the name of the Saviour written up by Pilate in mockery over his sacred head, he gives such glory and power that it has become the sign of all those pre-destined to reign for ever with him in heaven.

The Gradual is derived from Psalm lxxii, and foretells the triumph of Easter day: "Thou hast held me by my right hand; and by thy will thou hast conducted me; and with glory thou hast taken me up."

The soul of Jesus burned with holy zeal during his Passion as he beheld the ruin of so many souls. For love of man he fearlessly faced the enemies of humanity, the devils and their allies, the impious and the wicked, and was nearly overcome by their malice, for by the agony of the cross his blessed soul was separated from his body, which endured the humilia-tion of the grave. But in all this the omnipotent hand of God ever upheld his only-begotten Son, and led him on the way to eternal life, crowning him finally with the triumphal glory of his Resurrection and Ascension into heaven.

The Tract or *Psalmus in directum* is taken from Psalm xxi, in which are described first the anguish of Christ and his feelings of humility and desolation, and of his filial confidence in God, then the triumph of the Messianic redemption, and lastly the coming of a new generation, which is the Church, to whom the Gospel message shall be delivered.

The Gospel lesson from St Matthew (xxvi-xxvii) contains the whole narrative of the Passion of our Lord, from the Last Supper with his disciples to the placing of the seals on the sepulchre. The reading of it on this day is a very ancient Roman tradition, being attested by the *Ordines* of the ninth century.

The remembrance of the sufferings endured for our sakes by Jesus Christ should be constantly revived in our hearts, that it may awaken in them those feelings of love and gratitude of which St Paul speaks: "Christ has loved me, and has given himself for me. I live, but it is no more I who live, it is Christ who liveth in me. I live in his faith."

The Crucifixion should teach us three things above all others. Firstly, how great is the love which the Blessed Trinity has borne towards us, in having sacrificed for us Jesus, the only-begotten Son of God; secondly, how fearful a thing is sin, since it could not be atoned for except by the most bitter death of the Saviour; and thirdly, how high is the value of our own soul, which could only be bought with the blood of Jesus. St Paul ends his meditation on the Passion of Christ in these words: *Empti enim estis pretio magno; glorificate et portate Deum in corpore vestro.*

The Offertory comes from Psalm lxviii, which also refers to the Passion of our Lord: " My heart hath expected reproach and misery; and I looked for one that would grieve together with me, and there was none : I sought for one to comfort me, and I found none; and they gave me gall for my food, and in my thirst they gave me vinegar to drink."

Jesus spoke in the same accents of sorrow to St Gertrude and to St Margaret Mary Alacoque, expressing his great longing that souls especially dedicated to him—priests and religious—should enter into these feelings of his Sacred Heart and should make reparation and atonement with him and should thus console him by their love.

Both the Secret and the Post-Communion are borrowed from the Sunday within the Octave of Christmas, and are of a general character.

The antiphon for the Communion is from St Matthew (xxvi 42) : " Father, if this chalice may not pass away, but I must drink it, thy will be done." When the faithful drew near, during the singing of these words, to drink the blood of Christ from the chalice held by the deacon, they understood clearly that by receiving Communion they became partakers in his Passion. For in the Mass, not only does Jesus Christ renew in a wonderful manner his sacrifice, but we, too, especially by virtue of Holy Communion, become united to him as members to the head, in order to abase ourselves, to immolate ourselves, to offer up ourselves together with him and to die in his death, so as to live in his life.

This chalice of the Passion cannot pass away from us : we too must drink it, if we would carry out in our own lives the will of God.

MONDAY IN HOLY WEEK

*Collecta at St Balbina. Station at the Title " de fasciola ";
now at St Praxedes.*

The titular Church of Balbina on that side of the lesser Aventine which rises above the spacious ruins of the Baths of Caracalla is already known to us. A little way off stands the basilica *de fasciola,* which a very old tradition connects with St Peter, at the time when he sought, by leaving Rome, to escape from persecution. Near the first milestone on the Via Appia, the Apostle stopped to replace the bandage (*fasciola*) which covered the wound in his leg caused by the fetters that he had worn in prison. At that moment, Christ himself appeared to him as he was going towards Rome. *Domine, quo vadis?* St Peter inquired of his divine Master. *Eo Romam iterum crucifigi,* answered our Lord. The vision passed, and Peter understood from these words that it was in the person of his first Vicar that Christ was to be put to death in Rome, so, obedient to the implied command, he returned in all haste to the city.

We do not know, given the documents we now possess, what may have been the foundation for this pleasing legend, but it is certainly of very great antiquity, and it gathers support from the very name, *de fasciola,* given to the church as far back as the beginning of the fourth century.

Under the altar rest the bodies of the martyrs Nereus, Achilleus and Domitilla, which were first transferred thither from the neighbouring cemetery of Domitilla on the Via Ardeatina, when it fell into disuse and neglect after the time of Paul I (757-67). Still later, the whole region of the Via Appia, being then deserted on account of the malaria, the church of the *fasciola* also fell into ruin, hence the bodies of its martyrs were conveyed to the diaconal Church of St Adrian in the Forum.

When towards the end of the sixteenth century Cardinal Baronius became titular Cardinal of the basilica of the *fasciola,* he caused the mosaics of the triumphal arch erected in the time of Leo III (795-816) to be restored, and he again brought back from St Adrian to his own titular church the bodies of SS Nereus, Achilleus and Domitilla, raising above their tomb an altar of " cosmato " work which had stood originally in the Basilica of St Paul on the Via Ostiensis.

Our present Missal assigns to-day's station to the Church of St Praxedes, an arrangement which dates from the end of the Middle Ages, when the title *de fasciola* was completely abandoned.

The *titulus Praxedis,* on the Esquiline, appears for the first time in an inscription of the year 491, recording one of its priests, which was discovered in the cemetery of Hippolytus, on the Via Tiburtina. Paschal I (817-24), who was titular priest of this church, rebuilt it from the foundations, moving it, however, a little from its original site, and rendered it more venerable by bringing thither a great number of bodies of martyrs who had been buried in the now abandoned extramural cemeteries.

Besides the mosaics of the apse, those of the oratory of San Zeno are very important, where down to 1699 this martyred priest rested by the side of his brother Valentinus. An ancient representation of the Blessed Virgin is venerated here, as also a column of reddish jasper brought to Rome from Jerusalem in 1223, which tradition affirms to be the one to which our divine Redeemer was bound during his flagellation.

Under the high altar lies the body of St Praxedes, to whom

the basilica is dedicated, and in a crypt under the sanctuary are all the numerous bodies of martyrs removed by Paschal I from the cemeteries outside Rome; so that this basilica, by reason of its antiquity, its artistic monuments, and the sacred relics which it contains, may well be considered as one of the most famous sanctuaries of Christian Rome.

The Introit is taken from Psalm xxxiv, which also in the Greek Liturgy is connected with the Passion of Christ: "Judge thou, O Lord, them that wrong me; overthrow them that fight against me: take hold of arms and shield, and rise up to help me, O Lord, the strength of my salvation. Bring out the sword, and shut up the way against them that persecute me: say to my soul, I am thy salvation."

Christ, overwhelmed by the multitude and by the violence of his adversaries—those sinners whose guilt he, the immaculate Lamb of God, had in his compassion taken upon himself—not only calls upon his Father, protesting his own innocence, but also implores him to curb the bold attacks of Satan against the human race, and more especially against his mystical body, the Church. The Father hears the prayer of his Son, and comes to his assistance by crushing the head of the serpent beneath the weight of the cross and raising him up from death to a new life impassible and glorious.

The Collect is full of the sadness suggested by this holy season: "Grant, we beseech thee, almighty God, that we who fail through our infirmity in so many difficulties, may be relieved by the Passion of thy Son interceding for us." As Jesus offered himself voluntarily for us to his Father upon the cross, so in heaven he renews this sacrifice on our behalf each time that we desire it, and invoke to that end the merits of his Passion.

The Lesson is derived from Isaias (l 5-10), in which the prophet represents Christ as offering himself to his Father in confutation of those who were persecuting him, and, by his exact and detailed description of the sufferings of our Lord so many centuries before they actually occurred, Isaias has well deserved the title of " Proto-evangelist " which has been attributed to him. Christ, says the prophet, has delivered his body to the scourgers, his cheeks to those that smote them, and his face to those that spat upon him. But the Just One, assailed by the calumny of his enemies, has naught with which to reproach himself; so, bereft of all other help, he calls upon him who is the strength of the weak and the desolate, and who, when invoked by them in the hour of their need, causes all oppressors to tremble—namely, God.

If we may be allowed in a work such as this, which treats

of sacred subjects, to refer to a writer of romance, we would beg those among our readers who are familiar with the masterpiece of Manzoni to recall the impression produced on the mind of "Innominato" when his helpless victim on the night of her capture called on the holy name of God.

Isaias ends with these solemn words : "He that hath walked in darkness and hath no light, let him hope in the name of the Lord and lean upon his God." To lean upon God is to trust in his love; the whole spiritual life consists in this, and blessed is he who, understanding it, abandons himself without reserve entirely to God.

The Gradual comes from the same psalm as the Introit, and calls upon God to come to the help of his Christ. It is not to be thought, because God did not deliver Jesus from the death of the cross, that therefore his many prayers were unanswered. On the contrary, they showed, as those in the Garden of Olives, a natural shrinking from suffering, and thus proved the reality of his human nature. Moreover, these same entreaties were expressly subordinated to the will of his Father, who had made the sacrifice of his only-begotten Son the condition of the redemption of mankind. Moreover, these prayers concerned also the mystical body of the Saviour —that is, the faithful, whom Jesus desired above all things to rescue from the jaws of hell.

The prayer of the Redeemer was favourably received by his Father by reason of the dignity of the suppliant, as the Apostle so well explains. His desires were fully granted, for the wisdom of God caused the calumnies and persecutions of the Synagogue to redound to the greater glory of Christ in the day of his final victory and triumph.

There are now only six more days before the "Pasch"; therefore the Church appoints for the Gospel lesson of to-day the account from St John (xii 1-9) of the supper in the house of Lazarus, when Jesus came to Bethania six days before Easter. We should note that the Jews of Jerusalem celebrated this feast on the fifteenth of Nisan—that is, on the day following the death of our Lord, who, by partaking of the paschal supper on the evening of Thursday, the thirteenth of Nisan, anticipated by twenty-four hours the official ceremony of eating the lamb. It is probable that this anticipation, influenced in this case by the nearness of his death, was customary among the Galileans in order to avoid the dangerous crush of people in the Temple at the time when the paschal lamb was killed. It is well known that the men of Galilee used to go up fully armed to the paschal feast at Jerusalem, so for this reason the civil authorities did all they could to prevent occasions for quarrelling between Galileans and Jews.

During the supper, Mary (Magdalen) repeated the act of reverence which she had performed on the day of her conversion, and anointed the feet of Jesus with perfumes. Our Saviour, his mind full of the thought of his coming death, gave to this sign of veneration a significance in keeping therewith, accepting it as a loving action forestalling the embalming of his body. The more his heart was saddened by the baseness of his enemies, so much the more did he show himself affected by the smallest token of devotion on the part of his friends.

Jesus praises this disinterested affection, which was not withheld even by the excuse of benefiting the poor. "The poor you have always with you, but me you have not always." By this he teaches us to profit by the favourable occasions that grace offers us, for we shall have plenty of time in which to give to human affairs that attention which they rightly claim. When Jesus grants us some moments of intimate union with himself, let us ignore for a while our exterior occupations, let us forget ourselves and think of him alone. "The poor you have always with you." This is one of the most consoling promises of Christ, in which he commits to his Church a very precious treasure. As Jesus on leaving this earth to return to his Father gives himself to be with us in the Blessed Sacrament, so, too, he wishes to remain always present among us in the person of his poor.

The Offertory is from Psalm cxlii. In it the Just One begs for deliverance from the snares of his enemies, but he does not look for this deliverance in human aid, as do so many souls when in trouble, who by seeking creature consolation and relief lose all the spiritual benefits which pain and grief bring to the Christian sufferer. The true Christian turns to God alone in the hour of trial and temptation, and prays that by his interior light he will guide him to the accomplishment of his holy will.

The Secret is the same as that of the First Sunday in Advent, in which we ask that the Sacrament may so cleanse us by its power, that we may the more worthily celebrate *suum principium*—that is, the paschal feast—at which the first Eucharist was instituted.

The Communion is taken from Psalm xxxiv, and carries on the same idea which dominates the liturgy at this season. The Saviour, oppressed by the attacks of his enemies, calls upon his Father to bear witness to his innocence in face of the calumnies which assail him. "Let them blush and be ashamed together, who rejoice at my evils"—these words may be applied to the evil one and his followers, the Jews, who, standing by the cross, mocked at him and derided him—

" Let them be clothed with shame and fear who speak malignant things against me."

In the Post-Communion we beseech almighty God to grant us that fervour and spiritual hunger which will cause us to taste the inner sweetness of Communion and to experience its fruition. For, as bodily nourishment produces greater effect according to the health and vigour of the person who receives it, so the Blessed Sacrament produces greater fruit in those souls who come full of love and fervour to partake of it. This shows us how carefully we should prepare ourselves to receive the holy Sacraments.

In the Prayer over the people we ask God to help us that we may soon celebrate with fervent faith and loving hearts the commemoration of the greatest of all his mercies, that one by which he has deigned to " restore " us—that is, to make us live again through the shedding of his precious blood.

The Passion of Jesus is ever being renewed throughout the history of the Church, therefore it is necessary that there should always be loving souls who, by the perfume of their devotion, should make atonement to the divine Master for all the wrongs caused by his enemies. Happy are those who can make reparation in this manner, and the need for them is greater than ever in these days when disbelief and ungodliness are shaking all society to its foundations.

The precious and sweet-smelling ointment which these souls pour out at the feet of Jesus are their tears and their holy lives; these, by the power of good example, fill the Church of Christ with sweetness. The world condemns such contemplative lives as wasted and useless, and, like Judas, casts a doubt on the value of their sacrifice; but Jesus takes up their defence, and shows clearly that without doing injustice to more active and public service, these self-denying souls, devoted to prayer and penance, are indeed necessary to his Church.

TUESDAY IN HOLY WEEK

Collecta at Sta Maria in Portico. Station at St Prisca.

The present Church of Sta Maria in Portico stands about a hundred yards distant from the medieval diaconal church of that name, erected formerly in the porch of the palace of Galla, daughter of the consul Symmachus. The church and hospital of St Galla still show the exact site where, until 1618, stood the original diaconal church *in porticu Gallae*. This noble matron—before retiring from the world to lead the life of a religious in the still-existing convent of St Stephen

Kata Galla patricia near St Peter's—desired to turn her own house into a hospital and *xenodochium* for the poor. This she duly carried out,[1] dedicating the building to the great Mother of God, a representation of whom, executed in enamel on a plate of gold, dating from the fifth century, is still venerated on this spot.

Gregory VII (1073-85) who, in the ancestral castle of the Pierleoni at the foot of the Tarpeian rock, might indeed consider himself as born and bred under the shadow of the *titulus Gallae,* restored the church from its foundations and reconsecrated the high altar. Its venerable antiquity, however, did not protect it in the seventeenth century from the mania for restoring and remodelling all buildings in the classical style prevailing at that time; so the ancient painting at Sta Maria in Portico had to find a new resting-place near by.

Apart from the historic interest of the older church, it cannot actually be said that the shrine lost in any way in dignity or splendour, for the new basilica " in Campitelli "[2] is remarkable for its beauty and size, and is fully worthy of the great traditions of the Church of St Galla. Nor is this basilica altogether new, for it is built on the site of an ancient and dilapidated little church also dedicated in the Middle Ages to Sta Maria in Campitelli, which had the honour in 1217 of being consecrated by the hands of Pope Honorius III himself.

As regards the stational Basilica of St Prisca on the Aventine, the excavations made on the spot and the researches of De Rossi have but confirmed the tradition which connected the *domestica Ecclesia Aquilae et Priscillae* with the Apostles Peter and Paul, who are said to have received hospitality there. Indeed, in 1776, a Roman house was discovered near the church with paintings and other records of a Christian character, whilst among the ruins was found a bronze tablet offered in 226 by a city in Spain to Caius Marius Cornelius Pudentianus, a person of senatorial rank, who had been elected to that city as its patron. Now the relations between the founders of the Priscillian necropolis on the Via Salaria and the Pudenti of the *Vicus Patricius* are too well known, for the certainty of a house belonging to the Pudenti having existed on the Coelian on the site of the title of Aquila and Priscilla, not to throw a very favourable light on this ancient ecclesiastical tradition.

During the time of Pius VI (1775-99) there was also discovered near the basilica of St Prisca on the Coelian, an

---

[1] *Temp.* Pope John I (523-26).—Tr.
[2] Built by Pope Alexander VII in 1659.—Tr.

ancient oratory with paintings of the fourth century, representing the Apostles. A glass vase was also found, around which were engraved the heads of the Apostles, their names being inscribed above them, and, in addition, various fragments of mosaics, showing fishes of all kinds darting about in the water, symbolical of souls regenerated by grace through the waters of baptism.

Altogether a number of arguments help to support the Roman tradition which regards the title of Aquila and Priscilla on the Aventine as being one of the most ancient sanctuaries of the Eternal City, hallowed by the presence and ministry of St Peter and St Paul. Against this tradition, confirmed by documentary evidence, we have not as yet seen any valid argument brought forward to the contrary.

The Middle Ages recorded the venerable traditions of the title of Aquila and Prisca in a graceful inscription :

HAEC · DOMVS · EST · AQVILAE · SEV · PRISCAE · VIRGINIS · ALMAE
QVOS · LVPE · PAVLE · TVO · ORE · VEHIS · DOMINO
HIC · PETRE · DIVINI · TRIBVEBAS · FERCVLA · VERBI
SAEPIVS · HOCCE · LOCO · SACRIFICANS · DOMINO

It must be remembered, however, that the Prisca, virgin and martyr, whose body lies under the high altar of the church, is not the same as Prisca or Priscilla, the wife of Aquila, and disciple of the Apostle Paul.

In the Middle Ages there arose beside this title a celebrated Benedictine Abbey, which, in the eleventh century, was dependent on that of St Paul on the Via Ostiensis.

The Introit is derived quite exceptionally from St Paul's Epistle to the Galatians (vi 14). The cross is far from being to the Christian an occasion of shame; rather it is a sign of glory, since it is from the cross of Christ that there come to us salvation, life and resurrection.

Then follows Psalm lxvi : " May God have mercy on us and bless us; may he cause the light of his countenance to shine upon us, and may he have mercy on us." This is the most beautiful prayer that, in union with the Church, we can lift up to Christ crucified. He chose to die in the darkness of the awestruck earth, having himself become an object of malediction in the sight of the ineffable holiness of God; but, at the same time, his dying eyes are fixed on us in love, and that glance is a living and shining ray which enlightens the whole world.

The curse which he took upon himself on Calvary in obedience to his Father's will has merited for us an abundance of divine blessings, wherefore Christ crucified is

the true light of the world and the pledge of God's highest
graces. Let us then pray that Jesus may always turn from
the cross his suffering face towards us, so that he may deign
to remember all that he has suffered for us, and may show
us his infinite mercy; and that we too, looking upon the face
of the dying Jesus, may conceive a profound horror of sin
and a tender love for our crucified Lord, saying with St Paul:
Dilexit me et tradidit semetipsum pro me.

In the Collect we pray for grace so to celebrate the
mysteries of the Passion of our Redeemer, that we may
derive therefrom that fruit which the Church offers us in the
holy liturgy. We are not simply commemorating an historic
event. The works of Christ and his words contained in the
Gospel bear fruit whenever they are devoutly recalled, and
have the same divine power when the Church expounds them
to the Christian world to-day, as they had when they were
first done or spoken before the Jews. With what reverence
should we then listen to the words of the Gospel at holy Mass,
and how pure should be the heart and lips of the priest who
utters them!

The Lesson is taken from Jeremias (xi 18-20), who, on
account of the persecutions he suffered at the hands of the
corrupt priesthood of his time, is one of the prophetic types
bearing the greatest resemblance to Christ. In the passage
which the liturgy puts before us to-day, the prophet appeals
to God to judge between him and his enemies who have
devised counsels against him, saying: " Let us put wood in
his bread and cut him off from the land of the living."
Here the Fathers of the Church see a prophetic allusion to the
miracle of the Eucharist, in which the body of Christ is
hidden under the species of bread.

The Gradual is from Psalm xxxiv, in which Christ dis-
closes all the ingratitude of his enemies. He loved them so
much that in their sickness—the sins and passions which
afflict the soul—he clothed himself in sackcloth—that is, he
hid the glory of his divine nature underneath the lowliness
of our human nature, and afflicted his spirit with fasting.
Yet, in despite of this, they repaid his love with hate, so
Christ turns to his Father saying: " Judge thou, O Lord,
them that wrong me; overthrow them that fight against me:
take hold of arms and shield, and rise up to help me."

It may be observed here that when in holy Scripture the
divine judgement is invoked on the wicked, we should understand this as being either the final judgement of God on the
impenitent sinner, or, if the expression refers to our present
life, those physical and temporal ills with which he more often
visits the guilty in this world, in order to draw them from
their evil ways and to convert them, or to prevent them

from committing further sins which would render their eternal damnation more certain.

The Gospel was originally the narrative from St John (xiii 1-15) of the washing of the feet, afterwards reserved for Maundy Thursday. Our Lord here makes use, as was his wont, of a familiar image drawn from the daily life around him, in order to make his meaning clearer to the simplest among his hearers, saying to Peter : " He that is washed, *i.e.*, he that comes from the bath, needeth not but to wash his feet,'' so he who desires to celebrate worthily the Eternal " Pasch " with Jesus, and to become one with him, must first wash away even the least of his imperfections in the blood of the Lamb and in the ardour of his love.

It was only in later times that the story of the Passion of our Lord according to St Mark (xiv-xv) was introduced into the stational liturgy of to-day. According to the exegetes of the New Testament, the young man here mentioned, who was suddenly aroused by the uproar caused by the capture of Jesus, and who followed in the crowd clad only in a linen cloth,[1] is in all probability Mark, the actual writer of this Gospel, who, although he does not name himself openly, reveals his identity as its author by various signs. All the particulars of the story coincide in favour of Mark, and give a natural explanation to this incident.

Mark lived with his mother in Jerusalem, evidently in the less frequented part of the city, and for this reason his house was used by the first disciples as a place of meeting. When Jesus passed before the house, the youth was already in bed, and in accordance with the usual custom of Palestine, having laid aside his clothes, had wrapped himself in a large sheet, which, in this instance, as was usual among the wealthier classes, was woven from the finest linen. At the noise of the multitude, the young man awakes, and, hearing that Jesus was being led away captive, rushes out of the house just as he is and accosts the soldiers, possibly making use of threats. Some of them, having had a proof at Gethsemani that the disciples of the Nazarene could use arms if need be, attempted to seize him, but the young man, leaving the sheet in their hands, fled away naked.

St Gregory admonishes us that he who would escape the assaults of the devil must first strip himself internally, as the athletes stripped themselves outwardly before entering the circus; Satan must not be able to get hold of us by any of our affections and we must be willing to abandon freely to him all our worldly desires, so that we may rescue our souls from his clutches.

[1] Mark xiv 51-52.

The Offertory comes from Psalm cxxxix : " Keep me, O Lord, from the hand of the sinner; and from wicked men deliver me." God heard this prayer of the dying Saviour; and on the morning of Easter day gave him a new life, one no longer subject to suffering and to the weakness of the flesh, but glorious and immortal. " Christ being risen," cries the Apostle, " dieth no more. Death hath no longer any dominion over him." This is the victory of the crucified Redeemer, whose cry the Father has answered.

In the Secret we implore God that the sacrifice instituted to sanctify the solemn paschal fast may also serve to restore our will, turning it from evil to good.

Unlike the Greeks, who on days of abstinence refrain from offering the holy Sacrifice, Rome from earliest times never celebrated any fast without also offering the unbloody Sacrifice of the Mass. Therefore we find in the Missal for each day of abstinence—in Lent, on Ember days, on vigils, etc.—a Mass corresponding thereto, which, according to the liturgical spirit of our forefathers, consecrated the penance and marked the end of the fast. The only exceptions are Holy Saturday and the great vigils preparatory to the Sunday, which necessitated the " aliturgical Saturday "— that is, without any Mass—but the reason in these cases was that the Friday fast was prolonged uninterruptedly until the early morning Mass of the Sunday.

The Communion is taken from Psalm lxviii, which describes how the enemies of Jesus drank and sang as they planned to encompass his death, but he prayed to his Father and by his prayers hastened the blessed hour of mercy.

All things have their appointed times, nor can we alter them. There is a time of prosperity and a time of misfortune, a time of glory and a time of humiliation. It is God who in his divine providence gives us our appointed times of good and evil. We must therefore conform to his holy will and during the time of trial await patiently the hour when it shall please him to set us free. It is our duty then to pray with that end in view that we may be delivered from evil and not be led into temptation, but without anxiety and without losing our inward grace.

Qui crediderit, non festinet, Isaias says, and faith assures us that God's hour will surely come, even though it tarry. Let us then tranquilly await this hour, this *tempus beneplaciti,* as the Psalmist here calls it, and meanwhile our trust in God will sustain us and give us confidence that though all the world may fail us, yet God will never fail those who trust in him.

The Post-Communion is the same as that of Ember Saturday in Lent. In it we pray that by the merit of the holy

Sacrifice our evil passions may be rooted out from our hearts and the just desires of our hearts fulfilled. These desires are only just when they are in accordance with the just and holy will of God. When therefore in our prayers, instead of allowing ourselves to be guided by the Holy Ghost who dwells within us and, as St Paul says, prays within us *gemitibus inenarrabilibus,* we are led by our human desires to ask for those things which in the ruling of divine providence are not to our advantage, God, who is infinitely good, does not grant us what we in our blindness crave for, but that which he knows to be expedient for us. The prayer of faith is thus never useless and never inefficacious, but always obtains some degree of grace.

In the Collect of Benediction over the people before their dismissal—hence are explained the expressions of the early Church : *benedictione missae sint, fiant missae catechumenis,* etc.—we ask that the mercy of God may cleanse us from all the deceits of our old nature, so that we may be formed anew unto holiness by the paschal mystery. Indeed, in the death of Christ we all die to the Old Law, to sin and to the flesh, and by his resurrection we are called to a new life according to his example. Of him the Apostle writes : *quod mortuus est peccato, mortuus est semel, quod autem vivit, vivit Deo.* To live to God is the high destiny of all the " children of the Resurrection," as the Gospel calls them.

May the Lord cause the light of his countenance to shine upon us, and may he have mercy on us. Such is the beautiful Messianic psalm which the Church applies during these days to the triumph of the crucified one. For it is from the tree of the cross that Jesus, being lifted up as he said, draws all hearts to himself. It is from the cross that he turns his dying gaze on the human race, which from countless centuries passes before him, who, according to the words of St John, was deemed in the divine decrees to have been offered up from the beginning of the world, and who bestows his benediction on all who believe in him.

WEDNESDAY IN HOLY WEEK

General Morning Synaxis at the Lateran. Collecta at St Peter ad Vincula. Station at St Mary Major.

At the time of St Leo the Great, when the weekdays in Lent had not all as yet their own eucharistic liturgy, this Wednesday of Holy Week was, however, especially distinguished by its stational Mass; for we have a whole series of homilies by the great Pontiff delivered in *feria IV heb-*

domadae majoris, in which the author continues to develop before the people of Rome the history of the Passion of our Lord, which had been interrupted on the preceding Sunday.

This shows that there had been no intermediary synaxis between Palm Sunday and this Wednesday; indeed, the station on the Wednesday must evidently have been aliturgical from the first—that is, the Mass was omitted on that day, as on Good Friday; for we find traces of this ancient rule for many centuries in the *Ordines Romani.* They prescribe that on the *feria IV* of Holy Week, at the general assembly of the clergy, both of the city and the suburbs, which was held at the Lateran in the morning, and consequently before the synaxis on the Esquiline, only the solemn litany should be recited, which is now used exclusively on Good Friday. The Mass was reserved for the evening station in the Liberian Basilica.

During the most solemn weeks of the liturgical cycle at Rome, it was the rule that the synaxis of the Wednesday should be celebrated at St Mary Major, as though to ensure the protection of the blessed Virgin before undertaking any matter of special importance. In this particular instance, it is the new aspirants to the paschal baptism who are placed under her care, and to whom else could they be so surely entrusted as to her, the loving Mother, who in the noontide of Good Friday will be named Mother of Mercy and Advocate of the human race?

The Introit is from the Epistle of St Paul to the Philippians (ii 8-10, 11): " In the name of Jesus every knee should bow, of those that are in heaven, on earth and under the earth : for the Lord became obedient unto death, even the death of the cross : therefore the Lord Jesus Christ is in the glory of God the Father."

On the eve of the Passion the Church desires to confirm our faith by this grand hymn of triumph, that when we shall to-morrow see Jesus nailed to the cross between two thieves we may remember that it was by his obedience and humiliation that he won the triumph of the Resurrection and achieved the destruction of the kingdom of Satan.

In the Collect we ask that God would avert from us the scourges which our sins have deserved, and deliver us by the merits of the Passion of his Son. We cannot do anything more pleasing to God than offer him the merits of Christ's Passion, for as it is in his only-begotten Son that he is well pleased, for his sake he can refuse us nothing.

On this day, as formerly on all the more solemn occasions which have especially retained traces of the primitive liturgical order, we have two lessons from the prophets. In the first of these lessons (Isa. lxii 11; lxiii 1-7) the son of Amos foretells how Christ, his garments sprinkled with blood, overthrows the enemies of our souls. For his Passion conceals a mystery of ineffable humility and invincible power, while the degradations and torments which he underwent for love of us are the very weapons with which he struck down the pride and sensuality of man, and crushed the power of Satan.

The Gradual, derived from Psalm lxviii, speaks of the sorrows of the Sacred Heart of Jesus in his Passion : '' Turn not away thy face from thy servant.'' The Saviour had taken upon himself the burden of the sins of mankind, and had thereby incurred the penalty of being abandoned by God, who in justice turns away his face from the guilty sinner. This is the bitter torment, in some manner corresponding to the pain of loss which tortures the condemned in hell. '' Hear me speedily, for I am in trouble. Save me, O God, for the waters are come in, even unto my soul ''—that is, sin has filled my inmost soul with bitterness in such a manner that my heart is a prey to the deepest desolation, which even the hypostatic union with the person of the Word cannot allay. '' I stick fast in the mire of the deep ''—the iniquity of the whole world—'' and there is no sure standing.''

This abandonment which Jesus suffered on the cross is not to be understood in an absolute sense, since even in his terrible agony the blessed soul of the Redeemer enjoyed the beatific vision of God, but must be accepted in a relative sense, inasmuch as God, in order to abandon his only-begotten Son to the full extent of his sufferings, so disposed that this beatitude of the soul should not be experienced in the body.

In the Collect which follows, the thought of the Resurrection is intimately united to the commemoration of the Passion. Our faith teaches us that in Jesus Christ the divine and the human natures were united in one person, without confusion, but with perfect distinction of attributes. As man, therefore, he suffered and died, but his humanity, being hypostatically united to the Godhead, could not know the corruption of the grave, but was to receive the highest glory by rising from the tomb, the first-born among the dead, at once the cause and prototype of universal resurrection. '' O God, who wast pleased that thy Son should undergo for us the ignominy of the cross, that thou mightest drive away from us the power of the enemy; grant to us thy servants that we may obtain the grace of resurrection.''

This '' grace of resurrection '' is the spiritual resurrection of the soul by means of grace and its final salvation in glory. Without this result the Passion of Jesus Christ would be made void; as the Apostle says : *Ergo gratis Christus mortuus est?* We can therefore understand how the thought of the Resurrection completes that of the Passion, and why the Liturgy never separates these two holy mysteries which explain and fulfil one another.

The second Lesson, from Isaias (liii 1-12), has been finely described as the *Proto-evangelium,* because in it the Seer of Juda tells of the humiliations and sufferings of the Passion of Jesus many centuries before their accomplishment, and describes them in minute detail. The characteristic title of " Servant of Jehovah " is here given to the Messias; for since, by sinning, man had rebelled against the law of God, so in expiation of this rebellion the Redeemer must devote himself entirely to fulfilling the will of his Father. Christ is of God, as St Paul writes, *Christus autem Dei,* both as Son and as servant; nay, more, as victim. The divine rights of God over Jesus are thus perfectly and absolutely expressed, especially by the hypostatic union of the Word with the Saviour's human nature; by virtue of this union the humanity of Jesus is truly of God.

This title of " Servant of Jehovah " is carefully explained by the prophet throughout the lesson which is read to-day at the Mass. He presents the Messias to us in a new and un-expected light : his reign shall surely be triumphant and glorious, but it will begin in humiliation, and he must needs suffer many things and be nailed to the cross before he can enter into his glory. But why must the "Servant of Jehovah" suffer? To this Isaias answers : " Surely he hath borne our infirmities and carried our sorrows, and the Lord hath laid on him the iniquity of us all; and by his bruises we are healed. He shall not open his mouth, and he shall give the ungodly for his burial and the rich for his death. If he shall lay down his life for sin, he shall see a long-lived seed, and the will of the Lord shall be prosperous in his hand. By his knowledge shall this my just servant justify many, and he shall bear their iniquities."

The Tract comes from Psalm ci, and interprets the feelings of Jesus in his last agony, feelings of sorrow and humiliation, yet of complete confidence in God, who, when the appointed time has come, will deliver him and raise him up again to life. " O Lord, hear my prayer, and let my cry come to thee. Turn not away thy face from me : in the day when I am in trouble, incline thine ear to me. In what day soever I shall call upon thee, hear me speedily. For my days are vanished like smoke, and my bones are burnt up as in an oven. I am struck like grass, and my heart is withered : because I forgot to eat my bread. Thou, arising, O Lord, shalt have mercy on Sion; for the time is come to have mercy on it."

With what awe and reverence should we not meditate on these words of the Psalmist, which reveal to us the thoughts of our crucified Saviour. This book of prayer is the best commentary on the holy Gospel, for whilst the Evangelists speak chiefly of the exterior life and teaching of Jesus, the Psalter reveals to us the innermost feelings of his Sacred Heart.

To-day we read the Passion of our Lord, according to St Luke (xxii 1-7; xxiii 1-53), which reflects in a special manner the teaching of St Paul, and very closely agrees with his description of the institution of the holy Eucharist.[1] The words from Isaias—*et cum iniquis deputatus est*[2]—quoted by our Lord at the Last Supper refer to the passage previously read, which thus receives divine confirmation of its messianic interpretation.

The fact that the Apostles carried swords when they met together for the " Pasch " is explained by the enmity which existed between the Jews and the Galileans, for which reason the latter were always armed when they went up to celebrate the paschal festival at Jerusalem; and that the disciples did not wear their swords merely for show is seen from the circumstance that in the Garden of Gethsemani it became necessary for Christ to order Peter to replace his sword in its scabbard. The Church does not triumph by force of arms, but rather by the martyrdom of her sons.

On the way to Calvary Jesus comforts the compassionate women who weep over his sufferings, and warns them that their devotion to his Passion should not stop short at bare words of pity, but should be the beginning of a better life. Those who mourn over the death of the Redeemer should indeed labour to eradicate and banish from their hearts the sins which nailed him to the cross: *Si in viridi ligno haec faciunt, in arido quid fiet?* That is to say, if the divine Judge is so inflexible in punishing sin in the person of his own innocent Son, what treatment will he not mete out to the hardened sinner, when at the last judgement the hour has come for mercy to give place to his holy yet awful justice?

After the death of Jesus, at a moment when the disciples are still in hiding, Joseph of Arimathea and Nicodemus come forward, and these two, who until then had been timorous and had not dared to compromise themselves in the cause of Jesus, suddenly throw aside their precautions, and, fearlessly defying public opinion, are the first to render to the crucified Saviour the homage of their devotion. We must never judge our neighbour too harshly; grace can subdue the most re-

[1] 1 Cor. xi 23-25. [2] Isa. liii 12.

bellious heart, and transform it in a moment in accordance with the divine pleasure.

The Offertory is taken from Psalm ci : " O Lord—notwithstanding the multitude of the sins of humanity with which I have gladly burdened myself, and which render me unworthy of thy gaze—hear my prayer and let my cry come to thee—breaking down, as it were, the wall of brass which sin has raised between thee and sinful man—turn not away thy face from me."

In the Secret we pray that God would accept the gift which we offer, and would grant that we may obtain by pious affections those effects of the Passion of his divine Son, which we celebrate in the eucharistic mystery.

The Communion is also from Psalm ci : " I mingled my drink with weeping, for having lifted me up, thou hast thrown me down." In the Passion the divine nature of Jesus sustained his sacred humanity so as to render it the better able to endure. " I am withered like grass, but thou, O Lord, remainest for ever. Thou shalt arise and have mercy on Sion, for the time is come to have mercy on it." Truly the Lord shall arise to defend his Christ, at the dawn of the paschal feast. He will then heal all his wounds and fill him with the ecstasy of joy in the splendours of a new life. Sion, too, will share in his gladness, for the effects of the Resurrection are communicated also to the whole mystical body of Christ.

In the Post-Communion we beseech God that the Passion and death of Jesus which we commemorate in this mystery may fill us with the firm hope of attaining to eternal life in heaven. The death of Christ is the source of life. This is the grand fulfilment of that prophecy of Osee : *O mors, ero mors tua! morsus tuus ero, inferne.*"[1] It would have been easy for the Son of God to show himself master of death and not to have submitted to its sway, but he desired to triumph over it more completely, so, binding death and Satan to the foot of the cross, he made death the spring and fountain of eternal life for the whole human race.

The Blessing over the people is so beautiful that the Church uses this collect during the three following days at the conclusion of each hour of the divine office : " Look down, we beseech thee, upon this thy family, for which our Lord Jesus Christ hesitated not to be delivered up into the hands of wicked men and to undergo the torment of the cross." There is no better way of moving our heavenly Father to pity for us than by reminding him of the Passion of his only-begotten Son, and more especially of the immense love with which he loved us.

[1] Osee xiii 14.

The Crucifixion is the summary of Catholic belief. Christ crucified explains all the other mysteries of the faith, for it is in Jesus that God has loved us and destined us to future glory. The cross is the crown of all the works of God, and the masterpiece of his love. He is so well pleased with it—*et vidit cuncta quae fecerat et erant valde bona*—that he cannot hear it commemorated nor behold its image without being moved to pity towards us. Should not we, then, too, contemplate with boundless devotion Jesus Christ crucified and offer to the Father his sufferings and his merits in atonement for our sins?

MAUNDY THURSDAY

Station at the Lateran.

The Basilica of the Saviour, beside which the Popes had, from the fifth century onward, fixed their usual residence, is the scene of the solemn rites with which the Church commences on this day the celebration of the paschal feast. Originally there were three Masses, one in the morning for the reconciliation of public penitents, another for the consecration of the holy oils destined for Extreme Unction and baptism, and a third at the close of day in commemoration of the Last Supper and for the Easter Communion. It is easy, therefore, to understand why it was more convenient to hold the station at the Lateran than at St Peter's, which at that time was outside the city walls.

In our days the rites are less complicated, and, public penance having fallen into disuse, the holy oils are consecrated during the Mass of the Easter Communion.

The threefold synaxis, too, held formerly by our forefathers, had suggested a wise curtailment of the ceremonies, and we find from documents of the eighth century that the third Mass began directly with the Preface, omitting the lessons, psalms and prayers which usually precede the consecratory anaphora. For this reason the first part of the Mass for Maundy Thursday in our Missal has no Proper of its own, but has collected its matter from other Masses.

The Introit is the same as that of the preceding Tuesday. We must not allow ourselves to shrink from the mere thought of the cross. It is like a medicine which is bitter to the taste, but which is certain to restore health. St Paul says that in Jesus crucified *est salus, vita et resurrectio nostra.* He is our resurrection, because his death merits for us the grace of rising again from the sepulchre of our sins; he is our life, because for his sake the eternal Father gives us the Holy

Ghost, who is the vital source of all our spiritual life; he is our health, because, according to the word of Isaias, the blood which flows from his wounds and the bruises on his limbs, torn by the scourgings, are as balsam to heal our souls from all vices and evil passions.

The Collect is that appointed for to-morrow after the first lesson. It touches slightly on the mystery of predestination, calling to our minds how, at the time of our Lord's Passion, the thief obtained salvation, whilst Judas through despair rushed to his damnation. The different lot of these two fills us with awe and fear, for it teaches us that, in order to be saved, it is not enough to be mere spectators of the Passion of Jesus, but that we must renounce sin and the life we have been leading apart from God, so as to rise with Christ to a new life, entirely holy and conformed to his will.

In the Lesson, from the first Epistle to the Corinthians (xi 20-32), St Paul dwells on the institution of the Blessed Sacrament, and on the dispositions which are necessary in order to partake of it worthily. The same lesson has already been read in the office for the vigil of this day, but it is here repeated because its natural place is in the Mass of Maundy Thursday.

An abuse had crept in at Corinth on the occasion of the celebration of the common banquet, when the holy Eucharist was consecrated in accordance with the example of the Saviour and the earliest ordering of the Apostles. The richer members feasted on their own account, ignoring the poor and the late comers. This, observes the Apostle, is no longer the Lord's Supper, but bears a strong resemblance to those banquets which were customary among the religious societies of the pagans, who also met together for social intercourse and feasting. We do not, says St Paul, meet merely to satisfy the requirements of the body, but in order to preserve intact the sacramental significance of the Supper, at which we celebrate and take part in common in the sacrifice which commemorates the death of the Redeemer. Let each one, then, examine his own conscience, lest the Bread of Life, eaten unworthily, become the cause of condemnation and death.

The Mass, therefore, according to the teaching of the Apostle, is a true sacrifice, commemorating that of Calvary— that is, the death of our Lord. We should, then, take part in it with lively faith and gratitude if we desire to share in the effects of the redemption.

Every sacrificial rite ordains that those who participate in it should do so by consuming the victim. Among the ancient peoples this final banquet signified the intimate relationship which linked the victim to the worshippers, in whose name it was offered to the divinity. The victim is a substitute for him who offers the sacrifice, and the latter consumes the victim in order to be identified with that which legally represents him. Further, the sacrificial feast has a sacred character and symbolizes the reconciliation of the divinity with man, inasmuch as both are seated together as friends at the same table.

In the Mass the priest must necessarily partake of the sacred Victim through sacramental Communion. It is sufficient for the faithful to associate themselves with the sacrifice by a spiritual Communion, but the Church greatly desires and insistently teaches that they too should, as often as possible, take part in the sacrifice by the actual reception of Holy Communion in memory of the death of the Lord.

The Gradual is taken from St Paul's Epistle to the Philippians (ii 8-9) : " Christ became obedient for us unto death, even the death of the cross. Wherefore God also hath exalted him and hath given him a name which is above every name." The name given by God to Jesus is that of " Saviour." This name, unlike the names given to created beings, expresses not merely a hope, but the realization of the promise of salvation. The Redeemer appears as Jesus, Saviour, in the fullest and widest sense of its meaning, when on the cross he pours forth his blood for the redemption of the human race.

Then follows the Gospel from St John (xiii 1-15), with the account of the washing of the feet, which was evidently introduced at a later date, as it bears no reference to the eucharistic mystery. It was originally read on Tuesday in Holy Week.

Jesus washed the feet of his disciples, both in order to give us an example and lesson of the humility we ought to show to one another, and also to make us understand how pure we should be when we approach him. " He that is washed needeth not but to wash his feet." To be worthy of his friendship it is not enough to keep our souls free from mortal sin, but we must show our hatred of sin by uprooting from our hearts all that is displeasing to God.

The Secret has a literary beauty of its own, and deserves to be given in full : " We beseech thee, O holy Lord, Father almighty, eternal God, that our sacrifice may be made pleasing to thee by him who at what he instituted on this day taught his disciples to do this in memory of him, thy Son, Jesus Christ our Lord, etc."

On this day, as Pope Vigilius states in a letter to Profuturus of Braga, the following period, commemorating our Lord's Supper, is inserted in the prayer of consecration:

"Communicating and celebrating the most holy day on which our Lord Jesus Christ was delivered up for us; as also reverencing the memory, first, of the glorious and ever-virgin Mary, Mother of the same our God and Lord Jesus Christ, etc."

Also in the prayer which Innocent I, writing to Decentius of Gubbio, calls the *Commendatio Oblationis,* we commemorate to-day the Last Supper: "We therefore beseech thee, O Lord, to be appeased and to receive this offering which we thy servants, and also thy whole household do make to thee in memory of the day on which our Lord Jesus Christ delivered to his disciples the mysteries of his body and blood to be celebrated: order our days in thy peace and grant that we be rescued from eternal damnation and counted within the fold of thine elect. Through Christ our Lord. Amen.

"This our offering do thou, O God, vouchsafe in all things to bless, consecrate, approve, make reasonable and acceptable: that it may become for us the body and blood of thy most beloved Son, our Lord Jesus Christ.

"Who the day before he suffered for our salvation and that of all mankind—that is, on this day—took bread, etc."

Before the final doxology of the Canon, *Per quem haec omnia,* according to a very ancient rite confirmed by the Canons of Hippolytus—which, however, describe it as a ceremony that could be repeated in each Mass—the bishop blesses the oil for the sick, reserving the consecration of the chrism and of the oil for the catechumens until after the Communion.

This rite has already been described in the first volume, so we need only quote the beautiful hymn which was first introduced into the Gallican Liturgy, and later adopted in the Roman Pontifical, with which the liturgy of this memorable day hails the sacred chrism:

PART I[1]

HYMNUS	HYMN

O Redemptor, sume carmen temet concinentium.
   O Redemptor, etc.
	Hear our hymn, Redeemer Lord:
	 Thee we praise with one accord.
	   Hear our hymn, etc.

Audi, Judex mortuorum,
 Una spes mortalium,
 Audi voces proferentum
 Donum pacis praevium.
   O Redemptor, etc.
	Hear us, Judge of dead and living,
	 Hope of mortals, hear us singing.
	 Hear us, emblematic tribute
	 From the peaceful olive bringing.
	   Hear our hymn, etc.

---

[1] Part I is sung whilst the procession goes to fetch the oil for the chrism and the oil of the catechumens from the sacristy.—Tr.

Arbor foeta alma luce
Hoc sacrandum protulit :
Fert hoc prona praesens turba
Salvatori saeculi.

O Redemptor, etc.

Stans ad aram, immo supplex
Infulatus pontifex,
Debitum persolvit omne
Consecrato chrismate.
O Redemptor, etc.

Consecrare tu dignare,
Rex perennis patriae,
Hoc olivum, signum vivum,
Jura contra daemonum.
O Redemptor, etc.

Fruit of light the tree did yield
That gave this hallowed store :
Worshipping the world's Redeemer,
This we offer and adore.
Hear our hymn, etc.

There before the altar standing
Prays the mitred Pontiff lowly :
Duly he performs the rite,
To consecrate the chrism holy.
Hear our hymn, etc.

Consecrate thou, Christ eternal,
King of heaven our home,
This our chrism, a living Seal
Against the powers of doom.
Hear our hymn, etc.

PART II[1]

Ut novetur sexus omnis
Unctione chrismatis,
Ut sanetur sauciata
Dignitatis gloria.
O Redemptor, etc.

Lota mente sacro fonte
Aufugantur crimina :
Uncta fronte sacrosancta
Influunt charismata.

O Redemptor, etc.

Corde natus ex Parentis
Alvum implens Virginis,
Praesta lucem, claude mortem
Chrismatis consortibus.

O Redemptor, etc.

Sit haec dies festa nobis
Saeculorum saeculis :
Sit sacrata, digna laude,
Nec senescat tempore.
O Redemptor, etc.

That by this most sacred unction
Either sex may be renewed,
And our wounded glory rescued
Through the Spirit's plenitude.
Hear our hymn, etc.

First the hallowed fountain's waters
Cleanse the soul from taint of sin,
Then with oil the brows anointed,
And all graces flow within.
Hear our hymn, etc.

Son of the eternal Father,
Virgin-born, afford us light :
Who receive this holy unction :
Save us from Death's gloomy night.
Hear our hymn, etc.

May this day of festal gladness
Keep its holy joys in store.
Dignified with joyful praises,
Blooming now and evermore.
Hear our hymn, etc.

The Communion is derived from the Gospel lesson of the washing of the feet. Christ not only wishes to wash our feet, but has prepared for us a fount of regeneration in his precious blood, in which our souls shall be immersed and made wholly clean.

The Post-Communion is the following prayer : " We, who have been strengthened by the food of life, beseech thee, O

[1] Part II is sung whilst the vessels are being carried back to the sacristy.—Tr.

Lord our God, that what we do in the time of our mortal life
may bring us to life everlasting with thee. Through our Lord."

The Mass being finished, the sacred Host, reserved for
to-morrow's ceremonies, is carried to an altar specially prepared for it.

In the Middle Ages the Pope proceeded, at the end of the
Mass, to the Basilica of St Lawrence, known later as *Sancta
Sanctorum,* where, having laid aside his paenula, he washed
the feet of twelve subdeacons, whilst the cardinals, the
deacons and the *schola* sang Vespers. After this generous
gifts of money were distributed to the urban clergy, both of
the higher and lower ranks, as was then the custom on all
great solemnities, and, evening having now closed in, they all
went to dine in the Basilica or *Triclinium* of Pope Theodore,
which stood near the Oratory of St Silvester.

The pardoning of the penitents, the chrism of the Paraclete
on the brow of the newly baptized, the oil of consolation on
the limbs of the dying, the divine Eucharist in the hearts of
the faithful, all these ineffable mysteries of pity are dispensed
on this day of the Lord's Supper, on which he pours forth the
fulness of his heart, and, having always loved his own—*in
finem dilexit,* that is—he loved us with an unbounded love
even unto death, the death of the cross.

We quote from the Greek Liturgy the following passage
relating to to-day's feast :

Mysticam ad mensam omnes acce-
dentes cum tremore, cum anima
pura panem suscipiamus, neque
separemur a Domino, ut videamus
quomodo pedes lavet discipulor-
um, et faciamus quemadmodum
viderimus, invicem   subjecti,
pedesque singuli singulorum ab-
stergentes.   Christus enim sic
praecepit discipulis suis, sed non
audivit Judas, perfidus servus.

Drawing near with awe to the
mystical banquet, let us receive
the Bread with a pure conscience,
nor let us separate ourselves from
the Lord, that we may behold how
he washes the feet of his disciples.
Let us then do as we have seen
him do, and let us be subject the
one to the other, each washing the
other's feet; for thus did Christ
command his disciples to act, but
Judas, the faithless servant,
would not hearken.

GOOD FRIDAY

*Collecta at the Lateran.   Station at the Holy Cross in
Jerusalem.*

Christ had said, " *Non capit prophetam perire extra Hierusalem* " ;[1] for this reason the station is held to-day in the
basilica known as *Sancta Hierusalem,* to which the Pope

[1] " It cannot be that a prophet perish out of Jerusalem " (Luke xiii
33.)

formerly went barefoot, walking in procession from the Lateran. He swung, as he went, a censer filled with precious perfumes before the wood of the true cross, carried by a deacon, whilst the choir sang Psalm cxviii : *Beati immaculati in via.*

Originally, as a sign of deep mourning, this day was aliturgical, as were usually all the Fridays and Saturdays of the year in Rome. Thus, when towards the sixth century the rigour of the ancient rule was somewhat relaxed and the Friday stations of Lent were instituted, the Popes still continued for many centuries the ancient Roman usage, which excluded even the Mass of the Presanctified on this day. Therefore the present rite does not go back beyond the Middle Ages, and represents the order used in the titular churches in Rome, in which the Pope was never present.

The Adoration of the True Cross on Good Friday was taken, as we have already said, from the Liturgy of Jerusalem, where it was already in use towards the end of the fourth century. Indeed, for a long time, in the West also, this adoration formed almost the most important and characteristic part of the ceremony, the central point, as it were, of the whole Liturgy of the Parasceve. *Ecce lignum crucis:* this is the beginning of the *parousia* of the divine judge, and at the sight of the triumphal banner of redemption, whilst the Church prostrates herself low in adoration, the powers of hell flee away terror-stricken into the abyss.

At Rome in the Middle Ages the papal reliquary containing the true cross was sprinkled with perfumes, indicating thereby the sweetness of the grace which flows from the sacred wood, and the inner unction and spiritual balm which the Lord pours into the hearts of those who carry the cross for love of him.

According to the *Ordines Romani* of the eighth century, to-day's ceremony took place partly in the Sessorian Basilica and partly in the Lateran. Towards two o'clock in the afternoon the Pope and the palatine clergy moved in procession barefoot from the Lateran to the stational basilica, where the Adoration of the Cross took place, followed by the reading of the Passion according to St John, and the Great Litany for the various ecclesiastical orders and for the necessities of the Church. The procession then returned to the Lateran, singing as they walked the psalm *Beati immaculati in via.* On this day of sadness neither the Pope nor the deacons received Holy Communion, but the people were free to do so either at the Lateran, where one of the suburbicarian bishops celebrated, or at any of the titular churches in the city.

Towards the ninth century the rite was somewhat altered. The Adoration of the Cross was deferred until after the

Litany, which was followed by the *Pater Noster* together with the Communion of those who were present. The procession of the Blessed Sacrament did not take place at that point, the ceremony ending with the Pope's blessing—"*In nomine Patris et Filii et Spiritus Sancti*"—to which the assembly replied: "*Et cum spiritu tuo.*" Everyone then recited privately the Vesper psalms, after which all went off to break their fast.

In the twelfth century one of the seven suburbicarian bishops, whose turn it was, carried out the Good Friday ceremonies in the Lateran Basilica. The Pope did not take part in them as he continued to go to the Sessorian Basilica, whither both the true cross and the sacred Host were borne in procession from the Lateran for the Mass of the Presanctified; but it would seem that the people no longer received Communion on that day as in the early Middle Ages.

In the days of Honorius III (1216-27), the Pope, at break of day, used to sing the entire Psalter with his chaplains. Towards noon he proceeded with his Cardinals to the Oratory of St Lawrence, and, having opened the iron grating below the altar of Leo III (795-816), he took from underneath the two reliquaries containing the wood of the true cross, and the heads of the Apostles Peter and Paul, which, according to a somewhat late tradition, going back only to the tenth century, were preserved in that sanctuary.

The Cardinals then approached to kiss the holy relics, and the procession was formed to go to the Basilica of Holy Cross in Jerusalem. Before beginning the Mass the Pope retired to the neighbouring monastery to wash his feet and resume his ordinary sandals. The Mass being over, the procession returned to the Lateran, where, however, the usual banquet in the *Triclinium* did not take place, for on this day of mourning and penance the officials of the Lateran palace were offered only bread and herbs, even wine being excluded.

This order of ceremonies obtained in Rome almost down to the fifteenth century, when the rituals began to prescribe that the Pope should first recite the Psalter with his chaplains in his own rooms and then appear at a balcony to impart the indulgence to the people. At a fixed time the Pontiff recited the divine Office in choir, and after midday—before, that is, this stational procession to Sta Croce—he again appeared on the balcony, wearing a red cope and with a mitre on his head, and granted the indulgence once more to the people who crowded the piazza. This ceremony being ended, the Pope put off his sandals, and, together with the Cardinals, all walked in procession barefooted to the Sessorian Basilica.

The Mass of the Presanctified followed, with the rites described above, except that during the time of the French

Popes at Avignon it became the custom for the Blessed Sacrament to be carried to the altar by the Pontiff himself on the conclusion of the Adoration of the Cross, and not by one of the Cardinals who preceded the Pope as he entered the church from the *secretarium*. This is the rite followed in the present Roman Missal.

Notwithstanding all this complication of processions and ceremonies which we find in the Middle Ages, it is not a matter of difficulty to discern that the actual Mass of the Presanctified which has been handed down to us by the *Ordines Romani* of the sixteenth century, and which we still celebrate to-day, consists of three distinct parts that overlie one another like three successive strata. These are the so-called Mass of the Catechumens, the Adoration of the Cross and the Holy Communion.

The first preserves almost unchanged the type of the ancient aliturgical synaxes, or Masses at which the catechumens were present. There is neither Introit nor *Kyrie*, but three scriptural lessons are read, two from the Old Testament and one from the New. After each of the two lessons comes the responsorial chanting of a psalm (Tract), the first one terminating with a collect recited by the officiating priest. The third lesson, giving the account of the Passion according to St John (xviii, xix), is followed at once by the Great Litany for the various necessities of the Church (*Oremus, dilectissimi nobis,* etc.), which originally marked the end of the vigiliary Office preceding the Sunday and served as an introduction to the eucharistic liturgy.

Even now in the Mass the priest, after the Gospel—*i.e.,* immediately before the Offertory—salutes the people with the words *Dominus vobiscum,* and invites them to join in the collective prayer, *Oremus;* but the ancient litany having fallen into disuse, at least in the ordinary rite of the Mass, neither the priest nor the people, as a matter of fact, continue to pray at this point of the eucharistic *actio,* for the cantors alone sing the verse appointed for the Offertory.

It is only in the Good Friday ceremony that the ancient Roman rite survives intact; thus the primitive litany recited after the Gospel, which is mentioned even in the second century by Justin, cannot be said to have entirely dropped out of the liturgy of the Apostolic See, since it is still to be found in its original place on the solemn day of the Parasceve.

The eucharistic Canon and the Communion regularly followed the Litany in ordinary Masses. As, however, there was no Consecration on this day, the Pope in the ninth century passed over the Canon and went directly to the *Pater Noster,* which immediately preceded the Communion. This was the more regular order. Some centuries later, however, we find that the Adoration of the Cross, which originally took place before the Mass, had for some unknown reason been arbitrarily inserted between the Litany and the Communion, which somewhat disturbed the original ordering of the ceremony and produced a confusion of rites.

Some of the Popes, returning to the altar after the Adoration of the Cross, held that the Mass properly began at that moment, and so would have Psalm xlii recited, together with the Confession as in ordinary Masses. Afterwards, when the Popes of Avignon had introduced the procession of the Blessed Sacrament as a special devotion of their own, there gradually followed also the incensing of the oblations and of the altar, the washing of the hands, the secret prayers and the Elevation. In the fifteenth century this last ceremony took place when the Pope was reciting the *Pater Noster,* at the words *sicut in coelo . . .* but later it was deferred until after the Lord's Prayer, and immediately before the fraction of the Host, just as it used to be in the beginning.

The Synaxis of Good Friday has no Introit, as was originally the case before Pope Celestine instituted antiphonal singing in the Mass. Therefore, after a private prayer which each of the officiating clergy recites in a low voice prostrate before the altar, the lector, going up to the ambo, at once reads a passage from Osee (vi 1-6). The Lord, says the prophet, prefers the worship of a pure heart to all the legal purificatory rites of the Old Testament; such worship is shown in the realization of the divine truths by means of faith, and in the accomplishment of his holy will. To establish the New Covenant of Love he will destroy the Old Covenant of Fear; but the people of Israel have no cause to be alarmed, as, although for two days they shall be chastised by the divine justice in punishment for their sins, yet they shall arise to a new life on the third day and shall serve Jehovah in the company of the redeemed.

The Tract is from the Canticle of Habacuc (ch. iii). Never does the majesty of God appear more holy, more awful, and more glorious than on Calvary. It is there that the Blessed Trinity receives the perfect sacrifice offered by Jesus Christ in the name of humanity; it is there that the power of Satan is broken for ever. " Lord, I have heard thy hearing, and was afraid : I considered thy works and trembled. ℣. In the midst of two animals thou shalt be made known : when the years shall draw nigh, thou shalt be known : when the time shall come, thou shalt be shown. ℣. In the time when my soul shall be troubled : in anger thou shalt be mindful of mercy. ℣. God shall come from Libanus, and the Holy One from the shady and thickly covered mountain. ℣. His majesty hath covered the heavens : and the earth is full of his praise."

The responsorial psalm being ended, the priest invites the faithful to unite with him in prayer, saying : " Let us pray "; the deacon adds in the customary manner, " Let us kneel," and after a short private prayer the subdeacon says, " Arise." Then the officiating priest, in the name of all present, prays as follows : " O God, from whom Judas received the punishment of his guilt, and the good thief the reward of his confession ; grant us the effect of thy clemency, that as our Lord Jesus Christ, in his Passion, gave to each a different retribution according to his desert, so he would deliver us from our old sins, and grant us the grace of his resurrection : who liveth."

Next comes the lesson from Exodus (xii 1-11). The paschal lamb, outstretched with two sticks in the form of a cross and roasted whole, was a type of Christ crucified. In the utmost haste the sacrifice was eaten by the Israelites, their loins being girded and their staves in their hands as if about to set forth on a journey. This signifies that the road to heaven is a long one, that life is short and that we have no time to pause on our way to eternity. The lamb was eaten with wild lettuce and unleavened bread, to show us that in the Holy Eucharist we commemorate the death of Christ, and that penance and self-denial are the best preparation for receiving it worthily.

After the lesson the Tract (Ps. cxxxix) is sung, which tells us of the feelings of Jesus upon the cross. The entire human race has conspired against him, for, in sinning, we all have cried out : " *Reus est mortis.*" Alone he faces the hatred and fury of the whole world, wherefore he turns to his Father for succour. His prayer is lowly, but it is full of such immovable hope that, when dying upon the cross, he already sings the canticle of his resurrection.

" Deliver me, O Lord, from the evil man : rescue me from the unjust man. ℣. Who have devised wickedness in their heart ; all the day long they designed battles. ℣. They have sharpened their tongues like a serpent : the venom of asps is under their lips. ℣. Keep me, O Lord, from the hand of the sinner ; and from the unjust men deliver me. ℣. Who have proposed to supplant my steps ; the proud have hid a net for me. ℣. And they have stretched out cords for a snare for my feet ; they have laid for me a stumbling-block by the way-side. ℣. I said to the Lord, thou art my God : hear, O Lord, the voice of my supplication. ℣. O Lord, the strength of my salvation, overshadow my head in the day of battle. ℣. Give me not up from my desire to the wicked : they have plotted against me ; do not thou forsake me, lest at any time they should triumph. ℣. The head of them compassing me about; the labour of their lips shall overwhelm them. ℣. But the just shall give glory to thy name; and the upright shall dwell with thy countenance.''

With what reverence and awe should we not recite this prayer of our dying Saviour, making its sentiments our own, in such a way that the psalm may not be to us merely a record of his Passion, but the lifting up to God of each Christian soul, which renews in itself all the mysteries of our redemption.

The account of the Passion recorded by St John (xviii 1-40; xix 1-42) forms the third lesson, in which the teaching of Christ as conveyed in his words to Pilate is dwelt on with more detail than in the narratives of the other Evangelists. In accordance with the prophecy of the Psalmist—'' *Et vincas cum judicaris* ''—the divine nature of Christ shines out resplendent from the very answers that he gives to the Roman Governor. It is not a prisoner replying to a judge, but a teacher who, even in the Roman *praetorium* itself, preaches and teaches his sublime doctrine. He is the truth and is come into the world to give testimony to the truth, therefore he neglects no opportunity of showing himself to men, and of attracting them to himself by the manifestation of his glory.

As we have already said, the Mass for Good Friday has preserved in its entirety the ancient prayer in the form of a litany of which Justin Martyr speaks, which originally followed the reading of the Gospel at every Mass, just at the moment when the priest, turning towards the people before the Offertory, invites them to prayer, saying : *Oremus*. This litany, to which the whole people made answer by interjecting such exclamations as *Domine miserere, Kyrie eleison,* etc., in the form of a refrain, is still found in its proper place in the Eastern liturgies, but it has disappeared from the Roman Sacramentary, perhaps from the time of Gregory the Great.

The origin of this prayer can be traced in the liturgy of the synagogues, in which, after the scriptural reading, it was customary to pray for the various members of the Jewish community and its various needs; but the text, as contained in the Missal, shows by its particular terminology that it dates from the time of Leo the Great.

We find in it the term *ostiarius,* whose office was later filled by the *mansionarius;* monks, as in the Leonine Sacramentary, are called *confessores;* nuns, *virgines* and not *sanctimoniales;* prayer is made that the Roman Emperor may subdue all the barbarians, and the Roman Empire is considered as the only legitimately constituted temporal power, exactly as St Leo deemed it to be. The disciplinary rule of the catechumens is still in force, the world is torn by heresies, ravaged by pestilence, straitened by famine; innocent men are wrongfully detained in prison, slavery still disgraces the ancient civilization of Rome. All these circumstances at once recall the fifth century, therefore we attribute to the golden period of the Roman Liturgy the final and definite form of this majestic prayer which we may undoubtedly look upon as having originated in the time of the Apostles.

In early days the Litany was recited also apart from the eucharistic synaxis, and there is no reason why it should not be said privately by the faithful for the various spiritual and temporal necessities of the Catholic world. In reciting a prayer of such venerable antiquity, we seem to enter into a closer spiritual relationship with those early generations of martyrs and confessors for the faith, who used the self-same words before us, and thus obtained the graces needful to enable them to correspond to their high vocation of witnessing to this faith with their own blood.

THE GREAT LITANY

Oremus, dilectissimi nobis, pro Ecclesia sancta Dei : ut eam Deus et Dominus noster pacificare, adunare et custodire dignetur toto orbe terrarum : subjiciens ei principatus et potestates; detque nobis, quietam et tranquillam vitam degentibus, glorificare Deum Patrem omnipotentem.

Let us pray, dearly beloved, for the holy Church of God, that our Lord and God would vouchsafe to pacify, unite, and keep it, throughout the world; subjecting to it principalities and powers : and that he may grant us to lead a peaceful life, and to glorify God the Father almighty.

Oremus

Omnipotens, sempiterne Deus, qui gloriam tuam omnibus in Christo gentibus revelasti : custodi opera misericordiae tuae : ut Ecclesia tua toto orbe diffusa, stabili fide in confessione tui nominis perseveret. Per eumdem Dominum nostrum Jesum Christum.

℞. Amen.

Let us pray

Almighty and everlasting God, who hast revealed thy glory to all nations in Christ, watch over the works of thy mercy : that thy church spread over the whole world may persevere with steadfast faith in the confession of thy name. Through the same our Lord.

℞. Amen.

Oremus et pro beatissimo Papa nostro N., ut Deus et Dominus noster, qui elegit eum in ordine episcopatus, salvum atque incolumem custodiat Ecclesiae suae sanctae, ad regendum populum sanctum Dei.

Let us pray also for our most holy Pope N., that our God and Lord, who chose him to the pontifical order, may preserve him safe to his holy Church, that he may govern the holy people of God.

Oremus

Omnipotens, sempiterne Deus, cujus judicio universa fundantur :

Let us pray

Almighty and everlasting God, by whose judgement all things are respice propitius ad preces nostras, et electum nobis Antistitem tua pietate conserva : ut christiana plebs, quae te gubernatur auctore, sub tanto Pontifice, credulitatis suae meritis augeatur. Per Dominum nostrum Jesum Christum.

℞. Amen.

established, mercifully regard our prayers, and in thy clemency preserve to us the chief bishop whom thou hast chosen, that the Christian people, who are governed under authority from thee, may under so great a Pontiff increase in the merits of their faith. Through our Lord.

℞. Amen.

Oremus et pro omnibus Episcopis, Presbyteris, Diaconibus, Subdiaconibus, Acolythis, Exorcistis, Lectoribus, Ostiariis, Confessoribus, Virginibus, Viduis, et omni populo sancto Dei.

Let us pray also for all bishops, priests, deacons, subdeacons, acolytes, exorcists, lectors, porters, confessors, virgins, widows, and for all the holy people of God.

Oremus

Omnipotens sempiterne Deus, cujus Spiritu totum corpus Ecclesiae sanctificatur et regitur : exaudi nos pro universis ordinibus supplicantes : ut gratiae tuae munere, ab omnibus tibi gradibus fideliter serviatur. Per Dominum nostrum Jesum Christum.

℞. Amen.

Let us pray

Almighty and everlasting God, by whose spirit the whole body of the Church is sanctified and governed, graciously hear our supplications for all orders thereof; that, by the gift of thy grace, all in their several degrees may faithfully serve thee. Through our Lord.

℞. Amen.

Oremus et pro Christianissimo imperatore nostro N., ut Deus et Dominus noster subditas illi faciat omnes barbaras nationes, ad nostram perpetuam pacem.

Let us pray for our most Christian emperor N., that God and our Lord may render all barbarous nations subject to him, for our perpetual peace.

Oremus

Omnipotens sempiterne Deus, in cujus manu sunt omnium jura regnorum; respice ad Romanum benignus Imperium; ut gentes quae in sua feritate confidunt, potentiae tuae dextera comprimantur. Per Dominum nostrum Jesum Christum.

℞. Amen.

Let us pray

Almighty and everlasting God, in whose hand are the powers and the rights of all governments; look favourably on the Roman empire; that the nations which trust in their own fierce might may be overcome by the hand of thy power. Through our Lord.

℞. Amen.

Oremus et pro catechumenis nostris : ut Deus et Dominus noster adaperiat aures praecordiorum ipsorum, januamque misericordiae : ut per lavacrum regenerationis, accepta remissione omnium peccatorum, et ipsi inveniantur in Christo Jesu Domino nostro.

Let us pray also for our catechumens, that our God and Lord would open the ears of their hearts and the gate of mercy; that by the laver of regeneration having received the remission of all their sins, they too may abide in Christ Jesus our Lord.

Oremus ·

Omnipotens, sempiterne Deus, qui Ecclesiam tuam nova semper prole foecundas; auge fidem et intellectum catechumenis nostris, ut renati fonte baptismatis, adoptionis tuae filiis aggregentur. Per Dominum nostrum Jesum Christum.
℞. Amen.

Oremus, dilectissimi nobis, Deum Patrem omnipotentem, ut cunctis mundum purget erroribus, morbos auferat, famem depellat, aperiat carceres, vincula dissolvat, peregrinantibus reditum, infirmantibus sanitatem, navigantibus portum salutis indulgeat.

Oremus

Omnipotens, sempiterne Deus, moestorum consolatio, laborantium fortitudo, perveniant ad te preces de quacumque tribulatione clamantium : ut omnes sibi in necessitatibus suis misericordiam tuam gaudeant adfuisse. Per Dominum nostrum Jesum Christum.
℞. Amen.

Oremus et pro haereticis et schismaticis : ut Deus et Dominus noster eruat eos ab erroribus universis : et ad sanctam matrem Ecclesiam Catholicam atque Apostolicam revocare dignetur.

Oremus

Omnipotens, sempiterne Deus, qui salvas omnes et neminem vis perire, respice ad animas diabolica fraude deceptas : ut omni haeretica pravitate deposita, errantium corda resipiscant, et ad veritatis tuae redeant unitatem. Per Dominum nostrum Jesum Christum.
℞. Amen.

Oremus et pro perfidis Judaeis : ut Deus et Dominus noster auferat velamen de cordibus eorum ; ut et ipsi agnoscant Jesum Christum Dominum nostrum.

Almighty and everlasting God, who ever makest the Church fruitful with a new progeny, increase the faith and understanding of our catechumens; that, being born again in the font of baptism, they may be joined to the children of thy adoption. Through our Lord.
℞. Amen.

Let us, dearly beloved, beseech God the Father almighty to purge the world from all errors; to take away diseases; to keep off famine; to open prisons; to loose chains; to grant to travellers return; to the sick health; to mariners a port of safety.

Let us pray

Almighty and everlasting God, the consolation of the sorrowful, the support of the afflicted, may the prayers of those that cry to thee in any tribulation reach thy ears; that all may rejoice that thy mercy helped them in their need. Through our Lord.
℞. Amen.

Let us pray also for heretics and schismatics, that our God and Lord would deliver them from all errors, and vouchsafe to call them back to our holy mother, the Catholic and Apostolic Church.

Let us pray

Almighty and everlasting God, who savest all and wouldst not that any soul should perish, look down upon those souls who are deceived by the deceit of the devil; that, laying aside all the wickedness of heresy, the hearts of those who have gone astray may repent, and return to the unity of thy truth. Through our Lord.
℞. Amen.

Let us pray also for the perfidious Jews, that our God and Lord would remove the veil from their hearts; that they also may acknowledge our Lord Jesus Christ.

Omnipotens, sempiterne Deus, qui etiam Judaicam perfidiam a tua misericordia non repellis; exaudi preces nostras, quas pro illius populi obcaecatione deferimus; ut agnita veritatis tuae luce, quae Christus est, a suis tenebris eruantur. Per eumdem Dominum. Ry. Amen.

Almighty and everlasting God, who drivest from thy mercy not even the perfidious Jews, hear the prayers which we offer for the blindness of that people; that, acknowledging the light of thy truth, which is Christ, they may be delivered from their darkness. Ry. Amen.

Oremus et pro paganis: ut Deus omnipotens auferat iniquitatem a cordibus eorum; ut, relictis idolis suis, convertantur ad Deum vivum et verum, et unicum Filium eius Jesum Christum, Deum et Dominum nostrum.

Let us pray also for the pagans, that God almighty would remove iniquity from their hearts; that, forsaking their idols, they may be converted to the living and true God and his only Son, Jesus Christ, our God and Lord.

Oremus

Let us pray

Omnipotens, sempiterne Deus, qui non mortem peccatorum, sed vitam semper inquiris: suscipe propitius orationem nostram, et libera eos ab idolorum cultura: et aggrega Ecclesiae tuae sanctae, ad laudem et gloriam nominis tui. Per Dominum nostrum Jesum Christum. Ry. Amen.

Almighty and everlasting God, who ever seekest not the death but the life of sinners, mercifully receive our prayer; deliver them from the worship of idols, and join them to thy holy Church to the praise and glory of thy name. Through our Lord. Ry. Amen.

As in ordinary Masses, the Kiss of Peace and the presentation of the oblations on the altar followed immediately after the Litany, so also in to-day's ceremony the offering of the sacred gifts (presanctified) and the Communion should also follow after the Litany. It certainly was so in early times; but the original order of the ceremonies was altered, as was said above, when, towards the ninth century, the Adoration of the Cross began to be postponed until now, although it was in its origin, as we have already seen, a rite having no connection whatever with the Mass.

It cannot be denied, however, that this glorification of the holy cross at the most solemn moment of to-day's function is quite suitable and appropriate, since it is on this day that the triumph of the Redeemer began, when his cross was lifted up and planted on the height of Calvary. It is from this throne of love and of pain that Jesus with outstretched arms draws to himself the whole human race.

The ceremony of the Adoration of the True Cross was first instituted at Jerusalem, and is described in detail by Etheria about the year 385, in her *Peregrinatio*. From there it passed probably to Constantinople and to other cities of the Byzantine Empire, wherever relics of the true cross were

preserved. It was brought to Rome towards the end of the
seventh century by an Eastern Pope, Sergius I (687-701),
who must have introduced the rite as it was then carried out
by his compatriots.

This explains the circumstance that on this day the Pope,
during the procession from the Lateran to the Sessorian
Basilica, swung a censer before the casket containing the
relic of the true cross which was carried by a deacon, a
custom which is not found in any of the Latin liturgies,
whereas it is in common use in those of the Eastern rite, in
which the bishop often acts as thurifer. In like manner the
Greek Trisagion, which is sung to-day during the Adoration
of the Cross, clearly shows its origin from the Byzantine rite.

The ceremony, as time went on, was very much amplified,
additions being made from the Frankish liturgies, through
which channels customs which originally belonged to the
Spanish churches passed in their turn into the Roman ritual.

The rite, which we shall now describe, has as its object the
adoration of the glorious wood of the true cross which St
Helena had generously given to Rome. When, however, the
Roman Liturgy was no longer limited to the city itself, but
had been adopted by the whole Latin Church, since not all
churches and chapels possessed such a relic, a crucifix of
wood, iron or other metal was substituted for the true cross.
The priest, as he uncovered the crucifix, continued to say the
same words as those used by the Pope at Santa Croce in
Gerusalemme—" *Ecce lignum crucis* "—words which appear
very inappropriate when applied to a crucifix of silver or of
some other metal. The fact is that the ceremony was
arranged originally for the veneration at Rome of the relic
of the true cross presented by St Helena, which rite is still
in use, at least in the great patriarchal basilicas of the
Eternal City.

Whilst the priest performs the threefold ceremony of
unveiling the cross before the people, the following antiphon
is sung :

Ant.: " Behold the wood of the cross, on which hung the
Saviour of the world."

℟. " Come, let us adore."

The Adoration of the Cross is carried out by the clergy
after having first removed their shoes, which recalls the
ancient rule by which the Pope and the Cardinals on this day
walked barefooted in the stational procession. During the
adoration the singing of the Trisagion alternates with that
of the *Improperia*. This name is given to a number of
reproaches uttered by God against the Jewish people on
account of their ingratitude for the benefits they had received
from him. The inspiration of these verses is certainly scrip-

tural, but the text seems to be taken from the apocryphal Book of Esdras (i 13-24).

℣. " O my people, what have I done to thee? or in what have I grieved thee? Answer me. ℣. Because I led thee out of the land of Egypt, thou hast prepared a cross for thy Saviour."

Then one choir sings : " O holy God."

Another choir answers : " O holy strong one."

The first and second choir sing : " O holy immortal one, have mercy upon us."

The singing of this Trisagion during the Adoration of the Cross has a profound significance, for the death of Jesus is the perfect act of worship of the Holy Trinity fulfilled by the Pontiff of the New Testament. In truth, the infinite sanctity of God, his omnipotence, his eternal being, received the highest glory from the expiatory sacrifice of Calvary, from the divine Victim slain for the sins of the world. The Monophysite heretics attempted, indeed, to misinterpret the Trinitarian meaning of this Trisagion by craftily adding this invocation, " Thou who wast crucified for us," but this interpretation was condemned as being heretical, for it was not the three divine Persons who were crucified, but the second Person alone in his human nature.

℣. " Because I led thee out through the desert during forty years, and fed thee with manna, and brought thee into a land exceeding good, thou hast prepared a cross for thy Saviour."

The choirs answer in turn : " O holy God," etc.

℣. " What more ought I to have done for thee that I have not done? I planted thee for my fairest vineyard : and thou hast turned exceeding bitter to me; for thou gavest me vinegar to drink in my thirst, and pierced with a lance thy Saviour's side."

The choirs answer in turn : " O holy God," etc.

℣. " For thy sake I scourged Egypt with its first-born : and thou didst scourge me and deliver me up."

℟. " O my people, what have I done to thee?" etc.

℣. " I led thee out of Egypt, drowning Pharao in the Red Sea : and thou didst deliver me to the chief priests."

℟. " O my people, what have I done to thee?" etc.

℣. " I opened the sea before thee : and thou didst open my side with a spear."

℟. " O my people, what have I done to thee?" etc.

℣. " I went before thee in a pillar of cloud : and thou leddest me to the judgement-hall of Pilate."

℟. " O my people, what have I done to thee?" etc.

℣. " I fed thee with manna through the desert : and thou struckedst me with blows and scourges."

℟. " O my people, what have I done to thee?" etc.

℣. "I gave thee to drink the water of salvation from the rock : and thou gavest me gall and vinegar."

℞. "O my people, what have I done to thee?" etc.

℣. "For thy sake I struck down the kings of the Canaanites, and thou struckedst my head with a reed."

℞. "O my people, what have I done to thee?" etc.

℣. "I gave thee a royal sceptre : and thou gavest a crown of thorns to my head."

℞. "O my people, what have I done to thee?" etc.

℣. "I lifted thee up with great power : and thou didst hang me upon the gibbet of the cross."

℞. "O my people, what have I done to thee?" etc.

Before the dishonour of the cross we must not forget the divinity of the sacred Victim. Around the tree of shame thousands of angels stand, crying : "Holy, holy, holy." Let us unite our adoration to theirs and sing even now the hymn of triumph and of a blessed resurrection.

Ant. "We worship thy cross, O Lord, and praise and glorify thy holy resurrection; for behold, by the wood of the cross came joy into the whole world. *Psalm lxvi:* May God have mercy on us, and bless us : may he cause the light of his countenance to shine upon us, and may he have mercy on us."

Then follows the noble hymn composed by Venantius Fortunatus[1] in honour of the holy cross, at the time that Queen Radegonde received from Constantinople as a gift a small piece of the true cross, which she placed in her monastery at Poitiers, dedicated on this account to the holy cross.

Crux fidelis, inter omnes
arbor una nobilis :
nulla silva talem profert,
fronde, flore, germine.
Dulce lignum, dulces clavos,
dulce pondus sustinet.

Faithful Cross, O tree all beauteous,
Tree all peerless and divine !
Not a grove on earth can show us
Such a flower and leaf as thine.
Sweet the nails and sweet the wood
Laden with so sweet a load.

Pange lingua gloriosi
lauream certaminis,
et super crucis trophaeo
dic triumphum nobilem :
qualiter Redemptor orbis
immolatus vicerit.

Crux fidelis, etc.

Sing, my tongue, the Saviour's glory,
Tell his triumph far and wide;
Tell aloud the famous story
Of his body crucified :
How upon the Cross a victim,
Vanquishing in death, he died.
Faithful Cross, etc.

---

[1] *Circa* 530-609. Bishop of Poitiers.—Tr.

℣. De parentis protoplasti
fraude factor condolens,
quando pomi noxialis
in necem morsu ruit :
ipse lignum tunc notavit,
damna ligni ut solveret.
     Dulce lignum, etc.

℣. Hoc opus nostrae salutis
ordo depoposcerat :
multiformis proditoris
ars ut artem falleret :
et medelam ferret inde,
hostis unde laeserat.
     Crux fidelis, etc.

℣. Quando venit ergo sacri
plenitudo temporis,
missus est ab arce Patris
Natus, orbis Conditor :
atque ventre virginali
carne amictus prodiit.

     Dulce lignum, etc.

℣. Vagit infans inter arcta
conditus praesepia :
membra pannis involuta
Virgo mater alligat :
et Dei manus pedesque
stricta cingit fascia.

     Crux fidelis, etc.

℣. Lustra sex qui jam peregit,
tempus implens corporis,
sponte libera Redemptor
passioni deditus,
Agnus in crucis levatur
immolandus stipite.

     Dulce lignum, etc.

℣. Felle potus ecce languet :
spina, clavi, lancea,
mite corpus perforarunt;
unda manat et cruor :
terra, pontus, astra, mundus,
quo lavantur flumine !

     Crux fidelis, etc.

℣. Flecte ramos, arbor alta,
tensa laxa viscera,
et rigor lentescat ille,
quem dedit nativitas :

℣. Eating of the tree forbidden,
Man had sunk in Satan's snare,
When our pitying Creator
Did this second Tree prepare ;
Destined many ages later
That first evil to repair.
     Sweet the nails, etc.

℣. Such the order God appointed
When for sin he would atone ;
To the serpent thus opposing
Schemes yet deeper than his own.
Thence the remedy procuring,
Whence the fatal wound had come.
     Faithful Cross, etc.

℣. So when now at length the
     fulness
Of the sacred time drew nigh,
Then the Son, the world's Creator,
Left his Father's throne on high ;
From a Virgin's womb appearing,
Clothed in our mortality.
     Sweet the nails, etc.

℣. All within a lowly manger,
Lo, a tender babe he lies !
See his gentle Virgin Mother
Lull to sleep his infant cries !
While the limbs of God Incarnate
Round with swathing bands she
     ties.
     Faithful Cross, etc.

℣. Thus did Christ to perfect
     manhood
In our mortal flesh attain :
Then of his free choice he goeth
To a death of bitter pain ;
And a lamb, upon the altar
Of the Cross, for us is slain.
     Sweet the nails, etc.

℣. Lo, with gall his thirst he
     quenches !
See the thorns upon his brow !
Nails his tender flesh are rend-
     ing !
See, his side is opened now !
Whence to cleanse the whole
     creation
Streams of blood and water flow.
     Faithful Cross, etc.

℣. Lofty Tree, bend down thy
     branches,
To embrace thy sacred load ;
Oh, relax the native tension

et superni membra Regis
tende miti stipite.

Dulce lignum, etc.

℣. Sola digna tu fuisti
ferre mundi victimam :
atque portum praeparare
arca mundo naufrago :
quam sacer cruor perunxit,
fusus Agni corpore.

Crux fidelis, etc.

℣. Sempiterna sit beatae
Trinitati gloria :
aequa Patri, Filioque;
par decus Paraclito :
Unius, Trinique nomen
laudet universitas. Amen.

Dulce lignum, etc.

Of that all too rigid wood;
Gently, gently bear the members
Of thy dying King and God.
Sweet the nails, etc.

℣. Tree, which solely wast found
worthy
The world's Victim to sustain;
Harbour from the raging tempest !
Ark, that saved the world again !
Tree, with sacred Blood anointed
Of the Lamb for sinners slain.
Faithful Cross, etc.

℣. Blessing, honour, everlasting,
To the immortal Deity :
To the Father, Son and Spirit,
Equal praises ever be :
Glory through the earth and
heaven
To Trinity in Unity. Amen.
Sweet the nails, etc.

The adoration being ended, the deacon replaces the cross on the altar, and, together with the subdeacon, spreads upon the altar the cloths for the Communion. At this point in the ancient Roman rite the Levites brought to the Pope the casket containing the sacred Host consecrated at the Lateran on the preceding day. But when, in the fifteenth century, the pontifical functions took place, not at Rome nor in the stational basilicas, but in the narrower limits of the papal palace at Avignon, the Pontiffs of that period preferred to go themselves and to carry the Blessed Sacrament processionally from the altar where it had been placed.

As the procession returns, the following hymn, also by Venantius Fortunatus, which, however, has no connection with the eucharistic procession, is sung :

Vexilla regis prodeunt :
Fulget crucis mysterium,
Qua vita mortem pertulit,
Et morte vitam protulit.

Quae vulnerata lanceae
Mucrone diro, criminum
Ut nos lavaret sordibus,
Manavit unda et sanguine.

Impleta sunt, quae concinit
David fideli carmine,

Forth comes the standard of the
King :
All hail, thou Mystery adored !
Hail, Cross, on which the Life
himself
Died, and by death our life
restored !

On which our Saviour's holy side,
Rent open with a cruel spear,
Of blood and water poured a
stream
To wash us from defilement clear.

O sacred wood, in thee fulfilled
Was holy David's truthful lay,

Dicendo nationibus :
Regnavit a ligno Deus.

Which told the world that from a tree
The Lord should all the nations sway.

Arbor decora et fulgida,
Ornata regis purpura,
Electa digno stipite
Tam sancta membra tangere.

Most royally empurpled o'er,
How beauteously thy stem doth shine !
How glorious was its lot to touch
Those limbs so holy and divine !

Beata, cujus brachiis
Pretium pependit saeculi,
Statera facta corporis,
Tulitque praedam tartari.

Thrice blest, upon whose arms outstretched
The Saviour of the world reclined ;
Balance sublime, upon whose beam
Was weighed the ransom of mankind.

O crux ave, spes unica,
Hoc passionis tempore
Piis adauge gratiam,
Reisque dele crimina.

Hail cross ! thou only hope of man,
Hail on this holy Passion day !
To saints increase the grace they have ;
From sinners purge their guilt away.

Te, fons salutis, Trinitas,
Collaudet omnis spiritus :
Quibus crucis victoriam
Largiris, adde praemium.
Amen.

Salvation's spring, blest Trinity,
Be praise to thee through earth and skies :
Thou through the Cross the victory
Dost give ; oh, also give the prize.
Amen.

The Blessed Sacrament having been placed on the altar, there followed, in accordance with the *Ordines Romani,* the *Pater Noster* and the Holy Communion ; later, for greater reverence, other prayers were added, which gave this rite of the presanctified the appearance of a Mass. The priest, in fact, pours wine and water into the chalice which he places on the corporal, then, incensing the oblations, he says : " Let this incense which thou hast blessed rise up before thee, O Lord ; and let thy mercy come down upon us."

The incense is a symbol of the prayer and worship that we offer to God. Hence St John sees, in the Apocalypse, an angel near the altar in the temple, holding up before God a smoking thurible. He explains that the incense is the perfume of the meritorious deeds of the saints ; while the angels fulfil in heaven the office of mediators between God and ourselves : they tell him of our necessities and of our prayers, and bring down to us the mercies of God Almighty.

As the priest incenses the altar according to the usual rite, he says : " Let my prayer, O Lord, be set forth as incense in thy sight; the lifting up of my hands as the evening sacrifice. Set a watch, O Lord, before my mouth, and a door round about my lips; that my heart may not incline to evil words, to seek excuses in sin.''

In place of the ancient evening sacrifice of incense, of which Psalm cxl here speaks, the New Testament has substituted that of the cross on which Jesus with outstretched arms offers himself for us to the Father.

Giving the censer to the deacon, the priest says: '' May the Lord enkindle within us the fire of his love, and the flame of everlasting charity. Amen.

'' May we be received by thee, O Lord, in the spirit of humility and in a contrite mind; and so may our sacrifice be made in thy sight this day, that it may be pleasing to thee, O Lord God.''

To-day, as a sign of mourning, the offering of the eucharistic sacrifice is omitted. Instead we offer to God the merit of the bloody sacrifice of Calvary, with which we associate ourselves through humiliation and contrition of heart. Turning towards the people, he says: '' Brethren, pray that my sacrifice and yours may be acceptable to God the Father almighty.''

The entire anaphora of the consecration is omitted, the priest passing at once to the Lord's Prayer, which in the earliest times was the immediate preparation for Holy Communion. In the Roman Liturgy all consecratory anaphoras and the Lord's Prayer are preceded as a sign of respect by a brief formula or preface of preparation: '' Taught by the precepts of salvation and following the divine commandment, we make bold to say: Our Father who art in heaven,'' etc. Ry. '' But deliver us from evil.'' *Priest.* '' Amen.''

'' Deliver us, we beseech thee, O Lord, from all evils, past, present and to come: and by the intercession of the blessed and glorious Mary ever virgin, mother of God, with thy blessed apostles Peter and Paul, and Andrew, and all the saints, grant in thy mercy peace in our days; that assisted by the help of thy mercy, we may both be ever free from sin and secure from all disturbance. Through the same Lord Jesus Christ, etc.''

The celebrant, before the *fractio panis,* raises up in the sight of the people the paten with the sacred Host, so that they may gaze upon and adore the divine sacrament. He then breaks the Host over the chalice into three parts, the last of which he puts into the chalice to sanctify the wine and the water, which on this day are not consecrated, but merely represent the blood and the water which flowed from the pierced side of Jesus.

Before receiving the Host the priest recites the following

prayer : " Let not the partaking of thy body, O Lord Jesus Christ, which I, though unworthy, presume to receive, bring to me judgement and condemnation; but of thy mercy let it avail to the salvation of my soul and body, and as a saving remedy : who livest, etc.

" I will take the bread of heaven and will call on the name of the Lord.

" Lord, I am not worthy that thou shouldst enter under my roof; say but the word, and my soul shall be healed. (*Three times.*)

" May the body of our Lord Jesus Christ preserve my soul to life everlasting.   Amen."

According to the most ancient of the *Ordines Romani,* the people, too, received Communion on this day.   The participation in the divine mysteries on Good Friday had a special significance, as St Paul points out.   As the assistants, by partaking of the flesh of the victim, identified themselves with the sacrifice, so we, too, by partaking of the Communion, share in the merits of the death of our Lord.

After the Communion the priest says : " What we have taken with our mouth, O Lord, may we receive with a clean mind, and from a temporal gift may it become to us an everlasting remedy."

The Mass of the Presanctified being ended, the cloths and candlesticks are removed from the altar, as used to be done originally each time that Mass was finished.

In the Middle Ages the Pope, besides the usual *cursus* of the Office—which in the three last days of Holy Week still preserves unaltered the primitive type of the Roman Office, without the *Deus in adjutorium,* without the hymns, and without any responsorial doxology—recited in private on this day the entire Psalter.   This custom was followed by many of the laity, and is still observed in some of the religious orders.   The *Ordines Romani* prescribe that cooked food should not be served to-day in the papal palace, but only bread, herbs and water.

Jesus died for me.   He loved me with so great a love that he sacrificed his life for me, and, that I should not forget his love, he instituted the eucharistic sacrifice, which, commemorating that of Calvary, applies all its merits to my soul. For this reason the Church celebrates daily the death of Christ, because, as Eve came forth from the side of Adam as he slept, so the Church came forth to-day from the adorable Heart of Jesus on the cross.

This is the hidden mystery of to-day's liturgy.   Christ dies, and the Church is born.   He expires, stripped and bleeding, that the Church may be clothed in the robe of immortality and filled with the joy of eternal youth. In order that we may correspond with this excess of love—as the Gospel calls it—on the part of Jesus, we must strive to increase our devotion to the holy sacrifice and to the crucified Saviour, the sight of whose face should ever fill us with tender love and heartfelt gratitude. St Gertrude tells us that, whenever we ask our heavenly Father to look upon the face of Jesus on the cross, he is moved with pity towards us sinners and his anger is turned away from us.

We take the following antiphon from the Byzantine Liturgy :

Vitale Cor tuum, tamquam fons ex Eden scaturiens, Ecclesiam tuam, Christe, tamquam rationalem ortum adaquat : inde, tamquam ex praecipuo fonte se dividens in quatuor Evangelia : mundum irrigans, creaturam laetificans, gentesque fideliter docens venerari regnum tuum.

Thy life-giving heart, O Christ, as another fountain springing forth from Eden, waters thy Church like a spiritual garden. From this fountain-head the stream divides into four Gospels, irrigating the earth, filling all creatures with joy, and teaching the nations to adore thy power.

HOLY SATURDAY

Collecta at the Lateran for the Catechumens.

In olden days the paschal fast was very strict, extending from the evening of Good Friday until the dawn of Easter Sunday. In Rome not even children were dispensed from this fast. For this reason Mass was not celebrated on this day, as the whole Church was watching in devout expectation until the night should come in which the mystery of Christ's resurrection should be celebrated.

Early in the morning of Holy Saturday at the Lateran the archdeacon, having melted some wax, mixed it with chrism, blessed it and poured it into various small oval moulds, on which was impressed the figure of the mystical Lamb of God. These *Agnus Dei* were afterwards distributed to the faithful at the Mass on Saturday *in Albis,* as tokens and mementos of the paschal solemnity.

Out of Rome, in places where there still survived the ancient rite of the evening *Lucernarium* and of the blessing of the paschal candle, the wax from which the *Agnus Dei* were formed was that which remained over from the making of the great candle destined to light up the ambo on the night of Easter. As Rome, however, only consented later on to adopt this rite of the paschal *Lucernarium,* in order to conform to the custom which had been steadily spreading since the fifth century, of distributing the waxen *Agnus Dei* to the people, the making of them was entrusted to the archdeacon. We should note that in Rome these papal tokens had no connection at all with the paschal candle, as they had in other churches.

In the late Middle Ages the significance and advantages of these *Agnus Dei* are described in the following Leonine verses :

Balsamus et munda cera cum chrismatis unda
Conficiunt Agnum, quod munus do tibi magnum,
Fonte velut natum, per mystica sanctificatum,
Fulgura desursum pellit et omne malignum.
Peccatum frangit, ut Christi sanguis et angit.

Pregnans servatur, simul et partus liberatur.
Munera fert dignis, virtutem destruit ignis.
Portatus munde, de fluctibus eripit undae.
Morte repentina servat, Satanaeque ruina.
Si quis honorat eum retinet super hostem trophaeum.
Parsque minor tantum, tota valet integra quantum.

Agnus Dei, miserere mei.
Qui crimina tollis, miserere nobis.

Of balm and purest wax mixed with chrism
The precious Lamb is made, which now I give to you,
As though born at the font and blessed by secret prayer,
It shields you from the thunderbolt and from every harm.
It breaks the bonds of sin, and wars against the power of evil as does the Blood of Christ.
The woman in childbirth is preserved and safely delivered.
It gives grace to those who are worthy, and quenches flame.
Worn with devotion it saves from the dangers of the deep.
It preserves from sudden death and from Satan's snare.
He who holds it in honour shall triumph over the enemy.
And a small fragment of the *Agnus Dei* will have as much efficacy as the whole.
Lamb of God, have pity on me.
Thou who takest away the sins of the world, have mercy upon us.

For some centuries now the blessing of the *Agnus Dei* has been reserved to the Popes, by whom it is solemnly conferred at the beginning and in every successive fifth year of their Pontificate.

According to the *Ordines Romani,* at the hour of Terce on Holy Saturday the catechumens assembled once more at the Lateran in the Basilica of the Saviour, the men standing in a line on the right-hand side and the women on the left. The priest began by tracing the sign of the cross on their foreheads, then, laying his hands on the head of each, he recited the exorcism, *Nec te lateat, Satana,* which still forms part of the baptismal ritual for adults. After commanding Satan to depart and give place to the Holy Ghost, the priest, in memory of the Saviour whose *ephpheta* healed the blind, the deaf and the dumb, touched the ears and the nostrils of the catechumens with saliva, saying in turn to each one : " Be thou opened to the grace of the Holy Ghost, and do thou, O evil spirit, flee away; for the judgement of God is at hand."

The baptism of an adult in early days, when society was for the most part corrupt and idolatrous, implied a very real and determined conversion to God, and was usually the result of a fierce fight between the soul and the devil. The former struggled to free itself from the slavery to which Satan had reduced it, while the latter employed every temptation arising from the attractions of vice and the strength of the passions so as to prevent his prey from escaping. The moment in which the catechumen went down into the baptismal font was the decisive point of the fight, and, in imitation of the athletes of the stadium, who anointed themselves with oil before the contest, the Church also anointed her heroes with the blessed oil of the catechumens in order to prepare them for the struggle.

The solemn hour had now come. In reply to the question of the Pontiff, "Dost thou renounce Satan?" each of the candidates, with his forefinger pointing towards the West, the region of sunset, of shadows, and nocturnal darkness, said: "I renounce thee, O Satan, with all thy pomps and with all thy works." Then, turning to the East, the neophyte uttered the sacred formula of his consecration: "To thee do I dedicate myself, O Light uncreated."

After the priest had again laid his hand on the catechumens and pronounced another exorcism, there followed the solemn ceremony of the *redditio symboli,* in which the candidates made their profession of the Christian faith according to the form previously explained to them by the Pope at the station in *apertitione aurium* at St Paul on the Wednesday before Passion Sunday.[1]

The *Ordines Romani,* which describe the rites of the Christian Initiation as used in the eighth century, simplify this part of the ceremony very much. According to these the priest alone recited the Creed—which first took its place in the Liturgy as a baptismal formula of Catholic belief—whilst he was laying his hands on the catechumens. But St Augustine, in his *Confessions,* narrating the conversion of Victorinus the rhetorician, tells us that it was customary in Rome for the catechumens themselves standing in the ambo to recite, each in turn, the symbol in the presence of the faithful, thus declaring publicly their own personal belief.

When the time came for Victorinus to do this, continues the saint, the priests, out of consideration for his great fame, offered to receive his profession of faith in private, in order to spare him the publicity which it would otherwise entail.

---

[1] Wednesday " in Mediana."—Tr.

He refused the offer, saying that, as he had not feared formerly to conduct a school of rhetoric in public, so he would not now spare himself from declaring before the whole people his belief in the truths of Christianity. With these words he went up into the ambo, while a general cry of astonishment and joy repeating " Victorinus ! Victorinus !" greeted his appearance. Erect in the pulpit he recited his *Credo* amidst the emotion of the assembly, for, coming from his lips, that Creed was of a special significance, since it marked one more victory gained by the foolishness of the cross over the proud arrogance of the wisdom of the world !¹ It was a new *Apologia* for Christianity, a signal triumph of the Faith.

After a final prayer the catechumens were dismissed. *Catechumeni recedant; Filii charissimi revertimini in locis vestris, expectantes horam qua possit circa vos Dei gratia baptismum operari.*

As Christ rested in the grave during the whole of the Sabbath day, so the faithful were wont to wait in prayer and fasting until the evening star arose in the heavens, when they proceeded to the baptistery of the Apostles on the Via Salaria, or to the Vatican, where originally baptism was administered.

In the earlier *Ordines* no mention is made of any divine Office on Holy Saturday. Besides the prudence necessitated by the long fast and the coming strain of the night vigil, private prayer seemed better suited to the hours of waiting commemorative of the time during which the body of Christ lay in the tomb. The Psalter itself is the best interpreter of this mystery, for many of the psalms tell us of the feelings of Jesus, who calls upon his Father to bring him out of the darkness of the grave to the glory of his resurrection.

On the evening of the Parasceve the great Artificer—who by the mouth of Jeremias had called upon Israel to judge his work and the recompense it had received—he whose labour of redemption had been bought with the price of thirty pieces of silver—he had at last laid himself down to rest, and the disciples, bearing his body to the sepulchre, had sung, in accordance with the Jewish rite, the beautiful psalm *Qui habitat in adjutorio Altissimi,* with the prophetic words: " *In pace in idipsum dormiam et requiescam.*"

The sacrifice and the humiliation were still to be complete, so whilst the soul of Jesus announced the fulfilment of the redemption to the just in Limbo, his body, like a grain of wheat buried in the ground, had also to suffer the abasement of the tomb, so that none should be able to doubt the reality of his death, nor subsequently that of his resurrection. In-

¹ *Confess.,* Book VII, 2.

deed, that no doubt whatsoever should remain, all his friends depart from the sepulchre, and the wisdom of God chooses the Jews themselves to be official witnesses to the miracle about to be accomplished within it. The Sanhedrim affix their own seals and place their own guards, that no one may dare to tamper in any way with the tomb.

But at the dawn of the third day Christ rises triumphant over death; the Apostles proclaimed, and the Church for more than nineteen centuries has declared, that the Lord still lives, and the nations which have believed have become partakers of his resurrection by reason of their faith. And what of the people of Israel? Whilst the entire human race, in a pasch which knows no end, celebrates its triumph over death and hell, the synagogue still stands on guard before the door of the sepulchre, ready to draw its sword should Christ dare to break the seals of the Sanhedrim and to come forth in freedom from the tomb.

The space of time during which our Lord lay in the grave represents that of our present life, which is a period of expectation of our future perfect resurrection. We begin even here to " rise again " to grace, and for this reason we say on this night, as we celebrate the paschal solemnity : *Pascha nostrum immolatus est*—our pasch is immolated, not the pasch of Christ. But the festival is not yet complete : there still remain many things in us which sleep in the sepulchre of a corrupt nature, or are wrapped in the darkness of ignorance.

Faith indeed sustains us, and Hope assures us that one day all these miseries of our mortal nature will cease; but in the meantime we must be content to spend our mystical Holy Saturday in watching and waiting. This partial resurrection of the soul is granted to us as a foretaste of what is to come, just as our present ritual anticipates the celebration of the resurrection of Christ on the last day of Lent. This, as we know, is merely a concession to our weakness. We are still in Passiontide, and our Lent is not yet at an end. The true and perfect Easter will indeed come, and when it comes it will exceed all our conceptions. And when shall this be? When Christ shall cease to offer daily by the hands of his priests the eucharistic mysteries which commemorate his death and shall establish in heaven a new liturgy, the Liturgy of the universal and unending Easter.

APPENDIX

FOR the convenience of the faithful at Rome, who visit the stational churches in Lent in order to gain the indulgences, we add some prayers taken from the ancient Liturgy.

THE LITANY OF THE STATIONAL PROCESSION

THE INDULGENCES

In order to excite the devotion of the faithful towards the pious practice of visiting the stational basilicas in Rome on the days marked in the Missal, the Popes granted during the later Middle Ages certain indulgences, which were confirmed by Pius VI, and promulgated by a rescript of the Sacred Congregation of Indulgences on July 9, 1777 (Rescr. Auth. I, 313). They are as follows:

Plenary Indulgences.—On Christmas Day, Maundy Thursday, Easter and the Ascension.

Partial Indulgences.—(a) Thirty years and thirty quarantines on the Feasts of St Stephen, St John the Evangelist, the Holy Innocents, the Circumcision, the Epiphany; on the Sundays of Septuagesima, Sexagesima and Quinquagesima; on Good Friday and Holy Saturday; from Easter Sunday until Low Sunday; on the Feast of St Mark; on the three Rogation Days; on Whit Sunday; and during the Octave until the Saturday (inclusive).

(b) Fifteen years and fifteen quarantines on Palm Sunday.

(c) Ten years and ten quarantines on the First, Second and Fourth Sundays of Advent; on every day in Lent except those mentioned above; on the vigil of Whit Sunday; on the Ember Days except those in the Octave of Whit Sunday already noted.[1]

The Popes have granted to the Cardinals, to some Prelates and religious Orders, Communities and Congregations, the privilege of being able to gain the stational indulgences by visiting their own churches or chapels.

The manner and conditions of these visits vary, and are given in the respective rescripts.

The conditions usually required for gaining the stational

[1] *Cf.* Fr. Beringer, S.J., *Die Ablässe*, pp. 413-15, Paderborn 1895.

indulgences are Confession and Communion for the plenary, a state of grace or contrition for the partial, and, further, a visit to the stational church on the day named in the Roman Missal, together with a prayer for the intentions of the holy Father, for the exaltation of the Church, and for peace and concord among Christian nations. Occasionally, by Apostolic concession, some churches in the vicinity of the stational basilica partake of the privileges of the station, but it is not necessary for the faithful to visit all these churches where the station is celebrated; it is sufficient that they visit one, as long as they fulfil the other conditions prescribed.

Leo XII, in a *Motu Proprio* of February 20, 1827, granted *in perpetuo* to the faithful in Rome, each time that they should visit during Lent, with a contrite heart, the stational church named in the Missal, an indulgence of forty years and forty quarantines applicable to the souls in Purgatory; and to those who should pay such visits on three separate days he granted, on any day of their choice, when, having confessed and received Holy Communion, they should visit a public church, a plenary indulgence also applicable to the souls in Purgatory.

The same Pope also prescribed the manner in which confraternities and pious persons should make these stational visits. They had first of all to go to a public church, where prayers were recited before the Blessed Sacrament. From there they moved towards the stational basilica, repeating as they went along the *Miserere*, with five *Paters, Aves*, and *Glorias*, and also some other act of devotion in honour of the Saviour's Passion. Having reached the stational church the Litany of the Saints was recited with the verses and collects prescribed.

The whole of this rite, reminiscent of the ancient Roman stational processions, was described in a pamphlet specially published by the Vatican Press, and was for many years regularly carried out by the faithful at Rome. In time, however, the altered condition of things rendered processions through the public streets unsuitable, so, first, the station was celebrated inside the titular church with the same ritual and prayers as before. Later, by an indult of Leo XIII, the prayers were modified in accordance with the more distinctly liturgical character of the stational procession of to-day, instead of being left as it had been previously to the private devotion of the Confraternities.

When the procession started from the church where the *collecta* was held, to go to the church appointed for the station, the Litany of the Saints was sung:

ANTIPHONA	ANTIPHON
Sancta Maria et omnes sancti tui, quaesumus Domine, nos ubique adjuvent, ut dum eorum merita recolimus, patrocinia sentiamus, et pacem tuam nostris concede temporibus, et ab Ecclesia tua cunctam repelle nequitiam.	We beseech thee, O Lord, that holy Mary and all thy saints may everywhere aid us, that while we proclaim their merits we may perceive their protection: and do thou grant peace in our days, and ward off all evil from thy Church.

Kyrie eleison.	Lord have mercy on us.
Christe eleison.	Christ have mercy on us.
Kyrie eleison.	Lord have mercy on us.
Christe, audi nos.	Christ hear us.
Christe, exaudi nos.	Christ graciously hear us.
Pater de coelis Deus, *miserere nobis.*	God the Father of heaven, *have mercy on us.*
Fili Redemptor mundi Deus, *miserere nobis.*	God the Son, Redeemer of the world, *have mercy on us.*
Spiritus Sancte Deus, *miserere nobis.*	God the Holy Ghost, *have mercy on us.*
Sancta Trinitas, unus Deus, *miserere nobis.*	Holy Trinity, one God, *have mercy on us.*

Sancta Maria,	*ora pro nobis*	Holy Mary,	*pray for us*
Sancta Dei genitrix,	*ora*	Holy Mother of God,	*pray*
Sancta Virgo virginum,	*ora*	Holy Virgin of virgins,	*pray*
Sancte Michael,	*ora*	St Michael,	*pray*
Sancte Gabriel,	*ora*	St Gabriel,	*pray*
Sancte Raphael,	*ora*	St Raphael,	*pray*
Omnes sancti angeli et archangeli, *orate pro nobis*		All ye holy angels and archangels, *pray*	
Omnes sancti beatorum spirituum ordines, *orate*		All ye holy orders of blessed spirits, *pray*	
Sancte Joannes Baptista,	*ora*	St John the Baptist,	*pray*
Sancte Joseph,	*ora*	St Joseph,	*pray*
Omnes sancti patriarchae et prophetae, *orate*		All ye holy patriarchs and prophets, *pray*	
Sancte Petre,	*ora*	St Peter,	*pray*
Sancte Paule,	*ora*	St Paul,	*pray*
Sancte Andrea,	*ora*	St Andrew,	*pray*
Sancte Jacobe,	*ora*	St James,	*pray*
Sancte Joannes,	*ora*	St John,	*pray*
Sancte Thoma.	*ora*	St Thomas,	*pray*
Sancte Jacobe,	*ora*	St James,	*pray*
Sancte Philippe,	*ora*	St Philip,	*pray*
Sancte Bartholomaee,	*ora*	St Bartholomew,	*pray*
Sancte Matthaee,	*ora*	St Matthew,	*pray*
Sancte Simon,	*ora*	St Simon,	*pray*
Sancte Thaddaee,	*ora*	St Thaddeus,	*pray*
Sancte Matthia,	*ora*	St Matthias,	*pray*
Sancte Barnaba,	*ora*	St Barnabas,	*pray*
Sancte Luca,	*ora*	St Luke,	*pray*
Sancte Marce,	*ora*	St Mark,	*pray*
Omnes sancti Apostoli et Evangelistae, *orate pro nobis*		All ye holy apostles and evangelists, *pray for us*	
Omnes sancti Discipuli Domini, *orate*		All ye holy disciples of our Lord, *pray*	
Omnes sancti Innocentes, *orate*		All ye holy Innocents, *pray*	

Sancte Stephane,	*ora pro nobis*	St Stephen,	*pray for us*
Sancte Laurenti,	*ora*	St Lawrence,	*pray*
Sancte Vincenti,	*ora*	St Vincent,	*pray*
Sancti Fabiane et Sebastiane,	*orate*	SS Fabian and Sebastian,	*pray*
Sancti Joannes et Paule,	*orate*	SS John and Paul,	*pray*
Sancti Cosma et Damiane,	*orate*	SS Cosmas and Damian,	*pray*
Sancti Gervasi et Protasi,	*orate*	SS Gervase and Protase,	*pray*
Omnes sancti Martyres,	*orate*	All ye holy Martyrs,	*pray*
Sancte Silvester,	*ora*	St Sylvester,	*pray*
Sancte Gregori,	*ora*	St Gregory,	*pray*
Sancte Ambrosi,	*ora*	St Ambrose,	*pray*
Sancte Augustine,	*ora*	St Augustine,	*pray*
Sancte Hieronyme,	*ora*	St Jerome,	*pray*
Sancte Martine,	*ora*	St Martin,	*pray*
Sancte Nicolaë,	*ora*	St Nicholas,	*pray*
Omnes sancti Pontifices et Confessores,	*orate*	All ye holy bishops and confessors,	*pray*
Omnes sancti Doctores,	*orate*	All ye holy doctors,	*pray*
Sancte Antoni,	*ora*	St Antony,	*pray*
Sancte Benedicte,	*ora*	St Benedict,	*pray*
Sancte Bernarde,	*ora*	St Bernard,	*pray*
Sancte Dominice,	*ora*	St Dominic,	*pray*
Sancte Francisce,	*ora*	St Francis,	*pray*
Omnes sancti sacerdotes et Levitae,	*orate*	All ye holy priests and Levites,	*pray*
Omnes sancti monachi et eremitae,	*orate*	All ye holy monks and hermits,	*pray*
Sancta Maria Magdalena,	*ora*	St Mary Magdalen,	*pray*
Sancta Agatha,	*ora*	St Agatha,	*pray*
Sancta Lucia,	*ora*	St Lucy,	*pray*
Sancta Agnes,	*ora*	St Agnes,	*pray*
Sancta Caecilia,	*ora*	St Cecily,	*pray*
Sancta Catharina,	*ora*	St Catherine,	*pray*
Sancta Anastasia,	*ora*	St Anastasia,	*pray*
Omnes sanctae virgines et viduae,	*orate*	All ye holy virgins and widows,	*pray*
Omnes sancti et sanctae Dei, *intercedite pro nobis.*		All ye holy men and women, saints of God, *make intercession for us*	
Propitius esto, *parce nobis Domine*		Be merciful, *spare us, O Lord*	
Propitius esto, *exaudi nos Domine*		Be merciful, *graciously hear us, O Lord*	
Ab omni malo, *libera nos Domine*		From all evil, *deliver us, O Lord*	
Ab omni peccato,	*libera*	From all sin,	*deliver*
Ab ira tua,	*libera*	From thy wrath,	*deliver*
A subitanea et improvisa morte,	*libera*	From sudden and unprovided death,	*deliver*
Ab insidiis diaboli,	*libera*	From the snares of the devil,	*deliver*
Ab ira, et odio, et omni mala voluntate,	*libera*	From anger, hatred, and all ill-will,	*deliver*
A spiritu fornicationis,	*libera*	From the spirit of fornication,	*deliver*
A fulgure et tempestate,	*libera*	From lightning and tempest,	*deliver*
A flagello terraemotus,	*libera*	From the scourge of earthquake,	*deliver*
A peste, fame, et bello,	*libera*	From plague, famine, and war,	*deliver*
A morte perpetua,	*libera*	From everlasting death.	*deliver*

Per mysterium sanctae incarnationis tuae, *libera nos Domine* — Through the mystery of thy holy incarnation, *deliver us, O Lord*

Per adventum tuum, *libera* — Through thy coming, *deliver*

Per nativitatem tuum, *libera* — Through thy nativity, *deliver*

Per baptismum et sanctum jejunium tuum, *libera* — Through thy baptism and holy fasting, *deliver*

Per crucem et passionem tuam, *libera* — Through thy cross and passion, *deliver*

Per mortem et sepulturam tuam, *libera* — Through thy death and burial, *deliver*

Per sanctam resurrectionem tuam, *libera* — Through thy holy resurrection, *deliver*

Per admirabilem ascensionem tuam, *libera* — Through thine admirable ascension, *deliver*

Per adventum Spiritus Sancti Paracliti, *libera* — Through the coming of the Holy Ghost the comforter, *deliver*

In die judicii, *libera* — In the day of judgement, *deliver*

Peccatores, *te rogamus audi nos.* — We sinners, *beseech thee to hear us*

Ut nobis parcas, *te rogamus* — That thou wouldst spare us, *we beseech*

Ut nobis indulgeas, *te rogamus* — That thou wouldst pardon us, *we beseech*

Ut ad veram poenitentiam nos perducere digneris, *te rogamus* — That thou wouldst bring us to true penance, *we beseech*

Ut ecclesiam tuam sanctam regere et conservare digneris, *te rogamus* — That thou wouldst vouchsafe to govern and preserve thy holy Church, *we beseech*

Ut domnum apostolicum et omnes ecclesiasticos ordines in sancta religione conservare digneris, *te rogamus* — That thou wouldst vouchsafe to preserve our apostolic prelate, and all orders of the Church in holy religion, *we beseech*

Ut inimicos sanctae ecclesiae humiliare digneris, *te rogamus* — That thou wouldst vouchsafe to humble the enemies of holy Church, *we beseech*

Ut regibus et principibus christianis pacem et veram concordiam donare digneris, *te rogamus* — That thou wouldst vouchsafe to give peace and true concord to Christian kings and princes, *we beseech*

Ut cuncto populo christiano pacem et unitatem largiri digneris, *te rogamus* — That thou wouldst vouchsafe to grant peace and unity to all Christian people, *we beseech*

Ut nosmetipsos in tuo sancto servitio confortare et conservare digneris, *te rogamus* — That thou wouldst vouchsafe to confirm and preserve us in thy holy service, *we beseech*

Ut mentes nostras ad coelestia desideria erigas, *te rogamus* — That thou wouldst lift up our minds to heavenly desires, *we beseech*

Ut omnibus benefactoribus nostris sempiterna bona retribuas, *te rogamus* — That thou wouldst render eternal blessings to all our benefactors, *we beseech*

Ut animas nostras, fratrum, propinquorum, et benefactorum nostrorum ab aeterna damnatione eripias, *te rogamus* — That thou wouldst deliver our souls, and the souls of our brethren, relations and benefactors from eternal damnation, *we beseech*

Ut fructus terrae dare et conservare digneris, *te rogamus* — That thou wouldst vouchsafe to give and preserve the fruits of the earth, *we beseech*

Ut omnibus fidelibus defunctis — That thou wouldst vouchsafe to

requiem aeternam donare digneris,   *te rogamus audi nos*

grant eternal rest to all the
faithful departed,
            we beseech thee to hear us

Ut nos exaudire digneris,
                   te rogamus
Fili Dei,   *te rogamus*
Agnus Dei, qui tollis peccata
mundi,   *parce nobis Domine*

That thou wouldst vouchsafe graciously to hear us, *we beseech*
Son of God,   *we beseech*
Lamb of God, who takest away
the sins of the world,
                spare us, O Lord

Agnus Dei, qui tollis peccata
mundi,   *exaudi nos Domine*

Lamb of God, who takest away the
sins of the world,
        graciously hear us, O Lord

Agnus Dei, qui tollis peccata
mundi,   *miserere nobis*

Lamb of God, who takest away the
sins of the world,
                have mercy on us

Christe audi nos.
Christe exaudi nos
Kyrie eleison
Christe eleison
Kyrie eleison
Pater noster,   *secreto, usque ad*
℣. Et ne nos inducas in tentation-
em.
℟. Sed libera nos a malo.

Christ hear us,
Christ graciously hear us
Lord have mercy on us
Christ have mercy on us
Lord have mercy on us
Our Father,   *silently, as far as*
℣. And lead us not into tempta-
tion,
℟. But deliver us from evil.

PSALM L
Miserere

Miserere mei, Deus : secundum
magnam misericordiam tuam.
Et secundum multitudinem misera-
tionum tuarum : dele iniquitatem meam
Amplius lava me ab iniquitate
mea : et a peccato meo munda
me.
Quoniam, iniquitatem meam ego
cognosco : et peccatum meum
contra me est semper.
Tibi soli peccavi, et malum coram
te feci : ut justificeris in ser-
monibus tuis, et vincas cum
judicaris.

Ecce enim in iniquitatibus con-
ceptus sum : et in peccatis con-
cepit me mater mea.
Ecce enim veritatem dilexisti :
incerta et occulta sapientiae
tuae manifestasti mihi.

Asperges me hyssopo, et munda-
bor : lavabis me, et super nivem
dealbabor.

Auditui meo dabis gaudium et
laetitiam : et exultabunt ossa
humiliata.

Have mercy upon me, O God :
according to thy great mercy.
And according to the multitude of
thy tender mercies : blot out my
iniquities.
Wash me yet more from my iniquity : and cleanse me from my
sin.
For I acknowledge my iniquity :
and my sin is always before me.

Against thee only have I sinned,
and done evil in thy sight : that
thou mayest be justified in thy
words, and mayest overcome
when thou art judged.
For behold I was conceived in
iniquities : and in sins did my
mother conceive me.
For behold thou hast loved truth :
the uncertain and hidden things
of thy wisdom thou has made
manifest unto me.
Thou shalt sprinkle me with
hyssop, and I shall be cleansed :
thou shalt wash me and I shall
be made whiter than snow.
Thou shalt make me hear of joy
and gladness : and the bones
that were humbled shall rejoice.

Averte faciem tuam a peccatis meis : et omnis.iniquitates meas dele.

Cor mundum crea in me, Deus : et spiritum rectum innova in visceribus meis.

Ne projicias me a facie tua : et spiritum sanctum tuum ne auferas a me.

Redde mihi laetitiam salutaris tui : et spiritu principali confirma me.

Docebo iniquos vias tuas : et impii ad te convertentur.

Libera me de sanguinibus, Deus, Deus salutis meae : et exsultabit lingua mea justitiam tuam.

Domine, labia mea aperies : et os meum annuntiabit laudem tuam.

Quoniam si voluisses sacrificium dedissem utique : holocaustis non delectaberis.

Sacrificium Deo spiritus contribulatus : cor contritum et humiliatum, Deus, non despicies.

Benigne fac, Domine, in bona voluntate tua Sion : ut aedificentur muri Jerusalem.

Tunc acceptabis sacrificium justitiae, oblationes, et holocausta : tunc imponent super altare tuum vitulos.

Gloria, etc.

℣. Exaudi, Domine, supplicum preces.
℟. Et confitentium tibi parce peccatis.
℣. Respice, Domine, ad humilitatem nostram.
℟. Et non deseras nos in tempore tribulationis.
℣. Gregem tuum, Pastor aeterne, non deseras.
℟. Sed per beatos Apostolos tuos perpetua defensione custodias.

℣. Ostende nobis, Domine, misericordiam tuam.
℟. Et salutare tuum da nobis.
℣. Oremus pro Pontifice nostro N.
℟. Dominus conservet eum, et

Turn away thy face from my sins : and blot out all my iniquities.

Create in me a clean heart, O God : and renew a right spirit within my bowels.

Cast me not away from thy presence : and take not thy holy Spirit from me.

Restore unto me the joy of thy salvation : and strengthen me with a perfect spirit.

I will teach the unjust thy ways : and the wicked shall be converted unto thee.

Deliver me from blood, O God, thou God of my salvation : and my tongue shall extol thy justice.

Thou shalt open my lips, O Lord, and my mouth shall declare thy praise.

For if thou hadst desired sacrifice, I would surely have given it : with burnt-offerings thou wilt not be delighted.

The sacrifice to God is an afflicted spirit : a contrite and humble heart, O God, thou wilt not despise.

Deal favourably, O Lord, in thy good will with Sion : that the walls of Jerusalem may be built up.

Then shalt thou accept the sacrifice of justice, oblations, and whole-burnt offerings : then shall they lay calves upon thine altars.

Glory, etc.

℣. Hear, O Lord, the prayers of thy suppliants.
℟. And forgive the sins of them that confess to thee.
℣. Look, O Lord, upon our humility.
℟. And forsake us not in the time of tribulation.
℣. Forsake not thy flock, O eternal Shepherd.
℟. But through thy blessed apostles guard it with continual defence.
℣. Show us, O Lord, thy mercy.

℟. And grant us thy salvation.
℣. Let us pray for our Sovereign Pontiff N.
℟. The Lord preserve him and

vivificet eum, et beatum faciat eum in terra, et non tradat eum in animam inimicorum ejus.

℣. Fiat pax in virtute tua.
℟. Et abundantia in turribus tuis.
℣. Domine exaudi orationem meam.
℟. Et clamor meus ad te veniat.
℣. Dominus vobiscum.
℟. Et cum spiritu tuo.

give him life and make him blessed upon earth; and deliver him not up to the will of his enemies.

℣. Peace be in thy strength.
℟. And plenteousness in thy towers.
℣. O Lord, hear my prayer.
℟. And let my cry come unto thee.
℣. The Lord be with you.
℟. And with thy spirit.

Oremus

(Primo loco Collecta Missae Stationalis, omissa Conclusione.)

Ne despicias, omnipotens Deus, populum tuum in afflictione clamantem : sed propter gloriam nominis tui, tribulatis succurre placatus.

Ecclesiae tuae, quaesumus, Domine, preces placatus admitte : ut, destructis adversitatibus et erroribus universis, secura tibi serviat libertate.

Libera, quaesumus, Domine, a peccatis et hostibus famulos tuos tibi supplicantes : ut in sancta conversatione viventes, nullis afficiantur adversitatibus.

Deus, qui per immaculatam Virginis Conceptionem dignum Filio tuo habitaculum praeparasti : quaesumus; ut qui ex morte ejusdem Filii tui praevisa eam ab omni labe praeservasti, nos quoque mundos ejus intercessione ad te pervenire concedas.

Deus qui, miro ordine, Angelorum ministeria hominumque dispensas : concede propitius; ut, a quibus tibi ministrantibus in coelo semper assistitur, ab his in terra vita nostra muniatur.

Sanctissimae Genitricis tuae Sponsi quaesumus, Domine, meritis adjuvemur : ut, quod possibili-

Let us pray

(First is said the prayer of the stational Mass without the usual ending.)

O Almighty God, despise not thy people crying out in affliction, but for the glory of thy name be appeased, and succour those in tribulation.

Mercifully hear, O Lord, we beseech thee, the prayers of thy Church; that, overcoming all hostility and error, she may freely and securely serve thee.

Deliver, we beseech thee, O Lord, thy servants who implore thee from their sins and their enemies : that living in holy behaviour they may not be assailed by any adversities.

O God, who by the Immaculate Conception of the Virgin didst prepare a worthy dwelling-place for thy Son; we beseech thee that as by the death of the same thy Son, which thou foreknewest, thou didst keep her free from all stain, so by her intercession thou wouldst grant to us also to come with clean hearts to thee.

O God, who in a wonderful order dost direct the ministry of angels and men, mercifully grant that our life on earth may be protected by those who ever minister before thee in heaven.

Vouchsafe, O Lord, that we may be helped by the merits of the spouse of thy most holy tas nostra non obtinet, ejus nobis intercessione donetur.

Deus, omnium fidelium pastor et rector, famulum tuum N., quem pastorem Ecclesiae tuae praeesse voluisti, propitius respice : da ei, quaesumus, verbo et exemplo, quibus praeest proficere, ut ad vitam una cum grege sibi credito perveniat sempiternam.

Omnipotens, sempiterne Deus, qui vivorum dominaris simul et mortuorum, omniumque misereris quos tuos fide et opere futuros esse praenoscis : te supplices exoramus : ut pro quibus effundere preces decrevimus, quosque vel praesens saeculum adhuc in carne retinet, vel futurum jam exutos corpore suscepit, intercedentibus omnibus sanctis tuis, pietatis tuae clementia, omnium delictorum suorum veniam consequantur. Per Dominum nostrum Jesum Christum Filium tuum, qui tecum vivit et regnat in unitate Spiritus Sancti, Deus, per omnia saecula saeculorum.
℞. Amen.

℣. Exaudiat nos omnipotens et misericors Dominus.

℞. Et custodiat nos semper. Amen.

mother, so that what we cannot obtain of ourselves, may be given to us through his intercession.

O God, the Shepherd and ruler of all the faithful, mercifully look upon thy servant N., whom thou hast been pleased to appoint pastor over thy Church; grant, we beseech thee, that both by word and example he may edify those over whom he is set, and, together with the flock committed to his care, may attain everlasting life.

Almighty everlasting God, who hast dominion over the living and the dead, and art merciful to all who thou foreknowest will be thine by faith and works; we humbly beseech thee that they for whom we intend to pour forth our prayers, whether this present world still detain them in the flesh, or the world to come hath already received them stripped of their mortal bodies, may, by the grace of thy loving kindness, and by the intercession of all the saints, obtain the remission of their sin. Through thy Son Jesus Christ our Lord, etc.

℞. Amen.

℣. May the almighty and merciful Lord graciously hear us.

℞. And ever preserve us. Amen.

EUCHARISTIC MEDIEVAL HYMN IN ADORATION OF THE BLESSED SACRAMENT

Ave verum Corpus, natum
Ex Maria virgine,
Vere passum, immolatum
In cruce pro homine.

Cujus latus perforatum
Vero fluxit sanguine :
Esto nobis praegustatum
Mortis in examine.

O clemens, O pie,
O dulcis Jesu, Fili Mariae.

Hail to thee ! true Body sprung
From the Virgin Mary's womb !
The same that on the Cross was hung,
And bore for man the bitter doom !

Thou whose side was pierced, and flowed
Both with water and with blood,
Suffer us to taste of thee
In our life's last agony.

O kind, O loving one !
O sweet Jesu, Mary's Son !

ANTIPHON TO THE SACRED HEART OF JESUS
(From the Medieval Liturgy)

Ant. O quantum in Cruce spirant amorem caput tuum, Christe, inclinatum, manus expansae, pectus apertum! Fili Dei, qui venisti redimere perditos, noli damnare redemptos de valle fletus ad te clamantium; Jesu bone, exaudi gemitum, nec mensuram observes criminum : vulneratum Cor precamur tuum, pie Deus.

How great a love inspire in us, O Christ, thy hands outstretched upon the Cross, thy bowed head, thy wounded side! O Son of God who camest to save the lost, condemn not thy redeemed who call on thee from this valley of tears. Merciful Jesus, hear our sighs, nor consider the measure of our sins. By thy wounded Heart we implore thee, O pitiful God!

THE EUCHARISTIC HYMN

The primitive liturgy of early days, drawing its inspiration from the *gratias agens* and the hymn sung by Jesus at the Last Supper, gave to the eucharistic anaphora, or Canon of the Mass, the form of a lyric, after the manner of a hymn of thanksgiving. The one we give here for the use of the faithful when they visit the stational basilicas, is one of the most ancient, and in its general lines may be taken as showing the eucharistic hymn in use in the Church towards the end of the apostolic era. We have already spoken of it in Vol. I, and we introduce it here because it may serve for the private devotion of the faithful during Holy Mass.

Sac. Dominus vobiscum.
Pop. Et cum spiritu tuo.
S. Sursum corda.
P. Habemus ad Dominum.

S. Gratias agamus Domino Deo nostro.
P. Dignum et justum est.

Priest. The Lord be with you.
People. And with thy spirit.
P. Lift up your hearts.
People. We have lifted them up to the Lord.
P. Let us give thanks to the Lord our God.
People. It is meet and just.

Gratias tibi referimus, Deus,
Per dilectum puerum tuum[1]
Jesum Christum,
Quem in ultimis temporibus
Misisti nobis   .
Salvatorem
Et Redemptorem

We give thanks to thee, O Lord, through thy beloved Son Jesus Christ, whom thou didst send to us in these latter times that he might be our Saviour, our Redeemer and the messenger of thy will. He is thy inseparable Word

[1] In imitation of the Prophet Isaias, who gives to the Redeemer the title of " Servant of Jehovah," inasmuch as Jesus Christ accomplished his Father's will even unto death, and rendered him the supreme homage of obedience and adoration in the name of all creation, the Saviour is called the " Servant " of the Father in several very ancient liturgical writings, as being truly man, the first-born among all creatures. In our text he is also spoken of as God, so that his divine and his human natures in perfect oneness of person are perfectly distinct according to the unceasing teaching of Holy Church.

Et angelum voluntatis tuae
Qui est Verbum tuum inseparabile,
Per quem omnia fecisti
Et beneplacitum tibi fuit;
Misisti de coelo in matricem
 Virginis,
Quique in utero habitus incarna-
 tus est
Ex Spiritu Sancto
Et Virgine natus;
Qui voluntatem tuam complens
Et populum sanctum tibi ad-
 quirens,
Extendit manus, cum pateretur,
Ut a passione liberaret
Eos qui in te crediderunt.

by whom thou didst create all things, and in whom thou art well pleased. Thou didst send him from heaven into the womb of a virgin, wherein he took flesh by the power of the Holy Ghost; he was born of the Virgin and manifested himself (to the world) as thy son. He accomplished thy will and gained for thee a holy people, and that he might deliver from punishment those who believed in thee, he stretched forth his hands to suffer (the death of the Cross).

Qui cumque traderetur volun-
 tariae passioni,
Ut mortem solvat,
Et vincula diaboli dirumpat,
Et infernum calcet,
Et justos illuminet,
Et terminum figat,
Et resurrectionem manifestet,
Accipiens panem
Gratias tibi agens
Dixit: accipite, manducate:
Hoc est corpus meum,
Quod pro vobis confringetur.
Similiter et calicem
Dicens: hic est sanguis meus
Qui pro vobis effunditur;
Quando hoc facitis,
Meam commemorationem facitis.

When he went forth freely to his Passion that he might loose (the bonds) of death, break the chains of Satan, conquer hell, bring light to the just, perfect the work (of creation) and unfold the mystery of the resurrection, he took bread and gave thanks to thee, saying: Take, eat, this is my body which is broken for you. In like manner (he took) the chalice saying: This is my blood which shall be shed for you. As often as you shall do this, do it for a commemoration of me.

Memores igitur mortis
Et resurrectionis ejus,
Offerimus tibi panem et calicem,
Gratias tibi agentes
Qui nos dignos habuisti
Adstare coram te
Et tibi ministrare;
Et petimus
Ut mittas Spiritum tuum Sanctum
In oblationem sanctae ecclesiae;
In unum congregans, des omnibus,
Qui percipiunt, sanctis
In repletionem Spiritus Sancti
Ad confirmationem fidei in veri-
 tate,
Ut te laudamus et glorificemus
Per puerum tuum Jesum Christum,
Per quem tibi gloria et honor,
Patri et Filio cum Sancto Spiritu,
In sancta Ecclesia tua
Et nunc et in saecula saeculorum.
 Amen.

Mindful therefore of his death and resurrection, we offer to thee the bread and the chalice, giving thanks to thee that thou hast made us worthy to stand here before thee and to minister to thee at thy holy altar.

We beseech thee that thou wouldst send thy Holy Spirit upon (this) oblation of (thy) Holy Church, and making us one body, wouldst grant that all thy saints who partake (of this oblation) may be filled with the Holy Ghost and confirmed in the true faith, that we may praise and glorify thee through thy servant Jesus Christ, by whom are glory and honour to thee; to Father, Son, and Holy Ghost and to thy Holy Church now and to endless ages.

 Amen.

EASTER HYMN OF THE CHRISTIAN POET SEDULIUS
(*Fifth Century*)

Regnavit Dominus, plaudite gentes,
Vicit vita necem, tartara lignum.
Kyrie eleison.

The Lord hath reigned, rejoice all ye nations,
Life hath conquered death, the Cross hath triumphed over hell.
Kyrie eleison.

Servi supplicium pertulit haeres,
Laus tibi, Christe;
Vicit vita necem, tartara lignum.
Kyrie eleison.

The heir hath suffered in the place of the slave,
Laus tibi, Christe;
Life hath conquered death, the Cross hath triumphed over hell.
Kyrie eleison.

Fit nunc ille lapis spretus ab hoste
Jesus magna Deus quaestio mundi.
Kyrie eleison.

May Jesus, the stone cast aside by the foe,
Become, O God, the supreme desire of the world.
Kyrie eleison.

Cur frendent populi? concidat error!
Laus tibi, Christe;
Jesu magna Deus quaestio mundi.
Kyrie eleison.

Why do the nations rage? May error be confounded :
Laus tibi, Christe;
And Jesus, O God, become the supreme desire of the world.
Kyrie eleison.

Qui pascis propria carne redemptos,
Qui ditas roseo sanguine labra.
Kyrie eleison.

Thou who dost feed thy redeemed with thy flesh,
Who dost empurple our lips with thy blood.
Kyrie eleison.

Praesta perpetuae gaudia paschae;
Laus tibi, Christe;
Qui ditas roseo sanguine labra.
Kyrie eleison.

O grant us the joys of an unending Pasch,
Laus tibi, Christe;
Thou who dost empurple our lips with thy blood.
Kyrie eleison.

PRAYER TO THE BLESSED VIRGIN
(*From the Greek Liturgy*)

Sub tuum praesidium confugimus, sancta Dei Genitrix, nostras deprecationes ne despicias in necessitatibus nostris, sed a periculis cunctis libera nos semper, Virgo gloriosa et benedicta.

We fly to thy patronage, O holy Mother of God, despise not our petitions in our necessities; but deliver us always from all dangers, O glorious and blessed Virgin.

PART IV
BAPTISM BY THE SPIRIT AND BY FIRE
(THE SACRED LITURGY DURING THE EASTER CYCLE)

ΙΧΘΥΣ

CAELESTE · DEIFERI · PISCIS · GENVS · VIRES · SVMAS

MORTALES · INTER · DIVINIS · VNDAE · FONTIBVS · POTVM

PERPETVIS · AMICE · COR · FIRMES · SAPIENTIAE · DITISSIMAE · LYMPHIS

SALVATORIS · SANCTORVM · MELLIFLVIS · VTERE · ESCIS

DVLCE · EDE · PISCEM · PRAE · MANIBVS · FERENS

PISCE · PRO · VOTO · REFICERE

(EPIT. PECTORII II—III SAEC.)

INTRODUCTION

CHAPTER I

THE "EUCHARISTIA LUCERNARIS"

LIGHT, heat, and fire, but more especially fire, that element so necessary to life, so beautiful and yet so terrible, were considered amongst the ancient races as symbols of the divine Being; indeed, in some cases as the divinity itself.

God speaks to Moses from a burning bush; the fire of Jehovah consumes the victim on the altar and comes down from heaven at the prayer of Elias. In the writings of the prophets, the throne of the Most High is surrounded by fire, as by a wall of defence; the Cherubim spoken of by Ezechiel and the angels mentioned by Daniel are of fire. Flames, lightning, and thunder are described in the Apocalypse as making terrible even the throne of the gentle Lamb of God slain for the sins of the world. Our God is a consuming fire, the Scriptures tell us,[1] and, like his Word, all that surrounds him partakes of his nature; thus not only are the angels represented as flames of fire, but even the face of Moses, after long contemplation of the Godhead on Sinai, reflects the radiance of the divine Light.

This symbolism, which so clearly expresses the infinite sanctity of Jehovah, who by the ardour of his love purifies those souls which draw near to him, could not, of course, be ignored in the golden age of primitive Christian Liturgy. We find, for instance, in several of the ancient forms of eucharistic epiklesis the idea of the Holy Ghost descending like fire upon the altar, and taking possession, in the name of the Blessed Trinity, of the gifts offered up in sacrifice. Elsewhere it is a fiery angel who carries the sacred victim to the altar set up on high before the throne of God.

The conception of the Godhead, who by means of the fire of the Paraclete, or by the angel of the sacrifice, takes possession of and consumes the victim in the flame of his ineffable sanctity, is so common in the ancient liturgies that in the Spanish rite this part of the anaphora was very appropriately termed *Immolatio missae*, as though to express that this was truly the moment of the consummation of the sacrifice.

Besides the Mass, there was another liturgical rite which,

---

[1] Deut. iv 24; Heb. xii 29.

among the early Christians, recalled the idea of fire and sacrifice; we allude to the rite of the evening office, which was called λυχνικόν, or *Lucernarium,* from the lamp lighted by the Jews at the close of the sabbatical feast, which for the first Christians coincided with the beginning of the vigil before the Sunday.

That lamp lighted at the commencement of the vigiliary office held to commemorate the resurrection of our Lord, or in expectation of his final *parousia,* at once became symbolical of him who is justly called the " Splendour of the Godhead." Then, from the necessity of dispelling the darkness of night by means of that light, so as to carry out the sabbatical tradition of the Sanhedrim, the faithful conceived the idea of solemnly offering to God the light which was burned in his honour.

Considerably later, in addition to the light, incense was offered, this being suggested by Psalm cxl, which was recited by the first Christians at the night office, and in which the evening sacrifice of Calvary is likened to the smoke of the incense rising up before the throne of Jehovah. Altogether we have here a Jewish ceremony, which was raised by Christian feeling to a higher significance—that of Christ rising from the dead and dispelling the darkness in which mankind was enwrapped.

Among the Greeks the hymn Φῶς ἱλαρόν was well known, and St Basil appears to consider it of great antiquity.[1] Even before his time, the *Canones Hippolyti,* whether they represent the rule of the Church at Rome in the third century, which is very doubtful, or whether they originate from Alexandria,[2] make mention of the Office of the *Lucernarium* as marking the beginning of the solemn Saturday vigil; while the fact that it had formerly closed the Jewish Sabbath was soon forgotten.

The Apostolic Constitutions[3] also describe this λυχνικόν, so well known throughout the Church, that by the testimony of Etheria,[4] Prudentius,[5] St Ambrose,[6] St Jerome,[7] and St

---

[1] *Cf.* Probst, *Lehre und Gebet in den drei ersten christlichen Jahrhunderten,* pp. 283, 292.

[2] Cf. *Rev. Bénédict,* 241-46, 1900; S. Bäumer, *Histoire du Bréviaire.* Traduct. française par Dom Réginald Biron, vol. i, p. 74. Paris 1905.

[3] *Cf.* Bäumer, *op. cit.,* i., p. 125 *sqq.;* Funk, *Die Apostolischen Constitutionen,* p. 358.

[4] *Cf.* G. F. Gamurrini, *S. Sylviae Aquitanae peregrinatio ad Loca sancta. Editio altera, novis curis emendata.* Romae, ex Typis Vaticanis. 1888. pp. 46-47. *Cf.* Cabrol, *Etude sur la Peregrinatio Sylviae.*

[5] A. Prudentii, *Catemerinon, hymn. V. ad incensum Lucernae, P.L.,* XLIX, col. 813.

[6] *De Virginibus,* lib. III, c. iv; *P.L.* XVI, col. 237. *Cf.* Bäumer, *op. cit.,* i, 194.

[7] Epist. CVII *ad Laetam; P.L.* XXII, col. 875.

Paulinus,[1] we could easily reconstruct the chain of Catholic tradition concerning the *Hora incensi*,[2] *Eucharistia lucernaris*,[3] as it was called, and show that the Fathers of the Church are almost unanimous on the importance and liturgical meaning of this form of evening sacrifice, the origin of which must certainly be sought in that early ritual which the primitive Church inherited from the synagogue. The rabbinical origin of the lamp lit on the evening of the Sabbath having so soon fallen into oblivion, it seems especially necessary to examine carefully how this evening ceremony was regarded by the faithful in those early days.

Originally the evening synaxis formed the starting-point of the whole Christian ritual, when the Apostles, after the late sacrifice in the temple at Jerusalem, gathered the faithful together towards the end of the day in the house of some wealthy follower, where, having lighted the ritual lamp, they preached, prayed, and celebrated the eucharistic agape. It was perhaps in connection with the *Lucernarium* that we read in the Acts of the Apostles that at Troas, on the occasion of St Paul's preaching at the evening agape, the supper room was brilliantly lighted with a great number of lamps.[4]

It was not long, however, before Christian sentiment gave to this evening synaxis a meaning which connected it closely not only with the offering of the incense in the temple which took place at the same moment, but also with the eucharistic sacrifice of his Body and Blood offered up by the Saviour at that hour, first in the upper room, and afterwards on Calvary. The rite of the *Lucernarium* came originally from Jerusalem, and we know that there, in the fourth century, the evening office recalled the memory of the supper of our Lord with his disciples in the village of Emmaus.[5]

Psalm cxl, which tells of the crucified Redeemer who at the hour of the evening sacrifice stretched out his arms upon the cross and with prayers and tears celebrated the first Vespers of the New Law, was, and still is, the special vesper psalm among the Greeks. The ancient liturgies were in complete agreement as to this meaning which the Fathers attributed to it. Indeed, the whole of the vesper rite, as it was conceived in early Christian times, with the offering of the lighted candle or lamp, the singing of Psalm cxl, and the dominating thought of the cross and the Eucharist, must have produced an impression somewhat similar to that which we now feel on Good Friday during the Mass of the Pre-

[1] Uranius, *Epist. de morte Paulin.* IV; *P.L.* LIII, col. 862.
[2] St Ambrosii, *De Virginibus, loc. cit.*
[3] *Cf.* Martène, *De antiquis monachor. ritibus*, col. 925. Antwerp 1738.
[4] Acts xx 8.
[5] *Vita S. Melaniae junioris, Analect. Bolland.* viii, pp. 49-62. 1889.

sanctified, at which we commemorate the death of the Lord and, instead of offering up the usual daily sacrifices of the Eucharist, appeal directly by our hymns and our rites to the sacrifice offered up by Christ on Calvary, more than nineteen centuries ago.

If Jesus be the " Splendour of the Father," and if his sacrifice is likened by the Psalmist to the perfume of incense ascending to heaven, why should we not connect the thought of a devout oblation offered to God with the lighting of the lamp which ends the Jewish Sabbath and begins the Sunday synaxis? Why should we not render it still more fragrant with the smoke of the incense?

These ideas, which gradually developed amongst the early Christians, soon became general, and St Basil bears witness that the faithful used to reply in chorus to the hymn of the *Lucernarium* with the Trinitarian refrain : Αἰνοῦμεν Πατέρα, καὶ Υἰὸν, καὶ ἅγιον Πνεῦμα Θεοῦ ;[1] and Etheria depicts in brilliant colours the evening Office in the Anastasis at Jerusalem, when in the presence of the clergy, the monks and the entire people, the liturgical light was brought forth from the Holy Sepulchre, at the commencement of the *Lucernarium,* whilst the basilica, from the ceiling of which hung a great number of lamps, was brilliantly illuminated, *fit lumen infinitum.*[2]

The honour of being the first in the West to establish the daily recital of the divine Office belongs probably to Milan in the time of St Ambrose. According to his biographer Paulinus, *ejus celebritatis devotio . . . per omnes pene Occidentis provincias manet,*[3] no doubt on account of the immense influence then exercised throughout Italy, Gaul and Spain by this true patriarch, whose metropolitan jurisdiction included nearly half the West.[4] In his treatise *De Virginibus,* the great Bishop makes special mention of the *hora incensi,* which has left so deep a mark on the Milanese Vespers. To this day the Ambrosian *Lucernarium* consists of responsorial verses such as : *Quoniam tu illuminas lucernam meam, Domine ;* and *Exortum est in tenebris lumen rectis.* Although these Ambrosian *Lucernaria* are not all drawn from the Psalter, yet they generally contain some graceful allusions to the symbolical lamp which originally gave light to the vesper psalmody of Milan.

At Nola, Psalm cxxxi was probably dedicated to the evening liturgy, since Uranius, in his letter on the death of St Paulinus, tells us how the saint, who had always been

---

[1] *Cf.* Basilius, *De Spiritu Sancto,* c. xxix, n. 73; *P.G.* XXXII, col. 205.

[2] *Peregrinatio Sylviae,* pp. 46-7.

[3] *Vita S. Ambrosii,* n. 13; *P.L.* XIV, col. 34.

[4] *Cf.* Duchesne, *Christian Worship,* p. 33.

used to attend the Office of the *Lucernarium* and of the dawn with great regularity, being in his last agony, *quasi ex somno excitatus,* Lucernariae devotionis tempus *agnoscens, extensis manibus, lenta licet voce: " Paravi lucernam Christo meo,"* Domino *decantavit.*[1]

Cassian speaks of Vespers by the name of that which preceded them, that is : *Lucernaris hora.*[2] St Jerome writes to Laeta : *assuescat, lucerna accensa, reddere sacrificium vespertinum ;*[3] whilst the Council of Merida in 666 prescribes : *Post lumen oblatum, prius dicitur vespertinum, quam sonum.*[4]

The memory of this ancient " offering of light " is still preserved in the Mozarabic rite, for after the prelude of the threefold *Kyrie eleison* with the *Pater noster,* the deacon chants : *In nomine Domini nostri Jesu Christi, lumen cum pace.* The people answer *Deo gratias*[5] and then begins the true vesper office.

Prudentius is the writer who has described with the greatest understanding and delicacy of language the spirit of the sacred liturgy during this *Eucharistia lucernaris,* or Ἐπιλύχνιος Εὐχαριστία, as St Gregory of Nyssa calls it. It is a symbolical offering of light which the Church desires to consecrate at that hour to him who is the true Light, as is shown by the use of such phrases as *lumen offerre, oblationem solemnem reddere, lucerna accensa, reddere sacrificium,* and the like, which we find in the writings of the Fathers and in the various liturgies.

It has been questioned whether the magnificent hymns of the *Cathemerinon* of Prudentius were intended by the author to be used at the public liturgical prayer; but the sixth hymn *ad incensum lucernae* would alone suffice to prove that such was his intention, for this hymn was so popular in Spain that the Council of Toledo, in the year 400, was obliged to decree that this office should not be celebrated in country parishes unless a priest or a deacon presided at the ceremony. *Lucernarium nisi in Ecclesia non legatur; aut si legatur in villa, praesente episcopo vel presbytero vel diacono legatur.*[6] Prudentius speaks, not of a single candle, but of a great number of lamps hung from the vaulting of the church at the hour of the *Lucernarium,* so that it was compared to the vault of heaven, in which shines so great a multitude of stars. It is the holy *grex christianus* which offers to God the

---

[1] Uranius, *Epist. de morte Paulini,* n. 4; *P.L.* LIII, col. 862.
[2] *De Coenob. Instit.* lib. III, c. iii; *P.L.* XLIX, col. 126.
[3] *Ad Laetam,* Ep. CVII ; *P.L.* XXII, col. 875.
[4] Bäumer, *op. cit.,* i, 277.
[5] *Breviar, Mozarab.; P.L.* LXXXVI, col. 47-8. *Cf.* Duchesne, *op. cit.*
[6] Mansi, *Collectio Conciliorum,* vol. iii, col. 1000; Hefele, *Histoire des Conciles,* Trad. Leclercq, I, can. 9, p. 123.

splendour of light, all the more expressive since it is offered at the moment in which the sun is about to disappear and sink into the depths of the ocean.

Inventor rutili, dux bone luminis,
Qui certis vicibus tempora dividis,
Merso sole, chaos ingruit horridum;
Lucem redde tuis Christe fidelibus. . . .
O res digna, Deus, quam tibi roscidae
Noctis principio grex tuus offerat
Lucem, qua tribuis nil pretiosius ! . . .
Pendent mobilibus lumina funibus,
Quae suffixa micant per laquearia,
Et de languidulis fota natalibus
Lucem perspicuo flamma jacit vitro. . . .
Quamvis innumero sidere regiam
Lunarique polum lampade pinxeris,
Incussu silicis lumina nos tamen
Monstras saxigeno semine quaerere.
Ne nesciret homo spem sibi luminis
In Christi solido corpore conditam,
Qui dici stabilem se voluit petram,
Nostris igniculis unde genus venit.[1]

Profane literature can hardly boast of anything to compare with this hymn, which is one of the most beautiful of those composed by Prudentius. The framers of the Roman Liturgy, which, as we have seen, had originally no *Lucernarium*, admired it to such a degree that, not being able to adapt it to any part of its *cursus*, they desired to sing it at least once a year, and so introduced it into the paschal *vigilia*,[2] the only form of *Lucernarium* accepted by Rome since the fifth century.

The liturgical tradition of the Gallican churches is in complete accord with the churches of the East and with those of Spain, regarding the rite and significance of the *Lucernarium*. Thus, in the rule of St Caesarius for nuns, we find that Vespers included the *Lucernarium,* the *Duodecima* or twelve psalms, two lessons and a final hymn.[3] Just as with the Greeks, Psalm ciii formed an integral part of this evening rite, on account of the verse : *sol cognovit occasum suum,* a usage which we find also in Spain, and of which only a slight trace remains in the Benedictine liturgy.

St Isidore clearly distinguishes the rite of the *Lucernarium* from the vesper psalmody ;[4] whereas the *Regula Magistri,* although, in accordance with the Benedictine use, it reckons Vespers among the daily offices performed whilst the sun is still high in the heaven, yet continues to call that office by its

---

[1] *P.L.* XIX, col. 776.   [2] Cf. *P.L.* LIX, col. 678,
[3] *Cf.* Bäumer, *op. cit.,* i, 217, and note 4.
[4] Martène, *op. cit.,* 95.

ancient traditional name of *Lucernarium:* '*Adhuc altius stante sole, Lucernaria inchoentur.*[1]

St Gregory of Tours translates the *Eucharistia lucernaris* of the Greeks as *gratia vespertina;*[2] St Columbanus calls it, from the number of its psalms, the *Duodecima* or *initium noctis,*[3] while the " Life of St Brendan " records, as well as Psalm ciii, the gradual chants of which it was composed;[4] so that we are able, therefore, to assert that both in Gaul and in Ireland the most perfect agreement existed, both as to the rite and as to the meaning of this *Lucernarium.*

In the Antiphonary of Bangor, which was first transferred to Bobbio, and from there to the Ambrosian Library at Milan, Vespers include among the various traditional psalms also Psalm cxii (*Laudate pueri*) and the greater Doxology (*Gloria in excelsis*), followed by the *supplicatio* in the form of a litany, exactly as at Arles. We must make a special mention of the Bangor hymn : *Quando caerea benedicitur:*

Ignis creator igneus,
Lumen donator luminis,
Vitaque vitae conditor,
Dator salutis et salus.

Ne noctis hujus gaudia
Vigil lucerna deserat ;
Qui hominem non vis mori,
Da nostro lumen pectori.

Ex Aegypto migrantibus
Indulges geminam gratiam,
Nubis velamen extulis,
Nocturnum lumen porrigis.

A special collect said by the priest corresponds to this hymn : *ad caeream benedice:* . . . *In nocte Tu fuisti columna ignis, Domine* . . . *in ista nocte scuto fidei defendas nos, ut non timeamus a timore nocturno, qui regnas in saecula.*[5]

The absence of any allusion to Easter suggests that this hymn, together with the corresponding collect, represents merely the prayers at the usual daily *Lucernarium,* and bears no relation to the candle lighted at the great paschal vigil. This brings us to the consideration of the paschal candle itself, for the solemn vigil before Easter was preceded by

---

[1] *P.L.* LXXXVIII, col. 1004.
[2] *De Miraculis S. Juliani,* l. II, c. xx; *P.L.* LXXI, col. 813.
[3] *Regula Coenobialis.* Ed. Seebass, in *Zeitschrift f. Kath. Gesch.,* vol. xvii, pp. 215-33.
[4] *Acta Sanctorum Hiberniae,* p. 133 sqq. Bruges 1887.
[5] *Antiphonarium Bangor.* (Phototype edition, F. E. Warren in the collection of the *Henry Bradshaw Society,* London, vol. iv), vol. x, fol. 11. *Cf.* Bäumer, *op. cit.,* i, 241-2.

the *Lucernarium* at least from the fourth century onwards, and on such an occasion the praises of the paschal candle formed a conspicuous part of the ceremony.

The *Laus cerei,* as it was then called, is mentioned by St Jerome towards the year 378, on a certain occasion when Presidius, a deacon of Piacenza, wrote to beg him to compose one for him. The caustic Doctor replies by giving him a regular lecture in which he declaims against the abuse by which the deacons arrogate to themselves the right of chanting the *Laus cerei*[1] whilst the bishop and the priests remain silent before him. In conclusion St Jerome invites his correspondent to follow him into the solitude of Bethlehem, where he would cause him to hear some very different Easter hymns.[2]

St Jerome's censure of those deacons who, having up to that time tried their hand at the same subject, now brought into the *Laus cerei* not only the bees and the wax, but also the flowery meadows of the Georgics of Virgil, gives us reason to suppose that the use of the *Laus cerei* was quite common in the West. *Esto haec jucunda sint . . . quid ad diaconum, quid ad Ecclesiae sacramenta, quid ad tempus Paschae . . ., cum, tacente episcopo, et presbyteris in plebeium quodammodo cultum redactis, levita loquitur, docetque quod pene non didicit?*

St Jerome, being in haste to return to Rome, ended his letter with the remark that in the Holy Scriptures there is no mention of any oblations of honey and wax : *nusquam in Dei sacrificium mella, nusquam cerae usum, sed lucernarum lumina et oleo fotos videbis igniculos,* which proves, at least indirectly, that the Roman use did not favour the ambitious claims of the deacon of Piacenza.[3]

Notwithstanding the censures of St Jerome, the world continued to go its own way, so that Ennodius of Pavia (d. 521) himself composed two beautiful *Laus cerei,* in which the chastity of the working bee is used as a symbol of the virgin birth of the Redeemer[4] and the sacrificial meaning of the candle is thus expressed : *Domine, stupendi hujus opifex elementi, aliquam tibi a nobis reddi credimus . . .*

---

[1] The ancient and almost universal custom of giving to the deacon the honour of chanting the *Laus cerei* confirms the theory of the derivation of this paschal ceremony from the evening *Lucernarium* which was reserved to the deacon. Otherwise it would not be possible to explain how such an important office should be filled by the deacon during the first part of the paschal vigil. The fact that the *Praeconium Paschale* sung by the deacon took the literary form of a *Eucharistia* or Preface is a liturgical anomaly which is only explained by the history of the development of this paschal *Lucernarium.*

[2] *P.L.* XXX, col. 188; Duchesne, *op. cit.*

[3] *Cf.* Duchesne, *op. cit.*   [4] *P.L.* LXIII, col. 259-62.

particulam, quod totum nos cognoscimus debere. . . . *In hujus . . . sanctissimae noctis ministerio, hoc cereum lumen offerimus . . . consecramus . . . commendamus. . . . Proprium tibi est . . . quidquid in hoc cereo servorum tuorum prae-paravit obsequium; serenis in isto respice oculis, quod contulit coelum, fluenta, pudicitia. . . . Sumptam ex hoc contra pro-cellas vel omnes incursus fac dimicare particulam. . . . Si quis hinc sumpserit, adversus flabra ventorum, adversus spiritus procellarum, tua jussa faciens, sit illi singulare profugium, sit murus ab hoste fidelibus.*

The custom has continued until the present day, especially in Italy, where the faithful hold in veneration, as precious relics, the small particles of wax which fall from the paschal candle, the "*Lumen Christi.*"

St Augustine, too, records his verses *in laude quadam cerei*,[1] whilst we find from the fourth Council of Toledo, that those few churches outside Spain which had not yet intro-duced the special rite of the paschal *Lucernarium* were much interested in the ceremony, and asked the Spanish bishops to explain its meaning. *Lucerna et cereus in prae-vigiliis Paschae apud quasdam ecclesias non benedicuntur, et cur a nobis benedicantur inquirunt: propter enim gloriosum noctis ipsius sacramentum solemniter haec benedicimus ut . . . Resurrectionis . . . mysterium . . . in benedictione sanctificati luminis suscipiamus.*[2] The Fathers of the Council would indeed have been much embarrassed if the opposers of the *Lucernarium* had observed that the *Laus cerei* was utterly unknown in Rome at that date.

In the history of the development of the liturgy, Rome stands somewhat apart. As a rule the Holy See does not take the lead in instituting innovations, however pious, which infringe on the established and traditional rites : *Nihil innovetur, nisi quod traditum est.* Only in exceptional cases has Rome allowed herself to be drawn into accepting them, while safeguarding as far as possible her character of pre-server of the Catholic tradition. For this reason, Vespers did not form part of the Roman *cursus* until the seventh century, there being no mention of it in the *Indiculus* of the *Liber Diurnus*, and influenced by this the suburbicarian bishops, when they received their consecration at the hands of the Pope, took upon themselves the obligation of celebrat-ing the *vigiliae* daily.[3]

Gratian quotes a decretal attributed in the MSS. to

[1] *De Civitate Dei,* XV, c. xxii; *P.L.* XLI, col. 467.
[2] *Concil. Toledo* IV, can. 9. *Cf.* Mansi, *Collectio Concil.*, vol. x, col. 620.
[3] *Liber Diurnus Romanorum Pontificum*, c. iii, p. 77 (Ed. Sickel, 1899).

Gelasius I or Pelagius II, but which is certainly of the
sixth century, in which the clergy of a certain bishop called
Eleutherius were censured for being opposed to the introduction of vigils into their church, in spite of the fact that that
prelate had formally undertaken on the day of his consecration to establish them.[1]   The Pontiff makes no mention of
Vespers, which fact, together with the writings of St Jerome[2]
and of Pelagius,[3] leads us to suppose that this office was still
looked upon in Rome as being a private and voluntary
devotion, chiefly in use among ascetic persons.

The very freedom with which St Benedict arranged Vespers
in the *Cursus Monachorum,* in a different order from that
which was traditional,[4] seems to show that the tradition
itself was not supported by any official ecclesiastical authority.
For whilst in the case of the early morning Lauds the Saint
did not hesitate to change the whole plan of his psalmody in
order to bring it into conformity with the use of the Roman
Church : *Sicut psallit Ecclesia Romana,*[5] with regard to
Vespers, on the contrary, he acted with entire freedom.   The
liberty accorded to abbots by St Benedict[6] in matters of
liturgy would hardly have been possible had the Roman
cursus at that time been definitely established in each
separate part.

If there ever existed a city in which the chanting of divine
Office seven times a day aroused scant enthusiasm, that city
was Rome.   Until the eighth century the clergy considered
this *cursus* of psalmody as proper to the monasteries, and
did not take part in it except on the vigils of the principal
festivals, when, that is, the ancient traditions of the Roman
festal *vigilia* had been influenced by the new nocturnal *cursus*
of the monks, thus giving rise to a transitional liturgy of the
basilicas, partly monastic and partly episcopal.   The monks
therefore, whose office it was to perform the psalmody in the
Roman basilicas, did not adopt the Bendictine *cursus* until
somewhat late, for in the early Middle Ages their liturgy
could only have been that of the basilicas of which we are
now speaking, since their choirs constituted what we should
call the chapters of the Roman basilicas.

It is also remarkable that St Benedict, who must have been
familiar with the rites and significance of the *Lucernarium,*
which was in use in Campania and at Nola, should have
attributed no importance to it.   Merely because this ceremony
was unknown at Rome, he considered himself at liberty to

---

[1] *Friedberg,* vol. i, p. 316.
[2] *Ad Laetam.* Epist. CVII ; *P.L.* XXII, col. 875.
[3] *Ad Demetriadem; P.L.* XXX, col. 38.
[4] *Regula Monachorum,* c. xvii, xviii.
[5] *Op. cit.,* c. xiii.   [6] *Op. cit.,* c. xviii.

ignore it; in fact, he so arranged Vespers that they should not correspond in any way to the evening office of the Greeks, candles and lamps being thus excluded. In the Benedictine *cursus* Vespers form part of the day hours : *Vespera sic agatur, ut lumen lucernae non indigeant reficientes, sed luce adhuc diei omnia consummentur. Sed et omni tempore, sive coenae, sive refectionis hora, sic temperetur, ut luce fiant omnia.*[1]

The exclusion of daily Vespers from the Roman *cursus* of the fifth century explains why the *Laus cerei* was introduced so late into the paschal vigil. St Gregory, writing in 601 to Archbishop Marinianus of Ravenna, mentions the blessing of the paschal candle as being a rite peculiar to that city : *a vigiliis quoque temperandum, et preces quae super cereum in Ravennati civitate dici solent . . . quae circa paschalem solemnitatem a sacerdotibus* (St Jerome might well have rejoiced at this belated victory over the deacons—at Ravenna the bishop himself blessed the candle) *fiunt, per alium dicantur.*[2]

Although the *Liber Pontificalis* attributes the origin of the blessing of the candle to Pope Zosimus (about 417)[3] the biographer of Pope Theodore, who assigns to him this liturgical innovation,[4] appears to be the more reliable. The Gregorian Sacramentary, like the *Pontificalis*, makes no mention whatever of this paschal *Laus cerei*, and the *Ordo Romanus I*, which describes the rites as they were performed in the eighth (seventh) century, observes that they were used exclusively in the churches outside the city : *Et hic ordo cerei benedicendi, in suburbanis civitatibus agitur.*[5]

At the Lateran, in place of the *Lucernarium*, the following ceremony was carried out. On Maundy Thursday about None, a spark was struck from a flint, before the door of the basilica, and a candle lighted at it which was fixed on the top of a reed carried by the *mansionarius*. When the procession reached the altar, seven lamps were lighted from this candle and Mass was begun.[6] On Good Friday and on Holy Saturday the honour of carrying the candle in procession was given to the archdeacon or to the youngest among the bishops instead of to the *mansionarius*, whilst in the monasteries, as the *Ordo Romanus* tells us, this ceremony was performed by the sacristan, the *praepositus* and the abbot.

[1] *Op. cit.*, c. xli.
[2] *Epistolar.*, lib. XI, n. xxxiii; *P.L.* LXXVII, col. 1146. *Cf.* Duchesne, *op. cit.*, p. 252.
[3] *Lib. Pontif.* (Ed. Duchesne), i, 225.   [4] *Op. cit.*, i, 332.
[5] *P.L.* LXXVIII, col. 960.
[6] *Op. cit.*, col. 960 *sqq.*

Outside Rome the rite suffered other alterations. The flame obtained from the flint with the steel was kept in a secret place until the evening of Holy Saturday, when the paschal candle was lighted from it.[1] From this custom is derived the use which is still observed in the Basilica of St Paul at Rome. On the evening of Wednesday in Holy Week, after all the lamps around the tomb of the Apostle have been extinguished, a few are hidden in the interior of the *cella confessionis,* in the space between the papal altar and the sepulchral stone covering the martyr's sarcophagus, where they remain burning until Holy Saturday.

In Rome itself, therefore, there was originally no candle, no *Lumen Christi,* but only a procession *cum supplici silentio,* one candle set on a reed, and seven lamps. In accordance with this regulation, instead of distributing among the people particles of the paschal candle, the archdeacon of the Apostolic See used to prepare at the Lateran, during the morning of Holy Saturday, small mementos made of wax and oil with an imprint of the *Agnus Dei,* which were given to the faithful after Communion on Low Sunday : *et ex eis faciunt in domos suas incensum, ad suffumigandum pro qualicumque eis eveniente necessitate.*[2]

Later on, rites and prayers which were formerly distinct became strangely united and blended together, producing the ceremony that we have to-day, with the one reed, and the triple *Lumen Christi* preceding the blessing of the paschal candle. Further, the expression in the *Laus cerei: Incensi hujus sacrificium vespertinum,* which simply means the lighting of the candle as an oblation and act of homage to the risen Saviour, being misunderstood, suggested the idea of the grains of incense which now are placed in the candle in the form of a cross. Consequently, all that part of the paschal vigil which in the modern Roman Liturgy precedes the recitation of the twelve lessons is the result of the fusion of several rites and unaccustomed formulas in the place of the original prayer of the *Lucernarium,* which, in countries where the Frankish liturgy was in use, marked the commencement of the vesper psalmody throughout the year.

Perhaps originally the *Laus cerei* was the solemn *Lucernarium* peculiar to the paschal festival; but from the fifth century onwards we find that in Spain it was joined to the usual *benedictio lucernae* of the Saturday vigil. Thus two

----

[1] *Cf,* Duchesne, *op. cit.* From a letter of Pope Zachary (741-52) to St Boniface it appears that the custom of lighting the lamps on Holy Thursday, and keeping them hidden in a secret place until the Saturday, had been introduced also into Rome at that time. *Cf.* Jaffé, *Regesta Pontif. Roman.,* i, n. 2291.

[2] *P.L.* LXXVIII, col. 960 *sqq.*

Lucernaria were united just as they are now in the Roman rite.[1]

The *Consuetudines Cassinenses* of the eighth century record in the paschal vigil only the blessing of the candle and of the water;[2] whereas the custom of blessing the fire and the candle during the last three days of Holy Week is prescribed both in the Farfa copy of the *Consuetudines Cluniacenses*[3] and in those of St Bernard,[4] where mention is made of the *lapis pretiosus berillus,* from which the spark was produced.

The ancient Gallican Lectionaries, too, ordain for the paschal vigil first a *Praefatio ab initio noctis sanctae paschae,* followed by a collect in which it is easy to discern traces of the traditional *Eucharistia lucernaris.* Then follows the *benedictio cerei* with the hymn *Exultet,* a collect *post benedictionem cerae,* and another *post hymnum cerae.*[5]

In the Spanish rite the ceremony has become somewhat complex. The bishop, assisted by the abbots and the clergy, strikes the spark from the flint and blesses both the lamp and the five grains of incense; then the deacon sings two separate *Laudes* for the candle and for the lamp,[6] using for the latter the *benedictio lucernae* formerly attributed by Elipandus (783) to St Isidore of Seville. Here again we have two *Lucernaria,* the daily rite and that of paschal tide merged into one.

When the Roman Liturgy finally triumphed over the Gallican and Spanish rites, the beautiful and symbolical ceremony of the *Lucernarium* also disappeared, to survive only in the paschal vigil. Then the offering of incense during the daily singing of the *Magnificat* at Vespers came almost unconsciously to take the place of the ancient oblation of the *Lucernarium.* The vesper incense, although it is derived more directly from the evening sacrifice of the Old Testament, is yet suggested by the same thought which first conceived the *Lucernarium* as a symbol, both by its light and by its perfumes, of the sacrifice on Calvary, where the Pontiff of the New Covenant offered up his first oblation as a cloud of incense in the sight of God, amidst the splendours of his essential and infinite sanctity.

[1] *Cf.* P. Ewald, G. Löwe, *Exempla scripturae visigothicae,* Table II, III ; Mercati (and Bannister), *Studi e Testi,* Part 12, p. 40. Rome 1904.
[2] B. Albers, *Consuetud. Monasticae,* vol. iii, pp. 21-22. Montis Cassini, 1907.
[3] B. Albers, *Consuetud. Farfenses,* lib. I, p. 55.
[4] Herrgott, *Vetus disciplina monastica,* pp. 311, 313, 317.
[5] *P.L.* LXXII, col. 268 *sqq.*
[6] *P.L.* LXXXV, col. 437 *sqq; cf.* Duchesne, *op. cit.*

CHAPTER II

CONCERNING CERTAIN PASCHAL RITES OF THE MIDDLE AGES

ST BENEDICT by his own example, and in a special chapter of his Rule, pointed out to his monks the immense importance of Easter in the liturgical cycle, enjoining that a monk should regard it as the goal of his personal sanctification which, through the purity and sincerity of his life, should exemplify the continual resurrection of the soul in Christ's eternal Pasch. Faithful to the teaching of the great Patriarch, his spiritual family has always celebrated the paschal festival with great splendour of rites and prayers, in order to express also outwardly the interior dispositions of the Benedictine spirit before the mystery of the resurrection of Christ.

The poet Marcus, in his verses on the life of St Benedict, describes how, during Lent, the Saint, like the early Eastern Fathers, remained shut up in his stronghold of Monte Cassino, at the foot of which the people, recently brought by him to the knowledge of the faith, waited impatiently until he should show himself to them once more during the solemn night vigil of Holy Saturday.

> *Hic quoque clausum populi, te teste, requirunt*
> *Expectas noctis dum pia festa sacrae.*

By studying the various *Ordines Cassinenses*, we can reconstruct the whole history of the paschal liturgy at Monte Cassino.

In the ninth century the paschal *vigilia* began at None on Holy Saturday, and consisted of the ancient twelve lessons with alternate gradual responsories, amongst which were the traditional *Benedictiones* which follow the Lesson from the Book of Daniel. Contrary to the use of other churches in Spain, Gaul, etc., the blessing of the candle and of the water—stripped of every allusion to baptism as being unnecessary in a monastery, the abode of a *gens aeterna in qua nemo nascitur*—followed immediately after the lessons; then came the procession accompanied by the singing of a triple litany, going from the Basilica of St Martin first to that of St Peter, and then to the neighbouring one of St Benedict, where the Mass of the vigil was celebrated.

Towards the end of the same century—that is, in the time

of Abbot Bertarius—the bells were rung when the celebrant intoned the *Gloria in Excelsis*, and after the Epistle the abbot distributed candles to those present. Vespers having been sung, the choir moved in procession to the refectory, chanting the antiphon *Vespere autem sabbati*, and it was only when the priest had recited the collect that the officiating clergy laid aside their vestments. It is well known, indeed, that among the faithful of early days, the *Triclinium* and the refectory were regarded as having an important liturgical character, and the community meal, owing to the benedictions and prayers which accompanied it, brought to mind the first years of Christianity, when the eucharistic agape was the most complete and efficacious expression of the Church's unity of life.

The blessing of the monastery of Monte Cassino took place on Easter Sunday, and that of the adjoining buildings on the Monday following, the whole community being present at the ceremony. To the singing of litanies, the precious crosses and the relics of the saints were carried in procession, so that the whole monastery might be sanctified by their passing. On the Tuesday the liturgy was solemnized in a still more dramatic form. For among our forefathers it was not regarded as something to be hidden in sanctuaries and sacristies, but as the expression of the life and polity of the Christian people in all its fulness; and, as such, was brought out into the light of day, into the free air of the streets and squares, to be greeted by the joyful cries of the populace who came to meet the clergy with smoking censers.

Thus, also on Monte Cassino, the monks of the head monastery came down on that day from the heights to share the holy joys of Easter with their brethren of the monastery of the Saviour, which lay at the foot of the sacred Mount. The two communities met in the village of San Pietro, where the modern town of Cassino stands. The priests and other clergy of the two houses wore their finest vestments for the occasion, all the silver objects, the reliquaries, and the precious vessels were borne in procession, whilst the monks of both communities exchanged in a brotherly spirit the scriptural greeting: *benedictus qui venit in nomine Domini*. The two choirs then exchanged a fraternal embrace, and the monks of the *Salvatoris*, acting as hosts, led those of Monte Cassino to the chanting of the litanies into their Basilica of St Peter, where they together recited the Office of Terce.

The Mass had nothing unusual about it except the singing of the Greek responsories after the Epistle; which, however, being mentioned only towards the end of the ninth century— in the time, that is, of Bertarius—show a somewhat later

origin than that of the primitive Cassinese liturgy, and
appear to belong to a Hellenistic period, when the influence
of the Greeks who had settled in the neighbourhood made
itself felt more than once on the ritual of Monte Cassino.

After Mass, the procession again set forth and crossed the
public square, on its way to the monastery of the Saviour.
The two communities first entered the basilica of that name,
singing the litanies, and, after a brief stay, the monks
resumed their liturgical vestments and passed under the
arcades of the basilica. The abbot followed, carrying against
his breast the volume of the Gospels which had been beautifully illuminated by order of Bertarius, and proceeded to the
sanctuary, where a second Mass was celebrated.

The ceremonies did not, however, end with the divine
Sacrifice, for the monks, singing the *Te Deum,* then went in
procession to the refectory, and sat down to table together.
The meal being over, the two communities once more
exchanged the kiss of peace, after which the monks of Monte
Cassino returned joyfully to their monastic acropolis, where
beside the ancient tomb of St Benedict they led a life of
mingled prayer and work.

During the Octave of Easter the night offices at Monte
Cassino included, besides the traditional twelve psalms, also
eight lessons, together with the final reading of the Gospel :
it was therefore fitting that during these days of holy
rejoicing the meals should be somewhat less austere than at
ordinary times. Thus on Easter Day, and on the following
Tuesday, the regulations at Monte Cassino allowed four
courses, consisting of vegetables, herbs, and fish with two
cups of wine to the monks, who were somewhat weakened
by the rigours of the Lenten fast.   Flesh meat was always
strictly forbidden, but not poultry ; therefore, during Easter
week it sometimes made its appearance on the table, at an
opportune moment, to cheer and strengthen those whose
health had been tried by the long abstinence.

In the eleventh century, when the observances of Cluny
had been adopted by the greater number of the Benedictine
monasteries, the Easter liturgy attained its highest point of
magnificence and splendour. During the solemn vigils, the
whole church was lighted up, and, according to an ancient
custom in the Roman basilicas, the altar and the choir were
incensed after the third lesson of each nocturn.

On Easter Sunday, at the dinner which followed the Mass,
instead of each monk receiving, as on ordinary days, a certain
portion of food appointed for him, he was allowed to help
himself as he pleased from the large dish (*generalis*) which
was set before him. The first course consisted of fish, then
followed three other courses of vegetables and herbs, whilst

the lay-brothers, the deacons, and the priests filled the cups of the monks three times, in honour, as they said, of the Blessed Trinity,[1] so strong still was the conception of the liturgical character of the common meal among the clergy and religious communities.

In France, the procession to the Sepulchre on the morning of Easter Sunday was held in great reputation. At the third responsory of the vigils, the choir went with great ceremony, carrying candles, incense, and perfumes, to the Sepulchre, whither two deacons, or two boys dressed in white, with angels' wings, had preceded them, and were now sitting beside the altar awaiting them. As the procession drew near, the two angels, addressing those who took the part of the Marys, sang the words : *Quem quaeritis in sepulchro?—Jesum Nazarenum.—Surrexit; non est hic.* Then, raising the veil spread over the altar, which represented the Saviour's winding-sheet, they showed the holy women that the body of Jesus was no longer in the tomb.

Then followed a pleasing dialogue between Mary Magdalen, Mary the mother of James, Mary of Salome, and the choir. Mary Magdalen sang the first strophe of the sequence : *Victimae Paschali laudes immolent Christiani.* The mother of James followed with : *Agnus redemit oves, Christus innocens Patri reconciliavit peccatores;* Mary of Salome sang the third verse : *Mors et vita duello conflixere mirando; dux vitae mortuus regnat vivus.* Then two of the clergy from behind the pulpit addressing the Magdalen sang : *Dic nobis, Maria, quid vidisti in via?* and she replied : *Sepulchrum Christi viventis, et gloriam vidi resurgentis, angelicos testes, sudarium et vestes. Surrexit Christus spes mea, praecedens suos in Galileam.* At this joyful news the whole choir exclaimed : *Scimus Christum surrexisse a mortuis vere. Tu nobis, victor Rex, miserere;* and singing the *Te Deum* with one voice, they all returned together to finish the celebration of the interrupted morning vigil.

In other places, as at Soissons, for instance, the same rite was used when taking the Blessed Sacrament from the Sepulchre, and as the episode of the winding-sheet had become extremely popular, it ended by being one of the most important features of this dramatic representation of the resurrection. It was by no means unusual to paint or embroider on the sheet a picture of the sacred body of our Lord, as it was enwrapped by Joseph of Arimathea and

[1] *Cf.* Albers, *Consuetudines Farfenses,* pp. 55-59. I believe, however, that in my " History of Hugh I of Farfa " I have proved that the title of these usages should be corrected thus : *Johannis monachi Sancti Salvatoris. Consuetudines Cluniacenses* (1030-1039), *ex MSS. codice pharphensi,* saec. xi.

Nicodemus with linen bands before being laid in the tomb. These *sudaria* were greatly esteemed by the people, so much so that many ancient rituals enjoined that on Easter Sunday the winding-sheet should remain exposed to the veneration of the faithful from the early morning vigil until sunrise.

The Roman rite of the stations and of the evening processions during Easter week, as described in the various *Ordines* of the Middle Ages, gradually spread beyond the city boundaries, especially throughout Italy and France.

The Gelasian anniversary of the Easter Day of the preceding year—*Pascha annotinum*—was another occasion on which our forefathers showed their devotion to the mystery of the resurrection of Christ, the type not only of the resurrection of the Church by means of baptism, but also of the final resurrection of all flesh on the day of the great *parousia.* This custom soon died out in Rome, being rarely mentioned in documents after the eighth century, but it continued to be observed for some time longer in France, where it was celebrated with exactly the same rites as those of Easter Day itself.[1]

The resurrection of the human race, of which the feast of Christ's resurrection from the dead is a pledge to us each year as Easter comes round, was also brought before the eyes of the faithful in a striking manner by the white-robed band of neophytes, who each year added their number to the flock of Christ. In a certain sense they themselves formed the Church's Easter; therefore it is not surprising that the whole paschal liturgy, as seen in the Roman rite, is inspired by the idea that baptism gives to the soul a share in the resurrection of its Redeemer.

This, indeed, is the true meaning of the beautiful responsory of the vigil: *Isti sunt agni novelli qui annuntiaverunt Alleluia, modo venerunt ad fontes, repleti sunt claritate, Alleluia.* Even later, when, owing to the change in the outward condition of the Church, Tertullian's emphatic words: *Christiani non nascuntur, sed fiunt,* no longer expressed a truth; and when, consequently, from the seventh century onwards baptism was administered only to infants, the Roman liturgy not only kept intact the ancient baptismal ceremonial in use during the Byzantine period, but even enriched it. The *professio fidei* of the scrutinies, recited both in Greek and Latin, was retained, the use of Greek having been permitted originally on account of the many Byzantine officials in Rome. The Papal Court found it expedient to show a certain amount of consideration

[1] Cf. *Consuetud. Farfenses,* p. 61.

towards these latter, as is seen also by the bilingual lessons of the paschal vigil, and by the Greek processional responsories in the evening office which Rome left in their original place until after the eleventh century.[1]

The most characteristic, however, of the Easter ceremonies at Rome was the evening office. The second Vespers which we now have, which may be said to end the ceremonies, were then quite unknown in the Eternal City. In the ancient Roman rite, as even now among the Eastern Christians, Vespers are always a liturgical preparation for the festival day which follows, the ritual celebration of which ends with the Mass. In any case the vesper hour in early times was regarded as belonging chronologically to the following day, and not to the one which was drawing to a close.

Easter Day alone formed an exception to this rule; but this was a concession to the newly baptized, derived from Jerusalem. The Easter Vespers at the Lateran began with a kind of processional Introit, as is still the custom among the Greeks,[2] the clergy passing from the *pergula*—on which was erected the crucifix—to the sacred *vima*. The *schola* took up its position between the marble *plutei* set up before the altar; the deacons placed themselves in the sanctuary to the side of the *pergula*, whilst it was the privilege of · the bishops and Roman priests only to seat themselves around the Papal throne.

Meanwhile the *Kyrie eleison* was sung processionally, after which the proper Vesper Office began. At a sign from the archdeacon, the leader of the singers intoned the Alleluia antiphon, alternating it with each verse of Psalm cix; the second singer of the *schola* followed with another Alleluia from Psalm cx; then there entered a choir of boys, directed by a subdeacon, who sang the paschal psalm *Dominus regnavit* in responsorial form, leaving the closing Psalm cxi, the verses of which were also alternated with Alleluias, to the most experienced singers of the *schola*. Next followed the short responsory : *Pascha nostrum immolatus est Christus,* with the verse *Epulemur in azymis.* There was no hymn, as it was not until much later that hymnody was allowed at the divine office in Rome. The *Magnificat* was then sung and was followed by a collect, bringing to a close the first part of Vespers.

As at Jerusalem, where, after the office of the *Lucernarium,* it was customary to go in procession from the Anastasis to the Oratory of the Holy Cross, so, too, at the Lateran. From

---

[1] *Cf.* Duchesne, *Christian Worship.*   [2] Cf. *op. cit.*

the Basilica of the Saviour, which was the Anastasis of
Rome, the neophytes were conducted in procession on this
day to visit once more the baptistery and the adjoining
Oratory of the Holy Cross, the *Confirmatorium,* in order to
close that memorable day with a special prayer of thanksgiving, offered in the very places where, on the preceding
night, they had been born again in baptism to a Christian
life.

Singing the verse *In die resurrectionis meae,* the procession passed behind the apse of the Lateran, through the
porch and the *atrium* which led to the baptistery. There the
leader of the *schola* intoned the Alleluia with Psalm cxii, a
psalm very suitable to the occasion. Next came a Greek
choir which sang the paschal psalm: ὁ κύριος ἐβασίλευσεν;
then after the *Magnificat* and the collect, the procession
moved to the chapel of St John *ad vestem,* singing the
responsory: *Lapidem quem reprobaverunt,* and the psalms
In exitu, Venite exultemus, and the *Magnificat.* The
oratory was very small and actually adjoined the baptistery,
so the greater part of those taking part in the ceremony
remained in the baptistery during this third Vesper Office
owing to lack of space.

This procession to the Oratory of St John *ad vestem,* in
which, contrary to custom, there was no Greek choir,
represents a later addition to the ancient *statio ad fontes*
in the Roman Liturgy, made perhaps when the chapel
acquired greater importance in consequence of its claiming
to possess the robe of St John the Baptist. As a matter of
fact, there is no mention at all of this garment in the *Ordo
Romanus* of the MSS. of St Armandus, although it appears
in later documents.

The visit to the baptistery being concluded, the whole
company, singing the baptismal antiphon *Vidi aquam,* proceeded to the Oratory of St Andrew *in crucem,* where on
the preceding night the neophytes had received the *Confirmatio chrismalis.* Here also Vespers consisted of Psalms
cxiv and xciv only, with the *Magnificat* and the final collect.

After the recital of such a number of psalms and collects,
the higher clergy of Rome, invited by the notary or the
vicedominus, adjourned to the papal *Triclinium* to taste three
different kinds of wine, noted in the documents; Greek, *de
Pactis,* and *de Procoma,* so called probably from the country
of their origin. Afterwards in the time of Cencius Came-
rarius, the minor clergy also were admitted to this papal
compotatio;[1] and the archdeacon together with the *schola*

[1] "Quid Dominus Papa facere debet in die prima et secunda
Paschae," Watterich, *Pontificum Romanorum Vitae,* i, pp. 8-13.

sang a Greek song in praise of Easter, concluding with a toast in honour of the Pope.[1]

The assembly dispersed towards sunset, and the cardinals, together with their attendant clergy, went back to celebrate Vespers in their respective titles, where, following the example of generosity set by the Pope, they again invited the clergy to taste the wine from their own cellars. Such Christian liberty and holy rejoicing were natural to an age in which faith was the motive force of all the social life of the people; and in which the liturgy led the way and was the true expression both of the joys and the sorrows of the entire Christian family.

After the eighth century, this Easter ceremonial developed still further. When each urban title had its own baptistery, the titular priests at the end of the Lateran *Vigilia* took leave of the Pope, as he was going to bless the font in the baptistery, saying: *Jube, domne, benedicere,* to which the Pontiff replied: *Ite, baptizate omnes gentes in nomine Patris et Filii et Spiritus Sancti;* after which the cardinals went to administer baptism in their own titular churches.

On Easter morning, when Matins were ended, the Pope, having put on the sacred vestments in the Lateran chapel of St Lawrence—the only one which still remains of the ancient patriarchal buildings—opened the doors which hid the celebrated representation of the Saviour, and, kissing the feet, sang three times: *Surrexit Dominus de sepulchro, qui pro nobis pependit in ligno.* All those who were present joined in the singing, and the Pope exchanged the traditional paschal embrace with the clergy, beginning with the archdeacon down to the acolytes and the other officials of the patriarchal household, who then did the same among themselves. This custom of a general embrace on Easter Day is still in vogue among the Eastern peoples, and it certainly existed at Rome in the time of St Gregory the Great, for it is expressly mentioned by John the Deacon in his life of that holy Pope.

The weariness caused by the preceding vigil quite prevented the stational procession from getting as far as St Peter's on Easter Sunday, so the Basilica of St Mary Major,

---

[1] The words are as follows (*cf.* Watterich, *op. cit.,* i, p. 11):

Πάσχα ἱερὸν ἡμῖν σήμερον ἀνεδείκνυσθη,
Πάσχα καινὸν, ἅγιον Πάσχα, μυστικὸν Πάσχα,
Πανσεβάσμιον.
Πάσχα Χριστοῦ τοῦ λυτρωτοῦ
Πάσχα ἄμωμον, Πάσχα μέγα,
Πάσχα τῶν πιστῶν,
Πάσχα τάς πύλας ἡμῖν τοῦ παραδείσου ἀνέῳγε,
Πάσχα πάντας ἀναπλάττων βροτούς.
Χαινὸν Πάταν Χριστέ φύλαξον.

being nearer to the Lateran, very soon took its place, as it did also in later years on Christmas Day. The Papal Court repaired thither in great splendour, escorting the Pontiff, who wore the *regnum,* and rode a gorgeously caparisoned steed. In the Via Merulana they were met by a notary, who announced to the Pope the number of neophytes baptized at St Mary Major on the preceding night, and whilst the Pope gave thanks to God, the bearer of the good news was presented with a gold bezant by the *sacellarius.*

After the Mass the procession returned to the Lateran, where the higher dignitaries of the papal Court were invited to dine with the Pontiff, in the usual Leonine *Triclinium.* Eleven cardinals sat at the side of the Pope, whilst the *primicerius* took his place on a seat opposite to them. The roasted lamb was duly blessed, and the Pope, taking a morsel of it, placed it in the mouth of the *basilicarius,* saying to him : *quod facis, fac citius; sicut ille accepit ad damnationem, tu accipe ad remissionem.* When the meal was half over, a deacon read for a while, and then one or two paschal sequences were sung—this being the traditional place given up to hymnody in the ancient Roman Liturgy. After having received a last cup of wine from the hands of the Pontiff himself, the guests departed pleased and contented, each receiving his *presbyterium* in ready money, as well as an additional bezant of gold in his pocket.[1]

The paschal festival continued throughout the week, and stations were held at the most famous Roman sanctuaries, as though it were desired to present the neophytes to each of the patron Saints of the City. On the Monday morning they went to St Peter's, on the following days they visited in succession St Paul's, St Lawrence, the Apostoleion, etc. ; while in the afternoon Vespers were always celebrated in the Lateran according to the rite of the preceding Sunday. On the Saturday morning, as though to close the festivities, the station was celebrated once more in the Lateran Basilica, where the archdeacon distributed the *Agnus Dei* of blessed wax to the people.

The station of Low Sunday at the tomb of St Pancras, the fourteen-year-old martyr of the Via Aurelia, although it referred to the neophytes (*Quasi modo geniti infantes,* etc.) is really a later extension of the Octave of Easter, which originally closed with the Vespers of the Saturday, in the

---

[1] The documents make no mention of the monks of the four Lateran monasteries of St Pancras, St Andrew, SS Sergius and Bacchus, and St Stephen " in Orphanotrophio," whose duty it was to carry out the celebration of the Divine Office in the Basilica of the Saviour on ordinary days—on the more solemn occasions this Office was performed by the Pope, the clergy, and the whole Roman people.

same manner as that of Pentecost does now. It is remarkable that on the Friday and Saturday of Easter Week, the
procession, instead of going, after Vespers at the Lateran,
to the Oratory of the Cross, went to the Basilica of Holy
Cross in Jerusalem and to that of St Mary Major;[1] thus in
this pious pilgrimage we have one of the earliest traces of
the special dedication of Saturday in honour of the Blessed
Virgin.

How great a happiness was that which filled the life of a
Christian in those more vigorous days! A happiness of
which our age, although surrounded by all the comforts of
modern life, has lost the secret. For its springs are dried
up, and attacks are being made on Christian society, both
public and private, in order to break as far as possible every
natural bond of fellowship, and thus leave the individual to
face alone the dread power of an undenominational and
therefore atheistic state. Having then closed all outlets to
the instinctive aspirations of the man and the Christian,
modern civilization has only the pleasures of the cinemato-
graph and the music-hall to offer us, and these are very far
from being able to bring joy and solace to society, but rather
bear sad witness to the truth of that which St Peter Chry-
sologus with forceful eloquence repeated to the hot-headed
people of Ravenna : *Qui vult jocari cum diabolo, non potest
gaudere cum Christo.*

[1] *Cf.* Duchesne, *op. cit.*

CHAPTER III

THE FEAST OF ROSES IN THE ROMAN LITURGY

IN the *Ordines Romani* a solemn station and a very characteristic "Feast of Roses" is ordained for the Sunday after the Ascension, the Octave being of later date. This ceremony distantly recalls somewhat similar flower festivals among the pagans. The synaxis was held in the ancient Pantheon of Agrippa, and the Pope, who used to take part in it and offer the Holy Sacrifice, was in the habit also of delivering there a homily in which he announced to the people that the coming of the Holy Ghost was now close at hand.

In order to illustrate his words and to symbolize the descent of the Paraclete from heaven, a shower of roses was caused to fall from the opening in the centre of the roof upon the people, whilst the Pontiff was addressing them from the ambon, a figure *ejusdem Spiritus Sancti,* as is noted in the eleventh *Ordo Romanus.* Hence the name of "Feast of Roses" was usually adopted in Rome to describe the festival of Pentecost.

The stational Mass *ad Sanctam Mariam Rotundam,* as the Pantheon of Agrippa is called in the medieval documents, is one of preparation for the coming of the Holy Ghost, so much so that when in the fifteenth century an Octave was assigned also to the Ascension, it was considered necessary to add a collect, commemorative of this feast, to the eucharistic liturgy celebrated in the Pantheon in expectation of the coming of the Paraclete. However, though these *Rosalia* of the Pantheon are not devoid of poetry, the real and ancient preparation for Pentecost is that appointed for the vigil in the Missal, and its ceremonies are well worth describing.

The great feast of Pentecost, which marks the foundation of the Church, is a part of that liturgical inheritance which the first Christians of Jerusalem received from the synagogue. St Paul speaks of Pentecost in his first Epistle to the Corinthians (xvi 8) as of a feast well known to them, and Tertullian reckons it among those handed down by the Apostles. On this day, as on Easter Sunday, it was customary to pray standing, and solemn baptism was administered to the catechumens,[1] an observance which we

---

[1] Tertullian, *De baptism.* XIX; *P.L.* I, col. 1331.

find in all the churches forming part of the Roman patriarchate, whereas it is rarely, if ever, found in the liturgical traditions of the great Eastern Churches.

On the eve of Pentecost the station was in the Lateran, where the Easter vigil had also been celebrated. The tendency to raise Pentecost to the same level as the Easter solemnity was very soon apparent at Rome. In the fourth century the feast of the Holy Ghost marked the limit of the paschal festivities: the administration of baptism on that day took the place of the earlier ceremony on Holy Saturday for those catechumens who had been absent or sick, and the solemnity was prolonged by two or three extra days of festival.

The Octave so characteristic of the paschal festival is wanting altogether to that of Pentecost, as the latter is itself the continuation of the Feast of the Resurrection, so for this reason the fasts of the Ember days were fixed in the week following Whit-Sunday, when the rejoicings were ended and the time had come to put into practice the words of Christ in the Gospel: *Auferetur ab eis Sponsus et jejunabunt.*

Only later, towards the seventh century, was the idea of equalising Pentecost and Easter, also in regard to the Octave, completely accepted at Rome, and in consequence a whole series of stational Masses during the week was introduced, displacing the Ember day fasts, which down to the eleventh century were moved backwards and forwards throughout the whole month of June.

Gregory VII remedied, or at least tried to remedy, the disorder which had thus arisen. As a true Roman, he must have remembered, if only vaguely, that the summer Ember days came originally immediately after Whit-Sunday; therefore, without concerning himself about the reason of their having been displaced, which, as we have seen, was the prolongation of the festival throughout the week, he replaced them in their former position by means of a curious compromise. The Octave of Pentecost was solemnized with all the splendour of its Alleluias, but, after the stational Mass, the faithful were obliged to protract their fast until the hour of None—that is, until about three o'clock in the afternoon.

So much for the history of the feast. As to its liturgical and mystical significance, it should be noted that although the sacrament of baptism is entirely separate from that of confirmation, yet in ancient theological terminology the latter is called *Confirmatio,* because it sets a seal, as it were, on the rite of Christian initiation through baptism. The descent of the Holy Ghost upon the soul of the neophyte completes and gives stability to the work of his sanctification. By his sacramental *sphragis* as a soldier of Christ, the Paraclete confers on him a more defined and a more perfect likeness to Jesus, places the final seal upon him and completes his union with God. It was the same with the Church of the Apostles. Baptized though she was in the blood and the water which flowed on the evening of Good Friday from the pierced side of the Redeemer, she was not confirmed by the fire of the Paraclete until the morning of Pentecost, when, no longer now in infancy, she came forth for the first time in the sight of the Gentiles to proclaim by the mouth of Peter the accomplishment of the Messianic redemption.

The term *Confirmatio* is archaic but expressive. In the Spanish liturgy, the *Confirmatio Sacramenti* is, strictly speaking, the prayer which calls down the Holy Ghost upon the eucharistic offerings, in order that, having rendered pleasing to God the sacrifice of his Church, it may be made truly fruitful to all those who partake of it worthily.

By realizing the similarity which exists between the eucharistic epiklesis—*Confirmatio Sacramenti*—and the sacrament of confirmation, we shall be the better able to understand the expression *Confirmatio*. As in the former, so also in the latter, the descent of the Holy Ghost is invoked to ratify, fulfil, and give a definite character to that divine sonship in Christ which was conferred by the sacrament of regeneration. This link between the two sacraments—of baptism and confirmation—which in the East are still invariably administered together—explains why the ancient Eastern liturgy ordered that they should be solemnly administered not only on the vigil of Easter, but also on that of Pentecost.

In the early Middle Ages the sacred rite always took place at the Lateran, but in the twelfth century, when the ceremonies of the vigil of Pentecost were already anticipated on the afternoon of Saturday, the Pope used to go to St Peter's to recite the Vespers and Matins of Pentecost, thus reviving the ancient Roman tradition which prescribed that baptism should be administered *ad fontes sancti Petri* in the Vatican.

The rites of the vigil of Pentecost, as described in our present Missal, show traces of very great antiquity. The blessing of the candle is wanting, as Rome never adopted the evening *Lucernarium*, while the ceremony used on Holy Saturday at the lighting of the paschal candle was a later addition introduced from other countries. The lessons, instead of being twelve, are only six, in accordance with the Gregorian Rule. St Gregory had, it is true, also diminished by half the number of lessons in the paschal vigil, but these were again increased to twelve, owing to the ancient popular tradition, and also to the influence of the Gelasian Sacramentary, which was held in great esteem during the Carlovingian period.

There is nothing especially characteristic about the vigiliary Mass. The antiphons for the Offertory and the Communion in particular, quite independently of the Gospel, show a liturgical freedom which does not belong to the classical period; but the collects are very devotional,˙ and their delicacy and tenderness are in perfect harmony with the character of the Christian Pentecost, the feast of Love.

For, as the outpouring of the Holy Ghost is the supreme act of the Love of God for men, so the final and definite withdrawal of the soul from him, in the determined refusal of this love, constitutes that which the Gospel calls sin against the Holy Ghost. It is the Paraclete who determines in us the development of our supernatural life according to our divine Exemplar Jesus Christ. Each time, then, that we disfigure this divine work, or that we roughly hinder its progress, we are resisting the Holy Ghost, and for this reason St Paul warns his followers to beware of lukewarmness, lest they should sorely grieve the Paraclete.

Following the *Ordines Romani* on Whit-Sunday the station took place at St Peter's, the true and primitive cathedral of Rome, for the Lateran was originally regarded merely as the ordinary, everyday residence of the Pontiffs. On the great feast-days, on the occasion of Ordinations, and on the Ember vigils, the Roman stations were always at the Vatican. On Whit-Sunday there was a further reason for this, since St Peter held a foremost place in the festival, being the first of the Apostles after the descent of the Holy Ghost to announce the Gospel to the men of various nations assembled at Jerusalem.

As we have already said, the feast of Pentecost formerly closed the Easter *quinquagesima,* and was followed by a prolongation of at most two festival days, after which began the summer fast. When, however, it was desired to give to Pentecost in all respects the same importance as Easter, a stational cycle was arranged for it, which being somewhat laboured, and wanting in spontaneity, clearly shows that it belongs to a period later than that which is known as the golden age of the Roman Liturgy. In fact, on the Monday, the station should rightly have been at St Peter's, as it is on Easter Monday, but in order not to celebrate High Mass at the Vatican on two days in succession, the Esquiline Basilica of St Peter ad Vincula was chosen, although in olden days it never ranked with the Apostoleion of Narses, the Pantheon, St Anastasia, St Lawrence, or with any of those churches which are distinguished by having a station in Easter Week.

In honour of the titular saint of the Eudoxian Basilica, the first lesson of the Mass on Whit-Monday relates the discourse of St Peter in the house of the centurion Cornelius. The decisive moment is come. The preaching of the Gospel is addressed rather to the Gentiles than to the stubborn Jews; hence it falls to Peter to be the first to admit them into the fold of Christ. He converts Cornelius and his household to the faith, and by his orders they are baptized and permitted to form part of the new family, the spiritual Israel.

On the Tuesday the station should have been at St Paul's outside the Walls; but at Rome, in the month of June, it is too hot for the procession to walk as far as the second milestone on the Via Ostiensis. A more central church was therefore chosen, that of St Anastasia, the Court church during the Byzantine period; thus does diplomacy affect even the liturgy.

The Introit of Whit-Tuesday is taken from the apochryphal book of Esdras, rejected by Rome, but admitted by the Greeks, a circumstance which supplies us with a valuable chronological criterion in fixing approximately the date at which this stational Mass was composed.

The Gospel lesson, like the greater number of those appointed for this week, is only remotely connected with the feast of Pentecost, and comes from an Eastern source. It refers to the loving work of the Holy Ghost in the redemption of humanity, and in the sanctification of the soul, rather than to his historical and sacramental mission.

On the following Wednesday the Mass is at St Mary Major, no doubt in consequence of the Ember days, the station of Wednesday in Ember Week being always held at the Liberian Basilica. Perhaps, however, before the time of Gregory VII, the station was at St Lawrence outside the Walls, as on Wednesday in Easter Week. It is important to notice that the Gospel lesson for this day treats of the holy Eucharist, and gives to this period of the Roman liturgical cycle a foreshadowing of the feast of *Corpus Domini,* which later was celebrated midway in the week following the Octave of Pentecost.

Thursday in Rome was always aliturgical. Later the station *ad Apostolos* was celebrated on the Thursday after Pentecost just as it was after Easter, but, as the Liberian station of the Wednesday has displaced the earlier one at St Lawrence, a certain disorder arose among the ancient Roman commemorations. Our present Missal assigns to St Lawrence the station which should have been celebrated there on the previous day, and, to add to the confusion, the lesson relating the miracles of the deacon Philip in Samaria has been preserved, but quite out of its proper place. Originally this lesson bore reference—although erroneously—to the Apostle Philip, whose relics repose under the High Altar of the Apostoleion of Narses.

The series of the stations having once been altered, it was impossible to re-establish the former order. On the Friday we now have the station at the Twelve Holy Apostles, as on Thursday in Easter Week; whereas in the seventh century the Mass was on the Coelian at the ancient title of Pammachius.

The station of the Saturday brings us back to the Vatican, where the *Pannuchis* was celebrated and holy orders administered. The vigiliary rite is the one customary in Rome, but the choice of the scriptural lessons is in the nature of a compromise, for, out of the five which are read, only one is connected with Pentecost; all the others having reference to the harvest feasts. When in the seventh century the Ember fasts were displaced for some weeks on account of the Octave of Whit-Sunday, the Saturday station was celebrated at St Stephen on the Coelian Hill, a custom which continued down to the time of Gregory VII.

With the Octave of Whit-Sunday the Easter cycle definitely closes. Jesus Christ, risen from the dead and seated at the right hand of the Father, communicates his own divine life to the mystical members of his body through the outpouring of the gifts of the Holy Ghost. The Church who, until yesterday, like an infant bound in swaddling bands, was shut in by the narrow walls of the Upper Room, having now grown to her full stature, comes forth radiant with life and truth and makes her first appearance in the sight of all the world. The Holy Ghost, flowing through her pure veins like new wine, fills her with the living power of Christ and causes her to share in his ministry and in his work of redemption. For this reason St Paul was able to say with truth that his apostolic labours formed part of the mystery of the redemption, inasmuch as they completed that which was wanting to the passion of Jesus Christ for the salvation of the Church.

CHAPTER IV

ANCIENT HYMNODY DURING THE CELEBRATION OF THE NIGHT VIGIL

THE New Testament, far from abolishing the Old, replaced the figure by the reality, and by completing its teaching and grafting itself upon it, arose like a flower from the stem. The Christian liturgy from the first adopted the *Alleluia,* the psalms, and the canticles of the Synagogue; hence the psalter, on account of its eminently Messianic character, will always be in all ages the chief book of Catholic prayer and devotion.

However, for some time after the Ascension of our Lord into heaven, the rays of dogmatic revelation continued to shine upon the Church, especially through the teaching of St Paul, and this period was only brought definitely to a close by the Seer of Patmos, who, in the name of Jesus, has set the final seal upon that sacred and mysterious book begun long ages before in the name of the Creative Word: *In principio creavit Deus.* . . . *Amen: veni, Domine Jesu.*

The *lex credendi* being thus completed, the Liturgy, *i.e.,* the *lex supplicandi,* also had to be enriched with new formularies and rites which should fully set forth the "good news," rendering to God a perfect worship *in spiritu et veritate.* As a result of its primitive inspiration the ancient euchological literature often assumed a lyrical character with a preference for rhythmic forms. The rhythm was free, and was based on the succession of syllables and accents, with occasional rimed cadences, and with phrases and measures which balance each other in perfect harmony.[1]

On account, however, of the extemporaneous character of these very early liturgical compositions, and of the rule of the *arcanum* which hindered the diffusion of the sacred writings; above all, on account of the persecution of Diocletian, when in the *dies traditionis* the archives of the Church were confiscated and dispersed, only a very few euchological documents recording the early Christian prayers have come down to our days.

In the second century, when the gifts of the Holy Ghost were no longer poured forth so abundantly on the assemblies of the faithful as they had been in very early times, the Church, desiring to safeguard the deposit of the Catholic

---

[1] *Cf.* Cabrol, *Liturgical Prayer.*

faith which she had received, was obliged to defend the liturgy from any personal influence; consequently the extemporaneous and voluntary character of the ritual formularies became typical of heretical sects such as the Gnostics and the Montanists. So from that time the Catholics began to possess their own earliest collections of ritual prayers in MS. A brief account of the more important among the liturgical documents still existing will help us better to realize their value.

Besides the testimony of St Paul that, at Corinth, in the assemblies, ἕκαστος ψαλμὸν ἔχει, διδαχὴν ἔχει, ἀποκάλυψιν ἔχει,[1] in other passages of his Epistles the rhythm of his periods seems to evoke reminiscences of some liturgical hymn then in use among the faithful.

Of these we will give some examples :[2]

(Θεὸς) ἐφανερώθη ἐν σαρκί,	Manifestatum est in carne,
ἐδικαιώθη ἐν πνεύματι,	Justificatum est in Spiritu,
ὤφθη ἀγγέλοις,	Apparuit Angelis,
ἐκηρύχθη ἐν ἔθνεσιν,	Nunciatum est gentibus,
ἐπιστεύθη ἐν κόσμῳ,	Creditum est in mundo,
ἀνελήμφθη ἐν δόξῃ.	Assumptum est in gloria.

And again :[3]

Εἰ γὰρ συναπεθάνομεν καὶ συνζήσομεν·	Si commortui sumus et convivemus ;
Εἰ ὑπομένομεν, καὶ συνβασιλεύσομεν·	Si sustinebimus, et conregnabimus.
Εἰ ἀρνησόμεθα, κἀκεῖνος ἀρνήσεται ἡμᾶς·	Si negabimus, et ipse negabit nos.
Εἰ ἀπιστοῦμεν, ἐκεῖνος πιστὸς μένει,	Si infideles erimus, ille fidus permanet ;
Ἀρνήσασθαι γὰρ ἑαυτὸν οὐ δύναται.	Negare se ipsum non potest.

And addressing the Ephesians :[4] *Propter quod dicit:* (Who says it?)

Ἔγειρε, ὁ καθεύδων,	Exsurge qui dormis,
καὶ ἀνάστα ἐκ τῶν νεκρῶν,	et resurge a mortuis,
καὶ ἐπιψαύσει σοι ὁ Χριστός.	et illucebit tibi Christus.

It would probably be possible to find other traces of hymnody in the Acts of the Apostles[5] and in the Apocalypse,[6] but as these have already been examined and discussed by the exegetes,[7] it only remains for us now to try to discover the part which this kind of archaic hymnody formerly played in the history of the development of the divine Office.

---

[1] 1 Cor. xiv 26. [2] 1 Tim. iii 16.
[3] 2 Tim. ii 11-13. It is worthy of note that St Paul quotes this rhythm as being a "πιστὸς ὁ λόγος," well known to the faithful.
[4] Eph. v 14. [5] iv 24-30. [6] xix 6 *sqq.*
[7] Probst, *Liturgie der drei ersten christlichen Jahrhunderte.* Tübingen 1870. *Lehre und Gebet in den drei ersten christlichen Jahrhunderten.* Tübingen 1870.

The Odes of Solomon of the second century, recently discovered by Rendel Harris, the origin of which is not yet
altogether clear, deserve special mention. Almost as ancient
as these is the *Liber Psalmorum* of Marcion quoted in the
Muratorian Fragment, but this collection, like that of the
Psalms or Odes[1] of Basilides, is hardly known to us except
by name. Many other odes, besides the five attributed to
Solomon, are scattered throughout the Gnostic work *Pistis
Sophia*. Bardesanes and Ammonius collected in Syria an
entire psalter of one hundred and fifty psalms, enriched with
popular melodies, which was still in use at the time of St
Ephrem.

Of the Ὠδαί of Hippolytus mentioned on his marble seat
now in the Lateran Museum, we know nothing definitely; but
a Roman fragment against the heresy of Artemon, quoted by
Eusebius, certainly records Christian ψαλμοὶ καὶ ὠδαί composed
in the earliest ages of the Church in honour of the divine
nature of Christ.[2] Very similar to these must have been
the soteriological psalms suppressed at Antioch by Paul of
Samosata,[3] so that he might have instead songs sung by
women in his own praise: Ἐν μέσῃ τῇ Ἐκκλεσίᾳ . . . ψαλμ-
ῳδεῖν γυναῖκας παρασκενάζων.

St Dionysius of Alexandria also mentions a πολλῆς ψαλμῳδίας
which was popular in Egypt, and which was known to have
been composed by Bishop Nepos in the first half of the third
century.[4] Arius, especially, made use of psalmody in order
to propagate his errors; and he did this with greater success
because the melodies of these odes or songs of seamen, of
travellers and others took a great hold on the imagination of
the excitable Egyptian populace.

The discoveries made in Egypt among various fragmentary
papyri of apocryphal Gospels, rituals, and heretical treatises,
have also brought to light a few remains of these liturgical
odes. Amélinau has published that very interesting one from
the papyrus of Bruce: " Then he began to sing a hymn of
praise to his Father: I will give praise unto thee, etc. And
he bade his disciples answer three times: Amen, Amen,
'Amen. And he repeated again: I will sing a hymn of praise
to thee my Father and my God; for, etc., and at every verse
the disciples replied: O immutable God, such is thine
immutable will."[5]

Cf. Origen, *in Job*, xli, 19 *sqq.*; *P.G.* XII, col. 1050.
[2] Euseb., *Hist. Eccl.*, v, 28; *P.G.* XX, col. 512.
[3] *Op. cit.*, vii, 30; *P.G.* XX, col. 715.
[4] *Op. cit.*, vii, 24; *P.G.* XX, col. 693.
[5] *Cf.* Amélinau, *Notice sur le papyrus gnostique de Bruce*, pp. 160-
70. Paris 1891.

A papyrus in the collection of Archduke Ranier gives us the text of another hymn, most certainly earlier than the Arian controversy, the verses of which were used as refrains or acrostics to Psalm xxxii.[1] The worn place of the papyrus where the cantor used to place his finger shows that the scroll was for many years in liturgical use.

At length the Council of Laodicea (343-381) intervened in order to protect the Catholic spirit of the sacred Liturgy against the too great euchological influence of persons and of schools; and by means of Canons XV and LIX put an end to the ἰδιωτικοί ψαλμοί, ordering that the psalmody should be executed only by the κανονικοί ψάλται.[2] Thus a perfect balance was re-established, and a place of honour was assured to the euchology of the Old Testament in the divine Office; which otherwise would, in the East, soon have been submerged under the wealth of antiphons and tropes.

Besides the one hundred and fifty psalms divided into three sections of the Davidical psalter, other rhythmical compositions taken from the canonical books of both the Old and the New Testament were added to it in very early times. As a rule these canticles or odes are twelve in number, as follows :

1. Canticum Moysis (Exod. xv).
2. Canticum Deuteronomii (Deut. xxxii).
3. Canticum Annae (1 Reg. ii).
4. Canticum Habacuc (Habacuc iii).
5. Canticum Esaiae (Isa. xii).
6. Canticum Esaiae (Isa. xxvi).
7. Canticum Ezechiae (Isa. xxxviii 10-20).
8. Canticum Jonae (Jon. iii).
9. Canticum benedictionum (Dan. iii).
10. Canticum de Evangelio (Luc. i, *Magnificat*).
11. Canticum de Evangelio (Luc. i, *Benedictus*).
12. Canticum de Evangelio (Luc. ii, *Nunc Dimittis*).

To these are often added the apocryphal *canticum Manasse,* the *canticum Azariae* (Dan. iii), the *canticum Ezechiae* (Isa. xxxviii-ix), the *canticum Deborae* (Judges v 2), the *canticum Jeremiae* (Lam. v 1), and several other canticles which are still preserved in the Mozarabic and Benedictine liturgies. The latter contains, besides those already mentioned, the following canticles : Isaias xxxii 2, ix 2, v 2, xl 10, lxi 6; Jeremias xiv 17; Eccles. xiv 22, xxxi; Jeremias xvii; Wisdom iii, x; Isaias xxxix, lxi, lxii; Jeremias vii; Tobias xiii; Isaias lxiii; Osee vi; Sophonias iii.

---

[1] Socrat., *Eccl. Hist.*, vi, 8; *P.G.* LXVII, col. 688 *sqq.*; Philostorg., *Hist. Eccles*, ii, 2; *P.G.* LXV, col. 465.
[2] Mansi, *Collect. Concil,* vol. ii, col. 567, 574.

Verecundus, an author of the sixth century, discovered by Pitra,[1] mentions the tradition of the African Church, according to which Esdras is said to have collected in a single volume the canticles scattered through the Holy Scriptures, so that they might be sung in the same manner as the Psalms. The *Codex Alexandrinus* of the fifth century, in fact—after the Psalter and in addition to the twelve Canticles mentioned above, among which is the *Nunc Dimittis* taken from the Gospel—gives us also the penitential prayer of Azarias (Dan. iii 26 *sqq.*) and a ὕμνος ἑωθινός very free in style. In all there are fourteen songs or odes. The collection of Verecundus is more restricted, for it contains only the two canticles of Moses, that of the Lamentations, the *Benedictiones,* and those of Isaias (xxxviii 10), Habacuc, Manasses, Jonas, and Debbora.

Unlike the African Churches, to which belong the two collections we have mentioned, the Eastern Churches admitted as a rule only nine odes, which were sometimes recited in succession in the morning Office with the insertion of at most a few tropes.[2] St John Chrysostom bears witness that in his time, at any rate among the religious, the Canticle of Isaias (xxvi) and the *Benedictiones* were everywhere recited, the former in the night Office and the latter in the morning Office.[3]

The list of canticles given by Nicetas of Remesiana is almost identical with that of Constantinople, except in the precedence given to Isaias over Habacuc and in the addition of a canticle of Jeremias. I quote from Morin[4] the following comparative lists of canticles in use at Remesiana, Constantinople, Milan, and in Gaul.

As to Rome, its list *per hebdomadam* appeared so ancient and venerable even in the sixth century that St Benedict himself did not venture to alter it in his monastic *cursus.* He therefore ordered that his monks should recite each week in addition to the Psalter the traditional canticles of the Roman Church.

NICETAS	MILAN
Moses (Exod.).	Isaias (xxvi 9).
Moses (Deut.).	Anna.
Anna.	Habacuc.
Isaias (xxvi 9).	Jonas.

---

[1] *Spicileg. Solesmense,* vol. iv, p. 1.

[2] *Cf.* Pitra, *Jur. Eccles. Graec., Histor. et Monum.,* vol. i, 220, n. 17, in which the Office of Abbot Nilus on Mount Sinai is described. St Athanasius in his Epistle *Ad Marcellinum* merely mentions the rich melody : τῶν ψαλμῶν, καὶ ᾠδῶν, καὶ ἀσματῶν ῥήματα, *P.G.* XXVII, col. 40.

[3] Hom. XIV in 1 Tim. v; *P.G.* LXII, col. 576. Cf. *Quod nemo laeditur; P.G.* LII, col. 477.

[4] G. Morin, Le " *De Psalmodiae bono* " de *l'évèque Nicetas,* in *Rev. Bénédict.,* xiv, p. 389. 1897.

Habacuc.
Jonas.
Jeremias (?).
Benedictiones.
Elisabeth (Luc. i 46).

Moses (Deut.).
Moses (Exod.).
Zacharias (Luc. i 68).
Mary (Luc. i 46).
Benedictiones.

CONSTANTINOPLE

Moses (Exod.).
Moses (Deut.).
Anna.
Habacuc.
Isaias (xxvi 9).
Jonas.
Benedictiones (I part).
Benedictiones (II part).
Mary (Luc. i 46).
Ezechias.
Lamentations (v 1-22).
IV Esdras (viii 20-36).
Azarias (Dan. iii 26-45).

GAUL

Benedictiones.
Moses (Exod.).
Moses (Deut.).
Isaias (lx 1-14).
Isaias (lxi 10-lxii 7).
Anna.
Mary.
Isaias (xxvi 9).
Judith.

CURS. BENEDICT.

Benedictiones (Dominica).
Isaias (xii).
Ezechias (Isaias xxxviii).
Anna.
Moses (Exod.).
Habacuc.
Moses (Deut.).
Canticum de Evangelio ad Matut (Luc. i 68).
Canticum de Evangelio ad Vesperas (Luc. i 46).
Te decet laus ad vigil.

RULE OF ST CESARIUS

Canticum Moysis (Exod.).
Benedictiones.
(Te Deum).
(Gloria in Excelsis).
} Dominica ad Matut. Laudes.

ANTIPHONARY OF BANGOR

Cantic. Moysis (Deut. xxxii).
Cantic. Moysis (Exod.).
Benedictiones.
Canticum Benedictio S. Zachariae (Luc i).
(Te Deum).
(Gloria in Excelsis).

These lists of canticles would be incomplete if not collated with that of Rome as still contained in the Sacramentaries. It is in the primitive text of the paschal *vigilia* that we must more especially make our investigations. In the Gelasian Sacramentary, before the Gregorian alterations, the paschal lessons, whether in Latin or in Greek, were twelve in number, alternated by the collects and by the following canticles: *Cantic. Moysis* (Exod.), after the fourth lesson; *Cantic. Esaiae* (Isa. v); *Cantic. Moysis* (Deut.), and perhaps also the *Benedictiones* after the lesson from Daniel, since Psalm xli was sung immediately before the procession moved towards the baptistery. Such was the custom at Rome before the liturgical reform introduced by St Gregory the Great.

The *Ordo Romanus I,* on the other hand, which represents the papal liturgy of the sixth to the eighth century, orders six lessons only, both in Greek and in Latin, for the paschal vigil, but interspersed with the collects, and with the following canticles recited in both languages: *Moysis* (Exod.), *Cant. Isaiae* (Isa. v), and Psalm xli.[1] There is no mention of the *Benedictiones,* which, however, certainly followed the reading from Daniel at the end of the other solemn vigils of the year,[2] and from that date formed part of the *Ordo Missae* both in the Gallican and in the Mozarabic liturgy.[3]

In the Roman books the first *collecta* of the Mass on these days recalls the lesson from Daniel, and leads us to suppose that at one time, instead of the *Kyrie* and the litany, the canticle of the *Benedictiones* formed a link between the vigiliary Office and the Mass itself. On Feria VI of Holy Week the Roman Liturgy orders the canticle of Habacuc, *Domine audivi,* to be recited in the Mass after the lesson from Osee, this same canticle being the one appointed for the Matins of that day.

We learn, in fact, from the Rule of St Benedict that Rome, unlike the churches of Gaul and Ireland, already made use of a collection of canticles appointed for each day of the week. *In matutinis dominica die. . . . Benedictiones . . .; sabbato autem . . . canticum Deuteronomii . . . nam coeteris diebus canticum unumquodque die suo ex Prophetis, sicut psallit Ecclesia Romana, dicatur.*[4]

Nor was this all; for the collection must have been very much richer than those in use in the East, since for the third nocturn of the *vigiliae* preceding the Sunday, St Benedict leaves to the abbot the task of choosing the three canticles from the Prophets which compose it: *Tria cantica de Prophetarum*—this was the title written on the volume— *quae instituerit abbas; quae cantica cum alleluia psallantur.*[5] These canticles were not taken directly from the Bible, merely in accordance with the personal preference of the abbot, since there undoubtedly existed an entire collection, as we see from the title *Prophetarum,* and from ancient tradition. Therefore the same saint at the end of his *cursus* adds a warning that, should a different *cursus* be preferred, the rule is in any case to be observed that *psalterium cum canticis consuetudinariis per septimanae circulum psallant.*[6]

The Christian tradition of the first centuries which had inspired so many psalms and hymns in honour of the Blessed Trinity and of our Lord was not, however, entirely lost. The Eastern as well as the Western Churches maintained in

[1] *Ord. Rom. I; P.L.* LXXVII, col. 955-56.
[2] *Ord. Rom. IX, loc. cit.,* col. 1007; *Sacram. Greg.; P.L.* LXXVII, col. 61, 115, 129.
[3] *Cf.* Wagner, *Origine e sviluppo del Canto Liturgico.* Italian translation, pp. 96-7. Siena 1910.
[4] *Regul. S. Benedicti,* c. xii, xiii.
[5] *Op. cit.,* c. xi.   [6] *Op. cit.,* xviii.

liturgical use not only the New Testament canticles, but also certain hymns belonging to the traditional literature of early Christian times.

The three canticles of the Blessed Virgin, of Zachary and of Simeon, related by St Jude, are called *cantica de evangelio,* and we find them almost everywhere in use both in the Greek and in the Latin liturgies. The Alexandrian Biblical codex contains all three *cantica,* although the Greeks generally exclude from the lists that of Simeon, and it is also omitted by St Benedict.

The name given to the *Magnificat* by Nicetas of Remesiana, "Canticum Elisabeth,"[1] is unique with the exception of an allusion by Origen. The Eastern churches recited the Μεγαλύνει during the Sunday Matins, and, following their example, the Rule of Aurelian in Gaul also ordered that it should be said in the Office at dawn.[2]

The *Canticum Sancti Zachariae* in the East, in the Rule of St Benedict and in the Irish *Cursus* of Bangor forms part of Matins,[3] but that of Simeon fared otherwise, and although it was included in Vespers on Mount Sinai,[4] on the other hand it was not admitted to the various *cursus* of the monasteries in the West. However, it very soon came to be included in the Roman *Completorium,*[5] perhaps owing to the influence of the Eastern monasteries, which were very numerous in the Holy City, the more so because the *Nunc Dimittis* forms part of the evening prayer in the Apostolic Constitutions.

The Greater Doxology, or *Gloria in Excelsis,* notwithstanding its uncanonical origin, became far more important than the other scriptural canticles, and soon held a place in the morning liturgy. This is the traditional place allotted to it in the Apostolic Constitutions—one of the most ancient documents witnessing to its use—also in the Greek and Milanese liturgies, in the monastic liturgies of Cæsarius, of Aurelian, and of the Irish monastery of Bangor. Indeed in this latter monastery the *Gloria* was repeated at Vespers as being the most perfect triumphant hymn which humanity, redeemed in the precious Blood of the Lamb, raises each day to God at the time of the evening sacrifice.

The origin of the Greater Doxology is lost in the shadows of the past. Some students have identified it with the hymn

---

Cf. Morin, *op. cit.*

[1] *Cf.* Bäumer, *Hist. du Bréviaire,* i, 217.   [3] *Op. cit.,* 239.

[4] *Op. cit.,* 181. It was already added to the evening prayer in the Apostolic Constitutions; I, vii, c. 48; *P.G.* I, col. 1057.

[5] Amalarius mentions this, but in his time among the clergy Compline was already losing its ancient significance of a personal, almost private, prayer previous to retiring for the night's rest. *De Ord. Antiphon.,* 7.

to Christ *quasi Deo,* mentioned by Pliny in his letter to Trajan, and this would seem to be borne out by the *Apologia* of Aristides,[1] in which we read that the Christians " praise and glorify God every morning and at every hour of the day by reason of his great goodness towards them." Others have wished to connect it with the hymn πολυώνυμος, of which Lucian speaks, and certainly the external and internal arguments brought to prove this hypothesis render it very probable.

In fact the theological matter of the *Gloria in Excelsis,* its rhythm, the proofs cited above, the importance given to it in the fourth century even over the scriptural canticles, all combine to lead us to recognize in the Greater Doxology one of the earliest of the Christian hymns which sustained the faith of the infant Church amid the cares and dangers of persecution.

The text preserved in the Apostolic Constitutions[2] is spoilt by subordinationist tendencies, but in some points it seems to be more complete than the ordinary version. They are as follows :

CONSTIT. APOSTOL.		TEXT. VULG.
Δόξα ἐν ὑψίστοις Θεῷ, καὶ ἐπὶ γῆς εἰρήνη, ἐν ἀνθρώποις εὐδοκία.	Gloria in excelsis Deo, Et super terram pax, in homines pia voluntas.	Gloria in excelsis Deo, Et in terra pax hominibus bonae voluntatis.
Αἰνοῦμέν σε,	Laudamus Te,	Laudamus Te,
Ὑμνοῦμέν σε,	Canimus Te,	
Εὐλογοῦμέν σε,	Benedicimus Te,	Benedicimus Te
Δοξολογοῦμέν σε,	Glorificamus Te,	(Glorificamus Te)
Προσκυνοῦμέν σε,	Adoramus Te,	Adoramus Te
Διὰ τοῦ μεγάλου ἀρχιερέως, σὲ τὸν ὄντα Θεόν,	per Pontificem magnum, Te qui Deus es,	. . . .
Ἀγέννητον ἕνα,	Solus ingenitus,	. . . .
Ἀπρόσιτον μόνον,	Solus inaccessibilis,	. . . .
Διὰ τὴν μεγάλην σοῦ δόξαν.	propter magnam gloriam tuam.	Propter magnam gloriam tuam.
Κύριε, βασιλεῦ ἐπουράνιε,	Domine, Rex coelestis, ...	Domine, Deus, rex coelestis
Θεὲ πάτερ παντοκράτορ.	Deus, Pater omnipotens,	Deus, Pater omnipotens,
Κύριε, ὁ Θεός, ὁ Πάτερ τοῦ Χριστοῦ, τοῦ ἀμώμου ἀμνοῦ,	Domine, Deus Pater Christi, Agni immaculati	Domine, (Fili Unigenite Iesu Christe) Domine Deus, Agnus Dei, Filius Patris,
Ὃς αἴρει τὴν ἁμαρτίαν τοῦ κόσμου,	Qui tollit peccatum mundi,	Qui tollis peccata mundi
Πρόσδεξαι τὴν δέησιν ἡμῶν.	suscipe deprecationem nostram,	(suscipe deprecationem nostram). . . . .

---

[1] A Christian apologist of Athens, *cir.* 125, *temp.* Emp. Hadrian.— TR.

[2] *Constitutiones Apost.*, Bk. VII, c. 47; *P.G.* I, col. 1056-1057.

'Ο καθήμενος ἐπὶ τῶν Χερουβίμ.

Qui sedes super Cheru-bim.

Qui sedes (ad dex-teram Patris suscipe deprecationem nos-tram)

. . . .

Ὅτι σὺ μόνος ἅγιος,

Quoniam tu solus Sanc-tus,

Quoniam tu solus sanc-tus,

Σὺ μόνος κύριος

Tu solus Dominus

Tu solus Dominus,

Ἰησοῦς Χριστοῦ τοῦ Θεοῦ πάσης γεννητῆς φύσεως

Iesu Christi, Dei totius naturae creatae,

Tu solus altissimus Iesu Christe,

Τοῦ βασιλέως ἡμῶν

Regis nostri,

Cum Sancto Spiritu

Δι᾽ οὗ σοι δόξα, τιμή, καὶ σέβας.

Per quem Tibi gloria, honor et adoratio.

In gloria Dei Patris. Amen.

The rhythm is the one previously described, oratorical in form and based on the essential consonance of the accents, with due regard to the length of the phrases which often fall into rime. Its theological matter is precisely the same as that which we find in the prayers of the Διδαχή. The Holy Ghost is not even mentioned in it. Jesus is God and Lord of all creation, priest and victim of the Father, but the dignity of the divine Fatherhood is too strongly insisted upon for it to be possible that this hymn should have been composed after the Trinitarian controversies of the third century. God the Father is spoken of not only as ἀγέννητον, but also as ἀπρόσιτον μόνον; which, unless understood in a Catholic sense of the Word as Creator and Redeemer, would imply a degree of inferiority in the second Person of the Blessed Trinity, as being the one through whom the " Inaccessible " communicates with the finite.

It was not until much later that the Greater Doxology, excluded in Rome from the morning Office, was inserted by Symmachus (?) (498-514) between the litany and the collect in the Sunday Mass. It is nevertheless true that a tradition mentioned in the *Liber Pontificalis* attributes the inclusion of the *Gloria* in the midnight Mass of Christmas to Pope Telesphorus (died 154); but, apart from the anachronism of the Christmas festivity, celebrated as early as the first half of the second century, it is probable that the legend contains a confused and vague remembrance—but the only one as far as Rome was concerned—that formerly the Greater Doxology did really form part of the παννυχίς of that solemn day, as it did among the Greeks.

In any case it is certain that in the sixth century at Rome the *Gloria* had no longer a place in the morning Office; whence, notwithstanding the beginning, which recalls the song of the angels at the birth of the Redeemer, it was regarded rather as an Easter hymn, or triumphal ode, to be sung on the most solemn occasions. In the early Middle Ages the Pope recited it at Mass every Sunday, as being the day dedicated to the remembrance of the resurrection, and later also on the festivals of martyrs.

Priests on the other hand said the *Gloria* only on Easter Day and on the *natalis ordinationis,* the anniversary, that is, of the day on which they received their ordination to the priesthood.

Another ancient hymn which, in the Apostolic Constitutions, is appointed to be sung at Vespers, and in the Western liturgies has been accepted by the Benedictine *cursus,* is the *Te decet.* St Benedict enjoins that it be sung as a doxology after the reading of the Gospel on the vigils before the Sundays. Its liturgical use, therefore, is similar to that of the antiphon *post evangelium* of Milan, and of the various acclamations which, in the Mass, follow the Gospel in the Gallican and Mozarabic liturgies; in every place, in fact, where Eastern influences have been felt. Later on, in the twelfth century, the *Te decet* came to form part also of the papal *vigilia* as an alternative hymn instead of the *Te Deum* which concluded the first night Office on the days of double Office.[1]

The following is the text of this venerable doxology:

APOSTOL. CONSTIT.		BENEDICTINE TEXT.
Σοὶ πρέπει αἶνος·	Te decet laus,	Te decet laus,
Σοὶ πρέπει ὕμνος·	Te decet hymnus,	Te decet hymnus,
Σοὶ δόξα πρέπει τῷ Θεῷ καὶ Πατρί,	Te decet gloria Deo et Patri,	Tibi gloria Deo Patri,
Διὰ τοῦ Υἱοῦ, ἐν Πνεύματι τῷ παναγίῳ,	Per Filium, in Spiritu omnisancto,	Et Filio cum sancto Spiritu,
εἰς τοὺς αἰῶνας τῶν αἰώνων.	In saecula saeculorum.	In saecula saeculorum.
Ἀμήν.[2]	Amen.	Amen.

Far more famous than the above is the Western hymn *Te Deum,* composed by Bishop Nicetas of Remesiana at the end of the fourth century, which has been attributed in turn to St Ambrose,[3] to St Anicetus, to Sisibutus, and to St Abundius. St Benedict directs it to be sung at the end of the vigil previous to the Sunday;[4] but in the monastic Rules of Gaul[5] and Ireland it is described, on the contrary, as a *hymnus ad matutinos in dominicis diebus.*[6] Of later date

---

[1] *Cf.* Bäumer, *op. cit.,* ii, 51. The differences between the text of the Apostolic Constitutions and the Benedictine are found also in the present Greek version, which was probably modified during the Arian controversy.

[2] *Cf. Const. Apost,* VII, c. 48; *P.G.* I, col. 1057.

[3] *Cf.* Morin, *Rev. Bénéd.,* pp. 15-19, 1890; pp. 49-77, 337-345, 1894; p. 390, 1897; p. 399, 1898.

[4] *Regul.,* c. xi.   [5] *Cf.* Bäumer, *op. cit.,* i, 216-7.

[6] This is the place it occupies in the Antiphonary of Bangor (seventh century), first edited by Muratori, (*Anecd. Ambrosiana,* vol. iv, pp. 119

than the above-mentioned hymns, the *Te Deum* yields place to them also in originality of conception, for the first ten verses appear to be derived from the eucharistic hymn in the liturgy of Jerusalem; verses 11-13 and 24-26 are inspired by the *Gloria,* whilst the others are taken from the Psalms.

Originally, the hymn ended with verse 21 : *Aeterna fac cum sanctis tuis in gloria numerari,* but in the different Churches various other endings began to be added, which contributed to give the *Te Deum* a penitential character. In fact, in the Middle Ages it was chanted in times of great calamity, whilst on joyful and solemn occasions the *Gloria in excelsis* was sung.[1] About the year 525 the *Te Deum* had come to be universally used in the Western liturgy, like the *Gloria* and the *Benedictiones,* and served as a link between the παννυχίς and the Mass; for which reason the Bangor Antiphonary calls it the *hymnus quando communicant sacerdotes.*

The resemblance between the *Te Deum* and another ancient Ambrosian hymn (*Transitor.,* Dom. IV p. Epiph.) is so suggestive that we cannot refrain from giving the text of it here. Cagin, who has studied it carefully, considers that we may hold it to be of very great antiquity, partly for the reason that the Latin version, when compared with the melody, betrays a Greek original, for which the music was primarily composed.

" 1. Te laudamus, Domine Omnipotens,
  2. Qui sedes super Cherubim et Seraphim,
  3. Quem benedicunt Angeli, Archangeli,
  4. Te laudant Prophetae et Apostoli.

  5. Te laudamus, Domine, orando,
  6. Qui venisti peccata solvendo ;
  7. Te deprecamur magnum Redemptorem,
  8. Quem Pater misit ovium pastorem.

  9. Tu es Christus Dominus Salvator,
 10. Qui de Maria Virgine es natus ;
 11. Ab omni culpa libera nos semper."[2]

It is impossible not to observe the affinity which exists between this text of Greek origin and the hymn of Nicetas, which, although by its language it belongs to the great Latin stock, yet has a strong connection with the East, on account of the surroundings among which the author lived.[3]

---

sqq., Patavii 1713), and later by F. E. Warren, in the collection of the Henry Bradshaw Society, London, vol. iv, par. ii, 1893; vol. x, 1895.
[1] *Cf.* Cabrol, *op. cit.*
[2] *Paléograph. Musicale,* p. 18. 1897.
[3] *Cf.* Morin, in *Rev. Bénédict.,* xxiv, pp. 180 *sqq.* 1907.

Another canticle of very great importance in the Eastern Churches, already mentioned as being in the Alexandrian Bible, is the hymn of the *Lucernarium* cited by St Basil,[1] as a proof of the belief of the ancient Church in the divine nature of the Holy Ghost.

It has not in any way been proved that St Basil identifies this hymn with the one composed by the martyr Athenogenes as he ascended the funeral pyre. Yet, as he reproduces the texts of the Fathers, quoting them in chronological order, and as the evening hymn occupies a place between Origen and Gregory Thaumaturgus, it follows that it could not have been composed later than the third century.

We give here the text of this hymn of the *Lucernarium*, which is still held in great esteem among many Oriental peoples.

Φῶς ἱλαρὸν ἀγίας δόξης ἀθανάτου
  Πατρὸς οὐρανίου,
ἀγίου, μάκαρος, Ἰησοῦ Χριστέ,
ἐλθόντες ἐπὶ τὴν ἡλίου δύσιν,
ἰδόντες φῶς ἑσπερινὸν,
ὑμνοῦμεν Πατέρα καὶ Υἱὸν καὶ Ἅγιον
  Πνεῦμα, Θεόν.
Ἀξιόν δε ἐν πᾶσι καιροῖς

ὑμνεῖσθαί σε φωναῖς ὁσίαις,
Υἱὲ Θεοῦ, ζωὴν ὁ διδοὺς
Διὰ ὁ κόσμος σε δοξάζει.

Lumen hilare gloriae sanctae im-
  mortalis Patris coelestis,
Jesu Christe, Sancti, Beati,
Ad solis occasum qui pervenimus,
Nocturnum lumen videntes,
Patrem, Filium et Spiritum sanc-
  tum Deum canimus.
Justum quidem (est) omnibus mo-
  mentis
Piis Te canere vocibus,
Fili Dei, qui vitam largiris,
Unde mundus Te glorificat.

Although this hymn was always very popular among the Greeks, it would appear that the Latin liturgies never adopted it; indeed, even the Apostolic Constitutions seem not to have known of it.

Another gem of early Christian psalmody is the joyous hymn *Ubi caritas et amor,* which nowadays is used only at the washing of the feet on Maundy Thursday. The rhythm is free, being formed by the accentuation and proportion of the sentences.

" 1. Ubi caritas et amor—Deus ibi est.
  2. Congregavit nos in unum—Christi amor.
  3. Exultemus et in ipso—Jucundemur.
  4. Timeamus et amemus—Deum vivum.
  5. Et ex corde diligamus—Nos sincero.
  6. Simul ergo cum in unum—Congregamur,
  7. Ne nos mente dividamur—Caveamus.
  8. Cessent jurgia maligna—Cessent lites,
  9. Et in medio nostri sit—Christus Deus.
  10. Simul quoque cum beatis—Videamus

[1] St Basil, *De Spir. Sancto,* cxxix, n. 73; *P.G.* XXXII, col. 205.

11. Glorianter vultum tuum—Christe Deus.
12. Gaudium quod est immensum—Atque probum,
13. Saecula per infinita—Saeculorum. Amen."

The monastic liturgies of Cesarius and Aurelian add to the second nocturn of the winter vigils another beautiful apocalyptic hymn which has found its way also into the Mozarabic liturgy under the form of a responsory for the vigils (or matins) of Wednesday in Holy Week.[1]

" 1. Magna et mirabilia opera tua sunt,
  2. Domine Deus omnipotens.
  3. Justae et verae sunt viae tuae,
  4. Domine, rex gentium.
  5. Quis non timebit et magnificabit nomen tuum?
  6. Quoniam tu solus sanctus et pius,
  7. Et omnes gentes venient et adorabunt nomen tuum
      sub oculis tuis,
  8. Quoniam justitiae tuae manifestatae sunt."[2]

The varying form, and the free and graceful rhythm of this ancient Christian hymnody, resulting from the balance of its accents and the consonance of its measures, needed a degree of ability and literary taste not easily found in the ranks of the people. Therefore this type of hymnody suffered the same fate as that which befell the classical prosody of Greece and Rome when the ancient popular poetry was revived in later times under the auspices of St Ephrem the Syrian, St Hilary and St Ambrose. It was then that the tonic accent of the word superseded the importance hitherto given to the length of the syllable and thus originated the medieval poetry of the neo-Latin tongues.

[1] G. Morin, *Un texte prehiéronymien du Cantique de L'Apocalypse,* xv, 3-4. *L'hymne " Magna et mirabilia," Rev. Bénédict.,* xxvi, pp. 464-66. 1909.
[2] *Apocal.,* xv, 3-4.

THE SACRED LITURGY DURING THE EASTER CYCLE

THE HOLY VIGIL OF EASTER

Station at the Lateran (originally at St Peter).

TWO days have passed since we contemplated Christ upon the cross, bearing for us the malediction due to our sins. He has died a shameful death, delivered up as guilty to the inexorable justice of God, no less than to the fury of hell and the hatred of his enemies. He has died; and with him has died all mankind; for, as once, through the sin of Adam, it died to sanctity and innocence, so now in Christ and through Christ it dies to sin and to the Old Law, identifying itself by faith with the sacrifice and expiation of Jesus.

The time has come at last for this poor weakened humanity, torn and bruised in the divine person of the Crucified, having now made fitting satisfaction to God for its sins, to be restored to its former honourable state. Jesus on the cross yields himself up into the hands of the Father. The Father accepts the offering—a lifeless body covered with wounds and bruises—and pressing it to his heart, warms it with the fire of his very being, and communicates to it his own divine life. Jesus rises again from death at the dawn of the third day, and as he had associated the entire human race with himself in his atonement, so now he shares his triumph with his whole mystical body on whom he, as head, sheds the glory of his resurrection.

Thus Christ has died, as the Apostle says, by reason of our sins, and by rising again has destroyed the effects thereof and has established us once more in grace, in justice, and in the hope of glory. The resurrection of Christ, then, is our resurrection, for, as on the evening of Good Friday we all died with him on the cross, so on this night we also arise with him unto a newness of life in God.

For this reason the Church, especially in the West, has been accustomed from remotest times to reserve the solemn administration of baptism for the feast of Easter only; since in receiving it, as St Paul explains, the soul goes down into the font, as though to be buried with Christ and to rise again clothed in his sanctity to a new life of grace. There exists,

286

consequently, an intimate bond between the sacrament of baptism and the festival of Easter; hence the Church unites these two ideas—these two resurrections—in the solemn liturgy of this week in order to sing the triumph of the one Pasch, that of Christ the Head, and of his mystical body.

An ancient Eastern tradition maintained that the second coming of our Lord (which on account of the universal resurrection of the dead may be truly regarded as the perfect fulfilment of the Christian Pasch) would take place on the anniversary of the night in which he rose from the tomb. The faithful, therefore, assembled in the Church and kept watch in expectation of the *parousia;* but, when midnight had come and gone, and no one had appeared from heaven, they concluded that the end of the world would not come that year and so proceeded to celebrate Easter.

Be this as it may, the custom of spending the night between Holy Saturday and Easter Sunday in prayer is very ancient. Tertullian speaks of it as a law, the origin of which was unknown, and from which no one could be exempted. It was only in the later Middle Ages that the ceremony was definitely anticipated in the afternoon, and afterwards in the morning of Holy Saturday.

The most ancient account of the paschal vigil is that given us by Justin Martyr in his *Apologia,* in which the ceremony of baptism followed by the Mass must have been the very rites which we are now describing, since they followed upon a solemn and public fast, not only of the catechumens, but of the entire Christian community; a fast which, at that time, could only be identified with the general fast preceding the solemnity of the resurrection.

In the classical era of the sacred liturgy in Rome—that is, after the Gregorian period—the whole ceremony of the Easter vigil took place with much magnificence in the Lateran, as we learn from the earliest *Ordines Romani.* At first, however, baptism in Rome was connected with St Peter, and was therefore administered in the cemetery *ad nymphas ubi Petrus baptizabat,* between the Via Nomentana and the Via Salaria, in the Apostolic sanctuary *ad Catacumbas,* and more especially in the baptistery of St Damasus at St Peter's.

To this latter most probably refers that inscription read and copied in the ancient Roman assemblies which we have already quoted in the first part of this work: *Auxit Apostolicae geminatum Sedis honorem.* The importance of these verses consists in the connection which they establish between the Roman baptism and the Apostles Peter and Paul. This see is celebrated, the unknown poet tell us, because it is founded by the two Princes of the Apostles, but Christ has willed to glorify it yet more; for he to whom

he entrusted the door of his heavenly kingdom makes use
also in this temple of a second key which unlocks the outer
gates of heaven.

The sacred ceremony which we are now about to consider,
which aims at expressing by its brilliant and inspiring colours
the holy and tremendous reality of the resurrection of Christ
and of the Church, consists of three distinct parts. First, the
Office of the vigil, to which the blessing of the *Lucernarium*
is the prelude, then the administration of baptism, and, lastly,
the Mass. Originally, with the exception of baptism, the
ceremonies of the ordinary *pannuchis,* which in the third
century sanctified the night between Saturday and Sunday,
in each week, could not have been very different from those
which the Roman Missal prescribes to-day for the paschal
vigil.

Indeed, before monastic devotion about the fifth century
created the type of night Office contained in the Breviary, the
faithful of the earliest times in their ordinary Saturday vigils,
or on the anniversaries of the martyrs, in the crypts of the
cemeteries and in the urban titles, knew no other form of
vigiliary Office than that in accordance with which the solemn
liturgical preparation for Easter was drawn up. Thus the
present ceremony of the Missal *in Vigiliis Paschae* represents
and preserves unaltered the primitive type of night Office
according to the Roman use.

The first part of to-day's ceremony consists in the blessing
of the fire and of the paschal candle. It is, however, only an
alteration of the primitive *Eucharistia lucernaris,* and as
such is entirely foreign to the ancient liturgical tradition of
the Apostolic See, being altogether absent from the oldest
Ordines Romani. The cause of its having been brought into
Rome is due to that kind of compromise between the Gallican
uses and the Roman Liturgy which was agreed to in the first
Carlovingian period. The result of this fusion, thanks to the
new Frankish domination, was its eventual adoption in the
Holy City itself.

We have already spoken of the *Eucharistia lucernaris,* so
it is not necessary to recur to the subject. It is, however,
well to note—more especially with regard to this first part of
the Roman Liturgy in the Easter vigil—that the whole of
the present blessing of the fire, with its four alternative
collects, beautiful and inspiring though these may be, forms
a curiously mistaken interpretation of the rubric and of the
medieval terminology. As a matter of fact, these did not
refer to the fire, nor to the brazier of coals, still less to the
grains of incense. The object of the sacred rite was the
Lucernarium, or lighting of the evening candle, which, at
the commencement of the vigil, was to be lighted and placed

at the side of the book-stand as a symbolical offering of light, the candle being consumed in honour of him who is the " Light of Light," the enlightener of the darkness of the world.

This is what is meant by the *claritatis tuae ignem* spoken of in the first prayer, that *lumen quod a te sanctificatum atque benedictum est.* Indeed, this same collect which the rubric of the Missal now appoints for the blessing of the grains of incense in reality refers to a *nocturnum splendorem* which is to be lighted so that the *arcana luminis tui admixtione refulgeat.* In a word, it is the Paschal candle itself which is meant, from which, as Ennodius tells us, and as the same prayer in the Missal attests, the faithful' were formerly in the habit of taking home small fragments as blessed tokens : *In quocumque loco ex hujus sanctificationis mysterio aliquid fuerit deportatum, expulsa diabolica fraudis nequitia, virtus tuae majestatis assistat.* Nor has this custom died out entirely. Even in our own days, in many parts of Italy, the people still have a great devotion for the particles, no longer of the Paschal candle, but of the tapers of the *Lumen Christi,* which they enclose in little bags of silk and hang round the necks of the children. We cannot now trace how the resinous grains of incense came to take the place in the popular mind of the candle used at the vigil, seeing that the expressions *incensum, incensi sacrificium, incensum lucernae* undoubtedly denoted, from the fifth century onwards, the ritual lighting of the candle, which, from its place beside the ambo, was to shed its light in the Church during the holy night-watches.

The lighting of the triple candle by the deacon, as he chants the words *Lumen Christi,* appears to be an alternative rite which could be substituted for the *Lucernarium.* This ceremony may have reached Rome from the liturgy of distant Spain by way of the Gallican rites.

A third form of the *Eucharistia lucernaris* follows, the classical one formerly attributed to St Augustine. In any case it goes back to the fourth century at least, to a period, that is, when all that wealth of liturgical compositions in the form of anaphoras began to show itself, of which we find some curious examples in the Leonine Sacramentary.

St Jerome deplores the somewhat pagan phrases which several of the deacons introduced in his time into the paschal eulogy, by quoting Vergil's commendation of the chaste and diligent bee. Such themes continued to be developed on the occasion of the paschal vigil for many succeeding centuries, as is shown by the twelfth century scroll of the *Exsultet* of Bari.

The Roman form is distinguished by its sobriety and

unction. It is not wanting in lyrical beauty, and at times its inspiration is so forcible that it seems about to raise its author to the highest planes of Christian mysticism, as when he wishes to impress upon us the advantages which human nature has so abundantly derived from the present dispensation of the redemption of a world once lost through sin. We cannot doubt that the actual plan chosen by God in order to make manifest his glory through Jesus Christ, the Saviour of the human race, is that one which is the most worthy of the Godhead, the most glorious for Christ, and the most helpful to ourselves. In this sense we can say with the Church: *O felix culpa, o certe necessarium Adae peccatum,* for in the wisdom of God these evils have been on occasion the cause of so much good.

Therefore only a narrow mind, one which stops short at the mere idea of sin and its offence in God's sight, unable to comprehend the divine plan for the restoration of the world, and to realize God's power to draw the greatest good out of evil, only such a mind could cavil at the sentences quoted above. Taken out of their context, they no doubt dismay the devout soul—for which reason they were suppressed at Cluny—but if they are accepted in the spirit which inspires the whole composition, they express truthfully the cry of eager gratitude which bursts forth from the believing soul in contemplating the mystery of its redemption.

So, before the Last Judgement of Michelangiolo in the Sistine Chapel, a mind which feels in a lesser degree than the great Master the shudder of the *Dies irae, dies illa,* will be inclined to think the whole scene strange and exaggerated —a scene in which the holy Mother herself appears to tremble before the majesty of the Judge. In order to understand certain powerful results of genius, it is necessary first to feel their effects within oneself; and this is especially true of the sacred liturgy, for if we would truly appreciate it, it must become for us a living force within our souls.

HOLY SATURDAY

1. The "Eucharistia Lucernaris."

Form B[1] (*alternative*).

The priest salutes the people and recites several alternative forms of prayer, which originally bore reference to the lighting of the evening candle, and which were only later adapted to the blessing of the fire.

[1] These alternative collects are distinguished by the letters of the alphabet.

Priest: The Lord be with you.

    ℟ : And with thy spirit.

Priest: Let us pray.

O God, who by thy Son, who is the corner-stone, hast bestowed on thy faithful the fire of thy brightness; sanctify this new fire produced out of the flint, that it may be profitable to us; and grant us, through this Easter festival, to be so inflamed with heavenly desires, that with pure minds we may arrive at the festival of perpetual light. Through the same Christ our Lord. ℟ : Amen.

The prayer is suggested by the famous hymn of Prudentius for the *Lucernarium,* in which the spark struck from the flint is a symbol of our soul, which receives from Christ, the mystical corner-stone, the fire of charity, and the life of grace.

Form C (*alternative*).

The following prayer also is better suited to the blessing of the evening light according to the ancient use than to the blessing of the fire.

Prayer: O Lord God, Father almighty, unfailing light, who art the creator of all lights, bless this light, which is blessed and sanctified by thee, who didst enlighten the whole world; that we may be inflamed with that light, and enlightened with the fire of thy brightness : and as thou didst give light to Moses going out of Egypt, so enlighten our hearts and senses that we may deserve to arrive at life and light everlasting. Through Christ our Lord. ℟ : Amen.

Form D (*alternative*).

As we have already explained the symbolism of these prayers in the introduction to the fourth part of this work, it is unnecessary to dwell longer upon it. The liturgical misinterpretation and the disorder which exists among these alternative collects prove once more that they did not belong to the primitive liturgical tradition of Rome, and that they represent foreign additions, which, venerable though they may be, yet take away from the solemn simplicity of the Roman worship.

Prayer: Holy Lord, Father almighty, eternal God, vouchsafe to work with us who bless this fire in thy name, and in that of thy only begotten Son Jesus Christ, our God and Lord, and of the Holy Ghost; and help us against the fiery darts of the enemy, and enlighten us with heavenly grace : who livest and reignest with the same, thine only-begotten

Son, and the Holy Ghost, God, world without end. ℞ : Amen.

FORM E (*alternative*).

The following prayer, now used for the blessing of the five grains of incense which are afterwards placed in the form of a cross in the Paschal candle, originally represented another alternative blessing of the evening light. The mistaken interpretation occurred much later on, and was due to the word *incensum,* which originally signified the lighted candle, but which afterwards came to mean the grains of incense.

Prayer: May the abundant outpouring of thy blessing come upon this incense, we beseech thee, almighty God; and do thou, the unseen regenerator, lighten this splendour of the night, that not only the sacrifice which is offered up this night may shine with the hidden admixture of thy light; but in whatever place any portion of the mystery of this sanctification may be brought, the wickedness of satanic deceit may be driven away, and the power of thy majesty may be present. Through Christ our Lord. ℞ : Amen.

This prayer alludes to the ancient custom of distributing among the people the fragments of wax from the Paschal candle, to be kept as blessed tokens. We have seen that at Rome in the seventh century, on the morning of Holy Saturday, the archdeacon mixed the melted wax with the blessed oil, and pouring it into a mould, formed small medallions with the representation of the *Agnus Dei* stamped upon them. These were dispensed among the people on Low Sunday, and were kept by them to be burnt at home in time of sickness or during thunderstorms. This was the origin of the *Agnus Dei,* which are now blessed at stated times by the Pope himself.

After these first four prayers of the *Eucharistia lucernaris* which are now said by the priest at the entrance to the church before the brazier containing the new fire and the dish with the five grains of incense, the deacon puts on the white paschal dalmatic, and the procession advances towards the altar. In order to light the way—this was the original meaning of the ceremony—the deacon lights successively the three candles placed at the end of a reed, saying each time, as in the Mozarabic rite of the daily *Lucernarium:*

Deacon: The light of Christ.
  ℞ : Thanks be to God.

At Rome in the eighth century, before the clergy entered the Church to celebrate the vigil, the candle was lighted on the ambo and the lessons from the Prophets were begun. At a later period the deacon, having asked the priest's blessing, saluted the people, and himself chanted the collect which was used as an introduction to the blessing or *sanctificatio,* as it was termed, of the candle. After the collect followed the chanting of the beautiful eucharistic prayer, otherwise called by the general term " preface." The Sacramentaries contain various forms of this prayer, but from the time of St Jerome its theme was always the same, since, though in different words, the ideas remain unchanged.

FORM A᷄.—SANCTIFICATION OR BLESSING OF THE " LUCERN-ARIUM PASCHALE."

It was the duty of the deacon to light the candle at the night-watch, hence to him was reserved the " declamation " which, on the solemn occasion of the paschal vigil, formed part of this symbolic rite of the close of the Sabbath. It is unnecessary to add that the rite of the *Lucernarium* was also derived from the ceremonial of the synagogue.

Deacon: Sir, give me thy blessing.
Priest: May the Lord be in thy heart and on thy lips, that thou mayest worthily and duly proclaim his paschal praise : in the name of the Father, and of the Son, and of the Holy Ghost. Amen.

Then follows the famous form of the *Eucharistia lucernaris* of which we have spoken above. This composition of the deacon has a very special character, and liturgical tradition demanded that it should be read from a parchment scroll, which the deacon, standing in the ambo, gradually unrolled. It was usually illustrated, but the pictures were painted up-side down so that the people should be able to see them as the scroll was unfolded.

Deacon: Let the angelic choirs of heaven now rejoice; let the divine mysteries rejoice; and let the trumpet of salvation sound for the victory of so great a King. Let the earth also rejoice, made radiant by such splendour; and, enlightened with the brightness of the eternal King, let it know that the whole world's darkness is scattered. Let mother Church, too, rejoice, adorned with the brightness of so great a light; and may this temple resound with the loud voices of the people. Wherefore I beseech you, most dear brethren, who are here present in the wonderful brightness of this holy light, to invoke with me the mercy of almighty God. That he who hath vouchsafed to number me among his levites without any merit of mine would pour forth his brightness upon me and enable me to perfect the praise of this light,

Through Jesus Christ our Lord, his Son: who liveth and reigneth with him in the unity of the Holy Spirit, God, world without end. ℟ : Amen.

Deacon: The Lord be with you.
℟ : And with thy spirit.
Deacon: Lift up your hearts.
℟ : We have lifted them up to the Lord.
Deacon: Let us give thanks to the Lord our God.
℟ : It is meet and just.
Deacon: It is truly meet and right to proclaim with all affection of heart and mind and by the service of our voice the God invisible, the Father everlasting, and his only-begotten Son, our Lord Jesus Christ, who for us repaid to his eternal Father the debt of Adam, and by the pitiful shedding of his blood cancelled our ancient bond of sin. For this is the festival of the Pasch, in which is slain that true Lamb by whose blood the doorposts of the faithful are hallowed. This is the night in which thou didst first bring out of Egypt our fathers the children of Israel and lead them dry-foot through the Red Sea. This, then, is the night which cleansed the darkness of sin by the light of the pillar. This is the night which at this season throughout the whole world restores to grace and yokes to holiness those that believe in Christ, detaching them from worldly vice and the foulness of sin. This is the night in which Christ burst through the bonds of death and rose victorious from hell. For it would have been no boon to be born had we not had the boon of being redeemed. How wonderful the condescension of thy mercy towards us ! How incomparable the predilection of thy love ! That thou mightest ransom thy slave, thou gavest up thine own Son ! Oh, truly necessary was Adam's sin, that was blotted out by the death of Christ ! Oh, happy was his fault, that was worthy of so great a Redeemer ! Oh, how blessed is this night which alone was worthy to know the season and the hour in which Christ rose again from hell ! This is the night of which it was written : And the night shall be enlightened as the day : and the night is my light in my enjoyments. Therefore does the holiness of this night banish crime, wash away sin, and restore innocence to those that have fallen and gladness to those that are sad. It drives forth hate, it brings peace, it curbs haughtiness.

(Here the deacon fixes the five grains of blessed incense in the candle in the form of a cross, and proceeds :)

In the grace of this night, then, O Father, receive for an evening sacrifice this incense, which holy Church renders unto thee in the solemn offering of this candle of wax, wrought by bees, at the hand of her ministers. Now we know the glory of this column which God's bright flame kindles.

There is evidently a hiatus here, as the chain of thought is broken. As a matter of fact, this is the place where the allusion to the purity and diligence of the bees was cut out, which, however, we find in other forms of the *Exsultet* used out of Rome—

(Here the deacon lights the candle with one of the three candles on the reed.)

Though divided into parts, yet it suffers no loss from the light which it imparts. For it is fed from the melted wax which the mother bee wrought for the substance of this precious lamp.

(Here the lamps are lighted.)

O truly blessed is the night which despoiled the Egyptians and enriched the Hebrews ! the night in which things ' of heaven are joined to those of earth, things of God to those of man ! We therefore pray thee, O Lord, that this candle, which is hallowed in honour of thy name, may avail and fail not to scatter the darkness of this night. May it be received as a sweet savour and be mingled with the lights of heaven. May the morning star find its flame alight : that morning star which knows no setting; which came back from hell and shed its kindly light upon mankind. We therefore beseech thee, O Lord, grant a season of peace at this time of Easter gladness to us thy servants, and to all the clergy, to thy devout people, and especially to our most blessed Pope N. and to N. our bishop; and ever rule and guide and keep them under thy protection.

(The following passage is usually omitted since the Romano-Germanic Empire, founded by Charlemagne, has ceased to exist.)

Look down also upon our most devoted Emperor (*if he is not crowned say:* Emperor elect) N., and as thou, O God, foreknowest his desires by the unthinkable gift of thy loving-kindness and mercy, grant him, with all his people, the rest of everlasting peace and a heavenly victory. Through the same Lord Jesus Christ thy Son, who liveth and reigneth with thee in the unity of the Holy Ghost, God, for ever and ever. ℞ : Amen.

2. THE HOLY VIGIL.

The *Eucharistia lucernaris* being ended—which, as regards time and meaning, corresponded in part to a prelude to Vespers—it was immediately followed by the vigil. At Rome, during the first three centuries, this consisted exclusively of a series of extracts from the Scriptures interspersed with collects and the responsorial chanting of psalms. It was not until afterwards that monastic influence gave a different form and order to the divine Office.

A very ancient tradition reserved to the morning Office the singing of a series of prophetic odes handed down to the Church from the synagogue; and this is the reason why to-day, on the eve of Easter, the responsorial chants after the lessons are not taken from the Psalter, but from the ancient collection of matutinal odes. Indeed the vigil of Easter, as contained in the Roman Missal, is of capital importance, since it preserves almost intact the primitive type of the Roman vigil before the Sunday, followed by the Eucharistic sacrifice, as it was observed in the first centuries of the Church.

St Gregory reduced the number of the lessons to six; but after some time the traditional number of twelve again obtained in Rome from the Gelasian Sacramentary, which was universally followed both in Italy and in France. The collects which come after the lessons are noteworthy, because with clearness and brevity they explain their mystical significance, showing their connection with the sacrament of baptism.

The first prophecy is taken from Genesis (i 1-31 and ii 1-2), and describes the work of creation. The *cosmos* is the masterpiece of the wisdom of God, and everything is good because it is the work of his hands. Thus the world is like a great temple built by God himself to his own glory, and we, whilst making use, through his condescension, of the inferior creatures, should do so with respect and discretion, bearing in mind the end for which God has put them at our service.

The Saints loved all creatures, because in them they recognized a certain brotherhood with regard to God, who is the Father of us all; thus St Francis spoke of brother fire, brother wolf, and brother sun. When, therefore, the Scriptures attribute to God the words : " Let us make man to our image and likeness," the Fathers of the Church remark that this image and likeness bear a very deep and exact interpretation, for they may be understood of the raising up of the rational creature to a supernatural state by means of grace. It is grace which uplifts created nature in the fullest degree, and gives to it, as far as is possible for a creature, a sublime conformity with the divine nature, and it is in this sense that St Paul calls us *divinae consortes naturae*.

After the Lesson the whole assembly, at the invitation of the deacon, kneels down and recollects itself for a few moments in private prayer, after which the priest recites the collect.

Deacon: Let us kneel.

Subdeacon: Arise.

Prayer: O God, who didst wonderfully create man, and still more wonderfully redeem him; grant us, we beseech thee, to resist with strong mind the allurements of sin, that we may deserve to arrive at eternal joys. Through our Lord.

The redemption may be compared to a second creation, as, through it, man, who had become the slave of the devil, has been restored to his former dignity of a son of God. The senses especially are the means by which Satan draws us into sin, but reason enlightened by faith breaks the spell of this enchantment.

The second prophecy (Gen. v, vi, vii, and viii) is closely connected with the first, and therefore with the work of redemption. As in the beginning God had drawn the universe out of nothing, so now by means of the ark of Noe he preserves that part of it which he had chosen for its renewal. St Peter explains very clearly the meaning of the ark floating on the waters of the universal deluge. It is the symbol of the Church—that is, the company of all those who, through the waters of baptism, have been chosen to form the spiritual temple of the true God. As the ark of the Patriarch Noe was the means of renewing the life of the world, so now does holy baptism do away with the former order of things grown intolerable, and inaugurate the New Covenant of peace and love.

After the second lesson comes a collect which, by the spirituality of its conception, is indeed worthy of the golden period of the Roman Liturgy. We may accept at once, as a general rule, that all the collects which conclude the lessons during the paschal vigil are among the finest in the liturgy, and might well serve as foundations for a complete treatise on the mystery of the redemption of mankind.

Deacon: Let us kneel, etc.

Prayer: O God, unchangeable power and light eternal, mercifully regard the wonderful mystery of thy whole Church, and peacefully effect by thy eternal decree the work of human salvation : and may the whole world experience and see what was cast down, raised up; what was grown old, renewed; and all things return to a perfect state through him from whom they received their beginning, our Lord Jesus Christ thy Son : who liveth.

With God there is no alteration of design. Like a supreme artist he conceived the world as a whole, so that St Augustine says truly: *mutans opera, sed non mutans consilium.* . . . All this complexity of things belongs to one grand and single plan in which is made manifest the great goodness of almighty God.

The third prophecy (Gen. xxii 1-9) tells us of Abraham sacrificing his son Isaac and meriting by his faith the grace of becoming the prototype and patriarch of an infinite multitude of believers, to whom his blessing will come as an inheritance. This people is to descend from Abraham, not like the Jewish nation by carnal generation, but by the merit of faith in him whom the Chaldean patriarch had himself confessed, adoring from afar the Christ who was to come. The sacrifice of Isaac, the first-born son of Abraham, is also a type of the sacrifice of Jesus whom his Father delivered up to death for love of us. Christ, like another Isaac, accepts this decision with willing obedience, and taking upon his shoulders the wood of the cross, ascends the mount of sacrifice.

The following collect explains the symbolical tie which exists between the prophecy in the lesson and the paschal regeneration of the world, by means of faith and the waters of baptism.

Deacon: Let us kneel, etc.

Prayer: O God, the supreme Father of the faithful, who throughout the world dost multiply the children of thy promise, diffusing the grace of adoption, and by the paschal sacrament dost make Abraham thy servant the father of all nations, as thou didst promise; grant thy people worthily to enter unto the grace of thy vocation. Through our Lord.

The fourth prophecy, from Exodus (xiv 24-31, and xv 1), has been placed here either in order to serve as an introduction to the canticle of Moses, which originally formed part of the collection of odes to be sung at the morning Office, or because the miraculous passage of the Israelites through the Red Sea is a type of holy baptism. This incident was one of those belonging to the scriptural cycle alluded to in the prayers of the Jews, which inspired alike the composer of our *Commendatio animae,* and the painters of the catacombs. The Red Sea is a figure of Christian baptism through the blood of the Saviour. In those waters the devil and sin are destroyed, whilst a new race of believers arises therefrom safe and sound and rejoicing in youth restored.

Now follows as a Tract the famous Canticle of Moses, after the passage of the Red Sea. The hand of God, which weighed so heavily on the idolatrous and obstinate Egyptians, has shielded the people who trusted in him, with the tenderness of a mother.

The Collect interprets the symbolism of the preceding narrative, which, on account of its spiritual significance, is one of ever-abiding interest. By this we mean that the scriptural scenes here described are not merely chronicles of past events, but represent those things which, in a far higher and more real sense, take place among believing Christians even in our own time.

Deacon: Let us kneel, etc.

Prayer: O God, whose ancient miracles we see shining even in our days, since that which by the power of thy right hand thou didst confer upon one people by delivering them from Egyptian persecution, thou dost operate by the water of regeneration for the salvation of the Gentiles; grant that the fulness of the whole world may pass over to the children of Abraham, and the dignity of Israelites. Through our Lord.

The fifth prophecy comes from Isaias (liv 17, and lv 1-11) and refers to the calling of the Gentiles through faith and the waters of baptism. In order to reach so high a state, it is not necessary, as under the Old Law, to attain to legal righteousness, nor yet to be of the race of Israel; a lively faith in Christ our Redeemer, the universal guide and teacher of the nations, is all that is required of us. The mission of the Holy Ghost, emanating from our divine Saviour, will be fruitful and conclusive, as the rain and the dew which descend from above to refresh and fertilize the land. Jesus raised upon the cross will draw all men unto him.

In the Collect the connection which exists between the Old and the New Testament is dwelt upon. The Old was a consoling promise; the New through the universality of the Messianic sonship is its glorious fulfilment.

Deacon: Let us kneel, etc.

Prayer: Almighty and everlasting God, multiply to the honour of thy name what thou didst promise to the faith of our fathers, and increase the children of promise by holy adoption, that what the saints of old did not doubt would come to pass, thy Church may now acknowledge to be in great part accomplished. Through our Lord.

The sixth prophecy is derived from Baruch (iii 9-38), and is one of the most profound passages in the Bible. It resembles a searching examination of conscience. What has Israel gained by following after the power, the glory, and the culture of the heathen? These have all crumbled away; and the very men who upheld them have shown themselves incapable of solving the problems which so greatly perplex the human mind; whereas Israel is called to receive its spiritual teaching directly from him whom all creation obeys in fear and trembling. He has come down to converse with man, and has entrusted the deposit of his revealed truth to the hands of the Church, which was prefigured by the people of Israel.

The Collect draws attention to the universal character of the spiritual family of Israel. This was visibly the case in Rome, for when all these forms of prayer were drawn up the catechumens, who then went down into the baptismal font, were representative of the most varied nations of the known world.

Deacon: Let us kneel, etc.
Prayer: O God, who dost ever multiply thy Church by the calling of the Gentiles, mercifully grant that those whom thou dost wash by the water of baptism may be defended by continual protection. Through our Lord.

The seventh prophecy describes the tragic vision of Ezechiel (xxxvii 1-14). Israel is dead and its bones are scattered over a vast plain. It bemoans its present lot, but the Lord is ever faithful in fulfilling his promises. Through the prophet he will instil movement, spirit, and life into those dry bones, and from them he will bring together a countless army which will become his chosen people—the people of God. This change has an entirely spiritual signification. God will restore the ruins of Sion by means of the Gentiles, who, through baptism, will receive the grace of the Holy Ghost and will form the spiritual progeny of Abraham. The mystical resurrection of the nations by the pouring out of the gift of the Paraclete foreshadows in its turn the miracle of the final resurrection of the dead.

The Collect expresses the thought that both the Old and the New Testaments agree in making the mystery of the paschal redemption the central fact of the divine scheme for the salvation of the world. For this reason Easter is the chief festival of the year, and the starting-point from which the whole cycle of the Christian liturgy is developed.

Deacon: Let us kneel, etc.
Prayer: O God, who dost instruct us by the pages of both Testaments to celebrate the paschal sacrament, grant us to understand thy mercy, that by receiving these present gifts, our expectation of future ones may be secured. Through our Lord.

In the eighth prophecy, from Isaias (iv 1-6), which serves as an introduction to the celebrated morning ode taken from the hymns of the prophet, the subject is the abrogation of the Old

Covenant and the ratification of the New. The Lord will punish the treachery of Israel, and the manhood of the nation having been destroyed, seven women shall ask of one man to give them the protection of his name, whilst providing themselves for their own maintenance. When Israel shall have perished and when the many nations shall begin to seek the one spouse Jesus Christ, God will restore in a spiritual sense the ancient kingdom of Juda. He will purge away the stains of those that believe in him, and will purify them with the fire of the Holy Ghost. In this prophecy the sacraments of baptism and confirmation are clearly foretold.

Now comes as a tract the Canticle of Isaias (v 1, 2, 7), describing the Lord's vineyard; that barren and unprofitable vineyard which repaid all the careful attention of the master by bringing forth naught but thorns and bitter fruits. This vineyard is a type of the Jewish race.

Deacon: Let us kneel, etc.

Prayer: O God, who in all the children of thy Church hast manifested by the voice of holy prophets in every place of thy dominion that thou art the sower of good seed and the cultivator of chosen branches; grant to thy people, who are called by thee by the names of vineyards and corn, that the unsightliness of thorns and briers being removed, they may produce worthy and abundant fruit. Through our Lord.

The ninth prophecy, from Exodus (xii 1-11), is the same as the lesson on Good Friday. It describes the Mosaic rites of the immolation of the Lamb and those of the paschal feast. The Lamb is the type of Christ who washes away in his blood the sins of the world. It is sacrificed and eaten at a religious feast, to signify our incorporation in and union with our Redeemer through the Blessed Sacrament. The Jews were enjoined to eat the paschal lamb as men about to start on a long journey, thus showing us that the Holy Eucharist is our viaticum in the earthly pilgrimage which we are making through the desert of the world in order to attain to heaven.

Deacon: Let us kneel, etc.

Prayer: Almighty and everlasting God, who art wonderful in the dispensation of all thy works; let those whom thou hast redeemed understand that the creation of the world in the beginning was not a more excellent thing than the immolation of Christ our passover at the end of time : who liveth.

The tenth prophecy, which is from the Book of Jonas (iii 1-10), is identical with the lesson of the Mass for the Monday after Passion Sunday. As our Lord himself pointed out in the Gospel, Jonas is the type of Christ buried in the tomb, and rising once more to life and light. Jonas preaches repentance to the Ninevites, and they, touched by his words, order a general fast, in which not only the citizens, but even their flocks and herds are to take part. This paradox is typical of the Jewish mind, but it signifies that not the individual alone, but also society as such, should pay to God the homage due to him; which obligation can be fully carried out through the sacred liturgy.

We must never forget the ties which bind us to Christ and to his mystical body—the Church. An undue prominence given to the individual in religious matters is the result of the Protestant system. A Catholic, whilst neglecting nothing which can prepare his own soul to receive God's grace, becomes sanctified in the Church, through the Church, and with the Church, and this is effected chiefly by means of liturgical worship.

The Collect which follows extols the mystical unity of the Church in one faith and one love without any barrier of race or caste. The Church, from the very fact that she is Catholic, cannot be national.

Deacon: Let us kneel, etc.

Prayer: O God, who hast joined together divers nations in the confession of thy name, grant us both to will and to be able to do what thou commandest; that thy people being called to an eternal inheritance, may hold the same faith in their hearts and show the same godliness in their lives. Through our Lord.

The eleventh prophecy is taken from Deuteronomy (xxx 22-30) and contains the last words of Moses in which he rejects the people of Israel because of their unfaithfulness towards the Lord. He makes this protest in the most solemn manner, in the presence of the chief men of the tribes, and calls down all kinds of evil on this rebellious race. But what was the terrible sin of which they had been guilty? The whole scene is symbolical. Moses declares that their faithlessness would be seen after his death, even *in extremo tempore*— that is to say, in the last ages of the world when the Jews would deny Jesus Christ the greatest of all prophets, foretold by that same Moses who had commanded Israel to obey him as they had obeyed himself.

The famous Canticle of Moses from Deuteronomy (xxxii), which was appointed in the Hebrew liturgy for the Sabbath, now follows as a tract. Moses takes heaven and earth to witness his maledictions on a people from whom he has separated himself, knowing that one day they will be guilty of deicide.

Deacon: Let us kneel, etc.

Prayer: O God, the exaltation of the humble and strength of the upright, who by thy holy servant Moses wast pleased so to instruct thy people by the singing of thy holy canticle, that that renewal of the law might be also our direction; stir up thy power in all the fulness of the justified Gentiles, and give joy whilst thou dost diminish fear; that all sins being blotted out by thy remission, what was denounced in vengeance may be turned to our salvation. Through our Lord.

The twelfth prophecy brings the series of lessons to a close with the narrative of the three youths cast into the fiery furnace of Babylon for refusing to worship the golden statue of Nabuchodonosor (Dan. iii 1-24). The story was a favourite one with the painters of the catacombs, who used to reproduce it on the tombs and on the sarcophagi. It was a type of the heroic fortitude of the Christian martyrs.

Priest: Let us pray.

Prayer: Almighty eternal God, sole hope of the world, who by the preaching of thy prophets didst declare the mysteries of these present times; mercifully increase the devotion of thy people, for in none of thy faithful can any virtues increase but by thy inspiration. Through our Lord.

As the procession " descended " into the baptistery a tract (Ps. xli 2-4) was sung.

As the hart panteth after the fountains of waters; so my soul panteth after thee, O God. ℣. My soul has thirsted after the living God; when shall I come and appear before the face of God? ℣. My tears have been my bread day and night, whilst it is said to me daily : Where is thy God?

The word " descend " is consecrated by Roman tradition as represented by the Missal, since the papal baptistery of the Via Salaria, and perhaps also that of the Vatican, was a good deal below the level of the ground.

The use of water as a symbol of inward grace was very common in ancient times. As water cleanses, refreshes, and gives fertility to the earth, so the grace of the Holy Ghost produces all these effects in a spiritual manner in the soul.

After the tract, the priest, according to an old custom, chanted a collect explaining the mystical meaning of the psalm itself. In ancient psalters such prayers are very often found, but this one, based on Psalm xli, is the only one now remaining in the Missal.

Priest: The Lord be with you.

℞ : And with thy spirit.

Prayer: Almighty, everlasting God, look mercifully on the devotion of thy people who are born anew, who pant, as the hart, after the fountain of thy waters; and mercifully grant that the thirst of their faith may, by the mystery of baptism, sancify their souls and bodies. Through our Lord. ℞ : Amen.

Here ends the vigiliary rite. Meanwhile, outside, the dawn is appearing, the hour of Christ's resurrection, and the time has now come to administer the sacrament of baptism to the catechumens.

3. THE BLESSING OF THE FONT.

After an introductory Collect there follows the consecratory anaphora of the holy waters of baptism.

Priest: The Lord be with you.

℞ : And with thy spirit.

Prayer: Almighty, everlasting God, be present at these mysteries of thy great goodness, be present at these sacraments; and send forth the spirit of adoption to regenerate the new people whom the font of baptism bringeth forth; that what is to be done by the ministry of us thy servants may be accomplished by the effect of thy power. Through our Lord.

Priest: For ever and ever.

℞ : Amen.

Priest: The Lord be with you.

℞ : And with thy spirit.

Priest: Lift up your hearts.

℞ : We have lifted them up unto the Lord.

Priest: Let us give thanks unto the Lord our God.

℞ : It is meet and just.

Priest: It is truly meet and just, right and availing unto salvation, to give thee thanks always and in all places, O holy Lord, almighty Father, eternal God; who by thy invisible power dost wonderfully work the effect of thy sacraments : and though we are unworthy to perform such great mysteries, yet, as thou dost not abandon the gifts of thy grace, so thou inclinest the ears of thy goodness even to our prayers. O God, whose Spirit in the very beginning of the world moved upon the waters, that even then nature might receive the virtue of sanctification. O God, who by water didst wash away the crimes of a guilty world, and by the pouring out of the deluge didst signify the likeness of regeneration : that one and the same element might, in a mystery, be the end of vice and the beginning of virtue: look down, O Lord, on thy Church and multiply in her thy regenerations, who by the streams of thy abundant grace makest glad thy city, and openest the font of baptism over all the world for the renewal of the Gentiles; that by the command of thy majesty it may receive the grace of thy Son from the Holy Ghost.

(Here the priest divides the water in the form of a cross, as though to render it fruitful by the touch of his consecrated hands, as in the beginning the spirit of God moved over the waters of chaos.)

Who by a secret mixture of his divine power may render fruitful this water for the regeneration of men: to the end that those who are sanctified in the immaculate womb of this divine font, and born again new creatures, may come forth as heavenly offspring, and that all, however distinguished by age in time, or by sex in body, may be brought forth to the same infancy by grace, their mother. Therefore may all unclean spirits by thy command, O Lord, depart from hence: may all the malice of diabolical wiles be entirely banished: may no power of the enemy prevail here: let him not spread his snares about it, nor creep into it by stealth, nor taint it by his poison.

(Here he touches the water again with his hand as though to exorcise it.)

May this holy and innocent creature be free from all assaults of the enemy and cleansed by the removal of all wickedness. May it become a living fountain, a regenerating water, a purifying stream: that all those that are to be washed in this saving bath may obtain, by the operation of the Holy Ghost, the grace of a perfect cleansing.

(Here he makes the sign of the cross thrice over the font, saying:)

Wherefore I bless thee, creature of water, by the living ✠ God, by the true ✠ God, by the holy ✠ God; by that God who in the beginning separated thee by his word from the dry land, and whose Spirit moved upon thee.

(Here he divides the water with his hands in the form of a cross and throws some of it towards the four quarters of the earth, to call to mind the river which, issuing from Eden, was divided into four streams.)

Who made thee flow from the fountain of paradise, and commanded thee to water the whole earth with thy four rivers. Who changing thy bitterness in the desert into sweetness, made thee fit to drink; and produced thee out of a rock to quench the thirsty people. I ✠ bless thee also by Jesus Christ our Lord, his only Son; who in Cana of Galilee by a wonderful miracle, changed thee into wine. Who walked upon thee with his feet, and was baptized in thee by John in the Jordan. Who made thee flow out of his side, together with his blood; and commanded his disciples that such as believed should be baptized in thee, saying: Go, teach all nations, baptizing them in the name of the Father, and of the Son, and of the Holy Ghost. Do thou, O almighty God, mercifully assist us who observe this commandment; do thou graciously breathe upon us.

(The priest breathes thrice upon the water in the form of a cross, as the Holy Spirit once breathed upon the waters of creation, saying:)

Do thou with thy mouth bless these pure waters; that besides their natural virtue of cleansing the body, they may also prove efficacious to the purifying of the soul.

(Here he dips the paschal candle thrice into the water, according to a rite which was first used in Rome about the eighth century.)

May the power of the Holy Ghost descend into all the water of this font.

(Then breathing thrice on the water, in the form of the Greek letter Ψ, he adds:)

And make the whole substance of this water fruitful for regeneration.

(Here the candle is taken out of the water, and he proceeds:)

Here may the stains of all sins be washed out; here may human nature, created to thy image and reformed to the honour of its author, be cleansed from the filth of the old man; that all who receive this sacrament of regeneration may be born again, new children of true innocence. Through our Lord Jesus Christ, thy Son: who will come to judge the living and the dead and the world by fire. ℞: Amen.

The people are then sprinkled with blessed water from the baptismal font by the assistant priests, and some is taken away in a vessel by one of them for sprinkling in the houses of the faithful. This being done, some of the oil of the catechumens is poured into the font in the form of a cross, a rite which is not at all ancient and which did not originally form part of the Roman Liturgy, but was introduced gradually when, there being no longer any adult catechumens, the special meaning of the oil as used in their case ceased to have any particular point.

May this font be sanctified and made fruitful by the oil of salvation for those born anew in it, unto life everlasting. ℞: Amen.

(The holy chrism is then poured into the baptismal water to symbolize the grace of the Holy Ghost which renders it fruitful.)

May this infusion of the chrism of our Lord Jesus Christ, and of the Holy Ghost the Comforter, be made in the name of the Holy Trinity. ℟ : Amen.

(The third time the chrism and the oil of the catechumens are poured together into the water in the form of a cross.)

May this mixture of the chrism of sanctification, and of the oil of unction, and of the water of baptism, be made in the name of the Father, and of the Son, and of the Holy Ghost. ℟ : Amen.

The administration of baptism follows according to the usual rite.

At first, no doubt because the catechumens were chiefly adults, confirmation was administered immediately after baptism—its very name showed its close connection with the sacrament of spiritual regeneration—and also the first Holy Communion. As time went on, however, and as society gradually became christianized, and those who were presented for baptism were nearly all infants, the sacraments which complete the spiritual development of the Christian were postponed to a more mature age.

The *Ordines Romani* of the eighth century prescribe that the Pope, having baptized a certain number of the catechumens with his own hand, should leave the rest to the clergy whilst he withdrew to the neighbouring oratory of the Holy Cross to *consignare* the neophytes with holy chrism as they came up out of the water. It has already been noted that according to the ancient Roman use there were two separate anointings with the chrism; the first (*chrismatio*) was performed by a priest on the head of the neophyte as soon as he came from the font, but the second (*consignatio chrismalis*) was administered by the Pope himself on the forehead of the newly made Christian, and was the actual sacrament of confirmation.

During all this long ceremony the greater part of the people had not entered the baptistery, which indeed could not have contained them, but remained in the church with the lower orders of the clergy and the choir. Moreover, their presence would not have been convenient, seeing that baptism was given by immersion and that the font was surrounded by veils and curtains, so that Christian modesty should not be offended. In order to occupy this space of time devoutly, the litany was sung three times, in such a manner, however, that each invocation was repeated at first seven times, then five times, and lastly thrice. This is why we still sing the litany as the procession returns from the baptistery, but now the invocations are repeated only twice.

This litany as given in the Missal is somewhat shorter than that of the Rogation days. Besides the great liberty accorded to the liturgy by the Church as regards litanies down to the thirteenth century, a further reason for this is, that the litany for the Rogations is intended to be sung by the people processionally with refrains, and can therefore be prolonged according to the distance which has to be traversed, whereas the litany of Holy Saturday, which the clergy still sing prostrate on the ground before the altar, is a true *supplicatio litanica,* and consequently is not usually one of great length.

4. The Sacrifice of Easter Eve.

Holy Saturday still preserves, almost unaltered, the primitive type of the morning Mass which, during the first three centuries, closed the vigil of preparation for the Sunday. Indeed we may say that all the other Saturday night vigils throughout the year were derived from the solemn paschal *vigilia,* the only one which in Tertullian's time was of universal observance and obligatory on all the faithful without distinction.

The Mass has no Introit, as was the case, at least originally, with all vigiliary Masses; for, at Rome, the Introit was introduced only at a much later date, about the time of Celestine I (423-32), when, that is, the Mass was as a rule no longer preceded by the Office of the Vigil. Therefore, even now, the priest, immediately after the litany, proceeds to chant the Collect, which is a natural conclusion, as it were, to all the foregoing rite of the night-watch. The prayers which follow have no longer a catechetical character, but are purely eucharistic. Since, however, from the sixth century at least, the original connection existing between the twelve vigiliary lessons and the short Epistle and Gospel —which represent the latest form of the vigiliary prayers formerly preceding the Mass—had been forgotten, so at a later time, but in any case before the seventh century, there were added to the Collect the two customary lessons from the Epistles and the Gospels.

After the morning hymn *Gloria in excelsis,* which, in Rome, had a distinctly paschal significance, the Collect is chanted which originally was intended to serve as the conclusion of the litany.

The entire paschal liturgy in Rome was influenced by the thought of the sacrament of baptism. By virtue of its sacred laver the neophytes have been admitted to rise again from death with Christ. In order, therefore, to enter into the spirit of the liturgy of this week, it is necessary to bear always in mind the link which exists between the Pasch of Christ rising from the grave and the Pasch of the Church emerging from the font of baptism to a new and spiritual life.

Prayer: O God, who dost illustrate this most holy night by the glory of our Lord's resurrection; preserve in the new progeny of thy family the spirit of adoption which thou hast given; that, renewed in body and mind, they may exhibit in thy sight a pure service. Through the same Lord.

The Lesson is taken from St Paul's Epistle to the Colossians (iii 1-4). The life of the Christian is both death and life in Jesus Christ. It is death to corrupt nature and resurrection to grace; so that the soul which has risen with Christ must of necessity desire those things that are above.

For many centuries the Alleluia was so much a part of the Easter solemnity that, at Rome, in the time of Sozomen, it was not unusual among the people to curse their enemies by wishing that they might not live to hear the Alleluias sung at the coming Easter festival. St Augustine says that, in his day, the Alleluia was repeated during the whole of the fifty days from Easter to Pentecost. It was probably St Gregory the Great who extended its use in Rome to all Sundays except those in Lent. It is, however, possible that even in Rome in the fourth century the Alleluia came after the Gospel as it does among the Greeks, and that St Gregory placed it by anticipation after the Epistle on account of his homilies on the Gospel. Be this as it may, it is certain that the Alleluia which now is solemnly intoned by the priest after the Epistle would—as being more logical and natural—be more appropriately placed after the Gospel narrative of the resurrection of our Lord. This was probably its original and special place in the solemn Easter vigil.

Alleluia, Alleluia, Alleluia.
Psalm cxvii. Give praise to the Lord, for he is good: for his mercy endureth for ever.
Then follows the Alleluiatic Tract, which is sung in Rome at all the *pannuches* preceding the Sunday.
Praise the Lord, all ye nations; praise him, all ye peoples.
℣. For his mercy is confirmed upon us, and the truth of the Lord remaineth for ever.
At the Gospel no lights are carried, to which rite a symbolical interpretation has been given by medieval liturgists. However this custom may have originated, the paschal candle placed at the side of the ambo rendered other lights unnecessary for this evening.

The Gospel is from St Matthew (xxviii 1-7). When the
dawn of the first day of the week began to appear, the faithful women who had followed the Saviour came to his sepulchre in order to embalm his body with greater care than had
been possible on the evening of Good Friday, when they were
obliged to hasten, as the beginning of the Sabbath rest was
close upon them.

They found the stone rolled back from the entrance of the
sepulchre, and on going in, they learned from an angel that
the Lord had indeed risen, as he said.   It was not the
Apostles but simple women who, rendered courageous by
faith and love, braved the anger of the Sanhedrim and faced
the soldiers on guard at the tomb, and who, regardless of
the difficulty of moving the stone from the mouth of the
sepulchre, conceived the bold plan of completing the embalming of the body of the Lord.   Often does God make use of
the weakest instruments in order to confound our human
judgements, and reveals in some simple soul among the
people a degree of virtue which it would be difficult to find
in those who are highly placed in the ranks of the hierarchy.

Thus the Apostles received the first announcement of the
resurrection of their Lord from the holy women, and this preference shown to the devotion of woman was most fitting.
Woman had been the first to weep, and she was also to be
the first to rejoice; she who had brought the doom of death
to Adam, was now to be the first herald of the resurrection
to the Church.

The Offertory is not sung, because the paschal vigiliary
Mass is far more ancient than the introduction of such singing into Rome, but the host and the chalice are placed on the
corporal with the usual rites and the customary incensing of
the oblations.

In the Secret we pray God that he will favourably receive
the prayers of his people, together with the oblations, that
being initiated to the paschal sacrament through baptism and
Holy Communion, it may avail us for a healing remedy unto
everlasting life.

In the text of the anaphora the following commemoration
is inserted before the diptychs with the names of the Apostles
and of the bishops of Rome :

. . . Communicating and keeping the most holy night of
the resurrection of our Lord Jesus Christ according to the
flesh; as also reverencing the memory of the glorious and
ever Virgin Mary, mother of the same our God and Lord
Jesus Christ, etc.

The eucharistic sacrifice, which is, as it were, the completion of the rite of Christian initiation, is offered more

especially for the neophytes. Hence they are mentioned to-day in the prayer which Pope Celestine I is supposed to have called *Commendatio oblationum,* in the sense which we have already explained in Part III of this work.

Spreading his hands over the oblation, the priest says:

We therefore beseech thee, O Lord, graciously to receive this offering, made by us thy servants and by thy whole household; which we offer up to thee for those also whom thou hast vouchsafed to regenerate by water and the Holy Ghost, granting them remission of all their sins; and order our days in thy peace, and command us to be delivered from eternal damnation, and to be numbered in the fold of thy elect. Through Christ our Lord. Amen.

The Agnus Dei is not said, nor any Post-Communion, as these are of later origin. The absence of the petition *dona nobis pacem* must have been one of the causes that con-tributed during the late Middle Ages to the suppression of the kiss of peace which in the Roman rite always preceded the Communion.

Afterwards, when the whole of this vigiliary Mass was said by anticipation on the afternoon of Holy Saturday, Vespers were added to it, so that our present rite, after having com-memorated the night of the resurrection of our Lord for several hours consecutively, suddenly takes us back some twelve hours at least. This has become still more noticeable since by continuing to anticipate the paschal vigil we have ended by celebrating it in the morning of the preceding day. All these successive changes are mentioned only for their historic interest without any intention of criticizing adversely the modern ecclesiastical rite; indeed no true son of the Church would dare to find fault with that which the wise indulgence of our holy Mother has conceded.

After the Communion is sung in place of Vespers *Alleluia* three times followed by Psalm cxvi:

O praise the Lord, all ye nations; praise him all ye people.
For his mercy is confirmed upon us; and the truth of the Lord remaineth for ever.
Glory be. As it was.
Ant. Alleluia, Alleluia, Alleluia.

No little chapter, hymn or verse is said, but the celebrant immediately sings the beginning of the antiphon to the *Magnificat:*

In the end of the Sabbath—and the choir continues—when it began to dawn towards the first day of the week, came

Mary Magdalen, and the other Mary, to see the sepulchre, Alleluia.

The *Magnificat* is then sung, during which the altar and choir are incensed as is usual at Vespers. The antiphon is repeated, and lastly the priest recites as a Vesper-collect the ancient eucharistic prayer :

Pour forth upon us, O Lord, the spirit of thy love; that by thy loving-kindness thou mayest make to be of one mind those whom thou hast fed with paschal sacraments. Through our Lord.

The spirit of charity is one of the fruits of Holy Communion. It impels us to unite ourselves closely, not only with the incarnate Christ, but with the mystical Christ which is the Church, in such a manner as to stifle within ourselves the growth of an unrestrained egoism that leads us to seek *quae sua sunt,* and to live henceforth only in the spirit of the Church.

Priest: The Lord be with you.
℟ : And with thy spirit.

The deacon then dismisses the assembly :

Go, the Mass is finished. Alleluia, Alleluia.
℟ : Thanks be to God. Alleluia, Alleluia.

The paschal vigil is the symbol of the watch which we must keep in expectation of the divine judge. He has himself told us that he will come as a thief in the night, and as it is the salvation of our soul which is at stake, no care can be too great for us to take in order to prepare ourselves for that fateful hour on which our eternal happiness depends.

Our forefathers expected the longed-for *parousia* of the Redeemer to take place during the Easter watch. We do not know when he will come, but we know that it will be at an hour when we are least expecting it. Yet it is not the *parousia* alone which comes so suddenly, and for which we must always be prepared. Many times during the day our Lord visits us unexpectedly with his gifts of grace, and woe to us if we let them slip from us. They are not offered to us a second time if they meet with no acceptance. A measure of grace which God gives us and which we allow to elude us is like a precious treasure floating on the stream beside our vessel, which, unless we grasp it at once, will be carried away by the current, and we shall not find it again until we pass out into the ocean of eternity.

EASTER SUNDAY

Station at St Mary Major.

Throughout this paschal week the Roman Liturgy is entirely absorbed by two great thoughts, that of the resurrection of our Lord and that of the baptism of the neophytes. These are, as it were, two mysteries which mutually complete and explain each other. Each is a symbol of the other; the one is the prototype, the other the antitype; but neither can be understood if considered by itself, for the regeneration of souls to the life of grace through the sacrament of baptism, after a spiritual manner which yet is full of reality, is a new resurrection of Christ in his mystical body.

Even the stational feasts which occur in this week have a somewhat different character from those solemnized during Lent; there is no longer any mention of fasts and corporal penances, but instead, visits are paid to the great Roman basilicas, the white-clad band of neophytes being conducted thither as in a triumphal procession.

After the paschal vigil at the Lateran the first basilica to be visited is that of the Mother of God on the Esquiline, for it is fitting that to her, before any other, the joys of the resurrection should be announced, to her who more intimately than any other shared in the passion of Jesus. Moreover, the fatigues of the previous night, and the lengthy Vesper Office which was to be again celebrated in the Lateran baptistery, would scarcely have permitted the Pope to absent himself from the patriarchal palace for so long a time as would be required for him to go in procession to St Peter's, where the stational Mass should rightly have taken place on this solemn festival.

The Introit is derived from Psalm cxxxviii, which extols the knowledge and the presence of God that pervade the innermost part of our being. The antiphon has, however, been adapted to the paschal solemnity. Truly Christ fell asleep upon the cross, having yielded up his spirit to his Father, and now he awakens in the loving arms of the Almighty, who has accepted the spotless victim spontaneously offered to him, and, pressing him to his bosom, has revived within him the spark of his own divine life. Christ has indeed arisen from the dead.

" I have risen again and am still with thee, Alleluia : thou hast laid thy hand upon me, Alleluia : thy knowledge is become wonderful, Alleluia, Alleluia. Lord, thou hast proved me and known me: thou hast known my sitting down and my rising up."

Then follows the grand Collect: "O God, who on this day through thine only-begotten Son didst overcome death and open unto us the gate of everlasting life; as by thy preventing grace thou dost breathe on the desires of our hearts, so do thou ever accompany them with thy help. Through our Lord."

The resurrection of Christ foreshadows the resurrection of humanity. The members, seeing to-day that their mystical head has risen from the grave, are confirmed in the hope that one day they also shall be as he is.

The Lesson comes from the first Epistle of St Paul to the Corinthians (v 7-8). The old leaven must be purged out in order that the Pasch may be celebrated with the unleavened bread of sincerity and truth. Our Pasch is Christ, who by his sacrifice has brought to a close the Old Testament and has initiated the New. We, therefore, as he, must walk before God with the innocence and candour of children, having no longer anything in common with the sinful nature which once was ours. As the Son of God reflects clearly the splendour of the Father, so every Christian soul is called upon to reflect the divine goodness and beauty. This is the same thought as we find expressed by the Apostle in another place: "*Estote imitatores Dei, sicut filii charissimi.*"[1]

The Gradual is taken from the paschal Psalm cxvii: "This is the day which the Lord has made: let us be glad and rejoice therein." If indeed we sang with so much joy on Christmas Day that Jesus Christ was made flesh *de Spiritu Sancto ex Maria Virgine,* and was born to suffer and to die, how much more should we not rejoice on this day, on which God alone, without human co-operation, has given back life to Christ, and has regenerated him, as it were, to his own glory? For this great gift Christ renders joyful thanks in the words of the Psalmist: "Give praise to the Lord, for he is good; and his mercy endureth for ever." More especially is God good to each one of us, for he did not spare even his own Son so that we might become possessors of the wonderful treasures of his goodness. In Jesus he has manifested his inexorable justice; towards men he has made known his tender compassion.

The Alleluiatic verse is inspired by the words of the Apostle: "Christ our Pasch is sacrificed." He is called *Pascha nostrum* because he has given himself entirely to us. He does not wish to celebrate the Pasch alone, he wishes to keep it with us, in order that we, by associating ourselves

---

[1] Ephes. v 1.

with his passion, may take part also in his triumphant resurrection. He is not called merely *Pascha,* but *Pascha nostrum;* because, unless his death and resurrection become truly ours by our dwelling upon his mysteries and making them a part of ourselves by our spiritual life, his sorrows and his joys will not in any way profit us, just as the healing medicine cannot benefit a sick man until he has actually partaken thereof.

We should, probably, look for the origin of the Sequence (ἀκολουθία) in Byzantium, whence it was brought by Greek monks to the Abbey of St Gall, in Switzerland. The very long oriental *neums* on the Alleluia became wearisome and difficult of execution to the Latin cantors; so the monk Notker conceived the idea of substituting for all the vocalisations at the end of the Alleluia rhythmical texts, to which were to be adapted the same *neums* as those of the alleluiatic *jubilus.* It was in this way that the Sequence came into existence.

The paschal Sequence is attributed to Wipo (died 1050), chaplain at the courts of Conrad II and of Henry III. The text given in the Missal is not quite intact, as the whole of the fifth strophe has been suppressed, thus leaving the antistrophe incomplete.

The original expression *praecedet suos,* too, was changed at the time of the revision of the Missal by Pius V, doubtless by a paleographic oversight, into *praecedet vos,* as we now have it. The *Amen* and the *Alleluia* are also of later date.

SEQUENTIA

SEQUENCE

1. Victimae Paschali laudes immolent Christiani.

1. Forth to the paschal Victim, Christians, bring
Your sacrifice of praise.

2. Agnus redemit oves:
Christus innocens Patri reconciliavit peccatores.

2. The Lamb redeems the sheep;
And Christ the sinless One
Hath to the Father sinners reconciled.

2a. Mors et vita, duello conflixere mirando:
dux vitae mortuus, regnat vivus.

2a. Together, death and life
In a strange conflict strove:
The Prince of life who died,
Now lives and reigns.

3. Dic nobis, Maria, quid vidisti in via?

3. What thou sawest, Mary, say,
As thou wentest on the way.

3a. Sepulchrum Christi viventis:
et gloriam vidi resurgentis.

3a. I saw the tomb wherein the living One had lain;
I saw his glory as he rose again;

4. Angelicos testes, sudarium et vestes.

4. Napkin and linen clothes, and angels' twain.

4*a*. Surrexit Christus spes mea :
  praecedet vos in Galileam.

4*a*. Yea, Christ is risen, my hope, and he
  Will go before you into Galilee.

5. Credendum est magis soli
  Mariae veraci :
  quam Judeorum turbae fallaci.[1]

5. To Mary pure and true,
  Rather than to faithless Jew,
  Let credence full be given.

5*a*. Scimus Christum surrexisse a
  mortuis vere :
  tu nobis, victor Rex, miserere.
  Amen. Alleluia.

5*a*. We know that Christ indeed
  has risen from the grave :
  Hail, thou King of Victory !
  Have mercy, Lord, and save.
  Amen. Alleluia.

This Sequence is said every day during Easter week.

Like the hymnody of the Office the Sequence introduces into the liturgy a poetic element inspired by private devotion and not taken from the Scriptures, for which reason it was not included in the regular Roman liturgical books until much later. In the ceremonial of the papal court of the twelfth century, the place given to the Sequence was during the banquet or *symposium* of the clergy in the *triclinium* of St Leo, quite apart, that is, from the liturgy.

The paschal Sequence, in particular, being inserted in the Mass as a hymn preceding the Gospel, has lost much of its original dramatic character, which, in France, had so greatly endeared it to the people, as, when on the morning of this day it was sung alternately by the Apostles together, by Mary of Magdala alone, and finally by the whole choir.

The Gospel telling of the message of the angel to the holy women is from St Mark (xvi 1-7). The resurrection of Jesus Christ is a dogmatic fact for which we have abundant documentary evidence. It took place among persons who were for the most part hostile, as in the case of the Jews, or at least hard to convince, as were not only the Apostles but the women themselves. We cannot, therefore, put it down as auto-suggestion on the part of the first Christians, a delusion caused by their hopes, for they believed in the resurrection of Jesus in spite of themselves; they were not disposed to admit the fact, but were forced to do so by the evidence of their senses. They believed because they saw, because they actually touched him, because they ate and drank with him who had been dead and had risen again.

The Offertory comes from Psalm lxxv: " The earth trembled and was still when God arose in judgement, Alleluia."

As nature itself was associated with the curse of God on

---

[1] This strophe is missing in the present Missal.

the sin of Adam, therefore, as St Paul says, it awaits with longing the day of its redemption and of its liberation from the state of servitude and degradation in which it is held by the sinner. At the first announcement of the *parousia* of the risen Christ, the earth is shaken to its foundations, for the judgement of God upon the faithless world has already begun; but at the last day, when Christ shall come to judge finally the living and the dead, all creation will realize the presence of the Creator and will join with him in warring against the impious, as it is said in the Book of Wisdom: *et pugnabit cum illo orbis terrarum contra insensatos.*[1]

The Secret and the Preface are the same as in the preceding vigil, perhaps because originally this second Mass did not exist, and the paschal sacrifice was that which concluded the baptismal ceremony.

The initiation into the paschal mysteries, the Secret teaches us, is not meant to end with the liturgical cycle of Easter. The Pasch of Christ is eternal; for, having entered once into his glory, he cannot again descend from on high. The Christian, too, is called to share in the lasting quality of the resurrection, since in his spiritual life he is to show forth in his turn a steadfast and continual Pasch.

In the Preface to the consecratory anaphora, just before the diptychs, a commemoration is made of the resurrection of the Lord, as on the preceding night.

The Communion is derived from the words of St Paul, which have already been read in the Lesson: "Christ our Pasch is sacrificed. Therefore let us feast in the unleavened bread of sincerity and truth." Let us be nourished by him. Our Pasch would be profaned by any other food or any other nourishment. Christ sacrificed and become the food of the faithful, indicates his passion which we must engrave in our minds. The unleavened bread, unfermented and untouched by yeast, signifies the spirit of mortification which must permeate the life of every earnest Christian.

In the Post-Communion we are reminded that the Holy Eucharist is a pledge of the Communion of Saints, uniting the hearts of all the faithful in the spirit of love. This is why, in olden days, the faithful, at the moment of receiving Holy Communion from the hands of their bishop, gave him the kiss of peace, of which we find a last trace in our present custom of kissing the ring of the bishop. For the same reason priests used to send the Holy Eucharist to one another, because in the Blessed Sacrament Jesus gives us his own spirit, so that the multitude of those who receive him may, through his grace, who is their life, truly form *cor unum et anima una.*

---

[1] Wisdom v 21.

The Holy Eucharist is not only the commemoration of the death of our Lord, it is also a representation of him in his glory. Therefore, whilst it sows in us the seeds of death, that we may learn to die with Christ, it gives us at the same time a part and share in his resurrection.

EASTER MONDAY

Station at St Peter.

Whereas, among the early Christians, the feasts of Christmas, the Epiphany, and Pentecost lasted only three or four days, it was characteristic of the Easter festivities that they were prolonged for an entire week, not concluding until the Saturday *in Albis;* so that the neophytes might lay aside their white baptismal garments on the Sunday following. During this whole week Rome kept continuous festival; all business transactions were suspended; the law-courts were closed, marriage ceremonies were deferred; every morning the station was celebrated at one of the chief basilicas of the city, whilst in the afternoon the people again met together in the Lateran basilica in order to accompany the neophytes in procession to the baptistery and to the various oratories grouped around that sanctuary.

After yesterday's station at St Mary Major, we must to-day hasten immediately to St Peter's—whether because it is fitting to bring at once to the *Pastor Ecclesiae* those who are called in the liturgy *Agni novelli, qui annuntiaverunt Alleluia,* or because St Peter was the first among the Apostles to be privileged to see the risen Saviour. The scriptural lessons in the Mass and the responsory in the evening Office: " *Surrexit Dominus vere et apparuit Simoni* "[1] bear witness to the lively faith of the Apostle in whose house the Roman Church is desirous of renewing, as it were, to-day the paschal feast.

The Introit is taken from Exodus (xiii 5, 9) and also from Psalm civ, and is addressed to the neophytes: " The Lord hath brought you into a land flowing with milk and honey, Alleluia; and that the law of the Lord may be ever in your mouth, Alleluia, Alleluia." Psalm civ : " Give glory to the Lord, and call upon his name : declare his deeds among the Gentiles."

The Collect speaks of the paschal Sacrament as being closely bound up with the redemption of the world. The

[1] Luke xxiv 34.

spiritual Israel has come forth from the slavery of Egypt. May the Lord then protect this newly won liberty.

" O God, who at the paschal festival didst give thy saving remedies to the world; continue, we beseech thee, thy heavenly gifts to thy people; that they may both deserve to attain to perfect freedom, and advance onward to everlasting life. Through our Lord."

To-day Peter himself receives us in his own basilica. He therefore lifts up his voice and proclaims to the neophytes the glory of Christ's resurrection. (Acts x 37-48). The mission of Jesus, says the Apostle, needs no further justification. All the prophets bear witness to him—God has filled him with the Holy Ghost and with power; he has passed through the world healing the sick and doing good to all. The Jews have crucified him, but God has reversed their judgement, raising him again to life, as chosen and trustworthy witnesses are able to testify, who have even sat at supper with him after his resurrection. According to the unanimous teaching of the prophets, God has constituted Jesus Christ redeemer and universal judge, so that, in order to be saved, it is necessary to acknowledge him in this twofold capacity and to conform our lives to this belief.

The exposition of Christian doctrine concerning the Saviour is brief but complete and comprehensive, so much so that if each point were to be fully developed, we should have matter for a marvellous treatise of Christian Apologetics.

The Gradual comes from Psalm cxvii, as on the preceding day, and is as follows : " This is the day which the Lord hath made; let us be glad and rejoice therein. Let Israel now say that he is good, that his mercy endureth for ever. Alleluia, Alleluia."

The alleluiatic verse is from the Gospel of the paschal vigil (Matthew xxviii 2) : " An angel of the Lord descended from heaven, and coming, rolled back the stone, and sat upon it."

The Gospel from St Luke (xxiv 13-35), in which towards the end mention is made of the appearing of our Lord to Peter, refers really to the evening of Easter Sunday. As, however, there was no place in yesterday's evening Office for a Gospel lesson, it is read to-day instead, in the basilica dedicated to the Prince of the Apostles himself.

Cleopas was probably the cousin of our Lord; the other disciple is not named, but he has been identified by some with St Luke. These two disciples, although deeply grieved at the death of Jesus, yet at the same time deserved from him the reproach of being foolish and slow to believe the mystery of the cross. They are examples of that sentimental piety so common in our days, and are typical of those souls

who are eager for religious emotions, but have no wish
to understand the necessary and indispensable connection
between the sacrifice and the resurrection, between the cross
and its salvation.

Et cognoverunt eum in fractione panis. Did our Lord
consecrate the Holy Eucharist at Emmaus, and was it by
virtue of the sacrament that the eyes of the two disciples
were opened? It is probable that it was so, for the expression
fractio panis is conventional in St Luke's writings and refers
in general to the ritual breaking of the eucharistic bread.
Besides, it is said that Jesus *accepit panem, benedixit ac
fregit*, just as at the Last Supper.

As the Saviour at the Last Supper received the Eucharist
first himself, in all likelihood he did so again after his
resurrection. In this new state he truly drank the new fruit
of the vine together with the Apostles, as to-day at Emmaus,
since the mystery which had been prefigured on Maundy
Thursday had been already accomplished and the Messianic
era fulfilled. It is therefore probable that the two disciples
recognized the risen Saviour at the moment when they saw
him repeat the sacramental act of the preceding Thursday.

The Offertory is derived from the Gospel of St Matthew
(xxviii). "An angel of the Lord descended from heaven,
and said to the women, he whom you seek is risen, as he
said, Alleluia." The true dogmatic importance of the holy
sepulchre consists in this, that he who died is no longer
there; the tomb is empty, for Christ is risen.

The Secret is the same as on Easter Sunday.

The Communion is taken from the Gospel of the day:
"The Lord is risen, and hath appeared to Simon, Alleluia."

Our Lord appeared to Peter separately for several reasons
—to spare him humiliation on account of his denial; further,
because Peter was to be the chief support of the Catholic
faith, it was fitting that the resurrection which sealed the
Messianic mission of Christ should be revealed first to him.
Thus, the other Apostles, even before they had seen Jesus
with their own eyes, believed in his resurrection because of
the infallible teaching and testimony of Peter. Peter had
seen, he therefore bore witness, and the Church formed her
first creed, uniting her faith to that of the first Apostle and
saying: "The Lord is risen indeed and hath appeared to
Simon."

The Post-Communion is the same as that of yesterday. As
all the members of a household gather around the family
table, so the Holy Eucharist is the visible sign of the unity
of the Christian family and of the dogma of the Communion
of Saints. We all participate in the one sacrifice offered in
the name of the whole Catholic community by the hands of

our appointed pastors. Hence we see how the spirit of the Church inspires the faithful to communicate collectively and frequently, whether at the parochial, the capitular, or the episcopal Mass. The fruit which we derive from the Holy Table is a sense of intimate union of mind, heart, and will with Jesus Christ, with the Church, and with our brethren.

Surrexit Dominus et apparuit Simoni; this is the first act of faith which the Church repeats at the close of the first Easter Day, and it is Peter alone who has the divine commission to pass on to us infallibly the deposit of revealed truth, whilst the Catholic world, like the Apostles of old, fully accepts the faith of Peter.

In order to keep in mind the significance of this first appearance to Peter, the Pope in the Middle Ages was accustomed to go in solemn procession to celebrate the stational Mass at the tomb of the Prince of the Apostles.

In those centuries it was not unusual for the emperor, or some other king or prince, to be present in Rome for the Easter festival, and historians relate that on such occasions these sovereigns would hold the Pope's stirrup or the bridle of his steed in token of their devoted homage.

After the Mass the Pontiff put on the tiara, and returned in state to the Lateran, distributing large gifts of money to the cardinals, the inferior clergy, and the people who crowded the streets. Hardly had he passed over Hadrian's bridge when he was acclaimed by representatives of the Jewish colony, who begged in return the papal protection for their people. The Pope caused money to be distributed among them also, promising to mete out justice to them and to shield them from oppression.

The procession, which had stopped for a few minutes to receive the petitions of the Jews, again set forth for the Lateran, first ascending to the Capitol, and then descending into the Forum by the Clivus Argentarius. It passed under the triumphal arches of Septimius Severus and of Titus, leaving the Arch of Constantine on their right at the Meta Sudans, and, turning towards the Colossus of Nero,[1] entered the Sacra Via which led straight to the Lateran.

The sight of that splendid religious procession passing through the ruins of the former greatness of Imperial Rome must have been wonderfully dramatic. The Pontiff crowned with the tiara, the bridle of his steed held by the highest earthly sovereigns; the throng of bishops and cardinals in their richest vestments surrounding the Pope; the lower orders of the clergy coming out of all the churches as the Pontiff passed by, and greeting him with clouds of incense;

---

[1] A colossal gilded bronze statue of Nero as the Sun-God.—Tr.

the dense crowd of people along the way; all this must have brought to the minds of the onlookers that prophecy of Daniel foretelling that the little stone which detached itself from the mountain would crush the mightiest kingdoms and found an empire that should have no end.

After this triumphant progress no chant could have been more appropriate to the occasion than that which the cantors intoned before the gates of the Lateran, as the Pope descended from his steed: *Christus vincit, Christus regnat, Christus imperat.*

EASTER TUESDAY

Station at St Paul.

After visiting St Peter's, it was fitting that the neophytes should at once be brought to the Doctor of the Gentiles, beside whose tomb they had learnt the first rudiments of the new law of the Gospel. Therefore in the lesson from the Acts of the Apostles chosen for to-day, it is Paul who announces to the faithful the resurrection of the Saviour as Peter did on Easter Monday.

The Introit is drawn from Ecclesiasticus (xv 3-4) and is followed, as yesterday, by Psalm civ: " He gave them the water of wisdom to drink, Alleluia : she shall be made strong in them, and shall not be moved, Alleluia : and he shall exalt them for ever, Alleluia, Alleluia." Psalm civ: " Give glory to the Lord, and call upon his name; declare his deeds among the Gentiles."

The Collect refers to the new generation which has brought joy to the Church, and enlarged the ranks of the faithful: " O God, who givest increase to the Church with an offspring ever renewed; grant that thy servants may hold fast in their lives to the mystery which they have received in faith. Through our Lord."

Sacramentum vivendo teneant—that is, that they may realize all which baptism means, inasmuch as it communicates to us the very life of Jesus Christ himself. How grand and sublime is the rule of life set forth to-day with a solemn simplicity of language that recalls the omnipotent simplicity of the words of God. No human mind could rise to such heights and still less put before others with equal authority so sublime an ideal. This divine language, which not only formulates, but through grace accomplishes that which it announces, is the language of Christ alone. If the Church repeats it, it is in his name and by his authority, and the Catholic apologist can find in the very words of the sacred liturgy the proofs of the divine mission of the Church.

The Lesson, containing the magnificent discourse of St Paul in the synagogue at Antioch in Pisidia, comes from the Acts of the Apostles (xiii 16 and 26-33). The wicked, even when they rebel against the law of God, take their part in the wonderful plan which he has foreseen and ordered from all eternity for the salvation of souls. The malice of the sinner is entirely attributable to himself, but God permits it, and makes use of its effects in such a way as to draw from them a greater good. Thus from the spite of those who crucified our Lord, the wisdom of God has brought forth the redemption of the world and the fulfilment of the prophecies, the most important of which was the one which foretold the resurrection of the Saviour.

The Gradual throughout the whole of the Octave is taken from Psalm cxvii, to which there is added to-day a verse of Psalm cvi, referring to the catholicity of the Church who gathers in her sons from all the countries of the earth. This mark of the universality of the New Covenant is brought forward especially on this day on which the station is celebrated in the basilica of the *Doctor Gentium*—of him who was the most energetic exponent of this teaching. " This is the day which the Lord hath made : let us be glad and rejoice therein." Psalm cvi : " Let those now speak who have been redeemed by our Lord : whom he hath redeemed out of the hand of the enemy, and gathered out of the nations. Alleluia, Alleluia. The Lord is risen from the sepulchre, who for us hung upon a tree."

The alleluiatic verse is of non-scriptural origin.

The Gospel from St Luke (xxiv 36-47) describes the first appearance of Jesus to the Apostles. As the resurrection of our Lord is the central tenet of the Christian faith, so the divine wisdom, in order to take away all excuse for the unbelief of the synagogue, willed that the miracle should be proved beyond all possibility of doubt. The witnesses are not merely a few isolated women who, in a state of hysteria, treat as solid fact a dream emanating from their love of the Saviour, but more than five hundred persons who saw him after he had risen, amongst whom many, like the Apostles, were but little disposed to believe. They speak to Jesus, they see on his hands and feet the marks of the nails, and yet they are not convinced. At last the evidence of the fact overcomes their preconceptions and their reluctance to believe, and on Whit-Sunday they come forward before the world to fulfil their special mission of bearing witness to the " resurrection of Jesus Christ." Here we have another instance of the divine wisdom making use of the very weakness of his creatures in the furtherance of his designs for the salvation of mankind.

The Antiphon *ad offerendum* from Psalm xvii alludes to the baptismal waters created and blessed by the power of the most High, thus making even insensate matter to be of service for the sanctification of man who had first been turned away from his duty to God by the desire for earthly things.

"The Lord thundered from heaven, and the most High gave his voice : and the fountains of water appeared, Alleluia."

The Secret has no special character of its own. It speaks of "prayers and sacrifices," because originally each member of the faithful brought to the altar his or her contribution for the common sacrifice.

"Receive, O Lord, the prayers of the faithful with the offerings of sacrifices, that by these offices of piety and devotion we may pass to heavenly glory. Through our Lord."

At the Communion the powerful words of St Paul are again heard (Col. iii 1-2) : "If you be risen with Christ, seek the things that are above, where Christ is sitting at the right hand of God, Alleluia : mind the things that are above, Alleluia." The Holy Eucharist, whilst uniting us to the sacrifice and death of Christ, makes us also to share in the spirit of his resurrection.

The Post-Communion is as follows : "Grant, we beseech thee, almighty God, that the fruits of the Easter sacrament of which we have partaken may ever remain in our soul. Through our Lord."

The Church teaches us in this prayer that there are two kinds of Communion, the sacramental and the spiritual. By means of the first we partake actually of the body and blood of Christ, by means of the second we live by the spirit of the Holy Eucharist. This second Communion is the fruit and the consequence of the first. As the sacramental Communion can be received only at certain times and in certain places, our Lord unites the soul so intimately to himself in the Holy Eucharist that it lives by his spirit and breathes in unison with his heart. Such, in its highest sense, is the spiritual Communion of which the Church speaks in to-day's Post-Communion Collect, the effect of which endures even when the eucharistic species have been consumed within us.

WEDNESDAY IN EASTER WEEK

Station at St Lawrence without the Walls.

To-day we honour St Lawrence, the Cross-bearer of the Roman Church, as though to express our gratitude for the favour shown by him to the catechumens in bringing them to the grace of holy baptism.   The Introit and the Offertory of the Mass bear special reference to these new sons of the Church, the *Benedicti* of the divine Father, now brought into the heavenly kingdom of Jesus Christ and admitted to the participation of the bread of angels.

The Introit is from St Matthew (xxv 34), and joyfully acclaims the neophytes.   They are the *Benedicti*, those to whom the benediction of the Father is promised as a heritage. To this blessing is attached the possession of a kingdom, that is to say, the Church of Christ in its three aspects, the militant, the purificative, and the triumphant.   The being admitted into the Church by baptism signifies that we have taken the first step on the way of our predestination.   It rests then with us in no way to thwart God's wondrous design towards us.

"Come, ye blessed of my Father, receive the kingdom, Alleluia; which was prepared for you from the foundation of the world, Alleluia, Alleluia, Alleluia."

Psalm xcv : "Sing ye to the Lord a new canticle; sing to the Lord all the earth."

The Collect is the following : "O God, who dost gladden us with the yearly celebration of our Lord's resurrection; mercifully grant that by these festivals which we keep in time we may become worthy to attain to bliss that shall last for ever."   This is the truly noble ideal of the Christian festival; it is a holy time during which the soul, with deeper recollection, greater purity of life, and keener desire for heaven, prepares itself for the eternal feast.

Throughout this Easter week, with the exception of yesterday's station at St Paul's own basilica—Thursday's Mass is somewhat later—St Peter is given the honour of being the first to announce to the Romans the resurrection of the Lord.   The Apostle, who once trembled at the voice of a maidservant, shows fear no longer in the presence of the Sanhedrim and of the people, but boldly throws upon them the entire responsibility of the deicide.   Pilate, he tells them in to-day's lesson (Acts iii 13-19) judged that Jesus should be released; God the Father has raised him from the dead; but they have delivered him up and have denied him, refusing in any way to acknowledge him.

This is one of the most striking features of the preaching of the Gospel. The Apostles do not praise nor do they flatter their hearers; on the contrary, they reproach them with their sins, preaching the need of repentance and of a change of life. The world will find nothing in the Gospel to encourage the sensuality which naturally attracts it; yet, notwithstanding all the opposition between the spirit of the world and the principles of the Gospel, in less than three hundred years the pagan world will, in spite of itself, have bowed its head to receive the healing waters of Christian baptism. Next to the resurrection of Jesus Christ, this is the greatest of all the miracles which have confirmed our Faith.

The Gradual comes from Psalm cxvii: "This is the day which the Lord hath made: let us be glad and rejoice therein. The right hand of the Lord hath wrought strength: the right hand of the Lord hath exalted me. Alleluia, Alleluia."

The alleluiatic verse (Luke xxiv 34) dwells once more on the special significance of our Lord's appearing to Peter. "The Lord is risen indeed: and hath appeared to Simon."

The passages from the Gospels read during this Octave follow more or less the historical order of the events narrated therein. On this, the third ferial day of the week, is read the account of the third manifestation of the risen Saviour to the Apostles (John xxi 1-14), which in St Luke is combined with his appearance at Emmaus. On the preceding Monday the first manifestation was described, and yesterday the second.

Christ shows himself to the Apostles on the shores of Lake Tiberias. John, the virgin soul among the Apostles, sees him first, but Peter, the most ardent and the most impetuous, in the vigour of his faith throws himself into the water and is the first to reach the divine Master, whilst the others slowly follow in the boat. Having come to land they dine, Jesus feeding them with the broiled fish and with bread. *Piscis assus,* says St Augustine, *Christus est passus,* to signify that even the necessary concessions which we have to make to the weakness of our nature must be mingled with the spirit of mortification taught to us by Jesus Christ.

Yesterday the Offertory reminded the neophytes of the holy font in which they were regenerated; to-day, on the other hand, it calls to their minds the eucharistic banquet to which they have been admitted.

Psalm lxxvii: "The Lord opened the doors of heaven, and rained down manna upon them to eat: he gave them the bread of heaven: man ate the bread of angels, Alleluia."

The bread of angels becomes the food of man; not that heavenly things should be formed after the pattern of earthly ones, but in order that man through its life-giving power may be raised to emulate the sanctity of the angels.

The Secret points out that we, in order to celebrate worthily the joyful festival of Easter, offer to almighty God the eucharistic sacrifice; which, whilst it renders to him the fullest honour, at the same time wonderfully feeds and sustains his holy Church.

The Antiphon for the Communion is taken from the Epistle of St Paul to the Romans (vi 9). "Christ rising from the dead, dieth now no more, Alleluia; death shall no more have dominion over him, Alleluia, Alleluia." He is now no longer subject to death, and, like the tree of life in Eden, has become for those who believe in him the food of immortality; so that as many as shall eat of him shall live spiritually for ever and together with him shall be the true "'sons of the resurrection."

In the Post-Communion we beseech our merciful Lord that the paschal sacrifice, which has brought to an end the Old Covenant, may also begin in us a new life of active holiness.

"May we be cleansed, O Lord, we beseech thee, from our old nature; and may thy sacrament, which we reverently take, change us into newness."

Throughout the paschal season the Church displays a great veneration for the martyrs, of which the first evidence is seen to-day at the tomb of St Lawrence. The reason of this devotion is that the martyrs have a special claim to the glory of the resurrection, since they have participated more closely than others in the ignominy of the Cross.

THURSDAY IN EASTER WEEK

Station at the Twelve Holy Apostles.

To-day the stational feast is celebrated in honour of all the Apostles together. As, however, the high altar of the venerable *Apostoleion*, built as a memorial of the victory of Narses, preserves the relics of the Apostles Philip and James only, the Roman Liturgy, apparently mistaking Philip the Evangelist of Cesarea for the Apostle of the same name, appoints to be read to-day the account of the baptism of the eunuch of Candace, Queen of the Ethiopians, administered by the famous deacon.

This station of Thursday in Easter week, celebrated in a Byzantine basilica, carries us back to those times in Rome when, under the predominant influence of the Byzantines, the Roman Liturgy experienced a strong oriental bias.

The Introit is derived from the Book of Wisdom (x 20-21): "They praised with one accord thy victorious hand, O Lord, Alleluia; for wisdom opened the mouth of the dumb, and made the tongues of infants eloquent, Alleluia, Alleluia."

A verse from Psalm xcvii follows : " Sing ye to the Lord a new canticle; for he hath done wonderful things."

This wisdom which made the tongues of infants eloquent is the Christian faith which the Church's new recruits solemnly professed on Easter Eve.   Their example is inspiring, and the rapid spread of the Gospel among all the nations is the best argument in proof of the divine nature of this influence which turns the world to Christ.

In the Collect the Church lays stress on the unity of the Catholic faith among the multitudes of the nations that profess it.   This is the mark which distinguishes the true Church from the ancient national religions.   Many are the nations and the peoples, but only one creed, one hierarchy, one rule, one worship.

" O God, who hast united divers nations in praising thy name, grant that those who have been born again in the font of baptism may be joined by faith in their minds and by love in their deeds."   The unity of the Christian family was the supreme desire of our Redeemer.   The closer we cling to him, the more real will be our union on earth, for the unity of the mystical body of Christ is only disturbed when one member, leaving the divine centre, seeks *quae sua sunt, non quae Jesu Christi.*

The Lesson from the Acts of the Apostles (viii 26-40) with the narrative of the conversion of the treasurer of Candace, Queen of the Ethiopians, through the ministry of the deacon Philip, is chosen, as we have said, in honour of the Apostle Philip, some of whose relics are preserved under the high altar.   The passage from Isaias describing the sufferings of the " Servant of Jehovah " led to the conversion of the Ethiopian, for the Evangelist proved to him that the words of the Prophet could refer to none other than Jesus Christ.

This scene, in which Philip was taken up into the chariot of the influential Ethiopian official, and was the means of converting him as they drove along, reminds us of an anecdote from the life of St Francis de Sales.   He was in France on a diplomatic mission from his prince, when a Calvinist came up to him and, addressing him in an aggressive manner, said to him : " Monseigneur, I would like to know if the Apostles went about in a carriage as you do?" " Certainly they did, when the occasion presented itself." " Could you prove this from the Bible?"   " Certainly.   Do you not remember how the deacon Philip sat with the eunuch of the Queen of the Ethiopians in his chariot and converted him as they went along to the faith of Jesus Christ?" " That," interrupted the Calvinist, " was not Philip's chariot, but belonged to the Ethiopian Court."   " Precisely, as in my own case," replied the saintly Bishop of Geneva, "since I am poor and the carriage of which I am now making use is not mine, but has been placed at my disposal by the courtesy of the king." "Then, although you are a bishop, you are poor?" asked the Calvinist. "Yes, indeed," replied the Saint, "for your co-religionists at Geneva have seized the entire patrimony of my Church." The Calvinist, needless to say, was greatly impressed by this conversation.

The Gradual is taken, as usual, from Psalm cxvii. "This is the day which the Lord hath made: let us be glad and rejoice therein. The stone which the builders rejected is become the head of the corner: this is the work of the Lord, and it is wonderful in our eyes, Allelluia, Alleluia." This stone is Christ, as he himself told the Sanhedrim. Having been denied and rejected by the builders of Israel and cursed by them, it has become the foundation-stone of the Church.

The alleluiatic verse is as follows: "Christ is risen, who created all things, and had compassion upon the human race."

On Easter Day Jesus poured forth upon mankind the merits which he had gathered on Good Friday, calling upon all men to share in his resurrection, firstly by means of grace, and lastly by sharing in his eternal glory.

The liturgy proceeds in due order, though not with mere rigidity of method, for it is an art, not a mathematical science, and is inspired by the highest religious ideals. Thus, to-day, by sacrificing somewhat the exact chronological order, we have in the Gospel (John xx 11-18), after the manifestations of Christ to his Apostles, the account of his showing himself to Mary Magdalen, which should rightly have been read on Sunday morning. This was done out of respect for the Apostles, but, on the other hand, it was not possible to omit the consoling appearance of the Saviour to the poor penitent of Magdala—that story which touched Gregory the Great so deeply when he spoke of it in his homilies to the people of Rome.

How great is the power of a woman's love! The Apostles depart, but Mary remains faithful, and weeps beside the sepulchre of Jesus without thought of danger. She fears no enemy and dreads no difficulty. If the gardener has carried off the sacred body, let him tell the Magdalen of its secret resting-place and she herself will take it away.

This poor sinner has indeed loved much, therefore she has deserved that much be pardoned to her. Hence, before the Apostles, and even before Peter himself, she receives the grace of being the first to see the risen Saviour. "Go to my brethren," Jesus says to her, "and tell them that I go to the Father." Mary obeyed, and thus it became the privilege of the penitent of Magdala to announce the central doctrine of the Christian faith to the Apostles, to those, that is, whom the Lord appointed to be the infallible messengers of his Gospel. For this reason the Church ordains that the Creed is to be recited in the Mass on the feast of St Mary Magdalen as on the feasts of the Apostles.

The Offertory comes from Exodus (xiii 5) : " In the day of your solemnity, saith the Lord, I will bring you into a land that floweth with milk and honey, Alleluia." It was formerly customary, at least from the time of Tertullian, to present the neophytes after baptism with a blessed drink composed of milk and honey, in order to symbolize the spiritual fertility of this land planted by the right hand of God and made fertile by the waters of redemption. The milk signified the nourishment given to the soul by the sacraments, and the honey the sweetness to be found in the service of God.

The Secret reverts once more to the thought of baptism, which entails the continuous profession of the Gospel of Christ, and a corresponding amendment of life. " Favourably receive, we beseech thee, O Lord, the offerings of thy people; that being renewed by baptism and the praise of thy name, they may attain to everlasting bliss."

The Communion is from the first Epistle of St Peter (ii 9) : " Ye purchased people, declare his virtues, Alleluia, who hath called you out of darkness into his admirable light, Alleluia." This is an allusion to the calling of the Gentiles, who, as an acquired people, have been redeemed or bought back for Jehovah, whereas Israel is his true heir. The vocation of the Gentiles to the faith is therefore a greater and more gratuitous grace of God, inasmuch as the heathen could lay no claim to the spiritual inheritance of Abraham.

In the Post-Communion we pray thus : " Hear our prayers, O Lord, that the holy mysteries of our redemption may bring us help in this life, and also procure for us everlasting joys." The *sacrosancta commercia redemptionis,* of which the liturgy here speaks, is a happily expressed metaphor. *Commercium* means an exchange of goods. In our case Christ gives himself up to the divine justice as the price of our redemption from the slavery of sin, and the divine justice gives us to Christ.

Jesus, speaking of us to the Magdalen, says to her : " Go to my brethren and say to them, I ascend to my Father and to your Father." How consoling are these words, and how unspeakable is the intimate bond by which the resurrection of our Lord has linked humanity to himself ! Jesus is truly our brother, God is in very deed our Father. By the death of Christ we have gained far more than we had lost by sin, and it is in this sense that the deacon sings in the Easter *praeconium:* " O happy fault, that was worthy of so great a Redeemer."

FRIDAY IN EASTER WEEK

Station at St Mary " ad Martyres " (or " Martyra ").

As the station of yesterday was called simply *ad Apostolos,* so that of to-day was known as *ad Martyres,* and was intended by the Roman Church as a special tribute of veneration to her heroic sons, who, as the Apostle says, had not spared their life *ut meliorem invenirent resurrectionem.* The martyrs indeed seem to have a particular right to the glory of the resurrection on account of their perfect resemblance to Christ crucified; and many ancient liturgies kept a special feast in their honour in the very midst of the Easter festival. To-day's station *ad Martyres* remains as a last record of this early liturgical tradition, for, later on, the collective feast of the martyrs was transferred, even in Rome, to the middle of the month of May, and still later to the first day of November.

The Introit is drawn from Psalm lxxvii, and contains an allusion to the paschal feast of the neophytes, who, like the Israelites of old, have escaped from the slavery of Egypt across the Red Sea, which is a symbol of holy baptism. The enemy who was overwhelmed by the waves is Satan, or sin.

" The Lord brought them out in hope, Alleluia; and the sea overwhelmed their enemies, Alleluia, Alleluia, Alleluia. Attend, O my people, to my law; incline your ears to the words of my mouth."

The New Covenant has been sealed by the Easter sacrifice, which, being renewed daily on our altars, causes the spiritual value of Easter to endure for ever. It is necessary, therefore, for our works to be in accordance with our faith.

The Collect finely expresses the same thought: " Almighty and everlasting God, who in the covenant of man's reconciliation didst order the mystery of Easter; give grace to our souls, that we may follow up by our deeds what we outwardly celebrate." This is precisely the end which the Church has in view throughout the sacred liturgy, namely—to train the faithful and to obtain for them by her powerful intercession the grace of showing by their actions that sublime sanctity which she expresses in her rites.

The Lesson is derived from the first Epistle of St Peter (iii 18-22), in which he speaks of the death of Christ and his descent into Limbo, bringing to the Patriarchs who were detained in that close prison the announcement of the redemption he had won for them. Among those souls were some who had paid no heed to the warnings of Noe, when he predicted that his ark alone would withstand in safety the force of those waters. This prophetic figure is now about to become completely realized, for the ark of Noe is a type of the Church which proudly floats upon the purifying waters of baptism.

The tenet expressed in the article of the Creed *descendit ad inferos* is here clearly taught by the Apostle Peter, but his words must not be taken to mean that Christ preached in hell in order to convert those souls who had already been condemned for their sin of unbelief; for the state of the soul cannot change after death. Christ descended into the abode of the dead to announce both to the good and to the wicked the redemption now accomplished; to the good for their supreme consolation, to the wicked as a further reason for their condemnation.

Ancient Christian art took pleasure in representing the descent of Christ into Limbo, depicting him as a conqueror coming to take possession of a fortress which had long held out against him, but which he had at last taken by storm. The liturgy expresses the same idea at Matins on Holy Saturday: *Ille captus est qui captivum tenebat primum hominem; hodie portas mortis et seras pariter Salvator noster disrupit. Destruxit quidem claustra inferni et subvertit potentias diaboli.*

The Gradual comes as before from Psalm cxvii: "This is the day which the Lord hath made; let us be glad and rejoice therein. Blessed is he that cometh in the name of the Lord; the Lord is God, and he hath shone upon us. Alleluia, Alleluia."

The alleluiatic verse is from Psalm xcv, with the addition *a ligno,* confirmed by many of the early Fathers. "Say ye among the Gentiles that the Lord hath reigned from a tree." This is the throne from which Jesus makes his power to be known. He crushes death by his own death and gives to the Church grace to triumph over his enemies by being himself overcome by their deadly hatred. *Semen Christianorum est sanguis martyrum;* thus the cross has become the standard and the glorious device of almost every civilized nation of medieval Europe.

The short Gospel from St Matthew (xxviii 16-20) contains in a few words the whole history of the Church, the summary of her rights, and the explanation of her mission in the world: *Euntes docete;* this is the charter of her freedom to teach the Gospel everywhere independently of the civil power; *baptizantes,* this is her authority for administering to the faithful the holy sacraments of which baptism is, as it were, the door; *docentes servare omnia quaecumque mandavi*, this is the legislative and juridical power of the Church without which there can be no true authority; *ego vobiscum sum usque ad consummationem saeculi*, this is the assurance of the unfailing help that God will give her until the end of the world.

The Antiphon *ad offerendum* is taken from Exodus (xii 14) and refers to the baptismal rite by which the neophytes, having come forth from the Egypt of sin and idolatry, have made a new covenant with God. All through their lives the Easter festival shall be a reminder to them of the sacred engagement they entered into on that day. Moreover, in ancient times they used to celebrate on the first anniversary of their baptism a special feast in commemoration of the preceding Easter, the *Pascha annotinum* described in the Gelasian Sacramentary.

"This day shall be for a memorial to you, Alleluia; and you shall keep it a solemn feast to the Lord in your generations : an everlasting legal day, Alleluia, Alleluia, Alleluia."

The Secret then follows : " Be appeased, O Lord, we beseech thee, and receive these victims which we offer up to wipe out the sin of those who are now born anew, and to win for them speedy help from heaven." In order to understand fully the meaning of this prayer it is necessary to remember that the sacrifice of the cross, and consequently also the unbloody sacrifice of the altar, expiates the sins of the world and gives sanctifying efficacy to the sacraments. The Church alludes to-day in this Collect to the moment preceding the baptism of the neophytes *in remissionem peccatorum ;* and to their penitence and sorrow for sins committed —in those days they were all adults—she unites the oblation of the eucharistic sacrifice.

In the Communion, derived from to-day's Gospel, Jesus Christ entrusts the Church with the mission of carrying on his work of redemption unto the end of the world by means of his divine teaching and of the sacraments, of which she is the guardian and dispenser. Christ has attained to the highest power in heaven and on earth. In heaven he exercises it directly; on earth he confides it to the Church, which is thus his image—we might almost say with St Paul, the *pleroma,* or fulness, of Christ.

"All power is given to me in heaven and in earth, Alleluia; going, teach all nations, baptizing them in the name of the Father, and of the Son, and of the Holy Ghost, Alleluia, Alleluia."

The Post-Communion, too, has a special thought for the neophytes, who have just entered on a new life of sanctity. " Look down upon thy people, we beseech thee, O Lord, and

mercifully absolve them from temporal faults, whom thou
hast vouchsafed to renew with thy eternal mysteries."

During this week the Church repeatedly accentuates the
importance of our baptismal initiation. On each afternoon
of this Octave she conducts the neophytes in their white
robes again to the baptistery, and in to-day's Offertory she
desires that the date of their baptism may be a memorable and festive day throughout their lives. Indeed, she
establishes the *Pascha annotinum* in memory of the baptism
received by them at the Easter of the previous year.

It is impossible to impress too much on the minds of
Catholics of our time the realization of the holiness to which
they have been called by the sacrament of baptismal regeneration. The very promises made at the moment of
baptism are a token of this sanctity, for by them we have
pledged ourselves to renounce for ever Satan and all his
works and to aspire to being perfect even as our Father in
heaven is perfect. A merely negative goodness is not
enough; we must not aim only at being good, but at being
perfect, after the example of our divine Master. It is to
Christians especially that God has said: "Be ye holy, for I
am holy," and as children partake of the nature of their
father, so also we, who are the children of God, should make
it our chief care that the divine likeness in us should become
each day more perfect, according to the ineffable beauty of
our heavenly Father.

SATURDAY IN EASTER WEEK

Station at St John Lateran.

The conclusion to-day of the baptismal celebrations calls
the neophytes together again in the Lateran basilica beside
the font in which on Easter Eve they were born to newness
of life. These are the last moments of their spiritual infancy,
for to-morrow they will be weaned, as it were, and will take
their place among the rest of the faithful. Hence to-day's
stational liturgy seems to be influenced more than ever by
the thought of their purity and innocence, like a loving
mother carried away by the beauty of her new-born child.

On this day in the early Roman Liturgy the Pope used to
distribute to the people the *Agnus Dei* of blessed wax mixed
with sacred chrism, on which was impressed the image of the
Lamb of God. This custom, one of great antiquity, took
place during the Mass, whilst the *schola* of the cantors
chanted the invocation *Agnus Dei* before the Kiss of Peace
preceding the Communion.

In the fourteenth century the ceremony is thus described:

During the singing of the *Agnus Dei* the Pontiff distributes the waxen *Agnus Dei* to the cardinals and prelates, placing them in their mitres. At the end of the holy Sacrifice he proceeds to the *Triclinium* and sits down to table. During the meal an acolyte appears on the threshold with a silver bowl containing the *Agnus Dei*, and addresses the Pope in these words: *Domine, Domine, isti sunt agni novelli qui annuntiaverunt* Alleluia; *modo venerunt ad fontes, repleti sunt claritate,* Alleluia.

Having advanced to the centre of the hall, the cleric repeats the same words; then approaching still nearer to the Pontiff he once more proclaims his message in a louder voice and with greater emphasis, this time placing the bowl on the papal table. The Pope then begins to distribute the *Agnus Dei* amongst those of his household, to the priests, the chaplains, and the acolytes, and even caused some to be sent as gifts to the Catholic sovereigns of Europe.

The Introit from Psalm civ contains a reference to the neophytes who have come forth from the darkness of Egypt. "The Lord brought forth his people with joy, Alleluia: and his chosen with gladness, Alleluia, Alleluia. Give glory to the Lord, and call upon his name: declare his deeds among the Gentiles."

The Collect is as follows: "Grant, we beseech thee, O almighty God, that we who have celebrated the Easter festival may deserve by it to arrive at eternal joys." This is the true spirit of the liturgy—to attain to the eternal feast by means of the temporal.

Festa Paschalia . . . egimus. The intention of the ancient liturgy was to celebrate on this day the Octave of Easter, as this was considered to have begun on the evening of Holy Saturday, exactly eight days previously. The same rule holds good for Pentecost, hence even now the first Sunday after Pentecost is not considered as the Octave of the descent of the Holy Ghost. The Octave ends at Mass on the Saturday, so that *Dominica in Albis* (Low Sunday), on which—the Easter feast being terminated—the neophytes laid aside their white garments, only in later times became known as "*in Octava Paschae.*"

Constantly, during this paschal week, the ancient Roman Liturgy led back the neophytes *ad fontes,* to the Lateran baptistery, in order to impress vividly upon their minds the vows which they had entered into on the brink of that mystic pool. The Roman Church sang on this occasion the well-known verse of Ezechiel:[1] *Vidi aquam egredientem de templo*

---

[1] Ezechiel xlvii 1-9.

a latere dextero, and meant by so doing to teach us that the waters of holy baptism flow from the pierced side of Jesus, and that there is the sea in which *nos pisciculi secundum* Ἰχθύν *nostrum* are born anew.[1]

In to-day's Epistle (1 Peter ii 1-10) the Apostle explains to his first Christian converts the sublime dignity to which they have been raised by baptism. At one time the Gentiles were not regarded as a legitimate race, since they had no share, as the Jews had, in the divine promise. Now the sacrament of regeneration has made of them a holy nation, a chosen people, a kingly priesthood, on condition that they shall unite themselves spiritually to Christ by means of an active and living faith. It is not here so much a matter of material rites and outward solidarity as it was in the case of the Jewish people; God is a spirit, and he wills that his followers in Christ shall adore him above all in spirit and in truth.

Beginning from to-day, during the whole paschal time, the Gradual becomes an alleluiatic song of praise, for between each verse sung by the soloist the people interposed Alleluia.

Alleluia, Alleluia. *Psalm cxvii:* "This is the day which the Lord hath made, let us be glad and rejoice therein, Alleluia." *Psalm cxii:* "Praise the Lord, ye children, praise the name of the Lord." The children who are here called upon to praise the Lord are the neophytes who were present at the stational Mass in their white baptismal robes.

The Gospel from St John (xx 1-9) is chosen most opportunely because of the prominent part taken therein by Peter and John. Peter is the *Pastor* who throughout this week has reserved to himself the right of feeding the flock of the neophytes with his word. John is the co-titular patron of the Lateran baptistery, so that it is in his house, as it were, that the station is celebrated to-day.

John, the younger and the more ardent in his love, out-ran Peter on their hastening to the sepulchre of Jesus. Having reached the entrance of the tomb, he stooped down and looked in, but did not venture to enter, being held back by a sense of awe, which the scene of the miraculous event inspired. Then Peter came and in the fervour of his faith went in at once, being eventually followed by John. This shows us that love must always be inspired by faith, which precedes it, and that therefore those vague forms of sentimental piety which find so much favour in our day, but which are not founded on Catholic doctrine, can have no good influence on the actions of the individual; they are a kind of morbid superstition and not a sincere worship pleasing to God.

[1] Christ is our symbolical Fish, and we are the little fishes. Tertullian, *De Baptism., P.L.* I, col. 1306. It is well known that this Greek word forms the acrostic: "Jesus Christ, Son of God, Saviour."

The Offertory comes from the paschal Psalm cxvii. The Church has now given to the neophytes all that she possesses. They have been brought to her by their faith in almighty God who has enlightened them. It only remains for the Church at the termination of the Easter feast to call down upon them in the holy place the treasures of the divine blessing.

"Blessed is he that cometh in the name of the Lord: we have blessed you out of the house of the Lord: the Lord is God, and he hath shone upon us, Alleluia, Alleluia."

The first part of this beautiful verse from Psalm cxvii belongs to the sacerdotal choir, who thus greet the newly made Christians. Before these lay aside their white garments, the priests bless them. The neophytes then testify to the great favours which they have received from God during this week, and, full of gratitude, they all acknowledge his power.

Now that the paschal feast is drawing to a close, the Church seems to feel a certain regret in concluding the festivities. She resigns herself thereto outwardly, but insists that the soul shall inwardly celebrate a continuous Easter together with the continuous sacrifice of the paschal Lamb upon her altars. Such is the meaning of the Secret.

"Vouchsafe, we beseech thee, O Lord, ever to gladden us at these Easter mysteries, that the work of our renewal may abide and bring us to everlasting bliss."

The Antiphon for the Communion is very beautiful. The neophytes are now about to put off their baptismal robes, but their souls have assumed a spiritual garment which must never be laid aside. The figure seems a bold one, but we find it in St Paul's Epistle to the Galatians (iii 27) where Jesus Christ is compared to a vesture; for the Christian, now clothed in the merits of the Saviour, must live again his life, share his thoughts and his affections, and realize the desires of his heart.

"All you who have been baptized in Christ have put on Christ, Alleluia."

In the Post-Communion the Church shows herself anxious that the new Christians, whilst laying aside their symbolical garments, should carefully guard in their hearts that faith taught them with so much care during the long period of instruction. The holy Eucharist is the sign and sustenance of this faith, the *mysterium Fidei,* excelling all other, which fed in the breasts of the martyrs that sacred fire that was urging them to endure all things and to confess boldly the Catholic faith.

"Quickened by the gift of our redemption, we beseech thee, O Lord, that by the help of these means to eternal salvation, true faith may ever prosper."

The Holy Eucharist is not merely a pledge of our redemption, but embraces it in the widest significance of the word, for it not only commemorates the sacrifice of Calvary and applies its merits to our souls, but it is the seed of our glorious resurrection, and gives us by the possession of God himself a foretaste of the joys of heaven even during our exile here on earth.

Jesus appeared to his Apostles in the evening of Easter Day, and showed himself to them again after eight days, saying: "Peace be to you." When time is drawing to an end and the last day is at hand, he will appear once more to his Church, and by the gift of his peace will strengthen her against the final persecutions of Antichrist.

LOW SUNDAY (OR "DOMINICA IN ALBIS")

Station at St Pancras. In the morning; at SS Cosmas and Damian, in the afternoon.

According to an ancient Roman custom, dating at least from the time of St Gregory the Great, the basilicas of the martyrs outside the walls were never chosen as the object of the stational processions on account of their distance from the city, but on a solemn day like this—the Octave of Easter —on which everything is still eloquent of spiritual youth, an exception is made in honour of the tomb of a young martyr, the fourteen-year-old Pancras. His sepulchral basilica in the Via Aurelia was erected by Pope Symmachus (498-514), and later was restored by Honorius I (625-38) and Adrian I (772-95).

As was customary at Ravenna at the tomb of St Apollinaris, so at Rome solemn oaths used to be taken at the tomb of St Pancras, a custom which continued, as Gregory of Tours affirms, at least down to the thirteenth century. St Gregory the Great founded an abbey near the basilica,. which, however, in order to distinguish it from the one dedicated to St Pancras near the Lateran, was named after the martyr Victor. The Roman devotion to St Pancras in the time of St Gregory spread over the seas as far as the shores of England, and it is well known that when the monks of the Lateran were sent by Pope Gregory to evangelize that island, one of the first basilicas which they erected in that distant land was dedicated to St Pancras, the patron of their first Roman monastery.

According to the ancient Roman tradition Easter Week ended with the Vespers of yesterday, therefore the Collect of that day commemorated the conclusion of the paschal feast. Hence to-day the neophytes lay aside their white garments as a sign that the festival is over, and resume their ordinary dress, and the Church in the Collect at the Mass speaks of Easter as of a festival which has already taken place. For this reason the divine Office of to-day is not that of Easter Sunday, but of an ordinary Sunday, having regard, however, to the paschal cycle of the liturgy which is continued to the Saturday after Pentecost.

The Antiphon for the Introit which precedes Psalm lxxx is taken from the first Epistle of St Peter (ii 2), where he calls upon the neophytes to taste the delights which the Lord has freely prepared for them at the commencement of their Christian life.

" As new-born babes, Alleluia, desire ye the rational milk without guile, Alleluia, Alleluia, Alleluia." Psalm lxxx : " Rejoice to God our helper : sing aloud to the God of Jacob."

When the Lord comforts us with his consolations, let us accept them, as did Job, *de manu Domini.* If to us he gives milk and sweets, as to children, let us not despise them as though the more solid food of adults were more suitable to us. God knows best what we need, and it is a great secret of the spiritual life always to remain before God in the same dispositions of sincerity, humility, and confidence as when we were still in our spiritual infancy.

In the Collect we pray thus : " Grant, we beseech thee, almighty God, that we who have celebrated the Easter rites may, through thy bounty, ever cleave to them in our life and conversation." To bring our actions into harmony with the Easter rites means to live a life of resurrection and innocence.

The Lesson (1 John v 4-10) is especially directed against the *gnosis* which denied the divinity of our Lord, holding that the divine nature had united itself to his human nature at the moment of his baptism in the Jordan, and that it had left him on Calvary. St John is insistent in his teaching that the Word was hypostatically united to the human nature and not alone at his baptism ; *non in aqua solum, sed in aqua et sanguine;* that is, from the instant of his virginal conception in the most chaste womb of Mary. He who preserves this Catholic faith retains within himself the testimony of God, whilst God alone can infuse into the human heart this ray of his own unapproachable light.

The alleluiatic verse in place of the Gradual comes from the Gospel of St Matthew (xxviii 7) : " Alleluia, Alleluia. On the day of my resurrection, saith the Lord, I will go before you into Galilee. Alleluia."

This solemn and general manifestation was promised by our Lord, not so much for the sake of the eleven Apostles to whom he appeared several times at Jerusalem as for the sake of the multitude of his disciples and believers, to whom he did indeed show himself, as St Paul tells us, when they were assembled together to the number of over five hundred.

The verse from St John xx 26 is, as it were, a prelude to the Gospel that follows : " After eight days, the doors being shut, Jesus stood in the midst of his disciples, and said : Peace be with you, Alleluia."

The Gospel (John xx 19-31) tells us of two separate manifestations of Jesus to the Apostles : the first on the evening of Easter Day, when he instituted the sacrament of Confession, the other eight days later, when he showed his wounds to Thomas.   The fact that the power of re-mitting sins was given to the Apostles on the day of the resurrection itself is very significant.   That was a day of triumph and rejoicing : it was fitting, therefore, that on such a day the divine compassion should institute that Sacrament which takes away sorrow and mourning in this world and calls sinners to a new life of sanctity.

In memory of that fact Catholic tradition still imposes on the faithful the duty of receiving absolution from a priest before receiving their Easter Communion.   In Italy, the act of performing one's Easter duties is described in the language of the people, which is always so expressive and reflects their hereditary Catholic teaching, as " making one's Easter " ; so close is the connection which exists between the resurrec-tion of Christ and the sacrament of penance.

In ancient times the reconciliation of public penitents took place on Maundy Thursday and Good Friday.

Jesus appeared the second time in the supper-room to confute the unbelief of Thomas, who refused to believe un-less he both saw and felt the place of the wounds ; and God allowed this weakness in order that the remedy which cured it might serve as a preventive against the incredulity of all future generations.   There is no room for doubt concerning the resurrection of our Lord ; he was seen and also touched before being believed in by those who were far from being disposed to admit its truth.

The Offertory is the same as that of Easter Monday.   The Greek Church celebrates a special feast on the second Sunday after Easter in honour of the holy women—the " ointment-bringers," that is, the women who carried sweet spices to the sepulchre.   The Latin Liturgy intermingles their praises in all the Offices of Easter Week.

In the Secret we beg almighty God to receive the gifts which the Church makes to him rejoicing, that this paschal joy may be a token of that eternal happiness which we hope for in heaven.

A holy Christian joy, such is the characteristic of our faith ;

a joy which proceeds from the ineffable treasures, both moral and dogmatic, contained in the Gospel, from the holy Sacraments, from sanctifying grace, from the training received from our Mother the Church. Those who are outside her Communion cannot realize the fountain of inward spiritual joy which fills the soul more and more as it becomes more completely penetrated by the spirit of the Catholic Church. More joy, still more joy—this should be our watchword in a holy crusade against that morbid sentimentality which threatens to find its way into the devotion of the faithful. More joy—and in order to possess it, we must return to its true fountain-head, Catholic piety.

In the Communion (John xx 27) we repeat the words of our Lord to Thomas. By partaking of the sacrament we also touch by means of faith the wounds in Christ's hands and side, and confess his resurrection, inasmuch as we believe that the flesh with which we are spiritually nourished is not the lifeless body of the Crucified, but the glorious body of a God immolated indeed for us, but now risen and alive once more.

The Post-Communion is of a general character : " We beseech thee, O Lord our God, that thou wouldst make the most holy mysteries which thou hast granted to make our renewal sure, a healing remedy for us both now and always." St Thomas Aquinas expresses the same thought in his Antiphon : *O sacrum convivium.*

By means of the holy Eucharist our Lord makes us partakers of the whole *mysterium fidei,* both of his passion and of his resurrection. At the altar we receive the flesh of the victim that was slain, and thus are sown in our souls the seeds of death, of a spiritual death, that is to say, to our corrupt nature, to sin and to the spirit of the world. At the same time Jesus who remains under the eucharistic veil is Jesus truly risen, glorious and triumphant, who unites us to himself in order to give us a share in his joy, his victory, and his risen life. The Blessed Sacrament produces in us this double effect, accomplishing that which St Paul said to his first converts (Col. iii 3) : " You are dead, and your life is hid with Christ in God."

When, through the influence of the Byzantines, the *cultus* of the martyrs SS Cosmas and Damian became general in Rome, the Easter stations had already for a long time been distributed amongst the most renowned basilicas of the city, so that none remained for the Church dedicated to these martyrs by Felix IV (526-30) on the Sacra Via. Thus the station at this last mentioned basilica was fixed for the second Sunday after Easter.

This arrangement, however, did not last long. The second Sunday after Easter, with its Gospel of the Good Shepherd, turned men's thoughts naturally to St Peter, so a compromise was made with regard to SS Cosmas and Damian; the station of the second Sunday after Easter was held at the Vatican basilica, but at the same time it was arranged that on the afternoon of Low Sunday the Pope should go to St Cosmas and St Damian to celebrate there the evening station. According to the *Ordines Romani* the titular clergy of that church were in the habit on this occasion of preparing for the Pope and his suite a frugal meal consisting of bread, wine, butter, cheese, and herbs.

SECOND SUNDAY AFTER EASTER

Station at St Peter.

In the time of St Gregory the Great, to-day's station was held at St Peter's, near the tomb of the *Pastor ovium,* for it was there that the great Pope pronounced his magnificent homily on the Gospel of the Good Shepherd. His words were full of power and beauty: Jesus, "the shepherd and bishop of our souls," as St Peter calls him in the lesson for this Sunday (1 Peter ii 25), before confiding to him the charge of the universal Church, had desired that the Apostle should make it convincingly clear that his love for him was greater than that of all his fellow-Apostles.

Christ, therefore, founded the papal primacy on the unshakeable faith and intense love of Peter; and he, following in his Saviour's steps, did not hesitate to give his life for the flock entrusted to him, sealing his pastoral office with his own blood. So from earliest antiquity the Roman Church always pointed to the tomb of St Peter as a trophy of victory. There, indeed, a few steps from the *Confessio* of the Apostle, the first Pontiff proclaimed before the "divine" Nero and his court the divinity of Christ: *Tu es Christus Filius Dei vivi;*[1] and then, like a glorious conqueror, he stretched out his arms on the cross, as though to take Rome and the whole world under his protection.

The devotion to Jesus the Redeemer under the figure of the Good Shepherd was dear to the faithful from very early times. Abercius in the epitaph on his mortuary *cippus*[2] speaks of the Good Shepherd guarding his flock with everwatchful eyes. At the close of the apostolic era Hermas

[1] Matt. xvi 16.
[2] Discovered in 1882, and presented in 1887 by the Sultan of Constantinople to Pope Leo XIII. It is now in the Lateran Museum.—TR.

gives the name of " Pastor " to his mystical treatise on
penance, a subject which was being much discussed at that
time. At Rome, the Church on the Viminal, beside which
the Popes had their temporary abode, is dedicated to the
Good Shepherd, whose figure, Tertullian tells us, adorned
the eucharistic chalices and cups. So familiar was the representation of the Good Shepherd to the painters and
sculptors of the catacombs that we find it constantly reproduced on the *arcosolia* and *sarcophagi*. Indeed, at a time
when ancient Christian religious art from its very spirituality
was strongly averse from statues, an exception is made for
that of the Good Shepherd, of which we find several important
examples.

On this day the Greek Church gracefully commemorates
the holy women who went to the sepulchre to anoint the body
of Jesus. There is nothing to show that this custom was
ever adopted in the Roman Liturgy. Be this as it may,
there is such a tender charm in the thought, that we cannot
refrain from quoting this pleasing Greek distich in honour
of the holy " ointment-bringers " : .

Χριστῷ φέρουσιν αἱ μαθήτριαι μύρα
'Εγώ δὲ ταύταις ὕμνον ὡς μύρον φέρω.

Christo deferunt aromata discipulae,
Quibus, pro unguento, carmina fero.

The Introit is derived from Psalm xxxii. The resurrection
of Christ has come to fill the earth with his mercies, that is,
with the holy Sacraments, the blessings and the graces which
nourish within the Church a life of sanctity and mystical
renewal. It is the power of the divine word which has
wrought such great wonders. Nature alone would be wholly
unable to account for the marvellous fact of the conversion
of the pagan world to Christianity in so short a time, and
the divine organisation of the Catholic Church. Here is
clearly evident the finger of God, and to him alone is the
glory due.

In the Collect we are reminded that the humiliations of
Jesus were the steps, as it were, by which God descended
to a world lying prostrate in the dust and mire of sin, in
order to raise us up again to our first dignity of children of
God. Happily this sad state of things is now past, and
mourning has given place to the joy of Easter. We therefore
ask God to give us an abiding gladness, not indeed in the
enjoyment of the empty pleasures of the world, but of that
inner happiness with which the Holy Ghost fills the souls of
the saints. This joy, being wholly spiritual, causes us to

desire more truly, and so to attain more surely to heavenly bliss.

In the Lesson for to-day, taken from the first Epistle of St Peter (ii 21-25), it is Peter himself who speaks from his own temple, the Vatican basilica. He explains to the faithful the reason of this Easter feast in honour of the Good Shepherd, who gives his life for his sheep, and dwells upon the tenderest and most touching circumstances of this voluntary sacrifice of Christ, his patience under insults, his bruises, the love with which he poured forth from his wounds his healing blood to cure our souls of sin. Lastly, the Apostle points to Jesus Christ as " the shepherd and bishop of our souls."

The alleluiatic verse in lieu of the Gradual comes from St Luke (xxiv 35) and relates how the Apostles recognized Jesus in the breaking of bread. In this life we walk amid parables and mysteries; but at the moment when we place our feet upon the threshold of eternity, the sacramental veil is rent and God shows himself to us no longer under symbols and outward signs, but face to face in the splendour of his light, of which the Psalmist says : *Et in lumine tuo videbimus lumen.*[1]

The verse from St John (x 14), immediately preceding the Gospel, anticipates our Lord's representation of himself to us to-day as the kind and loving Shepherd. He is closely bound to his flock by love. He knows his sheep, that is, he loves them and orders all things for their welfare. They, too, know him, that is, they hear his voice inwardly, they have spiritual experience of his guidance, and they correspond to the interior motions of his grace, as it is written : " *Qui Spiritu Dei aguntur, hi sunt filii Dei.*"[2]

The Gospel from St John (x 11-16) breaks the cycle of the Easter lessons which are taken exclusively from St John's version of our Lord's last discourse in the supper-room. This exception to the ancient Roman order is fully justified by the characteristic and exceptional solemnity which causes it.

Moreover, the liturgical and traditional use of the Gospel of the Good Shepherd on the second Sunday after Easter is very old. Jesus, therefore, presents himself to us to-day as the " Good Shepherd " and tells us what will henceforth be his relationship with his flock. In the first place there will be a perfect understanding between the Shepherd and his sheep, the sanctity of whose souls will be based upon this interior life of intimate union with him. The soul will keep itself in a state of recollection in order to listen to the gentle

[1] Ps. xxxv 10.   [2] Rom. viii 14.

voice of the Good Shepherd when he speaks, for it is in this colloquy that it will know Jesus.

The number of Catholics is indeed limited compared to those who *non sunt ex hoc ovili*. We should note the gentle language in which our Lord speaks of those outside the Church—not a word of reproach but merely a statement of fact. Yet Christ has come to redeem all men, that, as in Adam all perished, so in Christ all may be saved. Therefore by means of his Church he goes in search of his wandering sheep. The labour is long and difficult, but we must never despair; for Jesus has foretold that the result will be successful. In spite of all the opposition of men and of devils *fiet unum ovile*, there shall indeed be but one fold under one Shepherd.

The Offertory is from the morning Psalm lxii: "O God, my God, to thee do I watch at break of day; and in thy name I will lift up my hands. Alleluia."

In the Secret we pray that the eucharistic oblation may bring down upon us abundant blessings, so that Holy Communion may effectually accomplish in us that intimate union with Christ immolated and triumphant, which it—the *sacramentum unitatis*—mystically symbolizes.

The Communion repeats the alleluiatic verse of the Good Shepherd. Jesus not only gives his life for his sheep, but daily renews on the altar his sacrifice for them. He desires indeed that in order to perpetuate the memory of his death, the faithful shall also nourish their souls on his body and blood sacrificed and offered for them, that they may become one with him.

In the Post-Communion we beseech almighty God that, having participated in the Sacrament which causes us to live through his own life, he will grant us the enjoyment in eternity of the grace we have to-day received. How wonderful is the thought that the best preparation for a holy Communion is that Communion which precedes it!

O thrice holy Basilica of the Vatican! enlarge thy mighty aisles, for thy hopes, since they are founded on the promises of Christ, can never fail.

The Good Shepherd will lead back to the fold those sheep also that have gone astray *et illas oportet me adducere* . . . and there shall be one fold and one Shepherd.

THIRD SUNDAY AFTER EASTER

The Roman lists no longer mention by name any special basilica for the celebration of the Sunday station. This would indicate that, the primitive assemblies in the cemeteries having been discontinued, on account of the insecurity of the suburban districts of Rome in the sixth century, either the place of the stational meeting was announced on each occasion, or that the station did not take place at all, in which latter case the Mass celebrated by the priests in their titular churches was substituted for it.

During this paschal time the first lesson of the Mass is taken regularly from the canonical Epistles, since the Church before Pentecost was entirely gathered about the Apostles in the supper-room, and it was only after the descent of the Holy Ghost that Paul was especially destined by God to carry the good news to the Gentiles.

The passage from the Gospels on the other hand is always derived from the discourse of Jesus at the Last Supper, whether because in that most beautiful address, which may be truly termed the testament of the Sacred Heart, he describes, as being within the limits of one prophetic vision, his death, his resurrection, his ascension to his Father and the descent of the Holy Ghost, so many different aspects, as it were, of the one mystery, that is, his redemption, the Christian Pasch—or because, owing to the length of the divine Office ᴄ Maundy Thursday, it was impossible to read this discourse ᴏn that memorable day.

The Introit comes from Psalm lxv, a very hymn of triumph. " Shout with joy to God, all the earth, Alleluia; sing ye a psalm to his name; give glory to his praise, Alleluia, Alleluia, Alleluia." This is the true glory of the Catholic liturgy, that it is expressed not in words alone—as Isaias reproached the Jews for doing—but in the actions of a life in which are reflected the glory and sanctity of the risen Christ.

In the Collect the Church speaks of the sublimity of the Christian calling, and of the high degree of sanctity required of us by this profession, which confers on us the very name of Christ himself. Let us, then, make our humble prayer to God that by the same mercy through which he has caused the light of truth to shine upon us, he may grant to us and to all those who have received the same baptism as ourselves the grace to act in accordance with its teaching.

In the Lesson (i Peter ii 11-19) the Apostle Peter addresses the infant Church. The persecution under Nero has already commenced, and the first weapons of which the enemies of the Church—for the most part Jews—make use are those of calumny and violence. The Christians reply to this show of hatred with silent endurance and the manifestation of all the highest virtues, after the example given to them by their divine Master. Through suffering and love, the way will be opened to truth and holiness, and these will finally triumph over popular prejudice. For the time being, however, it is necessary to respect and to be subject to legitimate authority, even that of Nero, without regard to the unworthy manner in which the power received from God is being exercised. The reign of God is not established on earth in the twinkling of an eye. The Christian lives in expectation; the hour will come at last in which God will "visit" with his grace the Empire of Rome—such is the consoling prophecy of Peter— and then Constantine will repair the harm wrought by the monster who now wears the imperial crown.

The alleluiatic verse is from Psalm cx, which is one of the Easter psalms. The Lord hath sent redemption to his people, who now belong to him by the twofold right of creation and of redemption. If, then, we belong to God, it is our duty to live for him.

In the verse before the Gospel taken from St Luke (xxiv 26-46) allusion is made to the great law of the kingdom of grace, that is, the necessity of the cross. It is a mysterious word, one containing an awful truth. It was needful that Christ should suffer first, and thus alone should enter into his glory. If, therefore, the Son of God himself submitted obediently to this law, how much the more shall not we be bound thereby, who aspire to attain to a glory which is not ours, but his?

The Gospel (John xvi 16-22) is an extract from the sublime address of our Lord to his disciples before his apprehension. Jesus announces that he is about to leave the world, and speaks of the short interval between his death and his resurrection. This period after his resurrection, during which he shows himself to his followers, is symbolical of our own life—it is the history of the Church militant. The unbelieving world has not seen him since the evening of Good Friday, but we who believe see him every day in the Holy Eucharist; we converse with him, and our life, as a brilliant noon-day, is illuminated by the rays which form his halo of glory. This joy, which comes from our nearness to Christ, cannot be taken from us, for it is purely an interior joy. It more than repays us for the suffering which the world inflicts on us as bearers of his name.

The Offertory from Psalm cxlv calls upon us to praise the Lord in that new life of resurrection to which he has raised us, an eternal life which knows no death. The verse has special reference to Christ, in whose life we participate by means of the Sacraments.

In the Secret attention is drawn to one of the most important effects of Holy Communion. This Sacrament is indeed the wine of the prophecy, which causes the virginal stem to bud. It extinguishes within us all worldly desires and inflames the heart with a holy love of heavenly things, engrafting in our souls a great longing for paradise.

The Communion, derived from to-day's Gospel, dwells on the faithfulness with which Jesus has maintained his promise. He said that we should see him again, and in truth not only do we see him, but we touch him; his blood flows in our veins and endues us with strength and youth and the unfailing joy which springs from a divine life.

In the Post-Communion we ask that the holy Eucharist, whilst filling us with a desire for eternal life, may also give us strength to attain thereto.

Heaven is the goal of our hopes, and for this reason the early Christian communities, following the teaching of St Peter in to-day's lesson, called themselves " pilgrims " : *Ecclesia Dei quae peregrinatur.*

The Gospel also voices this feeling, warning us that here on earth we shall meet only with sorrow and bitterness, whilst the world shall rejoice. But at last we shall look upon the beatific face of Jesus, when our joy shall have no end. This difference between the world and ourselves must not, however, cause feelings in our hearts of envy and contempt. We must not hate anyone, and it is our duty to endure evildoers in patience until the hour of their " visitation " also shall strike, that is, as St Peter tells us in his Epistle, when the grace of God shall triumph over their rebellious will.

FOURTH SUNDAY AFTER EASTER

Every Sunday between Easter and Pentecost is, we may say, a continuation of the paschal solemnity, hence both the Introit for to-day and the alleluiatic verse which follows the lesson from St James celebrate the Victor who in the strength of his arm has triumphed over death and sin.

The coming of the Holy Ghost, announced beforehand in the Mass, renders the difference between the Church and the spirit of the world absolute and irreconcilable. The Paraclete founds the Church in the spirit of unity, giving to her a single will, a single faith, and a single supernatural life in Christ Jesus, whilst the world becomes more and more hardened in its sin. Pentecost, therefore, is the supreme glorification of Christ and his mystical body, and it is in this sense that the Holy Ghost convinces the world of the sin of deicide, pronounces the final condemnation on the evil one, and renders justice to the Saviour, proclaiming him to be the only-begotten Son of God sitting at the right hand of his Father in heaven.

The Introit is taken from Psalm xcvii. " Sing ye to the Lord a new canticle "—of Christ inaugurating his new life of glory and triumph on the day of his resurrection. Nor is this exultation his alone, for all creation is embraced in this joyful renewal, and joins in celebrating the Redeemer's triumph. The Lord has proclaimed before the whole world that Just One, that Saviour whose secret had until now been revealed by the Prophets only to the Jewish people. The eternal Father manifested his only-begotten Son to the world in the sight of all upon a hill-top where Jews, Greeks, and Romans were gathered together, in order that all the peoples of the earth might now turn their eyes to the Crucified, hailing him as the universal Redeemer of the whole human race, and that no one nation should claim a monopoly of creed and worship.

In the Collect reference is made to the miracle accomplished by God through holy faith. It is by means of this faith that so great a multitude of believers professes one only creed, and holds one and the same hope of salvation. Since, therefore, the Lord shows by this unity of doctrine that he is the true arbiter of all hearts, we beg him so to direct our hearts that amidst the changes and chances of this mortal life, now joyful, now sorrowful, our affections may be set where true joy is to be found, that is, in God alone; for in this world indeed all things change, pass away, and fail us; God alone remains for all eternity.

The cycle of the Apostolic Lessons continues with another extract from the Epistle of St James (i 17-21). In this passage, the " brother " or cousin of our Lord, the first Bishop of Jerusalem, opposes to the speculations of the false *gnosis,* which even then attempted to defile the pure sources of Christian inspiration, the moral teaching contained in the Gospel, showing that faith to be vain which is merely a speculative theory and not a rule of action, which does not, that is, declare itself openly and bring forth the fruits of good deeds.

This assertion of St James condemns beforehand that Protestant theory which denies the necessity of good works and makes of religion merely an abstract scheme reasoned out in the schools instead of a living reality. Luther was well aware that his opinion was contrary to the teaching of St James, so, incited by his spleen, he deliberately struck his epistle out of the list of scriptural books, proclaiming it to be *straminea,* that is, a thing of no value. In later days also since the time of Luther the words of the " brother " of our Lord still maintain their original force and can be quoted as a test when one is desirous of knowing where the true Church of Jesus Christ is to be found.

It is necessary, then, to have both a true faith and also good works. A morality which is not founded on dogma is as a house built on the sand; it is like a foolish person who acts rightly but without knowing, or caring to know, that he does so. A faith on the other hand which denies the necessity of acting according to its precepts is such a monstrosity and contradiction that its appearance is of something impure and subversive.

The saying: *Crede firmiter et pecca fortiter* is Luther's very own. The Catholic Church alone, by the abundant and marvellous fruits of sanctity, charity, and zeal which she produces, proves herself to be in every place the one legitimate depositary of the life-giving message of Christ.

The Gospel (John xvi 5-14) is drawn as usual from the discourse at the Last Supper. It would seem as though our Saviour were grieved that we do not desire a closer intimacy with him, and that when he announces to us that he is about to leave us, we do not trouble to ask him : " Lord, whither goest thou?" He will, indeed, depart from us, but it is for our good; for, until he has attained at the right hand of his Father in heaven the fulness of glory which he merited through his passion, he will not be able to diffuse this glory upon each member of the mystical body of which he is the head.

It is the special mission reserved to the Holy Ghost to glorify Jesus by the outpouring of grace in the Church. In this way he will make reparation for the dishonour done to the Saviour by the world in condemning him to death, and in a certain measure will anticipate the final judgement on impenitent sinners by leaving them to their fate, and sanctifying those only who believe in Christ as the Redeemer of the human race.

The Offertory, with its flowing Gregorian melody, which is one of the most exquisite masterpieces of its kind, is identical with that of the second Sunday after the Epiphany. If on that day the whole world was invited to look with wonder upon the miracle of love which God had worked by the Incarnation of his Word, how much more should not we do so, now that he has given redeemed humanity a share in the grace, the resurrection, and the final glorification of Christ?

In the Secret we call to mind the relationship which the eucharistic sacrifice creates between earth and heaven, a connection which may be explained to the simple for their better understanding by comparing it to an act of purchase. We offer Jesus to God as the price of our redemption and he gives himself to us in exchange—his grace being the pledge. Such is the bond between ourselves and God. It is for us to see that we do not break the contract by failing in that interior imitation of Christ which is the foremost and essential condition of eternal salvation. The reason why this is so, is that we must participate and live in Christ through the union of our souls with him whom we embrace by faith and good works before we can offer him to the Father.

The Antiphon for the Communion from to-day's Gospel is a renewed menace to the world. When the Paraclete shall come, it announces, he will accuse the world of deicide, rectifying the injustice done to Jesus, and will judge those who pronounced that iniquitous condemnation. This judgement will not, however, be fully effective until the final one. The Holy Ghost is light and life. The sinner obstinately shuts his eyes and resists with all his power lest this light should shine upon him and this life should enkindle his soul and compel him to virtue. This, the holy Scripture tells us, is the first death, the forerunner of the second and final death, of which the Church speaks when she prays *a morte perpetua libera nos, Domine.*

In the Post-Communion we ask that the eucharistic sacrifice may atone for the sins of our past life and may strengthen us against possible perils in the future. Many of us realize too little the necessity we are under of doing penance for the sins which we have committed, even after having confessed them. Here the divine Sacrifice, by reason of its expiatory character, comes most opportunely to our aid. We should, therefore, hear Mass in this spirit of true penitence, and cause it to be offered by the priest sometimes for this intention, for by so doing we shall greatly shorten our time in purgatory.

To-day the distinctive characters of the Church and of the world are clearly defined. The spirit of Jesus communicates to the Church that supreme glorification which the Saviour merited for the head and the members of his mystical body— a glorification which now surrounds his members with grace and sanctity, and which will in due time give place to the supreme glory of heaven. The world on the other hand *in maligno est positus;* it is filled with the spirit of Satan—that is the spirit of hatred—and cannot therefore participate in any way in this divine life of love of which the Paraclete is the origin and vital source.

FIFTH SUNDAY AFTER EASTER

The Church calls the resurrection of our Lord *Pascha nostrum,* because after his triumph over death and sin, he poured forth upon his mystical body the fulness of his divine life, the gifts and graces of the Holy Ghost and the supreme

glory of life eternal; hence St Ambrose says that the whole
world rose again with Christ.   Therefore the Antiphon of the
Introit, the Offertory and the Communion are inspired to-day
by a fervent spirit of thanksgiving for so great a benefit, and
sing the victory of the risen Christ, the echoes of which resound throughout the whole world.

The Introit is derived from Isaias (xlviii 20) and sends a
cry of joy to the utmost ends of the earth, to those places
where, as in Africa and Oceania, the most savage tribes, who
appear to be a link between man and the brute creation, hear
preached to them the Gospel of the crucified Christ, the
Redeemer of mankind.

In the Collect we are reminded that God is the origin of
our being, therefore we implore him first of all to inspire us
with just and holy thoughts, and then to give us strength to
put them into practice.   Here we see how little credit we can
take to ourselves for the small amount of good that we do.
The first impulse, the determination of our free will, the
carrying out of the good resolution, all come from God,
and we as reasonable creatures contribute only the bare
co-operation of our wills with grace, and this, too, emanates
from God.   This truth which we learn in our Catholic
catechism should fill us with humble submission to God and
distrust of ourselves, for humility is the foundation of all our
relations with God.

The Lesson is a further passage from the Epistle of St
James (i 22-27) warning us against that false piety which
makes religion to consist in sentimental feelings or in outward rites, without any call for self-denial or effort on our
part.   True religion on the other hand is active and makes
itself known by good deeds, of which the Apostle mentions
several, such as the restraining of the tongue, charitable
works, and the like, and concludes by naming a general
virtue which is practically a condition for possessing all the
others, namely, to keep oneself apart from the spirit of the
world in order to live instead according to the spirit of the
Gospel.

It would be well that these words should be pondered on
by many Catholics of our day whose Christianity consists
merely in the fact of their having been baptized in the name
of Christ and in the careless performance of those acts of
worship which are termed not very appropriately " religious
duties."   This is often all that religion means to these so-
called practising Catholics; yet at their baptism they promised to renounce the devil and all his pomps, the spirit, that
is, of the world, which is nothing less than the glorification
of Satan.

They know that Jesus Christ himself absolutely refused to intercede for the world—*pro eis rogo, non pro mundo*—and that the spirit of the Gospel is the spirit of mortification, humility, charity, and purity ; yet how contrary to such a spirit is the life of many ! They have wellnigh forgotten their childhood's catechism, they are replete with the joy of life, and they think that God and the Church should be beholden to them because they lend their names to Catholic undertakings, and occasionally put in an appearance at parochial functions. What a strange delusion ! St James shows us that such persons deceive themselves and that their outwardly religious attitude is devoid of any real foundation. We should accustom ourselves to carry out our religious practices from conviction and not merely from habit, and we should bring all our acts, our intentions and our affections into harmony with this conviction.

The alleluiatic verse celebrates once more the triumphal victory of the Saviour over death, a victory all the more glorious since it was because of his painful death on the cross that Jesus rose from the tomb and shares his triumph with the whole of humanity. He has triumphed, not with the tremendous weapons of his divine nature, but in the weakness of his human nature. The devil has fought against him, the holy and sinless one, but has been rendered powerless and his weapons blunted, so that they have no longer any power against us.

In the verse before the Gospel we read in the words of our Lord, as in a parable, the course of our own life. Like Jesus we, too, come from God and have a mission in this world which we must fulfil. This mission is to save our souls and to return to God who made us. Life, then, is a journey ; whither does it lead us ? The river in its flood carries us swiftly to the ocean of eternity. We are going to God whether we will or no, the good and the bad alike, and life can have for us no other meaning than this—to seek God. To seek him, that is, as our Father and our Redeemer along the way of the Gospel, so that we may meet him again as a merciful judge in the hour of our last agony. If we wish to find him then, we must seek him now while it is day ; if we wait to seek him until life is declining and the shadows of death are closing around us, we run the risk of never finding him at all, either then or in eternity.

Christ's discourse on that last evening is continued in to-day's Gospel (John xvi 23-30). With his ascension into heaven, our elevation to the dignity of sons of God, through the outpouring of the Holy Ghost, becomes perfected and complete ; but from this radical change in our being there follows a fundamental alteration in our relationship to God.

II. 23

We are no longer merely subjects and servants, but sons, whose prayers have an inalienable right to the heart of their heavenly Father.

It is in this sense that our Lord says that it is not absolutely necessary for him to pray to the Father on our behalf, because the Father himself already loves us tenderly. Nevertheless, Jesus always prays for us in heaven, whether it be to testify thus to his love for us, or because he can never dissociate himself from us in our relations with God. If the Father loves us and adopts us as his children, if he predestines us to grace and glory, it is always in Christ and through Christ, whence it is that the Church concludes her consecratory hymn in the Canon of the Mass with the words : *Per ipsum, et cum ipso, et in ipso est tibi Deo Patri omnipotenti in unitate Spiritus Sancti omnis honor et gloria.*

The Offertory, from Psalm lxv (8-9, 20), is the same as that of the Wednesday of the " great scrutinies " previous to baptism. " The Lord hath not turned away my prayer in the day of tribulation," in the hour when it was said to the ministers of Satan : " This is your hour and the power of darkness."[1] The Lord hath restored me to newness of life, and my enemies can no longer boast of having moved my feet from the central position which I hold in the history of the ages. " O bless the Lord our God, ye Gentiles," who have a share in this great mercy, give him thanks and let his praises resound to the uttermost ends of the earth, making known to all the glory of the Redeemer.

In the Secret we beg God to receive the prayers of his faithful people which accompany the gifts they offer upon the altar in proof of their devotion. It was by means of these oblations that the people in olden days expressed their active participation with the priest in the holy Sacrifice. Now, owing to the lessened devotion of later times, the Church has thought fit to modify her primitive rule on this point, but in the early ages of Christianity everyone present, without exception, including even the Pope at Rome, brought each his own oblation to the altar, so that the sacrifice offered by the bishop or parish priest for the whole people should represent also materially the joint oblation of the entire community. At the Lateran one exception was made, and that was in favour of the little singers of the musicians' orphanage, who, however, were required to present the water for the chalice used at the Mass.

As time went on this custom was superseded by that of giving offerings in money to the celebrant—the so-called " alms " for the Mass. The faithful should realize the great importance of contributing individually to the expenses

[1] St Luke xxii 53.

of the Church which they attend, and should think of their offerings not merely as part of the funeral rites on the occasion of the death of a relative, but as part of their duty as Christians and as a consequence of the precept enjoined by God on the Israelites to contribute with their offerings towards the expenses of the sacrifices in the Temple and the maintenance of its ministers.

This obligation has become even more urgent in our days since successive governments have confiscated almost all the revenues of the Church, thus obliging her not only to provide for her daily expenses, but also to maintain all her very numerous charitable works, missions, and so on, entirely out of the contributions of the faithful.

The Communion is taken from Psalm xcv, and re-echoes the joyous cry of the Introit : " Sing ye to the Lord and bless the new name which he has won by his cross and passion." This name which is above every name, to which even the infernal powers must bend the knee in fear and trembling, is Jesus, the Saviour of mankind. When on the day of his Circumcision the divine Child received this name, it foretold the promise which has now been fulfilled, for on Easter morning the Saviour inaugurated a new day, an immortal day, which he alone has made, the Messianic era of the redemption.

We pray God in the eucharistic Collect to grant us as a fruitful result of Holy Communion a great hunger and thirst for heavenly things, for justice, truth, and high aspirations. Blessed are those souls who, like Daniel, live by these holy desires ! He who has kindled in them this holy flame, and aroused in their hearts this hunger and thirst for God, will never fail to satisfy them.

To go to the Father ! This is the whole significance and ordering of our life ; there is no other. To follow Jesus along the *via crucis* of the duties of our own state—this is the supreme sacrifice which the spirit of the Gospel commands. But how few souls there are who, like St Philip Neri, resolve never to pause by the way for the enjoyment of any single thing, never to seek rest for the soul in anything except the contemplation of the far-off goal of Heaven above !

APRIL 25. ST MARK

The Greater Litanies

Collecta at the Title of Lucina. Station at St Peter.

This great procession, which formerly went from St Lawrence in Lucina to St Peter's along the Flaminian

Way, over the Milvian Bridge, and, skirting the Tiber, continued as far as the *Ager Vaticanus,* took the place originally of the ancient festival of the *Ambarvalia,* or the pagan *Robigalia.* This latter feast occurred on April 25, when the young people of Rome used to go across the bridge to sacrifice to Robigus, the god who preserved the grain from blight. The Roman Church, adopting this popular festivity, raised its significance by teaching that it was not the favour of a heathen god, but a devout life, humble prayer, and the intercession of the saints, especially that of St Peter, the *Pastor ovium,* which would disarm the justice of God offended by our sins. This intercessory rite is called the " Greater Litanies," because it was of a much more solemn nature than the ordinary stational litanies. The route was very long, and there took part in the procession the whole population of Rome, divided into various companies. The rite must already have been fully established at the time of St Gregory, for the saint was in the habit of preaching a sermon in preparation for it on the preceding day. As this procession and the stational Mass at St Peter's always occurred at Eastertide, they had consequently a distinctly festal character, in which they differed from the processional litanies which took place during Lent, these being especially distinguished by their penitential nature.

At a later date during the Carlovingian period a *triduum* of penitential litanies was introduced at Rome, on the three days preceding the feast of the Ascension. The custom seems to have been first instituted at Vienné in France, on the initiative of Bishop Mamertus (about 470), and to have been accompanied by three days of fasting as in the Lenten season. This penitential observance, brought to Rome by the Franks, and still marked in the Roman Missal by the purple vestments and the omission of the *Gloria in excelsis,* is, however, at variance with the whole spirit of the ancient paschal liturgy at Rome, which is inspired by the purest joy and gladness. It is a later addition, made at a time when the barbarian invasions had interrupted the ancient classical tradition, which by order of the Councils had forbidden any fast whatever during the holy time of paschal rejoicing.

To return to the procession of the *Robigalia* on April 25, we should note that in the twelfth century there were two processions in Rome on this day : the one starting from the basilica of St Mark *in Pallacinis,* in which all the municipal bodies of the city took part; the other coming from the Lateran, composed only of the papal court and the chapters of the patriarchal basilicas.

The Pope having recited the Collect, a subdeacon took from the altar the stational cross, and presented it to be kissed by all present, after which the procession set forth

towards Sta Maria Nova in the Forum, where the first halt
was made. When the Pontiff was somewhat rested, they
proceeded to St Mark's, where there was another pause.
They next went towards the Mausoleum of Hadrian, the
third halting-place, and finally in the direction of the Vatican.
There was a last halt in the little basilica of Sta Maria dei
Vergari, close to St Peter's, whence the Pope went up into
the Vatican Basilica and celebrated the stational Mass, accepting when it was concluded the *presbyterium* of twenty *denarii
papienses*[1] *pro missa bene cantata.* The Vatican chapter on
this occasion made large gifts of money also to the cardinals,
deacons, subdeacons, acolytes, and cantors.[2]

Collecta at the Title of Lucina.

The ceremony began with a solemn Introit from Psalm xliii
26, recited regularly in Rome before each stational *Collecta.*
" Arise, O Lord, help us and redeem us for thy name's sake,"
not for any merits of our own, for we dare not put them
before thee, but because of thine infinite mercy. Then, after
the prayer of benediction upon the people said by the celebrant, the whole assembly formed a procession, following the
same route as that formerly taken in the case of the ancient
Robigalia.

The persistent survival of classical traditions in the
religious customs in use among the faithful at Rome helps
us to understand better the prudence and wisdom of the
Church, which preferred to give a spiritual significance to
observances implanted in the hearts of the people, rather
than suppress them harshly, and in this way was able to
assimilate and preserve them. The present writer has had
opportunities of verifying this, for he has found in some
villages in his diocese traces of undoubted pagan customs,
which now for many centuries have assumed among those
simple peasants a perfectly innocent signification.

He found, for instance, the classical festival of the *Rosalia*
at Civitella San Paolo, where on the solemnity of the
Kalendae Maiae (the first of May) maidens, the " basket-
bearers," carry in procession on their heads pyramid-like
baskets of flowers intertwined with silken ribbons. The
procession goes, as at the ancient Roman stations, to celebrate solemnly the eucharistic sacrifice in the Church of St
Lawrence outside the Walls, the pavement of which is then
strewn with roses and aromatic herbs. The meaning of the
custom has been changed and sanctified, for it is now the
celebration of the feast of the two Apostles St Philip and

[1] *Moneta civitatis Papiae, i.e.,* Pavia; originally called Ticinum and
later known as Papia.—Tr.
[2] Cf. *Ord. Rom. XI, P.L.* LXXVIII, col. 1047-8.

St James, but the actual rite is the same as that of the *Rosalia* of ancient Rome.

Again, at Leprignano, among the modern descendants of the ancient *Capenates*,[1] a procession takes place on April 25 in which walk all the boys and girls of the village, carrying figures made of sugared cake, which are afterwards blessed by the priest. These figures are evidently derived from those of which the pagans made use in the procession of the *Ambarvalia*, in order to keep off the " evil eye " of the god Robigus from the crops.

THE PROCESSION

During the first part of the route which went along the Via Flaminia, passing the cemetery of the martyr Valentine, the *schola* of the Cantors sang a number of antiphons which are preserved in the ancient collections, but have unfortunately fallen into disuse, as they are no longer included in the Roman Missal.

We give here an example of this forgotten hymnody :

Deprecamur te, Domine, in omni misericordia tua, ut auferatur furor tuus a civitate tua ista et de domo sancta tua, quoniam peccavimus. Alleluia.	We beseech thee, O Lord, by thine infinite mercy, to withhold thine anger from this thy city and from thy holy temple, for we have sinned against thee. Alleluia.

We know from the story of St Augustine and his forty monks that when they first reached the shores of England, as though to take possession of the country in the name of Christ, they at once formed a procession, and, headed by the crucifix, presented themselves before the king, singing the following beautiful antiphon :

Salvator mundi, salva nos supplices tuos; defende populum tuo sanguine redemptum; libera nos, Christe, a periculis, donans nobis vitam aeternam.	Saviour of the world, save those who cry to thee, defend the people redeemed by thy blood; deliver us, O Christ, from all dangers, and grant us eternal life.

The next antiphon may well have been inspired by the holy memories of the Flaminian Way and the cemeteries of the martyrs beside it.

Placet Jerusalem, civitas sancta, ornamento martyrum decorata, cujus plateae sonant laudes de die in diem.	How beautiful is Jerusalem,[2] the holy City, whose jewels are her martyrs, whose streets sound with praises from day to day.

---

[1] The inhabitants of Capena, a town in Etruria, near Rome, just under Mount Soracte—the modern San Martino.—TR.

[2] *i.e.,* Rome.

The first part of this antiphon was engraved by some pilgrim of old on the wall of the papal *cubiculum* in the cemetery of Callixtus on the Via Appia, at the very spot where the Popes of the third century lie buried with Sixtus II, near the resting-place of St Cecilia.

Benedicat nos trina majestas Domini; benedicat nos Spiritus Sanctus qui in specie columbae in Jordane fluvio super Christum requievit; ille nos benedicat, qui de caelis dignatus est descendere in terras et de suo sancto sanguine nos redemit; benedicat Dominus sacerdotium nostrum et introitum nostrum. Alleluia.

May the divine Trinity bless us; may the Holy Spirit who in the form of a dove rested upon Christ in the waters of Jordan, bless us; may he who deigned to come down from heaven to earth to redeem us by his sacred blood, bless us; may the Lord bless our priestly office and our going up into his holy temple. Alleluia.

THE LITANY

The Litany still preserves the very ancient type of prayer which ended the night vigil and served as a transition between the vigiliary Office and the offering of the holy sacrifice. The oldest part of the Litany is that which follows the invocation of the Saints, and may date, at any rate in its earliest form, from the third century. The invocation of the Saints was added in the early Middle Ages, and like the Canon of the Mass was suggested by the local memories of the great Roman martyrs. Other Churches and the celebrated monasteries of olden days had each their own litany, but the Roman form finally prevailed and was definitely adopted by almost all the Western Churches.

Kyrie eleison.
Christe eleison.
Kyrie eleison.
Christe audi nos.
Christe exaudi nos.

Lord have mercy.
Christ have mercy.
Lord have mercy.
Christ hear us.
Christ graciously hear us.

Pater de caelis Deus, *miserere nobis.*
Fili Redemptor mundi Deus, *miserere nobis.*
Spiritus Sancte Deus, *miserere nobis.*
Sancta Trinitas, unus Deus, *miserere nobis.*
Sancta Maria, *ora pro nobis.*

God the Father of heaven, *have mercy on us.*
God the Son, Redeemer of the world, *have mercy on us.*
God the Holy Ghost, *have mercy on us.*
Holy Trinity, one God, *have mercy on us.*
Holy Mary, *pray for us.*

When the procession drew near to the Vatican Basilica, the Litany, which served as prelude to the Mass, was intoned.

In memory of the ancient sevenfold litanies formerly used in the Roman Liturgy from the time of St Gregory, each invocation is still repeated twice, first by the cantors and then by the people in unison.

Sancta Dei Genitrix, *ora pro nobis*		Holy Mother of God,	*pray for us*
Sancta Virgo Virginum,	*ora*	Holy Virgin of virgins,	*pray*
Sancte Michael,	*ora*	St Michael,	*pray*
Sancte Gabriel,	*ora*	St Gabriel,	*pray*
Sancte Raphael,	*ora*	St Raphael,	*pray*

St Ambrose and the early Fathers mention the names of other angels, such as Uriel, etc., emanating from Jewish traditions, but Rome officially ignores them as apocryphal.

Omnes sancti angeli et archangeli,		All ye holy angels and archangels,	
	orate pro nobis		*pray for us*
Omnes sancti beatorum spirituum		All ye holy orders of blessed	
ordines,	*orate*	spirits.	*pray*
Sancte Joannes Baptista,	*ora*	St John the Baptist,	*pray*
Sancte Joseph,	*ora*	St Joseph,	*pray*
Omnes sancti patriarchae et pro-		All ye holy patriarchs and pro-	
phetae,	*orate*	phets,	*pray*

Then follow the diptychs of the Apostles in the same order as in the Roman Canon.

Sancte Petre,	*ora*	St Peter,	*pray*
Sancte Paule,	*ora*	St Paul,	*pray*
Sancte Andrea,	*ora*	St Andrew,	*pray*
Sancte Jacobe,	*ora*	St James,	*pray*
Sancte Joannes,	*ora*	St John,	*pray*
Sancte Thoma,	*ora*	St Thomas,	*pray*
Sancte Jacobe,	*ora*	St James,	*pray*
Sancte Philippe,	*ora*	St Philip,	*pray*
Sancte Bartholomaee,	*ora*	St Bartholomew,	*pray*
Sancte Matthaee,	*ora*	St Matthew,	*pray*
Sancte Simon,	*ora*	St Simon,	*pray*
Sancte Thaddaee,	*ora*	St Thaddeus,	*pray*
Sancte Mathia,	*ora*	St Matthias,	*pray*

Barnabas, as an Apostle and companion of St Paul, is put before the two Evangelists Luke and Mark, the disciples respectively of St Paul and St Peter. This preference is given to Barnabas also in the diptychs, where he is named immediately after Stephen and Matthew, whilst Luke and Mark are not mentioned at all.

Sancte Barnaba,	*ora*	St Barnabas,	*pray*
Sancte Luca,	*ora*	St Luke,	*pray*
Sancte Marce,	*ora*	St Mark,	*pray*
Omnes sancti apostoli et evange-		All ye holy apostles and evange-	
listae,	*orate*	lists,	*pray*
Omnes sancti discipuli Domini,		All ye holy disciples of our Lord,	
	orate		*pray*
Omnes sancti Innocentes,	*orate*	All ye holy Innocents,	*pray*
Sancte Stephane,	*ora*	St Stephen,	*pray*
Sancte Laurenti,	*ora*	St Lawrence,	*pray*
Sancte Vincenti,	*ora*	St Vincent,	*pray*

Fabian owes his celebrity to the circumstance that his feast occurs on the same day as that of St Sebastian, who was greatly venerated at Rome, and whose popularity was in consequence shared by the Pontiff.

Sancti Fabiane et Sebastiane,	*orate*	SS Fabian and Sebastian,	*pray*
Sancti Joannes et Paule,	*orate*	SS John and Paul,	*pray*
Sancti Cosma et Damiane,	*orate*	SS Cosmas and Damian,	*pray*

The fame of the two Milanese martyrs whose names come next is due to the interest aroused by the discovery of their bodies by St Ambrose.

Sancti Gervasi et Protasi,	*orate*	SS Gervase and Protase,	*pray*
Omnes sancti martyres,	*orate*	All ye holy martyrs,	*pray*

St Sylvester and St Martin were the first to receive public and liturgical honour of those who were not martyrs, but only *confessores* in the primitive signification of the word. The *cultus* of *Confessores*, that is, of those who had undergone imprisonment, exile, and such-like sufferings for the faith without having lost their lives thereby, was an extension of that paid to actual martyrs.

Sancte Silvester,	*ora*	St Sylvester,	*pray*
Sancte Gregori,	*ora*	St Gregory,	*pray*
Sancte Ambrosi,	*ora*	St Ambrose,	*pray*
Sancte Augustine,	*ora*	St Augustine,	*pray*
Sancte Hieronyme,	*ora*	St Jerome,	*pray*
Sancte Martine,	*ora*	St Martin,	*pray*

St Nicholas was added to the Litany in the Middle Ages, when devotion to him was very popular. He is the only representative of the Eastern Episcopate in the Roman litanies.

Sancte Nicolae,	*ora*	St Nicholas,	*pray*
Omnes sancti pontifices et confessores,	*orate*	All ye holy bishops and confessors,	*pray*
Omnes sancti doctores,	*orate*	All ye holy doctors,	*pray*
Sancte Antoni,	*ora*	St Antony,	*pray*
Sancte Benedicte,	*ora*	St Benedict,	*pray*
Sancte Bernarde,	*ora*	St Bernard,	*pray*
Sancte Dominice,	*ora*	St Dominic,	*pray*
Sancte Francisce,	*ora*	St Francis,	*pray*
Omnes sancti Sacerdotes et Levitae,	*orate*	All ye holy priests and levites,	*pray*
Omnes sancti monachi et eremitae,	*orate*	All ye holy monks and hermits,	*pray*
Sancta Maria Magdalena,	*ora*	St Mary Magdalen,	*pray*

The order here has been slightly altered. Originally the Roman martyrs Agnes and Cecilia came first, as in the Litany of Holy Saturday, and were followed by the Sicilian virgins Agatha and Lucy and then by the matron Anastasia.

Sancta Agatha,	*ora*	St Agatha,	*pray*
Sancta Lucia,	*ora*	St Lucy,	*pray*
Sancta Agnes,	*ora*	St Agnes,	*pray*
Sancta Caecilia,	*ora*	St Cecily,	*pray*
Sancta Catharina,	*ora*	St Catharine,	*pray*
Sancta Anastasia,	*ora*	St Anastasia,	*pray*
Omnes sanctae virgines et viduae, *orate*		All ye holy virgins and widows, *pray*	
Omnes sancti et sanctae Dei, *intercedite pro nobis*		All ye holy men and women, saints of God, *make intercession for us*	
Propitius esto, *parce nobis Domine*		Be merciful, *spare us, O Lord*	
Propitius esto, *exaudi nos Domine*		Be merciful, *graciously hear us, O Lord*	
Ab omni malo, *libera nos Domine*		From all evil, *deliver us, O Lord,*	
Ab omni peccato,	*libera*	From all sin,	*deliver*
Ab ira tua,	*libera*	From thy wrath,	*deliver*
A subitanea et improvisa morte,	*libera*	From sudden and unprovided death,	*deliver*
Ab insidiis diaboli,	*libera*	From the snares of the devil,	*deliver*
Ab ira et odio, et omni mala voluntate,	*libera*	From anger, hatred, and all ill-will,	*deliver*
A spiritu fornicationis,	*libera*	From the spirit of fornication,	*deliver*
A fulgure et tempestate,	*libera*	From lightning and tempest,	*deliver*
A flagello terraemotus,	*libera*	From the scourge of earthquake,	*deliver*
A peste, fame, et bello,	*libera*	From plague, famine, and war,	*deliver*

Everlasting death is the judgement of eternal reprobation due to the final obstinacy of the sinner.

A morte perpetua,	*libera*	From everlasting death,	*deliver*

The enumeration which follows of the different mysteries of the redemption is very important from the liturgical point of view, for it appears to have been derived from the primitive text of the eucharistic anaphora and of the anamnesis after the Consecration in which they are duly commemorated. In the Roman anamnesis there is no mention of the Nativity, but it is possible that the original text, like the Litany, contained it.

Per mysterium sanctae incarnationis tuae,	*libera*	Through the mystery of thy holy incarnation, *deliver us, O Lord,*	
Per adventum tuum,	*libera*	Through thy coming,	*deliver*
Per nativitatem tuam,	*libera*	Through thy nativity,	*deliver*

Per baptismum et sanctum jejunium tuum, *libera*

Through thy baptism and holy fasting, *deliver*

Per crucem et passionem tuam, *libera*

Through thy cross and passion, *deliver*

Per mortem et sepulturam tuam, *libera*

Through thy death and burial, *deliver*

Per sanctam resurrectionem tuam, *libera*

Through thy holy resurrection, *deliver*

Per admirabilem ascensionem tuam, *libera*

Through thine admirable ascension, *deliver*

Per adventum Spiritus Sancti Paracliti, *libera*

Through the coming of the Holy Ghost the Comforter, *deliver*

In die judicii, *libera*

In the day of judgement, *deliver*

Peccatores, *te rogamus audi nos*

We sinners, *beseech thee to hear us.*

Ut nobis parcas, *te rogamus*

That thou wouldst spare us, *we beseech*

Ut nobis indulgeas, *te rogamus*

That thou wouldst pardon us, *we beseech*

Ut ad veram poenitentiam nos perducere digneris, *te rogamus*

That thou wouldst bring us to true penance, *we beseech*

Ut ecclesiam tuam sanctam regere et conservare digneris, *te rogamus*

That thou wouldst vouchsafe to govern and preserve thy holy Church, *we beseech*

Here the meaning of " Ecclesiastical Orders " is still the one originally given to this expression, which signified the various ranks of those ministering at the altar, and not the religious corporations, of which our forefathers knew only one—that of the monks of St Benedict. There is no particular mention of the bishop of the diocese, for this type of litany is purely Roman, and at Rome the bishop is the Pope, the Apostolic Lord, as he was called in the early Middle Ages.

Ut domnum apostolicum et omnes ecclesiasticos ordines in sancta religione conservare digneris, *te rogamus*

That thou wouldst vouchsafe to preserve our apostolic prelate, and all orders of the Church in holy religion, *we beseech*

The overthrow of the enemies of the Church is next prayed for, not from hatred nor from revenge, but that they may repent and turn to God. Success and good fortune foster pride and do not tend to bring souls back to God; whereas on the other hand disaster, adversity, and sorrow humble the spirit and cause it the more easily to realize its own weakness.

Ut inimicos sanctae ecclesiae humiliare digneris, *te rogamus*

That thou wouldst vouchsafe to humble the enemies of holy Church, *we beseech*

Ut regibus et principibus christianis pacem et veram concordiam donare digneris, *te rogamus*

That thou wouldst vouchsafe to give peace and true concord to Christian kings and princes, *we beseech*

Ut cuncto populo christiano pacem et unitatem largiri digneris, *te rogamus*

That thou wouldst vouchsafe to grant peace and unity to all Christian people, *we beseech*

Ut omnes errantes ad unitatem Ecclesiae revocare, et infideles universos ad Evangelii lumen perducere digneris, *te rogamus*	That thou wouldst vouchsafe to recall all wanderers to the unity of the Church, and to lead all unbelievers to the light of the Gospel, *we beseech*

The "holy service" mentioned below signifies in very ancient liturgical language the priestly office, the λειτουργία of the Greeks. This expression recalls that of the primitive eucharistic anaphora in which immediately after the Consecration the priests who were jointly celebrating the divine mysteries gave humble thanks to God for having granted them the grace of surrounding his holy altar and dedicating themselves to his holy service. The *nosmetipsos,* therefore, of the litanies, inasmuch as it is distinguished from the *cuncto populo christiano,* and is in the plural number, may well be a last echo of this venerable and traditional prayer.

Ut nosmetipsos in tuo sancto servitio confortare et conservare digneris, *te rogamus*	That thou wouldst vouchsafe to confirm and preserve us in thy holy service, *we beseech*
Ut mentes nostras ad coelestia desideria erigas, *te rogamus*	That thou wouldst lift up our minds to heavenly desires, *we beseech*
Ut omnibus benefactoribus nostris sempiterna bona retribuas, *te rogamus*	That thou wouldst render eternal blessings to all our benefactors, *we beseech*
Ut animas nostras, fratrum, propinquorum, et benefactorum nostrorum ab aeterna damnatione eripias, *te rogamus*	That thou wouldst deliver our souls, and the souls of our brethren, relations and benefactors from eternal damnation, *we beseech*
Ut fructus terrae dare et conservare digneris, *te rogamus*	That thou wouldst vouchsafe to give and preserve the fruits of the earth, *we beseech*
Ut omnibus fidelibus defunctis requiem aeternam donare digneris, *te rogamus*	That thou wouldst vouchsafe to grant eternal rest to all the faithful departed, *we beseech*
Ut nos exaudire digneris, *te rogamus*	That thou wouldst vouchsafe graciously to hear us, *we beseech*
Fili Dei, *te rogamus*	Son of God, *we beseech*
Agnus Dei, qui tollis peccata mundi, *parce nobis Domine*	Lamb of God, who takest away the sins of the world, *spare us, O Lord*
Agnus Dei, qui tollis peccata mundi, *exaudi nos Domine*	Lamb of God, who takest away the sins of the world, *graciously hear us, O Lord*
Agnus Dei, qui tollis peccata mundi, *miserere nobis*	Lamb of God, who takest away the sins of the world, *have mercy on us*
Christe audi nos.	Christ hear us.
Christe exaudi nos.	*Christ graciously hear us.*
Kyrie eleison.	Lord have mercy on us.
Christe eleison.	Christ have mercy on us.
Kyrie eleison.	Lord have mercy on us.
Pater noster, *secreto*	Our Father, *silently*

℣. Et ne nos inducas in tenta-
tionem.
℞. Sed libera nos a malo.

℣. And lead us not into temptation,
℞. But deliver us from evil.

There next comes Psalm lxix, which was added to the
Litany in the Middle Ages and well illustrates the condition
of fear and anxiety in which the penitential litanies of the
Rogations were first instituted by St Mamertus at Vienne.

Psalm lxix

Deus in adjutorium meum intende :
Domine, ad adjuvandum me fes-
tina.
Confundantur et revereantur, qui
quaerunt animam meam.

Avertantur retrorsum, et erubes-
cant qui volunt mihi mala.

Avertantur statim erubescentes,
qui dicunt mihi, Euge, euge.

Exsultent et laetentur in te omnes
qui quaerunt te, et dicant semper : Magnificetur Dominus :
qui diligunt salutare tuum.
Ego vero egenus et pauper sum :
Deus adjuva me.
Adjutor meus et liberator meus es
tu : Domine ne moreris.
Gloria, etc.

O God, come to mine assistance :
O Lord, make haste to help me.

Let them be confounded and
ashamed, that seek after my
soul.
Let them be turned backward, and
blush for shame, that desire
evils unto me.
Let them be straightway turned
backward, blushing for shame,
that say unto me, 'Tis well, 'tis
well.
Let all that seek thee rejoice and
be glad in thee ; and let such as
love thy salvation say always,
the Lord be magnified.
But I am needy and poor : O
God, help me.
Thou art my helper and my deliverer : O Lord, make no delay.
Glory be, etc.

The following versicles, although of varied origin, show
distinctly the type of ancient prayer or diaconal litany which
is still seen in the Greek Liturgies, and was used in Rome
almost down to the seventh century.

℣. Salvos fac servos tuos.
℞. Deus meus, sperantes in te.
℣. Esto nobis, Domine, turris
fortitudinis.
℞. A facie inimici.
℣. Nihil proficiat inimicus in
nobis.
℞. Et filius iniquitatis non ap-
ponat nocere nobis.
℣. Domine, non secundum peccata
nostra facias nobis.
℞. Neque secundum iniquitates
nostras retribuas nobis.
℣. Oremus pro pontifice nostro N.

℞. Dominus conservet eum, et
vivificet eum, et beatum faciat
eum in terra, et non tradat eum
in animam inimicorum ejus.

℣. Save thy servants.
℞. Who hope in thee, O my God.
℣. Be unto us, O Lord, a tower
of strength.
℞. From the face of the enemy.
℣. Let not the enemy prevail
against us.
℞. Nor the son of iniquity have
power to hurt us.
℣. O Lord, deal not with us
according to our sins.
℞. Neither requite us according
to our iniquities.
℣. Let us pray for our sovereign
Pontiff, N.
℞. The Lord preserve him, and
give him life, and make him
blessed upon earth, and deliver
him not to the will of his
enemies.

℣. Oremus pro benefactoribus nostris.

℟. Retribuere dignare, Domine, omnibus nobis bona facientibus propter nomen tuum vitam aeternam. Amen.

℣. Oremus pro fidelibus defunctis.

℟. Requiem aeternam dona eis, Domine; et lux perpetua luceat eis.

℣. Requiescant in pace.

℟. Amen.

℣. Pro fratribus nostris absentibus.

℣. Let us pray for our benefactors.

℟. Vouchsafe, O Lord, for thy name's sake, to reward with eternal life all those who do us good. Amen.

℣. Let us pray for the faithful departed.

℟. Eternal rest give unto them, O Lord, and let perpetual light shine upon them.

℣. May they rest in peace.

℟. Amen.

℣. For our absent brethren.

St Benedict also orders in his *Cursus* that the commemoration of the absent should be made amongst the others at the end of each hour of the divine Office.

℟. Salvos fac servos tuos, Deus meus, sperantes in te.

℣. Mitte eis, Domine, auxilium de sancto.

℟. Et de Sion tuere eos.

℣. Domine exaudi orationem meam.

℟. Et clamor meus ad te veniat.

℣. Dominus vobiscum.

℟. Et cum spiritu tuo.

℟. Save thy servants who hope in thee, O my God.

℣. Send them help, O Lord, from the holy place.

℟. And from Sion protect them.

℣. O Lord, hear my prayer.

℟. And let my cry come unto thee.

℣. The Lord be with you.

℟. And with thy spirit.

THE SACERDOTAL PRAYER

The various collects which follow are all of the early Middle Ages, but here they are out of their proper place. The processional litany formed a single ceremony with the Mass, which had therefore neither Introit nor *Kyrie*, the celebrant immediately reciting the Collect which formed the conclusion of the Litany. We should note that the latter was not, as now, a separate and isolated rite, for the procession was a preliminary to the solemn celebration of Mass at St Peter's.

Let us pray.

"O God, whose property is always to have mercy and to spare, receive our petition; that we and all thy servants who are bound by the chains of sins, may by the compassion of thy goodness mercifully be absolved."

"Graciously hear, we beseech thee, O Lord, the prayers of thy suppliants, and pardon the sins of them that confess to thee, that in thy bounty thou mayest grant us both pardon and peace."

"In thy clemency, O Lord, show unto us thine unspeakable mercy, that thou mayest both loose us of all our sins and deliver us from the punishments which we deserve for them."

"O God, who by sin art offended and by penance pacified, mercifully regard the prayers of thy people making supplication to thee, and turn away the scourges of thine anger, which we deserve for our sins."

"Almighty, everlasting God, have mercy upon thy servant N. our sovereign Pontiff, and direct him according to thy clemency into the way of everlasting salvation, that by thy grace he may both desire those things that are pleasing to thee, and perform them with all his strength."

"O God, from whom are holy desires, right counsels and just works, give to thy servants that peace which the world cannot give; that our hearts being devoted to the keeping of thy commandments, and the fear of enemies being removed, the times, by thy protection, may be peaceful."

"Inflame, O Lord, our reins and hearts with the fire of thy Holy Ghost, that we may serve thee with a chaste body, and please thee with a clean heart."

"O God, the Creator and Redeemer of all the faithful, give to the souls of thy servants departed the remission of all their sins; that through pious supplications they may obtain the pardon which they have always desired."

"Prevent, we beseech thee, O Lord, our actions by thy holy inspirations, and carry them on by thy gracious assistance; that every prayer and work of ours may begin always from thee, and through thee be happily ended."

"Almighty and everlasting God, who hast dominion over the living and the dead, and art merciful to all whom thou foreknowest shall be thine by faith and good works; we humbly beseech thee that they for whom we intend to pour forth our prayers, whether this present world still detain them in the flesh, or the world to come hath already received them out of their bodies, may, through the intercession of all thy saints, by the clemency of thy goodness, obtain the remission of all their sins. Through our Lord."

℣. Dominus vobiscum.
℟. Et cum spiritu tuo.
℣. Exaudiat nos omnipotens et misericors Dominus.
℟. Amen.
℣. Et fidelium animae per misericordiam Dei requiescant in pace.
℟. Amen.

℣. The Lord be with you.
℟. And with thy spirit.
℣. May the almighty and most merciful Lord graciously hear us.
℟. Amen.
℣. And may the souls of the faithful departed, through the mercy of God, rest in peace.
℟. Amen.

THE STATIONAL MASS IN THE VATICAN BASILICA

As we have already said, the Litany when regarded as a peculiar rite for the imploring of God's mercy in time of public calamity always ended in Rome, from the time of St Gregory, at the Vatican Basilica beside the tomb of the *Pastor ecclesiæ*, the special Patron of the Eternal City. The other stations at St Mary Major, St John Lateran and St Peter's on the three days preceding the Ascension are of later date, and represent a fusion of Roman and Frankish customs.

The Introit of to-day's Mass—which cannot, however, be ancient, for the Litany always replaces the Introit in all processions—expresses the confidence of the Just One who knows that his prayer has been favourably heard by God. The Antiphon is from Psalm xvii : He heard my voice from his holy temple, Alleluia : and my cry before him came into his ears, Alleluia, Alleluia. I will love thee, O Lord, my strength; the Lord is my firmament, and my refuge, and my deliverer. Glory be, etc.

In the Collect, which recalls the circumstances in which the Rogations were instituted, we declare our humble confidence in God under the stress of the afflictions which oppress us, and invoke the help of his arm. The real evil, nay, the root of all evil, is sin. All other sufferings may be penitential in their nature, and in God's hands often become a means to the conversion of souls.

The Lesson, taken from St James (v 16-20), has been chosen very appropriately. It treats of the efficacy of prayer, to which, as to a golden key opening the treasury of the divine heart, our Lord has promised unfailing power. Nor is it only the prayers of the saints which prevail, while those of the ordinary man have no result, for the Apostle dwells particularly on the fact that Elias when he drew down and withheld rain from the land by his prayer, was a man of a like nature with ourselves. That which is needed for prayer to be effectual is that it be constant and full of faith.

We quote here this beautiful passage from the Epistle of St James :

" Dearly beloved : Confess your sins one to another, and pray one for another, that you may be saved. For the continual prayer of a just man availeth much. Elias was a man passible like unto us ; and with prayer he prayed that it might not rain upon the earth, and it rained not for three years and six months : and he prayed again, and the heaven gave rain, and the earth brought forth her fruit. My brethren, if any of you err from the truth, and one convert him, he must know, that he who causeth a sinner to be converted from the error of his way, shall save his soul from death, and shall cover a multitude of sins.''

The alleluiatic verse is from Psalm cxvii, and is well suited to the Easter season. '' Alleluia, give praise to the Lord, for he is good; for his mercy endureth for ever.''

The Gospel, which comes from St Luke (xi 5-13), is in complete harmony with the character of to-day's litany or public and solemn penitential intercession, which aims at obtaining from God through fervent prayer and strong faith the mercy which we have not deserved by reason of our sins. In a special manner we seek to obtain for the coming feast of Pentecost the ''good Spirit,'' which God grants to those who fear him.

'' At that time : Jesus said to his disciples, Which of you shall have a friend, and shall go to him at midnight, and shall say to him, Friend, lend me three loaves, because a friend of mine is come off his journey to me, and I have not what to set before him; and he from within should answer and say, Trouble me not, the door is now shut, and my children are with me in bed; I cannot rise and give thee. Yet if he shall continue knocking, I say to you, Although he will not rise and give him because he is his friend; yet because of his importunity he will rise, and give him as many as he needeth. And I say to you, Ask, and it shall be given you; seek, and you shall find; knock, and it shall be opened to you. For everyone that asketh, receiveth; and he that seeketh, findeth; and to him that knocketh, it shall be opened. And which of you, if he ask his father bread, will he give him a stone? or a fish, will he for a fish give him a serpent? Or if he shall ask an egg, will he reach him a scorpion? If you, then, being evil, know how to give good gifts to your children, how much more will your Father from heaven give the good Spirit to them that ask him?''

This shows us how highly we should value prayer. Even in the middle of the night, and even to the extent of seeming importunate, our prayers should rise to God, because our miseries and our weaknesses are so numerous, and because God has decreed that his grace shall be granted to us only on the wings of prayer. *Ascendit oratio, et descendit Dei miseratio,* as St Augustine of Hippo taught his people.

The Offertory is taken from Psalm cviii : '' I will give thanks to the Lord exceedingly with my mouth, and in the midst of many I will praise him, because he hath stood at the right hand of the poor, to save my soul from persecutors, Alleluia.''

The " poor man " of whom the Psalmist here speaks is Christ. The Lord has delivered his soul from the hands of the Jews and has raised him from death. The " many " in whose midst the Saviour will sing his hymn of praise represent the Catholic Church, so different from the ancient Jewish religion, which was kept within the narrow limits of Palestine by its exclusively national character.

The Secret is of general application. In it we ask that the eucharistic offerings may " loose the bonds of our wickedness "—one of the chief effects of Holy Communion is that of subduing our evil passions—and may render the divine mercy favourably disposed towards us, by first satisfying the justice of God.

The Communion is derived from the Gospel of to-day: " Ask, and you shall receive; seek, and you shall find; knock, and it shall be opened to you; for everyone that asketh, receiveth; and he that seeketh, findeth; and to him that knocketh, it shall be opened. Alleluia."

In the Post-Communion we entreat God that the eucharistic banquet which comforts us in our tribulation may also be a token of future consolation. The sacred bread is truly a food of sorrow and of tears, because it commemorates the passion of Christ and ours also with him. It contains nevertheless the germ of our future glory in the final resurrection, and is the pledge of that other heavenly food with which God will nourish the blessed in the beatific vision.

What are the things which we must fervently ask of God in prayer? St Augustine tells us that we must not expect to receive those things which are not promised to us in the Gospel. God has not promised to give us those temporal favours which we, perhaps, might ask for in our childish judgement—for in comparison with the maturity of eternal life we all are children—but he wishes, above all, that we should ask of him, and he desires to give us in the first place the *Spiritum bonum* of which the Gospel speaks to-day, which is the motive and source of all the other spiritual gifts with which he is desirous of enriching our souls.

This " good Spirit " is the Paraclete, and it is from him that come all other gifts, inasmuch as he is Love, and Love is the great motive by which friendship is shown through gifts. Therefore, with God, Love is his first gift. God gives his Holy Spirit to the humble, to the pure, and to those that fear him.

Such are the best dispositions in which to prepare for the feast of Pentecost. The Paraclete, as he himself has said in the Book of Wisdom, withdraws himself from the deceitful and the hypocritical, and the eternal Wisdom cannot enter a soul which is evil or a heart enslaved by sin. Therefore the Spirit of God will not dwell with the carnal man, but finds his resting-place with the humble and the pure of heart.

MONDAY AFTER THE FIFTH SUNDAY AFTER EASTER

Station at St Mary Major. The Rogations.

As we have said above, the *triduum* of penitential litanies before the feast of the Ascension was first instituted at Vienne by St Mamertus, about the year 470, and was accompanied by fasting and abstention from servile work. The custom spread with great rapidity, and became very popular. Since, however, a period of penitence and mourning in the very midst of the paschal season seemed at Rome to be an exceedingly inopportune contradiction, it was not adopted in the Roman Liturgy until long afterwards; that is, during the Frankish period, under Leo III (795-816) and then only by way of exception, and not as a regular observance to be repeated year by year.

The custom of the Gallican Churches was afterwards definitely accepted at Rome, but in the form of a compromise; the fast was abolished, and only the three days' processsion of St Mamertus was retained, together with the Mass, which, however, is the same as that celebrated in Rome at the Greater Litany. It should be noted that these Frankish Rogations formed part of the official ritual at Rome only at a much later period, for the *Ordines Romani* ignore them completely.

The stational church of St Mary Major recalls the ancient *litania septiformis* or penitential procession instituted by St Gregory the Great in order to pray for the cessation of the plague.

AT THE PROCESSION

When we call to mind that our Lord's first miracle at the wedding feast of Cana was worked at the intercession of the Blessed Virgin, whose prayer alone was able to move her divine Son to anticipate his own appointed time for manifesting himself to the world through his miracles, we should be filled with confidence in the powerful patronage of Mary. How many times has not this blessed Mother repeated in our favour the prayer which she uttered on behalf of the bridal pair at Cana : *Vinum non habent,* and our souls have been filled with the wine of divine love, whilst we have repeated the words of the chief steward of the feast : *" Tu autem servasti bonum vinum usque adhuc !"*

The procession and the Mass follow exactly the same order as already described for April 25, the Roman *Ambarvalia*.

TUESDAY AFTER THE FIFTH SUNDAY
AFTER EASTER

Station at St John Lateran. The Rogations.

This intermediary station at the Lateran is in itself a proof of the late introduction of the Rogations into the Roman Liturgy. The Lateran Basilica is no longer called the Basilica of the Saviour, but of St John the Baptist, to whom is thus given the place immediately after the Blessed Virgin and before the Apostle Peter.

St John the Baptist is the type of that penitence which disposes us to ask for and to obtain grace. The stational solemnity of to-day aptly recalls him to us, for unless the waters of penance purify the soul, the Paraclete will never be able to sanctify it by his presence, for it is written : *Non permanebit Spiritus meus in homine in aeternum, quia caro est.*

Severe penance, rigorous fasting, the rough hairshirt, the savage solitude of the desert—these are the means by which the Baptist kept his soul free from the least taint of sin, and it is against such a background as this that his figure stands out as the greatest among the children of Adam. What a lesson for us who treat our rebellious and sinful bodies with so much leniency, and who have all the more cause for severity since we are far from approaching the purity of the Baptist, who was sanctified even from his mother's womb.

The procession and the Mass both to-day and to-morrow are the same as on April 25.

WEDNESDAY BEFORE THE ASCENSION

Station at St Peter. The Rogations.

This station at the Vatican Basilica on the last day of the Rogations was probably instituted, not only out of veneration for the tomb of the Apostle, but also in order to assimilate as far as possible the lesser litanies to the greater ones of April 25 which ended at the Basilica of St Peter. The motives of this fitting if tardy assimilation are certainly important, but evidently no account was taken of the slight liturgical anomaly which ensued in having two stations at St Peter's on two successive days.

The Litany of the Saints which is sung during this *triduum* is one of the most precious jewels of ancient euchology. In its present form, which dates from the tenth century at least, the long list of apostles, martyrs, priests, confessors, and virgins reminds us of the succession of saints whom the early artists loved to represent in mosaic on the naves of their basilicas. These names are the glory of the Church; the thought of them fills us with hope. Although the heavenly Jerusalem rejoices now over her many noble citizens, yet these were fostered in the bosom of the Church militant, and every crown that they wear, every throne that they adorn in heaven, has cost the Church bitter strife, acute sorrow, and blood freely shed. Such is the rich holocaust which the faithful offer to Christ, in return for his own sacrifice on Calvary.

THE VIGIL OF THE ASCENSION

The Mass of the vigil of the Ascension, noted in some Roman lists of the middle of the seventh century, though it is not of very early origin, since it is out of harmony with the ancient conception of the papal liturgy which considered the fifty days between Easter and Pentecost as a festival season, yet is older than the procession of the Rogations, introduced at Rome under Leo III.

The post-Gregorian origin of this Mass is shown by the absence of any proper hymns and prayers; with the exception of the two lessons, the rest is borrowed from the Mass of the preceding Sunday.

In the Lesson (Eph. iv 7-13) St Paul teaches us that the gifts of God differ in regard to each individual soul, and that this variety aims at the unity and perfection of the mystical body of Jesus Christ, which demands to that end an infinite diversity of means and active functions. This fact not only causes us to be generous towards dispositions and talents differing from our own, but also obliges us to respect in each one the special grace or office with which Christ has endowed him, and not to desire to bend all others to our own will and caprice.

" Brethren : To every one of us is given grace according to the measure of the giving of Christ. Wherefore he saith, Ascending on high, he led captivity captive; he gave gifts to men. Now, that he ascended, what is it, but because he also descended first into the lower parts of the earth? He that descended is the same also that ascended above all the

heavens, that he might fill all things.   And he gave some
to be apostles, and some prophets, and other some evangelists, and other some pastors and doctors, for the perfecting
of the saints, for the work of the ministry, for the edifying
of the body of Christ; until we all meet into the unity of
faith, and of the knowledge of the Son of God, unto a perfect
man, unto the measure of the age of the fulness of Christ."

In the Gospel (John xvii 1-11) we have the final prayer of
Jesus at the Last Supper.   The human mind strives in vain
here below to attain to the sublime height of the beatific
vision from which the Redeemer looks back upon us and
calls us lovingly to follow him.   To know God and his
Christ—that is the supreme bliss; but, in order to know him
in the splendour of his glory, we must first know him through
the veils of faith, that, as the brightness of his glory is the
very life of the blessed in heaven, so the light of faith may
be the life of the faithful soul during this mortal pilgrimage.

Jesus prays for me!   How this thought should fill each
one of us with hope!   Jesus prays so that I may never be
separated from him, so that I may have nothing in common
with the spirit of the world.   Should not I then conceive a
great dread of this evil world which the merciful Redeemer
himself distinctly refused to make the object of his prayer?

ASCENSION DAY

Station at St Peter.

The liturgical festival of the Ascension, whilst less ancient
than that of Pentecost, is yet one of the oldest of the cycle,
and although we find no documentary evidence of its existence before Eusebius,[1] the feast was already so universally
observed at that time that St Augustine was able to attribute
its institution to the Apostles themselves.   The chief characteristic of the festival in olden days was a solemn procession
which took place about midday in memory of the Apostles
accompanying our Lord out of the city to the Mount of
Olives.   At Rome, the Pope, after the night Office was concluded, and after Mass had been celebrated at the altar of
St Peter, was crowned by the cardinals, and towards the
sixth hour was accompanied by bishops and clergy to the
Lateran.

On this day Jesus was taken up into heaven in the sight
of his faithful disciples, who, however, continued to gaze
heavenwards, striving to catch sight once more of their

---

[1] *De Sol. Pasch.*, c. v, *P.L.* XXIV, 699.

divine Master; but such contemplative life, wholly absorbed in the beatific vision of Paradise, is reserved for those who have already passed into the Church triumphant. They indeed have their reward *in mercede contemplationis,* as St Augustine expresses it in a famous homily, which the liturgy in the Breviary appoints to be read on the feast of St John the Evangelist. Our calling, on the other hand, must be *in opere actionis;* wherefore the liturgy in to-day's Introit repeats in one of the most beautiful of the Gregorian melodies the words of the Angels to the Apostles: "Ye men of Galilee, why wonder you, looking up to heaven? Alleluia: he shall so come as you have seen him going up into heaven, Alleluia, Alleluia, Alleluia."

Ita veniet. This is our comfort in the sorrows and separations of life. Jesus has left us, but he will certainly come back to us. The expectation of his coming should be the pulse of our inner life, whilst with our hearts turned to him and the eyes of our faith fixed on heaven, we eagerly await his return.

The Collect, too, is full of beauty. Our Redeemer has gone to prepare a place for us in heaven. He is our head, and it is only by a kind of violence that his mystical members are compelled still to remain as pilgrims here on earth. Since we are unable to follow him at once to heaven, we must dwell there with him in our thoughts, our affections, and our desires, so that although we are exiles in the body we may be able to say with St Paul, *conversatio nostra in coelis est.*

The Lesson is taken from the Acts of the Apostles (i 1-11) and gives an account of our Lord's Ascension into heaven. Jesus ascends from the Mount of Olives, from the place where his passion began, in order to teach us that the cross is the one and only way to Paradise. He promises the Apostles that he will send to them the Paraclete, but only after his triumphal entry into his kingdom, because it was fitting that the fulness of glory should be shed on the members from their head. Before disappearing from their sight, Jesus blesses his Apostles, so as to assure them in the secret places of their hearts of his unfailing assistance, intimate and unseen. It is there that he establishes, by the power of the Holy Ghost, the temple in which he comes to dwell with his heavenly Father.

The angels dissuade the Apostles from remaining to gaze up to heaven, because our present life is a time for work and not for repose. Now we sow, later we shall reap. We sow in toil and sorrow, we shall reap in joy and gladness. We must therefore work, but in this, too, there is a rule to be observed. We must work as do the angels, when they exercise their loving ministry of watching over us. They assist us

and are always at our side, but at the same time they fix
their gaze on Paradise, seeking their happiness in the contemplation of the beauteous countenance of the Eternal
Father, *in quem desiderant Angeli prospicere.*

The alleluiatic verse is from Psalm xlvi : God is ascended
with jubilee ; and the Lord with the sound of the trumpets of
the angelic hosts, who acclaim him as their leader and
Saviour, and render him thanks, since by means of the redemption of man, he has filled the gaps in their ranks caused
by the lapse of the fallen angels.

A circumstance which added to the splendour of the
Ascension was that the holy Prophets and Patriarchs, who
rose from their sepulchres at the moment of the death of our
Lord upon the cross, and appeared to many in Jerusalem, in
all probability accompanied him in this glorious triumph.

The verse immediately preceding the Gospel is derived from
Psalm lxvii : The Lord who showed himself on Sinai, now
ascends on high, and leads captivity captive ; that is, he
triumphs over sin and the devil, whose power he treads underfoot. The followers of Christ need have no fear of Satan ;
he is chained like a savage animal, and can harm only those
who foolishly put themselves within his reach.

The Gospel, relating the story of the Ascension, comes from
St Mark (xvi 14-20). It tells at once the history not only of
the forty days which our Lord spent with his Apostles after
the resurrection, but also of the later days of the Church's
more immediate life and work. The disciples are imbued
with the power of working miracles in confirmation of their
divine mission, and go forth to preach the Gospel in all parts
of the world. Jesus from heaven gives efficacy to their
words, and thus the Church, like her divine Master whose
beneficent work she carries on, spreads everywhere her
saving influence : *pertransiit benefaciendo et sanando.*

Nor must it be thought that this picture applies only to the
apostolic ages, for the Church is the same now as she was
then. There exists no corporal nor spiritual work of mercy
to which she does not also now devote herself, especially
through the agency of her marvellous religious orders. As
to the gift of miracles, this, too, is a grace which has never
failed her. Indeed this gift is in such close connection with
her mark of sanctity, that in her wisdom the Church insists
that before inscribing any one of her members on the roll of
the saints, the wonders obtained through his intercession
shall first be judicially examined, discussed and approved.
Moreover, there are always a great number of these apostolic
processes before the Sacred Congregation of Rites, which is
the competent tribunal for these causes.

The Offertory is drawn from Psalm xlvi : " God is ascended

in jubilee, and the Lord with the sound of trumpet, Alleluia."
On the day of the Incarnation the angels proclaimed his glory
only in heaven : *Gloria in excelsis Deo;* the gift most fitted
on earth whilst the Saviour was in poverty and humiliation,
was that of peace between God and man : *et in terra pax
hominibus bonae voluntatis.* But to-day the grand work of
redemption being completed, the glory of heaven is reflected
also upon earth, since the barrier of separation has been
removed and the two families of men and angels have become
one. Thus whilst Jesus Christ, *caput hominum et angelorum,*
is seated in glory at the right hand of the Father, the members
of his mystical body, in which he continues to live and work,
remain here on earth. As then the Saviour unites in himself
these two attributes, that of the glorious head in heaven and
that of the members who labour on earth, so likewise the
Church is militant here below, but has already through her
head begun the blessed life of Paradise.

In the Secret we call to mind that the sacred gifts are
offered on this day in commemoration of the glorious Ascension of Christ, which is the consequence of his passion. Therefore we pray God to make the path to heaven easier for us by
removing all stumbling-blocks which lie in the way so that
we may safely reach the longed-for goal. It is to be noted,
however, that we do not at all ask here that the soldiers of
Christ should be withdrawn entirely from the battle, to spend
their time in a place of safety—by no means, for this life is
a season of warfare—but we do ask that God will guard our
steps against the only real harm and danger that can threaten
us, which is that of offending him.

In the eucharistic anaphora or Preface which introduces the
Trisagion, there is inserted during the whole Octave of the
Ascension the commemoration of this sublime mystery, in
accordance with the Roman custom, mentioned by Pope
Vigilius in writing to Profuturus of Braga : " Who after his
resurrection appeared and showed himself to all his disciples ;
and while they beheld him was lifted up into heaven, so that
he might make us partakers of his Godhead."

This is the meaning of to-day's feast, and the end which
Christ desires to compass by ascending into heaven. He
fully attains this desire on the approaching feast of Pentecost,
when together with the Holy Spirit he bestows on us his own
divine life, his own Sacred Heart.

We also commemorate to-day's solemnity within the
Action before the apostolic diptychs in the words : " Communicating and keeping the most holy day, on which thine
only-begotten Son our Lord set at the right hand of thy glory
the substance of our frail human nature which he had taken
to himself,"

The Communion is taken from Psalm lxvii : " Sing ye to the Lord, who ascendeth above the heaven of heavens to the east, Alleluia." The " heaven of heavens " here signifies the very throne of the Godhead, of which the sacred humanity of Christ takes possession to-day. He ascends in the East because all the works of God are full of light and splendour, and the Church has never had, like some modern theosophists, two doctrines, one secret for the initiated, and one open for the people at large. God works in full daylight. Jesus Christ dies on a hill-top, in the presence of a whole people, on the great day of the Parasceve of the Jews at Jerusalem itself. He rises again and lets himself be seen and touched not only by the Apostles, but by the holy women and even by as many as five hundred persons at one time. To-day he ascends to heaven from the heights of the Mount of Olives in the presence of at least eleven persons besides his holy Mother and his brethren.

In the Eucharistia or prayer of thanksgiving, we beseech the divine clemency to grant that the visible sign of God's grace, that is, Holy Communion, may produce within us its full effect. In other words, we ask that the material incorporation with the victim of the eucharistic sacrifice may unite us spiritually to Christ.

The supreme glorification of the head who is this day enthroned at the right hand of the Father in heaven affects the members also, like the precious balsam which, as Psalm cxxxii tells us, descended from the head of Aaron on to his flowing beard and on to his gorgeous pontifical vestments. This spiritual unction is the gift of the Holy Ghost, which Christ obtains to-day from heaven for his Church. Hence the connection between the Ascension and Pentecost is very close, nor can we understand the one without the other.

SUNDAY AFTER THE ASCENSION

Station at St Mary "ad Martyres."

The celebration of the Octave of the Ascension dates only from the fifteenth century, hence in the earlier Roman documents this Sunday is called simply *dominica de rosa*. The station is assigned to the church of *Sancta Maria rotunda*, the ancient sanctuary of the martyrs, once the *Pantheon* of Agrippa. The Pope himself celebrated the Mass there and delivered the homily, announcing to the people the speedy coming of the Holy Ghost. Further, in order to illustrate his words more effectually, a shower of roses *in figura ejusdem Spiritus Sancti* was scattered from the central opening in the roof upon the people as he preached. Even to this day the Mass, in which only a commemoration is made of the Ascension, is altogether preparatory to the approaching feast of Pentecost; the Epistle from St Peter being descriptive of the various gifts of the Holy Ghost, while the Gospel contains the promise of Christ to his Apostles at the Last Supper, that he would not fail to send the Paraclete to them.

The Introit is derived from Psalm xxvi : " Hear, O Lord, my voice with which I have cried to thee, Alleluia : my heart hath said to thee, I have sought thy face; thy face, O Lord, I will seek : turn not away thy face from me, Alleluia, Alleluia." This grand Introit, which teaches us so insistently to seek always the face of God, that is, to have him always present in our thoughts and in our desires, suggested to-day's station at Sta Maria " ad Martyres." It was here that in the Middle Ages, in a coffer locked with thirteen keys, was kept the representation of the Holy Face which Dante calls *la Veronica nostra*,[1] which in his time had already been transferred to the Vatican Basilica.

In the Collect we ask God—to whom is subject the free determination of our will—to grant us a will devoted to him; that is, which desires him alone; and not only to desire him, but to put into practice this resolve of serving him by means of a good life and virtuous deeds. In this connection it is customary to say with some shrewdness and much truth that hell is paved with good intentions, that were never carried out by those who made them. St Philip Neri was wont to repeat in that playful manner which distinguished him : " Deeds, not words, but deeds " !

In the Lesson, St Peter (i iv 7-11) on the morrow of the burning of Rome under Nero and on the eve of the human pyres in the *Circus Vaticanus*, warns the faithful to watch and pray. The gifts which God gives to each one are intended for the common good of all, for we are but stewards of the manifold treasures of our heavenly Father. It is in this spirit that we should make use of the graces we have received, employing them in the service of our brethren. One man has one talent, another has another; no one talent is complete in itself, but each completes the other, when used for the benefit of the entire Christian community. When we practise charity towards one another in this manner, the current of our mutual love serves to purify us from the guilt of our shortcomings and prepares us to meet the judgement of God.

The alleluiatic verse comes from Psalm xlvi : " Alleluia, Alleluia. The Lord hath reigned over all the nations; God

---

[1] *Paradiso*, xxxi, 104.

sitteth on his holy throne. Alleluia." He has crushed his rebel subjects, that is, those apostate angels who at the dawn of creation refused to acknowledge him in his human nature as their head. He has caused this human nature to be seated on his holy throne, which to-day is called his, because it belongs to him by virtue of the hypostatic union with his divine nature, and the merits of his passion and death.

The verse before the Gospel is from St John (xiv 18) : " I will not leave you orphans ; I go and I come to you ; I will return to you soon with my grace, through my Holy Spirit and in my Eucharist, and your heart shall rejoice. Alleluia." This then is the source of all Christian joy—the continuous union with Jesus Christ through the sacraments of the Church.

The Gospel is taken from St John (xv 26, 27 ; and xvi 1-4). The mission of the Paraclete is to bear witness to the sanctity of Christ against the world which once condemned him to death. The Apostles and the Church are associated with him in this mission, since by their holiness and their fearless preaching, and by their practising the highest virtues under the most terrible trials, whether in the dungeon, at the stake, or upon the scaffold, they give unfailing testimony to the divine nature of the crucified Saviour.

The Offertory is the same as that for Ascension Day. As the sound of the trumpet accompanies Jesus on his way heavenwards, so this same sound will accompany him on the day of his second coming, when the dead shall rise from their graves and go forth to meet him. The trumpets of the angels also represent the preaching of the Gospel by the bishops and pastors of the Church. Indeed these are called in the Apocalypse the " Angels " of the respective Churches over which the Holy Ghost himself placed them, to feed the flock redeemed by Christ with his own blood.

In the Secret we beg that not only may the spotless offering of the Eucharist be for us a fount of purification, but that this cleansing in the waters of redemption may give renewed strength to our limbs so that we may be able to climb with alacrity the path to heaven. The ascent is steep, the air is rarefied and exhausting, so a sound heart is necessary. We shall certainly need the bread of the strong which infuses vigour into the weak. This bread is that which was placed before Elias when he was about to climb the rocky heights of Sinai;[1] it is the body of Christ himself.

The Communion is from our Lord's prayer at the Last Supper (John xvii 12-15) : Father, while I was with them, I kept them whom in thy inscrutable predestination thou

---

[1] Called also Horeb (3 Kings xix 6-8).—Tr.

entrustedst to me; none of them is lost but the son of perdition, and he only because he has obstinately willed it, despite all the efforts of my loving heart to save him. Now I come to thee; I pray not that thou shouldst take them out of the world, but that thou shouldst keep them from the evil spirit of the world.

This, then, is the will of God, that we should live, not indeed apart from the world, but apart from the spirit of the world. It is not necessary, nor would it always be permissible, to withdraw oneself from the society of one's fellowmen in order to live alone and so to flee from all danger. A Christian man, and especially a priest or a religious, lives in the world as long as God wills, but without belonging to it, or sharing in its spirit. Such a one is in the world as is a ray of the sun which enlightens and warms this sad earth without being stained by the crimes committed in its light.

In the Post-Communion we pray God to grant us the true eucharistic spirit, which is that of heartfelt and loving gratitude for the wondrous gifts which he has given us, and of humble and close union with Jesus in the Blessed Sacrament, in such a manner that he may live in us and that we may no longer live for ourselves, but for him.

The eucharistic spirit then is one of union with Christ, of humility, sacrifice, and silent recollection. These are the true effects of Holy Communion and the gifts of grace which the Church begs for from the Holy Ghost in the ancient consecratory anaphora : *ut quotquot ex hac altaris participatione sacrosanctum Filii tui Corpus et Sanguinem sumpserimus, omni benedictione coelesti et gratia repleamur.*

THE NIGHT VIGIL OF PENTECOST

Station at St John Lateran.

Although the sacrament of Baptism is entirely distinct from that of Confirmation, yet the latter takes its name of *Confirmatio* from the fact that the coming down of the Holy Ghost into the soul of the neophyte completes the work of his supernatural regeneration. Through its sacramental character it confers on him a more perfect likeness to Jesus Christ, impressing on his soul the final seal or ratification of his union with the divine Redeemer.

The word *Confirmatio* was used in Spain to denote also the invocation of the Holy Ghost in the Mass, *Confirmatio Sacramenti.* Hence the existing analogy between the epiklesis— that part of the Mass which begs from the Paraclete the fulness of his gifts upon those about to receive Holy Communion—and the sacrament of Confirmation, which in olden days was administered immediately after Baptism, shows very clearly the deep theological meaning hidden in the word *Confirmatio* as applied to this sacrament.

The link which unites these two sacraments explains why the ancient liturgies, and the Roman in particular, from the time of Tertullian, appointed the night vigils of Easter and Pentecost to be set apart for their solemn administration. In ancient times the sacred rite took place on this night in the Lateran exactly as on Easter Eve; but in the twelfth century, when the ceremony had already been anticipated on the afternoon of Holy Saturday, the Pope went at sunset to celebrate solemnly Vespers and Matins at St Peter's.

In private Masses the lessons, the Litany, etc., are omitted, and the Introit is recited as on the Wednesday after the Fourth Sunday in Lent on the occasion of the great baptismal scrutinies. The passage is from Ezechiel,[1] in which Christian baptism and the descent of the Holy Ghost on the faithful is clearly pre-announced. Literally the prophecy foretells the future lot of Israel, who, too, is destined to have a part in the kingdom of the Messias : *ubi intraverit plenitudo gentium tunc Israel salvus fiet;* but it may also be applied to every believing soul, to those whom the Apostle calls the *Israel Dei,* as distinguished from the Israel according to the flesh.

Inasmuch as the outpouring of the Holy Ghost is the supreme act of the love of God for man, so the final and definite act by which the soul turns away from God is called " sinning against the Holy Ghost." It is the Holy Ghost who determines within us the development of our spiritual life in accordance with our divine exemplar, Christ, and each time that this development is hindered, we resist the Holy Ghost, wherefore the Apostle exhorted his first followers not to grieve the divine Spirit who dwells in our souls and who is himself its supernatural life.

WHITSUN EVE

The vigiliary rite of Pentecost consisted, according to the original Roman type, of twelve lessons from the holy Scriptures—the Prophecies—as on Easter Eve. These were read in Greek as well as in Latin and were interspersed with the chanting of the prophetic " Odes " or Tracts, and of the pontifical collects. St Gregory reduced the number of the lessons to six, this number being retained unaltered, even when in the eighth century the lessons of the great paschal

---

[1] Ezech. xxxvi 23-26.

vigil were again increased to the symbolical number of twelve, consequent on the influence of the Gelasian Sacramentary, which returned to Rome with honour during the Frankish period.·

The first prophecy of to-night's vigil corresponds to the third of the Easter vigil and describes the sacrifice of Abraham. Isaac was offered up as a holocaust, but his life was not sacrificed upon the altar, for the Lord was satisfied with the willing offering of himself and made him the father of an innumerable people. Thus Jesus did not remain in the sepulchre as the victim of death, but was raised by his Father to a glorious life on the third day, and was made the firstborn of the redeemed and the head of the numberless family of the elect.

The collects which follow the prophecies are the same as in the Gregorian Sacramentary, except that the last one is out of place; for, originally, it was said after Psalm xli, which thus terminated the actual vigil. Moreover, the collect which formerly followed the sixth prophecy from Ezechiel has fallen into disuse through the negligence of the amanuenses.

After the first prophecy the priest recites this prayer : " O God, who in the deed of thy servant Abraham hast given to mankind an example of obedience; grant us both to break the stubbornness of our wills, and in all things to fulfil thy righteous commands. Through our Lord.''

The second prophecy corresponds to the fourth of Easter Eve; its teaching is embodied for us in the striking prayer which follows : " O God, who by the light of the New Testament hast expounded the miracles wrought in the first ages of the world, so that the Red Sea was an image of the sacred font, and the deliverance of the people from Egyptian bondage did prefigure the sacraments of the Christian people; grant that all nations who have now obtained the privilege of Israel by the merit of faith, may be born again by partaking of thy Spirit. Through our Lord.''

The third prophecy corresponds to the eleventh of the paschal vigil and introduces the great canticle of Deuteronomy which formed part of the Sabbath Office in the Synagogue. Then comes this beautiful prayer : " O God, the glory of the faithful and the life of the just, who by Moses thy servant didst teach us to sing sacred hymns; bestow on all nations the gift of thy mercy by granting them happiness and taking from them fear; so that the punishment with which they are threatened may turn to everlasting salvation. Through our Lord.''

The fourth prophecy with the Canticle of Isaias corresponds to the eighth of Holy Saturday.

The prayer helps us clearly to understand its mystical meaning: " O almighty and eternal God, who by thy only Son hast shown thyself the husbandman of thy Church; mercifully cultivate every branch which bringeth forth fruit in the same thy Christ, who is the true vine, that it may bring forth more fruit; let not the thorns of sin prevail against thy faithful, whom thou hast brought out of Egypt by the font of baptism; but like a vineyard, let them be strengthened by the grace of thy Spirit and bear abundant fruit for ever. Through the same Lord."

The fifth prophecy corresponds to the sixth of Easter Eve, and is followed by the prayer: " O God, who hast commanded us by the mouth of thy prophets to leave the things of this world, and to hasten after those that are eternal; grant that, by thy heavenly inspiration, we thy servants may fulfil what we know thou hast commanded. Through our Lord."

The sixth prophecy corresponds to the seventh of the paschal vigil, and has this appealing prayer: " O Lord God of hosts, who dost restore what is fallen down and keep what thou hast restored; increase the number of those who are to be renewed by the sanctification of thy holy name; that all who are washed in holy baptism may ever be governed by thy inspiration. Through our Lord."

This last prayer, which has a distinct baptismal character, at first immediately preceded the Litany which was sung as the procession descended to the baptistery. We say " descended " because this is the expression still used in the rubric of the Missal. As to its origin, it is well to bear in mind that since both the Lateran and the Vatican baptisteries were more or less on the same level as the two basilicas, it is possible that this word " descend " originally had reference to some baptistery in one of the cemeteries, for instance, in that of Priscilla, where as a matter of fact several subterranean baptisteries have been discovered.

THE PROCESSION TO THE BAPTISTERY

As the procession descends to the baptismal font, the Tract (Psalm xli 2-4) is chanted, as on Holy Saturday. " As the hart panteth after the fountains of waters; so my soul panteth after thee, O God. ℣. My soul has thirsted after the living God; when shall I come and appear before the face of God? ℣. My tears have been my bread day and night, whilst it is said to me daily: Where is thy God?"

Priest: The Lord be with you.

℞ : And with thy spirit.

℣ : Let us pray.

Prayer: " Grant we beseech thee, O almighty God: that

we who celebrate the solemnity of the gift of the Holy
Spirit, being inflamed with heavenly desires, may thirst after
the fountain of life. Through our Lord."

(The font is then blessed.)

The consecratory anaphora of the baptismal waters, the
ceremonies and rites of Christian Initiation, are all precisely
as those of the paschal vigil.

After the baptism the procession returns to the basilica
and the vigiliary Mass is celebrated. It has no Introit. The
ancient morning hymn *Gloria in excelsis* immediately follows
the Litany, which terminates the night Office, and is thus
restored to its original function, that of serving as a transition from the night vigil to the holy sacrifice of the Mass.

The Collect has reference to baptism : " Grant, we beseech
thee, O almighty God, that the splendour of thy brightness
may shine forth upon us ; and the light of thy light may by
the illumination of the Holy Ghost confirm the hearts of
those who have been born again by thy grace. Through
our Lord."

This light is faith, and it is the interior grace of the Holy
Ghost which effectually gives us the comprehension of the
things of God.

Then follows the Lesson (Acts xix 1-8) with the narrative
of the administering of Baptism and Confirmation by St Paul
at Ephesus to twelve of the former disciples of St John the
Baptist.

We may note here that according to the best exegetes
the expression used sometimes by St Luke, in the Acts of
the Apostles, of baptizing " in the name of Jesus " does not
necessarily imply that the Apostles in administering the
sacrament of baptism did not name all three persons of the
Blessed Trinity, according to the form taught them by their
divine Master, but, as St Thomas thought might have been
done, by special privilege that of Jesus alone. It merely
signifies that in contradistinction to the baptism of John,
baptism with the Trinitarian form is precisely the one
instituted by Christ and that which makes us spiritually one
with him.

The Blessed Trinity is invoked in baptism to denote that
by virtue of this sacrament the eternal Father raises us to
the dignity of adopted sons ; Jesus unites us so intimately
to himself that we become the mystical members of his body ;
the Holy Ghost then descends upon us and communicates to
us that divine life which befits the sons of God, the brethren
of Jesus Christ, and all the members of his mystical body.
The perfect worship of the Blessed Trinity is therefore the
first consequence of our initiation as Christians, and for this
reason the sacred liturgy celebrates immediately after the

Octave of Pentecost a solemn feast in honour of the most holy Trinity, the central mystery of all Catholic theology.

The alleluiatic verse is drawn from Psalm cxvii, and is followed by the Tract (Psalm cxvi) as on Easter Eve.

At the Gospel candles are not carried as usual, for the ceremony took place at night when the ambo was sufficiently lighted up by the great candle (*Eucharistia lucernaris*) which was blessed and lighted by the deacon at sunset on the preceding Saturday, at the commencement of the vigiliary Office. The custom was derived from that of the Synagogue and has been already described. Moreover, the Greek, the Ambrosian, and the Mozarabic rite of Toledo all keep the Office of the *Lucernarium* which daily precedes the singing of vespers.

The Gospel from St John (xiv 15-21) treats of the coming of the Holy Ghost and of his office as comforter and leader of souls in the way of truth. Jesus calls the Paraclete the "Spirit of truth," to show that he proceeds not from the Father alone, but also from the Word who is the truth of the Father and who proclaims him fully, so much so that St Luke in the Acts of the Apostles calls him simply the "Spirit of Jesus." It is well known that the Greek schismatics deny the loving procession of the Paraclete from the Father and the Son, as from a single living principle, which denial is contrary to the manifest teaching of the Gospel—" He shall receive of mine "[1]—and also to that of the Fathers both Eastern and Western.

For many centuries the Church used every means, Œcumenical Councils, apologists, embassies, to recall the Greeks to Catholic unity, but all was in vain. When, however, the sin against the Holy Ghost reached its full measure, the justice of God delayed not to strike the Church and the Byzantine Empire. On Whit-Sunday of the year 1453, the army of Mohammed II entered Constantinople and slew the Emperor and the Patriarch, as also the clergy and a great number of the populace who were thronging the Church of St Sophia. That grand Basilica of Justinian, which for nine centuries had been the scene of so many betrayals of the Catholic faith, was profaned by slaughter and turned into a Turkish mosque.

The Offertory is derived from Psalm ciii: "Send forth thy Spirit, and they shall be created; and thou shalt renew the face of the earth: may the glory of the Lord endure for ever, Alleluia."

The creation no less than the redemption is an act of God's love, and for this reason is attributed to the Holy Ghost,

---

[1] John xvi 14.

who is described in the Book of Genesis as " moving over
the waters " of chaos. It was the love of God which gave life
to primordial matter and drew from it the various orders of
creatures. So in the New Covenant the coming of the Holy
Ghost gave life to the body of the Church, and enabled it to
begin its mission, the continuation of that of Christ.

In the Secret we beseech God to sanctify the gifts we offer
and by the merits of the sacrifice to cleanse our hearts with
the fire of the Holy Ghost from all stains of sin. The
Paraclete is love and with the fire of his love destroys every
evil, wherefore Jesus said in speaking of Mary of Magdala :
" Many sins are forgiven her, because she hath loved much."[1]

According to the traditional Roman custom the commemoration of to-day's feast is introduced into the anaphora
and is repeated throughout the Octave of Pentecost : " Who
going up above all the heavens, and sitting at thy right hand,
on this day sent forth the Holy Ghost, as he had promised,
on the children of adoption. Wherefore does the whole world
rejoice with exceeding great joy all the earth over." The
whole world rejoices, and well it may, for it is the Holy Ghost
himself who transforms and raises the faithful follower of
Christ to the dignity of a son of God, and this not by an
outward or legal adoption, as is customary among men, but
because God shares with him his own life and his own
sanctity by means of his divine Spirit.

Also at the beginning of the Apostolic diptychs in the
Preface within the Action mention is made of the mystery
of Pentecost : " Communicating and keeping the most holy
day of Pentecost, whereon the Holy Ghost appeared to the
Apostles in countless tongues."

. In the prayer in which the priest commends to God the
donors of the offerings and which ends the first part of the
diptychs—*prius ergo oblationes commendandae sunt,* wrote
Pope Innocent I in his famous letter to Decentius of Gubbio
—the neophytes are named, who on this night received
baptism and confirmation, and who were therefore about
to make their first Communion at the Mass : " We therefore
beseech thee, O Lord, to be appeased, and to receive this
offering which we, thy servants, and also thy whole household, do make unto thee on behalf of these also whom thou
hast vouchsafed to bring to a new birth by water and the
Holy Ghost, giving them remission of all their sins."

The antiphon for the Communion is very appropriate to this
season. On this last festival of the paschal cycle is repeated
the cry of Jesus which he uttered on the last day of the feast
of Tabernacles, when the priests went to draw water from the

---

[1] Luke vii 47.

fountain of Siloe.[1] The water of grace of which Jesus here speaks is a symbol of the Holy Ghost, and more especially of the waters of baptism, which he endows with their life-giving virtue. This is why the Latin Church solemnly administers the sacrament of baptism on the Eve of Pentecost as well as on Easter Eve.

In the Post-Communion we beg that the Holy Spirit may purify our hearts by the flames of his love, by the gift of contrition and by holy zeal. Nor should these flames, which burn out our vices and cleanse our souls, inspire us with fear. The Paraclete tempers their fierceness with the cool and refreshing dew of his consolations, that interior dew which nourishes the flowers and the fruits of holiness.

WHIT-SUNDAY

Station at St Peter.

On this day Christ, risen from the grave and seated at the right hand of the Father, communicates his own divine life to the members of his mystical body through the outpouring of the Holy Ghost. So the Church, which until this moment has been confined within the narrow walls of the upper room, like an infant in its cradle, having attained its full development, now first appears before the world, glowing with holiness and truth. The Holy Spirit, which flows to-day through her pure limbs, fills her with the life of Christ, associating her with his teaching and with his work of redemption, whence St Paul has well said that the apostolic labours of those who preach the Gospel have their share in this very work; indeed, the Saviour told the same Apostle on the road to Damascus that it was he himself who was being persecuted and who suffered in the members of his Church.

Peter is the leader around whom gathers the little flock of Sion on this first Christian Pentecost, and he inaugurates to-day his pontifical primacy when he announces for the first time the Gospel message to the representatives of the various nations, without distinction of race or nationality, of country or State. It is Peter, too, who in the name of the whole Church protests against the false and vulgar accusation of drunkenness brought against the Apostles, and, lastly, it is he who consequent on that first sermon converts and baptizes the first three thousand neophytes, who thus are added to the household of Christ.

For this reason the station, unlike that of Easter Sunday, is held to-day at the Vatican Basilica where the Pope used

---

[1] John vii 37-39.

formerly to celebrate the first Vespers, the night vigil and the Mass. According to the Roman rite for the greater solemnities of the year, the night Office of the vigil on this occasion was duplicated; it was carried out first in the crypt where the tomb of the Apostle was venerated, and afterwards at the high altar. At this latter celebration, which was the more solemn of the two, the Canons sang the first lesson, the Cardinals the second, and the Pope himself the third. After the Mass the Pontiff was crowned with the *regnum,* and returned in procession to the Lateran.

The Introit, which is taken from the Book of Wisdom (i 7), should be heard, in order to be fully appreciated, together with the majestic and joyful melody which the ancient Gregorian music has allotted to it. It is well known that all the present texts of the Missal and of the Breviary have beautiful melodies attached to them. As no one, for instance, would desire to judge of a opera simply by reading the *libretto* of the author, but would also wish to hear the music and see the full effect of the *mise-en-scène,* so, in order thoroughly to appreciate the sense of beauty and inspiration, the powerful influence produced by the sacred liturgy on Christian people, it is necessary to see it performed in the full splendour of its architectural setting, of the clergy in their vestments, of the music, the singing, and the ritual, and not to judge of it merely from a curtailed and simplified presentment.

" The Spirit of the Lord hath filled the whole earth, Alleluia ; and that which containeth all things hath knowledge of the voice, Alleluia, Alleluia, Alleluia."

This is said especially of the wisdom and goodness of which God has given us such striking proofs in the creation, but it applies still more to the supernatural order to which he has raised us. The Lord has poured forth his Paraclete upon all Christians ; the preaching of the Gospel by means of which the Holy Ghost initiates the believer to the intimate secrets of the Godhead has resounded throughout all countries to the uttermost ends of the earth, and to-day, by means of her catechism, a simple-hearted old peasant woman knows more with regard to God and her last end than all the ancient sages of Greece and of Rome.

The beautiful Antiphon is from Psalm lxvii : " Let God arise, and let his enemies be scattered ; and let them that hate him flee before his face."

This martial song is well suited to the descent of the Holy Ghost. He is come to vindicate the innocence of Jesus, and this he does by filling the Church with such surpassing sanctity that it becomes, as it were, a fire prefiguring the final judgement on the enemies of God. He who does not

believe nor love is already judged by the Paraclete. Such
a one has of his own self rejected his salvation.

The Collect is as follows : " O God, who on this day didst
instruct the hearts of the faithful by the light of the Holy
Spirit; grant that by the same Spirit we may relish what is
right, and ever rejoice in his consolation. Through our
Lord."

The Church here asks for two things. The first that we
may have that desire for the things of God which denotes a
certain spiritual wellbeing, and is the result of the interior
life maintained by the Paraclete in our souls. The second
that we may receive the consolation of the Holy Spirit, who
is called the Paraclete, precisely because Jesus has given
him to us, so that through his spiritual consolations he may
strengthen us to endure the warfare of the Christian life and
may keep us back from seeking comfort in the hurtful
pleasures of our fallen nature.

In the Lesson (Acts ii 1-11) is described the miraculous
descent of the Holy Ghost upon the Apostles. We should
carefully note the circumstances in which it took place. The
eleven disciples had prepared themselves by a retreat of ten
days in company with and under the motherly care of the
Blessed Virgin. They lived together in great peace and
harmony, under the authority and rule of Peter. About the
third hour of the day they were in prayer, when the Holy
Ghost descended upon them in the form of tongues of fire.
All these things should teach us a spirit of recollection,
tender devotion to the Blessed Virgin, perfect obedience to
the Vicar of Christ, a great love of peace and brotherly
concord, even to the sacrificing of our own too susceptible
personality, and an untiring zeal for prayer.

Such are the best conditions for obtaining the gift of the
love of God; and this is demanded of us too, so that through
the Holy Ghost we may become Apostles to the benefit of our
fellow-men.

The alleluiatic verse comes from Psalm ciii, as does also
the Offertory of Whitsun Eve. The Holy Ghost " renews
the face of the earth," because from being sons of Adam
who sinned, he raises us to the highest dignity of sons of
God himself. The reign of sin and the rule of servitude
being ended, the Messianic era begins. Nature itself seems
to hasten by its desires that day in which it will be freed
from the shame to which the sinner now subjects it when he
uses it for his evil ends and bends it to serve his passions.
St Paul with powerful imagery describes creation yearning
with far-seeing gaze for its deliverer. *Exspectatio enim
creaturae revelationem filiorum Dei exspectat.* The day of
reckoning will come at length, when all nature shall rise up

in arms and together with its Creator shall take vengeance on its unrighteous oppressor. *Et armabit creaturam ad ultionem inimicorum, et pugnabit pro illo orbis terrarum contra insensatos.*

This rehabilitation of creation, however, has already begun, since Christ *mundum volens adventu suo piissimo consecrare,* as the Church expresses it in the Martyrology for Christmas, ordained that the earth should be the scene of the mysteries of his life, his passion, and his death. He has also raised matter to the dignity of being the means through which the grace of the Holy Ghost is given to the faithful in the sacraments and sacramentals. Thus nature, which at first by its allurements tempted and led man astray and was therefore involved in his curse, is consecrated afresh by the Paraclete in the New Covenant and co-operates in the sanctification of those who use it rightly with faith and gratitude to God its Creator.

The verse before the Gospel is both by its wording and its rhythm one of the finest of the whole Gregorian Antiphonary. The liturgy makes use of it in the consecration of new altars, when five small candles placed in the form of a cross, each standing on as many grains of incense, are lighted on the altar-stone, which has already been anointed with the sacred chrism. The whole altar then appears to be wrapped in flames, recalling the heavenly fire which in the Old Covenant sometimes consumed the victims of the holocaust.

" Come, O Holy Spirit, fill the hearts of thy faithful;" and such are all Christians, for they have been definitely consecrated by baptism in the name of the Blessed Trinity to the glory of the Father, and of the Son, and of the Holy Ghost. "Kindle in them the fire of thy love," or rather, be thou thyself this inextinguishable flame which destroys in our hearts all the dross, all the refuse, all that which is not pure gold and does not serve, as St Paul says, to the building up within us of a divine and spiritual temple.

The rubric prescribes that while this devout invocation to the Holy Ghost is being sung all should kneel.

The Sequence which is given in our present Missal is attributed by some to Innocent III, but it replaces another of great beauty : " *Sancti Spiritus adsit nobis gratia,* which is mentioned in the *Ordines Romani* of the fifteenth century. The author of this latter prose composition was the famous monk Notker, of whom it is related that when Innocent III in 1215 heard his melodious and deeply devotional work, he marvelled that the author had not already been canonized. Here is the celebrated composition, which at one time found a place in the Roman Missal. It should be noted that it is a piece of rhythmical and musical prose in imitation of that

kind of composition which originated at Byzantium. The
words by themselves are not so impressive, they should be
heard with their musical setting.

> Sancti Spiritus
> Adsit nobis gratia,
>   Quae corda nostra sibi
> Faciat habitaculum,
>   Expulsis inde cunctis
> Vitiis spiritualibus.
>   Spiritus alme, illustrator hominum,
> Horridas nostrae mentis
>   Purga tenebras.
> Amator, sancte sensatorum
>   Semper cogitatuum,
> Infunde unctionem tuam
>   Clemens nostris sensibus.
> Tu, purificator omnium
>   Flagitiorum, Spiritus,
> Purifica nostri oculum
>   Interioris hominis,
> Ut videri supremus
>   Genitor possit a nobis,
> Mundi cordis quem soli
>   Cernere possunt oculi.
> Prophetas tu inspirasti, ut praeconia
> Christi praecinuissent inclita.
> Apostolos confortasti, ut trophaeum
> Christi per totum mundum veherent.
> Quando machinam per Verbum suum
> Fecit Deus coeli, terrae, maris,
> Tu, super aquas foturus eas, numen
> Tuum expandisti, Spiritus.
> Tu animabus vivificandis
> Aquas foecundas.
> Tu adspirando da spiritales
> Esse homines.
> Tu divisum per linguas mundum
> Et ritus adunasti, Spiritus.
> Idololatras ad cultum Dei revocas,
> Magistrorum optime.
> Ergo nos supplicantes tibi
> Exaudi propitius, sancte Spiritus,
> Sine quo preces omnes cassae
> Creduntur et indignae Dei auribus.
> Tu, qui omnium saeculorum sanctos
> Tui numinis docuisti instinctu,
> Amplectendo spiritus,
> Ipse hodie Apostolos Christi
> Donans munere insolito
> Et cunctis inaudito saeculis
> Hunc diem gloriosum fecisti.

May the Holy Spirit with his grace assist us,
That our hearts may become his dwelling-place,
All evil inclinations thence cast out.
Kindly Spirit, enlightening all men,
Drive far away the dark shadows from our minds,
Thou who delightest in the humble and meek,
Mercifully let thy holy unction

Down upon our senses fall.
O Holy Spirit, who dost wash all sins away,
Cleanse the vision of our inmost being
That we may behold our Father above,
Upon whom the pure in heart alone may gaze.
Thou didst inspire the prophets of old to sing
The great mysteries of Christ their redeemer.
Thou didst give strength to the holy Apostles
To carry his ensign throughout the wide world.
When God by his Word called out of nothing
The heavens, the earth, and the seas,
Thou, O Spirit, didst hover over the waters
And, giving them life, didst render them fruitful.
By thy breath, O Paraclete, thou grantest to us
Thy children in spirit and truth to become.
Thou, O Spirit, hast now made into one
The world divided by language and custom.
Thou dost reclaim, O best of all teachers,
The idolatrous heathen to the worship of God.
Mercifully hear us who cry unto thee,
O Holy Spirit, without whose gracious help
Our prayers are but vain and unworthy of answer.
Thou who hast taught through the ages thy Saints
And with thine own divine self ever filled them,
To-day hast enriched with a gift unheard of before
The Apostles of Christ and made ever glorious this festival
day.

The following is the text of the Sequence incorporated in the Roman Missal at the reform of Pius V :

Veni, Sancte Spiritus,
Et emitte caelitus
  Lucis tuae radium.

Holy Spirit, Lord of light,
From thy clear celestial height
  Thy pure beaming radiance give.

Veni, Pater pauperum,
Veni, dator munerum,
  Veni, lumen cordium.

Come, thou Father of the poor !
Come with treasures which endure !
  Come, thou light of all who live !

Consolator optime,
Dulcis hospes animae,
  Dulce refrigerium.

Thou of all consolers best,
Visiting the troubled breast,
  Dost refreshing peace bestow.

In labore requies,
In aestu temperies,
  In fletu solatium.

Thou in toil art comfort sweet,
Pleasant coolness in the heat,
  Solace in the midst of woe.

O Lux beatissima,
Reple cordis intima
  Tuorum fidelium.

Light immortal, light divine,
Visit thou these hearts of thine,
  And our inmost being fill.

Sine tuo numine,
Nihil est in homine
  Nihil est innoxium.

If thou take thy grace away,
Nothing pure in man will stay;
  All his good is turned to ill.

Lava quod est sordidum,
Riga quod est aridum,
  Sana quod est saucium.

Heal our wounds, our strength renew,
On our dryness pour thy dew,
  Wash the stains of guilt away.

Flecte quod est rigidum,	Bend the stubborn heart and will,
Fove quod est frigidum,	Melt the frozen, warm the chill,
Rege quod est devium.	Guide the steps that go astray.

Da tuis fidelibus,	Thou, on those who evermore
In te confidentibus,	Thee confess and thee adore,
Sacrum septenarium.	In thy sevenfold gifts descend.

Da virtutis meritum,	Give them comfort when they die,
Da salutis exitum,	Give them life with thee on high,
Da perenne gaudium.	Give them joys which never end.
Amen. Alleluia.	Amen. Alleluia.

This Sequence is repeated daily throughout the Octave.

The Gospel is derived from St John (xiv 23-31). If any man truly loves Jesus in such a measure that the fire of this divine love has consumed in him all irregular and earthly affections, then the kingdom of God can attain its full and lasting development in his heart. The Blessed Trinity takes up its mystical abode in him through a firm and intimate union of his soul with God. The bond of this union between the soul, the bride of Christ, and the Bridegroom is the Holy Ghost, who by the superabundance of his gifts disposes the chosen soul for the blessed day of her espousals with God. Such a state, the mystics tell us, is highly exalted and few are the souls that attain thereto, for the many are wanting in generosity in giving themselves wholly to God and in allowing themselves to be freely borne upon the wings of his Spirit to heights far beyond our poor mortal nature.

Jesus goes on in the Gospel to speak of the mission of the Paraclete among the faithful. He is to complete the spiritual training of the Apostles and by the unfailing help which he gives to the Church *docens,* to impress a permanent character on the preaching of the Gospel of the Kingdom established for the salvation of souls.

The Apostles are full of sorrow because the hour of Christ's leaving them draws so near. Their judgement is obscured by a purely human reasoning, for they fail to rise above it to the higher regions of faith, so as to behold Christ's sacred humanity glorified by the Father. This glorification of the head implies also that of the members, therefore the Apostles should have rejoiced instead of grieving at their Master's going.

We need not dwell upon the circumstances of his leaving this world, that is to say, the hatred of Satan shown by his inciting his followers to put Jesus to death. No leaf falls from the tree without God's permission. Christ was not overcome by the rage of the devil, who of himself had no power nor right over him. The death of Christ was not by will of the Jews nor of Satan, their father, but because he of his own free will took upon himself the sins of the whole world, offering himself to God on the altar of the cross, a voluntary and pleasing victim, a sacrifice of adoration to the sanctity of the Father.

The Offertory is from Psalm lxvii. That which took place in the upper room at Jerusalem—the first Christian church—was not of a transitory order; it was the beginning of a lasting covenant of love and redemption, since by means of the Apostles God gave to the rest of the faithful this shining σφραγίς, that is, this spiritual and precious seal which is the pledge of our adoption as sons of God. The Christian people thus become a royal race. They offer to the Lord gifts worthy of him—this is the moment of the Offertory—and these very gifts are symbolized by the oblations which are now being brought to the altar, and by virtue of which the sacrifice of the people is united to that of Christ, just as in the chalice the water becomes mingled with the wine.

The Secret is the same as that of the Eve. In it we ask of God two things : firstly, that the fire of the Holy Ghost may consume the holocaust of our hearts, which, through his gift of compassion, are now wholly consecrated to God and, as a continual sacrifice, beat for him alone. Secondly, we ask that the same Holy Ghost may descend upon the offerings which we have now laid on the altar, so that the feeling of earnest devotion with which he himself inspires us may make this Holy Eucharist a sacrament efficacious and profitable for our sanctification.

During the entire Octave of Pentecost the commemorations of the Holy Ghost, of which we have already spoken in the Mass of the vigil, are inserted in the Canon. On this occasion the memory of that first Christian Pentecost in the upper room on Mount Sion is all the more touching when we call to mind the special work performed by the Holy Ghost on Calvary. Then in the fire of his ineffable sanctity he consumed the divine victim who *per Spiritum Sanctum semetipsum obtulit immaculatum Deo.*

For this reason the Fathers when they invoked the Paraclete in the ancient eucharistic epikleses prayed that he would descend upon the altar and overshadow the sacred gifts as *testis passionum Christi tui.* This is always the mission of the Holy Ghost : *Ille testimonium perhibebit de me.* He who had a full understanding of the ineffable martyrdom of the Crucifixion, since he had sanctified it in his love, must now bear witness thereto before the world. This he does by strengthening in our souls the effects of the redemption through the outpouring of his gifts of grace.

The Communion is taken from the Lesson (Acts ii 2-4) : A sound was heard as of a mighty wind coming. The Apostles were filled with the Holy Ghost, and began to speak of the wonderful works of God. The mighty wind is a symbol both of the force and of the gentleness of the action of the Holy Ghost; of force, for who can stand against God? of gentleness, because this action does not in any way violate our free will, for it is God himself who shapes and directs it according to his pleasure. He does not influence us against our will—that would be doing it violence—but moves us to desire that which is right.

The Post-Communion is similar to that of the vigiliary Mass. The Holy Ghost is likened to a gentle dew which, whilst it cleanses the stains of our hearts, renders them fruitful of good actions. Without this dew our hearts would be like a land scorched by the sun; the fierce fire of our passions dries up within us every pure spring, and leaves them as a stony desert where no blade of grass can grow. Then comes the Holy Ghost and quenches these evil flames, the burning soil of the heart receives the kindly dew from heaven, and the Paraclete sows therein the seed of every great and noble virtue.

Tertullian describes the Christian as formed of a body, a soul, and the Holy Ghost. The phrase is somewhat paradoxical, but must be interpreted in the sense intended by its author. The Holy Ghost it is who by his grace actually raises the soul to the supernatural state of an adopted child of God. It is the working of the Paraclete which determines all our meritorious acts, in such a manner that when we call upon Jesus, when we mourn at his feet, when we suffer, when we work for God, it is always the Holy Ghost who prays, who mourns, who works in us. He, too, *testimonium reddit spiritui nostro quod sumus filii Dei;* indeed it is actually the *Spiritum Filii sui* which God has infused into us, in order that we may share together with Christ the grace of being his well-beloved children. This same Spirit, which dwells in us during our life and impels us towards heaven, does not cease to work in us at our death. At the last day he requires the restoration of his mystical temple within the Christian soul, and this *propter inhabitantem Spiritum ejus in nobis.*

MONDAY IN WHITSUN WEEK

Station at the Apostles, at the Eudoxian Title " ad Vincula."

Originally the feast of Pentecost brought to an end in Rome the fifty days of the Easter celebrations and introduced the fast of the Ember Days of the summer quarter. Afterwards it became customary to continue the festivity for two more days, the Monday and the Tuesday, and, finally, after the time of St Leo the Great it was extended like the Octave of Easter through the entire week. In order to conform to this deliberate design of making the two feasts equal, the station to-day should have been at St Peter's; but, in order to avoid having two stations at the Vatican on successive days, the ancient Basilica *ad Vincula* was preferred, which in olden times was dedicated to the two Princes of the Apostles, and where the chains of St Peter are still venerated.

The Introit, which St Thomas Aquinas made famous in later days through his Office of Corpus Christi, comes from Psalm lxxx, and has reference to the neophytes who yesterday tasted the cup of milk and honey given to them after their baptism and first communion. " The Lord fed them with the fat of wheat "—this signifies the Holy Eucharist, which together with his divine nature gives us also the sacred humanity of Christ, the choicest part of the abundant wheat, which here symbolizes the human race.,

We pray in the Collect that God would grant to his people the gift of the Holy Ghost even as he had done to his Apostles. The coming of the Paraclete into the soul pre-supposes the gift of faith and is intended to enrich it with another most precious grace, that of peace. This is the peace that Jesus calls *pax sua;* for the Paraclete, as he proceeds from the Father, proceeds also from the Son. This peace is the bond which unites the soul to God; in other words it is love, it is sanctifying grace. Hence St Paul, in enumerating the fruits of the Holy Ghost, rightly named in the first place peace, and then the joy which immediately proceeds from it.

The Lesson, from the Acts of the Apostles (x 42-48), is a portion of St Peter's discourse in the house of the centurion Cornelius. It is a decisive moment. The time has come to decide whether the new religion shall remain a Jewish spiritual movement within the gates of Israel or whether, by breaking down the barriers of nationalism, Christ shall be proclaimed to the whole world without distinction or monopoly of race. God himself decides this great question by a miracle and pours forth his Spirit upon the Gentiles. The evangelization of the heathen world is specially reserved to Paul, the Apostle of the eleventh hour. But, as the first step must be taken by the head of the Church, it is Peter who plays the most important part on this occasion. Paul holds an honoured place, but the principle of authority is affirmed. Peter, by God's command, is the first to preach the Gospel to the Gentiles, who to-day are admitted to holy baptism on his responsibility.

The alleluiatic verse, drawn from the Acts, tells of the

Apostles "speaking in divers tongues the wonderful works of God." The rest is as in yesterday's Mass.

The Gospel (John iii 16-21) is taken from the words of our Lord to Nicodemus, when he spoke with him by night, and told him that it was necessary for a man to be born again spiritually of water and of the Holy Ghost. The Holy Ghost is love, wherefore to his power is attributed also the Incarnation of the Son of God in the womb of the Blessed Virgin for the redemption of mankind. To-day's Gospel makes clear to us the ill-will of the world, which scornfully refuses to love God in return for his love, and sinning thus against the Holy Ghost, renders itself deserving of final reprobation. The contrast is overwhelming—on the part of God, light, truth, holiness and love; on the part of man, voluntary blindness, malice, darkness and falsehood. Should this not fill us with a horror of the spirit of the world?

The Offertory is the same as that of Easter Tuesday. The Lord thundered from heaven in his indignation against Satan, who held the human race in bondage. The earth trembled, the mountains opened, and the fountains of water appeared. These are the waters of baptism; nature is once more made the servant of man, and by the grace of the Sacrament becomes the instrument of his inward purification.

The prayer over the oblations is very grand : " In thy mercy, O Lord, we beseech thee, hallow these gifts; receive this spiritual victim which we offer up; and make of us, too, an eternal gift to thee. Through our Lord."

The Communion is from the Gospel of St John (xiv 26) and contains the promise of the coming of the Holy Ghost together with the assurance of his special help, so that the Church may lose nothing of the divine deposit of truth entrusted to her. Therefore, in the history of Catholic doctrine, beyond the New Testament Scriptures and the sacred tradition of the Church, there have been neither facts forgotten nor truths newly discovered. The Holy Ghost still gives life and strength to the preaching of the Gospel of the Kingdom, to which nothing can be added and from which nothing can be taken away.

In the Post-Communion we beseech God to defend us by the merits of heavenly mysteries from the rage of our enemies. Indeed, if the blood of a lamb sprinkled on the doors of the Israelites sufficed to save them from the sword of the Angel of Death, how much more efficacious will not be the blood of Christ, which we have just received in Holy Communion?

The grace granted to the Gentiles of receiving the gifts of the Holy Ghost even before they were baptized was a sign altogether extraordinary, but necessary at that moment in order to decide the Church to open her doors to all nations. Nevertheless, this outpouring of the grace of the Paraclete, the effect of that form of spiritual baptism known to theologians as the baptism of desire, did not in any way dispense those first converts from receiving in the usual manner the baptism of water as ordained by Christ.

The Incarnation and Redemption, being the work of divine love, are attributed to the Holy Ghost, inasmuch as the fire of the Paraclete sanctified and consumed the sinless victim offered on the cross for the salvation of men. To-day's Gospel, in order to impress this thought more clearly on our minds, shows the immense contrast between God and man. God so loves the world that, in order to save it, he sacrifices his only-begotten Son, whilst mankind repays this supreme love with utter ingratitude and obstinately chooses darkness rather than light.

TUESDAY IN WHITSUN WEEK

Station at St Anastasia.

The titular church of St Anastasia, once the Court church during the Byzantine period, is chosen for to-day's station instead of the Basilica of St Paul, as the latter is too far out for a procession at this season of the year, when the sun's rays already fall scorchingly on the Eternal City. The Introit, too, of the Mass, emanating from the Apocryphal books of Esdras, which were altogether discredited in Rome, seems to point to a Greek origin, or at least to Greek influence, and thus supplies us with a valuable date for determining when the Octave of Pentecost first assumed the importance which is now given to it in the Missal.

The Introit (4 Esdras ii) is as follows: " Receive the joy of your glory, Alleluia; giving thanks to God, Alleluia; who hath called you to a heavenly kingdom, Alleluia, Alleluia, Alleluia." The Christian must indeed fully realize the dignity of his state, and never permit himself a thought unworthy of his rank as a son of God the most High.

To this is added a verse from Psalm lxxvii: " Attend, O my people, to my law; incline your ears to the words of my mouth."

Then comes the Collect: "Grant, we beseech thee, O Lord, that the power of the Holy Ghost may be ever present to us, mercifully cleansing our hearts and keeping them from all harm. Through our Lord." What succinct eloquence and depth of meaning do we not find in the ancient prayers of the Church! The purification which is spoken of here is brought about by the fire of divine love which burns and consumes in our heart all that is not pure gold : in other words, all that is not given to God.

The Lesson, from the Acts of the Apostles (viii 14-17), is very important from the dogmatic point of view, since it shows that whilst the deacons or any other could administer the sacrament of Baptism, yet the Apostles and their successors alone could administer that of Confirmation. Besides this great dogmatic fact we must note also the liturgical value of the expression : *Oraverunt pro ipsis ut acciperent Spiritum Sanctum.* This prayer was not merely one said privately previous to the administration of the sacrament of Confirmation, but, as the ancient liturgies tell us, a true sacramental epiklesis which accompanied the imposition of the hands of the Apostles, and in all probability also the anointing on the head with the sacred chrism of the Paraclete *in quo signati estis,* as the Apostle says to his flock.

The alleluiatic verse is the same as that for the Communion of yesterday : " Alleluia, Alleluia. The Holy Ghost shall teach you whatsoever I shall have said to you, Alleluia." All the rest is as on Whit-Sunday.

The Gospel lessons throughout this week all speak to us of Christ's love for the human race and represent our divine Redeemer under the most attractive figures ; now as the compassionate shepherd, and again as the worker of miracles who heals the paralyzed and those stricken with fever. At first it is hard to see the connection between these Gospel lessons and Whitsun Week ; but as this Octave was more or less introduced in Rome during the Byzantine period, and as in the Greek rite the Sundays after Easter have for their Gospels passages telling of the Good Shepherd, the paralytic, etc., so it is probable that when the Apostolic See had finished its own series of Easter lessons taken exclusively from our Lord's discourse at the Last Supper, as given by St John, it turned to the Greek liturgy in order to supply those required for the Octave of Pentecost.

To-day's Gospel (John x 1-10) speaks of the supreme mission of Jesus Christ, sent by God and consecrated by the plenitude of the grace of the Holy Ghost for the redemption of the world. He who presents himself before men and assumes to himself this office of teacher without a like heavenly call will be doing but a useless and harmful work, whereas nothing will be able to resist the powerful influence of the Gospel message, destined to bring everlasting life to all who believe.

Our Lord is here placed before us under the touching symbol of the Good Shepherd. He gives us the rules by which we may discern the only true religion from false sects.

In the first place the founders and propagators of these latter are robbers who have stealthily made their way into the fold of another where they had no right to enter and have destroyed many of the flock. They have not entered by the door, but have crept in another way—that is, by illicit means, by fraud and hypocrisy. There is no confidence nor affection between them and the sheep; they have thrust themselves upon them by violence, and have not gained them by love. The lives of such would-be reformers have been shameful; they have indeed driven the flock, and have not gone before them to lead them by the example of a holy life. The end of such attempts at reform has been an immense disaster and a hecatomb of souls.

From these indications given to us in the Gospel can we not clearly discern the origin, character and history of all heresies, from the *gnosis* of early days down to the modernism of our own times? Jesus alone is the Good Shepherd who draws our hearts to his own by the union of sacred love. He goes before us teaching us by his example, and leading us to the rich pastures of the holy sacraments and of his divine grace.

The Offertory is identical with that of Wednesday in Easter Week. The manna which feeds the faithful is of heavenly origin and strengthens us that we may live and strive for heaven. The Eucharist is called the " bread of angels "; because, as in heaven, the saints feed on the clear vision of God in the light of his glory, so on earth we attain to a foretaste of this happiness in Holy Communion through the light of our faith.

The Secret distinguishes between the Sacrifice of the Mass and Holy Communion. The oblation of the Sacrifice is intended to obtain for us from God the grace of interior sanctification, so that by thus receiving our Lord more worthily, our Communion may be the more fruitful.

Having received through Holy Communion the gifts of the Holy Ghost we recall in the antiphon the promise made to us by Christ at the Last Supper. " The Spirit," he said, " who proceedeth from the Father, he shall glorify me." We ourselves are witnesses of this glorification; indeed, we do more than bear witness, for we have an active part therein, since we have seen how at the invocation of the divine power upon the oblations laid on the altar there is accomplished the miracle of their transubstantiation into the Body and Blood of Jesus Christ our Lord. That which the words of the Gospel have already taught us: " This is my body, this is my blood " is now confirmed by the Holy Ghost, for his grace is poured out on us at the moment of our communion with the victim immolated on the altar. It follows that the

Blessed Sacrament, whilst it causes us to share in the saving death of Christ, unites us at the same time with the Holy Ghost in his perfect life of sanctity and glory.

The Post-Communion expresses in different words the same idea which recurs so constantly during to-day's Mass—that the grace of the Holy Ghost is the means through which we receive remission of our sins. The sense of this is clear. Sin is like a frost which contracts and hardens the heart. When we sin, it is as though we introduced into the construction of our spiritual edifice waste material, wood and sticks in the place of gold and stone. The fire of the Holy Ghost descends and consumes all this rubble, which takes up space for no purpose. The ice melts, and the heart is cleansed from its stains. Once more we recall to mind that which the Saviour said of the Magdalen : " Many sins are forgiven her, because she hath loved much."[1]

During the Octave of Pentecost the Church celebrates more especially the glories of the grace of the Holy Ghost and his secret work of sanctification in the mystical body of Christ. Thus to-day she repeats in the verse for the Communion the words of our Lord : " The Spirit who proceedeth from the Father, he shall glorify me," and this glorification consists chiefly in our sanctification and in the growth of the Kingdom of God in our souls.

EMBER WEDNESDAY IN WHITSUN WEEK

Station at St Mary Major.

In spite of the solemn Ember fast of the summer quarter to-day's stational Mass bears a distinctly festal character and recalls the time when, a little later than St Leo the Great, a solemn Octave having been granted to the festival of Pentecost similar to that of Easter, the fast was postponed for a few weeks. During several centuries the two Roman traditions disputed the supremacy, but finally in the eleventh century Gregory VII, whilst at the same time preserving the festal tone of the Office of the Octave, re-established the Ember Days in their proper place, that is, immediately after Tuesday in Whitsun Week.

The station is at St Mary Major, as is the rule in Rome whenever the scrutinies of the candidates for Holy Orders are to take place. The Mass with its two lessons from the Acts of the Apostles preserves a record of the ancient stational Masses of the fourth and sixth Ferias throughout the year, when, before the Gospel, two other lessons were read, one

[1] Luke vii 47.

from the Old Testament and one from the New. It is important to notice that many centuries before the institution of the feast of Corpus Christi, the Roman Liturgy had already directed the thoughts and devotion of the people to this mystery of love immediately after the solemnity of Pentecost, hence the Introit and the Gospel of to-day refer in an especial manner to the Blessed Sacrament.

The Introit is taken from Psalm lxvii, which is itself inspired by the canticle of Debbora (Judges v) : " O God, when thou didst go forth in the sight of thy people, making a passage for them, dwelling amongst them, Alleluia : the earth was moved, the heavens dropped, Alleluia, Alleluia. Let God arise, and let his enemies be scattered : and let them that hate him flee from before his face."

As the column of cloud and of fire preceded Israel in the desert, so now the Holy Ghost is the guide of our souls in the desert of this world. There is no longer an exterior sign, but the inward guidance of the Paraclete, turning our minds to God.

After the *Kyrie eleison,* instead of the *Gloria in Excelsis,* the first Collect is recited, in which we earnestly beg for the graces of the Comforter, so that we may not only understand but still more practise the truth, which is holiness.

" May our hearts be enlightened, O Lord, we beseech thee, by the Comforter, who proceedeth from thee ; and may he guide us unto all truth, even as thy Son promised : who liveth . . . in the unity of the same."

In the first lesson (Acts ii 14-21) the prophet Joel,[1] in the passage quoted by St Peter, describes in one great prophetic vision the inauguration and the consummation of the Messianic Kingdom. This must not be taken to mean that on the day of Pentecost the Apostles believed and preached that the final *parousia* was imminent. This was not possible, for they had received from our Lord the gift of understanding the Scriptures, and could not therefore be deceived into believing the end of the world to be near at hand, which after twenty centuries of Christianity has not yet come to pass.

The words of Joel simply mean that the Kingdom of the Messias, that is, the Church, which lives through the ages, represents the final and definite state of redeemed humanity, which period will be immediately followed by the universal judgement. In other words the gifts of the Holy Ghost poured out upon the Apostles on the day of Pentecost were not reserved exclusively for that day. Pentecost is only the beginning of the reign of the Holy Ghost, and the Church in

[1] Joel ii 28-32.

all ages, but more especially in those days when she will
have to sustain the final combat with Antichrist, will always
be strengthened by the graces of the Comforter.

The alleluiatic verse follows from Psalm xxxii: "By the
word of the Lord the heavens were established; and all the
power of them by the spirit of his mouth."

In imitation of that which was customary at night vigils
when the morning hymn *Gloria in Excelsis* marked, as it
were, the passage from the night prayer to the eucharistic
Sacrifice at dawn, to-day the *Gloria* is separated from the
Kyrie, and comes immediately after the alleluiatic verse., All
that precedes it therefore belongs to the Office of the vigil
and what follows forms an integral part of the Ordinary of
the Mass.

The Collect proper to the Mass is very fine. " Grant, we
beseech thee, almighty and merciful God, that the Holy
Ghost may vouchsafe to come and dwell within us, and make
us a temple of his glory. Through our Lord." The inspiration of this prayer is due to St Paul, who reasons thus : If by
means of the Paraclete, whom God has infused into our
hearts, we are become his temple, to what a high degree of
sanctity should we not mould our actions? It is needful that
every movement of our heart should express this inward and
spiritual worship, the *rationabile obsequium* that we render
to God.

The gift of miracles conferred on the Apostles and
especially on Peter, of which we read in the second lesson
(Acts v 12-16), is an effect of the grace of the Holy Ghost:
and this is the reason why there are so many allusions during
this Octave to the miraculous healing of the sick. Besides,
corporal diseases are symbols of spiritual maladies, which
are healed by the power of the divine Paraclete. The Lord
grants to Peter the gift of working even greater wonders
than the other Apostles, as though to ratify his supreme
Office and to confirm his primacy over the whole Church.

To-day, in accordance with the ancient Roman rite, two
lessons are read before the Gospel; therefore the two chants,
the Gradual and the alleluiatic verse, which in the Missal are
ordinarily placed together just after the Epistle, are reinstated
in their original places : the Gradual after the first lesson,
usually from the Old Testament, and the alleluiatic verse (the
Tract) after the second lesson—derived from the New Testament. Then comes the third scriptural lesson, chosen from
one of the Gospels, and it is probable that before the time of
St Gregory there was also a final chant, an Alleluia, an
Amen, a *Gloria Patri* or such like. It is quite possible that
this was the original place of the Sunday Alleluia as it still
is with the Greeks; and that the holy Pontiff displaced it,

and caused it to be sung in anticipation after the Epistle
on account of the homilies on the Gospel which he was
accustomed to preach.

The Gospel is from St John (vi 44-52), in which the Saviour
after the miracle of the multiplication of the loaves promises
to the people of Capharnaum the eucharistic bread from
heaven which gives life to the soul. The difference pointed
out by Christ between the temporal gifts of the Old Law and
this heavenly Food is chiefly a question of efficacy. In spite
of so many worldly advantages, Christ says to the Jews,
your fathers are dead. They were faithless and sensual and
they turned away from Jehovah, preferring stagnant waters
to living springs. Being merely earthly, they desired merely
earthly benefits and these melted away in their grasp. The
holy Eucharist, on the contrary, is a wholly spiritual food,
and is to be received spiritually—that is, in the spirit of faith.
It prepares us, not indeed for the enjoyment of a sensual and
earthly life—since it associates us with the sacrifice of the
death of Christ—but for our participation in the fulness of
his grace.

The Offertory, from Psalm cxviii, is the same as that of
Ember Wednesday in Lent. It speaks of all the benefits
gained by the soul in meditating on the word of God : " I
will meditate on thy commandments which I have loved
exceedingly "; this prayer kindles the sacred fire in our
hearts; " and I will lift up my hands to thy commandments." Such are the firm and practical resolutions which
must always follow our meditations on the eternal truths, for
if our consideration is merely speculative, it resembles a tree
thickly covered with foliage and flowers, but entirely devoid
of fruit.

In the Secret we pray God to accept the sacrifice and to
grant that our actions may truly correspond to the perfect
worship which we offer to him at the sacred altar through
the rites of the Church. In other words, we desire that the
death of Christ which we commemorate in the holy Eucharist
may be always shown forth also in our own lives. This is
the meaning of that beautiful prayer in the *Stabat Mater:
Fac ut portem Christi mortem.*

The Communion (John xiv 27) is the following : " My peace
I leave you, my peace I give you." This interior peace is
Christ himself, who by his death establishes us in peace with
God. The token of this peace is the Holy Ghost who sets on
our hearts the seal of our adoption as sons of God to which
the Father has raised us.

In the Post-Communion we ask that the pledge of salvation which we have received on earth by the grace of the
Sacrament may be fully redeemed in heaven. Glory is but

a fuller and more complete outpouring of grace; for as the seed potentially contains the tree, so grace is the prelude to the clear and perfect vision of glory.

The contrast between to-day's fast and the Gospel lesson in which Jesus offers himself as the bread of eternal life is very opportune. Man does not live by bread alone, but has an absolute need of the Word of God, without whom this earthly existence is as a day without light, an empty pretence of life, a gloomy image of death.

THURSDAY IN WHITSUN WEEK

Station at St Lawrence without the Walls.

The late origin of the whole Octave of Pentecost and of this Thursday in particular is clearly shown by the uncertainty of the Roman tradition concerning the stational Mass of to-day. In fact, the Gregorian Antiphonary, like the Würzburg Capitulary of the Gospels (middle of the seventh century), ignores it altogether. The present Missal fixes the station at St Lawrence without the Walls, where it would have taken place yesterday, just as on Wednesday in Easter Week, had not the ancient station at St Mary Major, which was traditional at Rome on Ember Wednesday, prevented it.

Other early Roman stational lists, ignoring the omission of St Lawrence, indicate to-day's station as being *ad Apostolos*, as on Thursday in Easter Week, which is confirmed by the selection of the lesson from the Acts of the Apostles, with the account of the wonders worked in Samaria by the deacon Philip, erroneously identified with the Apostle of the same name, who is venerated in the Church below the Quirinal.

The Gospel, too, which relates the sending forth of the twelve Apostles, is thereby connected rather with the titular saints of the early stational Church than with the Octave of Pentecost.

The whole of to-day's Mass, with the exception of the Epistle and the Gospel, is taken from that of Whit-Sunday.

The passage from the Acts (viii 5-9) describes how the deacon Philip confirmed his preaching of the Gospel at Samaria by a number of miracles which filled all the people with joy. This joy, of which the Sacred Scriptures speak, is a gift of the Holy Ghost granted to those who surrender themselves in a docile spirit to the action of grace, without resisting or impeding its inner working. If the world nowadays is more than ever before restless and eager for amusements, it shows that it has none of the joy and consolation of the divine Paraclete, of which it has become unworthy by its resistance to his grace. Christian joy is the outward sign of spiritual health; if it be wanting, then the soul's fervour has cooled, and must be re-awakened by prayer. *Tristatur aliquis vestrum? Oret . . . psallat,* is the counsel of St James.

It is a remarkable fact, and one which ought to be a salutary lesson to us all, that in the Holy Scriptures we often find that the persons most disposed to correspond to grace are not always the Israelites, the priests, nor the doctors of the law, but the accursed Samaritans, the publicans, and the women of the lowest class. This comes from that hidden pride which sometimes results from the knowledge of having led a life free from great disorders. We then presume on our own strength as though we had no need of God's mercy to uphold us, whilst greater sinners feel deeply the wretchedness of their state, and in their profound humility draw nearer to the throne of God's mercy and move him to a greater pity for them.

In the Gospel (Luke ix 1-6) we read of our Lord sending out the Apostles to preach the Word without any material necessaries. God's providence will care for them and will supply them with that which they may require rather than that they should take thought for their own needs when they might be devoting themselves entirely to his work. Not that our divine Master here forbids all thought of material interests, for the fact that he commands his Apostles to accept hospitality willingly whenever offered, proves the contrary, but he wishes to discourage in the preachers of the Gospel all attachment and excessive care for their own interests, in order that they may abandon themselves with confidence to his heavenly care. They are therefore not forbidden to use all diligence in providing for their livelihood—the purse of the company of the Apostles presided over by Jesus Christ was kept by Judas, and Paul worked assiduously to support himself and his companions—but it is essential that the preacher of the Gospel should not make such provision his chief care.

EMBER FRIDAY IN WHITSUN WEEK

Station at the Twelve Holy Apostles.

The station actually appointed in the Roman Missal certainly agrees with the Würzburg Capitulary of the Gospels, but towards the middle of the seventh century it was celebrated at the house of the martyrs John and Paul on the Coelian Hill, which was turned into a titular church

by the Senator Bisantius and his son Pammachius.   The
change in the stational basilica took place when the summer
Ember Days were assigned to the week after Pentecost.

The Spirit in which the Church solemnizes her feasts is one
of intense spiritual joy.   The Introit to-day contains, as it
were, the summary of a great ascetic treatise on Christian
joy.   " Let my mouth be filled with thy praise, Alleluia "
this is the supernatural origin of the grace of prayer; " that
I may sing, Alleluia "; this is the action and condition of
prayer inspired by love, since *cantare amantis est,* as St
Augustine says.   " My lips shall rejoice when I shall sing
to thee, Alleluia, Alleluia "; this is the inward consequence
of this prayer of love.

Thus this verse of the Introit is a song of love, in which
the soul overflowing with divine love expresses in melody all
that it feels.   The words are those of Psalm lxx, which continues thus : " In thee, O Lord, have I hoped, let me never
be put to confusion ; deliver me in thy justice, and rescue me."

The Collect follows, in which the Church, bereaved of her
Spouse and forlorn among her foes, turns with unshaken
faith to the Paraclete, the Heavenly Comforter.   " Grant
unto thy Church, we beseech thee, O Lord, that she may be
gathered within the fold of the Holy Ghost, and in nowise
troubled by attack from the foe.   Through our Lord."

The Lesson, from Joel (ii 23-27), is fully in keeping with the
character of a country festival which, according to the Roman
tradition, originally distinguished the Ember Day fasts.   These
of the summer season were regarded as a solemn thanksgiving for the ingathering of the harvest, and it is for this
reason that both to-day and to-morrow the lessons in the
Missal consist of most comforting passages from the Scriptures, telling of the promise of Jehovah to the people of
Israel that they should possess fertile fields and abundant
harvests as a reward for their faithful observance of the Law.

The Prophet here foretells the coming of the Holy Ghost—
doctorem justitiae—and calls to mind those early days of
Creation when the Spirit of God moved over the primordial
waters and under the figure of a spring of living water refreshed and fertilized the earth.   Such mystical symbols well
express the gentle and efficacious action of the Paraclete in
the souls of the faithful.

The alleluiatic verse is derived from the Book of Wisdom
(xii 1): " Alleluia, Alleluia.   Oh, how good and sweet, O
Lord, is thy spirit within us, Alleluia."   Towards us he is
sweet indeed, for without violating our free will he moves us
irresistibly to love God, but to the obstinate and impenitent
sinner, on the other hand, he is terrible, for an undying fire

avenges on them the honour of a love which has been slighted and denied.

The Gospel, from St Luke (v 17-26), with the story of the man sick of the palsy, shows us our Lord healing the physical and spiritual infirmities of the Jews. It is specially connected with the feast of Pentecost, for the Holy Ghost has an intimate part in these miracles, inasmuch as they are visible proofs of the infinite love with which the Paraclete filled the divine heart of Jesus on our behalf.

Moreover, it was through the infusion of grace, which is the special work of the Holy Ghost, that the sins of the paralytic man were forgiven him. He is a figure of our poor human nature degraded by sin and passion. It has voluntarily renounced its liberty, fettering its spiritual faculties with the bands of vice, thus causing them to grow rigid through neglect. The friends of the sick man are ministers of God's mercy, who, making use of every means, even letting him down through the roof with all his burden of sinful habits and laying him at the feet of the Saviour, present to him the helpless sufferer. The Lord sees their faith and for their sake forgives the sick man all his sins and cures him of his malady.

The Greeks commemorate this miracle on the Third Sunday after Easter.

Those amongst us who have received the priestly ministry from the Holy Ghost must therefore never relinquish hope, no matter how desperate the position may appear to be. Even though the sick man has not faith, it is sufficient that the pastor should have it, when, having exhausted all other means, he presents this soul to the Saviour in his prayers.

The Offertory comes from Psalm cxlv : " Praise the Lord, O my soul : in my life I will praise the Lord : I will sing to my God as long as I shall be. Alleluia." Our present life, seen under an aspect which is often put before us in the Holy Scriptures, resembles a radiant day, during which we can work manfully for the greater glory of God, and for the increasing of our own merits. Death is the dark night, wherein rest succeeds to labour. That which is done, is done. With what intensity should we not then work for God during the brief day of our life on earth !

In the Secret we beg that as in the Old Law fire from heaven consumed the sacrifices of the Patriarchs in order to show that they were pleasing and acceptable to God, so the Holy Ghost, who is the consuming fire of sanctity and love, would descend upon the oblation of his holy Church and render the eucharistic sacrifice pleasing to God and profitable to all Christian people.

The Communion is taken from St John (xiv 18) : " I will

not leave you orphans; I will come to you again, Alleluia; and your heart shall rejoice, Alleluia.'' Christ comes to us again when he bestows upon us his own Spirit; he comes to us also in Holy Communion, and lastly he comes to us a third time when, together with the Father and the Paraclete, he takes up his abode in the temple of our soul. The fruit of this threefold return of Christ to the soul is each time the same; it is that which St Paul calls the inward joy of the Holy Ghost.

In the Post-Communion we pray that the sacred mysteries of the altar, which we have just celebrated in obedience to our Lord's command, may become a remedy which shall strengthen our weakness in the hard trials that beset us. It is then, in order to carry out the injunction of the Saviour: '' Do this for a commemoration of me,''[1] which he expressed on the supreme night of his betrayal, that we offer the holy Sacrifice. It is in this spirit of obedience that we must all, priests and laity alike, each in his own manner, celebrate or assist in celebrating the mystery of the death of Christ. '' The Lord has so commanded us,'' some of the martyrs of old replied to the judge, and it is not permissible for us to allow a day of obligation to pass without offering to him the eucharistic sacrifice. This divine precept has been sealed, as have all the other Gospel precepts, by the blood of many martyrs. We may, for example, commemorate here those heroic priests of France who during the Revolution, when it was forbidden to say Mass under pain of death, cheerfully ascended the steps of the guillotine, their only crime being that of having offered up the Holy Sacrifice in obedience to the command of their Lord and Master Jesus Christ.[2]

EMBER SATURDAY IN WHITSUN WEEK

Station at St Peter.   (Station at St Stephen on the Coelian Hill.)

The fact that the Ordinations and to-night's vigil took place, as documents of the fifth century prove, at St Peter's, greatly tended to affirm the Roman belief that all ecclesiastical power was derived from the Apostle to whom God entrusted the keys of the kingdom of heaven; but when, in the seventh century, the Ember fast of the summer quarter was post-

[1] Luke xxii 19.
[2] It will not be out of place to associate here with the memory of these heroes of France those other glorious martyrs of our own land, whether priests or lay-folk, who in penal times underwent an even more terrible death as the climax of bitter and cruel sufferings endured for the faith.—Tr.

poned for some weeks on account of the solemn Octave of Pentecost, the station was transferred from St Peter's to St Stephen on the Coelian Hill. This change, however, was not regarded very favourably, consequently in the eleventh century a return was made to the primitive usage.

Of the five scriptural lessons which precede the *Gloria in Excelsis* of the Mass, some refer to the feast of Pentecost and some to the "fast of the fourth month," as St Leo the Great calls it; they represent a kind of compromise or fusion of the two rites. Formerly the vigil lasted throughout the night, and twelve lessons were read, both in Greek and in Latin; but in the time of St Gregory the Great the vigil was shortened and brought within more reasonable limits, as we now find it in our present Missal.

The Introit is derived from the Epistle to the Romans (Rom. v 5): "The charity of God is poured forth in our hearts, Alleluia: by his Spirit dwelling within us, Alleluia, Alleluia," and is followed by Psalm cii: "Bless the Lord, O my soul; and let all that is within me bless his holy name." In order to gain the love of man, whom by his grace he has raised to a divine sonship, God has poured forth his charity into his heart, and this charity of the Blessed Trinity is the Paraclete himself.

The *Kyrie eleison* follows, and then instead of singing the *Gloria in Excelsis,* the Collect, with its especially Trinitarian character, is recited. The Wisdom of which it speaks is the Word of God, the Providence is the eternal Father.

Oremus	Let us pray
Mentibus nostris, quaesumus, Domine, Spiritum Sanctum benignus infunde; cujus et sapientia conditi sumus, et providentia gubernamur. Per Dominum.	In thy bounty, O Lord, we beseech thee, pour into our minds the Holy Ghost, by whose wisdom we were made and by whose providence we are guided. Through our Lord.

The first Lesson is taken from the prophecy of Joel (ii 28-32) and contains the passage quoted by the Apostle Peter in his first address to the Jews on the morning of Pentecost. It speaks of the pouring out of the Holy Ghost on the universal Church, introducing at once the Messianic era and the last age of the world, which leads to the final *parousia* and the destruction of the present *Kosmos*. "Thus saith the Lord God: I will pour out my spirit upon all flesh, and your sons and your daughters shall prophesy; your old men shall dream dreams, and your young men shall see visions. Moreover, upon my servants and handmaids in those days I will pour forth my spirit. And I will show wonders in heaven;

and in earth, blood, and fire, and vapour of smoke. The sun shall be turned into darkness, and the moon into blood, before the great and dreadful day of the Lord doth come. And it shall come to pass that every one that shall call upon the name of the Lord shall be saved."

In order thoroughly to understand the sacred vigiliary rite we must again call to mind that the reading of each lesson was usually followed by the singing of a responsorial psalm; then, at the invitation of the priest or deacon: *Oremus, Flectamus genua,* the faithful knelt in private prayer. The deacon then gave the sign to rise: *Levate,* that they might accompany in spirit the prayer of the priest. This prayer was called *Collecta,* inasmuch as the priest "collected" or gathered together in one short formula the desires and wishes of the whole assembly and presented them thus united to Almighty God.

The alleluiatic verse is from St John (vi 64): "Alleluia. It is the spirit that quickeneth: but the flesh profiteth nothing." That is to say, nature left to itself is incapable of meriting eternal life; but if the body becomes the obedient instrument of the soul burning with love and zeal for God, then the flesh also shares both in the merits and in the glorious reward to which that soul attains.

The psalmody concludes with this Collect:

<table>
<tr><td>Oremus</td><td>Let us pray</td></tr>
<tr><td>Illo nos igne, quaesumus, Domine, Spiritus Sanctus inflammet, quem Dominus noster Jesus Christus misit in terram et voluit vehementer accendi : Qui tecum.</td><td>May the Holy Ghost, O Lord, we beseech thee, enkindle us with that fire which our Lord Jesus Christ cast upon the earth and desired exceedingly to be kindled : who liveth. . . .</td></tr>
</table>

The second Lesson (Lev. xxiii 9-21) does not refer in any way to the gift of the Holy Ghost, which has been the guiding thought of the liturgy throughout this week. It must doubtless have been one of the ancient group of vigiliary lessons selected for the fast of the fourth month— the year at that time began with the month of March—before the institution of the Octave of Pentecost. The Jewish Pentecost, described in this passage from Leviticus, was a festival of thanksgiving for the ingathering of the harvest, which corresponds closely to the original character of the summer Ember Days according to the tradition of the Roman Liturgy. There had originally been at this season a classical country festival to which Christianity had given a devotional significance.

"In those days: the Lord spoke to Moses, saying, Speak to the children of Israel, and thou shalt say to them, When you shall have entered into the land which I will give you, and shall reap your corn, you shall bring sheaves of ears, the first-fruits of your harvest, to the priest, who shall lift up the sheaf before the Lord, the next day after the Sabbath, that it may be acceptable for you, and shall sanctify it. You shall count therefore from the morrow after the Sabbath, wherein you offered the sheaf of the first-fruits, seven full weeks, even unto the morrow after the seventh week be expired, that is to say, fifty days; and so you shall offer a new sacrifice to the Lord, out of all your dwellings, two loaves of the first-fruits, of two-tenths of flour leavened, which you shall bake for the first-fruits of the Lord. And you shall call this day most solemn and most holy. You shall do no servile work therein. It shall be an everlasting ordinance in all your dwellings and generations, saith the Lord almighty."

The tithes and the first-fruits are offered to the Lord in order to testify that he is the ruler of the universe, and that the good things which we receive from him are to be used by us to his greater glory.

Then comes a second alleluiatic verse chosen from the prophecies of Job (xxvi 13): "Alleluia. His spirit hath adorned the heavens." The beauty of nature reveals to us the ineffable love of God for his creatures, whence Dante rightly sang in the *Divina Commedia* of: "the love which moves the sun and the stars."[1]

The following is the third Collect:

Oremus	Let us pray
Deus, qui ad animarum medelam, jejunii devotione castigari corpora praecepisti, concede nobis propitius et mente et corpore tibi semper esse devotos. Per Dominum.	O God, who for the healing of our souls hast commanded us to chasten our bodies by fasting and devotion, grant in thy mercy that we may be ever devoted to thee in mind and body. Through our Lord.

When the body fasts, the heart, the soul, and the will must fast too, abstaining from everything unworthy of the dignity of sons of God to which we have been raised by holy baptism.

The third Lesson, from Deuteronomy (xxvi 1-11), also refers to the first-fruits of the harvest, which were offered to the Lord fifty days after the Pasch. It should be noted, however, that the first sheaf of ripe barley had already been brought to the temple on the sixteenth of Nisan—that is, on the second day of the Jewish Pasch; so that these two sacrifices marked, as it were, the beginning and ending of the fifty holy days of the Pasch to which was afterwards given by the Hellenists

[1] *Paradiso* xxxiii, last line: " L'amor che muove il sole e l'altre stelle."—Tr.

the name of Pentecost, which name has been preserved also in the Christian liturgy.

"In those days : Moses said to the children of Israel, Hear, O Israel, what I command thee this day. When thou art come into the land which the Lord thy God will give thee to possess, and hast conquered it, and dwellest in it ; thou shalt take the first of all thy fruits, and put them in a basket, and shalt go to the place which the Lord thy God shall choose, that his name may be invocated there : and thou shalt go to the priest that shall be in those days, and say to him, I profess this day before the Lord thy God, who heard us, and looked down upon our affliction, and labour, and distress ; and brought us out of Egypt with a strong hand, and a stretched-out arm, with great terror, with signs and wonders, and brought us into this place, and gave us this land flowing with milk and honey. And therefore now I offer the first-fruits of the land which the Lord hath given me. And thou shalt leave them in the sight of the Lord thy God, adoring the Lord thy God ; and thou shalt feast in all the good things which the Lord thy God hath given thee."

It is easier to take sorrow from the hand of God, than happiness. Sorrow brings back many souls to the faith, whereas prosperity causes many to forget God. We should imitate the calmness of mind evinced by Job, who accepted from God's hands with equal thankfulness both joy and sorrow ; nor can these ever prove unwelcome to us if we remember that they come *de manu Domini*.

The third alleluiatic verse emanates from the Acts of the Apostles (ii 1). "When the days of Pentecost were accomplished, they were all sitting together." Here we notice the spirit of concord and brotherly love, which is a most favourable disposition for receiving the gifts of him who is called "the God of peace and of love."

The fourth Collect follows :

Oremus

Praesta, quaesumus, omnipotens Deus, ut salutaribus jejuniis eruditi ab omnibus etiam vitiis abstinentes, propitiationem tuam facilius impetremus. Per Dominum.

Let us pray

Grant, we beseech thee, almighty God, that we, who have been disciplined by healthful fasting, may also abstain from vice and the more readily win thy mercy. Through our Lord.

The fourth Lesson (Lev. xxvi 3-12) recalls the promises made by God to his people if they remained faithful to the observance of the Law. We should remember, however, that, although it is sin which makes men unhappy, even in a material sense, and with a dull and carnal race such as were the Jews, it is useless to hold forth any but material advantages, yet the true end of life is not happiness on this earth : indeed for the Christian this present life is but a continuation of the *Via Crucis* of Jesus Christ, while he looks for true and complete satisfaction in heaven alone.

" In those days : the Lord said to Moses : Speak to the children of Israel, and thou shalt say to them : If you walk in my precepts and keep my commandments and do them, I will give you rain in due season ; and the ground shall bring forth its increase, and the trees shall be filled with fruit. The threshing of your harvest shall reach unto the vintage, and the vintage shall reach unto the sowing time ; and you shall eat your bread to the full, and dwell in your land without fear. I will give peace in your coasts : you shall sleep, and there shall be none to make you afraid. I will take away evil beasts ; and the sword shall not pass through your quarters. You shall pursue your enemies, and they shall fall before you. Five of yours shall pursue a hundred others, and a hundred of you ten thousand : your enemies shall fall before you by the sword. I will look on you and make you increase : you shall be multiplied and I will establish my covenant with you. You shall eat the oldest of the old store ; and new coming on, you shall cast away the old. I will set my tabernacle in the midst of you, and my soul shall not cast you off. I will walk among you, and will be your God, and you shall be my people : saith the Lord almighty."

Here is repeated, as on Whit-Sunday, the invocation to the Holy Ghost : " Come, O Holy Spirit, fill the hearts of thy faithful ; and kindle in them the fire of thy love."

The fifth Collect is then recited :

Oremus	Let us pray
Praesta, quaesumus, omnipotens Deus, sic nos ab epulis carnalibus abstinere, ut a vitiis irruentibus pariter jejunemus. Per Dominum.	Grant, we beseech thee, almighty God, that we may so abstain from fleshly feasts that we may fast also from the vices which assail us. Through our Lord.

The fifth Lesson is the same as that of Ember Saturday in Advent which closes the vigiliary Office and contains the story of the three youths who were thrown by Nabuchodonosor into the fiery furnace at Babylon. This was such a favourite theme amongst the early Christians that we see it represented in thousands of pictures and sculptures of the first four centuries. The canticle which comes after it, known as the *Benedictiones,* served as a sort of transition between the vigiliary Office and the Mass itself, but to-day, perhaps because of the paschal Alleluia which precedes it, it has lost its original responsorial character and has been abbreviated and reduced to the single opening verse. On the other Ember Saturdays, however, we find it in full.

" Alleluia.   Blessed art thou, O Lord, the God of our fathers, and worthy to be praised for ever."

The *Gloria in Excelsis* which follows was also originally a transitional hymn between the night vigil and the Mass, but here it is out of its proper place, since it separates the lesson and the canticle of Daniel from this striking Collect which bears special reference to the three Babylonian youths who were miraculously delivered by an angel on account of their heroic fidelity in not prostrating themselves before the golden statue set up by the king.

Oremus	Let us pray
Deus, qui tribus pueris mitigasti flammas ignium, concede propitius, ut nos famulos tuos non exurat flamma vitiorum. Per Dominum.	O God, who didst allay the flames of fire for the three children, mercifully grant that the flame of vice may not consume us thy servants. Through our Lord.

The flames which try the followers of Jesus are the passions, the fire of sensuality, of pride, and of self-love. He who has faith passes unhurt through this furnace; he who has not faith, succumbs.

The Epistle is from that of St Paul to the Romans (v 1-5), and describes in short vigorous sentences the whole essence of Christian life; regeneration by means of faith in Jesus Christ, hope in the future inheritance of heavenly glory which belongs to us as being sons of God, and lastly charity, which is poured forth in our hearts by the Holy Ghost.

" Brethren : Being justified by faith, let us have peace with God, through our Lord Jesus Christ; by whom also we have access through faith into this grace wherein we stand, and glory in the hope of the glory of the sons of God.   And not only so, but we glory also in tribulations; knowing that tribulation worketh patience, and patience trial, and trial hope, and hope confoundeth not; because the charity of God is poured forth in our hearts by the Holy Ghost, who is given to us."

After the Epistle, the Tract (Psalm cxvi) is recited, as is the rule on Ember Saturdays and on solemn vigils preceding the Sunday, excepting on Ember Saturday in Advent.   "O praise the Lord, all ye nations : and praise him together all ye people.   For his mercy is confirmed upon us : and the truth of the Lord remaineth for ever."

Originally the *Tractus* was the festive psalmody of the Roman Church, before the introduction of the alleluiatic verse in the time of St Gregory.   The ferial Masses had no Tract, but it is found on the Ember Saturdays, as these Masses were in their origin true Sunday Masses and bore a festal character. Psalm cxvi coming after the Ordinations is a true hymn of thanksgiving to God. In the seventh century the Gospel lesson which followed the *Tractus* on this day was taken from St Matthew (xx 29-34) and gave the narrative of the two blind men who were cured of their blindness by our Lord; but when the liturgy of the Ember Days was finally fused with that of the Octave of Pentecost, the passage in which St Luke describes the healing of the mother-in-law of Peter—possibly the original one—was preferred, since the station was celebrated at the *domus Simonis* of the Vatican.

To-night the Sequence, not forming part of the alleluiatic verse, is not followed by the final Alleluia.

The Gospel is the same as that of the Thursday after the Third Sunday in Lent. Jesus enters the house of Simon, and at the request of the Apostles, heals his mother-in-law. St Francis de Sales remarks in relation to this incident that the sick woman does not herself ask to be healed; she is indifferent as to whether she is well or ill, as long as she is doing the will of God. Others obtain the grace of restoration to health for her, and she receives it with equal tranquillity of mind, and at once makes use of her recovered strength to receive Jesus and his Apostles into her house and minister to their needs.

The Offertory of the Ember Saturdays is, with the exception of Ember Saturday in Advent, always the same—an antiphon from Psalm lxxxvii, in keeping with the night hour of the Mass: *In die clamavi et nocte coram te.*

The Secret is the following:

Secreta	*Secret*
Ut accepta tibi sint, Domine, nostra jejunia, praesta nobis, quaesumus; hujus munere sacramenti purificatum tibi pectus offerre. Per Dominum.	That our fasts may be received by thee, O Lord, grant, we beseech thee, that we may offer up to thee a heart made clean by the gift of this sacrament. Through our Lord.

We find here again expressed the beautiful thought that our aim must be to unite ourselves to the oblation of Christ, immolating our own nature in the fire of God's love.

The Communion (John iii 8) contains a last allusion to the Octave of Pentecost and to the paschal season which is now fast drawing to its close. The joyous song of Alleluia, too, at least according to the ancient Gregorian rite, is about to disappear and vanish in the skies.

" The Spirit breatheth where he will; and thou hearest his voice, Alleluia: but thou knowest not whence he cometh, nor whither he goeth, Alleluia, Alleluia, Alleluia." These words in the Greek text of the original really refer, not to the Holy Ghost, but to the wind; yet as our Lord, in explaining to Nicodemus the intangible and supernatural character of the grace of the Holy Ghost, made use of the figure of the wind, it was not altogether arbitrary of the Roman Liturgy to apply this verse to the conclusion of the Whitsuntide solemnities.

This is the Post-Communion :

Postcommunio	*Post-Communion*
Praebeant nobis, Domine, divinum tua Sancta fervorem; quo eorum pariter et actu delectemur et fructu. Per Dominum.	May thy holy mysteries, O Lord, impart to us divine fervour, by which we may delight both in their celebration and in their fruit. Through our Lord.

True fervour, spiritual enjoyment, and real progress in the way of perfection, such is the threefold fruit for which the Church inspires us to ask after Holy Communion. It often happens that persons abstain from receiving Holy Communion, for the reason that they do not feel any fervour or spiritual desire. It is as though one were to refuse food because one felt weak, whereas this is an additional reason for seeking nourishment. Fervour and devotion follow the reception of Holy Communion, but are not an essential part of our preparation for the sacrament. The Church teaches us that for frequent or even daily Communion, all that is required is purity of conscience and a right intention, and the word of the Church should suffice to cause us to put aside any over-scrupulous hesitation. Moreover, as to spiritual desire, it is as well not to give too much importance thereto, for in prayer we should seek not the fulfilment of our own will but that which God wishes.

The Sacrifice of the Mass fittingly brings the holy season of Easter to an end. Our redemption is now accomplished, and the Holy Ghost has come as though to insure its lasting efficacy by means of the sacramental character which he impresses on our souls. This is the special prerogative of the divine Paraclete; his work is always definite, complete, and final, like a conclusion which follows inevitably and irrevocably on its premises. This is the reason why sins against the Holy Ghost can never find pardon; for they are the outcome of the final hardening of the soul in utter hatred of Supreme Love.

EUCHOLOGICAL APPENDIX

I.—ARCHAIC TYPES OF PRAYER, INSPIRED BY THE EUCHARIST, USED AT THE LOVE-FEASTS (AGAPE)

From " The Teaching of the Twelve Apostles " (Διδαχὴ, ch. ix and x, end of first century).

Περὶ δὲ τῆς εὐχαριστίας, οὕτως εὐχαριστήσατε· Πρῶτον περὶ τοῦ ποτηρίου·

Εὐχαριστοῦμέν σοι, Πάτερ ἡμῶν, ὑπὲρ τῆς ἁγίας ἀμπέλου Δαβὶδ τοῦ παιδός σου, ἧς ἐγνώρισας ἡμῖν διὰ Ἰησοῦ τοῦ παιδός σου· σοὶ ἡ δόξα εἰς τοὺς αἰῶνας.

Περὶ δὲ τοῦ κλάσματος·

Εὐχαριστοῦμέν σοι, Πάτερ ἡμῶν, ὑπὲρ τῆς ζωῆς καὶ γνώσεως, ἧς ἐγνώρισας ἡμῖν διὰ Ἰησοῦ τοῦ παιδός σου· σοὶ ἡ δόξα εἰς τοὺς αἰῶνας. Ὥσπερ ἦν τοῦτο τὸ κλάσμα διεσκορπισμένον ἐπάνω τῶν ὀρέων καὶ συναχθὲν ἐγένετο ἔν, οὕτω συναχθήτω σου ἡ ἐκκλησία ἀπὸ τῶν περάτων τῆς γῆς εἰς τὴν σὴν βασιλείαν· ὅτι σοῦ ἐστιν ἡ δόξα καὶ ἡ δύναμις διὰ Ἰησοῦ Χριστοῦ εἰς τοὺς αἰῶνας·

Μηδεὶς δὲ φαγέτω μηδὲ πιέτω ἀπὸ τῆς εὐχαριστίας ὑμῶν, ἀλλ᾽ οἱ βαπτισθέντες εἰς ὄνομα Κυρίου· καὶ γὰρ περὶ τούτου εἴρηκεν ὁ Κύριος: Μὴ δῶτε τὸ ἅγιον τοῖς κυσὶ (Matt. vii 6).

Μετὰ δὲ τὸ ἐμπλησθῆναι. οὕτως εὐχαριστήσατε·

Εὐχαριστοῦμέν σοι, Πάτερ ἅγιε, ὑπὲρ τοῦ ἁγίου ὀνόματός σου, οὗ κατεσκήνωσας ἐν ταῖς καρδίαις ἡμῶν καὶ ὑπὲρ τῆς γνώσεως καὶ πίστεως καὶ ἀθανασίας. ἧς ἐγνώρισας ἡμῖν διὰ Ἰησοῦ τοῦ παιδός σου· σοὶ ἡ δόξα εἰς τοὺς αἰῶνας. Σύ, Δέσποτα παντοκράτορ, "ἔκτισας τὰ πάντα" (Apoc. iv 11) ἕνεκεν τοῦ ὀνόματός σου· τροφήν τε καὶ ποτὸν ἔδωκας τοῖς ἀνθρώποις εἰς ἀπόλαυσιν, ἵνα σοι εὐχαριστήσωσιν, ἡμῖν δὲ ἐχαρίσω πνευματικὴν τροφὴν καὶ πότον καὶ ζωὴν αἰώνιον διὰ τοῦ παιδός σου. Πρὸ πάντων εὐχαριστοῦμέν σοι, ὅτι δυνατὸς εἶ· σοὶ ἡ δόξα εἰς τοὺς αἰῶνας. Μνήσθητι,

IX.—*And concerning the giving of thanks (Eucharist), do it in this manner.*

First over the Chalice:

We give thee thanks, O God our Father, because of the holy vine of thy servant[1] David, which thou hast made known to us through thy servant[1] Jesus. To thee be glory for ever and ever.

Next over the Broken Bread:

We give thee thanks, O God our Father, because of the life and knowledge[2] which thou hast revealed to us by thy servant[1] Jesus. To thee be glory for ever and ever. As the elements of this bread now broken were scattered upon the mountains, and being gathered together have become one whole, so do thou gather together thy Church into thy kingdom from the ends of the earth; for thine is the glory and the power through Jesus Christ, world without end.

Let no one eat nor drink of that over which you have given thanks,[3] except those who have been baptized in the name of the Lord: for to that end the Lord hath said: "Give not that which is holy to the dogs" (Matt. vii 6).

X.—*And after you are filled,[4] give thanks in this manner:*

We render thee thanks, O holy Father, because of thy holy name, which thou hast caused to dwell in

---

[1] παῖς, which also means *child* or *son*.

[2] γνῶσις.

[3] *i.e.*, at the Eucharist.

[4] *i.e.*, at the Agape.

Κύριε, τῆς ἐκκλησίας σου τοῦ ῥύσασθαι αὐτὴν ἀπὸ παντὸς πονηροῦ καὶ τελειῶσαι αὐτὴν ἐν τῇ ἀγάπῃ σου, "καὶ σύναξον" αὐτὴν ἀπὸ τῶν τεσσάρων ἀνέμων (Matt. xxiv 31), τὴν ἁγιασθεῖσαν εἰς τὴν σὴν βασιλείαν, ἣν ἡτοίμασας αὐτῇ ὅτι σοῦ ἐστιν ἡ δύναμις καὶ ἡ δόξα εἰς τοὺς αἰῶνας. Ἐλθέτω χάρις καὶ παρελθέτω ὁ κόσμος οὗτος. "Ὡσαννὰ τῷ υἱῷ Δαβίδ" (Matt. xxi 9). Εἴ τις ἅγιός ἐστιν, ἐρχέσθω· εἴ τις οὐκ ἔστι, μετανοείτω. "Μαρὰν Ἀθά," ἀμὴν (1 Cor. xvi 22).

our hearts, as also because of the knowledge,[1] the faith and the immortality which thou hast revealed to us by thy servant[2] Jesus. To thee be glory for ever and ever. Thou, O Almighty Lord, 'hast created all things' (Apoc. iv 11), for thy name's sake. Thou hast given to men meat and drink, that they, rejoicing therein, may render thee thanks; and to us thou hast granted spiritual meat and drink, and eternal life through thy Servant.[3] Above all do we thank thee because thou art omnipotent. Glory be to thee for ever. Forget not, O Lord, to free thy Church from all adversity, and to perfect her in thy love. 'Gather from the four winds' (Matt. xxiv 31) this Church which thou hast sanctified, and give her the kingdom which thou hast prepared for her, for thine is the power and the glory, world without end. May thy grace come and this world pass away! 'Hosanna to the Son of David' (Matt. xxi 9). If anyone be holy, let him draw nigh! If anyone be unholy, let him repent! Maran-atha,[3] Amen (1 Cor. xvi 22).

These beautiful prayers formed part of the ritual of the love-feasts of the early Christians in Palestine. Perhaps, even in those days, the Eucharist was separated, for fear of abuses, from the Agape, or meal taken in common. But, though kept distinct from the Sacrament, the love-feast became its symbol, as it were, and thus the phraseology of the prayers of blessing and of thanksgiving at its conclusion was inspired by the thought of the Eucharist, as we find to this day among religious communities. As regards the chalice of benediction, the subject of the first prayer, it is the carrying on of an ancient Jewish tradition by which in some of the ancient Christian Churches it was preserved together with a loaf of the " bread of blessing," also called the " bread of exorcism."

As is seen in the hymn *Gloria in excelsis*, the first text of which appears to date from the beginning of the second century, so also in the preceding prayers, the author of them

---

[1] γνῶσις. [2] παῖς.

[3] *Maran-atha*, explained by St Jerome and St Chrysostom as signifying, " The Lord is come "; by others as, " May the Lord come "—*i.e.*, as Judge.—TR.

is concerned to show forth clearly the human nature and the priestly mission of Christ, to whom therefore—drawing his inspiration from the well-known expression of Isaias—he gives with evident satisfaction the title of " Servant of Jehovah."

II.—THE EARLIEST TYPE OF PRAYER IN THE RHYTHM OF AN ANAPHORA

(From the Epistle of St Clement to the Corinthians, Ep. I ad Corinth., c. lix, seq).

Continuo orantes ac supplicantes precabimur, ut opifex omnium rerum numerum electorum suorum constitutum in toto mundo conservet integrum, per dilectum puerum Jesum Christum, per quem nos vocavit de tenebris in lucem, de ignorantia in cognitionem gloriae nominis sui . . . qui humilias arrogantiam superborum . . . qui intueris in abyssos, inspector operum hominum. . . .

Rogamus te, Domine, ut sis adjutor et exauditor noster. Eos nostrum qui in tribulatione sunt, libera ; humilium miserere, lapsos eleva, inopibus succurre, infirmos sana, errantes populi tui converte : nutri esurientes, solve captivos nostros, erige imbecilles, consolare pusillanimes, cognoscant omnes gentes quod tu es Deus solus, et Jesus Christus puer tuus, ac nos populus tuus et oves pascuae tuae.

Tu perennem mundi constitutionem per effectus manifestasti ; tu, Domine, orbem terrae fundasti, fidelis in omnibus generationibus, justus in judiciis, admirabilis in fortitudine et magnificentia, sapiens in condendo, ac prudens in creatis stabiliendis . . . benignus et misericors, dimitte nobis iniquitates et injustitias et peccata et delicta nostra.

Ne imputes omne peccatum servorum tuorum et servarum, sed purifica nos in veritate tua et dirige gressus nostros, ut in pietate et justitia et simplicitate cordis ambulemus, et agamus quae bona et beneplacita sunt coram te ac coram principibus nostris.

Immo, Domine, ostende faciem tuam super nos, ut bonis fruamur in pace, ut tegamur manu tua potenti et ab omni peccato liberemur brachio tuo excelso, ac libera nos ab iis qui nos oderunt injuste.

Da concordiam ac pacem, et nobis et omnibus habitantibus terram, sicut dedisti patribus nostris pie te invocantibus in fide et veritate, qui oboedientes sumus nomini tuo omnipotenti, omnique virtute pleno, et principibus et praefectis nostris in terra.

Tu, Domine, dedisti eis potestatem regni per magnificam et inenarrabilem virtutem tuam, ut cognoscentes gloriam et honorem quem tu iis tribuisti, nos subjiciamus ipsis, voluntati tuae non adversantes ; quibus da, Domine, sanitatem, pacem, concordiam, firmitatem, ut imperium quod tu iis dedisti, sine offendiculo administrent. Tu, enim, Domine, caelestis Rex saeculorum, filiis hominum das gloriam et honorem et potestatem eorum quae in terra sunt. Tu, Domine, dirige consilium eorum secundum id quod bonum et beneplacitum est in conspectu tuo, ut potestatem a te datam in pace et mansuetudine pie administrantes, propitium te habeant.

Qui solus haec et plura bona nobiscum agere potes, tibi confitemur per pontificem ac patronum animarum nostrarum, Jesum Christum, per quem tibi gloria et majestas et nunc et in generationem generationum et in saecula saeculorum. Amen.

III.—EXAMPLE OF A PRAYER IN THE FORM OF A LITANY

(From the Milanese Liturgy according to the Biasca Missal)

Divinae pacis et indulgentiae munere supplicantes, ex toto corde et ex tota mente. Precamur te, Domine, miserere.

Pro ecclesia tua sancta catholica, quae hic et per universum orbem diffusa est. Precamur te, Domine, miserere.

Pro Papa nostro (illo) et omni clero ejus, omnibusque sacerdotibus ac ministris. Precamur te, Domine, miserere.

Pro famulo tuo (illo) imperatore et famula tua (illa) imperatrice et omni exercitu eorum. Precamur te, Domine, miserere.

Pro pace Ecclesiarum, vocatione gentium et quiete populorum. Precamur te, Domine, miserere.

Pro plebe hac et conversatione ejus, omnibusque habitantibus in ea. Precamur te, Domine, miserere.

Pro aërum temperie ac fructuum et foecunditate terrarum. Precamur te, Domine, miserere.

Pro virginibus, viduis, orphanis, captivis ac poenitentibus. Precamur te, Domine, miserere.

Pro navigantibus, iter agentibus, in carceribus, in vinculis, in metallis, in exsiliis constitutis. Precamur te, Domine, miserere.

Pro iis qui diversis infirmitatibus detinentur, quique spiritibus vexantur immundis. Precamur te, Domine, miserere.

Pro iis qui in sancta tua Ecclesia fructus misericordiae largiuntur. Precamur te, Domine, miserere.

Exaudi nos, Deus, in omni oratione atque deprecatione nostra. Precamur te, Domine, miserere.

Dicamus omnes, Domine miserere, Kyrie, eleison, Kyrie, eleison, Kyrie, eleison.

This prayer is typical of the tradition of the synagogue, and was recited at the end of the synaxis, after the scriptural lessons, just as is still done in the Roman Liturgy, in the Mass of the Presanctified on Good Friday. This Ambrosian Lenten litany, belonging to a period when prayers were still offered for those among the brethren who were condemned to exile, to penal servitude, to the mines, etc., certainly dates back to the early days of the fourth century at least. The Pope alone is prayed for by name, for he was probably at that time still the only metropolitan in Italy. Together with him intercession is made for all the clergy, whether bishops, priests, or deacons.

IV.—EUCHARISTIC HYMN FROM THE AMBROSIAN LITURGY[1]

Te laudamus, Domine omnipotens,
  Qui sedes super Cherubim et Seraphim.
Quem benedicunt Angeli, Archangeli,
  Et laudant Prophetae et Apostoli.
Te laudamus, Domine, orando,
  Qui venisti peccata solvendo.

Te deprecamur magnum redemptorem,
  Quem Pater misit ovium pastorem;
Tu es Christus Dominus Salvator,
  Qui de Maria Virgine es natus.
Hunc sacrosanctum calicem sumentes,
  Ab omni culpa libera nos semper.

V.—EUCHARISTIC ANTIPHON DERIVED FROM THE GREEK, IN USE AT MILAN AND AT LYONS

Venite populi ad sacrum et immortale mysterium et libamen agendum; cum timore et fide accedamus, manibus mundis poenitentiae munus communicemus; quoniam Agnus Dei propter nos Patri sacrificium propositum est. Ipsum solum adoremus, ipsum glorificemus, cum angelis clamantes : Alleluia.

VI.—FROM THE ARMENIAN LITURGY FOR MAUNDY THURSDAY

Thou who art seated in majesty in the four-sided chariot of fire, O ineffable Word of God, who didst come down from heaven for the sake of thy creatures, to-day didst deign to sit at table with thy disciples! The Cherubim and Seraphim and the high princes of the celestial hosts stood around thee full of wonder and awe, singing together in harmony : Holy, holy, holy is the Lord of hosts.

VII.—FROM THE SAME

After the Kiss of Peace, before beginning the Anaphora

Christ is about to manifest himself to us. He who is himself the essence of being, God, is here about to raise his tabernacle amongst us. We have already heard the proclamation of peace. We have already heard the sacred greeting. Enmity being laid aside, Charity reigns in all. Arise, O ministers of God, open your lips and celebrate

---

[1] The text must have been derived originally from the Greek. In the Ambrosian Missal it has been preserved in the form of a *transitorium* for Septuagesima.

in unison the consubstantial, indivisible Godhead to whom the Seraphim sing the *Trisagion*.

All ye faithful who stand around this royal and sacred altar, regard with awe Christ your King enthroned upon it, surrounded by the heavenly hosts. With our eyes raised to heaven we pray saying : Remember not our sins, but in thy mercy pardon us. We bless thee, O Lord; together with the Angels and the Saints we glorify thee.

VIII.—CANTICLE FOR HOLY COMMUNION

(From the Armenian Liturgy)

O holy Church, Mother of the Faith, bridal chamber of the spiritual nuptials,

Thou art the home of the immortal Bridegroom which he hath adorned with everlasting splendour.

Thou art a new and marvellous heaven raised up from glory to glory ;

Thou dost regenerate us by means of holy Baptism, and we become thy children, glorious as the day.

Thou dost give us this sanctifying Bread to eat and this sacred Blood to drink.

Thou dost raise us to inaccessible heights, even to the company of the incorporeal spirits.

Come then, O children of the New Sion, draw nigh to the Lord with pure hearts.

Taste and see how gentle and yet how strong is our Lord.

The tabernacle of old was a figure of thee, O Church of Christ; thou, in thy turn, art a figure of the celestial tabernacle.

He burst the adamantine gates, thou overthrowest to the foundations the gates of hell.

He overcame the Jordan, thou dost overcome the flood of universal wickedness.

Josue was the captain of the first tabernacle; thy captain is Jesus, the only-begotten Son of the eternal Father.

This bread is the body of Jesus Christ; this chalice is the Blood of the Covenant.

Behold the most profound of all mysteries is revealed to us; God himself is made manifest.

This is the same Christ, the Divine Word, who sits at the right hand of the Father.

He is sacrificed here among us and takes away the sins of the world.

May he be blessed for evermore, with the Father and the Holy Ghost, Now, and always, and throughout all the ages to come.

IX.—EASTER HYMN

ATTRIBUTED TO VENANTIUS FORTUNATUS

1.

Salve, festa dies,
Toto venerabilis aevo ;
Qua Deus infernum
Vicit, et astra tenet.

1.

Welcome, festival day !
Thrice hallowed for ever and
  ever ;
God, who hath conquered hell,
Openeth a path to the skies.

2.

Ecce renascentis
Testatur gratia mundi,
Omnia cum Domino
Dona redisse suo
    Salve, festa, etc.

2.

Lo ! the fair beauty of earth,
From the slumber of winter awaking,
Showeth how all God's gifts
Now with their Maker revive.
    Welcome, etc.

3.

Namque triumphanti
Post tristia tartara Christo,
Undique fronde nemus,
Gramina flore favent.
    Salve, festa, etc.

3.

Christ in his triumph doth rise,
Who hath vanquished the devil's
  dominion :
Gay is the woodland with leaves,
Bright are the meadows with
  flowers.
    Welcome, etc.

4.

Qui crucifixus erat
Deus, ecce per omnia regnat,
Dantque Creatori
Cuncta creata precem.
    Salve, festa, etc.

4.

He who once hung on the cross
Now reigneth in boundless dominion :
All things created on earth
Worship the Maker of all.
    Welcome, etc.

5.

Christe, salus rerum,
Bone conditor atque Redemptor,
Unica progenies
Ex deitate Patris,
    Salve, festa, etc.

5.

Jesu, the health of the world,
Creator of man and Redeemer,
Son of the Father supreme,
Only-begotten of God !
    Welcome, etc.

6.

Qui genus humanum
Cernens mersisse profundo,
Ut hominem eriperes,
Es quoque factus homo;
    Salve, festa, etc.

6.

Yea, it was thou, blessed Lord,
Who, discerning humanity's
  sorrow,
Humbledst thyself for our race,
Taking our flesh for thine own.
    Welcome, etc.

7.

Funeris exequias
Pateris, vitae auctor et orbis;
Intras mortis iter,
Dando salutis opem.
    Salve, festa, etc.

7.

Mourning they laid thee to rest,
Who art author and life of creation :
Treading the pathway of death,
Life thou bestowedst on men.
    Welcome, etc.

8.

Tristia cesserunt
Infernae vincula legis,
Expavitque chaos
Luminis ore premi.
    Salve, festa, etc.

8.

Burst are the gates of the Law,
The chains of its bondage are
  broken,
Darkness and chaos and death
Flee from the face of the light.
    Welcome, etc.

9.

Pollicitam sed redde
Fidem precor, alma potestas:
Tertia lux rediit:
Surge, sepulte meus.
    Salve, festa, etc.

9.

God of all pity and power,
Let thy word be assured to the
    doubting:
Light on the third day returns:
Rise, Son of God, from the tomb!
    Welcome, etc.

10.

Non decet ut humili
Tumulo tua membra tegantur;
Non praetium mundi
Vilia saxa premant.
    Salve, festa, etc.

10.

Ill doth it seem that thy limbs
Should linger in lowly dishonour;
Ransom and price of the world,
Veiled from the vision of men.
    Welcome, etc.

11.

Solve catenatas
Inferni carceris umbras,
Et revoca sursum
Quidquid ad ima ruit.
    Salve, festa, etc.

11.

Loosen, O Lord, the enchained,
The spirits imprisoned in dark-
    ness,
Rescue, recall unto life
Those who are rushing to death.
    Welcome, etc.

12.

Redde tuam faciem,
Videant ut saecula lumen;
Redde diem, qui nos,
Te moriente, fugit.
    Salve, festa, etc.

12.

Show us thy face once more,
That the ages may joy in thy
    brightness,
Grant us thy daylight again,
Veiled by thy death from our eyes.
    Welcome, etc

13.

Inferus insaturabiliter
Cava guttura pandens,
Qui rapuit semper,
Fit tua praeda, Deus,
    Salve, festa, etc.

13.

Hell that hath lain in wait
With gaping jaws and unsated,
She that was ever the wolf
Now is thy prey, O our God.
    Welcome, etc.

14.

Rex sacer, ecce tui
Radiat pars magna triumphi,
Cum puras animas
Sacra lavacra beant.
    Salve, festa, etc.

14.

Lo! how these shine, holy King,
As the prize of thy triumph before
    thee,
Souls in the sacred font
Blest and made clean unto thee.
    Welcome, etc.

15.

Candidus egreditur
Nitidis exercitus undis,
Atque vetus vitium
Purgat in amne novo.
    Salve, festa, etc.

15.

Now from the cleansing wave
Goeth forth a white-garmented
    army,
Stain of the ancient crime
Purged in thy new stream of
    grace.
    Welcome, etc.

16.

Fulgentes animas
Vestis quoque candida signat,
Et grege de niveo
Gaudia pastor habet.
    Salve, festa, etc.

16.

Garments of white betoken
The glory on souls thou bestowest :
Joy hath the Shepherd now,
Seeing his flock white as snow.
    Welcome, etc.

X.—ANCIENT GREEK FRAGMENT OF AN ACROSTIC HYMN DISCOVERED ON AN EGYPTIAN PAPYRUS[1]

1. . . . ut vitam adipisci posses immortalem.
2. Tu sententiam terribilem illam impiorum evasisti, ut ames.
3. Ad regias venisti nuptias, illas inquam nuptias . . . ne vultus concidat.
4. Ne amplius aequivoca proferas verba. . . .
5. Veniunt aliqui ovinam induti pellem, qui tamen intus lupi probantur . . . a longe namque.
6. Cum sanctis vitam ducere satage; vita imbui stude; contende ut ignem effugias.
7. Omni custodia spem illam quam didicisti serva, spem quam Magister tui gratia constituit.
8. Venit Deus innumeras secum ferens benedictiones. Ter ille mortem vicit. . . .
9. Qui ob ipsum passus est Jesus, aiebat : trado corpus meum, ne tu morti sis obnoxius.
10. Quam gloriosa sunt divina proposita! In omnibus ille veluti exemplar patitur, ut gloriosa tu vita potiaris.
11. Ipse in Jordane mersus est : mersus est ut exemplum praeberet, ipse qui unda est purificans.
12. In monte permansit et horridi obnoxius fuit tentationi.
13. Labora nunc et hereditatem tibi compares; nunc certe, quia tempus adest tibi, ut iis dones qui fame opprimuntur.
14. Dicit Deus : ciba advenam, peregrinum pasce et miserum, ut ignem valeas effugere.
15. Pater ad passionem illum misit qui aeternam adeptus est vitam, cui potestas in mortem collata est.
16. Ipse suis servis Evangelium predicavit, dicens : inops regnum possidebit, manet ei pars haec in hereditate.
17. Flagellis in exemplum caesus est, ut omnium animos erigat . . . ut mortem destruat.
18. Ut post mortem resurrectione potiaris; ut lumine aeternitatis perfrui possis; ut a Deo luce donari valeas.
19. O requies afflicti, o choree. . . . Veh! ignis horridus hominis nequam.
20. Gratiae ope tu libere pervenisti, aurem praebe igitur preci pauperis, mitte arroganter loqui.
21. Terribilis . . . est ignis; in aeternum terribilis; terribilis est iniquo ignis.
22. Dabit Christus . . . et coronas sanctis, sed homini nequam . . ignem.

---

[1] B. P. Grenfell and A. S. Hunt. *The Amherst Papyri, being an Account of the Greek Papyri in the Collection of Lord Amherst.* Part I, pp. 23-28 and plate II. London, 1900.

23. . . . psalmodiae cum sanctis concentus in aevum animas pascunt.
24. Noli eorum quae didicisti oblivisci, et consequi valeas quae ipse
promisit. . . .

It is very pleasant to dwell upon the hymns of the early
Christian muse, so unstudied, yet so attractive by their very
simplicity, and by the fact that they draw all their inspiration
from Holy Scripture, and are all filled with an intense love of
Christ, which dominates the whole life of his Saints.